THE
WHOLESALE-
BY-MAIL
CATALOG®
1992

THE WHOLESALE-BY-MAIL®
Catalog 1992

BY THE PRINT PROJECT

Lowell Miller, Executive Producer

Prudence McCullough, Editor

HarperPerennial

A Division of HarperCollins*Publishers*

The Wholesale-by-Mail Catalog® is a resource for use by the general public. Companies in this catalog are listed at the sole discretion of the editors, and no advertising fees are solicited or accepted.

First HarperPerennial edition published 1992

Designed by Cassandra J. Pappas

LIBRARY OF CONGRESS CATALOG CARD NUMBER 89-45135

ISSN 1049-0116
ISBN 0-06-273061-4

91 92 93 94 95 AT/HAD 10 9 8 7 6 5 4 3 2 1

CONTENTS

Introduction vii
Using This Book viii
The Listing Code xi

Animal Supplies 1
Appliances, Audio, TV, and Video 19
Art, Antiques, and Collectibles 44
Art Materials 57
Auto, Marine, and Aviation Equipment 78
Books, Periodicals, and Recordings 101
Cameras, Photographic and Darkroom Equipment, Optics, Film,
    and Services 135
Cigars, Pipes, Tobacco, and Other Smoking Needs 147
Clothing, Furs, and Accessories 155
    Mother and Child 188
    Footwear 197
Crafts and Hobbies 204
Farm and Garden 238
Food and Drink 258
General Merchandise, Buying Clubs, Great Sales, and Good Values 281
    Packaging and Storage 300
Health and Beauty 306
Home 316
    Decor 317
    Furnishings 344
    Kitchen 358
    Linen 371
    Maintenance and Building 381
    Table Settings 391
Jewelry, Gems, and Watches 411
Leather Goods 420
Medicine and Science 429
Music 446
Office 465

Computing   489
Sports and Recreation   504
Surplus   532
Tools, Hardware, Electronics, Energy, Safety, Security, and
   Industrial Goods   538
Toys and Games   556
Travel   562

The Complete Guide to Buying by Mail   573
   Feedback   616
   Chart   618
   Company Index   619
   Product Index   627

INTRODUCTION

We're happy to bring you *The Wholesale-by-Mail Catalog® 1992*, the ninth edition of *the* consumer's guide to mail-order values. This updated edition lists companies that sell goods and services at 30% below list or comparable retail—the traditional definition of "wholesale." (Of course, not everything will be discounted 30%—sometimes the savings are greater, and sometimes they're near list, but every firm has been included because at least a portion of the offerings meet our criteria.) Using *The Wholesale-by-Mail Catalog® 1992*, you can save considerable sums on all kinds of purchases: cruises, tambourines, specialty hardware, greenhouses, ethnic spices, deerskin gloves, sailboards, TV scripts, software, fruit crate labels, nurses' shoes—the list is almost endless. Before you send for a catalog or place an order, be sure to read the explanations of the Listing Code (beginning on page xi), which will help you understand and use this book. For more detailed information on mail-order shopping, see "The Complete Guide to Buying by Mail," beginning on page 573.

Enjoy your reading and shopping, and please let us know about your experiences with the firms listed here. Turn to "Feedback," page 616, if you'd like to contact us.

THE PRINT PROJECT
Lowell Miller, Executive Producer
Prudence McCullough, Editor

USING THIS BOOK

___

The Wholesale-by-Mail Catalog® *1992* is a consumer guide to buying by mail that's designed to be used by all catalog shoppers, from novice to seasoned veterans. No matter what your status is, the following will help you get the most from the book:

"FIND IT FAST"

This new feature, immediately preceding the listings in most chapters, provides an at-a-glance guide to different types of products featured in that section. For example, if you're looking for firms selling contact lenses and eyeglasses, you can check the "Find It Fast" box in the "Medicine and Science" chapter instead of reading through all of the listings. The "Find It Fast" feature is designed to supplement the Product Index in the back of the book, as well as the "See Also" section (see below) at the end of each chapter.

"SEE ALSO"

Each firm is listed in the chapter that best reflects its business focus, and *cross-referenced* in the "See Also" sections at the end of other chapters, as appropriate. For example, Gohn Bros. is listed in the "Clothing" chapter, because that's its strong suit. Because Gohn also sells horse blankets, you'll find it cited in the *See Also* section at the end of the "Animal Supplies" chapter. Since the *See Also* section can often direct you to valuable sources, don't overlook it!

PATIENCE

Since companies are constantly revising their catalogs and printing new ones, we ask you to be patient while waiting for literature to arrive. Specifically, please allow *six to eight weeks* for delivery, unless the firm's listing indicates a longer possible delay. If the catalog doesn't arrive within the designated period, write or call the company—and contact us (see "Feedback," page 616, for information). Please remember that some products, such as flower bulbs and highly perishable foods, can be ordered only at certain times of the year.

PRICE QUOTES

Some firms do not issue catalogs at all. Most of these operate under a price-quote system: You tell them the exact make and model number of the item you want and they give you the price and shipping cost. Price quotes are given by mail and phone. Businesses that operate this way are clearly indicated in the listings. (Be sure to check the "Special Factors" notes at the end of each listing as well as the core information.) Price-quote firms often have the lowest prices on such goods as appliances, audio and TV components, and furniture; they usually sell well below both the standard manufacturers' suggested list prices and the less formal minimum prices that some manufacturers try to enforce. Before writing or calling for a price quote or making a purchase in this way, remember to read the "Price Quotes" section of "The Complete Guide to Buying by Mail." In addition, see "The Grey Market" in the introduction to the "Cameras" chapter for information on several types of goods that are often sold on a price-quote basis.

MINIMUM ORDERS

In a few cases, the very best buys are available from firms that require a minimum order in dollars or goods (although most of the companies in this book impose no such restriction). Don't be put off by a minimum requirement. Minimum requirements are usually not ironclad: Most firms will accept orders below the minimum, although an extra "handling fee" is often imposed for the privilege. Be sure to check the catalog, though, for the last word on this. If you want something that's a real bargain, chances are you have friends or work associates who'll want it as well. Even if you can't find a buying partner, remember that a great bargain can also be a great gift. If appropriate, stock up on a special product—doing so may also keep you one small step ahead of inflation.

A CAVEAT

The Wholesale-by-Mail Catalog® 1992 is compiled as a resource for consumers, to help you to find the bargains available by mail. *Never* order goods directly from this book, even if prices are given in the listing. *Always* contact the company first to get a catalog or a current price quote, and be sure to follow specific ordering and payment instructions. *Please do not request extra discounts or wholesale prices, unless the listing states that these are available.* All of the information in this book is based on our research and fact-checking as of press time, and is subject to change.

THE LISTING CODE

Some of the information in the listings is presented in a simple coded form at the head of each entry, formatted as follows:

1. Company name, mailing address, and phone number
2. Literature form: catalog, brochure, flyer, leaflet, price list, etc.; the price, followed by "refundable" or "deductible" if you can redeem the price by placing an order; *SASE:* send a long (business-sized), self-addressed, stamped envelope; "Information": price quote or information is given over the phone and/or by letter (when there is no catalog)
3. Save: the percentage of savings you may expect on the *suggested list* or *comparable retail prices* of the goods and/or services. The percentage is often an average and usually applies to some, but not all, goods. *Please don't deduct this percentage from the order total* unless so instructed in the listing text
4. Pay: methods of payment accepted for orders (catalog fees should be paid by check or money order unless listing states otherwise):
    (a) personal check
    (b) MO: bank or postal money order
    (c) IMO: bank or postal international money order
    (d) certified check: includes certified check, teller's check, cashier's check, or bank draft
    (e) Access: Access credit card
    (f) AE: American Express credit card
    (g) CB: Carte Blanche credit card
    (h) CHOICE: CHOICE credit card
    (i) DC: Diners Club credit card

(j)   Discover: Discover credit card
(k)   EC: Eurocard credit card
(l)   MC: MasterCard credit card
(m)   Optima: Optima credit card
(n)   Universal: AT&T's Universal credit card
(o)   V: VISA credit card

5.   Sells: type of goods sold
6.   Store: address and hours of the firm's retail location or other outlets, if applicable

$ THE DOLLAR CODE

The dollar-code symbol represents our opinion of the overall worth of the firm to the average bargain hunter. We take into account the quality of the goods, quantity of the offerings, depth of the discount, and, when information is available, the quality of the service.

$$$$ is a top rating; $ is the lowest. A low rating may reflect a limited number of products and does not mean the company is a poor source for those products. (For example, if a firm doesn't accept credit cards, it will usually receive a lower rating than a similar firm offering the convenience of payment by plastic.) Whenever possible, the rating reflects our opinion of that firm compared to others within the same product category. And we don't list companies to which we'd have to give a "poor" rating.

☎   THE PHONE SYMBOL

This means the firm accepts orders over the phone, usually charged to a credit card. Many WBMC firms have toll-free order lines (800 numbers), over which you can usually get price quotes and information as well.

🍁   THE MAPLE LEAF

This symbol means the firm will ship goods to Canada. Canadian shoppers should check current import restrictions and tariffs before placing an order, and request shipping charges or an estimate before finalizing the order. *Please note:* U.S. firms generally request payment for goods *and* catalogs in U.S. funds.

🇺🇸   THE FLAG SYMBOL

A small "Old Glory" on the symbol line means the firm will ship goods to APO and FPO (U.S. military) addresses. For more information, see "Shipments Abroad," page 594.

✔ THE DISCOUNT SYMBOL

If a checkmark appears at the top of the listing, the firm is offering a special discount or offer to readers of *The Wholesale-by-Mail Catalog®* *1992.* For more information, see "WBMC Reader Offers," page 577.

THE COMPLETE GUIDE TO BUYING BY MAIL

Our updated guide to buying by mail, in the back of this book, can help you with questions on everything from sending for catalogs to interpreting warranties. If a problem arises with a mail-order transaction, look here for help in resolving it. You'll find additional consumer information in the chapter introductions.

THE
WHOLESALE-
BY-MAIL
CATALOG®
1992

ANIMAL SUPPLIES

Livestock and pet supplies and equipment,

veterinary instruments and biologicals,

live-animal referrals, and services

Americans spend more each year on cat food than they do *baby food*, according to recent statistics. The steady growth of pet ownership testifies to the pleasures of companionship in an increasingly "single" society, and keeping an animal can have other pluses: stroking domestic animals seems to have genuinely therapeutic benefits for people suffering from hypertension and Alzheimer's disease. In fact, pets are now widely used in therapy programs for nursing-home patients, hospitalized children, and psychiatric patients. (For further reading on this topic, see *Pet Therapy: A Study and Resource Guide for the Use of Companion Animals in Selected Therapies*. Request the current price of the publication and ordering information from Humane Society, Pikes Peak Region, P.O. Box 187, Colorado Springs, CO 80901.)

Most of us, who adopt pets for less pragmatic reasons, are unaware of the long-term costs of ownership: You can spend several thousand dollars in food, health care, and other necessities over the lifetime of the average cat or dog. While buying pet food by mail is seldom cost-effective because of the shipping costs, there are many products you *can* get for less: collars and leashes, cages and carriers, feeding dishes and devices, grooming tools, beds, and even medications. The firms listed here carry products for a wide range of animals—from hamsters and ferrets to horses and barnyard animals—and all can save you money.

While pets are acquired on impulse, deliberating over the selection can help you choose the animal that best suits your personality and lifestyle. If you're planning a pet adoption, consult *Getting More for Your Money,* by the Better Business Bureau. The book includes a section on selecting cats, dogs, fish, and birds. (Send a self-addressed, stamped envelope and request for the publications list to the Council of Better Business Bureaus, Inc., 4200 Wilson Blvd., Suite 800, Arlington, VA 22203, Attn.: Publications Dept.) Dog fanciers undecided on breed can turn to *The Perfect Puppy—How to Select Your Dog by Its Behavior,* by Ben and Lyn Hart (W.H. Freeman, 1988). The authors assess popular breeds on the basis of such criteria as playfulness, tendency to bark, ease of obedience training, congeniality with other dogs, and patience with children. If birds interest you, see *The Basic Bird Book,* by Elizabeth Randolph with Douglas G. Aspros, D.V.M. as consultant (Ballantine Books, 1989), for a comprehensive guide to choosing and caring for a bird.

Mastering the basics of pet care can save you considerable sums in a variety of ways—in salon costs, the price of obedience school, and sometimes even on vet fees. There's no lack of books and magazines on the topic: *The Common Sense Book of Kitten and Cat Care* and *The Common Sense Book of Puppy and Dog Care* (Bantam Books), by Harry Miller, are excellent reference works. The advice of the late Barbara Woodhouse is especially valuable to owners of uncooperative canines, and can be found in *Encyclopedia of Dogs and Puppies* and *Dog Training My Way* (Berkley Books), as well as *No Bad Dogs* (Summit Books, 1982). *The Complete Dog Book,* by the American Kennel Club, Inc., is a highly praised general reference that dog owners may want to add to their own libraries. There are scores of guides to the care of fish, birds, reptiles, and more exotic creatures; the Simon & Schuster Guides (Fireside), on cats, fish, dogs, birds, horses, and other animals are especially helpful and easy to use. Consult your local library or bookstore for available titles.

If you're among the owners of this country's 50 million pet birds, tell your vet about the Avian Referral Service, which helps vets get advice on bird problems. Your vet should write to AAHA, Avian Referral Service, P.O. Box 15899, Denver, CO 80215, for more information. If *wild* birds are your pleasure, you may enjoy membership in the National Bird-Feeding Society, which entitles you to a newsletter on the care and feeding of wild birds. Membership costs $15 a year; for more information, send a self-addressed, stamped envelope to National Bird-Feeding Society, 1163 Shermer Rd., Northbrook, IL 60062.

Despite the best care, pets invariably fall prey to sickness and accidents at some time during their lives, and the ensuing vet bills can be staggering. You might consider insurance: The Animal Health Insurance Agency, 24 Delay St., Danbury, CT 06810, insures cats and dogs under ten years old against illness and injury; Veterinary Pet Insurance, 400 N. Tustin Ave., Santa Ana, CA 92705, imposes an age limit on new applicants (the animal must be 11 or younger). Write for details, rates, and restrictions.

Several of the firms listed here retain veterinarians who can answer questions on products and use, but they're not allowed to give specific medical advice. If your pet is ailing, consult a vet, and *always* seek professional guidance if you plan to administer any vaccines or medications to your animal yourself. There are other ways to safeguard your pet's well-being: Keep the number of a local 24-hour service that handles medical emergencies posted near the phone, and become familiar with symptoms and the first-aid measures you may have to take in order to transport the animal to the clinic. The "Angell Memorial Guide to Animal First Aid," published by the American Humane Education Society and MSPCA, is a great primer on first aid for pets. The 22-page guide tells you how to restrain and handle an injured animal, bind a wound, and deal with burns, drowning, heat stroke, problem deliveries, choking, shock, poisoning, and many other crises. Rosters of toxic household substances and plants are included, as well as a list of tips to help prevent accidents and injuries. The booklet costs $1; request it by title from the American Humane Education Society, 350 South Huntington Avenue, Boston, MA 02130.

Finally, when your pet reaches old age you should prepare yourself for the inevitable. Although it's always difficult to lose a beloved animal, the process may be eased with some guidance. Among other resources, you may find help in the brochure, "The Loss of Your Pet," from the American Animal Hospital Association (AAHA). Request the pamphlet from Member Services, AAHA, P.O. Box 150899, Denver, CO 80215-0899.

FIND IT FAST

FISH • **Daleco, Pet Warehouse, That Fish Place**
HORSES • **Dairy Association, Jeffers, Kennel Vet, Master Animal, UPCO, Wholesale Veterinary**
LIVESTOCK • **Dairy Association, Jeffers, Kansas City, Northern Wholesale, Omaha Vaccine, Wholesale Veterinary**
PETS (DOGS AND CATS) • **Dog's Outfitter, Kennel Vet, Master Animal, Pet Warehouse, R.C. Steele**
TRAPS • **Tomahawk Live Trap**

DAIRY ASSOCIATION CO., INC.

**DEPT. B1
LYNDONVILLE, VT 05851-
 0145
800-232-3610
802-626-3610
FAX: 802/626-3433**

Brochure and Price List: free
Save: up to 35%
Pay: check or MO
Sells: livestock treatments and leather balm
Store: mail order only

$$ ☎ 🍁(see text) ▇

Generations of herd farmers know Dairy Association Co., Inc., for its Bag Balm ointment. The firm, which was founded in 1900, also sells Hoof Softener and Tackmaster leather conditioner—all at excellent savings.

Bag Balm, which was formulated to soothe the chapped, sunburned udders of cows, is also recommended by horse trainers for cracked heels, galls, cuts, hobble burns, and other ailments. It can be used on sheep, goats, dogs, and cats as well, and is touted as a softener for weatherbeaten, chapped hands. A ten-ounce can, over $5 elsewhere, costs $4.35 here; a 4½-pound pail costs $29. Dilators and milking tubes for injured udders are also available. Green Mt. Horse Products, a division of Dairy Association, produces Hoof Softener—made of pine oil, lanolin, and vegetable oils, it helps to keep hoofs pliable and sound ($4.15 per pint). The firm's Tackmaster is TLC for leather—a one-step, all-around conditioner, cleaner, and preservative—cheaper than similar products at $1.85 for four ounces.

Canadian readers, please note: Contact Dr. A.D. Daniels Co. Ltd., N. Rock Island, Quebec, for prices and ordering information.

Special Factors: Price quote by phone or letter; shipping is included; phone orders are accepted for C.O.D. payment.

DALECO MASTER BREEDER PRODUCTS

3340 LAND DRIVE
FORT WAYNE, IN 46809
219/747-7376

Catalog: $4, refundable (see text)
Save: up to 40%
Pay: check, MO, MC, V
Sells: tropical fish supplies and aquarium specialties
Store: mail order only

$$$ ☎ 🍁(see text)

Daleco publishes a catalog/reference book entitled "The Aquarists Supply Manual," which is packed with useful information for the owner of fresh and saltwater fish. The catalog costs $4 if mailed bulk rate, $6 by first-class mail (to U.S. addresses only), and is refundable with a $50 order.

Daleco has been selling aquarium supplies since 1966, and discounts tank filters, aquarium heaters, lights, tank stands, air and water pumps, foods, water test kits, UV water sterilizers, water conditioners, reef trickle filter systems, and related goods. Among the brands represented are Aquanetics, Aquarium Products, Aquarium Systems, Eugene Danner, Dupla, Ebo-Jager, Energy Savers, Hagen, Hawaiian Marine, Hikari, Jungle Laboratories, Kordon, Mardel, Marineland, Perfecto, Sees, Tetra, Vortex, and WISA. The products are selected for serious hobbyists and breeders, for whom the catalog's "Fish Problem Solver" and "Fish Disease" charts should prove useful. The Manual is worth the $4 for the information alone, but the prices are good—savings run up to 40%. Shipping and handling are free on orders over $25 shipped in the contiguous U.S. The catalog comes with a voucher entitling you to $4 off your first order over $50—don't overlook it when you order.

Canadian readers, please note: The Manual costs $6 (in U.S. funds) via surface mail, $9 via airmail.

Special Factors: Price quote by phone or letter; shipping included on orders over $25; authorized returns are accepted.

THE DOG'S OUTFITTER

**P.O. BOX 2010
HAZLETON, PA 18201
717/384-5555**

Catalog: free
Save: up to 50%
Pay: check, MO, MC, V
Sells: vet, kennel, groomer, and pet supplies
Store: mail order only

$$$ ☎

Despite the fact that the Dog's Outfitter catalog is geared to professionals, it has one of the best selections of products for pet *owners* around. The firm has been in business since 1969, and is exclusive in name only—the catalog is full of things for cats, and there's even a page devoted to the needs of ferrets. A full range of pet products is sold here, including grooming tools, shampoo, flea and tick collars and insecticides, cages, gates and doors, training aids, feeding and watering equipment, nutritional supplements, collars and leads, pet beds, carriers, toys and bones, and even books and gifts. The brands include A&W, Bio-Groom, Dubl Duck, General Cage, Havahart, Lambert Kay, Oster, PetAg, Resco, Ring 5, Speedy, André Tisserand (shears), Twinco, and Zodiac.

We saw several items pet owners might appreciate: molting combs for dogs and cats, no-tears pet shampoo, herbal flea collars, pet doors to fit *screen* doors, a variety of yard scoops, all types of feeding bowls and crocks, "small animal" nurser kits, reflective collars and leads, dog parkas, bulk rawhide bones, and toys in boxes of 50. There are gifts, pet jewelry (for owners), note cards, and books (Arco, Howell, T.F.H.), and grooming videos from Oster and Animal Academy training tapes.

Unlike many animal-supply discounters, The Dog's Outfitter has its own warehouse and does not drop ship. The minimum order is $50 and shipping is included on most items, which becomes a meaningful bonus if you're buying something heavy—other firms ship even gallons of pet shampoo freight collect, which can add as much as $5 to the price.

Special Factors: Satisfaction is guaranteed; price quote by phone or letter; shipping is included on most items; authorized returns of new and unused goods are accepted within 10 days for exchange, refund, or credit; minimum order is $50; C.O.D. orders are accepted.

J-B WHOLESALE PET SUPPLIES, INC.

**289 WAGARAW RD.
HAWTHORNE, NJ 07506
201/423-2222
FAX: 201/423-1181**

Catalog: free
Save: up to 50%
Pay: check, MO, MC, V, AE, Optima
Sells: vet, kennel, and pet supplies
Store: same address; Monday to Friday 9–6,
Thursday 9–9, Saturday 10–5, Sunday
11–4

$$$ ☎ ♦ 🇺🇸

J-B Wholesale Pet Supplies stocks "over 6,500 different items for showing, grooming, training, breeding," and other animal-related functions. J-B is staffed by professional animal handlers who can give you informed buying assistance, and who've kennel-tested all of the products the company sells.

The 100-page catalog features a wide range of goods for cats and dogs, with the emphasis on the latter: vaccines, remedies for common health problems, vitamins and nutritional supplements, repellents and deodorizers, shampoos and grooming products, beds and mats, flea and tick control products, cages, kennels, pet doors, grooming tables and dryers, leashes and leads, feeding devices, rawhide bones, and rubber toys. Every major manufacturer is represented, and J-B's own line of grooming aids—shampoo and coat conditioners and tints—is also featured. You can send for the catalog, or call for prices and availability on specific name-brand items.

Special Factors: Satisfaction is guaranteed; price quote by phone or letter; returns are accepted within 7 days for exchange, refund, or credit; minimum order is $25; orders are shipped worldwide.

JEFFERS VET SUPPLY

**P.O. BOX 100
DOLTHAN, AL 36302-0100
800-JEFFERS
FAX: 205/793-5179**

Catalog: free
Save: up to 50%
Pay: check, MO, MC, V
Sells: vet and livestock supplies
Store: 419 Inez Rd., Dolthan, AL; also Old
    Airport Rd., West Plains, MO; every day
    7–6, both locations

Jeffers publishes a 128-page catalog heavy on supplies for livestock farmers and anyone who keeps a horse, but which also features goods for cats, dogs, and even rabbits. The firm has been in business since 1976, and welcomes any questions you may have about its goods.

Livestock farmers who raise cattle (including dairy), swine, sheep, goats, and poultry should see the catalog for the antibiotics and sulfa drugs, biologicals, wormers, milking equipment, incubators, and other necessities. A sizable chunk of the catalog is devoted to equine supplies—biologicals and nutritional supplements, grooming tools and products, farrier supplies, stable equipment, and tack—including several pages of saddles. Equine videotapes by Al Dunning, and Richard Shrake are also available.

The line of goods for "companion animals" is similarly geared for professionals, although there are a number of products—training devices, collars, cages, clippers, etc.—that pet owners might find useful. Savings run up to 50% on list and regular retail prices, and some quantity discounts are offered on some items.

Special Factors: Satisfaction is guaranteed; price quote by phone or letter; quantity discounts are available; returns are accepted for exchange, refund, or credit.

KANSAS CITY VACCINE COMPANY

**P.O. BOX 5713
KANSAS CITY, MO 64102-
5713
816/842-5966**

Price List: free
Save: up to 35%
Pay: check, MO, certified check
Sells: vet supplies and biologicals
Store: 1611 Genesee St., Kansas City, MO;
Monday to Friday 8:30–4

$$$ ▰

Dairy farmers, herders, and veterinarians have relied on Kansas City Vaccine for its comprehensive stock of supplies and equipment since 1912. The price list, geared to medical/commercial needs, is published twice yearly.

You'll find products for cattle, horses, sheep, hogs, poultry, dogs, and cats here—vaccines, antitoxins, flea and tick treatments, grooming tools, wormers, stethoscopes, soaps, tattoo markers, nutritional supplements, and other related items. The brands include Chaparral, Franklin, Happy Jack, Havoc, Kopertox, Lindane, Norden, Oster, Red-Kote, Resco, Ritchey, Sunbeam, Trax-M, and Tylosin, among others. Kansas City Vaccine is ideal for the vet or animal handler, since most of the products are for professionals.

Special Factors: Price quote by phone or letter; vaccines and biologicals are sent where ordinances permit; quantity discounts are available; minimum order is $10.

THE KENNEL VET CORP.

DEPT. WBMC
P.O. BOX 835
BELLMORE, NY 11710
516/783-5400
FAX: 516/783-7516

Catalog: $1 (see text)
Save: up to 70%
Pay: check, MO, MC, V, AE, Discover,
Optima
Sells: vet, kennel, and pet supplies
Store: 1811 Newbridge Rd., Bellmore, NY;
Monday to Friday 9–5, Saturday 10–4

$$$$ ☎ 🍁 ▦

If you own or raise dogs, you'll find Kennel Vet's compact, 84-page catalog great reading. This firm beats other companies' discount prices on products for dogs, cats, horses, and has been in business since 1971.

Kennel Vet offers vaccines and biologicals, remedies for common health problems, vitamins and nutritional supplements, repellents and deodorizers, droppings composters, shampoos and grooming products, flea and tick control products, cages, kennels, pet doors, grooming tables, dryers, leashes, leads, feeding devices, rawhide bones and rubber toys, and other goods. The brands represented include Adams, Classic, Doskocil (carriers), Gem-Line, General, Holiday, Johnson, Lambert Kay, Lawrence (brushes), Mid-West, Mycodex, Natra-Pet, Norden, Oster, Redi, Rich Health, Ring 5, St. Aubrey, Sulfodene, Vet-Kem, and others. Kennel Vet also sells pet food from Eukanuba, Iams, and Science Diet, by mail as well as in the store. And the book department includes veterinary manuals, books on dog breeds, and a selection on cats, birds, and horses—all at a discount.

Be sure to mention WBMC when you send for the catalog ($1) and when you order, since readers of this book are entitled to $2 off their first order.

Special Factors: C.O.D. orders are accepted; authorized returns are accepted; shipping is included on orders of $60 or more (with some exceptions—see the catalog); vaccines and biologicals are sent where ordinances permit; orders are shipped worldwide.

MASTER ANIMAL CARE

LAKE RD.
P.O. BOX 3333
MOUNTAINTOP, PA
   18707-0330
717/384-3600
FAX: 717-384-3500

Catalog: free
Save: up to 40%
Pay: check, MO, MC, V, Discover
Sells: dog and cat supplies and biologicals
Store: mail order only

$$ ☎

Master Animal Care specializes in dog and cat health supplies, selling them at highly competitive prices. The "Master Animal Care" catalog, which includes helpful information on health care and vaccinating procedures, includes products for both cats and dogs. You'll find 56 pages of grooming tools, a range of cages, feeding devices, training aids, leashes and leads, and related goods, at prices up to 40% below list. Master usually features the latest innovations in pet products, which have included airline-approved cages in designer colors, timer-operated feeding dishes that keep two meals fresh, natural and biodegradable cleaners and disinfectants, and hot-oil skin treatments for dogs and cats. But it's also a good place to save on a carton of rawhide bones!

Special Factors: Satisfaction is guaranteed; price quote by phone or letter; returns are accepted for exchange, refund, or credit.

NORTHERN WHOLESALE VETERINARY SUPPLY, INC.

P.O. BOX 2256
ROCKFORD, IL 61131-
   0256
800-356-5852
FAX: 402/731-9829

Catalog: free (see text)
Save: up to 50%
Pay: check, MO, MC, V, Discover
Sells: vet, kennel, and pet supplies
Store: mail order only

$$$ ☎ 🍁

Northern Wholesale offers vets, breeders, and livestock farmers savings of up to 50% on thousands of products. Northern Wholesale, which has been in business since 1970, is geared for the animal-care professional but offers goods for pet owners as well.

The 128-page catalog we reviewed was devoted to veterinary care products for cattle, sheep, rabbits, horses, and swine, including vaccines and biologicals, nutritional supplements, surgical instruments, identification products, horse tack, feeding devices, and manuals. The pet products were principally medicinal, but grooming tools and preparations, carriers and cages, leashes and leads, flea and tick treatments, and a number of other items were shown as well. The brands available through Northern Wholesale include Absorbine, AgriLabs, Carnation, DC&R, Groom-Rite, Lambert Kay, Norden, Orvus, Oster, Pfizer, Rubbermaid, Squibb, Stewart, Sunbeam, Theralin, and Vet-Kem, and prices we spot-checked were among the lowest on widely used dairy farming supplies.

Special Factors: Quantity discounts are available on some items; veterinarian is on staff; C.O.D. orders are accepted.

OMAHA VACCINE COMPANY, INC.

3030 L ST.
OMAHA, NE 68107
800-367-4444
402/731-9600
FAX: 402/731-9829

Catalog: free
Save: up to 50%
Pay: check, MO, MC, V, Discover
Sells: vet, kennel, and pet supplies
Store: same address; Monday to Friday 8–6, Saturday 8–5, Sunday 11–5

$$$

Omaha Vaccine Company's 104-page "Master Catalog," published several times yearly, offers products for livestock, horses, and household pets. Established in 1965, Omaha Vaccine does much of its business with livestock producers and veterinarians, but has branched into the consumer market with new catalogs.

Omaha Vaccine's Master Catalog features vaccines and biologicals, medications, surgical implements, grooming tools, wormers, nutritional supplements, flea and tick products, cages and carriers, leads and leashes, and horse tack, among other goods. Omaha also publishes two specialty catalogs: "Best Care," a 52-page catalog "about dogs and cats," and "First Place," a 48-page catalog for "horse and rider." The horse catalog should be especially useful to the noncommercial owner, since it offers a comprehensive selection of tack, saddles, vet manuals, and a number of videotapes (from "Emergency First Aid" to special-interest tapes on dressage, cross-country riding, and calf roping). Pet owners should request "Best Care," since it's devoted to the needs of dogs and cats and the whims of their keepers.

Special Factors: Price quote by phone; some pharmaceutical products are available by prescription only (shipment is subject to local ordinances); shipping is included on many items; C.O.D. orders are accepted; minimum order is $30.

PET WAREHOUSE

P.O. BOX 20250, DEPT. BMC
DAYTON, OH 45420
800-443-1160
FAX: 513/252-7388

Catalog: $1
Save: up to 60%
Pay: check, MO, MC, V
Sells: pet supplies
Store: mail order only

$$$ ☎ ♦ ▬

The 96-page color catalog from Pet Warehouse is one of the best we've seen for the typical pet owner, who doesn't need breeding equipment or a wall-sized aquarium. The Pet Warehouse sells supplies for cats, dogs, birds, and fish, and there's even a page of goodies for "small animals"—hamsters, gerbils, and mice.

Whether you have a freshwater or marine aquarium, or even a pond, this firm can supply you with filters, air pumps, heaters, feeders, lighting, maintenance equipment and water conditioners, tank decorations and plants, fish medication, food, and other fish goods (but no tanks). The brands include Aquarium Pharmaceuticals, Eheim, Hagen, Kordon, Marineland, Penn Plax, Perfecto, Rainbow Lifeguard, and Tetra, among others. The bird owner can choose from over a dozen different Hagen and Next-to-Nature cages to suit all kinds of birds, as well as cage accessories and bird toys, nests, feeders, an extensive selection of bird food, and dietary supplements and medication. For dogs and cats, there are beds, collars and leashes, feeding devices, grooming supplies and implements, flea and tick repellants, nutritional supplements, cages and carriers, pet doors, litter boxes and scooper, and toys. Name brands are represented here as well, and if you want to read up on pet care or breeds, the Pet Warehouse can provide T.H.F. titles on a wide range of topics.

Special Factors: Price quote by phone or letter; minimum order is $10; orders are shipped worldwide.

R.C. STEELE CO.

BOX 910-WC
1989 TRANSIT WAY
BROCKPORT, NY 14420-
 0910
800-872-3773

Catalog: free
Save: up to 50%
Pay: check, MO, MC, V
Sells: vet, kennel, groomer, and pet supplies
Store: 1989 Transit Way, Brockport, NY;
 Monday to Wednesday 9–7:30, Thursday
 and Friday 9–8:30, Saturday 9–6, Sunday
 12–5

$$$ ☎ ♦

R.C. Steele Co., which was founded in 1959, is the wholesale division of Sporting Dog Specialties. Steele's prices are excellent—sometimes as much as 50% less than comparable retail—and the only drawback is the firm's $50 minimum order.

R.C. Steele makes saving fun with its 68-page color catalog, which features canine products and equipment—cages, pet doors, insecticides, feeding equipment, droppings composters, training dummies and jumps, leashes and leads, grooming supplies and tools, and manuals. There are great buys on rawhide bones, which are sold in case lots at a fraction of full retail, and all types of pet beds, at about half the going rate. The catalog we reviewed had several pages of books from Arco, Denlinger, Howell, T.F.H., and other publishers, as well as videotapes from the American Kennel Club (breed shows), Doral, Oster (grooming), and Volhard (obedience). R.C. Steele also offers a small but well-chosen selection of products for cats, as well as a page of aquarium supplies. And every catalog includes a number of items that will capture your imagination: a rawhide frisbee, the Quick Muzzle for Cats, gold-plated link chokes and leads, fruit-flavored rawhide treats, and a ball that plays "You Are My Sunshine" when it's bounced were among those we found in the catalog we reviewed.

Special Factors: Authorized returns are accepted; minimum order is $50.

THAT FISH PLACE

237 CENTERVILLE RD.
LANCASTER, PA 17603
800-233-3829
717/299-5691
FAX: 717/295-7210

Catalog: $2
Save: up to 50%
Pay: check, MO, MC, V
Sells: aquarium and fish supplies
Store: same address; Monday to Thursday
10–8, Friday and Saturday 10–9, Sunday
12–5

$$$$ ☎ ♦ 🇺🇸 (see text)

We learned about That Fish Place from an aquarium hobbyist, who praised the company's selection, pricing, and service. That Fish Place has been selling aquarium supplies since 1973, and stocks the works: aquariums, air pumps, cleaners, feeders, filters, lighting, heaters, fish food, medication, plants, ornaments, water conditioners, and much more. Supplies for dogs and cats are also sold.

That Fish Places publishes a 178-page catalog, which is packed with everything from acclimators to worm feeders, from such manufacturers as Aquanetics, Blue Ribbon, Driftwood Arts, Eheim, Fritz, Hagen, Hikari, Iwaki, MarineLand, Penn Plax, Tetra, Whisper, and Zema. The catalog also features several pages of items for ponds—filters, plants, fountains, etc.—as well as supplies for birds, cats, and dogs. Scores of books on fish species and care are available, and the catalog includes information that can help you determine what might be ailing your fish or aquarium. As our reader said, the discounts are excellent—up to 50% on list—and quarterly sales brochures can save you even more.

That Fish Place will send its catalog (usually $2) to WBMC readers free of charge, so be sure to mention this book when you requesting the catalog. This WBMC reader offer expires February 1, 1993.

Special Factors: Price quote by phone or letter; Authorized, unused returns are accepted (a 15% restocking fee may be charged); minimum order is $15 for dry goods, $25 for live plants; orders are shipped worldwide.

TOMAHAWK LIVE TRAP COMPANY

P.O. BOX 323-WBM
TOMAHAWK, WI 54487
715/453-3550
FAX: 715/453-4705

Catalog: $3.95 (see text)
Save: up to 50%
Pay: check, MO, MC, V
Sells: humane animal traps
Store: Tomahawk, WI; Monday to Friday 8–5; also Coburn Company, Whitewater, WI; and Plow & Hearth, Orange, VA

$$$ ☎ ♣ ▦

Tomahawk's box traps are used by the U.S. Army Medical Corps, state and federal conservation departments, dog wardens, universities, and others who want to catch a critter without endangering its pelt or life. It may be ironical that the founders of this firm once operated a fur farm, and developed the traps to cope with their own runaways. The success of the traps put an end to the farm, a conclusion that should please animal-rights activists.

Tomahawk, which was established in 1930, makes traps for 58 different animals. They'll help you trap everything from mice (about $13) to large dogs (about $172), as well fish and turtles, birds, beavers, grackles, raccoons, skunks, bobcats, jackrabbits, and cats. There are rigid and collapsible styles, transfer cages, station wagon and carrying cages, several with sliding doors (for shipping animals), and special sizes can be made to order. You can order the comprehensive, 56-page catalog ($3.95), which includes tips on trapping animals, a list of common foods that can be used to lure over 20 species, and trap dimensions and specifications. If you're familiar with the firm's traps, you can send a self-addressed, stamped envelope for the brochure and price list only.

Special Factors: Price quote by phone or letter; quantity discounts of 50% are available on orders of six or more of the same trap; C.O.D. orders are accepted.

UNITED PHARMACAL COMPANY, INC.

P.O. BOX 969, DEPT. WBM
ST. JOSEPH, MO 64502
816/233-8800
FAX: 816/233-9696

Catalog: free
Save: up to 50%
Pay: check, MO, MC, V, AE, Discover
Sells: vet, kennel, and pet supplies
Store: 3705 Pear St., St. Joseph, MO;
  Monday to Friday 7:30–6, Saturday
  7:30–5

$$$$ ☎ 🍁 ▀

UPCO, established in 1952, publishes a 160-page catalog of thousands of products for dogs, cats, birds, and horses. The stock runs from hay racks to catnip-filled fur fish, making UPCO a valuable source for both pet owners and professionals.

UPCO's veterinary line includes antibiotics, wormers, medical instruments, nutritional supplements, skin treatments, insecticides, grooming aids, and related goods. Horse owners should check the dozen pages of medications and supplements, farrier supplies, and tack. Dog and cat owners will appreciate the savings on leashes and leads, collars, feeders, books, toys, feeding dishes and stations, pet doors, and other goods. Professional groomers should note the selection of grooming products for show dogs. UPCO also has a selection of bird cages and supplies and some products for hamsters, gerbils, guinea pigs, ferrets, and rabbits. The manufacturers represented include Absorbine, Borden, Dubl Duck, Farnam, Happy Jack, Lambert Kay, Nylabone, Oster, St. Aubrey, and Zema, to note a few. And hundreds of books and manuals are available that cover the care and breeding of a variety of animals.

Canadian readers, please note: Payment must be made in U.S. funds, and vaccines are not shipped to Canada.

Special Factors: Quantity discounts are available; C.O.D. orders are accepted; returns are accepted within 20 days; minimum order is $10.

WHOLESALE VETERINARY SUPPLY, INC.

**P.O. BOX 2256
ROCKFORD, IL 61131
800-435-6940**

Catalog: free
Save: up to 50%
Pay: check, MO, MC, V
Sells: vet, livestock, and pet supplies
Store: 4801 Shepherd Trail, Rockford, IL;
Monday to Friday 8–6, Saturday 8–4

$$$ ☎ ♦ ▰

Wholesale Veterinary Supply publishes a 112-page catalog that offers several thousand products for cats, dogs, rabbits, cattle, and horses, at prices of up to 40% on full retail. Wholesale Veterinary Supply was established in 1971, and it keeps abreast of new developments in research and preventive medicine.

The firm's professional products include vaccines and biologicals, nutritional supplements, surgical instruments, and grooming tools and preparations. In addition, Wholesale Veterinary's catalog offers cages and carriers, leashes and leads, flea and tick treatments, and a wide range of other products for pets and livestock (cattle, swine, sheep, and poultry). Reference works on veterinary care are available, as well as a collection of videotapes on equestrian topics. You'll also find leather-care products, flashlights, knives, disinfectants and cleaning products, work shoes and boots, and related goods. Well-known manufacturers—Absorbine, Andis, Farnam, Fortex, Holiday, Lambert Kay, Oster, Roche, Sergeant's, Shaw's, WAHL—are represented, as well as hard-to-find labels and imports.

Special Factors: Price quote by phone or letter; C.O.D. orders are accepted; authorized returns are accepted within 30 days; vaccines and biologicals are sent where ordinances permit; minimum order is $30.

SEE ALSO

Cabela's Inc. • dog beds; hunting dog training equipment • *SPORTS*
Central Tractor Farm & Family Center • livestock handling equipment; vet products • *FARM*
Defender Industries, Inc • pet life preservers • *AUTO*
Gander Mountain, Inc. • hunting and fishing gear • *SPORTS*
Gohn Bros. • horse blankets • *CLOTHING*
Mellinger's Inc. • live pest controls, fly traps, bird feeders, etc. • *FARM*
Weston Bowl Mill • bird feeders and bird calls • *GENERAL MERCHANDISE*

APPLIANCES, AUDIO, TV, AND VIDEO

Major, small, and personal-care appliances; sewing machines and vacuum cleaners; audio components and personal stereo; TV and video equipment

The firms in this chapter offer every conceivable electronic or battery-run device, including white goods (washers, dryers, refrigerators, and ranges), brown goods (TVs, air conditioners, etc.), small kitchen and personal-care appliances, pocket calculators, phones and phone machines (autodialers, answerers, line switchers, etc.), sewing machines, vacuum cleaners, and floor machines. Some of these companies also sell blank audiotapes and videotapes, luggage, cameras, typewriters, computers, pens, and video games. Thanks to stiff price competition across the country, discounts routinely run from 15% to 40%—more on extremely popular brands, and less on high-end audio and video components.

While the price is important, it's just one of many purchase considerations. You may improve your decisions with help from the Better Business Bureau, which publishes a number of "Booklets on Wise Buying". Pamphlets on appliance service contracts, air conditioning, home computers, microwave ovens, phones, and video equipment are all available. You can get them from your local BBB, or send a stamped, self-addressed envelope for the complete listing of pamphlets and an order form to the Council of Better Business Bureaus, Inc., 4200 Wilson Blvd., Suite 800, Arlington, VA 22203, Attn.: Publications Dept.

Consumer Reports magazine is valuable for its monthly reviews of name-brand products, as well as its yearly *Buying Guide,* which summarizes scores of the reviews. In addition to dispassionate assessments of product performance and guides to features, the CR reviews often include both suggested list and "benchmark" retail selling prices. *Consumer Reports* also features news on product recalls, deceptive selling practices, health issues, money management, and related topics of concern to every consumer. For subscription information, see the current issue or write to Consumers Union, 256 Washington St., Mount Vernon, NY 10553.

Manufacturers of appliances and electronics are also a source of information, since most publish brochures on specific models, which they'll send upon request. You can often find the manufacturers' address on product packaging, and the consumer contacts and addresses of hundreds of major corporations are listed in *Consumer's Resource Handbook,* which is available from the Consumer Information Center (see the listing in "Books").

Planning to purchase a refrigerator, freezer, or air conditioner? The Association of Home Appliance Manufacturers (AHAM) publishes guides to the features and specifications of refrigerators and freezers in the *Consumer Selection Guide for Refrigerators and Freezers*. Air conditioners are examined in *Consumer Selection Guide for Room Air Conditioners,* which includes the "Cooling Load Estimate Form." This worksheet will help you determine how many BTUs your home or room requires, something you should find out *before* you decide on the model you want. Send a check or money order for $1.50 for each title requested to AHAM, Public and Consumer Relations Dept., 20 N. Wacker Dr., Chicago, IL 60606.

Since even small appliances and light bulbs can consume large amounts of energy over time, determining how much power you're using when you flip the switch will help you figure out wise use of the appliances you own—and help you make energy-efficient purchases in the future. To compute the hourly cost of an appliance, find its *wattage* and divide that figure by 1,000 to find the *kilowattage,* which you can multiply by the price of a *kilowatt hour* (kWh) charged by your utility company. (The wattage of an appliance can usually be found in the same place as its model and serial number, or can be obtained through the manufacturer.) For example, a 600-watt vacuum cleaner has a kilowattage of 0.6 (600 divided by 1,000). Run in New York City, where the price per kilowatt hour is 12.4303¢, the operating cost per hour is 7.46¢. If you have cheaper rates at night, reserve as much high-consumption use (ironing, running the dishwasher and dryer, self-cleaning the oven) for evening hours.

In addition to price and energy consumption, try to find out as much as possible about a product's repair record before you buy. *Consumer Reports* periodically undertakes surveys of repair shops, and reveals which brands seem to be turning up most frequently. Unfortunately, models in the same line can vary widely in performance, so undifferentiated reviews of brands may not provide accurate reflections of individual models. But you can conduct your own interviews: Workers at appliance repair centers usually know about lemons and troublesome brands, and will often share their information. And don't overlook your friends, who are probably happy to share both their horror stories and the tales of their best buys.

The next-best thing to keeping something out of the shop is having it in, under warranty. The electronics boom of the mid-1980s has helped to popularize the sale of service contracts (erroneously termed "extended warranties"), which kick in when the manufacturers' warranties expire. Extended warranties are often pushed on big-ticket items at the point of sale on in-store purchases, but they're also sold by mail-order vendors. (Some credit-card companies provide similar protections, free of charge, for products purchased with their cards.) Extended warranties are honored by the seller, not the manufacturer, at the seller's repair center. Are they worth the money? According to one analyst who examined the warranties, service contracts, and repair records of color TVs, air conditioners, refrigerators, washers, and ranges in a National Science Foundation/MIT study, the answer is no. The bottom line is price: In many cases, the *probable* repair bill is lower than the cost of the service contract. But if you've had a post-warranty appliance breakdown, you may feel that a contract is worthwhile insurance. If you decide to buy one, get answers to these questions:

- Does the service contract duplicate the manufacturer's warranty coverage?
- Does the service contract cover parts and labor?
- Is the company selling the contract stable, and is its service department reputable? (Contact the local Better Business Bureau for information on its record.)
- Could you troubleshoot or repair the appliance yourself? Contact the manufacturer (many have 800 lines staffed by technicians who can provide advice on making repairs) or your local repair center before bringing in a malfunctioning product—it may be something you could fix at home.
- What's your *own* history of appliance and electronics breakdowns? If machines seem to enjoy long and healthy lives in your care, you may not need the insurance.

Good maintenance and care will help extend a product's performance. VCRs, which appear susceptible to breakdown, will work better longer if you keep the heads clean, ease wear and tear by using a rewinder, and follow the manufacturers' use and care instructions carefully. Audio components also reward good treatment, and you'll find a battery of cleaning solutions and devices for LPs and CDs available from The Audio Advisor, Lyle Cartridges, and several other firms in this chapter.

If you run into trouble with a *major appliance* and can't get it resolved, you may be able to get help from the Major Appliance Consumer Action Panel (MACAP). MACAP, which is sponsored by AHAM (see above), can request action from a manufacturer and make recommendations for resolution of the complaint. (The Panel's advice is not binding, but it resolves over 80% of the cases it handles.) You can turn to MACAP with problems about dishwashers, ranges, microwave ovens, washers, dryers, refrigerators, freezers, garbage disposals, trash compactors, air conditioners, water heaters, and dehumidifiers. If your complaint concerns one of these appliances, and your attempts to get the problem resolved with the seller and the manufacturer have been futile, write to Major Appliance Consumer Action Panel, 20 N. Wacker Dr., Chicago, IL 60606. Your letter should state the manufacturer's name, model number of the appliance, and date purchased, and should include *copies* of relevant receipts and correspondence. You can also call 800-621-0477 for information.

Grey-market (parallel-import) products are sometimes sold by appliance discounters, but we've made every effort to avoid listing grey-marketers. (For more on the issue, see the chapter introduction of "Cameras.")

For listings of additional firms selling appliances and electronics, see "General Merchandise," "Office" (including the "Computing" subchapter), and "Tools."

FIND IT FAST

APPLIANCES • **Bernie's, Cole's, Dial-A-Brand, Harry's, LVT, Percy's, Irv Wolfson**

AUDIO • **Audio Advisor, Bernie's, Crutchfield, Harry's, Illinois Audio, J & R, Lyle Cartridges, S & S Sound City, Wholesale Tape, Wisconsin Discount**

OFFICE MACHINES AND PHONES • **Crutchfield, J & R, LVT, Percy's, S & S Sound City**

SEWING MACHINES • *Derry's, Discount Appliance, LVT, Sewin' in Vermont, Singer Sewing Center, Suburban Sew 'N Sweep*
TV AND VIDEO • *Bernie's, Cole's, Crutchfield, Dial-A-Brand, Harry's, J & R, LVT, S & S Sound City, Wisconsin Discount*
VACUUM CLEANERS • *AAA-All Factory, ABC Vacuum Cleaner, Bernie's, Derry's, Discount Appliance, Harry's, LVT, Midamerica, Oreck, Singer Sewing Center, Irv Wolfson*

AAA-ALL FACTORY, INC.

**241 CEDAR
ABILENE, TX 79601
915/677-1311**

Flyer: $2, refundable
Save: up to 75%
Pay: check, MO, MC, V, Discover
Sells: vacuum cleaners, floor shampooers and polishers
Store: same address; Monday to Friday 8:30–5

$$$ ☎ ♦ ▅

You can save on some of the best names in the cleaning business at AAA-All Factory, which offers discounts of up to 75% on list prices. AAA has been in business since 1975, and sells supplies and accessories as well as floor machines.

The latest models in canister, upright, convertible, and mini vacuums are available, by Eureka, Filter Queen, Hoover, Kirby, Oreck, Panasonic, Regina, Rexair (the Rainbow), Royal, Sanitaire, and Tri-Star. Both home and commercial lines of vacuum cleaners, floor buffers, and rug shampooers are stocked, and bags and belts for machines by these makers are also available. The flyer we reviewed also featured Singer's Magic Press ironer, and a listing of very inexpensive reconditioned Kirby vacuum cleaners.

Canadian readers, please note: Only U.S. funds are accepted.

Special Factors: Satisfaction is guaranteed; price quote by phone or letter; layaway plan is available; C.O.D. orders are accepted; returns are accepted within 10 days; orders are shipped worldwide.

ABC VACUUM CLEANER WAREHOUSE

6720 BURNET RD., WM91
AUSTIN, TX 78757
512/459-7643

Price List: free
Save: up to 50%
Pay: check, MO, MC, V, AE, Discover
Sells: vacuum cleaners
Store: same address; Monday to Friday 9–6,
Saturday 9–5

$$$ ☎ ▩

ABC purchases from overstocked distributors and passes the savings—up to 50% on the suggested retail or usual selling price—on to you. ABC has been in business since 1977, and sells machines by Filter Queen, Hoover, Kirby, Oreck, Panasonic, Riccar, Royal, Thermax, and Tri-Star. The popular Rainbow, by Rexair, is sold at a discount, as well as all of its accessories and parts. And top-of-the-line Eureka and Hoover machines are available, as well as built-in cleaning systems. See the price list for bags, filters, and accessories and attachments for selected models. ABC also offers repair services by mail—call for information if you're having trouble getting your machine repaired locally.

Special Factors: Price quote by phone or letter; no seconds or rebuilt models are sold; C.O.D. orders are accepted.

THE AUDIO ADVISOR, INC.

225 OAKES S.W.
GRAND RAPIDS, MI 49503
800-669-4434
616/451-3868
FAX: 616/451-0709

Catalog: SASE (see text)
Save: up to 20% (see text)
Pay: MO, MC, V, AE, Discover
Sells: high-end audio components
Store: mail order only

 $$ ☎ 🍁 ▩

The Audio Advisor sells high-end audio components—no video—and stocks many hard-to-find audio items. The firm has been satisfying the needs of audiophiles since 1979, at discounts of up to 20%. (We've bent our "30% minimum" requirement here, since this is "deep discounting" in the high end of audio.) Terms of the sales policy are spelled out clearly in The Audio Advisor's brochure, and the firm's staff welcomes any questions you may have. *No grey-market goods are sold here.*

The Audio Advisor sells state-of-the-art audio equipment, including CD players, turntables, digital processors, tuners, receivers, amps, preamps, speakers, headphones, and the cables and connectors needed to create a superlative system. And since maintenance is critical with more sensitive, high-end equipment, the Advisor offers a full range of care products: Tweek, LAST cleaners, vacuum tubes, CD and laser lens cleaners, and VPI and Nitty Gritty record-cleaning machines. Dedicated audiophiles are concerned about power spikes, and protect their equipment with line filters, surge suppressors, and power regulators—all of which are sold here. And the Audio Advisor even provides a selection of recordings (LP and CD) to do justice to your investment in equipment, from such labels as Chesky, Delos, Dorian, Mobile Fidelity, Proprius, Reference, Sheffield Labs, Telarc, Water Lily, and Wilson Audio.

Special Factors: Price quote by phone or letter; *please do not call for the catalog.*

BERNIE'S DISCOUNT CENTER, INC.

**821 SIXTH AVE., D-5
NEW YORK, NY 10001-
6305
212/564-8758
212/564-8582
FAX: 212/564-3894**

Catalog: $1, refundable (see text)
Save: 30% average
Pay: check, MO, MC, V, AE, Optima (see text)
Sells: appliances, TV and audio components, office machines
Store: same address; Monday to Friday 9–5:30, Saturday (except July and August) 11–3:30

$$$ ☎ 🍁(see text)

Bernie's has been in business since 1948, and sells "pluggables"— everything from electric brooms to fax machines—at 10% to 15% above dealers' cost (an average of 30% off list). Although a catalog is available for $1 (refundable with a purchase), it shows just a smattering of the stock at Bernie's, and you're better off calling for a price quote. One of the city's best sources for discounted electronics and appliances, Bernie's tries to carry the top-rated goods listed in popular buying guides, and *Bernie's does not handle grey-market goods.*

Bernie's offers electronics (audio, TV, and video equipment) by Aiwa, Brother, Fisher, JVC, Mitsubishi, Panasonic, Quasar, RCA, Ricoh, SCM, Sony, and Toshiba. White and brown goods (shipped in the New York City area only) are available, as well as microwave ovens and small and personal-care appliances (shipped nationwide) by Airtemp, Amana, Bionaire, Black & Decker, Braun, Caloric, Clairol, Eureka, Farberware, G.E., Hamilton Beach, Hitachi, Hoover, Hotpoint, Interplak, Jenn-Air, KitchenAid, Krups, Magic Chef, Maytag, Mr. Coffee, Modern Maid, Norelco, Oster, Panasonic, Presto, Remington, Sanyo, Simac, Sunbeam, Sylvania, Tappan, Teledyne (Water Pik and Instapure), Toastmaster, Wearever, Welbilt, West Bend, Whirlpool, White-Westinghouse, and other manufacturers.

Please note: Purchases charged to American Express cards are shipped to billing addresses only, and MasterCard and VISA are accepted for *in-store* purchases only.

Canadian readers, please note: Orders are shipped to Canada via UPS only.

Special Factors: Price quote by phone or letter; store is closed Saturdays in July and August.

COLE'S APPLIANCE & FURNITURE CO.

**4026 LINCOLN AVE.
CHICAGO, IL 60618
312/525-1797**

Information: price quote
Save: up to 40%
Pay: check, MO, MC, V, Discover
Sells: appliances and home furnishings
Store: same address; Monday and Thursday 9:30–9, Tuesday, Friday, and Saturday 9:30–5:30 (closed Wednesday and Sunday)

$$ ☎

Cole's, founded in 1946, sells electronics (TV and video), appliances, and home furnishings at discounts of up to 40%. If you're pricing something from a major manufacturer, call Cole's for a price quote—

especially if you live in the mid-West and are trying to save on shipping costs.

Special Factor: Price quote by phone or letter.

CRUTCHFIELD CORPORATION

I CRUTCHFIELD PARK, DEPT. WH CHARLOTTESVILLE, VA 22906-6020
800-336-5566

Catalog: free (see text)
Save: up to 55%
Pay: check, MO, MC, V, AE, CB, CHOICE, DC, Discover, Optima
Sells: car and home stereo components, video products, and phone equipment
Store: same address; also 153 South Main St., Harrisonburg, VA; Monday to Saturday 10–6, Friday 10–8, both locations

$$$$ ☎ ♦ ▆

Crutchfield publishes an informative, 120-page catalog of home and car audio components and video equipment that's loaded with buying tips and product specifications on featured goods, which Crutchfield prices at up to 55% below list price. Crutchfield's other catalogs, "Personal Office," a collection of electronics for home office and small business, and "Security," 20 pages of security devices for home and car, are great resources for anyone shopping for these goods. In fact, we shopped for a fax machine recently and found Crutchfield's catalog more helpful in comparing features than the articles in service magazines. Crutchfield's prices on the models we were shopping were quite competitive, even compared to New York City discounters. And good prices are just one of the pluses—Crutchfield backs everything it sells with a guarantee of satisfaction, and the staff can provide extensive support. Installation walk-throughs over the phone, car stereo kits for genuinely customized audio installation, and consumer service manuals are among the benefits of buying here. Crutchfield, which was established in 1974, is a factory-authorized repair station for most brands, and *does not sell grey-market goods*.

Crutchfield's car audio components line, which includes equipment for pickup trucks and hatchbacks, features goods by Alphasonik, AR, Carver, Cerwin Vega, Clarion, Infinity, JBL, Jensen, JVC, Pioneer,

Proton, Pyle, Sanyo, Sherwood, and Sony. Crutchfield also sells radar detectors, CB radios, and scanners by BEL, Cobra, Midland, and Whistler, as well as dozens of types of car antennas, and Crimestopper alarm systems to protect it all.

The home audio portion of the catalog includes pages of features comparisons of current models of receivers, CD players, cassette decks, and speakers, and shows amps, tuners, turntables, cartridges, equalizers, portable and personal audio, headphones, remote controls, speaker stands, cassette cabinets, and Discwasher maintenance products. The brands include Advent, AR, Audio-Technica, Bose, Cerwin Vega, Dual, Infinity, JVC, Kenwood, NHT, Ortofon, Phillips, Pioneer, Proton, Shure, and Sony. You'll also find camcorders and video components from JVC, Phillips, Pioneer, and Sony offered here.

Crutchfield's "Personal Office" catalog offers PCs and peripherals, fax machines, word processors, transcribers, personal copiers, phone machines, and related office equipment and supplies—all sold at a discount. The brands include AT&T, Canon, Cobra, Epson, Everex, Franklin, Hewlett-Packard, Logitech, Panasonic, PhoneMate, Ricoh, Sharp, Sony, Sota, and Tatung. Popular business software for DOS systems is also available at savings of up to 40% on list prices.

The newest Crutchfield catalog, "Security," offers well-chosen security products for home and car. You'll find locks, motion-sensing lights, whole-house security systems, smoke detectors and fire extinguishers, and auto anti-theft devices and systems by Audiovox, Crimestopper, DesignTech, Dicon, Espion, First Alert, Schlage, Serpico, Universal, and X-10. The catalog is packed with tips on evaluating and installing security devices, which should free you from the costly clutches of a professional security company.

Please note: The Crutchfield catalogs are free to readers of this book. Be sure to identify yourself as a WBMC reader when you request your copy, and specify the catalog you want by name: "Audio/Video," "Personal Office," or "Security."

Overseas customers: Request an "International Order Fact Sheet."

Special Factors: Satisfaction is guaranteed; shipping is included; returns are accepted within 30 days; orders are shipped worldwide (via Federal Express).

DERRY'S SEWING CENTER

**430 ST. FERDINAND
FLORISSANT, MO 63031
314/837-6103**

Brochure: $1 (see text)
Save: up to 40%
Pay: MO, MC, V
Sells: sewing machines and vacuum
   cleaners
Store: same address; Monday to Friday
   10–7, Saturday 10–4

$$ ☎ ♦ ▇

Replacing an outmoded sewing machine will cost less at Derry's, which carries models (sewing and overlock) by Babylock, Necchi, Simplicity, Singer, and Viking. Savings run up to 40%, and parts for new and older machines are available as well. Derry's has been in business since 1979, and provides in-warranty service on the Necchi, Simplicity, and Singer sewing machines. You can send for the brochure ($1 and a long, stamped, self-addressed envelope), but if you know the model you want, it's easier to call for a price quote. Derry's also sells Panasonic vacuum cleaners and bags.

Special Factors: Price quote by phone or letter; orders are shipped worldwide.

DIAL-A-BRAND, INC.

**57 S. MAIN ST.
FREEPORT, NY 11520
516/378-9694**

Information: price quote
Save: 30% average
Pay: check, MO, MC, V
Sells: appliances, TVs, and video equipment
Store: same address; Monday to Saturday
   9–6

$$ ☎

Dial-a-Brand, which was founded in 1967, has earned the kudos of institutions and individuals with its wide range of appliances and popular electronics. Dial-a-Brand offers discounts averaging 30%, and does not sell grey-market goods. Call of write for prices on air conditioners, TVs, video equipment, microwave ovens, and large appliances. Dial-a-Brand ships chiefly within the New York/New

Jersey/Connecticut area, but deliveries are made nationwide. (Note that freight charges may offset savings on outsized or heavy items shipped long distances—be sure to get a firm quote or estimate before you place your order.)

Special Factors: Price quote by phone or letter; returns are accepted for exchange if goods are defective or damaged in transit; minimum order is $100.

DISCOUNT APPLIANCE CENTERS

2908 HAMILTON ST.
HYATTSVILLE, MD 20782
301/559-6802

Information: price quote
Save: up to 60%
Pay: check, MO, MC, V, AE, CHOICE, DC
Sells: vacuum cleaners and sewing machines
Store: mail order only

Discount Appliance Centers offers sewing machines, vacuum cleaners, and accessories and supplies for both at good discounts. The firm has been in business since 1965, and doesn't have a catalog—please *write* for prices and availability information, since quotes are given over the phone as staff time permits.

Discount Appliance Centers offers the latest models in vacuum cleaners by Airway, Electrolux, Eureka, Filter Queen, Hoover, Kirby, Mastercraft, Oreck, Panasonic, Royal, Sanitaire, and Tri-Star, as well as bags, belts, and attachments. Write for prices on sewing machines by Bernina, Consew, Elna, Juki, Necchi, New Home, Pfaff, Riccar, Singer, and Viking.

Discount Appliance Centers is offering readers of this book a 10% discount on all orders (deducted from the goods total only). Identify yourself as a WBMC reader when you order. This WBMC reader discount expires February 1, 1993.

Special Factors: Price quote by letter only with SASE; minimum order is $25.

HARRY'S DISCOUNTS & APPLIANCES CORP.

**8701-18TH AVE.
BROOKLYN, NY 11214
718/236-3507
FAX: 718/236-5150**

Information: price quote
Save: 30% average
Pay: check, MO, MC, V
Sells: electronics and appliances
Store: same address; Monday to Friday
9–5:30

$$

Harry's, founded in 1952, stocks a wide range of appliances and electronics at savings that average 30% and doesn't sell grey-market goods. Harry's can deliver every Hitachi line, Sony TVs, and small appliances and air conditioners by Black & Decker, Emerson, G.E., Hitachi, Oster, Sunbeam, Toastmaster, and other manufacturers. Fisher audio components, Eureka vacuum cleaners, and many other appliances and electronics lines are stocked as well.

Special Factors: Price quote by phone; outsized items are shipped by truck only within the five boroughs of New York City, Long Island, and parts of New Jersey.

ILLINOIS AUDIO, INC.

**12 E. DELAWARE PL.
CHICAGO, IL 60611
800-621-8042
312/664-0020**

Price List: free
Save: up to 40%
Pay: MO, MC, V
Sells: audio and video equipment and components
Store: mail order only

$$$ ☎

Illinois Audio has been selling audio components since 1971, and sums up its competitive position on the price list: "If You See a Better Price, Call Us!" Illinois Audio discounts components 20% to 40%, and does not sell grey-market goods. The price list itemizes a fraction of the available goods, which include car and home components by ADC, Aiwa, AKG, Alison, AR, Audio Source, Audio-Technica, Azden, DBX, Dual, JBL, Jensen (auto audio), JVC, Kenwood, Koss, Marantz, Monster Cable, Panasonic, Pioneer, Onkyo, Sansui, Sennheiser,

Sherwood, Shure, Sony, Teac, Technics, and Wharfdale. Blank audiotape and videotape from Fuji, Maxell, Sony, and TDK are available in cases (ten cassettes). Illinois Audio's sales policy is stated clearly in its brochure.

Special Factors: Price quote by phone or letter; all goods are new, shipped in factory-sealed cartons with U.S. manufacturers' warranties; authorized returns are accepted (a restocking fee may be charged).

J & R MUSIC WORLD

59-60 QUEENS-
 MIDTOWN
 EXPRESSWAY
MASPETH, NY 11378
800-221-8180
718/417-3737
212/732-8600
FAX: 718/497-1719

Catalog: free
Save: up to 50%
Pay: check, MO, MC, V, AE, Discover
Sells: audio, video, computers, small appliances, etc.
Store: 23 Park Row, New York, NY; Monday to Saturday 9–6:30, Sunday 10–5

$$$ ☎

We know a number of bargain hunters who swear by J & R over all other New York City electronics discounters: J & R has deep discounts and selection, especially in the audio and video departments, and the service department is generally considered very good.

You can call for the catalog or price quotes on current lines of TVs, VCRs and video equipment, audio components and equipment, computers and peripherals, phones, fax machines, radar detectors, cameras, personal appliances, and even pens and watches. Every major brand name is represented here, from Acoustic research to Yamaha, and everything sold by J & R is guaranteed to be brand new and factory fresh.

Special Factors: Satisfaction is guaranteed; price quote by phone or letter; minimum order is $25.

LVT PRICE QUOTE HOTLINE, INC.

■

BOX 444-W92
COMMACK, NY 11725-
0444
800-582-8884
516/234-8884

Brochure: free
Save: up to 30%
Pay: check, MO, certified check
Sells: appliances, vacuum cleaners,
electronics, and office machines
Store: mail order only

$$ ☎

LVT, established in 1976, gives you instant access to over 4,000 products from over 75 manufacturers, at savings of up to 30% on suggested list or full retail prices. The brochure includes a roster of available brands, and price quotes are given on individual items. *LVT does not sell grey-market goods.*

First read LVT's brochure for details on ordering and shipping policies, then call with the manufacturer's name and exact model number for a price quote on major appliances, bread-making machines, microwave ovens, air conditioners, vacuum cleaners, washers and dryers, TVs, video equipment, phones and phone machines, calculators, typewriters, scanners, radar detectors, copiers, fax machines, and word processors.

The brands available include Acme, Admiral, Airtemp, Amana, AT&T, Bearcat, Bel-Tronics, Best, Braun, Caloric, Canon, Carrier, Casio, Cobra, Code-A-Phone, Creda, Dacor, Eagle, Emerson, Eureka, Excellence, Fedders, Fisher, Franke, Freedom Phone, Friedrich, Frigidaire, Gaggenau, G.E., Gibson, Go-Video, Hewlett-Packard, Hitachi, Hoover, Hotpoint, Insinkerator, Jenn-Air, JVC, Kelvinator, KitchenAid, KWC, Leisure, Magic Chef, Maxon, Maytag, Miami Carey, Miele, Mitsubishi, Modern Maid, Mont Blanc, Murata, Panasonic, Phone-Mate, Quasar, Rangaire, RCA, Record a Call, Regency, Ricoh, Rolodex, Roper, Samsung, Sanyo, Scotsman, Sharp, Smith Corona, Sony, Southwestern Bell, Speed Queen, Sterling, Sub-Zero, Sylvania, Tappan, Texas Instruments, Thermador, Toshiba, U-Line, Uniden, Victor, Viking, Welbilt, Whirlpool, Whistler, White-Westinghouse, Wolf, and Zenith.

Special Factors: Price quote by phone or letter; UPS shipping, handling, and insurance are included in quotes; all sales are final; all goods are sold with manufacturers' warranties; phone order lines are open Monday to Saturday 9–6, EST.

LYLE CARTRIDGES

**115 SO. CORONA AVE.
VALLEY STREAM, NY
    11582
800-221-0906
INQUIRIES AND NY
    ORDERS 516/599-1112
FAX: 516/561-7793**

Catalog: free with self-addressed, stamped envelope
Save: up to 60%
Pay: check, MO, MC, V, AE, Discover, Optima
Sells: phono cartridges, replacement styli, and accessories
Store: same address; Monday to Friday 9–5

$$$$ ☎ 🍁 ▆

Lyle Cartridges has been in business since 1952 and is one of the best sources we've found for the cartridges and replacement styli (factory original) that bring your music to life. If you're sticking by your LPs despite CDs, you'll really appreciate this reliable, well-informed source.

Lyle stocks phono cartridges and replacement styli by Audio Quest, Audio-Technica, Bang & Olufsen, Dynavector, Grado/Signature, Monster Cable, Ortofon, Pickering, Shure, Signet, Stanton, and Sumiko. Record-care products by Discwasher, LAST, and Ortofon are stocked, as well as Tweek's contact enhancer. Lyle is the first source to consult if you have to replace arm parts, since you may be able to save on both labor and material costs. Prices of these parts are up to 60% less than list or comparable retail, and orders are shipped worldwide.

Special Factors: Price quote by phone or letter with self-addressed, stamped envelope; authorized returns are accepted; defective goods are replaced; minimum order is $15, $25 with credit cards.

MIDAMERICA VACUUM CLEANER SUPPLY CO.

666 UNIVERSITY AVE.
ST. PAUL, MN 55104-4896
612/222-0763
FAX: 612/224-2674

Information: Price quote
Save: 25% plus
Pay: check, MO, MC, V, AE, Discover, Optima
Sells: vacuum cleaners, floor machines, and appliance parts
Store: same address; Monday to Friday 9–5:30, Saturday 9–3

Midamerica, which was established in 1952, also sells vacuum cleaners and floor machines at up to 50% below list. Midamerica used to publish an enormous catalog of appliance parts and supplies, and even though it's no longer available, the firm is a valuable source for the do-it-yourself appliance owner who knows what part is needed for a repair.

Call or write for a price quote on parts and accessories for vacuum cleaners, floor machines, blenders, coffee makers, irons, shavers, mixers, pressure cookers, and toasters. Brand-new vacuum cleaners by Avac, Beam, Bissell, Eureka, Hoover, MagNuM, Mastercraft, Optumus, Oreck, Panasonic, Progress (Mercedes), Rexair (Rainbow), Royal, Sharp, Shop-Vac, and Simplicity are available, as well as central vacuum systems, bags, belts, lights, and related products.

Special Factors: Price quote by phone or letter; quantity discounts are available; consult your appliance manual before attempting repairs; minimum order is $15; orders are shipped worldwide.

ORECK CORPORATION

100 PLANTATION RD.
NEW ORLEANS, LA
70123-9989
504/733-8761
FAX: 504/733-6709

Catalog: free
Save: up to 25%
Pay: check, MO, MC, V, AE, DC
Sells: vacuum cleaners, rug shampooers, and supplies
Store: mail order only

$

Oreck, established in 1963, makes excellent floor machines that are used extensively by hotels and institutions. In addition to vacuum cleaners and floor polishers, the 16-page catalog offers useful housewares and appliances.

Oreck's best-selling vacuum cleaner, the XL988, is a powerful, eight-pound upright with an effective edge-cleaning device and a 25-foot cord. The "top-fill" mechanism keeps the vacuum operating at optimum suction until the bag is completely full, and it's designed to be repaired by the user—replacement parts are available. Oreck also sells a "hypoallergenic power team" tank vacuum with a filtration system, mini-vacs with disposable dust bags, a stick/tank convertible vacuum, heavy-duty canister models for commercial and institutional use, rug shampooers, and floor buffers and polishers, as well as bags (in case lots). Oreck's catalogs always feature special buys on its most popular models, which bring the price down 25% or more. And they also offer other useful goods, such power-failure lights, emergency spotlights, air purifiers, kitchen work islands, and multi-band radios (which are not deeply discounted).

Special Factors: Satisfaction is guaranteed; returns are accepted within 30 days.

PERCY'S, INC.

19 GLENNIE ST.
WORCESTER, MA 01605
508/755-5269
FAX: 508/797-5578

Information: price quote
Save: up to 40%
Pay: MO, certified check, MC, V, Discover
Sells: large appliances, audio and TV components, office machines, etc.
Store: same address; Monday to Friday 9–9, Saturday 9–5

$$$ ☎ 🇺🇸 🍁

Percy's has been selling appliances of all types since 1926, at prices 3% above wholesale cost, or up to 40% below list. *Percy's sells no grey-market goods.*

You can call or write for a price quote on washers, dryers, dishwashers, refrigerators, freezers, ranges, standard and microwave ovens, TVs, video equipment and tapes, audio components, copiers, fax machines, radar detectors, dehumidifiers, disposals, and other appliances. The brands available at Percy's include Bose, Caloric, Fisher, Frigidaire, G.E., Hitachi, Hotpoint, Jenn-Air, Litton, Magic Chef, Magnavox, Maytag, Mitsubishi, Panasonic, Quasar, RCA, Sharp, Sub-Zero, Thermador, Toshiba, Whirlpool, White-Westinghouse, and Zenith. Please note that Percy's *does not sell small appliances,* and *does not publish a catalog.*

Special Factor: Price quote by phone or letter.

S & S SOUND CITY

58 W. 45TH ST.
NEW YORK, NY 10036-
 4280
212/575-0210
FAX: 212/221-7907

Brochure: free (see text)
Save: up to 50%
Pay: check, MO, MC, V, Discover
Sells: audio, TV, and video components, phone, and home-office machines
Store: same address; Monday to Friday 9–7, Saturday 9–6

$$ ☎ 🍁 🇺🇸

S & S Sound City has been in business since 1975 selling TVs and video equipment, audio components, radios, telephones, microwave ovens, and air conditioners. The inventory includes goods from AT&T, G.E., Harman Kardon, Hitachi, JVC, Minolta, Mitsubishi, Panasonic, Quasar, RCA, RSharp, Sony, Southwestern Bell, Toshiba, and Yamaha. S & S sent us a holiday brochure that showcased popular gift selections; call or write for a price quote if you're shopping out of season or you don't see the item you want in the brochure.

Special Factors: Price quote by phone or letter; returns are accepted within 7 days; special orders are accepted.

SEWIN' IN VERMONT

84 CONCORD AVE.
ST. JOHNSBURY, VT 05819
800-451-5124
802/748-3803

Brochure and Price List: free
Save: 35% average
Pay: check, MO, MC, V
Sells: sewing machines and accessories
Store: same address; Monday to Friday 9–5, Saturday 9–1

If you're shopping for a name-brand sewing machine or serger but don't want to pay top-of-the-line prices, give Sewin' in Vermont a call. The firm carries several of the best American and European brands at prices 15% to 40% below list: Bernina, Elna, New Home, Singer, and Viking sewing machines, and sergers from various manufacturers. These devices have professional features and can be bought here for less than half the suggested retail, but savings average around 35%. Professional irons and presses are also available. The knowledgeable sales staff can help you choose the right equipment for your needs; call the 800 number for information and price quotes.

Special Factor: Price quote by phone or letter.

SINGER SEWING CENTER OF COLLEGE STATION

**1669 TEXAS AVE.
COLLEGE STATION, TX
77840
800-338-5672
FAX: 409/696-9262**

Brochure: $3 (see text)
Save: 40% average
Pay: MO, MC, V, AE, Discover, Optima
Sells: sewing machines, sergers, and vacuum cleaners
Store: same address; Monday to Thursday 10–8, Friday and Saturday 10–5; also Pittsburg Sewing Machine Warehouse, 602 Broadway, Pittsburg, KS; Monday to Saturday 9–5, Thursday 9–8; Sewing Machine Warehouse, Willowbrook Ct., 17776 Tomball Pkwy., Houston, TX; Monday and Thursday 10–8, Tuesday, Wednesday, Friday, Saturday 10–6

Singer Sewing Center, in business since 1976, sells sewing machines, sergers, and vacuum cleaners. Call for a price quote on models by Babylock, Bernina, Elna, Necchi, Singer, Pfaff, and other well-known manufacturers. All of the machines sold here are new, and layaways are accepted—inquire for information.

Special Factors: Price quote by phone or letter; layaway plan is available; C.O.D. orders are accepted; minimum parts order is $25; orders are shipped worldwide.

SUBURBAN SEW 'N SWEEP, INC.

**8814 OGDEN AVE.
BROOKFIELD, IL 60513
800-642-4056
708/485-2834**

Brochure: free
Save: up to 50%
Pay: check, MO, MC, V, AE, Discover
Sells: sewing machines
Store: same address; Monday to Saturday
9–5

$$ ☎ ▆▆▆

Suburban Sew 'N Sweep, Inc. has been selling sewing machines since 1975, and although a brochure is available, you can call for a price quote on sewing and overlock machines by New Home, Singer, White, and other top brands. Discounts vary from model to model, but run up to 50%. Suburban Sew 'N Sweep is an authorized dealer for several major brands.

Special Factors: Price quote by phone; C.O.D. orders are accepted.

WHOLESALE TAPE AND SUPPLY COMPANY

**P.O. BOX 8277
CHATTANOOGA, TN
37411
800-251-7228
615/894-9427
FAX: 615/894-7281**

Catalog: free
Save: up to 50%
Pay: check, MO, MC, V, AE, Discover
Sells: audio and video tapes, duplication
services, etc.
Store: 2255 Center St., Suite 102,
Chattanooga, TN

Wholesale Tape, which has been selling audio/visual supplies and services worldwide since 1977, publishes a catalog featuring blank audio and video cassettes, reel-to-reel tapes in all configurations, duplicating machines, and accessories. The firm manufactures audio-tapes for professional duplication and six types of tape are available, in clear, white, and black shells (housing), in standard tape lengths (12 to 122 minutes). Custom tape lengths are available, and quantity discounts are offered. Wholesale Tape also sells professional-quality audio and video recording tape from Agfa, Ampex, Maxell, Memorex, and TDK. Tape duplication machines are offered, including models by Sony and Telex.

If you need an audiotape or videotape copied but don't have the necessary equipment, you may be interested in Wholesale Tape's duplicating services. You can have just one copy made, but the best prices are on orders of 50 or more copies. Custom labels can be produced, and cassette boxes, albums, shipping envelopes, and storage units are also sold.

Special Factors: Satisfaction is guaranteed; price quote by phone or letter; quantity discounts are offered; C.O.D. orders are accepted; minimum order is $20; orders are shipped worldwide.

WISCONSIN DISCOUNT STEREO

2417 W. BADGER RD.
MADISON, WI 53713
800-356-9514
608/271-6889

Information: price quote
Save: up to 70%
Pay: MO, MC, V
Sells: audio and video components
Store: same address; Monday to Friday 8–8, Saturday 9–5; also six other locations (see text)

$$ ☎

Wisconsin Discount Stereo, which began doing business by mail in 1977, carries most of the major brands of electronics but doesn't publish a catalog, so you must call for a price quote. WDS offers audio components, portable stereo, car audio, TVs, and video equipment by Aiwa, Bearcat, Blaupunkt, Bose, Brother, Casio, Clarion, Cobra, Craig, Fisher, Hitachi, JVC, Kenwood, Magnavox, Onkyo, Panasonic, Phillips, Pioneer, Quasar, RCA, Sanyo, Seiko, Sharp, Sherwood, Sony, Teac, Toshiba, Zenith, and other manufacturers. The savings can run as high as 70%, but generally average 35%.

Special Factors: Price quote by phone preferred; C.O.D. orders are accepted; returns are accepted within 10 days (a restocking fee may be charged).

IRV WOLFSON COMPANY

3221 W. IRVING PARK RD.
CHICAGO, IL 60618
312/267-7828
FAX: 312/267-7154

Information: price quote
Save: 30% plus
Pay: check, MO, MC, V, Discover
Sells: domestic- and foreign-current appliances, TVs, etc.
Store: same address; Monday and Thursday 9–9, Tuesday, Wednesday, Friday, Saturday 9:30–5:30, Sunday 12–4

$$ ☎

Irv Wolfson Company has been selling 220-volt/50-cycle appliances and electronics since 1953, at prices 7% over cost (an average of 35% to 40% below retail prices). Wolfson also carries domestic-current goods, home furnishings, built-in appliances, Franke sinks, and KWC faucets. but it does not sell grey-market goods. There is no catalog, so you can call for prices on foreign-current TVs and video equipment, white goods, microwave ovens, air conditioners, kitchen appliances, vacuum cleaners, personal-care appliances, electric blankets, and other goods for the home. The brands include Akai, Amana, Caloric, G.E., Grundig, Hitachi, JVC, Magic Chef, Maytag, Modern Maid, Oster, Panasonic, Phillips, Sanyo, Sony, Speed Queen, Sub-Zero, Whirlpool, White-Westinghouse, and other manufacturers. "Stepdown" autotransformers, current converters, and plug adapters are also stocked. The customer service department can help you if you're ordering goods to be used abroad.

Special Factor: Price quote by phone or letter.

SEE ALSO

A Cook's Wares • food processors and other appliances • *HOME: KITCHEN*
Crystal Sonics • auto audio • *AUTO*
Defender Industries, Inc. • marine electronic • *AUTO*
E & B Marine Supply, Inc. • marine electronics • *AUTO*
Fivenson Food Equipment, Inc. • commercial restaurant equipment • *HOME: KITCHEN*

Goldberg's Marine Distributors • marine electronics • *AUTO*

Kaplan Bros. Blue Flame Corp. • Garland commercial stoves • *HOME: KITCHEN*

Main Lamp/Lamp Warehouse • lamps and ceiling fans • *HOME: DECOR*

Skipper Marine Electronics, Inc. • marine electronics • *AUTO*

Solo Slide Fasteners, Inc. • professional irons, steamers, industrial sewing and overlock machines, etc. • *CRAFTS*

Staples, Inc. • office machines, small refrigerators • *OFFICE*

Thread Discount Sales • sergers, overlock machines, and related equipment • *CRAFTS*

Yachtmail Co. Ltd. • marine electronics • *AUTO*

ART, ANTIQUES, AND COLLECTIBLES

Fine art, limited editions, antiques, and collectibles

Buying antiques and collectibles by mail can be something of an adventure, since the wares are usually one-of-a-kind and subject to prior sale. The firms listed here offer everything from Victoriana to fruit crate labels, including patchwork quilts, vintage advertising posters and ephemera, limited-edition porcelain figures and plates, and contemporary posters and graphics. Although buying from "dealer" sources means you're usually getting the piece at a lower price than you'd pay at retail, don't buy with the expectation of reselling at a profit, unless you're sure of what you're doing. Investment potential notwithstanding, the best reason to acquire a piece of art or collectible is for the pleasure of ownership. And be sure to buy antiques from firms that have liberal return policies.

Getting to know the market is one of the pleasures of collecting, and there are hundreds of reference books and guides available to give you the necessary grounding. The indefatigable Kovels compile some of the numerous guides to prevailing market prices for antiques and collectibles, as well as directories of sources for the collector—mail-order dealers, restoration services, publications, and other useful data.

But there's no substitute for old-fashioned legwork when it comes to learning about your field of interest. You can learn volumes by seeing objects firsthand, at flea markets, antique shops, art galleries, museums, and auction previews. And don't just look—*ask questions*. Dealers enjoy an appreciative customer, and will usually share their invaluable tips on the market if you convey appreciation of their wares.

A collection of any merit usually requires the protection of archival quality materials. University Products, Inc. (in the "Packaging" section of "General Merchandise") is an excellent source for display binders, albums, boxes, and restoration materials for art works, books, manuscripts, photographs, textiles, posters, and postcards. The firm's archival products catalog includes goods for mounting, display, and storage.

FIND IT FAST

ANTIQUES • **Antique Imports**
ART BRONZES • **Excalibur**
ENAMELLED BOXES • **Friar's House**
FRUIT CRATE LABELS • **Original Paper Collectibles**
LIMITED EDITION COLLECTIBLES • **Atlantic Bridge, Friar's House, Saxkjaers**
NOSTALGIC PRINTS • **Gallery Graphics**
POSTERS • **Cinema City, Miscellaneous Man, Museum Editions, Rick's Movie Graphics**

ANTIQUE IMPORTS UNLIMITED

**P.O. BOX 2978-WBMC
COVINGTON, LA 70434-
2978
504/892-0014**

Price List: see text
Save: up to 60%
Pay: check, MO, MC, V
Sells: antiques and collectibles
Store: mail order only

Antique Imports, in business since 1981, markets a range of antiques and ephemera through two catalogs. The firm sells at "dealer" prices—up to 60% below what's being charged for comparable goods in antique shops. Don't miss the jewelry listings—the value of the gemstones alone often exceeds the prices of the pieces themselves.

The "Antique and Collectible Jewelry" catalog features old jewelry, charms, and watches, and usually includes exceptional values. A sample copy costs $3, a year's subscription of 10 to 12 issues, $30. The "Antiques and Collectibles" catalog (3 to 5 issues, $3 per copy or $20 for a year of issues) offers glassware, china, metalware, coins, stamps, and related miscellany. The catalogs we reviewed included a late Victorian diamond and ruby snake ring for $305, a Georgian pewter half-pint beer mug with scroll handle for $75, a Scottish letter opener of brass and agate for $30, an Italian 18K gold chain link bracelet with a diamond charm for $70, and a Victorian bisque "pudding doll" for $20. (The catalog notes that the doll, about an inch long, would have been put into a cake and pudding and confer luck—or a broken tooth—on the person who found it.) All of the foregoing are subject to prior sale.

Please note that the catalogs are not illustrated, but Antique Imports Unlimited accepts returns within three days.

Special Factors: All goods are one-of-a-kind items, subject to prior sale; listing second choices is recommended; UPS is *not* used; returns are accepted within 3 days for exchange, refund, or credit; minimum order is $75.

CINEMA CITY

P.O. BOX 1012-HK
MUSKEGON, MI 49443
616/722-7760

Catalog: $3, refundable
Save: 30% average
Pay: check, MO, MC, V
Sells: movie posters and ephemera
Store: mail order only

$$$ ☎ ❦ ▤

Movie posters circa 1975 and later are the specialty at Cinema City, which has been selling to collectors and dealers since 1976. There are thousands of movies listed in the 48-page catalog, from *A Bridge Too Far* ($15 for a set of 12 stills) to *Ziggy Stardust* (27″ by 41″ poster, $25). Press kits, scripts, and lobby cards are available for some of the titles. The catalog is arranged alphabetically by movie title, and includes a glossary of terms and guide to the poster sizes. (Posters are sent rolled if Cinema City received them "flat," but folded materials are stiffened to minimize damage and shipped that way.)

Cinema City adds to its gigantic inventory with each new movie release, and once you're on the mailing list, you'll receive periodic updates—including offerings of autographed posters and photos. While those tend to be pricey—a *Top Gun* poster signed by Tom Cruise fetches $90 at this writing—most of the 27″ by 41″ posters cost about $15, and some are less expensive. In fact, Cinema City usually beats the going rate by at least 30%, and sometimes prices its posters as much as 75% less (savings depend on scarcity and market for a title or item).

While most of the films listed in the catalog we saw were made for the U.S. market, Cinema City does handle materials for foreign films and limited-release items. You can send inquiries on these, as well as queries on films made before 1975, but include a self-addressed, stamped envelope if you want to receive a reply.

Canadian readers, please note: Only U.S. funds are accepted.

Special Factors: Price quote by phone or letter with SASE; orders are shipped worldwide.

EXCALIBUR BRONZE SCULPTURE FOUNDRY

85 ADAMS ST.
BROOKLYN, NY 11201
718/522-3330
FAX: 718/522-0812

Catalog: $10, refundable (see text)
Save: 25% average
Pay: check, MO, MC, V
Sells: art bronze sculptures and furniture
Store: same address

$$$ ☎ ♦ ▬

Excalibur Bronze Sculpture Foundry has been casting the works of sculptors and artists across the country since 1967. (Services include mould making, precision sand and ceramic shell casting, enlarging, chasing, patinating, etc.) But we've listed the firm because of its bronze reproductions of renowned sculptures and its delightful furniture.

For $10, you'll receive a portfolio with three catalogs: "The Excalibur Collection" shows a 20"-tall replica of Rodin's "Burgher of Calais," which costs $1,260 with the discount (regularly $1,800), Antoine-Louis Barge's "Theseus and the Centaur," which costs $1,400 (usually $2,000), and Emile Bourdelle's "Monumental Hand," $840 from $1,200. Scores of reproductions of Remingtons, Art Noveau and Art Deco figures, lamps, vases, and mirrors are shown in "The Decorative Arts Collection," at prices beginning at under $200. And the "Hommage à Diego Collection" shows scores of the type of "art" lamps and cocktail tables featured prominently in shelter magazines—wrought metal bases embellished with birds, leaves, hoofs, turtles, and other playful touches, topped with thick slabs of glass—inspired by the work of Diego Giacometti. There are handsome pieces, including a pair of caryatids (male and female) as lamps and andirons, a neo-Grec "moon lady" topping a torchere, a "shrub with bird" table lamp, and others in abstract forms. Again, prices are serious—from just under $1,000 for a lamp to nearly $10,000 for some of the tables—and that's *with* the discount.

Please note that the $10 catalog/portfolio fee is refundable only with a purchase, but you can call or write directly about specific pieces or custom work.

Excalibur Bronze is offering readers a discount of 30% on all orders. Be sure to identify yourself as a WBMC reader when you order, and deduct the discount from the cost of the goods only. This WBMC reader discount expires February 1, 1993.

Special Factor: Orders are shipped worldwide.

GALLERY GRAPHICS, INC.

227 MAIN ST.
P.O. BOX 502
NOEL, MO 64854
417/475-6116
FAX: 417/475-6494

Catalog: $5, refundable
Save: 50% plus
Pay: check or MO
Sells: art prints and stationery
Store: mail order only

$

Gallery Graphics, in business since 1979, sells reproduction antique prints, note cards, and Christmas cards, which feature nostalgic themes. The firm's "Antique Classic Collection" features copies of sentimental turn-of-the-century lithographs, advertising posters, and magazine illustrations, priced at $2 and $3.25. Nostalgic themes also appear in the line of blank note cards, and memo and tack boards and decorative flue hole covers are also available. The prints may be ordered in shrink wrapping at an additional charge, and many are offered matted and framed. This source is geared to the resale buyer; please note that the minimum order is $100 (on first orders).

Special Factors: Deduct the cost of the catalog from your first order; authorized returns are accepted; minimum first order is $100 ($75 on reorders); orders are shipped worldwide.

MISCELLANEOUS MAN

P.O. BOX 1776-W92
NEW FREEDOM, PA
  17349
717/235-4766
FAX: 717/235-2853

Catalog: $5
Save: up to 75%
Pay: check, MO, MC, V
Sells: rare and vintage posters and labels
Store: mail order only

$$$$ ☎ 🍁 ▤

George Theofiles, ephemerologist extraordinaire, is the moving force behind Miscellaneous Man. He founded his firm in 1970, and trades in vintage posters, handbills, graphics, labels, brochures, and other memorabilia, all of which are original—no reproductions or reprints are sold.

Each Miscellaneous Man catalog offers an average of about a thousand items, including theater and movie publicity materials, collections of colorful product labels, broadsides, and posters. Posters are the strong suit, representing everything from "aviation" to "weaponry": patriotic themes (including both World Wars, other conflicts, and related topics), sports of all sorts, wines and spirits, food advertising, labor, publishing, fashion, African-Americana, the performing arts, and travel, among others themes. Some of the posters are offered mounted on linen or conservation paper, and Mr. Theofiles can refer you to a service if you want your poster mounted after purchase (proper backing helps to preserve the poster, and doesn't detract from its value). Collections of unused broom handle labels, antique seed packets, luggage stickers, cigar box labels, and other such detritus have appeared in previous catalogs. Size and condition are noted in the catalog entries, and photos of individual items may be purchased for $2.

Miscellaneous Man's prices are usually at least 30% below the going rate, and regular customers receive sale catalog with further reductions. If you're about to purchase a vintage poster elsewhere, give Miscellaneous Man a call first. We've found that although the prices are sometimes comparable (especially on scarce or rare posters), Miscellaneous Man can charge 30% to 75% less than New York City sources—and the selection is always much better.

Special Factors: Price quote by phone or letter; stock moves quickly—order promptly and list second choices; layaways are accepted; returns are accepted within 3 days; minimum order is $50 with credit cards.

MUSEUM EDITIONS NEW YORK LTD.

12 HARRISON ST., 3RD FLOOR
NEW YORK, NY 10013
212/431-1913

Catalog: $5, refundable
Save: up to 50%
Pay: check, MO, MC, V
Sells: fine contemporary art reprints
Store: same address; Monday to Friday 9–5 (by appointment only)

$$$ ☎ 🍁 🇺🇸

Museum Editions, established in 1982, produces a stunning 32-page color catalog of reproductions of the posters used to announce exhibits in museums and art galleries. If your taste runs to modern and contemporary art, you'll have a field day deciding what to choose for your walls.

Modern masterpieces by Klee, Pissarro, O'Keeffe, Rothko, Hopper, Hockney, Hiroshige, Glaser, Katz, and Randy Green are among those shown in previous catalogs, along with examples of photography and photorealism, flora and fauna, and other posters depicting scores of varied subjects. Prices average $15 to $25, and custom framing is available; inquire for information.

Special Factors: Catalog is free to corporate buyers (send request on letterhead); cost of catalog is redeemable with retail orders.

ORIGINAL PAPER COLLECTIBLES

700-W CLIPPER GAP RD.
AUBURN, CA 95603

Brochure and Sample Label: free with *long*, self-addressed, stamped envelope
Save: up to 75%
Pay: check or MO
Sells: original, vintage labels
Store: mail order only

$$$ 🍁 🇺🇸

William Wauters began his business in 1970, when fruit crate labels were among the hot collectibles in antique and curio shops nationwide. The fact that Original Paper Collectibles has thrived over the years attests to the enduring appeal of the label designs, as well as a seemingly inexhaustible supply. At this writing, Mr. Wauters offers labels originally intended for brooms, cigar boxes, flour sacks, soda pop, canned fruits and vegetables, and produce—apples, pears, lettuce, oranges, asparagus, lemons, and other fruits and vegetables. Old used stock certificates, all of which have illustrations, are also sold. And collectors of African-Americana will find a selection of nearly a dozen labels depicting black characters.

The collections offer the best per-label prices, and Mr. Wauters tells us that dealers routinely double his prices when they resell. The price list we received described the most popular collection of fruit crate labels that included orange, apple, asparagus, lemon, pear, lettuce, cherry, grape, and carrot varieties—150 for $25, postpaid. (A vintage poster gallery in New York City charges that much for a *single* label.) Sliding discounts of 10% to 35% are given on orders of $100, $250, and $500. If you're searching for a specific label, you may find it among the listings of individual labels, which are grouped by size and type. And if you're looking for something to cover the walls, ask here—decorators are invited to inquire about damaged labels, which can be used as wall treatments!

Please note: Payment for orders should be made to William Wauters, *not* Original Paper Collectibles.

Special Factors: Satisfaction is guaranteed; price quote by letter with SASE; quantity discounts are available; orders are shipped worldwide.

RICK'S MOVIE GRAPHICS, INC.

**P.O. BOX 23709-WM
GAINESVILLE, FL 32602-
3709
904/373-7202**

Catalog: $3
Save: up to 60%
Pay: check, MO, MC, V
Sells: current and vintage movie posters
Store: mail order only

$$$ ☎ ♦ ▤

Today's collectibles become tomorrow's investments—sometimes. The possibilities of appreciation no doubt attract some of the people who buy movie posters, but most of us just want mementos of favorite flicks. Rick's Movie Graphics has been serving both kinds of customers since 1985, and publishes a 96-page, illustrated catalog packed with current releases and "vintage" posters dating back to the 1950s. (Sales catalogs are mailed quarterly.) The listings are coded to indicate whether the posters have been rolled or folded. At an average price of $15 (10% to 30% below the going rate), the new releases deliver a lot of visual bang for the buck. Prices on vintage posters are higher here, but dealers usually charge so much more that the savings through Rick's can reach 30% to 65% in this category.

The catalog we reviewed offered French posters, including *Blue Velvet* and *One Flew Over the Cuckoo's Nest,* British posters of *The Rocky Horror Picture Show,* The Who's *Quadrophenia,* and *No Nukes,* and Belgian posters of *Modern Times* and *Rear Window.* We found *Goldfinger, Funny Girl,* and *Manhattan* among hundreds of titles under the "back in stock" banner, and whole pages devoted to Rocky, Indiana Jones, Star Trek, James Bond, Disney, Batman, Friday the 13th, and other series. The catalog shows just a fraction of the inventory, and new titles and collections are constantly added to stock. If you don't see what you're looking for, send your requests with a self-addressed, stamped envelope.

Please note: Only U.S. funds are accepted.

Special Factors: Price quote by phone or letter; returns are accepted within 5 days for exchange, refund, or credit; orders are shipped worldwide.

COMPANIES OUTSIDE THE U.S.A.

The following firms are experienced in dealing with customers in the U.S. and Canada. We've included them because they offer goods not widely available at a discount in the U.S., because they have a better selection, or because they may offer the same goods at great savings.

Before ordering from any non-U.S. firm, please consult "The Complete Guide to Buying by Mail," page 573, for helpful tips. We recommend paying for orders from foreign firms with a credit card whenever possible, so you'll have some recourse if you don't receive your order. For more information, see "The Fair Credit Billing Act," page 612.

ATLANTIC BRIDGE COLLECTION CORP. LTD.

DEPT. WBM-92
BALLYBANE
GALWAY
IRELAND
011-353-91-53657
FAX: 011-353-91-53443

Catalog: $2
Save: up to 40%
Pay: check, IMO, MC, V, AE, Access
Sells: porcelain collectibles, tableware, crystal, and handcrafts
Store: same address (call for directions)

$$$ ☎ 🍁 ▀

Some of the most popular porcelain figurines and collectibles can be found at Atlantic Bridge Collection, which offers new issues for collectors of Anri, Belleek, Beswick, Coalport, Goebel, Irish Dresden, Lladró, Royal Doulton, Spode, and Wedgwood. Atlantic Bridge, which has been in business since 1972, also sells Royal Crown Derby paperweights and miniature cottages, Beatrix Potter nursery figures, pewter giftware, collectors' tea pots, Caithness paperweights, and Peter Rabbit nurseryware. The 32-page catalog we reviewed showed place settings of selected dinnerware patterns from Aynsley, Minton, Royal Albert, Royal Doulton, and Wedgwood, as well as crystal giftware and suites by Galway, Tipperary, and Waterford. We found especially good values on crystal vases and candlesticks, as well as a delightful collection of Irish specialties and handcrafts that include Claddagh jewelry, gifts engraved with coats of arms, double-damask linen and Nottingham lace tablecloths, and Aran handknits for men and women. Prices are given in U.S. dollars, and bonuses and special discounts are often available.

Special Factors: Satisfaction is guaranteed; price quote by phone or letter; minimum order is $25 with credit cards; orders are shipped worldwide.

THE FRIAR'S HOUSE

BENE'T ST.
CAMBRIDGE CB2 3QA
ENGLAND
011-44-223-60275
FAX: 011-44-223-264110

Catalog: free
Save: 25% average
Pay: check, IMO, MC, V, AE, DC, Access, Optima
Sells: porcelain collectibles, tableware, and handcrafts
Store: same address; Monday to Saturday 9–5:30, Sunday (in summer only) 11–4

The Friar's House publishes a 16-page color catalog that shows highlights of its stock, which includes fine china and crystal place settings and gifts, and a wide range of fine British handcrafts. Lines from Aynsley, Edinburgh, Portmeirion, Royal Brierley, Royal Crown Derby, Royal Doulton, Royal Worcester, Waterford, and Wedgwood are all available. Nursery china—Bunnykins and Beatrix Potter goods from several firms—is also offered.

The Friar's House, which has been in business since 1976, offers some of the most popular lines of collectibles, from Coalport, Lladró, Royal Crown Derby, and Royal Doulton. The appealing naturalistic animal statuettes from Albany of England, Border Fine Arts, Heredities, and North Light are available, as well as enameled boxes and gifts by Crummles, Swarovski crystal whimsies, lovely vases and paperweights from Caithness Glass, and rustic dwellings in miniature from Brambley Hedge, David Winter Cottages, and Lilliput Lane. The Friar's House also sells the "Enchantica" line of fantasy figures from Holland Studio Craft—wizards, elves, dragons, and goblins.

Special Factor: Price quote by phone, letter, or fax.

SAXKJAERS

53 KØBMAGERGADE
1150 COPENHAGEN K
DENMARK
011-45-331-10777
FAX # 011-45-333-27210

Catalog: $2 (by air), refundable
Save: 40% plus
Pay: check, IMO, MC, V, AE
Sells: collectible porcelain editions and gifts
Store: same address; also Krystalgade 3,
1172, Copenhagen

$$$

Saxkjaers, a family business founded in 1904, is the definitive source for collectors' plates issued by Bing & Grøndahl, Hummel, and Royal Copenhagen. The yearly issues of Christmas plates will stir even the tamest acquisitive instincts, but it's an affordable habit if indulged in through Saxkjaers. The firm's catalog shows the current Royal Copenhagen Christmas plate (and lists editions as early as 1908), as well as the complementing cup-and-saucer set and Christmas ornament. As Europe's foremost Hummel representative, Saxkjaers sells the Hummel commemoratives at great discounts—the current annual plate retails for $188 ($118 here), and the Century issue, "Let's Tell the World," sells in the U.S. for $1,250, but just $595 here. Bing & Grøndahl plates are available from 1895 to the current year, as are Mother's Day plates from both firms, and china bells, thimbles, and other special issues at savings of at least 40% on the U.S. prices. Although appreciation is possible—the 1895 B&G plate now sells for $8,000—common sense cautions against treating limited editions as investments.

The catalog also shows Royal Copenhagen figurines, vases, and dinnerware, Bing & Grøndahl dinnerware, George Jensen silverware and gifts, Danish dolls and elves, jewelry, and even down comforters. Prices at Saxkjaers include surface postage and insurance against all problems; airmail shipping is available at a surcharge.

The Saxkjaers family runs the entire company, and welcomes all comers with a cup of coffee, so stop by if you find yourself in Copenhagen (downtown, "opposite the old round Tower—impossible to miss"). Saxkjaers is efficient as well as hospitable—letters and inquiries are answered the day they're received, and all efforts are made to ensure your happiness with your order.

Special Factors: Satisfaction is guaranteed; shipping (surface mail) and insurance are included; orders are shipped worldwide.

SEE ALSO

Beverly Bremer Silver Shop • heirloom and estate silver pieces • *HOME: TABLE SETTINGS*

Caprilands Herb Farm • collectors' dolls • *FARM*

Editions • first editions and rare books • *BOOKS*

The Emerald Collection • figurines and collectibles • *HOME: TABLE SETTINGS*

Forty-Fives • original 45's from 1950 to the current year • *BOOKS*

Mandolin Brothers, Ltd. • vintage fretted instruments • *MUSIC*

Pages/Booktraders, Ltd. • rare and out-of-print books • *BOOKS*

Plexi-Craft Quality Products Corp. • acrylic display pedestals • *HOME: FURNISHINGS*

Rainbow Music • vintage guitars and amps • *MUSIC*

Rogers & Rosenthal • figurines and collectibles • *HOME: TABLE SETTINGS*

The Scholar's Bookshelf • remaindered university-press art books • *BOOKS*

Script City • movie posters, entertainment collectibles • *BOOKS*

Shannon Duty Free Mail Order • collectible porcelain figurines • *HOME: TABLE SETTINGS*

Skandinavisk Glas • collectible porcelain and crystal objets d'art • *HOME: TABLE SETTINGS*

United Supply Co., Inc. • Shorewood art reproductions (educational materials) • *ART MATERIALS*

University Products, Inc. • archival-quality collection storage, mounting, and display materials • *GENERAL: PACKAGING*

ART MATERIALS

Materials, tools, equipment, and supplies for the fine and applied arts

You don't *have* to starve to be an authentic artist, but the cost of good tools and supplies almost ensures it—unless you can buy them at discount. We've found that small art stores usually sell at list, and seldom knock off more than 10%, except on quantity purchases. But discount mail-order firms usually offer savings of at least twice that. The firms listed here offer supplies and materials for fine arts and some crafts: pigments, paper, brushes, canvas, frames, stretchers, pads, studio furniture, vehicles and solvents, silk-screening supplies, carving tools, and much more.

Since different materials can profoundly affect the quality and direction of your work, familiarize yourself with what's on the market through catalogs and artists' magazines. The catalogs from New York Central Art Supply and Daniel Smith, both listed in this chapter, provide a wealth of information. For a comprehensive assessment of the properties and uses of almost every medium available today, see *The Artists' Handbook of Materials and Techniques* (Viking Press, 1981). The book can be found in libraries and is sold by several firms in this chapter. The *Handbook,* considered indispensable by many artists, can introduce you to techniques that may broaden your artistic horizons.

Concern about the safety of art materials has prompted legislation to warn consumers of potential problems (the Art Materials Labeling Act of 1988, effective November 18, 1990). Congress has also asked the Consumer Products Safety Commission to create standards for the art materials industry, and banned the use of hazardous materials by children in the sixth grade or younger. This is important legislation, since the list of substances found in widely used materials has included toluene, asbestos, chloroform, xylene, n-hexane, carbolic acid, trichlorethylene, and benzene, to note just a few. Even with reformulation and warnings, art materials can still pose some hazards. Good studio protocol can minimize much of the exposure:

- Select the least toxic and hazardous products available.
- If your work creates dust or fumes, use a quality, OSHA-approved respirator suitable to the task. (There are masks to filter organic vapors, ammonia, asbestos, toxic dusts, mists and fumes, and paint spray.)
- Use other protective gear as applicable: protective gloves reduce the absorption of chemicals through the skin, earplugs give protection against hearing damage from loud machinery, and safety goggles help to prevent blinding accidents.
- A good window-exhaust system is vital to reducing inhaled vapors. You need to have a real airflow when working with fume-producing materials—not just an open window.
- Keep children and animals out of the work place, since chemicals reach higher levels of concentration in their systems.
- Don't eat, drink, or smoke in the work area, or before cleaning up.
- Keep the appropriate safety equipment on hand to deal with emergencies: an eyewash station if caustic materials are being used, a first-aid kit, a fire extinguisher if combustible materials are present in the work place. (Direct Safety Company, listed in "Tools," stocks all of these as well as respirators, gloves, and earplugs.)
- Ask your school board to make sure the least toxic and hazardous products are used in the classroom.

For further reading, consult *Artist Beware: The Hazards and Precautions in Working with Art and Craft Materials,* by Michael McCann (Watson-Guptill Publications, 1979). *Health Hazards Manual for Artists* (Nick Lyons Books, 1985), a smaller book by Mr. McCann, includes specifics on materials commonly used by children. Both are sold by Ceramic Supply of New York & New Jersey (listed in this chapter). Mr. McCann, who is a chemist and an industrial hygienist, also founded the Center for Safety in the Arts. The organization deals with art-safety issues in *Art Hazards News,* a four-page newsletter published ten times a year. For current subscription rates and more information, write to Center for Safety in the Arts at 5 Beekman St., Suite 1030, New York, NY 10038, or call 212/227-6220.

For firms that sell related products, see "Crafts and Hobbies" and "General Merchandise," and don't overlook the listings in "Surplus."

FIND IT FAST

CERAMICS AND POTTERY • **Ceramic Supply of New York**
CHILDRENS AND EDUCATIONAL ART SUPPLIES • **Dick Blick, Sax, United Supply**
FINE ARTS • **Art Express, Art Supply Warehouse, Cheap Joe's, Jerry's Artarama, New York Central, Pearl Paint, Daniel Smith, Utrecht**
FRAMES • **American Frame, Daniel Smith, Stu-Art, Utrecht**
GRAPHIC DESIGN • **Flax, A.I. Friedman, Utrecht**
MAILING TUBES • **Yazoo**
PAPER AND PRINTMAKING • **New York Central, Daniel Smith**
SILKSCREENING • **Crown Art**

AMERICAN FRAME CORPORATION

1340 TOMAHAWK DR.
MAUMEE, OH 43537-3553
800-537-0944
FAX: 419/893-3553

Catalog: free
Save: up to 50%
Pay: check, MO, MC, V, AE, Optima
Sells: sectional frames, mat board, acrylic picture glass
Store: same address; Monday to Friday 9–5

$$$ ☎

American Frame, in business since 1973, sells *wood* sectional frames—a great way to get the look of a custom framing job, at do-it-yourself prices—as well as metal sectional frames in a wonderful selection of colors. We checked local art-supply stores and found American Frame's prices were lower, by 35% to 50%.

The ten-page catalog features frame sections in basswood, mahogany, oak, and cherry. They're offered in a variety of stains, some with gilding and some with linen liners. The profiles and dimensions of the sections are shown in detail, and each wood frame (two pairs of sections) is sent with corner insets for assembling each section, spring clips to hold the mounted art work securely in place, and wall protectors to keep the frame from lying directly against the wall. (Assembly requires attaching one end of the spring clips to the frame with screws, which are provided, and gluing the joints. No clamps are required, and instructions are given in the catalog itself.)

The metal frames are offered in a choice of seven profiles, to accommodate ordinary flat work, standard canvases, and extra-deep canvases. There are ten colors in the metallics line and 18 shades in the enameled colors, including pewter, evergreen, wine, salmon, jade, and cocoa, among others. The metal frame sections are sold in pairs and come with assembly hardware.

Crescent board—acid-free mat, mounting, and foam core—is sold in groups of ten or more sheets, depending on the item. The mat board is offered in over 100 colors in the 32″ by 40″ size, and no cutting is done. Rolls of polyester film are available, as well as acid-free acrylic picture "glass" (cut to order in dimensions up to 22″ by 28″).

Special Factors: Price quote by phone or letter; shipping is included on orders over $500.

ART EXPRESS

P.O. BOX 21662
COLUMBIA, SC 29210
800-535-5908
FAX: 803/750-1492

Catalog: free
Save: up to 60%
Pay: check, MO, MC, V, AE, Discover
Sells: art supplies and equipment
Store: mail order only

Art Express publishes a 72-page catalog that features a well-chosen selection of name-brand art tools and equipment, at discounts averaging 40%. The inventory includes papers and board, canvas, brushes, mediums and solvents, pens, portfolios, paint, Art Bin artists' cases, inks, pastels, pencils, airbrushing equipment, Martin easels, light boxes, Logan mat cutters, and Artograph opaque projectors. Among the other names represented are William Alexander, Arches, Badger, Bienfang, Canson, Fabriano, Fredrix, Grumbacher, Holbein, Isabey, Le Franc & Bourgeois, Liquitex, Luma, Raphaël, Rembrandt, Rives, Shiva, Speedball, Strathmore, and Winsor & Newton. Several pages of books and videotapes on art technique, history, and related topics are available. If you don't see what you're looking for, write or fax Art Express with product information—the item might be in stock.

Special Factors: Price quote by letter or fax; quantity discounts are available; institutional accounts are available; orders are shipped worldwide.

ART SUPPLY WAREHOUSE, INC.

**360 MAIN AVE.
NORWALK, CT 06851
203/846-2279
FAX: 203/849-0845**

Catalog: free
Save: 40% average
Pay: check, MO, MC, V
Sells: art supplies
Store: same address; Monday to Saturday
9:30–5:30; also 14 Imperial Pl.,
Providence, RI; and 81 45 Baltimore Blvd.,
College Park, MD

$$ ☎ 🍁(see text) ▆▆

Art Supply Warehouse, founded in 1979, publishes a 76-page catalog of art materials and equipment at an average of 40% off list prices. The firm also pays shipping on orders sent within the continental U.S.

The stock at Art Supply Warehouse includes oil and acrylic paints, pigments, fixatives, and solvents by Bellini, Blockx, Bocour, Deka, Grumbacher, Holbein, Liquitex, Paasche, Pelikan, Rembrandt, Shiva, Robert Simmons, Weber, Winsor & Newton, and other firms. The catalog shows oil pastels, chalks, colored pencils, markers, inks, pens, brushes, palette knives, and other tools. Paper and board by Bainbridge, D'Arches, Strathmore, Westport, Whatman, Winsor & Newton, and other firms is offered, for watercolors, illustrating, pen and ink work, drawing, calligraphy, and general use. Check the prices on stretched and roll canvas by Fredrix, as well as stretchers, easels, art boxes, and related studio gear. Supplies and equipment for other creative pursuits are sold, including airbrushing, drafting, sumi-e, silkscreening, and textile arts, and Art Supply Warehouse also carries the Northlight Books series of manuals.

Canadian readers, please note: Payment must be made in U.S. funds.

Special Factors: Satisfaction is guaranteed; price quote by phone or letter; returns are accepted; quantity discounts are available; shipping is included on orders sent within the continental U.S.

DICK BLICK CO.

**P.O. BOX 1267-WM92
GALESBURG, IL 61401
309/343-6181**

Catalog: $3
Save: up to 30%
Pay: check, MO, MC, V
Sells: name-brand and proprietary art
supplies
Store: Plainville, CT; Roswell, GA; Decatur,
Galesburg, Moline, Peoria, Springfield, and
Wheaton, IL; Iowa City, IA; Dearborn, MI;
Emmaus and Wilkes-Barre, PA; and
Henderson, NV

$$$ ☎ 🍁 ▆

Dick Blick, an arts-and-crafts supplier geared to schools, lists tens of thousands of items in its thick compendium of supplies and equipment. Blick, which was established in 1911, has everything in general art and craft supplies: Liquitex paints, Shiva pigments, Crayola crayons and finger paints, drawing tables and other art furniture, paint brushes, kraft paper, canvas, scissors, and adhesives. The catalog includes silk-screening materials, display lighting, printmaking equipment, wood-carving tools, molding materials, kilns, glazes, copper enamels, decoupage supplies, lapidary equipment, leather-working kits, dyes, macrame materials, weaving tools and equipment, blackboards, and much more. Over 20 pages of the catalog are devoted to films, slides, videotapes, manuals, and books on arts and crafts. The quality house-label goods offer real savings, and the selection is unbeatable.

Special Factors: Price quote by phone or letter on quantity orders; quantity discounts are available; minimum order is $10 with credit cards.

CERAMIC SUPPLY OF NEW YORK & NEW JERSEY, INC.

**10 DELL GLEN AVE.
LODI, NJ 07644
201/340-3005
FAX: 201/340-0089**

Catalog: $4
Save: up to 40%
Pay: check, MO, MC, V
Sells: sculpture, pottery, glazing, and crafts supplies and equipment
Store: same address; Monday to Friday 9–5, Saturday 9–12; also 534 La Guardia Pl., New York, NY; Monday to Friday 9–5, Saturday 10–5

$$ ☎ 🍁 ▤

Ceramic Supply of New York & New Jersey serves parts of both its name states with free delivery on orders of $100 or more, and offers good values on glazes, brushes, and a wide range of lightweight ceramics supplies that can be shipped worldwide at nominal expense.

The indexed, 150-page catalog from Ceramic Supply devotes most of its space to supplies and equipment for ceramics: gas and electric kilns (including some that run on household current), raku and fiber kilns, glazes, resists, mediums, brushes, airbrushing tools, slip-casting equipment, potters' wheels, armatures, grinders, and related goods. The manufacturers include Alpine, Amaco, Brent, Kemper, Kimple, North Star, Shimpo, and Skutt, among others. The catalog we received included color charts of glazes, underglazes, and other finishes by Duncan and Mayco which we found so enticing, we're going to redo the bathroom—in tiles we've glazed ourselves. (Ceramic Supply sells both glazed and bisqued tiles of varying sizes and shapes, which can provide the determined hobbyist or remodeler the basis for a custom bathroom or kitchen.) Dozens of types of clay are offered, from white Grolleg porcelain to "economy" clay made of odds and ends of other clays, and there are lots of other modeling materials—FIMO plastic, Sculpey, Van Aken Plastelene (used to make Gumby and the inmates in Pee Wee's Playhouse!), wax, and water-based clay.

Even if you're not a potter or sculptor, the catalog may interest you for its other goods: music box movements in scores of tunes and other music box parts, lights for ceramic Christmas trees, hard-to-find lamp parts, clock movements and parts, jewelry findings, studio furniture, and safety equipment. Don't overlook the reference section, which features books on sculpture, ceramics, art hazards, and related topics, and videotapes and filmstrips.

Special Factors: Price quote by phone or letter; returns are accepted within 10 days (a restocking fee may be charged); orders are shipped worldwide.

CHEAP JOE'S ART STUFF

300A INDUSTRIAL PARK RD.
BOONE, NC 28607
800-227-2788

Catalog: free
Save: up to 45%
Pay: check, MO, MC, V, Discover
Sells: art supplies and equipment
Store: Boone Drug Co., 113 E. King St., Boone, NC

$$ ☎ 🇺🇸

There *is* a Joe here at Cheap Joe's, and he makes his presence felt throughout his 24-page catalog in photographs and pithy sayings, like "An artist is known by the critics he praises," and "Old age and treachery will overcome youth and skill." Cheap Joe is the first company president to tell us that his firm may be the *smallest* of its kind in the field, and that it's not his goal to see it get very big. But with his prices, he may get there anyway—savings of 30% are routine, and quantity pricing can deepen the discounts to 70% on at least a few items.

The catalog we reviewed offered Arches and Canson paper, paint from Da Vinci, Holbein, and Winsor & Newton, paintbrushes from Jack Richeson, Robert Simmons, Whitney, Wilton, and Winsor & Newton, shrink-wrap systems, Logan mat cutters, adhesives, foamcore, Artograph projection equipment, Fredrix canvas, and books and videotapes on painting and art theory. Joe told us that he'll be adding his own line of watercolor brushes, as well as Isabey brushes and Daler-Rownay paints and brushes. Cheap Joe set up shop in 1986, and his real reason for wanting to keep his company small is staying in touch with his artist customers. He's a serious watercolorist himself, and welcomes your questions and suggestions about materials and equipment.

Special Factors: Satisfaction is guaranteed; price quote by phone or letter; shipping is included on orders delivered to U.S. addresses east of the Mississippi River; quantity discounts are available.

CROWN ART PRODUCTS CO., INC.

■

90 DAYTON AVE.
PASSAIC, NJ 07055
201/777-6010
FAX: 201/777-3088

Catalog: free
Save: up to 50%
Pay: check, MO, MC, V, AE, Optima
Sells: silk-screening supplies and materials
Store: same address; Monday to Friday
9–4:30, Saturday 11:30–6

$$ ☎ ♣ 🇺🇸

Crown Art has been making and selling silk-screening supplies and equipment since 1974, under the guidance of a silk-screen artist who's developed several products for the craft. If you're within commuting distance of the store in New Jersey, you may be interested in taking a silk-screening workshop or lessons at Crown.

The company's 16-page catalog features Crown's products: simple silk-screening kits for textiles and paper ($32), water-based "3-D" paints, Voilà squeeze fabric dyes and Crown Aqua and Crown Opaque textile inks, Airotex airbrush ink, Posterelle ink for paper, and even "puffy" and metallic inks. Ready-to-print customized silk screens, screen printing stretcher strips, and photo emulsion chemicals are available. Prices are very reasonable, and if you're an art teacher, printer, or dealer, contact Crown for information on its special discount program.

Special Factors: Price quote by phone or letter on special sizes and volume orders; minimum order is $25 with credit cards.

FLAX ARTIST'S MATERIALS

**1699 MARKET ST., DEPT.
1FRW
P.O. BOX 7216
SAN FRANCISCO, CA
94120
415/468-7530
415/552-2355 (SAN
FRANCISCO)
FAX: 415/468-1940**

Catalog: $5 (see text)
Save: up to 30%
Pay: check, MO, MC, V, AE
Sells: art and graphic design materials
Store: same address; Monday to Friday
9–6:30, Saturday 10–6; also 510 East El
Camino Real, Sunnyvale, CA; Monday to
Saturday 10–6

$$

Flax Artist's Materials was founded in 1939 by members of the same family that established the Sam Flax art stores (well known on the East Coast), but has no affiliation with that business. Though both firms sells supplies and equipment for the fine arts, drafting, and graphic design, Flax Artist's Materials discounts *everything* it sells in its two California stores.

Flax's big, five-dollar catalog shows goods at list prices, but the free quarterly sales catalogs offer savings of up to 30%. Art professionals should find the investment worthwhile, since there are all sorts of uncommon tools and supplies listed in the big book, in addition to the usual roundup of paper, canvas, pigments, vehicles, brushes, and the like. Flax's strength is graphic design and commercial art products: the newest colors from Pantone, realistic fake edibles for food shots, airbrushing supplies and equipment, the sleekest studio furniture and storage units, layout tools and supplies, markers in every possible color, professional templates, portfolios and presentation binders, sumi supplies, brushes for decorative paint finishes (graining, mottling, stippling), frames, and even a small selection of conservation supplies are available. Choice goods show up in the sale catalogs, though not everything is sold at a discount.

Special Factors: Price quote by phone or letter; minimum order is $25 from the big catalog.

A.I. FRIEDMAN

44 W. 18TH ST.
NEW YORK, NY 10011
212/243-9000
FAX: 212/929-7320

Catalog: $5 (see text)
Save: up to 40% (see text)
Pay: check, MO, MC, V, AE, Optima
Sells: graphic arts supplies and tools
Store: same address; and 25 W. 45th St.,
New York, NY; Monday to Friday 9–6,
both locations; also Caldor Plaza, Port
Chester, NY; Monday to Friday 10–9,
Saturday 10–6, Sunday 12–5

If you're a professional graphic designer or artist, you'll want to add A.I. Friedman to your short list of suppliers. The firm, which has been in business since 1929, serves the "creative community" with the best in tools and equipment. You can send $5 for the 324-page catalog, but it's free to design professionals requesting it on letterhead.

The catalog itself is an object lesson in good design, making it easy to find what you want amid the studio furniture, drawing instruments, markers, paint, brushes, paper and board, airbrushing supplies, audio/visual equipment, frames, and reference books. Friedman offers goods not found in every art supply catalog: light boxes, dry-mounting presses, the *complete* Pantone line, precision drawing and drafting tools, a large selection of templates, and complete photostat systems. Among the manufacturers represented are Agfa Gevaert, Bainbridge, Canson, Chartpak, D'Arches, Dr. Ph. Martin's, Grumbacher, Iwata, Koh-I-Noor, Kolinsky, Lamy, LeRoy, Letraset, Liquitex, Luxo (lamps), Mont Blanc, Mutoh, Osmiroid, Paasche, Pelikan, Stacor, Staedler-Mars, Strathmore, 3M, Winsor & Newton, and Zipatone.

The catalog prices are not discounted, but if your order totals $50 or more, discounts of 20% to 40% are given. (Some items aren't discounted, including the Agfa products.) Call or write for a quote on specific items.

Special Factors: Price quote by phone or letter; institutional accounts are available; minimum order is $50 (see text); orders are shipped worldwide.

JERRY'S ARTARAMA, INC.

**P.O. BOX 1105-WMC
NEW HYDE PARK, NY
11040
516/328-6633
FAX: 516/328-6752**

Catalog: $2.50
Save: 33% average
Pay: check, MO, MC, V, Discover
Sells: art supplies and equipment
Store: 248-12 Union Tpk., Bellerose, NY;
also 270 S. Federal Hwy. (U.S. 1),
Deerfield Beach, FL; Monday to Saturday
9:30–6, Sunday 11–5, both locations

Jerry's Artarama publishes a 102-page compendium of materials, tools, and equipment for commercial and fine arts that includes both studio basics and imported goods that are seldom discounted elsewhere. Jerry's was established in 1968, and carries over 10,000 different items.

The catalog we reviewed offered pigments, brushes, vehicles and solvents, studio furniture, lighting, visual equipment, canvas and framing supplies, papers, and other goods, with an extensive section of oil, watercolor, and acrylic painting supplies. Jerry's also sells supplies for drawing, the graphic arts, drafting, calligraphy, print-making, sumi-e, airbrushing, fabric painting, marbleizing, and professional framing. There are some "generic" brands, but most are well known: Bill Alexander, Alvin, Badger, Blockx, Conté, Deka, D'Arches, Fabriano, Fredrix, Grumbacher, Holbein, Isabey, Iwata, Koh-I-Noor, Langnickel, Neolt, Paasche, Bob Ross, Robert Simmons, Stabilo, Stacor, Strathmore, Winsor & Newton, and X-Acto are among the many represented. Don't miss the dozen pages of publications, which include technique manuals, color guides and wheels, and workshop videotapes—all of which are discounted.

Special Factors: Satisfaction is unconditionally guaranteed; price quote by phone or letter; color charts and product specifications are available on request; quantity discounts are available; minimum order is $20, $50 with phone orders; orders are shipped worldwide.

NEW YORK CENTRAL ART SUPPLY CO.

62 THIRD AVE.
NEW YORK, NY 10003
212/477-7705
FAX: 212/475-2542

Catalog: $3 (see text)
Save: up to 40%
Pay: check, MO, MC, V, AE, DC, Discover, Optima
Sells: art supplies and equipment
Store: same address (art materials); Monday to Saturday 8:30–6:15; also 102 Third Ave., New York, NY (framing and studio furniture); Monday to Saturday 9:30–6:15

$$$ ☎ ◆ ▬

New York Central, which has been supplying artists since 1905, is well-known for its stock of fine papers. The firm publishes four catalogs: the "General" catalog ($3), listing over 10,000 items for the fine and applied arts; the 96-page "Fine Art" catalog (free) of paints, pigments, mediums, solvents, brushes, and canvas; "Fine Papers" ($3), over 2,000 papers and related goods; and "Printmaking and Drawing" ($2), supplies and materials for silkscreening, batik, drawing, textile painting, calligraphy, and other crafts.

The 220-page general catalog, "a complete resource of materials for artists, designers, architects, draftsmen, engineers, graphic arts, students, teachers, sculptors, hobbyists and photographers," offers mat board, paper and pads, canvas, stretchers, graphic arts tools and design aids, paints and mediums, markers, brushes, easels, airbrush equipment, frames, and books, to cite a sample. The brands include Alvin (drafting furniture), Bainbridge, Berol, Chartpak, Conté, D'Arches, Deka, Fredrix, Grumbacher, Hyplar, Keuffel & Esser, Koh-I-Noor, Letraset, Luxo, Mars-Staedtler, Osmiroid, Pantone, Stabilo, Strathmore, and Winsor & Newton, among others. The general catalog includes a number of color charts, making it a good reference tool.

Special Factors: Price quote by phone or letter; specify the catalog desired; institutional accounts are available; quantity discounts are available; minimum order is $25; orders are shipped worldwide.

PEARL PAINT CO.

**308 CANAL ST.
NEW YORK, NY 10013
800-221-6845
212/431-7932**

Catalog: free
Save: up to 70%
Pay: check, MO, MC, V
Sells: art supplies
Store: same address; also 42 Lispenard St., New York, NY (architectural furniture showroom); Monday to Saturday 9–5:30, Thursday 9–7, Sunday (except July and August) 11–4:45, both locations; also Tampa, North Miami, Miami, and Ft. Lauderdale, FL; Atlanta, GA; Cherry Hill, Woodbridge, and Paramus, NJ; East Meadow, NY; and Alexandria, VA

$$$ ☎ ❧(see text)

Gotham artists have been flocking to Pearl Paint since 1933 for good prices on tools and supplies, and since then Pearl has opened stores in four other states as well (locations are listed in the catalog). Since the catalog represents just 2% of available stock, call or write if you're looking for something that's not listed.

Pearl sells fine-arts materials, tools, equipment, and materials for every possible craft, offering pigments, brushes, vehicles and solvents, stretchers, papers of all kinds, canvas, manuals, studio furniture, and much more. The available brands include Alvin, Aquatec, Bainbridge, Bellini, Deka, Fabriano, Grumbacher, Holbein, Iwata, Lascaux, Letraset, Liquitex, Paasche, Pantone, Pelikan, Pentel, Sculpture House, Sennelier, Robert Simmons, Staedtler, and Winsor & Newton, among others. Pearl also stocks fine writing instruments, house paint, tints, and finishes, including gilding and "faux" finishing supplies.

Canadian readers, please note: Orders are shipped by UPS only.

Special Factors: Quantity discounts are available; specials are run on selected items; minimum order is $50.

SAX ARTS & CRAFTS

2405 S. CALHOUN RD.,
DEPT. 92WBMC
NEW BERLIN, WI 53151
414/784-6880
414/784-1176

Catalog: $4, refundable
Save: up to 50%
Pay: check, MO, MC, V, AE
Sells: arts and crafts supplies
Store: mail order only

$$$ ☎ 🍁

Sax Arts & Crafts publishes a 464-page "resource of art and craft materials and equipment for the classroom and studio." The color catalog ($4) serves both educator and professional artist, and is notable for the range of supplies—everything from craft sticks to kilns—and for keeping up to date in the crafts field. The catalog identifies products that have been certified "safe" or nontoxic by the Art and Craft Materials Institute, a feature that should be helpful in selecting products for use by children.

Sax sells tools and materials for everything from marbling fabric and paper to oil painting: paper lithography, "friendly" plastic for making jewelry, airbrushing, drawing, paper collage and tissue craft, paper sculpture, papermaking, etching, framing and matting, drafting, calligraphy, scratch art, ceramics, copper enameling, engraving, weaving, rug making, bead work, basketry, fabric painting, mosaics, and wood burning. Among the names represented are Amaco, Bockingford, Canson, Chromacryl, Cra-Pas, Crayola, Crescent, D'Arches, Deka, Fabriano, Fimo, Fredrix, Liquitex, Paasche, Pelikan, Pentel, Prang, Prismacolor, Shiva, Speedball, Strathmore, Whatman, and Winsor & Newton.

The catalog featured a number of items we haven't seen elsewhere, like fluorescent modeling clay, erasable felt-tip pens, balsa foam (cuts with a toothpick, prints like a woodblock), a kiln that works in a microwave oven, silhouette paper, and Venetian glass tile. And there are 40 pages of books, manuals, videotapes, and cards on art-related topics. Prices are competitive, but the real savings are on quantity purchases.

Special Factors: Satisfaction is guaranteed; price quote by phone or letter; authorized returns are accepted for exchange, refund, or credit; institutional accounts are available; minimum order is $10.

DANIEL SMITH

**4130 FIRST AVE. SOUTH
SEATTLE, WA 98134-2302
800-426-6740 (U.S. AND
   CANADA)
206/223-9599
FAX: 206/223-0672**

Reference Catalog: $5 (see text)
Save: 25% to 30% average
Pay: check, MO, MC, V, AE
Sells: fine-arts supplies and equipment
Store: same address; Monday to Saturday
   9–6, Sunday 12–5

$$$

Daniel Smith's catalogs are designed by artists, for artists, and are appreciated as much for their book reviews, discussions of the properties of different materials, and sheer physical appeal as much as their offerings. Daniel Smith has been recommended to us by more than one artist impressed by the company's line of materials and responsive service department, although the prices aren't rock bottom.

The color Reference Catalog presents an extensive collection of paper from Arches, Canson, Fabriano, Lana, Magnani, Pentalic, Rising, Strathmore, and other manufacturers, for watercolors, printmaking, drawing, bookmaking, and other applications. This catalog has listed specialty papers we haven't seen elsewhere, including banana paper from the Philippines, Mexican bark paper, genuine papyrus, and Japanese "fantasy" paper embedded with ginkgo leaves. The Reference Catalog is published annually and costs $5, but the sale catalogs are free on request.

Watercolor painters may find inspiration in Daniel Smith's own Metallic Watercolors, as well as dry and moist colors from Grumbacher, Holbein, Maimeri, Schmincke, Sennelier, and Winsor & Newton. Daniel Smith sells acrylic, oil, gouache, tempera, and casein paints by several of these firms, as well as its own line of oil paints, including luminescent colors. Brushes for all painting media are available by Daniel Smith and Grumbacher, Isabey, Strathmore, and Winsor & Newton. Canvas, Nielsen frames, airbrush equipment, solvents, pastels, colored pencils, calligraphy pens, printmaking materials, and other tools and supplies are also stocked, as well as a fine collection of studio furniture, portfolios, easels, and reference books.

Canadian readers, please note: Only U.S. funds are accepted.

Special Factors: Satisfaction is guaranteed; price quote by phone or letter; authorized returns are accepted for exchange, refund, or credit; minimum order of paper is $25; orders are shipped worldwide.

STU-ART SUPPLIES, INC.

2045 GRAND AVE., DEPT. W-92
BALDWIN, NY 11510-2999
516/546-5151

Catalog and Samples: free
Save: up to 50%
Pay: check, MO, MC, V
Sells: sectional frames and framing supplies
Store: same address; Monday to Saturday 9–5

$$$ ☎ ♦ ▤

Stu-Art sells sectional frames and framing materials—everything you'll need to do a professional job. The firm has been supplying galleries and institutions since 1970, and it offers the best materials, a range of sizes, and savings of up to 50% on list prices.

Nielsen metal frames are offered in nine profiles, for flat-stretched canvas and dimensional art (deep) mounting, in a stunning array of metallic finishes, soft pastels, and deep decorator colors. Acid-free single and double mats are sold in rectangles and ovals. The catalog includes precise specifications of the frames, and samples of the mats. Stu-Art also sells nonglare and clear plastic (which can be used in place of picture glass), unfinished ash sectional frames, and shrink film and dispensers. If you have to get work framed, see the catalog before handing it over to a framing shop—you may decide you can do the job yourself.

Special Factors: Shipping is included on UPS-delivered orders over $300 net; price quote by phone or letter; authorized returns are accepted (a restocking fee may be charged); minimum orders is $15 on sectional frames, $25 on other goods.

UNITED SUPPLY CO., INC.

■■■■■■■

**BOX 9219
FORT WAYNE, IN 46899-
9219
800-322-3247**

Catalog: $3, refundable
Save: up to 40% (see text)
Pay: check, MO, MC, V
Sells: art and crafts supplies
Store: 3736 Wells St., Fort Wayne, IN;
   Monday to Thursday 8–6, Friday 8–5,
   Saturday 9–4

United Supply's 224-page catalog is a good source for supplies and tools for a variety of fine arts, as well as crafts. United Supply has been in business since 1960, and prices its goods an average of 25% below list. Quantity discounts are available on many items, as well as United Supply's volume discounts of 5% on orders over $500, up to 20% on orders over $5,000.

Painters are well served here with tempera, watercolors, gouache, acrylics, alkyds, and oils, as well as canvas, paper, brushes, easels, and other goods. Airbrushing equipment, craft tissue and paper, button machines, balloons, yarn crafts, weaving equipment, stenciling supplies, scratchboard, printmaking equipment, "friendly" plastic, clay, copper enameling supplies, jewelry findings, and many other kinds of art and crafts supplies are available. The brands include Amaco, Arches, Badger, Canson, D'Arches, Deka, Fabriano, Grumbacher, Koh-I-Noor, Liquitex, Paasche, Pelikan, Pentel, Rembrandt, Shiva, Speedball, Strathmore, Winsor & Newton, and Zipatone.

United Supply also sells books and manuals, postcards, Shorewood art reproductions, videotapes, and "art education programs" filmstrips and slide sets on technique, art history, and art appreciation.

Special Factors: Satisfaction is guaranteed; shipping is included on many items; quantity discounts are available; authorized returns are accepted within 30 days for exchange, refund, or credit.

UTRECHT ART AND DRAFTING SUPPLY

**33 35TH ST.
BROOKLYN, NY 11232
718/768-2525
FAX: 718/499-8815**

Catalog: free
Save: up to 70%
Pay: check, MO, MC, V
Sells: art supplies
Store: 111 Fourth Ave, New York, NY; Monday to Saturday 9–6; also 1250 "I" St., N.W., Washington, DC; 332 S. Michigan Ave., Chicago, IL; 333 Massachusetts Ave., Boston, MA; 15 E. Kirby St., Detroit, MI; and Spruce St. off S. Broad, Philadelphia, PA

Utrecht has been selling supplies and equipment for painting, sculpture, and printmaking since 1949, and manufactures some of the best-priced oil and acrylic paints on the market. The 48-page catalog describes the production process and quality controls used in making Utrecht's paint, and features Utrecht's acrylics, oils, watercolors, gesso, and other mediums and solvents. Utrecht also sells a full line of professional artists' materials, including canvas, stretchers, frames, pads, paper, brushes, books, easels, flat files and taborets, pencils, drafting tools, and much more. In addition to the Utrecht label, materials by Arches, Bainbridge, Bienfang, Canson, Chartpak, Claessens, D'Arches, Deka, Eberhard Faber, Grumbacher, Koh-I-Noor, Kolinsky, Liquitex, Niji, Pentel, Rembrandt, Speedball, Strathmore, Vermeer, Winsor & Newton, and other manufacturers are featured in the catalog. Utrecht's prices are competitive, and the best buys are on the house brand and quantity purchases.

Canadian readers, please note: Only U.S. funds are accepted.

Special Factors: Institutional accounts are available; quantity discounts are available; minimum order is $40; orders are shipped worldwide.

YAZOO MILLS, INC.

P.O. BOX 369
NEW OXFORD, PA 17350
717/624-8993
FAX: 717/624-4420

Price List: free
Save: 50% plus
Pay: check, MO, MC, V
Sells: shipping tubes
Store: mail order only

$$ ☎ 🍁

Yazoo Mills takes its name from the Mississippi town where it was founded in 1902, but since moving to Pennsylvania in 1936 has run its plant from New Oxford. Yazoo manufactures paper tubes for shipping and industry—carpet "cores," cable reels, copy paper tubes, even heavy blast casings for the mining industry—Yazoo makes them all.

Yazoo also manufactures and sells shipping tubes in the sizes most popular among artists. They're offered in lengths from 12″ to 60″, in diameters of 2″ to 8″. (The larger sizes are "heavy duty" or "extra heavy duty.") The tubes are sold by the case—48 in a carton of 2″ by 12″ tubes, 20 of 3″ by 24″, and 7 of the heavy-duty 5″ by 48″—and they come with plastic plug inserts for the ends. The prices, which include shipping, are so low that if all you need are two mid-sized tubes, it's probably worth buying from Yazoo. For example, a case of 3″ by 36″ tubes costs $23.60, or $1.18 apiece; a *discounter* we checked was selling the same size for $9.95 each! The tubes can be used for storage as well as shipping art and other objects; although they're made of recycled paperboard, they're not acid-free.

Yazoo does much of its manufacturing to job specifications, and can give you quotes on custom sizes or colors.

Special Factors: Price quote by phone or letter; shipping is included; minimum order is one carton of stock tubes; C.O.D. orders are accepted.

SEE ALSO

A to Z Luggage Co., Inc. • artists' portfolios • *LEATHER*
Dharma Trading Co. • tools and materials for fabric painting and dyeing •
   Crafts
Innovation Luggage • artists' portfolios • *LEATHER*

The Potters Shop Inc. • books on pottery and ceramics • *BOOKS*
Print's Graphic Design Book Stores • books and manuals on the graphic
 arts • *BOOKS*
Thai Silks • silk fabrics for fabric painting • *CRAFTS*
Utex Trading Enterprises • silk fabrics for fabric painting • *CRAFTS*

AUTO, MARINE, AND AVIATION EQUIPMENT

Parts, supplies, maintenance products, and services

You'll find a wide range of parts and supplies for cars, motorcycles, RVs, trucks, and vans in this chapter—mufflers, shocks, tires, batteries, and much more. Some companies also stock products for vintage cars, and one offers products for the "general pilot." You can even buy salvaged parts through several of the firms here, which are priced as much as 70% below the "new" cost. You can also buy cars, trucks, and vans, through services offered by American Auto Brokers and other firms. Here are some additional information sources to help you make the best selection when buying a new or used car or tires:

- *The Car Book,* by Jack Gillis (HarperCollins), is an annual guide that rates current domestic and imported models on their performance in crash tests, as well as such factors as fuel economy, preventive maintenance costs, repair costs, and insurance rates. The edition we reviewed included valuable information on evaluating warranties, service contracts, insurance, tires, children's car seats, and used cars. The comprehensive, easy-to-understand "Complaint" chapter should help you resolve difficulties, and the "Checklist" at the back of the book will help you ask the right questions. *The Car Book* is available in bookstores or from The Center for Auto Safety, 2001 S St., N.W., Suite 410, Washington, DC 20009 (send a long, self-addressed, stamped envelope for the publications list and ordering information).
- *Consumer Reports* publishes reliable vehicle ratings each year, as well as offering the Consumer Reports Auto Price Service.

The Auto Price Service provides a computer printout showing both list price and dealer's cost for the model you specify, and the same data for each factory-installed option. If the CR Auto Test Division has recommended optional equipment for your model, the options are also listed. And the service also provides guidelines on negotiating the lowest possible price. At this writing, one report costs $11; two are $20; three, $27; and each additional report thereafter, $5. See the current *Consumer Reports* for information, or write to Consumer Reports Auto Price Service, Box 8005, Novi, MI 48376.

- The Better Business Bureau publishes "Tips on Buying a New Car" and "Tips on Tires." Send a self-addressed, stamped envelope to the Council of Better Business Bureaus, Inc., 4200 Wilson Blvd., Suite 800, Arlington, VA 22203, Attn.: Publications Dept., and request the list of available brochures and ordering information.

You can save hundreds or even thousands of dollars when buying your car, but squander as much in bad driving habits over a lifetime. The following tips will conserve funds and fuel, keeping your wallet fatter and the air cleaner:

- Drive at 55 miles per hour or less, whenever possible. You'll go about 20% farther on the same tank than you do when traveling at 70 mph.
- Don't burn fuel you don't have to: Don't leave the car in idle for more than a minute (turn it off), don't use air conditioning unless it's really necessary, and keep the car free of excess weight.
- Have the wheels aligned at least once a year, and switch to radials, which maximize mileage.
- Check your tire pressure monthly, using a gauge (the old pencil style is inexpensive and reliable, and stows easily in the glove compartment). If you're driving on underinflated tires, you're using more gas than necessary—as much as 2% of your bill at the pump could be waste. Take the reading when the tires are cold, using guidelines provided by the car manufacturer.
- Follow other care instructions outlined in your car manual, including scheduling tuneups and changing oil and filters.

Getting stranded far from home with a disabled car is a worry that induces many drivers to join auto clubs. Service and survival may be a compelling reason to join an auto club, but most of the organizations provide far more than emergency towing. The best-known club, the American Automobile Association (AAA), boasts nearly 30 million members among its affiliates and offers a wide range of membership benefits. The AAA of New York, for example, provides travel-planning services, lodging and car rental discounts, no-fee travelers' checks, special services for travel abroad, personal accident insurance, assistance in solving license problems, and other benefits. The package of services varies from affiliate to affiliate; to find the AAA club nearest you, call 800-336-4357. Other clubs worth contacting for rates and services are Amoco Motor Club (800-782-7887), and Exxon Travel Club (713/680-5723).

Boating, although a less routine form of transportation, can absorb enormous sums of money—insurance, dock fees, upkeep, new equipment. You can save 30% *routinely* on the cost of maintenance products, gear, and electronics by buying from the maine suppliers listed here, who sell every type of coating, tool, and device you'll need to keep your vessel afloat. You'll find exhaustive selections of electronics, hardware, and instruments, as well as galley accoutrements and foul-weather clothing. Even landlubbers should take a look at these catalogs for the well-designed slickers and oiled sweaters—and the handsome teak bath and kitchen fixtures designed for yacht installations are equally useful on terra firma.

If you're private pilot who'd like to save on some of the gear and electronics you need while flying high, see the listing Marv Golden, an aviation discounter. Like the marine suppliers, this firm also sells goods of interest to the landlocked, at savings of up to 35%.

FIND IT FAST

AVIATION • **Marv Golden**
BOATING SUPPLIES AND EQUIPMENT • **Defender, E & B, Goldbergs', Skipper Marine, West Marine, Yachtmail**
CAR AUDIO • **Crystal Sonics**
CAR PARTS • **Cherry Auto, Clark's Corvair, Edgewood National, IMPCO**
CARS, TRUCKS, JEEPS • **American Automobile Brokers**
FARM EQUIPMENT PARTS • **Central Michigan**
MOTORCYCLE PARTS • **Capital Cycle**
RACING EQUIPMENT • **Racer Wholesale**
TIRES • **Belle Tire, Euro-Tire, Teletire, Titan Rubber**

AMERICAN AUTOMOBILE BROKERS, INC.

24001 SOUTHFIELD RD., SUITE 110
SOUTHFIELD, MI 48075
313/569-5900
FAX: 313/569-2022

Information: price quote
Save: see text
Pay: check or MO (see text)
Sells: cars, trucks, vans, and jeeps
Store: mail order only

$$ ☎

When it comes to buying a car, two of the biggest negatives are paying all that money and knowing that you shelled out more than you had to. One way to come out on top, and maybe even a little ahead, is to make sure you get a quote from American Automobile Brokers, whose price includes dealer prep and delivery from the factory to a dealership near you by train or truck (for domestic vehicles). The savings you can realize through American Automobile Brokers depend on the prices in your area, but enough customers have been buying cars, trucks, and vans to keep the firm in business since 1972.

If you're shopping for a domestic model, you can get quotes on vehicles by General Motors, Ford/Lincoln-Mercury, and Chrysler Corp. (AMC), and the foreign makes include Alfa Romeo, BMW, Honda, Isuzu, Mercedes, Mitsubishi, Porsche, Saab, Toyota, and other manufacturers. (American Automobile Brokers doesn't sell Hyundais, Peugeots, or Yugos.) The procedure is simple: Call or write with complete details about the vehicle and options desired, or send a self-addressed, stamped envelope for American Automobile Brokers' price-quote form. You get *one free quote;* extra quotes cost $3 each. Send a self-addressed, stamped envelope both when requesting the form and when sending it back for the quote. You can shop your local dealers, then get a quote here, or get the quote first and use it as a bargaining tool when you're out on the lot.

Special Factors: Price quote by phone, letter, or American Automobile Brokers quote form with SASE; checks and money orders are accepted for deposit only, balance payable by certified check, cashier's check, or wire transfer.

BELLE TIRE DISTRIBUTORS, INC.
<hr>

WHOLESALE DIV.
3500 ENTERPRISE DR.
ALLEN PARK, MI 48101
313/271-9400
FAX: 313/271-6793

Catalog: free
Save: up to 35%
Pay: check or MO
Sells: radial tires
Store: same address; also Detroit, Farmington, Grand Rapids, Madison Heights, Novi, Plymouth, Port Huron, Roseville, Sterling Heights, Troy, West Bloomfield, and Woodhaven, MI; and Toledo, OH

$$ ♣

If you're in the market for tires, Belle can save you up to 35% on the list prices of radials by Bridgestone, Firestone, B.F. Goodrich, Goodyear, Kelly Springfield, Michelin, Pirelli, Uniroyal, and Yokohama. Belle, which has been in business since 1922, charges $5 to $20 per tire for shipping, depending on the destination. Call or write for prices of specific models, or see the brochure.

Special Factors: Price quote by phone or letter; only new tires are sold, no retreads; orders are shipped worldwide.

<hr>

CAPITAL CYCLE CORPORATION
<hr>

P.O. BOX 528
STERLING, VA 22170-0528
703/444-2500
FAX: 703/444-9546

Catalog: free
Save: up to 65%
Pay: check, MO, MC, V, AE
Sells: BMW motorcycle parts and accessories
Store: 1508 Moran Rd., Sterling, VA; Monday to Friday 8:30–6, Saturday 9–5

$$$ ☎ ♣ ▤

Capital Cycle is the nation's definitive source for replacement parts for BMW motorcycles, with an inventory of over 8,000 genuine, original parts, which are priced up to 65% below what the dealers are charging. Capital Cycle, which has been in business for 20 years, publishes a small, seasonal catalog featuring specials and much-requested items.

Capital offers genuine BMW motorcycle parts, manufactured from 1955 through the current year. The catalog includes only a fraction of the enormous inventory, including engine parts and electronics, carburetors, fuel tanks, mufflers, pipes, clutches, gears, steering bearings, shocks, springs, handlebars, mirrors, brakes, tires, rims, forks, fenders, fairings, locks and keys, paint, seats, switches and relays, tachometers, voltmeters, lights, tools, and decals. Parts books and factory repair manuals for BMW cycles are offered, as well as a selection of BMW car parts.

Capital Cycle also publishes the only motorcycle parts catalog we know of that also offers down quilts (2½ pounds of pure goose down, $279 in full size) and a rental villa in Jamaica (private beach, cook/housekeeper, "delicious cuisine"; rentals begin at $540 per week).

Canadian readers, please note: Only U.S. funds are accepted.

Special Factors: Price quote by phone or letter; quantity discounts are available; UPS ground shipping is included; repair services are available by mail; authorized returns are accepted within 30 days (a 15% restocking fee may be charged); minimum order is $20; orders are shipped worldwide.

CENTRAL MICHIGAN TRACTOR & PARTS

2713 N. U.S. HWY. 2
ST. JOHNS, MI 48879
517/224-6802

Information: price quote
Save: up to 50%
Pay: check, MO, MC, V
Sells: used and salvaged tractor parts
Store: mail order only

$$$ ♦

This firm, also known as Tractor Salvage, can save you up to 50% on parts for tractors and combines. It stocks used, reconditioned, and rebuilt parts, all of which are backed by a 30-day guarantee.

Central stocks everything from starters to cylinder blocks for machines made by almost every major manufacturer. Some of the goods are reconditioned, some are rebuilt; a rebuilt part is overhauled completely and you can expect it to function as well and for as long as a new one. Central maintains want lists for parts not in stock. Call between 8 and 5:30, Monday to Friday, or 8 and 4:30 on Saturdays.

Special Factor: Price quote by phone or letter.

CHERRY AUTO PARTS

5650 N. DETROIT AVE.
TOLEDO, OH 43612
800-537-8677
IN OH 800-472-8639
419/476-7222
FAX: 419/470-6388

Information: price quote
Save: up to 70%
Pay: check, MO, MC, V
Sells: used and rebuilt foreign-car parts
Store: same address; Monday to Friday 8:30–5, Saturday 8:30–12; also 17770 Telegraph Rd., Romulus, MI (Detroit area); Monday to Friday 8:30–5, Saturday 9–12

Why pay top dollar for new car parts if you can get perfectly good ones, used, for up to 70% less? Cherry Auto Parts, "The Midwest's Leading Foreign Car Dismantler," can supply you with used and rebuilt foreign-car components at up to 70% less than the cost of the same parts, new.

Cherry Auto has 45 years of experience in the car parts business, and can provide you with rebuilt cylinder heads, engines, starters, alternators, drive axles, turbos, and other vital parts. If you drive an Acura, Alfa Romeo, Audi, BMW, Chrysler Imports car (Challenger, Champ, Colt, Conquest, Raider), Datsun (Nissan), GEO, Honda, Isuzu, Jaguar, Lancia, Mazda, Mercedes, Merkur, MG, Mitsubishi, Peugeot, Porsche, Renault, Saab, Spectrum, Sprint, Subaru, Toyota, Triumph, Volkswagen, Volvo, or other foreign car, you may save up to 70% on your parts bills by getting them here. Cherry can access two nationwide computerized parts-locating networks to trace hard-to-find parts promptly.

Special Factors: Price quote by phone (preferred) or letter; "all parts are guaranteed in stock at the time of quotation, guaranteed to be the correct part, and in good condition as described"; minimum order is $15.

CLARK'S CORVAIR PARTS, INC.

RTE. 2
SHELBURNE FALLS, MA
01370
413/625-9776

Catalog: $4
Save: up to 40%
Pay: check, MO, MC, V
Sells: Corvair parts
Store: mail order only

$$$ ☎ 🍁 ▀▀▀

Clark's Corvair Parts publishes an inventory of over 4,500 Corvair parts in an indexed, 400-page catalog every other year, with small supplements to update it periodically. Clark's, in business since 1973, is indispensable source for the Corvair owner, since it stocks parts that are nowhere else.

Clark's can save you up to 40% on original and replacement General Motors parts, reproductions, and goods by Champion, Chevrolet, Clevite, Delco, Gabriel, Gates, General Motors, Loctite, Michigan Bearings, Moog, Permatex, Sealed Powers, TRW, and hundreds of other suppliers. The exhaustive inventory includes brakes, cables, lights, air filters, body parts and panels, carburetor and engine parts, gauges, gas tanks, manuals, pistons, points, seals, rims, specialty tools, paint, reproduction upholstery, trim, carpets, and many other parts and supplies. If you're looking for a specific part, you can call for a quote—but the catalog is a valuable reference tool.

Special Factors: Price quote by phone or letter; returns are accepted; C.O.D. orders are accepted; minimum order is $10.

CRYSTAL SONICS

1638 SOUTH CENTRAL
AVE., #C4
GLENDALE, CA 91204
818/240-7310

Catalog: $2
Save: up to 60%
Pay: check, MO, MC, V, AE
Sells: auto audio
Store: same address; Monday to Friday 9–6, Saturday 10–3

$$ ☎ 🍁 ▀▀▀

Crystal Sonics, in business since 1977, publishes an informative directory of discount auto audio components at savings of up to 60%.

Past catalogs have featured guides to audio terminology and extensive product specifications, as well as listings of sound systems, amps, speakers, baffles, security devices and alarms, antennas, wires and cables, hardware, installation kits, and related paraphernalia. Crystal Sonics represents Allsop, Alphasonik, Art Audio, Audio Control, BEL, Boston Acoustics, Clarion, Discwasher, Fujitsu Ten, Harada, Hirschmann, Hot Wires, Infinity, JBL, Klasse, Panasonic, Phoenix Gold, Pioneer, Sony, Streetwires, TDK, Triad, and XTC. The firm has a large facility at which installations of audio systems are made, and if you live within a reasonable distance from Glendale, it's probably worth the trip.

Please note: Not all goods shown in the catalog are available in the retail store, and vice versa.

Special Factors: Authorized returns of new, unaltered, unused goods are accepted within 14 days; minimum order is $50 with credit cards; orders are shipped worldwide.

DEFENDER INDUSTRIES, INC.

**255 MAIN ST.
P.O. BOX 820
NEW ROCHELLE, NY
10802-0802
914/632-3001
FAX (U.S. AND CANADA):
800-654-1616
FAX: 914/632-6544**

Catalog: $3, refundable
Save: up to 60%
Pay: check, MO, MC, V
Sells: marine supplies, gear, equipment, and clothing
Store: The Marine Discount Supermarket, 321 Main St., New Rochelle, NY; Monday to Friday 9–5:45, Thursday 9–8:45, Saturday 9–4:45 (call for hours, November-February)

$$$

Defender has been selling marine hardware and equipment since 1938, and backs its claim to have "the largest selection in the USA at the very lowest prices" with a 244-page catalog that just about proves it. It features page after page of boat maintenance supplies, resins and coatings, winches, windlasses, cordage, communications devices, foul-weather gear, books, tools and hardware, optics, galley fittings, navigation equipment, and electronics. You'll find sailboat hardware from Harken and Schaefer, Barient and Lewmar winches, Evinrude and Tohatsu outboard engines, and lines of marine electronics from Apelco, Datamarine, Humminbird, Impulse, King, Lowrance, Raytheon, Signet, and Sitex. We've also seen Shakespeare antenna, Babb and Maxxima radios, optics from Fujinon, Minolta, and Steiner, Avon and Achilles inflatable boats and liferafts; NYNEX mobile phones, Henri Lloyd, Musto, and Patagonia boating wear, Sebago and Timberland shoes, Force 10 cookers, and Taylor Made boat tops and covers among its pages—and that's a fraction of what's available. In addition to equipment, Defender is a national leader in boat-building supplies: fiberglass, xynole, epoxy and polyester resins, and other boat construction and maintenance materials are stocked in depth.

Many of the goods sold here have other applications—the cookstoves and coolers for camping, the teak and oak racks and trays for the home, caulks and wood finishes for general home maintenance, hardware and tools for the workshop—and there are deck shoes, sunglasses, first-aid kits, foul-weather jackets, lamps and lanterns, watches and clocks, folding chairs, tarps, and much more. Defender also offers a range of custom services, such as life raft repacking and repair, rigging services, and canvas goods to order (seat covers, pool covers, car covers, etc.).

Defender's wholesale division, Atlantic Main Corp., specializes in small boat marine hardware and safety gear. Among other items, this firm sells the "Horseshoe Harness," an alternative to the Lifesling that costs about half as much. Atlantic Main is also the U.S. agent for Holt Allen sailboat hardware. For details, contact Atlantic Main at 319 Main St., New Rochelle, NY 10801.

Special Factors: Price quote by phone, fax, or letter; returns are accepted within 20 days (a restocking fee may be charged); minimum order is $15, $25 with credit cards; orders are shipped worldwide.

E & B MARINE SUPPLY, INC.

**P.O. BOX 3138
EDISON, NJ 08818-3138
800-533-5007
FAX: 201/819-9222**

Catalog: free
Save: up to 60%
Pay: check, MO, MC, V, AE, Discover
Sells: marine supplies, gear, and equipment
Store: 50 outlets in AL, CT, FL, GA, MA, MD, MI, MS, NJ, NY, PA, RI, and VA (locations are listed in the catalog)

E & B Marine, founded in 1946, "consistently maintains the boating industry's lowest discount prices," which has helped to establish the firm as "the nation's leading retailer of quality marine supplies."

E & B offers a full range of products for power boating and sailing, boat maintenance and repair, safety, communications, and navigation, all at a discount. The brand names include Apelco, Aqua Meter, Boatlife, Bow t' Stern, Chelsea, Eagle, Humminbird, Icom, Igloo, Impulse, Interlux, Intermatic, Kidde, Micrologic, Pettit, Polaris, Ray Jeff, Raytheon, Ritchie, SeaFit, SeaRanger, Standard, and Stearns, among others. Water skis and Achilles inflatables are stocked, as well as boating apparel and sportswear. New products are featured in every catalog, and many items are useful on land as well—clothing, safety equipment, and hardware. Savings vary, but are typically 10% to 25%, and up to 60% on sale items and specials.

Special Factors: Authorized returns are accepted within 90 days; minimum order is $15, $25 on phone orders.

EDGEWOOD NATIONAL, INC.

623 MERIDIAN EAST,
DEPT. WBM
PUYALLUP, WA 98371
206/927-3388

Information: price quote by phone or letter
Save: up to 40%
Pay: check, MO, MC, V
Sells: parts for 4WD vehicles
Store: same address

$$$ ☎ ♦

Edgewood National discontinued its catalog several years ago, but it does a brisk mail business on an inquiry (price quote) basis. Edgewood was established in 1964.

The specialty here is four-wheel-drive vehicles, for which Edgewood stocks "after-market accessories"—both hard parts and what the manager calls "tinsel," or extras. This is the source to call if you need drive train components, an engine or parts, a suspension, and the like. These are brand-new parts (not reconditioned), comparable to those by the original manufacturer, and savings can reach 40% on some items. The staff is helpful and informed, so it's worth a toll call to discuss your needs and get prices.

Special Factors: Price quote by phone or letter; authorized returns are accepted (a restocking fee may be charged).

EURO-TIRE, INC.

**567 RTE. 46 WEST
FAIRFIELD, NJ 07004
800-631-0080
IN NJ 201/575-0080**

Brochure: free
Save: up to 50%
Pay: check, MO, MC, V, AE, Optima
Sells: auto tires, wheels, and shocks
Store: 500 Rte. 46 East, Fairfield, NJ;
   Monday, Wednesday, Thursday 8:30–5,
   Tuesday and Friday 8:30–7, Saturday
   8:30–3:30; also East 290, Rte. 4, Paramus,
   NJ; and 393 West Ave., Stamford, CT;
   Tuesday, Wednesday, Friday 8:30–5,
   Monday and Thursday 8:30–7, Saturday
   8:30–3:30, both locations

$$$ ☎ 🍁 🇺🇸

Euro-Tire's specialty is European tires and auto components, which are sold at up to 50% off list prices. Domestic car tires and products are also available. The brochure includes tips that should help you select the best tire for your car and driving needs, and Euro-Tire's informed staff can also assist you if you have quesstions.

The firm has been selling tires since 1974, and currently offers Bridgestone, Continental, Dunlop, Goodyear, Kléber, Michelin, Pirelli, Semperit, Vredestein, and Yokohama. Shock absorbers by Bilstein, Boge, and Koni are priced an average of 34% below list, and the brochure lists light alloy wheels for 13 car makes by BBS, Centra, MSW, and Ronal. Euro-Tire's concise brochure gives complete details on its sales and warranty policies, as well as its wheel mounting services offered at its facilities in Connecticut and New Jersey.

Special Factors: Price quote by phone or letter; no seconds or retreads are sold; returns are accepted within 30 days (see the catalog for details); minimum order is $25; orders are shipped worldwide.

GOLDBERGS' MARINE DISTRIBUTORS

**P.O. BOX 3040
EDISON, NJ 08818-3040
800-BOATING**

Catalog: free
Save: up to 60%
Pay: check, MO, MC, V, AE, Discover
Sells: marine supplies, gear, and equipment
Store: 12 W. 37th St., New York, NY; also
Whitman Plaza Shopping Center, 3rd and
Oregon Aves., Philadelphia, PA

$$$[mo] ☎ 🍁 ▧

Goldbergs' has been a marine supplier since 1946, and offers thousands of products at discounts of up to 60%, and even more in the sales catalogs. the firm sells everything from anchors to zinc collars, including rope, bilge pumps, fishing tackle, rigging, knives, lifeboats, life preservers, navigation equipment, boat covers, winches, and even kitchen (galley) sinks. The brands are the best in boating—SeaRanger electronics, Taylor Made buoys, PowerWinch windlasses and winches, motors, and Stearns life preservers are just a few of the items we saw in the catalog. The emphasis is on pleasure-boat equipment, but much of the sailing apparel—French fishermen's sweaters, sunglasses, boots, Sperry boating shoes, slickers—has landlubber appeal. A selection of stylish galley gear, teak bulkhead racks, and other yacht accessories rounds out the substantial catalog.

Special Factors: Price quote by phone or letter; authorized returns are accepted within 10 days (policy is stated in the catalog); minimum order is $10.

MARV GOLDEN DISCOUNT SALES, INC.

**8690 AERO DR., SUITE 102
SAN DIEGO, CA 92123
619/569-5220
FAX: 619/569-4508**

Flyer: free
Save: up to 35%
Pay: check, MO, MC, V, AE, Discover, Optima
Sells: equipment for the "general aviation" pilot
Store: same address; Monday to Friday 7–6, Saturday 8–3, PST

Marv Golden Discount Sales has been in business since 1983, offering the general-aviation pilot savings of up to 35% on headsets, electronics, and accessories. The firm sends out a flyer of specials, but you can call for quotes on such items as David Clark headsets, Astrotech digital clocks, Casio pilots' watches, Jeppesen charts and binders, genuine U.S. Air Force kneeboards, Aerox oxygen systems, and flight bags and other accessories. Intercoms by Flightcom, Sigtronics, Soft Comm, Telex, and other manufacturers are available, as well as computers from Jeppesen and Navtronic, and 720-channel transceivers from Icom, King, Narco, and Terra. Call Marv Golden if you don't see what you're looking for in the flyer, since it may be available.

Special Factors: Satisfaction is guaranteed; price quote by phone or letter; shipping is included on prepaid orders; quantity discounts are available; authorized, unused returns in original packaging are accepted within 30 days for credit; C.O.D. orders are accepted; orders are shipped worldwide.

IMPCO, INC.

**909 THOMPSON ST.
HOUSTON, TX 77007-
5630
800-243-1220
713/868-1638
FAX: 713/869-0186**

Catalog: free
Save: 30% average
Pay: check, MO, MC, V
Sells: OEM Mercedes-Benz diesel parts
(see text)
Store: same address; Monday to Friday 9–6

$$ ☎ ♦ ▆

Owners of diesel Mercedes-Benz cars made between 1977 and 1985 can get "original equipment manufacturer" (OEM) parts for them here, at average savings of 30%. IMPCO has been in business since 1984 and sells only first-quality parts through its 48-page color catalog.

Whether you're overhauling a wreck, or just want to replace the wiper blades, IMPCO provides with a full range of body parts, from front fender moldings to trunk seals, as well as electrical parts and supplies, bulbs, cooling and heating system components, upholstery materials, filters, brake parts, suspension and drive-line parts, window switches, accessories, tools, and Owner's Workshop manuals. If you're overhauling your car, check out IMPCO's engine rebuilding kits, as well as the exhaust systems. IMPCO also sells Meguiar's car-care products, Lexol leather cleaner and conditioner, and engine additives by Lubro Moly and Red Line. If you're looking for a part or Mercedes-Benz product not listed or have any questions, just call IMPCO.

Special Factors: Satisfaction is guaranteed; price quote by phone or letter; authorized, unused returns (except tools, manuals, and electronics) are accepted within 30 days for exchange, refund, or credit; minimum order is $20 on phone orders; C.O.D. orders are accepted; orders are shipped worldwide.

RACER WHOLESALE

**10390 ALPHARETTA ST.,
SUITE 620
ROSWELL, GA 30075
404/998-7777
FAX: 404/993-4417**

Catalog: free
Save: up to 70%
Pay: check, MO, MC, V, Discover
Sells: auto racing safety equipment
Store: mail order only

$$$ ☎  🍁 ▦

Racer Wholesale has been serving the professional and serious amateur auto racing markets since 1985, offering safety equipment and accessories at savings of up to 70% on list prices. The company's 32-page catalog shows professional driving and crew suits from AutoPro, Bell, Pyrotect, Racequip, and other manufacturers, as well as gloves, boots, helmets, belts, harnesses, window nets, arm restraints, fire extinguishers, and other safety products. Auto equipment is also available, including K & N filters and accessories, Flowmaster mufflers, Oberg filters and heavy-duty oil coolers, Aeroquip hoses and connections, fueling accessories, towing equipment, Wink wide-view mirrors, battery cutoff switches, and related products. List and discounted prices are both given in the separate price sheets, sales flyers with closeouts are sent periodically, and Racer Wholesale has a policy of "guaranteed lowest prices"—see the catalog for details.

Special Factors: Price quote by phone or letter; authorized, unused returns (except special orders) are accepted within 15 days for exchange, refund, or credit (a restocking fee may be charged); C.O.D. orders are accepted; orders are shipped worldwide.

SKIPPER MARINE ELECTRONICS, INC.

**3170 COMMERCIAL AVE.
NORTHBROOK, IL 60062
800-621-2378**

Catalog: free (see text)
Save: up to 30%
Pay: check, MO, MC, V
Sells: marine electronics
Store: same address; also 20307 South Western Ave., Torrance, CA; and 5053 N.W. 10th Terrace, Ft. Lauderdale, FL

$$$ ☎ ♦ ▆

Skipper Marine Electronics, in business since 1963, is a factory-authorized dealer and service center for every line of electronics it sells, and it never carries grey-market goods. Prior to delivery, Skipper can adjust and calibrate electronics for you, without impairing the warranties. You can discuss your equipment needs and get tips on installation from one of Skipper's staff technicians.

The 120-page, color catalog consolidates the "buying guides" Skipper used to publish, but it's still packed with notes on product functions and valuable features. You'll find VHF marine radios, fishing and powerboat instruments, sailboat instruments, navigation instruments, and miscellaneous electronics among the offerings, from Apelco, Cybernet, Datamarine, Eagle, Echotec, Furuno, Humminbird, Impulse, Interphase, King Marine, Lowrance, Micronar, Raytheon, Si-Tex, Signet, Uniden, Unimetrics, and Wesmar. If you don't find what you're looking for, or you have a question about the services Skipper offers, call for information.

Special Factors: Price quote by phone or letter; authorized returns are accepted; shipping is included; C.O.D. orders are accepted.

TELETIRE

17642 ARMSTRONG AVE.
IRVINE, CA 92714
800-835-8473
714/250-9141
FAX: 714/261-5473

Brochure: free
Save: 30% average
Pay: check, MO, MC, V, Discover
Sells: tires and wheels
Store: mail order only

$$$ ☎

Teletire's brochure addresses issues that befuddle many car owners, such as how often their tires should be rotated, and the secret meaning of speed ratings. In addition to getting an education, the brochure showcases a great selection of tires and wheels. Teletire boasts a multi-million-dollar inventory of tires for passenger cars, trucks, vans, and RVs, and also stocks road wheels. Models by BBS, Bridgestone, Continental, Dunlop, Enkei, Fittpaldi, B.F. Goodrich, Michelin, Pirelli, and Quantum are available, but if the tires or wheels you're looking for aren't listed in the brochure, call or write for a price quote. Teletire, which began doing business in 1969, is affiliated with Telepro (see the listing in "Sports").

Special Factors: Price quote by phone or letter; unused, undamaged returns are accepted within 30 days (a restocking fee may be charged).

TITAN RUBBER INTERNATIONAL

**ONE BRYAN DR.
WHEELING, WV 26003-
0137
800-443-8473
FAX: 304/233-4561**

Information: price quote
Save: up to 50%
Pay: check, MO, MC, V, Discover,
SearsCharge
Sells: performance tires and wheels and
auto parts
Store: same address; Monday to Friday 8–5;
also 86 locations in the East and Mid-
West

$$$ ☎ 🍁

Titan Rubber International has 86 outlets across the country, and doesn't publish a catalog—but will provide technical assistance by phone to help you make the best selection of tires for your vehicle and driving style. Titan has beem in business since 1959, and sells at prices up to 50% below the going rate.

If you're in the market for high-performance and RV tires and performance wheels, call for availability and quotes on models by American Racing, BBS, Dunlop, Falken, B.F. Goodrich, Goodyear, Michelin, MSW, Patriot, Pirelli, Ronal, RW, Sentry, and Weds. These are first-quality goods—no seconds or retreads—and they're all sold with the manufacturers' warranties. Tire and wheel packages for a number of vehicles may be available—inquire for information. And tubes, weights, valves, and batteries are also offered.

Special Factors: Price quote by phone or letter; no catalog is available; quantity discounts are available.

WEST MARINE PRODUCTS

Catalog: free
Save: up to 50%
Pay: check, MO, MC, V
Sells: marine supplies and equipment
Store: 18 outlets on the West Coast

P.O. BOX 1020
WATSONVILLE, CA 95077
800-538-0775
FAX: 408/728-2736

$$$ ☎ ♦

West Marine Products publishes 124-page color compendium of marine electronics, hardware, and maintenance products for sailboats and powerboats. The comprehensive selection of gear and materials includes epoxies and finishes, cordage, anchors, windlasses, buoys, horns, seacocks, winches, electronics, communications devices, navigation instruments, safety equipment, lumber, hardware, kerosene lamps, boating clothing, marine optics, inflatable boats, and a complete line of galley gear. There are scores of manufacturers represented, including Apelco, Barient, Cannon, Datamarine, Harken, Interphase, Lewmar, Magellan, Marinco, Navico, Patagonia, Ritchie, Schaefer, Stearns, Steiner, Taylor Made, and Weems & Plath, among others. Savings run up to 50%, and many top brands are available. West Marine has over 5,000 items in stock that didn't make it into the catalog, so if you don't see what you're looking for, call and ask.

Special Factors: Satisfaction is guaranteed; price quote by phone or letter.

COMPANIES OUTSIDE THE U.S.A.

Yachtmail, a well-known yacht chandler, is experienced in dealing with customers in the U.S. and Canada. Yachtmail offers goods not widely available at a discount in the U.S. and it has a better selection of certain goods than do domestic discounters.

Before ordering from any non-U.S. firm, please consult "The Complete Guide to Buying by Mail," page 573, for helpful tips. We recommend paying for orders from foreign firms with a credit card whenever possible, so you'll have some recourse if you don't receive your order. For more information, see "The Fair Credit Billing Act," page 612.

YACHTMAIL CO. LTD.

ADMIRAL'S COURT, THE
QUAY
LYMINGTON, HANTS
SO41 9ET
011-44-590-672784
FAX: 011-44-590-670089

Price List: free
Save: up to 50%
Pay: check, IMO, MC, V, Access
Sells: yachting equipment and electronics
Store: same address; Hamble Point Marina, School Lane, Hamble, and Port Hamble Marine, Satchell Lane, Hamble, Hants; Monday to Sunday 9–5, all locations

$$$

Yachtmail was founded in 1966 and specializes in cruiser-yacht gear and inflatables, but the firm also sells navigation instruments, winches, pumps, lights, clocks, barometers, and other boating goods. Yachtmail can often beat U.S. discount prices on English brands, even with shipping—so don't overlook this source if you're buying British.

Yachtmail has told us that the most popular items with U.S. buyers are Autohelm and Navico autopilots, Avon life rafts, satellite navigators, echo sounders, log speedometers, and sextants. Yachtmail has been cited for its low prices on Avon dinghies, which are usually 30% less here than in the U.S. The price list we received also itemized Lewmar and St. Anchorman winches, EPIRBs, bilge pumps, anchors, compasses, flares, binoculars, life jackets, foul-weather clothing by Douglass Gill, Henri Lloyd, Musto, and Splashdown, and other useful goods. Orders are generally shipped by airmail or air freight. The price list includes only a sample of what's available from Yachtmail, and if you're looking for a British-made item not mentioned, inquire—it may be available.

Special Factors: Price quote by phone or letter; certain items are unsuitable for mailing; orders are shipped worldwide.

SEE ALSO

Allyn Air Seat Co. • air-filled seat liners for motorcycles, cars, and trucks •
  SPORTS
The Audio Advisor, Inc. • high-end auto audio • APPLIANCES

Bart's Water Ski Center, Inc. • boat mounts and hardware for water-skiing equipment • *SPORTS*

Bass Pro Shops • boating gear and electronics • *SPORTS*

Bennett Brothers, Inc. • infants' car seats • *GENERAL MERCHANDISE*

BRE Lumber • lumber and flooring for marine use • *HOME: MAINTENANCE*

Cabela's Inc. • boat seats, covers, electronics, etc. • *SPORTS*

Cambridge Wools, Ltd. • sheepskin car covers • *CRAFTS*

Campmor • inflatable boats • *SPORTS*

Central Tractor Farm & Family Center • replacement tractor and engine parts; shop manuals • *FARM*

Crutchfield Corporation • auto audio • *APPLIANCES*

Danley's • marine binoculars • *CAMERAS*

Direct Safety Company • wheel chocks, traffic control equipment, auto emergency kits, etc. • *TOOLS*

E.T. Supply • aircraft replacement parts • *SURPLUS*

Gander Mountain, Inc. • boat seats, covers, electronics, motors, etc. • *SPORTS*

Leather Unlimited • Harley-Davidson personal accessories • *LEATHER*

LVT Price Quote Hotline, Inc. • radar detectors, scanners, CBs, etc. • *APPLIANCES*

Manufacturer's Supply • parts for motorcycles, snowmobiles, 3WDs, etc. • *TOOLS*

Mardiron Optics • marine optics • *CAMERAS*

Northern Hydraulics, Inc. • wheels and parts for ATVs, minibikes, etc. • *TOOLS*

Overton's Sports Center, Inc. • marine equipment and electronics • *SPORTS*

Pagano Gloves, Inc. • deerskin motorcycle jackets • *CLOTHING*

Sailboard Warehouse, Inc. • sailboard car racks • *SPORTS*

R.C. Steele Co. • life preservers and auto safety harnesses for pets • *ANIMAL*

WearGuard Corp. • mechanics' overalls, shoes, safety vests, etc. • *CLOTHING*

Wisconsin Discount Stereo • auto audio • *APPLIANCES*

BOOKS, PERIODICALS, AND RECORDINGS

Publications in all media, cards and stationery, and prerecorded films and videotapes

Why pay list prices for books or videotapes, or full rates for magazine subscriptions, when you can get them all by mail at discounts of 8% to 80%? The firms in this chapter can save you hundreds of dollars a year on your own reading and entertainment buys, as well as on the books, tapes, and movies on your gift lists. Looking for stationery, cards, and gift wrapping and ribbon? They're here as well, also competitively priced.

You'll help yourself resist bookstore forays that result in impulse purchases by keeping notes on the titles friends have asked for, as well as those that interest you, and checking for them when the discount catalogs arrive. You don't even have to wait for a catalog to save, since virtually any currently published title is available from BookWorld (listed here) at a discount of 8% to 25%. Consult *Books in Print,* at your library, to see whether a book is still being published. If you're looking for an out-of-print title, check the catalogs from Editions and Strand (listed here) to see if it's among their secondhand stock. Your best savings will be on remaindered books, which are routinely discounted 50% to 80%—and thanks to the manifold lapses of judgment in the publishing world, there are lots of intriguing remainders out there.

Most of us let our books take care of themselves, but real collections represent investments requiring proper storage and display. University Products (listed in the "Packaging" section of "General Merchandise") offers a wide range of conservation supplies, including acid-free book-jacket covers, manuscript cases and folders, rare-book boxes, record sleeves, interleaving sheets, and archival-quality repair materials.

Don't overlook the "See Also's," especially if you're looking for a how-to or self-help type of publication. You'll find gardening guides among the firms in "Farm and Garden," cookbooks offered by firms selling gourmet ingredients, books on color theory sold by art-supply houses, and so on. Many of the firms listed in WBMC also offer video-tapes on their specialties, usually at discount prices. And if you're looking for software, see the "Computing" section of the "Office" chapter.

FIND IT FAST

ART AND CRAFTS • **Dover, Potters Shop, Print's Graphic Design**
ASTRONOMY • **Astronomical Society**
CARDS AND STATIONERY • **American Stationery, Current, Rocky Mountain, Trumble Greetings**
CHILDREN'S • **Butternut Books**
COOKBOOKS • **Jessica's Biscuit**
GOVERNMENT PUBLICATIONS • **Consumer Information Center, Superintendent of Documents**
MAGAZINE SUBSCRIPTIONS • **American Family, Magazine Marketplace, Publishers Clearing House**
RECORDS, TAPES, CDS • **Barnes & Noble, Berkshire, Bose Express, Coronet, Discount Books & Video, Forty-Fives, Kicking Mule, Metacom, Musiquarium, Script City**
SCREENPLAYS • **Script City**
UNIVERSITY PRESSES • **Scholar's Bookshelf**
USED BOOKS • **Editions, Pages/Booktraders, Strand, Tartan**
VIDEOTAPES • **Astronomical Society, Barnes & Noble, Bose Express, Discount Books & Video, Metacom, Script City**

AMERICAN FAMILY PUBLISHERS

P.O. BOX 62111
TAMPA, FL 33662-2111
800-237-2400

Information: inquire
Save: up to 70%
Pay: check or MO
Sells: magazine subscriptions
Store: mail order only

$$$

American Family Publishers is a magazine clearinghouse that offers subscriptions to dozens of popular periodicals at rates that are usually much better than those offered by the publishers themselves. In addition to savings, every time you order you'll be entered into the current sweepstakes, which doesn't happen when you buy your magazines at the newsstand.

A recent American Family mailing included offers for *Business Weeks, Life, Popular Science, Road & Track, TV Guide, New Woman, Baseball Digest, Time, Sports Afield, Jet,* and *The Family Handyman.* Periodically, American Family features books—*The Columbia University Complete Home Medical Guide,* Rodale's home-improvement series, cookbooks, and other popular reference books have appeared in past mailings, all offered on the company's buying program that allows you to spread payments over four months.

Special Factors: Satisfaction is guaranteed; inquire for information.

THE AMERICAN STATIONERY CO., INC.

100 PARK AVE., DEPT. 4
PERU, IN 46970
800-822-2577
FAX: 317/472-5901

Catalog: free
Save: up to 35%
Pay: check, MO, MC, V, Discover
Sells: personalized stationery
Store: mail order only

$$$ ☎ ▤

The American Stationery Co. offers a good selection of personalized stationery at prices up to 35% below those charged by other firms for comparable goods and printing. The company has been in business since 1919, and also produces "The American Wedding Album," a 40-page color catalog with actual samples of wedding invitations and accessories—at savings similar to those offered on the stationery line.

American Stationery's correspondence selections include embossed sheets and notes in four colors, deckle-edged and plain sheets and envelopes in white and pastels, and heavyweight Monarch sheets, erasable sheets, business envelopes, and "executive" stationery of heavyweight, chain-laid paper. We've found great buys here, including a "typewriter box" of 100 printed sheets and the same number of printed envelopes for $14.95, which was similar in quality to one selling elsewhere for nearly twice the price. Stationery for children, personalized memo pads, bill-paying envelopes, bordered postcards, stationery sets, gummed and self-sticking return-address labels, and related goods are shown in the color catalog.

Special Factors: Satisfaction is guaranteed; returns are accepted for replacement or refund.

ASTRONOMICAL SOCIETY OF THE PACIFIC

390 ASHTON AVE.
SAN FRANCISCO, CA
94112
415/337-1100
FAX: 415/337-5205

Catalog: two first-class stamps
Save: up to 50%
Pay: check, MO, MC, V
Sells: books, posters, slides, and videotapes on astronomy topics
Store: mail order only

$$$ ✦(see text) ▆

The Astronomical Society of the Pacific is a not-for-profit organization that was founded in 1889 to support astronomical research and improve the public's appreciation of science, especially astronomy. To this end, ASP publishes a variety of materials: videotapes, books, charts and maps of the heavens, and slides. The 32-page catalog features an intriguing collection that includes *Universe,* an award-winning video commissioned by NASA and narrated by William Shatner, *Seven Days in Space,* a 1986 film about a week aboard the space shuttle; a four-tape audio recording of Stephen W. Hawking's *A Brief History of Time,* and the Royal Observatory of Canada's *Observer's Handbook.* There are breathtaking posters of the planets, a "moon phase calendar" for the whole year, computer programs that can simulate travel through the galaxy, and several slide sets covering nebulas and galaxies, the moon, Mars, the solar system, Supernova 1987A, and even the universe of radio waves.

ASP's prices are reasonable but don't seem particularly low ($29.95 for videotapes and $8.95 for posters), until you check the catalogs of supplies for educators selling similar publications. There are school sources charging an astonishing $300-plus for a *single* videotape. So even if you're not in the market for ASP's publications yourself, let your school board or PTA know about this source.

Canadian readers, please note: Only U.S. funds are accepted.

Special Factors: Satisfaction is guaranteed; returns in "as-new" condition are accepted for exchange, refund, or credit; institutional accounts are available; orders are shipped worldwide.

BARNES & NOBLE BOOKSTORES, INC.

■■■■■■■■■

126 FIFTH AVE., DEPT.
861F
NEW YORK, NY 10011
201/767-7079

Catalog: free
Save: up to 80%
Pay: check, MO, MC, V, AE, CB, DC
Sells: books, records, audiotapes, videotapes, and reading accessories
Store: same address; Monday to Friday 9:45–6:15, Saturday 9:45–6, Sunday 10–5; other locations nationwide

$$$ ☎ 🍁 ▤ (see text)

Barnes & Noble, founded in 1873, considers itself "America's best source of remainders, publisher's overstock and exclusive reprints—all at bargain prices"—up to 80%. In addition, the catalogs feature hundreds of records, audiotapes, videotapes, and calendars, also considerable discounts.

The typical Barnes & Noble catalog is 48 to 72 pages of best-sellers, reference works, publishers' overstock, and the firm's own reprints (*A History of Transylvania* and *Zen for Americans* were among recent offerings). The areas of interest include history, mystery, the arts science, literature, film, medicine, satire, juvenilia, current fiction, linguistics, religion, reference, crafts, and photography. The catalogs also offer a large selection of audiotapes and CDs (classical music, jazz, drama, and language tapes), and videotapes from Louis Malle's *My Dinner with André* to *The Story of English,* from the PBS series. Stunning art books, calendars, lighted globes, beechwood bookshelves, book embossers, book ends, cassette cases and cabinets, and book lights have all appeared in past catalogs.

Canadian and APO/FPO readers, please note: Inquire for shipping charges, and allow extra time for order processing.

Special Factors: Satisfaction is guaranteed; institutional accounts are available; returns are accepted; minimum order is $15 with credit cards.

BERKSHIRE RECORD OUTLET, INC.

RR 1, RTE. 102 PLEASANT ST.
LEE, MA 01238-9804
413/243-4080

Catalog: free
Save: 33% plus
Pay: check, MO, MC, V, Access
Sells: classical recordings
Store: same address; Monday to Saturday 11:30–5:30 (call first)

$$$ ☎ 🍁

If you're an LP holdout who loves classical music, Berkshire has what you've been looking for. The 159-page, quarterly catalog lists thousands of classical overstocked and remaindered recordings—LPs, tapes, and compact discs—at savings of 33%-plus on the original prices. It's organized alphabetically by label—from Abbey to Zephyr—and within that, by price groups. Each entry is coded to indicate whether the recording is available in stereo, mono, quadraphonic, or reprocessed stereo (or in digital or analog CD), and the country of origin is noted if the recording is an import. Berkshire is a gold mine for the classical music lover, although sound tracks, ethnic music, folk songs, and poetry readings do appear. If you're just looking for a good recording of a favorite concerto or movement, you may be overwhelmed by the selection. If you're unsure of your choices find someone who can advise you, since Berkshire isn't keen on second thoughts, saying "we respectfully ask that you do not attempt to amend your order once it is submitted."

Special Factors: Price quote by phone or letter; minimum order is $15 with credit cards.

BOOKWORLD SERVICES, INC.

■■■■■■

**1933-W WHITFIELD
 LOOP
SARASOTA, FL 34243
800-833-0720 (ORDERS
 ONLY)
813/758-8094
FAX: 813/ 9396**

Information: price quote
Save: up to 30%
Pay: check, MO, MC, V, AE
Sells: in-print books
Store: mail order only

$$$

If you never leave a bookstore empty-handed, you'll appreciate BookWorld for its access to virtually any book in print, and its prices—8% to 30% below publishers' rates. (The discounts apply to books on the New York Times best-seller list.)

BookWorld has 29 years in the book-selling business, but its computer-linked warehouses that give it a real edge in knowing whether a particular volume is available. The company's own database can scan its inventory of 135,000 titles in seconds, and if BookWorld doesn't have what you want, the warehouse stock can be scanned. Discounts vary, depending on the book, but apply to nearly every title.

Please note: There is no catalog; call or write for a price quote.

Special Factors: Price quote by phone or letter with SASE; institutional accounts are available; C.O.D. orders are accepted; orders are shipped worldwide.

BOSE EXPRESS MUSIC

**50 W. 17TH ST.
NEW YORK, NY 10011
800-233-6357**

Catalog: $6, refundable
Save: up to 35%
Pay: check, MO, MC, V, AE
Sells: audiotapes, CDs, laser discs, and
videotapes
Store: mail order only

Bose Express Music gives you access to backlisted and current music and video releases at a discount through its 240-page catalog, which includes discount coupons worth about $50. The compendium of over 50,000 titles costs $6 (refundable with your first order), which will also bring you a year of monthly updates and specials.

The big catalog gives list prices for every tape, CD, and video title sold by Bose Express, which include rock, pop, R&B, gospel, sound tracks, opera, classical, and Broadway show tunes. Rock videos, workout tapes, and new and old movies are also available, and the selection is diverse—we found Kiri Te Kanawa sharing space with Metallica.

Since cost of shipping, handling, and insurance is just $3.95 per order, splurging on gifts and your own audio/video library seems almost justified. The discount coupons in the large catalog reward orders of several items with freebies and extra savings, so don't overlook them.

Special Factors: Price quote by phone or letter; returns of defective goods are accepted within 10 days for exchange, credit, or refund; orders are shipped worldwide.

BUTTERNUT BOOKS

WELL ASSOCIATES, INC.
RD1, BOX 121A
MORRIS, NY 13808
607/263-5620

Catalog: $2
Save: 15% plus (see text)
Pay: check or MO
Sells: children's books (see text)
Store: mail order only

$$ ☎ 🍁 ▀

Butternut Books is a division of WELL Associates, an educational consulting firm that's been in business since 1985. WELL's objectives include the promotion of language development and literacy, and Butternut Books—which is devoted to good children's literature—is a natural outgrowth of those goals.

Butternut's book list represents the choices of the president of the firm, an education professional, who's chosen these particular titles because they meet the "Whole Language" approach to learning, are interesting to children, offer appealing story lines, and are well-illustrated. The catalog is organized alphabetically by title and notes the intended age group for each book and the publishers' prices, but doesn't include descriptive copy. Among those in the catalog we reviewed were several of our favorites—Vera Williams' *A Chair for My Mother,* Ludwig Bemelmans' *Madeline,* and McCloskey's *Blueberries for Sal.* Many of Butternut's choices are winners of Caldecott and Newbery awards, and if you need help with your selection, the firm can advise you and even develop lists of books by theme or idea—a very helpful service for educators. In addition to the juvenile literature, which runs from preschool to young adult, Butternut also sells professional resource books.

Prices are discounted 15% on orders of $50 or more (no discounts on the professional books), and selected sale titles are featured monthly at savings of 30%, 50%, and as much as 70% off list. Butternut is devoted to helping you make the best choices for your needs, whether you're buying for family, friends, play group, or school.

Please note: Orders are shipped via UPS only.

Special Factors: Institutional accounts are available; minimum order is $50 (see text).

CONSUMER INFORMATION CENTER

**P.O. BOX 100
PUEBLO, CO 81009**

Catalog: free
Save: see text
Pay: check or MO
Sells: consumer publications
Store: mail order only

$$$ ▰

The government's Consumer Information Center was established in 1970 "to help federal agencies promote and distribute useful consumer information." Many of the pamphlets and manuals in the Center's 16-page quarterly catalog are free, and cover such topics as careers and education, child care, federal benefits and laws, food handling and nutrition, health, home building and buying, energy conservation, appliances and electronics, home improvement and safety, travel, hobbies, and money management. You can subscribe to *FDA Consumer* through the Consumer Information Center's catalog, and order pamphlets that help you to learn about ultrasound, find out about Social Security, get tips on buying a mobile home, and obtain government records under the Freedom of Information Act, among other things.

Write for the catalog, if only to order the "Consumer's Resource Handbook," a guide to effective complaint procedures. It lists the best sources of help if you have a problem as a consumer: contacts, addresses, and phone numbers of the customer relations departments of hundreds of major corporations, Better Business Bureau offices worldwide, trade associations, consumer protection offices, and federal agencies. There are over 90 pages of valuable information in the Handbook, at the best possible price—free.

Please note: A Spanish-language catalog of dozens of federal consumer guides in Spanish is also available.

Special Factor: A handling fee is charged on all orders.

CORONET BOOKS & CDS/CASSETTES

**311 BAINBRIDGE ST.
PHILADELPHIA, PA 19147
215/925-2762
FAX: 215/925-1912**

Catalog: free
Save: up to 30% (see text)
Pay: check, MO, MC, V
Sells: CDs, audiotapes, and music videos
Store: mail order only

$$ ☎ 🍁

Coronet sells CDs, audiotapes, and music videos through a straight-forward catalog that lists the 15,000 available recordings under the artists' names, and includes the manufacturers' code number and Coronet's price. The firm really covers the bases, offering rock, pop, rhythm and blues, jazz, country, big bands, movie soundtracks and Broadway shows, and even 1,500 classical music titles. Rock is the featured player, running from ABC and Paula Abdul to ZZ Top. There are lots of great oldies, as well as current releases—Earth, Wind & Fire, Aerosmith, Vanilla Ice, 38 Special, Lou Reed, INXS, Stevie Ray Vaughn, and Indigo Girls are a few of the artists we found, with all or most of their general releases.

The performers represent mainstream favorites, and it's hard to resist making out a list while you're reading through the catalog—Coronet has the tapes you meant to get after you read the reviews, but somehow never got around to buying. Savings run up to 30% on list prices, and shipping is free if you buy ten or more items.

Special Factors: Price quote by phone or letter; shipping is included on orders of 10 or more items; orders are shipped worldwide.

CURRENT, INC.

**THE CURRENT
  BUILDING
COLORADO SPRINGS,
  CO 80941
303/593-5990**

Catalog: free
Save: up to 45%
Pay: check or MO
Sells: stationery, cards, and gifts
Store: mail order only

$$$ ☎ 🇺🇸

Current, in business since 1950, publishes an 88-page color catalog of stationery and cards in appealing designs, ranging from animal and nature scenes to quilt motifs and other Americana. All-occasion and holiday cards are available, as well as notes, stationery, gift wrapping, ribbon, recipe cards and files, toys, games, home organizers, calendars, memo boards, note pads, and other gifts. Prices are very reasonable, and discounts are given based on the number of items ordered.

Special Factors: Satisfaction is guaranteed; sliding discounts of 20% and more are offered on orders of 12 or more items; returns are accepted.

DAEDALUS BOOKS, INC.

**P.O. BOX 9132 (WBM)
HYATTSVILLE, MD 20781-
0932
800-395-2665**

Catalog: free
Save: up to 90%
Pay: check, MO, MC, V, AE, Optima
Sells: new and remaindered literary
  publications
Store: mail order only

$$$$ ☎ ♦ 🇺🇸

Daedalus, founded in 1980, offers fine books from trade publishers and university presses at 50% to 90% off publishers' prices. These remainders have been culled from thousands to appeal to literary readers looking for culture on the cheap. Daedalus isn't *just* remainders, though—about half the catalog is devoted to current titles that are discounted about 10%. And the witty, clearheaded descriptions of each book are reading pleasures in themselves.

The holiday catalog we reviewed offered a number of choice selections: *The Art of Florence,* a stunning two-volume set in a slipcover ($295 from $385), *The New Yorker Book of War Pieces* ($3.98 from $12.95), E.B. White's classic, *The Second Tree from the Corner* ($6.98 from $19.95), and the Willa Cather diary ($7.95 from $10.95). The categories include literature and general interest, visual and performing arts, philosophy, history, feminism, politics, and the social sciences. A gift certificate from Daedalus, presented with the latest edition of the catalog, should delight any serious reader.

Canadian readers, please note: Payment must be made by credit card, a money order drawn in U.S. funds, or a check drawn on a U.S. bank.

Special Factors: Price quote by phone or letter; institutional accounts are available; returns are accepted within 30 days; minimum order is $10 with credit cards; orders are shipped worldwide.

DISCOUNT BOOKS & VIDEO, INC.

P.O. BOX 928
VINELAND, NJ 08360-0928
800-448-2019
609/691-1620

Catalog: free
Save: up to 90%
Pay: check, MO, MC, V
Sells: remaindered books, CDs, audiotapes, and videotapes
Store: mail order only

$$$

Discount Books & Videos has been selling publishers' overstock and remaindered publications at savings of up to 90% since 1984, and also discounts books, audiotapes, and videotapes. The 64-page catalog we reviewed offered bargains on books about American history and politics, music, Judaica, health and nutrition, philosophy, law, crafts, cooking, computers, social sciences, medicine, and other fields of interest. Fiction, literature, criticism, and scholarly texts are featured, including technical books and textbooks. You'll find several pages of tapes and CDs of music—classical, jazz, rock, and opera—and motivational and self-help tapes. Scores of videotapes are also available, including comedy classics, old favorites from the 40s and 50s, sports highlights, instructional, and educational videos. Quantities of many of the books are limited, so order promptly.

Special Factors: Satisfaction is guaranteed; returns are accepted within 30 days for refund or credit; institutional accounts are available; minimum order is $15 with credit cards.

DOVER PUBLICATIONS, INC.

31 EAST 2ND ST.
MINEOLA, NY 11501
516/294-7000

Catalog: free
Save: up to 50% (see text)
Pay: check or MO
Sells: Dover publications
Store: same address; Monday to Friday
9–3; also 180 Varick St., 9th Floor,
New York, NY; Monday to Friday 9–4:30

$$$

Many of the firms listed in this book sell a selection of Dover books, but if you deal with the publisher directly you can buy any in-print Dover publication. Dover has over 40 years of publishing experience, and its books are noted for their good construction and materials, as well as their content. Dover's catalogs feature paperbacks on crafts and hobbies, Americana, mathematics and physics, American Indian arts, architecture, cooking, games, travel, music, and many other topics. Dover publishes "Pictorial Archives," featuring designs and graphics, typography, banners and scrolls, borders, etc., as well as the "Clip-Art Series" of copyright-free art that can be used in newsletters, ads, menus, and the like. Dover's postcard sets run from NASA shots to Tiffany windows, and there are stickers, coloring books, and posters as well.

Dover's facsimiles and reprints of rare and valuable texts include a facsimile of William Blake's *Songs of Innocence,* an 1864 illustrated catalog of Civil War military goods, and the earliest known cookbook, *Cookery and Dining in Imperial Rome,* by Apicius, to cite a few. Dover's reprint of the catalog of Gustav Stickley's Mission furniture designs is a standard among antiques dealers, and is probably more widely read now than it was when originally published.

Dover also publishes "Listen & Learn" language tapes, as well as bird song tapes and musical scores by Scriabin, Liszt, Scott Joplin, Couperin, Ravel, Bizet, Brahms, and other greats. The prices are easily up to 50% less than those charged for comparable publications, and the books themselves are made for long use. Dover doesn't *have* to discount its books because they're well-priced to begin with!

Canadian readers, please note: The shipping surcharge on orders sent to Canada is 20%.

Special Factors: Satisfaction is guaranteed; returns are accepted within 10 days for refund.

EDITIONS

DESK WM
BOICEVILLE, NY 12412
914/657-7000
FAX: 914-657-8849

Catalog: $2
Save: up to 40%
Pay: check, MO, MC, V
Sells: old, used, and rare books
Store: 153 Rte. 28, Shokan, NY; daily 10–5

$$$$ ☎ ♦ ▆

Editions is one of our favorite sources for used and out-of-print books, which are often we 30% to 50% less expensive here than elsewhere—and the service is great. Editions has been selling by mail since 1948, and operates a weekend store that's stocked with a separate book inventory—worth a stop if you're traveling in the area.

The 64-page monthly catalogs include *partial* listings from a range of categories. For example, the January catalog may list poetry titles from Eliot to Neruda, and February's issue will run from Powys to Wyse. Each issue lists about 10,000 titles, most priced under $20, from categories that include fiction, literature, history, the social sciences, natural history, travel, women, soldiers and war, the Irish, Americana, British history, theater, philosophy and religion, food, labor, espionage, sports, antiques, gardening, animals, publishing, and Judaica. And it's always interesting to see what ends up in the "Miscellaneous Subjects & Nonsense" section.

Real bargains turn up at Editions, like the collection of Weegee photographs priced at $58 that was offered by a local book dealer for nearly $100, without the dust jacket.) We've also found a number of original hardcover titles, in fine condition, at prices lower than those of their paperback editions. Collectors and researchers may wish to see the catalogs for the first editions and books from the Heritage Press and Lakeside Press, as well as the occasional listings of regimental histories, genealogies, and books on local history.

Special Factors: Inquiries by letter only; returns are accepted within 3 days; minimum order is $25 with credit cards.

FORTY-FIVES

P.O. BOX 358
LEMOYNE, PA 17043-0358

Catalog: $2 and SASE (see text)
Save: up to 50%
Pay: check or MO
Sells: original-label 45rpm records
Store: mail order only

$$ 🍁 ▀▀▀

Forty-Fives has been selling vintage and current 45's since 1979, and its closely typed 18-page price list will summon memories you might have thought lost to time. If one of your favorites happened to be "We Gotta Get You a Woman," by Runt, you can get it as a WBMC bonus by ordering just $15 in records here—or another of four titles currently available. The catalog lists records released from 1950 through the current year by title and artist and includes a condition rating. The records are grouped by price, which is the only reason you will find Barbra Streisand back-to-back with Pink Floyd. Most of the records are Top 40, AM hits of their day, and prices are very low—80% cost $1 each, and the remainder cost up to about $20. A small selection of LPs is available as well, and a separate country & western price list is available—send $1 and request it by name.

Please note that Forty-Fives asks you to order without enclosing payment; you'll be billed for the records that are still available when your order is received. Orders of $15 or more qualify for the bonus 45—see above. Mention WBMC when you order to be sure to receive the extra record.

Special Factors: Price quote by phone or letter; note ordering instructions and pay only when billed for records; minimum order is $5; orders are shipped worldwide.

EDWARD R. HAMILTON, BOOKSELLER

FALLS VILLAGE, CT 06031-5000

Catalog: free
Save: up to 90%
Pay: check or MO
Sells: closeout and remaindered books
Store: mail order only

$$$

Hamilton's monthly tabloid catalog lists *thousands* of bargain books in every conceivable category, at savings that average of 50% to 70% off the publishers' prices. The 48-page catalog appeals to the bargain-hunting bookworm who likes to explore old bookstores—it's the literary equivalent of shelves and stacks of volumes—art, humor, poetry, fiction, literature, photography, self-help, reference, business, crafts, psychology, history, film, science, cooking, sports, and biography are all featured. Hamilton's offerings are all new, remainders, closeouts, or publishers' overstock. Past best-sellers show up here frequently, as well as imports and other books no other remainder source seems to have. Our experiences with Hamilton have been faultless; the shipping is prompt, and refund checks for out-of-stock titles often arrive before the order itself!

Special Factors: Satisfaction is guaranteed; returns are accepted; prepaid institutional orders are accepted.

JESSICA'S BISCUIT

THE COOKBOOK PEOPLE
BOX 301
NEWTONVILLE, MA 02160
617/965-0530
FAX: 617/527-0113

Catalog: $2, refundable with first order
Save: up to 80% (see text)
Pay: check, MO, MC, V
Sells: cookbooks and food reference
Store: mail order only

$$$ ☎ ♦ ▰

Jessica's Biscuit is so discreet about sweetening its luscious catalog with sale books that you might overlook them at first. But they're here—scores in the regular catalog, and 40 pages of savings in the sale issues. Jessica's Biscuit is the source we turn to for specialty cookbooks and updates on the culinary convulsions of the taste dictators. In addition to national cuisines, Jessica's Biscuit offers books with recipes for vegetarian, macrobiotic, microwave, diabetic, low-salt, sugar-free, low-cholesterol, wheat-free, fiber-rich, kosher, and low-cost dishes. There are regional books for everything from soul food to Amish fare, as well as volumes devoted to muffins, tofu, pizza, biscuits, corn, mushrooms, barbecuing, cheesecake, beans, children's food, chili, garlic, and potatoes. Related topics, including canning and preserving, outfitting a working kitchen, buffets, wines, cake decorating, and entertaining in style are covered as well. Savings on the sale titles average 45% and run as high as 80%, and you can deduct the $2 catalog fee from your first order.

Special Factors: Satisfaction is guaranteed; returns are accepted.

KICKING MULE RECORDS, INC.

■■■■■■■■■■■■

**P.O. BOX 158-W
ALDERPOINT, CA 95411-
     0158
707/926-5312
FAX: 707-926-5250**

Catalog: free
Save: up to 70% (see text)
Pay: check, MO, MC, V, Discover
Sells: Kicking Mule and other recordings
Store: mail order only

$$$ ☎ 🍁 ▀

Kicking Mule was recommended to us by a reader for "mostly blues, folk albums with good acoustic guitar, banjo, mandolin, and dulcimer." The firm was established in 1972, features records, tapes, books, and teaching tapes under its own label, but also offers "Lark in the Morning" and other video music lessons and recordings of guitar, banjo, and dulcimer from Flying Fish, Rounder, Schanachie, and Sugar Hill. The 48-page catalog is written by people who really love music—for one, they list all the songs on an album by title. Other catalogs seem to feel that's a waste of space; at Kicking Mule, they know you'll *have* to hear Seth Austen play "Carbolic Rag" as well as the Tennessee Waltz on "Appalachian Fiddle Tunes for Guitar," and Dave Miller's "Star Trek Blues" guitar solo. All this, and prices that average 25% to 40% below list with specials and volume pricing to deepen the discounts to as much as 70% on selected items. (At this writing, records under the firm's label are priced at $4, and a grabbag selection of ten guitar LPs costs just $20.)

Kicking Mule is offering readers a discount of 10% on their first order. Be sure to identify yourself as a WBMC reader when you order, and deduct the discount from the cost of the goods only. This WBMC reader discount expires February 1, 1993.

Special Factors: Price quote by phone or letter; quantity discounts are available; orders are shipped worldwide.

MAGAZINE MARKETPLACE

**6523 N. GALENA RD.
PEORIA, IL 61644
309/691-4610**

Information: inquire
Save: up to 75%
Pay: check or MO
Sells: magazine subscriptions
Store: mail order only

$$$

Magazine Marketplace sells nonfiction books and subscriptions to general and special-interest magazines at savings of up to 75% on the publishers' rates, and guarantees lowest to-the-general-public prices. Our most recent Marketplace mailing included the chance to win $7 million in a sweepstakes, as well as bargains on subscriptions to *Family Circle, Compute, Fortune, Working Mother, Organic Gardening, Mirabella,* and *Outside* among the scores of publications. Bonuses and premiums are a regular feature, as well as the sweepstakes.

Special Factors: Satisfaction is guaranteed; inquire for information.

METACOM, INC.

ADVENTURES IN CASSETTES
DEPT. D370
5353 NATHAN LANE
PLYMOUTH, MN 55442
800-328-0108
FAX: 612/557-0424

Catalog: free
Save: up to 30%
Pay: check, MO, MC, V, AE, Discover
Sells: audiotapes, CDs, and videotapes
Store: mail order only

$$

Metacom, better known as Adventures in Cassettes, offers audiotapes of the comedy classics of Abbott and Costello, Fanny Brice, Burns and Allen, Fibber McGee and Molly, Jack Benny, and other radio luminaries, as well as mysteries and dramas of the era. Past catalogs have featured Arch Oboler's "Lights Out, Everybody," "War of the Worlds," the Lone Ranger, the Green Hornet, Hopalong Cassidy, and other favorites. And you can recall kinder, gentler Saturday mornings at will with the videotapes of cartoon greats, including the finest moments of Casper the Friendly Ghost and Felix the Cat.

Metacom's music choices include a wide selection of top-of-the-charts rock and country hits from past years. The selection of language and motivational tapes can help you learn German or French, stop smoking, improve your memory, lose weight, or achieve other goals. Prices of the tapes are comparable to those charged by other discount houses, running from $3.98 to $9.98 each, and quantity discounts and bonuses may be offered.

Special Factors: Satisfaction is guaranteed; returns are accepted within 30 days for exchange, refund, or credit; minimum order is $15 with credit cards.

MUSIQUARIUM USED CD CLUB

**DEPT. WBMC
P.O. BOX 7151
ROCHESTER, MN 55903**

Brochure: $2, refundable (see text)
Save: up to 30%
Pay: check or MO
Sells: used CDs
Store: mail order only

$$

Musiquarium can help you capitalize on the CDs in your collection through its used CD club. Through this forum, individuals can list and price CDs they'd like to sell, at the nominal cost of one stamp for each two titles offered for sale. Musiquarium doesn't charge any commission, just $7.50 for club membership, which runs for six months and includes three issues of the newsletter listings ($12 for a year, with six issues). You can preview the service by sending $2 for the current newsletter and details on joining the club (deductible from the price of membership if you join).

The listing we received included hundreds of CD titles in a number of categories: mainstream rock of every decade from the 50s to the 90s, "alternative" rock (from A House to Yen), heavy metal, country, easy-listening, jazz, R & B, soul, soundtracks, and miscellany. (There was just one offering under the "classical" music heading, but this category may become better represented as membership grows.) The prices members charge one another are better than the $3 or $4 they'd receive from a dealer, but well under the price of new CDs—they average $8.50 each, at this writing.

Special Factor: Sales of discs are made between members on an "honor" basis.

PAGES/BOOKTRADERS, LTD.

**801 SOUTH IRWIN AVE.
GREEN BAY, WI 54301
414/437-9566**

Catalog: free
Save: up to 50%
Pay: check, MO, MC, V, AE, Discover, Optima
Sells: new, used, and out-of-print books
Store: same address; Tuesday to Friday 10–5, Saturday 10–4

Pages/Booktraders Ltd. has run its Green Bay bookstore since 1982, and offers selections from its shelves of new, used, and hard-to-find books through a ten-page catalog. While some new titles are sold at or near publishers' prices, out-of-print and rare book titles may be priced 50% below what other book dealers are charging.

The catalog we received listed books on architecture and the arts as well as literature (where we found Dick Francis and William Shakespeare), "collectibles" (including Frank Baum's *The Army Alphabet*), "things that go bump in the night"—Barker, Doyle, King, Koontz, Lovecraft, et al. "Wisconsin and the packers," a collection of works on the history of the state and its legendary football team, "the great outdoors" (including the fishing great *Trout Madness*), world history, the Civil War, mythology, and a range of other topics. The stock includes illustrated books and first editions, and the descriptions note the condition of the books. Pages/Booktraders also offers a book search service for $3 a title, and says that "we can't guarantee finding a book although we do find about half." If you've had no luck with the free search services, you might try again here for this nominal fee.

Special Factors: Price quote by phone or letter; authorized returns are accepted within 7 days for exchange, refund, or credit; orders are shipped worldwide.

THE POTTERS SHOP INC.

**31 THORPE RD.
NEEDHAM, MA 02194
617/449-7687**

Catalog: free
Save: up to 75%
Pay: check or MO
Sells: books and videotapes on ceramics and pottery, ceramics tools
Store: same address; Monday to Thursday 9:30–5:30, Friday 9:30–2

$$ ◆ ▬

The Potters Shop, established in 1977, sells books and videotapes on ceramics and pottery at discounts of at least 15%, and as much as 75% on sale titles. The brochure we received listed hundreds of books and tapes, many of them obscure or hard-to-find imports. You'll find works on technique, historical surveys, profiles of individual potters, ceramics of the East, health and business for the production potter, and even a selection of books for children. Among the videotapes (all VHS) are workshops on raku, form, and technique, and bamboo and Dolan tools are also available. The Potters Shop also searches for books, maintains want lists, and buys used books on the subject. If you find yourself in Needham, stop in at the shop; the books are there, as well as the pottery of local artisans.

Special Factors: Price quote by phone or letter; orders are shipped worldwide.

PRINT'S GRAPHIC DESIGN BOOK STORE

**3200 TOWER OAKS BLVD.
ROCKVILLE, MD 20852-
    4216
800-222-2654
301/770-2900
FAX: 301/984-3203**

Catalog: free
Save: up to 50% (see text)
Pay: check, MO, MC, V, AE
Sells: books on the graphic arts
Store: mail order only

Print Magazine, which serves the graphic-design community, runs a mail-order bookstore that offers well-chosen manuals, color charts, and other aids and reference materials on a range of design-related topics. All of the books are discounted, typically 20%, but we found some tagged at 30% and 50% below their published prices.

The 16-page color catalog offers annuals, clip-art collections, and books on advertising, graphic design, trademarks and logos, computer-based graphics and desktop publishing, illustration, studio protocol, photography, color, and the Pantone color manuals and fanfold color guides. Among the 140-odd titles in the catalog we reviewed were *Visual Thinking, How to Check and Correct Color Proofs, Studio Secrets for Graphic Artists,* and *Homage to the Alphabet: A Typeface Sourcebook.* You can subscribe to *Print Magazine* through the catalog, and our mailing included an entry form to the magazine's annual regional design competition.

Canadian readers, please note: Only U.S. funds are accepted.

Special Factors: Satisfaction is guaranteed; undamaged returns are accepted within 15 days for exchange, refund, or credit; institutional accounts are available.

PUBLISHERS CLEARING HOUSE

101 WINNERS CIRCLE
PORT WASHINGTON, NY
11050
516/883-5432

Information: inquire
Save: up to 50%
Pay: check or MO
Sells: magazine subscriptions
Store: mail order only

$$$ ♣

Publishers Clearing House acts as an agent for magazine publishers, offering subscriptions to popular and special-interest magazines at savings of up to 50% on regular rates. PCH guarantees lowest to-the-public prices, and a recent mailing featured 119 periodicals, including *Parents Magazine, Reader's Digest, Consumer Reports, Organic Gardening, Changing Times, McCall's, TV Guide, Ski, Time,* and *People.* The mailings usually include bonuses, premiums, and sweepstakes, and you can spread payments for your magazines over four months. We've had excellent service with PCH over the years, and the only time a problem occurred, the firm responded quickly and resolved it.

Special Factors: Satisfaction is guaranteed; inquire for information; installment plan is available.

ROCKY MOUNTAIN STATIONERY

11725 CO. RD. 27.3
DOLORES, CO 81323
303/565-8230

Samples and Price List: $1 with double-stamped, self-addressed envelope
Save: up to 50%
Pay: check or MO
Sells: handmade note cards
Store: mail order only

$$ ▤

Rocky Mountain Stationery is run by Rose Ruland, an artist who presses flowers and leaves from her garden and the surrounding wilds of the Rockies and uses them to create note cards. The cards are small and quite lovely, the flowers artfully arranged on pastel parchment card stock. Ms. Ruland also creates unusual oil "paintings" on cards; the samples we've received show a good eye for color and design.

Rocky Mountain's "Nature" and "Just a Note" series are sold in collections of 12 in assorted colors, with envelopes. Each card collection costs $8.95, compared to $2 and up for *individual* cards of the same type sold in gift shops. Please note: Send $1 and a #10 double-stamped, self-addressed envelope for the samples and price list.

Special Factors: Satisfaction is guaranteed; returns are accepted.

THE SCHOLAR'S BOOKSHELF

51 EVERETT DR.
PRINCETON JUNCTION,
NJ 08550

Catalog: free
Save: up to 75%
Pay: check, MO, MC, V
Sells: scholarly and university press books
Store: mail order only

$$$ ☎ ◆ ▤

University presses still produce highbrow texts for scholars, but many are of interest—and accessible—to nonprofessionals as well. Virtue notwithstanding, these books sometimes suffer the same fate as their commercial counterparts—remaindering. The Scholar's Bookshelf turns publishing misfortune into intellectual excitement 14 times a year, offering a wide variety of university press and scholarly imprint remainders at an average of 30% off published prices, though savings can run up to 75%.

The 64-page catalog is packed with concise descriptions of volumes on American literature and drama, music, the Civil War, architecture and urban planning, archaeology, art history (ancient to modern), photography, world history and politics, psychology, philosophy, religion, Judaica, and the sciences. The issue we reviewed included all of Joseph Campbell's *The Masks of God* series, the West Point Military History series, Michel Foucalt's *The History of Sexuality,* and other facsimiles, illuminated manuscripts (reproductions), and special editions.

Special Factors: Returns are accepted within 30 days for exchange, refund, or credit; minimum order is $10, $15 with credit cards; orders are shipped worldwide.

SCRIPT CITY

**8033 SUNSET BLVD.,
  SUITE 1500-HR
HOLLYWOOD, CA 90046
213/871-0707
FAX: 213/871-9260**

Catalog: $2, refundable
Save: up to 50% (see text)
Pay: check, MO, MC, V, AE, Discover, CB, DC
Sells: TV and movie scripts, theme gifts, etc.
Store: mail order only

Scripts are the featured players in this catalog, which includes more than 10,000 screenplays used on movie sets, early drafts (which may include lost scenes), and scripts from TV shows, movies, and miniseries. Script City sells copies beginning at under $20, while at least one competitor charges $40 to $50 for the same titles. The movie categories include Academy Award winners and nominees, late releases, drama/mystery, horror/sci-fi, comedy, action/adventure, and "assorted favorites." The early drafts should be of interest to students of the cinema who are exploring the evolution of a work. (For example, *Die Hard,* originally entitled *Nothing Lasts Forever,* and Tim Burton's *Batman* both underwent considerable revision before finally making it to the screen.) A short list of treatments (synopses of 30 to 40 pages preceding the screenplay) and storyboards (drawings or photos showing shot sequences) is given, and there are hundreds of scripts for TV shows, pilots, series, and movies.

Much of the catalog is devoted to books, software, audiotapes, and videotapes for the aspiring screenwriter, including vital directories and insiders' guides. Lobby cards, movie posters, publicity photos, and theme T-shirts are all offered. Many of these items aren't discounted, but it's nice to know where you can find a "thirtysomething" nightshirt if you want one.

Please note: Instructors in the field are entitled to a 10% educators' discount; inquire on your institution's letterhead for details.

Special Factors: Quantity discounts are available; authorized returns are accepted within 7 days for exchange, refund, or credit; institutional accounts are available; orders are shipped worldwide.

STRAND BOOK STORE, INC.

**828 BROADWAY
NEW YORK, NY 10003
212/473-1452
FAX: 212/473-2591**

Catalog: free
Save: up to 80%
Pay: check, MO, MC, V, AE, Discover, Optima
Sells: new, used, and remaindered books
Store: same address; Monday to Saturday 9:30–9:25, Sunday 11–6; also 159 John St., New York, NY; Monday to Sunday 10–9

Manhattan's legendary Strand Book Store boasts eight miles of books—more than two million volumes—and is believed to be the largest dealer of used and out-of-print books in the U.S. Strand set up shop in 1929, and publishes a number of catalogs that feature samples of its staggering inventory.

The "Specials" catalog, published several times a year, lists thousands of works that run from Simon Schama's *Citizens* to Gerdy's three-volume set of *Art Across America* (list price $425, here $295). This catalog includes critique and commentary, biographies, books on art, architecture, philosophy, crafts, politics, food, drama, and other fields of interest. The "Review" catalog, available to institutional accounts, lists new releases at 50% off publishers' prices. (Request this catalog on your institution's letterhead.)

You have to visit to do justice to the Strand, and to find the pricing "accidents"—books ticketed at a few dollars that are worth many times that. (Veteran book collectors who frequent the store can usually produce a few examples.) Strand also has a Rare Books department, with first, fine, and scarce editions, as well as fine bindings and books signed by the author.

Special Factors: Satisfaction is guaranteed; price quote by phone or letter; specify catalog desired and request by postcard or letter; want lists are maintained; book collections are purchased; institutional accounts are available; returns are accepted; minimum order is $20 with credit cards; orders are shipped worldwide.

SUPERINTENDENT OF DOCUMENTS

U.S. GOVERNMENT PRINTING OFFICE WASHINGTON, DC 20402-9325 202/783-3238

Catalog: free
Save: up to 30% (see text)
Pay: check, MO, MC, V
Sells: Federal government publications
Store: same address; also U.S. Government bookstores in AL, CA, CO, FL, GA, IL, MA, MD, MI, MO, NY, OH, OR, PA, TX, WA, and WI (see the catalog for locations)

$$$ ☎ ♦ ▓

This is probably the only book catalog in the country that could run a subscription offer to *Special Warfare* right before the 1987 Folklife Annual, followed by *Building a Better America,* George Bush's address to Congress at the beginning of his presidency. These are among the latest hits from the Superintendent of Documents, whose 48-page catalog offers everything from *Walnut Notes,* a manual for the walnut farmer, to the 54-page *Narcotics Identification Manual.* Back in print is the government's "all time best seller," *Infant Care,* in an updated edition that costs $4. *The Complete Guide to Home Canning* ($11), *A Citizen's Guide to Radon* ($1), *Health Information for the International Traveler* ($5), and the three-volume *Back-Yard Mechanic* ($7), all caught our attention.

Uncle Sam has taken the time to put together "Making Bag Lunches, Snacks, and Desserts," compile *Letters of Delegates to Congress, 1774–1789,* and help you realize the American dream with the 54-page *Starting and Managing a Business from Your Home* ($1.75). None of the books or pamphlets is free, but many cost under $10 and are real treasure troves of useful information. (Quantity discounts of 25% on orders of 100 of the same title—with some exceptions—are available.) Subscriptions to consumer magazines published by the government can be ordered through the catalog, and there are calendars and a number of posters of American artists' work as well as space shots and maps.

Special Factors: Quantity discounts are available; authorized returns due to Government error are accepted within 6 months for exchange or credit; institutional accounts are available; orders are shipped worldwide.

TARTAN BOOK SALES

500 ARCH ST., DEPT. N14
WILLIAMSPORT, PA 17705
800-233-8467, EXT. 461
IN CANADA 800-666-
9162, EXT. 461
FAX: 717/326-6769

Catalog and Brochure: free
Save: up to 74%
Pay: check, MO, MC, V
Sells: used books
Store: same address (Brodart Outlet Bookstore); Tuesday through Friday 10–6, Saturday 10–4

$$$ ☎ 🍁 🇺🇸

Tartan, a direct-mail division of Brodart Co. that began business in 1960, sells hardbound books that have had short-term library circulation. Only undamaged, unsoiled, popular adult fiction and nonfiction books are offered—no paperbacks, juvenile titles, or reference texts.

Danielle Steele's *Daddy,* published at $19.95, sold here for $5.98; Stephen King's *Four Past Midnight* was $6.49 from $22.95; and Louis L'Amour's *Education of a Wandering Man* cost $4.98, from $16.95. These were among scores of titles listed in a recent catalog, which also featured other popular fiction, mysteries, romance novels, Westerns, science fiction and adventure, biographies, and self-help books. This is a great way to get hardbound books for little more than you'd pay for the paperback editions. Further savings are available through special offers, such as the "potluck books" special of five books for $6 or ten titles for $9—your choice of general category, Tartan's choice of title.

Tartan is offering readers a discount of 25% on their first order. Be sure to identify yourself as a WBMC reader when you order, and deduct the discount from the cost of the books only. This WBMC reader discount expires February 1, 1993.

Special Factors: Returns are accepted if an error was made in filling the order; quantity discounts are available; institutional accounts are available; orders are shipped worldwide.

TRUMBLE GREETINGS, INC.

P.O. BOX 9800-M146
BOULDER, CO 80301
800-525-0656
IN CO 303/530-7768
FAX: 303/530-5124

Catalog: $1, refundable (see text)
Save: up to 40% (see text)
Pay: check, MO, MC, V, AE
Sells: Leanin' Tree cards and gifts
Store: Museum of Western Art and Gift Shop, 6055 Longbow Dr., Boulder, CO; Monday to Friday 8–4:30

$$$ ☎ 🍁

People may not sit down and write long letters much anymore, but there are lots of us who stay in touch with distant friends and relations by sending cards on a regular basis. At $1.50 and $2 a card, though, that can get expensive. Trumble Greetings has a solution.

Trumble brings you Leanin's Tree cards, which are genuinely wholesome and appealing, as well as the company's line of mugs, prints, and other gifts. The catalog (which costs $1, but comes with a $2 refund coupon) features over 200 "everyday" card designs. Nature and Western themes dominate, but Native Americans, Americana, cats, whales and dolphins, flowers and gardens, folk art, teddy bears, and similar motifs also abound. Many of the cards are offered blank, but there is a wide selection with printed sentiments that celebrate friendship and birthdays and convey sympathy, appreciation, or regret.

The highest price you'll pay per card, at this writing, is $1.50; assortments of eight and ten cost $9.95 and $11.95, and some of the designs are also available as matted art prints for $8.95 (frames are available for $11.95). Trumble Greetings, which has been in business since 1949, offers discounts for roughly every $25 you buy, from 10% off on orders totaling $24.01 to $49.00, up to 40% off on orders reaching $99.01 or more (driving the card price down to 90¢). If you're not much on sending cards, check the art prints, "Sidekick Prints," and mugs with some of the Leanin' Tree's most popular images—outlaw dogs in cowboy hats is a favorite. The discounts apply to everything sold here, including the mugs, and Trumble urges you to combine orders with friends and coworkers to get the best prices possible.

Special Factors: Satisfaction is guaranteed; price quote by phone or letter; quantity discounts are available; returns are accepted for exchange, refund, or credit; orders are shipped worldwide.

SEE ALSO

Art Express • art-related books, manuals, and videotapes • *ART MATERIALS*

Art Supply Warehouse, Inc. • art-related books and manuals • *ART MATERIALS*

Sam Ash Music Corp. • sheet music • *MUSIC*

Astronomics/Christophers, Ltd. • star charts and manuals on astronomy • *CAMERAS*

Bailey's, Inc. • books on logging, chain saw use and maintenance, etc. • *TOOLS*

Baron/Barclay Bridge Supplies • books, cards, and teaching aids for bridge • *TOYS*

Bass Pro Shops • boating and fishing books and videotapes • *SPORTS*

Bike Nashbar • manuals on bicycle repair • *SPORTS*

Dick Blick Co. • films, slides, videotapes, and manuals on arts and crafts • *ART MATERIALS*

Bruce Medical Supply • books on vitamins, health care, and medical topics • *MEDICINE*

Butterbrooke Farm Seed Co-Op • booklets on gardening topics • *FARM*

Campmor • field guides, survival and outdoor guides • *SPORTS*

The Caning Shop • books on seat weaving, upholstery, basketry • *CRAFTS*

Capital Cycle Corporation • factory-repair manuals for BMW cycles • AUTO

Caprilands Herb Farm • books on herbs and gardening, making wreaths, and cooking • FARM

Central Tractor Farm & Family Center • shop manuals for farm equipment, books on the history of farm implements and equipment • FARM

Ceramic Supply of New York & New Jersey, Inc. • artists' manuals and books on crafts • ART MATERIALS

Cheap Joe's Art Stuff • art-related books, manuals, and videotapes • ART MATERIALS

Cheap Shot Inc. • reloading manuals • SPORTS

Cherry Tree Toys, Inc. • manuals on wood projects and toy making • CRAFTS

Circle Craft Supply • books and manuals on arts and crafts • CRAFTS

Craft King, Inc. • craft project books • CRAFTS

Custom Golf Clubs, Inc. • texts on golf club making and repair, golfing, etc. • SPORTS

Cycle Goods Corp. • texts on bicycling, repair, and maintenance • SPORTS

Daleco Master Breeder Products • books on fish and saltwater fish care and breeding • ANIMAL

Defender Industries, Inc. • manuals and videotapes on boating, seamanship, racing, etc. • AUTO

Dharma Trading Co. • books on textile dyeing, painting, batiking, etc. • CRAFTS

The Dog's Outfitter • books and videotapes on dogs, cats, horses, etc. • ANIMAL

Eastcoast Software • educational, business, and entertainment programs • OFFICE: COMPUTING

EduCALC Mail Store • computer books and programs • OFFICE: COMPUTING

Elderly Instruments • folk, rock, and esoteric recordings, songbooks, history, and manuals • MUSIC

The Fiber Studio • books on knitting, spinning, dyeing, and weaving • CRAFTS

Gallery Graphics, Inc. • nostalgic-theme notes and cards • ART, ANTIQUES

Gander Mountain, Inc. • videotapes on hunting and fishing topics • SPORTS

Giardinelli Band Instrument Co., Inc. • records and books on music • MUSIC

Gohn Bros. • Amish and country cookbooks, quilting books • *CLOTHING*

Goldberg's Marine Distributors • manuals and videotapes on boating, seamanship, racing, etc. • *AUTO*

Marv Golden Discount Sales, Inc. • aviation flight guides and binders • *AUTO*

Great Northern Weaving • books on shirret, rug weaving, and rug braiding • *CRAFTS*

H & R Company • reference books on computing and technical topics • *SURPLUS*

IMPCO, Inc. • Mercedes-Benz car maintenance manuals • *AUTO*

Jerry's Artarama, Inc. • books and videotapes on fine arts and crafts • *ART MATERIALS*

The Kennel Vet Corp. • large selection of books on breeds of dogs, cats, and horses, vet manuals • *ANIMAL*

E.C. Kraus Wine & Beermaking Supplies • books on wine- and beer-making • *FOOD*

Lone Star Percussion • books on drumming and percussion recordings • *MUSIC*

Mandolin Brothers, Ltd. • music books, audiotapes, videotapes, and sheet music • *MUSIC*

Mass. Army & Navy Store • survival manuals and outdoor guides • *SURPLUS*

Master Animal Care • veterinary handbooks • *ANIMAL*

Mellinger's Inc. • reference books on gardening, farming, landscaping, and food preservation • *FARM*

Metropolitan Music Co. • manuals and plans for making and repairing stringed instruments • *MUSIC*

National Educational Music Co., Ltd. • music software • *MUSIC*

The Natural Baby Co., Inc. • children's books • *CLOTHING: MOTHER AND CHILD*

New England Cheesemaking Supply Co. • publications on making cheese • *HOME: KITCHEN*

Newark Dressmaker Supply, Inc. • patterns, books, and guides on needlework and other crafts • *CRAFTS*

Northern Wholesale Veterinary Supply, Inc. • books on care and breeding of livestock, dogs, and cats • *ANIMAL*

Omaha Vaccine Co., Inc. • books on care and breeding of horses, livestock, dogs, and cats • *ANIMAL*

Orion Telescope Center • star charts and manuals on astronomy • *CAMERAS*

Overton's Sports Center, Inc. • windsurfing books and videotapes • *SPORTS*

Patti Music Corp. • sheet music • *MUSIC*

Pet Warehouse • books and manuals on dogs, cats, birds, and fish • *ANIMAL*

Pueblo to People • books and tapes on Central and South America and Third World issues • *GENERAL MERCHANDISE*

Porter's Camera Store, Inc. • books and videos on photography • *CAMERAS*

Retired Persons Services Inc. • health-care manuals • *MEDICINE*

Sailboard Warehouse, Inc. • windsurfing books and videotapes • *SPORTS*

Sax Arts & Crafts • art-related books, manuals, and videotapes • *ART MATERIALS*

Scope City • star charts, books, manuals • *CAMERAS*

Shar Products Company • sheet music, classical music videotapes, and audio cassettes • *MUSIC*

R.C. Steele Co. • AKC videotapes of dog shows, manuals for pet professionals • *ANIMAL*

Straw Into Gold, Inc. • Folkwear patterns and books on fiber crafts • *CRAFTS*

Sultan's Delight, Inc. • cookbooks featuring Middle Eastern and Greek cuisine • *FOOD*

That Fish Place • books on aquariums, fish, and related topics • *ANIMAL*

Turnbaugh Printers Supply Co. • texts on printing • *OFFICE*

Turner Greenhouses • books on gardening • *FARM*

United Pharmacal Company, Inc. • books and manuals on the care and breeding of a variety of animals • *ANIMAL*

United Supply Co., Inc. • art-related books, manuals, and videotapes • *ART MATERIALS*

University Products, Inc. • preservation supplies for book collections, references (books and videos) on archival conservation • *GENERAL: PACKAGING*

Veteran Leather Company, Inc. • guides to leatherworking • *CRAFTS*

Walnut Acres Organic Farms • natural foods and vegetarian cookbooks • *FOOD*

Weinkrantz Musical Supply Co., Inc. • student music books and cassettes • *MUSIC*

West Manor Music • small selection of music manuals • *MUSIC*

Wholesale Veterinary Supply, Inc. • veterinary texts and Farnam videos • *ANIMAL*

Wholesale Tape and Supply Company • blank audiotapes and videotapes, cases, accessories, etc. • *APPLIANCES*

The Wine Enthusiast • books and videotapes on wine • *FOOD*

CAMERAS, PHOTOGRAPHIC AND DARKROOM EQUIPMENT, OPTICS, FILM, AND SERVICES

Equipment, supplies, and services

The camera market is highly competitive, and even major electronics outlets with small camera departments can usually offer meaningful discounts on list prices. In addition to cameras, bulbs, and film, large camera houses carry lighting equipment, screens, film editors, splicers, batteries, projection tables, lenses, filters, adapters, cases, darkroom outfits, and chemicals, and custom photofinishing services—at discounts averaging 40%. Even if you don't need custom work done, you can have your film processed, enlargements made, slides duplicated, and other services done by a discount mail-order lab for half the price charged by a drugstore or retail outlet.

Even at a discount, photographs will cost you something—and they may have a great personal value as well, as the chief document of an individual history. So keep them out of "magnetic" photo albums, which are made with polyvinyl-film that gives off vinyl chloride gas, and cardboard pages that exude peroxide vapors. Both can cause deterioration of slides and prints. Some conservationists believe that an entire generation of family photos is being destroyed by toxic albums and by being stored in garages, attics, and basements. (Photographs should be kept in temperate, relatively dry areas, out of light as much as possible.) To preserve your pictures, use archival-quality materials—acid-free albums and storage boxes, Mylar sheet protectors, "safe" slide sheets, etc. These and other conservation materials are available from University Products, listed in the "Packaging" section of "General Merchandise."

THE GREY MARKET

Grey-market goods, also known as "parallel" or "direct" imports, are products are intended for sale in other countries. They're usually imported outside manufacturer-approved distribution channels, without authorization of the U.S. trademark owner. Grey-market goods are usually less expensive than their "authorized" counterparts, and although they may be just as good, they may also be produced under different quality-control standards, contain ingredients not approved for such use in the U.S., or have a warranty that is not honored in the U.S.

Unfortunately, many of the firms selling grey-market goods to consumers failed to inform them of the fact, and problems arose when products didn't perform properly, or couldn't be repaired in the U.S. Consumers turned to the U.S. manufacturers, who had no legal obliigation to service the goods, but who often tried to make good to preserve a positive image. (The manufacturers then turned to the courts to solve the problem.)

Grey-market goods are of concern because of potential hazards: The door of a luxury car, "reinforced" by the importer with a broomstick in order to appear to meet U.S. safety standards; the batteries that will be leaking into the kids' toys because they were left in a hot warehouse for a month; the perfume spray propelled by Freon and the night cream adulterated with an illegal dye—all are examples of grey-market goods that could cause harm.

Champions of parallel imports say they promote competition and keep prices down, but we think the possible problems make them hard to recommend. So we have not *knowingly* listed grey-marketers in this edition of WBMC. We can't make any guarantees, and companies can change selling policies, so if you want to be sure a firm is an authorized distributor of a product, call the manufacturer. Ask the mail-order company whether the warranty is honored by the service centers of the *U.S. manufacturer.* And make your purchase by credit card, which gives you certain protections under the Fair Credit Billing Act. See page 612 for more information.

BINOCULARS • *Astronomics/Christophers, Danley's, Mardiron, Orion, Scope City*
CAMERAS • *Ewald-Clark, Porter's, Solar Cine, Westside Camera*
PHOTO PROCESSING • *Ewald-Clark, Owl Photo, Skyline, Solar Cine*
TELESCOPES • *Astronomics/Christophers, Mardiron, Orion, Scope City*

ASTRONOMICS/ CHRISTOPHERS, LTD.

2401 TEE CIRCLE, SUITE 106-W92
NORMAN, OK 73069
800-422-7876
(TELESCOPES)
800-356-6603
(BINOCULARS AND SPOTTING SCOPES)

Catalogs: $1 and SASE
Save: up to 50%
Pay: check, MO, MC, V, AE, Discover
Sells: telescopes and optics
Store: same address; Monday to Friday 9:30–5, Saturday by appointment

$$$ ☎ 🍁

Astronomics/Christophers sells telescopes and birding equipment made by the best firms in the business at up to 50% below list, and its stock includes complete lines for astronomical photography. The firm's information-packed birding and astronomical catalogs are sent free if you specify which one you want, and send $1 and a self-addressed, business-sized envelope. Astronomics/Christophers was established in 1970, and sells no grey-market goods.

Astronomics sells optics and accessories by Astromedia, Bausch & Lomb, Bushnell, Celestron, DayStar, Dover, Edmund, Kowa, Leica (Leitz), Lumicon, Meade, Mirador, MotoFocus, Nikon, Optolyth, Questar, Sky Publishing, Swarovski, Swift, TeleVue, Vernonscope, and Zeiss. If you're looking for a telescope, choose from catadioptric, refractor, and reflector models, as well as lenses, mirrors, eyepieces, tripods, photo adapters, visual and photographic filters, equatorial mounts and wedges, spotting scopes for bird watching, and many other items. Astronomical and bird-watching binoculars are also offered, and Astronomics/Christophers offers a great collection of books and star chart, manuals, slides, maps, atlases, and other reference tools.

Special Factors: Price quote by phone or letter; shipping is included on prepaid orders delivered within the continental U.S.; minimum order is $25; orders are shipped worldwide.

DANLEY'S
■■■■■■■■■

P.O. BOX 4401-WM
HALFMOON, NY 12065
518/664-2014

Catalog and Price List: free
Save: up to 50%
Pay: check, MO, MC, V
Sells: optics and accessories
Store: mail order only

Danley's offers stargazer, bird watcher, hunter, and spectator a comprehensive selection of top-of-the-line optics for sports, marine use, and other specialized functions at up to 50% off list prices. Danley's, in business since 1960, stocks complete lines of binoculars and spotting scopes by Bausch & Lomb, Bushnell, aus Jena, Kowa, Leica (Leitz), Mirador, Nikon, Steiner, Swift, and Zeiss, as well as accessories. Standard and compact models, sports binoculars, armored models for field work, waterproof styles for marine use, zoom lenses, theater glasses, and telescopes are all available, as well as tripods by Bausch & Lomb, Tiltall, and Velbon.

Canadian readers, please note: Only U.S. funds are accepted.

Special Factors: Price quote by phone or letter with SASE; layaway plan is available; authorized returns are accepted.

EWALD-CLARK

ATTN: DON
17 W. CHURCH AVE.
ROANOKE, VA 24011
703/342-1829
FAX: 703/345-9943

Information: price quote (see text)
Save: 30% average
Pay: check, MO, MC, V, AE
Sells: cameras, darkroom equipment, optics, services
Store: same address; Monday to Friday 8:30–5:30; also 2140 Colonial Ave., Roanoke, VA; Monday to Friday 8:30–7, Saturday 9–5; and 213 Draper Rd., Blacksburg, VA; Monday to Friday 9–7, Saturday 9–5:30

Ewald-Clark is a full-service photography center that has over 40 years of experience in the field. In addition to cameras, lenses, darkroom equipment, and finishing services, Ewald-Clark sells binoculars and video cameras. Discounts run from 2% to 40%, and average 30% off list prices.

Among the available brands are Amphoto, Beseler, Bogen, Bronica, Canon, Fuji Professional, Gitzo, Gossen, Gralab, Hasselblad, Hoya, Ilford, Kodak, Logan, Lumedyne, Mamiya, Minolta, Nikon, Novatron, Pelican, Polaroid, Quantum, Ricoh, Tamrac, Tamron, Tiffen, Tokina, Toyo, and Vivitar. There is no catalog—call or write for a price quote on specific models. You can also inquire for rate and specifications on custom photofinishing services.

Canadian readers, please note: Shipments to Canada are subject to hazardous materials regulations.

Special Factors: Price quote by phone or letter with SASE; orders are shipped worldwide.

MARDIRON OPTICS

**THE BINOCULAR PLACE
4 SPARTAN CIRCLE, DEPT.
  WBMC
STONEHAM, MA 02180
617/938-8339**

Brochure and Price List: double-stamped
  SASE
Save: 40% average
Pay: check or MO
Sells: binoculars, spotting telescopes, and
  astronomical telescopes
Store: mail order only

$$$ ♦ ▇

Mardiron, in business since 1945, sells binoculars, telescopes, and opera glasses from a select group of manufacturers at savings of up to 45% on list prices. The full line of Steiner binoculars is featured—marine, aeronautical, and other models—which are used by 40 military forces worldwide. Binoculars, spotting scopes, and astronomical telescopes by Swift are offered. Mardiron will send you manufacturers' brochures and price lists—specify whether you're interested in binoculars, spotting scopes, or astronomical telescopes—for a double-stamped, self-addressed envelope. If you know the model you're looking for, you can write or call for a price quote.

Special Factors: Price quote by phone or letter with SASE; shipping is included.

ORION TELESCOPE CENTER

DEPT. WBM
P.O. BOX 1158
SANTA CRUZ, CA 95061
IN CA 800-447-1001
408/464-0466
FAX: 408/464-0446

Catalog: free
Save: up to 40%
Pay: check, MO, MC, V
Sells: telescopes, binoculars, and accessories
Store: 2450 17th Ave., Santa Cruz, CA; Monday to Saturday 10–5:30; also 10555 S. De Anza Blvd., Cupertino, and 3609 Buchanan St., San Francisco, CA; Monday to Saturday 10–5:30, Thursday 10–8, Sunday 10–5, both locations

 $$ ☎ 🍁 ▀▀▀(see text)

Orion brings you stellar savings on top-quality telescopes and accessories through an informative, 64-page catalog that includes sidebars on telescope selection and sky watching, as well as complete product descriptions. Orion, in business since 1975, stocks astronomical and terrestrial telescopes. The models including spotting, reflector, refractor, guide, finder, and "deep sky" scopes by Celestron, Edmund, Meade, Orion, and TeleVue. (If you visit Orion's stores, you'll also find goods by Bushnell, Fujinon, Optolyth, Pentax, Swift, and Zeiss.) Camera adapters, filters, lenses, optical tubes, tripods, eyepieces, star charts, books, and other accessories are available, and Orion also carries binoculars—deep-sky, sport, folding, waterproof, and armored models.

Please note: Orion ships only to the U.S. and Canada.

Special Factors: Satisfaction is guaranteed; price quote by phone or letter for institutional orders.

OWL PHOTO

**701 E. MAIN
WEATHERFORD, OK
73096
405/772-3353**

Mailers: free
Save: up to 40%
Pay: check, MO, MC, V
Sells: film processing and reprinting services
Store: mail order only

$$$

Owl Photo offers reasonably priced film processing services by mail, and will send you self-mailers on request. The firm will develop your color and black-and-white film for prices competitive with discount drug store processing, and you can also order reprints and fresh film—a price list comes with the mailer. Owl uses Kodak paper and chemicals, and guarantees your satisfaction or your processing costs and postage will be refunded.

Special Factors: Satisfaction is guaranteed; returns are accepted for refund or credit.

PORTER'S CAMERA STORE, INC.

**P.O. BOX 628
CEDAR FALLS, IA 50613
319/268-0104
FAX: 800-779-5254**

Catalog: free (see text)
Save: 35% average
Pay: check, MO, MC, V, Discover
Sells: cameras and darkroom equipment
Store: 323 Viking Rd., Cedar Falls, IA;
Monday to Saturday 9:30–5:30

$$$$

Porter's has been selling cameras and darkroom equipment since 1914, and publishes a 116-page tabloid catalog packed with an enormous range of photographic products, at prices up to 67% below list. Both amateurs and professionals will appreciate the buys on cameras and lenses, filters, darkroom equipment, film, bags and cases, batteries, studio equipment, chemicals, paper, and much more. The brands run from Agfa to Vivitar, the sales policy is clearly detailed in the catalog, and Porter's has even deputized one of its staff to answer your questions about equipment. If you're in Cedar Falls, drop by the warehouse outlet store where you'll find everything tagged at catalog prices—a welcome departure from the two-tier policies prevailing at most discount stores.

Canadian readers, please note: The catalog costs $3 in *Canadian funds,* but orders must be paid in U.S. funds. The catalog describes purchasing procedures and includes a shipping rate chart.

Please note: The catalog costs $10 in U.S. funds if sent to an address without a U.S. or Canadian postal code.

Special Factors: Price quote by phone or letter; authorized returns are accepted; institutional accounts are available; orders are shipped worldwide ($100 minimum order).

SCOPE CITY

679 EASY ST.
SIMI VALLEY, CA 93065
805/522-6646
FAX: 805/582-0292

Catalog: free (see text)
Save: up to 45%
Pay: check, MO, MC, V, AE, Discover, Optima
Sells: telescopes, binoculars, and other optics
Store: same address; Monday to Friday 9–6, Saturday 10–6; also 3132 Pacific Coast Hwy., Torrance; 3033 S. Bristol, Costa Mesa; 10076 Magnolia Ave., Riverside; 4766 Clairemont Mesa Blvd., San Diego; and 14324 Ventura Blvd., Sherman Oaks, CA; also 2216 Paradise Rd., Las Vegas, NV

Scope City has been selling telescopes, binoculars, spotting scopes, and other optics since 1976. The catalog shows telescopes and accessories by Celestron, Edmund, Meade, Parks, Questar, Simmons, and TeleVue, as well as field and specialty binoculars by Kronehof, Leica (Leitz), Meade, Optolyth, Parks, and other manufacturers. Scope City also offers lenses, eyepieces, adapters, mirrors, celestial charts, slides, manuals, and other reference tools. Most of the prices are discounted, and savings of up to 45% are possible on selected telescope components.

Special Factors: Satisfaction is guaranteed; returns are accepted within 30 days for exchange, refund, or credit; orders are shipped worldwide.

SKYLINE COLOR LAB

9016 PRINCE WILLIAM ST., DEPT. WBMC MANASSAS, VA 22110 703/631-2216 FAX: 703/631-8064

Catalog: free
Save: up to 30%
Pay: check, MO, MC, V, AE
Sells: film processing
Store: same address; Monday to Friday 9–6, Saturday 8–2

$$ ▇▇▇(see text)

Skyline Color Lab, whose parent firm has been in business since 1945, is a full-service professional and commercial mail-order lab that offers film and slide processing, negative duplication and slide copying, prints, and photographic packages (portraits and weddings) at competitive prices. Skyline's 24-page catalog lists the available services and prices, includes directions for cropping, and features a helpful glossary of terms like "internegative," "dodging," and "push/pull processing." Skyline is an affiliate of ABC Photo Service, formerly listed in this book.

Skyline will process your color or black-and-white film (roll or sheet), produce contact sheets, make prints and enlargements (from 3½" by 5" to 48" by 144"), and create murals and photographic displays (from 40" square to 48" by 96"; larger sizes are available on a custom basis). A wide range of custom services is offered, including "push" processing to compensate for underexposed film, glass mounts for slides, slide remounting, duplicate negatives and negatives made from slides or transparencies (internegatives), a choice of finishes for enlargements (canvas, pebble, matte, or luster), dry mounting of prints (on art board, foam core, or "gator" foam), mounting on canvas panels or canvas stretchers, and printing in Duratrans and Duraflex, two materials that are ideal for photographic display. Skyline has also put together economical print packages, including a "relative's special"—one 8" by 10", two 5" by 7", and 24 wallet-sized prints—perfect for sending to friends and family—as well as wedding album packages. Complete details of the firm's sales policy and guarantees are given in the catalog.

Please note: Deliveries to APO/FPO addresses must be prepaid.

Special Factors: Price quote by phone or letter; liability for damaged or lost film is limited to replacement with unexposed film; minimum order is $25; C.O.D. orders are accepted (for delivery within continental U.S.); orders are shipped worldwide.

SOLAR CINE PRODUCTS, INC.

**4247 SOUTH KEDZIE AVE.
CHICAGO, IL 60632
312/254-8310**

Catalog: free
Save: up to 40%
Pay: check, MO, MC, V, DC, Discover
Sells: photo equipment, supplies, and services
Store: same address; Monday to Friday 8:30–5, Saturday 9–1

$$$ ☎

Solar Cine's 24-page catalog gives a sample of the thousands of items carried by the company—a full range of photographic equipment and accessories from a large number of manufacturers. Solar Cine has been supplying professionals and serious amateurs since 1937, and stocks a full range of still and movie equipment, including videotapes and video batteries. Cameras, lenses, studio lights, light meters, tripods, and darkroom materials are available from Canon, Fuji, Kalimar, Kiwi, Kodak, Minolta, Pentax, Polaroid, Smith-Victor, and Yashica, among others. Scores of books on photography for beginners and professionals are available, as well as electronics and processing services (movies, slides, reprints, and prints). The services are described in the catalog; for more information on cameras and equipment, call or write for a price quote.

Special Factor: Price quote by phone or letter.

WESTSIDE CAMERA INC.

2400 BROADWAY
NEW YORK, NY 10024
212/877-8760
FAX: 212/877-7423

Catalog: $5 (see text)
Save: 30% average
Pay: check, MO, MC, V, AE
Sells: photo equipment and supplies
Store: same address; Monday to Saturday
8–7, Saturday 10–6

$ ☎ ♣

Westside has been selling photography goods since 1972 and features a comprehensive line of darkroom equipment and supplies that should satisfy both hobbyists and pros. The catalog costs $5, but if you know the model or item you want, you can call or write for a price quote.

Westside carries cameras and photo equipment (including video), darkroom supplies, frames, straps, carrying bags, and film products by Agfa, Beseler, Bogen, Canon, Cokin, Dax, Fuji, Gitzo, Hasselblad, Holson, Ilford, Kodak, Leica, Minolta, Nikon, Olympus, Pentax, Polaroid, Ricoh, Sprint Chemistry, Tamrac, Tiltall, Vivitar, Yashica, and other firms. There is a full line of related goods, such as the R.O.R. optical lens cleaner, which can be seen in the catalog.

Special Factors: Price quote by phone or letter; minimum order is $25.

SEE ALSO

American Science & Surplus • lenses and optics • *SURPLUS*
Berry Scuba Co. • underwater cameras • *SPORTS*
Cabela's Inc. • binoculars, spotting scopes, and sunglasses • *SPORTS*
Central Skindivers • underwater cameras • *SPORTS*
Harry's Discounts & Appliances Corp. • blank videotapes •
   APPLIANCES
S & S Sound City • blank videotapes • *APPLIANCES*
20th Century Plastics, Inc. • vinyl slide protectors • *OFFICE*
University Products, Inc. • archival-quality storage materials for
   photographs, slides, film, negatives, microfiche, etc. • *GENERAL:*
   PACKAGING
Wiley Outdoor Sports, Inc. • binoculars, spotting scopes, etc. • *SPORTS*

CIGARS, PIPES, TOBACCO, AND OTHER SMOKING NEEDS

Cigars, chewing tobacco, cigarette tobacco, snuff, pipes, and smoking accessories

It's not easy being a smoker today, but if you're going to light up, you might as well do it at a discount. The companies listed here sell cigars, pipe tobacco, chewing tobacco, shredded tobacco for cigarette rolling, pipes, and other smoking accessories at savings of up to 75%. If your current smoke is a name-brand cigar, look here for off-brand versions sold at a fraction of the prices of the originals, as well as the famous labels themselves, which are often available at a discount.

The right to smoke outside the home is being challenged by the ordinances being passed all over the country to limit smoking in public places. While the Surgeon General's objective of a "smoke-free society by the year 2000" won't be realized, at least one message seems to have registered with Americans: Smoking poses serious hazards to your long-term health. The tobacco industry has responded to our enlightenment by, among other tactics, trying to sell us on "smokeless" tobacco, (spending on advertising and promotion of this form of nicotine increased more than 20% in 1989, according to the FTC). But if you can switch, you can stop entirely.

QUITTING

Millions have quit smoking, and while some have been helped by hypnosis and nicotine-impregnated gum, most have succeeded with willpower alone. If you want to overcome nicotine addiction, you can get help from many sources:

Clinics: The American Cancer Society's local chapters run "Quit Smoking Clinics," usually free of cost. Contact your chapter for more information, or write to the American Cancer Society, 261 Madison Ave., New York, NY 10016.

Literature: The American Lung Association publishes two booklets, "Freedom from Smoking in 20 Days" and "A Lifetime of Freedom from Smoking," which are available from local chapters or from the American Lung Association, 1740 Broadway, New York, NY 10019.

Self-hypnosis: The behavior-modification message in self-help audiotapes can give a boost to the smoker committed to quitting, and tapes are usually cheaper and more convenient than live therapy. Metacom, in "Books," sells a line of self-improvement tapes at good prices.

Nicotine gum: Nicotine-impregnated chewing gum releases a dose of nicotine as it's chewed, helping to ease cigarette cravings. The gum won't make quitting easy, but can help you get through the first weeks. The gum has its drawbacks, and it's not inexpensive. If you'd like to try it, contact your physician (it's sold by prescription only) and ask about alternatives—including support groups and local programs. If you use the gum, you can have your prescription filled at a discount by one of the pharmacies listed in "Medicine."

Smoking poses other health hazards, one of which is fire. Smoking-related deaths in the home exceed those caused by arson, electrical or heating malfunctions, and kitchen accidents. And tobacco is actually poisonous; the residues left in cigarette filters and cigar stubs have proven toxic to small children and pets who've eaten the contents of ashtrays. Eliminating those risks are part of the benefits of quitting.

FAMOUS SMOKE SHOP, INC.

55 W. 39TH ST., DEPT. WB92
NEW YORK, NY 10018
800-672-5544
212/221-1408
FAX: 800-768-7443
FAX: 212/921-5458

Catalog: free
Save: up to 60%
Pay: check, MO, MC, V
Sells: cigars, tobacco, smoking accessories, and pens
Store: same address; Monday to Friday 7–6, Saturday 8–2

$$$$ ☎ ♦ ▆▆

The draw here is a super selection of branded and generic cigars and tobacco, offered through the 40-page catalog. Famous Smoke Shop has serving smokers since 1939 and can offer you the same privilege the firm's faithful enjoy: a private charge account.

The firm represents the most prominent cigar makers in the world with a vast stock of fine, hand-rolled cigars of every taste, length, size, and shape. Famous Smoke Shop imports and distributes dozens of brands, including Bering, Canaria D'Oro, Cuesta-Rey, Dom Domingo, Don Diego, Arturo Fuente, La Habanera, Hoya de Monterrey, Macanudo, Montecruz, Partagas, Primo del Rey, Punch, Royal Jamaica, Temple Hall, Troya, H. Upmann, and Zino Davidoff, among others. Unbranded house cigars, described as equivalent in quality to their famous counterparts, are sold at savings of up to 50% (compared to the name-brand versions), and miniature cigars from several leading cigar makers are available. Pipe tobacco from Amphora, Borkum, Captain Black, Dunhill, Erinmore, MacBaren, James Russell, Wessel, and other producers is also carried. Specials and cigar collections are featured regularly, and the catalog includes helpful tips on choosing cigars.

Famous Smoke Shop also sells smoking accessories, and sells Maglite flashlights and pens by Cross, Mont Blanc, and Waterman at up to 40% off list prices.

Special Factors: Satisfaction is guaranteed; price quote by phone; returns are accepted; minimum order is one box; C.O.D. orders are accepted; orders are shipped worldwide.

WALLY FRANK LTD.

63-25 69TH ST.
MIDDLE VILLAGE, NY
11379
718/326-2233
FAX: 718/326-0453

Catalog: free
Save: 45% average
Pay: check, MO, MC, V, AE, DC, Discover
Sells: cigars, pipes, and tobacco
Store: mail order only

$$$ ☎

Wally Frank offers cigar and pipe smokers a wide selection of famous-label cigars, tobacco, and privately produced smoke-alikes, priced to save you up to 50% on list or regular prices. Wally Frank has been in business since 1930 and publishes a 48-page color catalog that shows cigars by Don Diego, Dunhill, Lancer, Martinez, Montecruz, Partagas, Te-Amo, H. Upmann, and other firms, as well as Frank's generic equivalents, "irregulars," and closeout specials. In addition, a quarter of the catalog we reviewed was devoted to pipes—briar, Delft (ceramic), meerschaum, corn cob, and lava block, by Comoy's, Peterson, and Weber–in a large selection of bowl shapes and stem styles, beginning at under $5. You can fill your pipe with tobacco from Amphora, Balkan Sobraine, Borkum, Captain Black, MacBaren, and Murrays, or Wally Frank's own economy blends. Pipe-cleaning tools, pouches, racks, cigar and tobacco humidors, cigar cutters, and lighters are available, all at savings. And flavored chewing tobaccos and snuff are offered.

Special Factors: Satisfaction is guaranteed (see the catalog for details); returns are accepted; pipe service and repairs are available; shipping is included on orders over $50.

MAGNUM

500 INDEPENDENCE AVE.
S.E.
WASHINGTON, DC 20003
202/544-6858

Brochure and Price List: free with SASE
Save: up to 50%
Pay: check or MO
Sells: cigar cutter
Store: mail order only

If you smoke cigars, you probably don't need to add controversy to your life—but if you do, Magnum has the ticket: a cigar cutter set into in a .44 magnum shell casing. This conversation starter has a blade of surgical steel that "makes a smooth cut, eliminating damaged wrappers, shredded ends, and loose tobacco." The "44 Magnum" comes in a drawstring pouch, and you can have it shipped directly to your gift recipients with your card enclosed. The price Magnum is charging for the cutter is up to 50% below the list price of cutters of similar quality. Send a stamped, self-addressed envelope for the brochure, or call for more information.

Canadian readers, please note: Only U.S. funds are accepted.

Special Factor: Satisfaction is guaranteed.

MARKS CIGARS

8TH AND CENTRAL
OCEAN CITY, NJ 08226
800-257-8645
609/399-0935

Catalog: free
Save: 25% average
Pay: check, MO, MC, V, AE
Sells: cigars
Store: same address; Monday to Sunday 7
A.M.–9 P.M.

This firm has been praised by readers for its prices, which average 25% off regular retail, and for its good service. Marks Cigars, in business since 1947, represents dozens of manufacturers that include Canaria D'Oro, Don Diego, Arturo Fuente, F.D. Grave, Henri Wintermans, Hoyo de Monterrey, Macanudo, Montecruz, Partagas, Primo del Rey, Punch, Royal Jamaica, Te-Amo, Tesoro, and H. Upmann, among others. The catalog descriptions note the country of origin, ring size, length, and wrapper color of each cigar. If you're looking for a cigar not listed, call or write—it may be in stock.

Special Factor: Price quote by phone or letter with SASE.

IWAN RIES & CO.

**19 SO. WABASH
CHICAGO, IL 60603
800-621-1457
312/372-1306
FAX: 312/372-1416**

Catalog: free
Save: up to 60% (see text)
Pay: check, MO, MC, V, AE, CHOICE, Discover, Optima
Sells: cigars, pipes, and tobacco
Store: same address; Monday to Friday 9–5:30, Saturday 9–5

$$$ ☎ ❧ ▅▅▅(see text)

When Iwan Ries moved its shop off the street level a few years ago, it also changed its selling strategy. The company took its 135 years of experience as tobacconists into the discount mail-order arena, producing a 16-page color catalog full of buys, as well as periodical sales flyers with more smoking bargains.

Iwan Ries features its own pipe tobacco blends and what the firm believes to be "the largest selection of pipes in the country"—over 20,000. They include meerschaums and briars from pipemakers worldwide, including Alpha, Artigiana, Butz-Choquin, Dunhill, Jobey, Peterson, Savenilli, and Seville. The prices can reach thousands of dollars for a rare collectors' pipe, but most of the pipes in the catalog are priced under $50, and there are many under $20. In addition to the house blends, Iwan Ries sells both domestic and imported pipe tobacco from dozens of companies—call for a price on your favorite. As for cigars, the thrifty connoisseur should be pleased by the prices and the selection: Ashton, Baring, Canarias D'Oro, Davidoff, Don Diego, Dunhill, Flor de Canarias, Arturo Fuente, Griffin, Hoyo de Monterrey, Macanudo, Montecruz, Partagas, Pleiades, Primo del Ray, Punch, Royal Jamaica, Schimmelpennick, Te Amo, Tresado, H. Upmann, and Zino cigars are all available. Everything in the catalog is discounted, but the flyers offer further savings and bonuses. If you're in Chicago, drop by the store for a free pipe polishing and a sample of the house blend.

Members of the armed forces, please note: Iwan Ries offers free shipping to members of the armed forces whose orders total $22.50 or more.

Special Factors: Satisfaction is guaranteed; price quote by phone or letter; returns are accepted for exchange, refund, or credit; orders are shipped worldwide.

FRED STOKER & SONS, INC.

P.O. BOX 707
DRESDEN, TN 38225-0707
800-243-9377
901/364-5419
FAX: 901/364-3322

Catalog: free
Save: up to 50%
Pay: check, MO, MC, V
Sells: tobacco products and sweet potato plants
Shop (bonded warehouse): Rte. 1, Dresden, TN; Monday to Friday 8–5

$$$ 🇺🇸

Mr. Fred "Famous Since 1940" Stoker sells homegrown at down-home prices—chewing, smoking, and snuffing tobacco priced up to 50% less than comparable products sold elsewhere. The 12-page catalog lists flake and chewing tobacco in bourbon, "old hickory," honey, apple, butternut, wild cherry, coffee, pineapple, wintergreen, chocolate mint, and other flavors in containers of 5, 10, or 20 pounds. Stoker offers 21 types of plug tobacco in twists, in a choice of air or fire cure, as well as other sweet chews, moist and dry snuff, and cigars—boxes of smokes from the Caribbean. You can buy clipping cigar tobacco, as well as long shredded tobacco for roll-your-own cigarettes, and rolling machines and cigarette papers. Domestic and imported pipe tobacco blends are sold, as well as tobacco pouches, humidors, and other pipe accessories.

Mr. Stoker also presides over "Fred's Plant Farm," which sells tobacco seeds (Burley or Madole, $2 per packet) and 16 varieties of yams and sweet potato plants. These plant slips are well-priced—$18 to $20 a bushel in early spring, and from $7 per 25 plants to $175 for 5,000 later in the year. (Mr. Stoker estimated his 1990 yields at an average of 520 bushels an acre.) Old-fashioned sorghum-flavored table syrup and popping corn round out the offerings.

Special Factors: Inquire for information on quantity discounts; shipping is included on local deliveries and all plant orders; plants are shipped April 15 to July 1; C.O.D. orders are accepted.

THOMPSON CIGAR COMPANY

■■■■■■■

5401 HANGAR CT., DEPT. 7836
TAMPA, FL 33634
813/884-6344
FAX: 813/882-4605

Catalog: free
Save: up to 30%
Pay: check, MO, MC, V, AE, DC, Discover, Optima
Sells: cigars and tobacco
Store: mail order only

$$ ☎ ▬

Thompson Cigar has been selling cigars since 1915, and currently publishes a 48-page catalog that's packed with both national-brand and private-label cigars, at prices up to 30% below comparable retail. The names include Cuesta Rey, Hoyo de Monterrey, Macanudo, Montecruz, Partagas, Royal Jamaica, H. Upmann, and many other makers—both Thompson's own line and the national-brand smokes. The catalog descriptions note the country of import, ring size, length, and relative strength (very mild to heavy). Pipe tobacco blends are stocked, and you'll also find a tempting selection of smoking accessories and gifts: handsome humidors, handmade pipes, cigar cutters, smokers' candles, and ashtrays. The catalog we reviewed showed a number of gifts, including a replica of a Civil War Cavalry saber, U.S. Marine tin soldiers, watches, and belt buckles—including one pewter model that declares "God, Guns and Guts Made America Free," with the Second Amendment on the back of it—for just $9.95.

Special Factors: Satisfaction is guaranteed; price quote by phone or letter.

SEE ALSO

Sultan's Delight, Inc. • Middle Eastern tobacco, brass waterpipes • *FOOD*

CLOTHING, FURS, AND ACCESSORIES

Clothing, furs, and accessories for men, women, and children

The firms listed here sell a wide range of clothing for men, women, and children—Amish clothing from Indiana, lingerie from New York City's Lower East Side, swimsuits that have qualified for the Olympics, executive suiting for both sexes, easy-access clothing, custom-made deerskin coats and jackets, and much more—at savings of up to 90%.

If you're considering buying a fur, take a look at these books: *How to Buy and Maintain a Fur Coat* (Harmony Books, 1986), by Leslie Goldin and Kalea Lulow, which includes information about quality construction characteristics of different furs, and their suitability for different types of wear, and *How to Buy a Fur That Makes You Look Like a Million,* by Viola Sybert (Villard Books).

Clothing that's made in the U.S.A. must bear labels providing specific information on cleaning and care. The Federal Trade Commission has compiled "What's New About Care Labels," a booklet defining the terms used in the labeling that answers a number of typical consumer questions. For a copy, request it by title from the Federal Trade Commission, Public Reference Office, Washington, DC 20580. If you want to make the best of what you own, you'll appreciate *Taking Care of Clothes,* by Mablen Jones (St. Martin's Press, 1982). It can help you evaluate clothing before purchase, and give tips on stain removal, laundering, dry cleaning, ironing and pressing, storage, and caring for leather, fur, and other special materials. You can also get it from the horse's mouth: The Neighborhood Cleaners' Association (NCA) publishes the "Consumer Guide to Clothing Care," a brochure of tips on the care and cleaning of different fabrics and trims. Send a long, self-addressed, stamped envelope to NCA, 116 E. 27th St., New York, NY 10016, for the pamphlet.

FIND IT FAST

BRIDAL • *I Do I Do*
HATS • *Manny's Millinery*
MEN'S CLOTHING • *Jos. A Bank, Paul Fredrick, Huntington, Lee-McClain, Quinn's Shirt Shop, Saint Laurie*
SHEEPSKIN, DEERSKIN, AND FUR • *Arctic Sheepskin, Custom Coat, Deerskin Place, Pagano Gloves*
SPORTSWEAR • *Sportswear Clearinghouse*
SWIMWEAR • *The Finals*
UNDERWEAR AND HOSIERY • *Chock, D & A, Goldman & Cohen, National Wholesale, Petticoat Express, Showcase of Savings, Smart Saver*
WOMEN'S CLOTHING • *Jos. A Bank, Chadwick's, Images, Thos. Oak, Anthony Richards, Saint Laurie, Ultimate Outlet*
WORK CLOTHING • *Cahall's, Gohn, Sara Glove, Todd, WearGuard, Workmen's Garment*

ARCTIC SHEEPSKIN OUTLET

**565 CO. RD. T, BOX WB
HAMMOND, WI 54105
715/796-2292
FAX: 715-796-2295**

Brochure: $2
Save: up to 60%
Pay: check, MO, MC, V, Discover
Sells: sheepskin clothing and accessories
Store: 30 miles east of St. Paul on I-94 at the Hammond exit; Monday to Saturday 9–5, Thursday 9–8

Arctic Sheepskin Outlet was founded in 1987 by the energetic Joseph Bacon, whose venture into mail-order skylights and insulated glass panels has proven a great success. (See the listing of Arctic Glass & Window Outlet in the "Maintenance" chapter of "Home" for more on that business.) His Outlet features sheepskin favorites—slippers, mittens, hats, car seat covers, rugs, etc.—from the largest sheepskin tannery in the world. Savings vary from item to item; we found rubber-soled sheepskin moccasins in other catalogs selling for just a few dollars more than Arctic's price of $34.95, but the car seat covers are real buys at $49.95, as are mittens for $14.95, kids' slippers for $8.95, and a "Marlboro Man" coat for just $129. There are also hats with earflaps, sheepskin headbands, rugs ($39.95), and bicycle seat covers. All purchases are covered by Arctic's "money-back guarantee."

Arctic Sheepskin Outlet is offering readers a discount of 10% on their first order. Be sure to identify yourself as a WBMC reader when you order, and deduct the discount from the cost of the goods only. This WBMC reader discount expires April 1, 1993.

Special Factors: Satisfaction is guaranteed; price quote by phone or letter; returns are accepted for exchange, refund, or credit; minimum order is $5; orders are shipped worldwide.

JOS. A. BANK CLOTHIERS, INC.

25 CROSSROADS DR. OWINGS MILLS, MD 21117-5499 800-284-3225 FAX: 301/356-5741

Catalog: $1
Save: up to 30%
Pay: check, MO, MC, V, AE
Sells: men's and women's career clothing and sportswear
Store: 40 stores in 21 states (locations are listed in the catalog)

Bank's business is executive suiting, which it serves with separate catalogs for men and women. Fine tailoring details and prices up to 30% below comparable goods—but not "discount"—distinguish the company's offerings.

The men's catalog features suits, jackets, pants, accessories, weekend separates, and underwear. The suits are handsomely executed in fine wool worsteds, among them pin and chalkline stripes, glen plaids, and herringbones. Chesterfield and cashmere topcoats, tuxedos and formal wear, blazers, tweed jackets, and complementing pants and shirts are sold. Swatches are available on the suits and sports coats. Braces, silk ties, shoes, pajamas, and underwear are sold as well.

The offerings in the women's catalog include fine business ensembles in the "relaxed traditional" style—belted suits, double-breasted coatdresses, and wool gabardine skirts paired with Chanel-style jackets were a few examples from the catalog we reviewed.

Much of the women's clothing is offered in petites and talls, as well as regular sizes. Scarves, belts, jewelry, bags, and coordinated weekend separates are also available.

Bank's garments often compare well to similar garments sold elsewhere for more money. Dressy jackets are often priced at $175 to $225 in other catalogs, but here we found examples of the same styles in the same fabrics at about $150. Please remember that Bank is more noteworthy for its selection of fine apparel than for its prices, and *do not ask for discounts*.

Special Factors: Satisfaction is guaranteed; returns are accepted for exchange, refund, or credit.

CAHALL'S DEPARTMENT STORE

CAHALL'S BROWN DUCK CATALOG
P.O. BOX 450-WM
MOUNT ORAB, OH
 45154
513/444-2094

Catalog: $1
Save: up to 40%
Pay: check, MO, MC, V, Discover
Sells: working clothing and footwear
Store: 112 S. High St., Mount Orab, OH;
 Monday to Saturday 9–6

$$$ ☎ 🍁 ▀

The Cahall family opened its department store on April 20, 1946, and took the leap into mail order in 1987, with the "Brown Duck Catalog" of heavy-duty apparel and footwear. You'll find your favorites—jeans, shirts, jackets, and overalls—here at savings of up to 40% on suggested list or retail prices.

The 32-page catalog offers the popular lines of Carhartt, Five Brothers, Hanes, Key, Jerzees, Levi, OshKosh, Wrangler, and other well-known manufacturers. A third of the catalog we reviewed featured an excellent selection of work shoes and boots for men and women from LaCrosse and other names, in hard-to-find sizes. (If you don't see the style you're looking for in the catalog, call—it may be available.) Heavy-duty socks, work gloves, bandannas, T-shirts, hats, and even a nail apron are available as well.

Special Factors: Satisfaction is guaranteed; price quote by phone or letter; returns are accepted for exchange, refund, or credit; orders are shipped worldwide.

CHADWICK'S OF BOSTON, LTD.

ONE CHADWICK PLACE
BOX 1600, DEPT. WBMC
BROCKTON, MA 02403
508/583-6600

Catalog: free
Save: up to 50%
Pay: check, MO, MC, V, AE, Discover
Sells: women's clothing and accessories
Store: mail order only

$$$ ☎ ◆ ▅

Chadwick's publishes "The Original Women's Off-Price Catalog," full of pretty-but-professional outfits for office, smashing cocktail dresses for evening, and weekend separates and activewear. Chadwick's has been in business since 1983, and features labels like Averroe, Bagatelle, David N, J.G. Hook, Kenar, Elliott Lauren, Prestige, Reed Hunter, and Tahari ("Alternatives"). Past offerings have included silk dresses, challis skirts with sweater jackets, Henley shirts, denim skirts, intarsia-knit sweaters, and reefer coats. Jewelry, belts, bags, shoes, and other accessories are also available.

The clothing is offered in a range of fashion colors, and sizes run from 4 to 14 (16 and 18 in some items, and petite sizes are available). Most of the separates cost between $25 and $40, and the accessories are also well-priced.

Special Factors: Satisfaction is guaranteed; returns are accepted for exchange, refund, or credit.

CHOCK CATALOG CORP.

74 ORCHARD ST., DEPT.
WBMC
NEW YORK, NY 10002-
4594
212/473-1929
FAX: 212/473-6273

Catalog: $1
Save: up to 35%
Pay: check, MO, MC, V
Sells: hosiery, underwear, sleepwear, and infants' clothing
Store: same address; Sunday to Thursday 9–5, Friday 9–1

$$$ ☎ ◆ ▅

Chock, known to generations of New Yorkers as Louis Chock, is a family operation selling unmentionables. Chock was established in

1921, and currently publishes 64-page catalog packed with good values on name-brand underthings for men, women, children, and infants.

Chock carries duofold thermal underwear for the whole family, women's stockings and panty hose by Berkshire, Hanes, and Mayer; underpants by Carter's, Calvin Klein, Lollipop, and Vanity Fair; and Louis Chock sleepwear for women. The men's department includes lines by BVD, Hanes, Jockey, Calvin Klein, Manshape, and Munsingwear, as well as pajamas and robes from Botany, Cannon, Knothe, Martex, and Oscar de la Renta; and socks by Burlington, Camp, Christian Dior, and Supp-hose. Men's sizes run up to XXXX (58 to 60). Chock's children's department stocks Carter's layette items and nursery needs, cloth diapers and crib linen, Hanes underwear for boys, Carter's underwear and sleepwear for boys and girls, and Trimfit socks for both.

Special Factors: Satisfaction is guaranteed; price quote by phone or letter; unopened returns with manufacturer's packaging intact are accepted within 30 days; orders are shipped worldwide.

CUSTOM COAT COMPANY, INC.

**P.O. BOX 69
BERLIN, WI 54923
414/361-0900**

Catalog: free
Save: up to 35%
Pay: check, MO, MC, V
Sells: deerskin clothing and tanning services
Store: 227 N. Washington St., Berlin, WI;
Monday to Friday 8–5, Saturday 8–3
(8–12 noon, May–August)

$$$ ☎ 🍁

Custom Coat, established in 1939, offers a service hunters will find useful: The firm will tan your green hides, color them, and create custom clothing and accessories from the leather. The same items can be made up in stock deerskin, and the prices for the services and finished goods are exceptionally reasonable. Custom Coat's 30-page color catalog shows deerskin vests, town-and-country jackets and coats, classic wrap coats, safari and bush jackets, fringed and Western models, and sports coats, as well as riding, motorcycle, and bomber jackets. Bags and gloves—driving, shooting, hunting, and dress gloves for men and women—are offered, as well as a selection of mittens for children. Change purses, keycases, billfolds, cigarette cases, golf-club covers, and smooth-soled moccasins are also offered. The garments can be ordered in custom sizes, lengths, details, and linings. Green deer, elk, and moose hides are accepted for curing and coloring, but no fur work is done.

Special Factor: Tanning rates, guides to shipment of skins, number of hides needed per garment, and other information is listed in the catalog.

D & A MERCHANDISE CO., INC.

**22 ORCHARD ST.
NEW YORK, NY 10002
212/925-4766**

Catalog: $2
Save: up to 35%
Pay: check, MO, MC, V
Sells: underwear and hosiery
Store: same address; Sunday to Thursday
9–5, Friday 9–3

D & A, home of "The Underwear King," has been selling name-brand lingerie, socks, hosiery, and underwear for men, women, and boys since 1947. You'll find solid discounts on first-quality goods here: men's underwear by BVD, Camp, duofold, Jockey, and Munsingwear, and socks by Burlington, Camp, Christian Dior, Interwoven, and Supp-hose. Also available are Botany and State of Maine robes and pajamas, Career Club shirts, and Totes rain boots, and boys' underwear by BVD and Hanes. The women's underwear department offers lines by Bali, Carnival, Chicas, Christian Dior, Do-All, Exquisite Form, Formfit Rogers, Jockey for Her, Lilyette, Lily of France, Lollipop, Lorraine, Maidenform, Olga, Playtex, Poirette, Smoothie, Strouse Adler, Warner's, and other manufacturers, and hosiery by Berkshire, Burlington, Camp, Danskin, Hanes, Trimfit, and Wigwam.

Special Factors: Satisfaction is guaranteed; price quote by phone or letter; returns in original packaging are accepted within 30 days for refund or credit; C.O.D. orders are accepted.

THE DEERSKIN PLACE

283 AKRON RD.
EPHRATA, PA 17522
717/733-7624

Brochure and Price List: $1, refundable
Save: up to 50%
Pay: check, MO, MC, V
Sells: deerskin clothing and accessories
Store: same address; Monday to Saturday 9–9, Sunday (September–December) 12–5

$$ ☎ ♦ ▤

The Deerskin Place, in business since 1969, features clothing and accessories of deerskin, cowhide, and sheepskin at prices up to 50% less than those charged elsewhere for comparable goods. Among the offerings are fingertip-length shearling jackets for $275, fringed buckskin-suede jackets at $169, and sporty deerskin handbags for about $70. The Deerskin Place offers moccasins and casual shoes, knee-high suede boots, and crepe-soled slip-ons for men and women (from $16), deerskin wallets, clutches, coin purses, and keycases (from about $5), mittens and gloves for the whole family, beaded belts (under $6), and many other accessories.

The Deerskin Place is offering readers of this book a 10% discount on orders of $150 or more. Be sure to identify yourself as a reader when you order, and deduct the discount from the goods total only. This WBMC reader discount expires July 1, 1993.

Special Factors: Satisfaction is guaranteed; inquire before ordering if unsure of color, size, etc.; returns are accepted; C.O.D. orders are accepted; orders are shipped worldwide.

F.R. KNITTING MILLS, INC.

DEPT. WBMC
P.O. BOX 4360, FLINT
**   STATION**
FALL RIVER, MA 02723
800-446-1089
IN MA 508/679-5227
FAX: 508/677-4266

Catalog: free
Save: up to 40%
Pay: check, MO, MC, V, Discover
Sells: sweaters and knitwear
Store: 69 Alden St., Fall River, MA

$$ ☎  ♣

The "F.R." in this company's name stands for Fall River, where the firm was founded in 1911. Fall River was a thriving textile center then, and the Knitting Mill carries on in the same tradition—manufacturing knitwear and clothing for the whole family. You can buy through the color catalog and save up to 40% on the prices charged in department stores for the same goods.

You'll usually find such wardrobe staples as turtlenecks, crews, V-necks, cardigans, rugby styles, polo shirts, turtlenecks, and vests for men, women, and children. Brightly colored cotton sweaters are invariably on offer, including Shaker knits, cable-front crews, and stripes and intarsia designs. Dresses, knitted skirts and pants, and even home accessories have been featured in past catalogs.

Special Factors: Satisfaction is guaranteed; returns are accepted.

THE FINALS, LTD.

21 MINISINK AVE., DEPT.
**   WB**
PORT JERVIS, NY 12771
914/856-4456

Catalog: free
Save: up to 60%
Pay: check, MO, MC, V, AE
Sells: swimwear and athletic apparel
Store: 487 Broadway, New York, NY; also
   3314 M St., N.W., Washington, DC

$$ ☎ ♣

The Finals, in business since 1976, is serious about swimwear: It's outfit a number of U.S. swim teams, and can offer you the same great combination of style, comfort, and practicality that the pros get, at a world-class price. The firm makes its suits from a blend of Antron nylon and Lycra, a fabric that's ideal for the demands of competition-level use. Sleek, form-fitting tank suits for women ($22 and up) and men's briefs ($14 and up) are offered in a variety of colors and styles, as well as shirts and suits for lifeguards and surfers. "Second Skin" separates for bicycling and working out are available, as well as running and track wear, and standard shirts, shorts, warm-ups, and sweats. The catalog also shows singlets and shorts in unisex sizes, tote bags and duffels, swimming goggles, caps, fins, buoys, tubes, kickboards, and related gear.

Special Factor: Satisfaction is guaranteed.

PAUL FREDRICK SHIRT COMPANY

140 W. MAIN ST., DEPT. WM92
FLEETWOOD, PA 19522
215/944-0909

Catalog: $1
Save: up to 50%
Pay: check, MO, MC, V, AE, DC
Sells: men's dress shirts and accessories
Store: mail order only

$$$ ☎ 🍁 🇺🇸

Private labels have emerged as a successful marketing technique in the clothing business, providing specialty and department stores with good-quality garments identified with only the store name—and a fat markup. As a consumer, you can't comparison-shop private labels since they don't have brand names. The only way to beat the price is to go to the manufacturer—and pay "factory direct" prices.

Paul Fredrick is the mail-order division of a shirt manufacturer that's been selling to designers and better stores since 1952. If you're in the market for fine-quality men's shirts, Paul Fredrick is the place to stop. The firm's 24-page color catalog shows a $36 shirt that compares favorably in material, construction, and detail to dress shirts in other catalogs and stores that are selling for nearly twice the price. Fredrick's shirts are offered in fine fabrics—pinpoint Oxford cotton, Cambridge Oxford cotton, and Egyptian cotton broadcloth—with a range of tailoring options: French and barrel (buttoned) cuffs, and straight, Windsor, English tab, and buttondown collar styles. Colors and patterns include stripes, miniature checks, and pastels, and sizes run from 14½" to 18½" neck, 32" to 37" sleeve. Three-letter monograms (on the left sleeve cuff) cost $5. Men's jewelry cuff links, leather belts, and Italian silk neckties are also sold here.

Special Factors: Satisfaction is guaranteed; returns are accepted.

GOHN BROS.

**105 S. MAIN
P.O. BOX 111
MIDDLEBURY, IN 46540
219/825-2400**

Catalog: $1
Save: up to 40%
Pay: check or MO
Sells: general merchandise and Amish specialties
Store: same address; Monday to Saturday 8–5:30

$$$ 🍁 🇺🇸

Other firms add fax machines and 800 lines, but Gohn Bros. is staying firmly rooted in a world where bonnet board and frock coats were stock items in the general store. Gohn has been in business since 1904, and sells both of those items—and many other practical goods—at prices up to 40% below comparable retail. Many home sewers know Gohn for the yard goods staples and notions, such as the all-cotton Sanforized blue denim ($4.89), muslin ($1.98), chambray shirting ($2.59), quilting thread (98¢), cotton percale and quilting prints, pillow tubing, all-cotton sheeting, tailor's canvas, haircloth, mosquito netting, embroidery floss (25¢ per skein), and wool overcoating (at under $12 per yard).

At least half of Gohn's stock lists are devoted to work-tailored, sturdy Amish clothing, including men's cotton chambray work shirts ($14.98), cotton denim broadfall pants ($14.98), men's underwear, cotton dress socks (89¢), Carolina shoes, rubber galoshes and footwear by LaCrosse and Tingley, work gloves, felt hats, and handkerchiefs. Much of the clothing is available in large sizes, and many of the items in the men's department are also offered in boys' sizes.

If you're assembling a layette, see the catalog for good buys on the basics—diapers, receiving blankets, sleepers, pacifiers, baby pants, and other goods by Curity and Gerber. Nursing bras are available, and women's underwear and hosiery are offered at low prices.

Special Factors: Satisfaction is guaranteed; C.O.D. orders are accepted.

GOLDMAN & COHEN INC.

**55 ORCHARD ST.
NEW YORK, NY 10002
212/966-0737**

Information: price quote
Save: up to 60%
Pay: check, MO, MC, V, AE, Discover
Sells: women's underwear
Store: same address; Monday to Thursday
9–5, Friday 9–3, Sunday 8–5:30

$$

Goldman & Cohen doesn't publish a catalog, but will quote prices over the phone and by mail on its stock of popular lingerie and hosiery lines. The firm was founded in 1954, and sells at discounts of up to 50% on suggested list prices. Women's intimate apparel is available from Bali, Barbizon, Carnival, Christian Dior, Exquisite Form, Lilyette, Maidenform, Olga, Playtex, Vanity Fair, Warner's, and other well-known manufacturers and designers. You can ask for price quotes on loungewear by these firms, as well as Hanes panty hose. Goldman also carries a full line of nursing and maternity foundations and sleepwear, and the firm's experienced saleswomen can help you ensure a proper fit, and choose the garments appropriate for your own needs.

Special Factors: Price quote by phone or letter; no phone orders or inquiries are accepted on Sunday; orders are shipped worldwide.

HUNTINGTON CLOTHIERS

**1285 ALUM CREEK DR.
COLUMBUS, OH 43209-
9985
800-848-6203**

Catalog: free
Save: up to 50% (see text)
Pay: check, MO, MC, V, AE, CB, DC
Sells: executive menswear
Store: same address; Monday to Friday
10–6, Saturday 10–5, Sunday 12–5

$$$

The 84-page catalog from Huntington Clothiers illustrates all the basics of a conservative wardrobe, from pinstriped suits to pima cotton boxer shorts. Prices are very competitive with those of old-line haberdashers; some items cost as much as 50% less here than their equivalents in other catalogs.

Huntington offers its own line of shirts in a variety of fabrics, including Oxford cloth (with buttondown and plain collars), pima cotton solids, Sea Island cotton, Egyptian cotton broadcloth, and cotton/poly blends. We saw shirts in the catalog we reviewed that were selling for under $20 each that were comparable to those in other catalogs that commanded $50. (Monogramming is available for $4.) Huntington also sells neckwear—foulards, silk rep stripes, and linen solids and paisley ties—at similar savings, and executive suits that run the gamut from grey chalk stripes and gabardines to poplin and seersucker summer suits to tuxedos. Jackets and blazers are shown, as well as trousers, sportswear separates, walking shorts, lisle cotton polo shirts, rugby shirts, cotton and wool sweaters, belts, suspenders, underwear, and even shoes are shown.

Special Factors: Satisfaction is guaranteed; returns (except monogrammed goods) are accepted for exchange, refund, or credit.

I DO I DO BRIDAL SALON

1963 86TH ST.
BROOKLYN, NY 11214
718/946-0011

Information: price quote (see text)
Save: up to 50%
Pay: check, MO, MC, V
Sells: gowns for the bridal party
Store: same address

$$$ ☎ ♦ ▀

The process of getting married should make married life seem like a piece of cake, considering the trials of the typical wedding. They also exact a financial toll: the cost of dressing the wedding party for "the big day" can easily amount to $10,000. Before you go the city hall route, contact I Do I Do, a Brooklyn bridal salon that sells gowns for the entire bridal party at 30% to 50% below list prices.

The procedure is simple: Make your gown selection from the ads and editorial pages of *Bride's* or *Modern Bride,* and send I Do I Do the pages with photos of what you want for a price quote. Allow as much time as you'd give to a local salon—you'll probably have to wait about three months before the gowns are delivered, and you'll have to arrange alterations yourself. I Do I Do requires a 50% deposit, as well as the complete measurements of each person being outfitted.

Brides and members of the wedding who live in the New York City area can visit the shop for the same savings, *and* personal attention.

Special Factor: Price quote by phone or letter with SASE.

IMAGES

317 ST. PAUL AVE., 1ST FL.
JERSEY CITY, NJ 07306
201/653-6599

Catalog: free
Save: up to 40%
Pay: check, MO, MC, V, AE
Sells: women's fashions
Store: mail order only

$$$ ☎

Images is the most recent entry we know of in the field of discount fashion catalogs. The firm is actually a manufacturer of up-to-the-minute women's fashions, which it brings to market in a 32-page color catalog. The issue we saw offered a swing coat in wool/cashmere for $198, a chic navy poly/wool coatdress for $88, a handsome "steamer" coat at $169, a wool jersey sweaterdress for $39, and a challis dress teamed with a suede vest for $129. The sizes run 4–16 in missy, and some styles are offered in petite and tall sizing as well.

Please note: Orders are shipped via UPS.

Special Factors: Satisfaction is guaranteed; returns are accepted for exchange, refund, or credit.

LEE-MCCLAIN CO., INC.

RR 6, BOX 381-A
SHELBYVILLE, KY 40065-
9017
502/633-3823

Brochure: free
Save: up to 40%
Pay: check, MO, MC, V
Sells: executive menswear
Store: U.S. 60 W., Shelbyville, KY; Monday to Saturday 8–4:30

$$

Lee-McClain, which has been manufacturing fine suits and separates for men since 1933, offers you the same apparel marketed in better stores at up to 40% below suggested retail prices. Lee-McClain's clothing is sold under the "Strathmore" house label, and the brochure features a small collection of suits, and jackets. The conservative, classic styling features slightly fitted, two-button jackets with center vent and straight-leg pants. Suits begin at $195, and fabric choices include cashmere and blends, camel's hair, wool worsted, flannel, gabardine, pinstripes, herringbones, glen plaids, hopsacking, and other weaves. It's hard to beat $225 for a fine camel's hair sports coat, or $59 for slacks in wool worsted.

Special Factors: Swatches are available upon request; list all measurements when ordering; shipping is included.

MANNY'S MILLINERY SUPPLY CO.

63 W. 38TH ST.
NEW YORK, NY 10018
212/840-2253
FAX: 212/944-0178

Catalog: $2
Save: 33% average
Pay: check, MO, MC, V, AE
Sells: hats, millinery supplies, gloves, bridal trimmings
Store: same address; Monday to Friday 9–5:30, Saturday 9–4

We were very pleased to discover Manny's among the shops in New York City's "trimmings" district, which has more sequins, tassels, and decorative add-ons per square foot than a Las Vegas floor show. Manny's offers some of that glitter, but the company's specialty is women's hats, millinery supplies, and bridal accessories.

About half of the 32-page catalog is devoted to hats, many of which are trimmed. Hundreds of styles are shown, in parisial, milanette, genuine Milan straw, felt, and fabric, and scores of "frames," or fabric-covered forms, are offered. The satin frames are suitable for bridal outfits, and the buckram frames provide a base for limitless flights of fancy. Stunning bridal headpieces, which can be used to decorate the hats and headpieces, and lace parasols, fans, satin and velvet gloves, edged veils, and even ring pillows are shown in the catalog. In addition, Manny's offers over a dozen jeweled or beaded hatpins, pearl and sequin trim, bugle-bead appliqués and trims, fringe, fabric flowers, rhinestone buttons, and even feathers—loose and in boas.

Professional millinery supplies and equipment are available, including horsehair braid, hat stretchers, display heads and racks, hat boxes and travel cases, netting, and cleaning products. Savings vary from item to item, but average 33% below regular retail.

Please note: If you're buying hats only, the minimum order is 3; if you buy 1 or 2 hats, you must also buy $15 in assorted items (frames, trims, etc.); if you're buying assorted items only, the minimum order is $25.

Special Factors: Price quote by phone or letter; minimum order on certain items (see text); orders are shipped worldwide.

NATIONAL WHOLESALE CO., INC.

**400 NATIONAL BLVD.,
DEPT. WX
LEXINGTON, NC 27292
704/249-0211**

Catalog: free
Save: up to 50%
Pay: check, MO, MC, V, AE
Sells: women's hosiery, loungewear, and underwear
Store: Lexington and Wilmington, NC; Monday to Saturday 9–9, Sunday 1–5:30

$$ ☎ 🍁 🇺🇸

National Wholesale offers just about any woman, regardless of height (from 5') or girth (to 60" hips), savings of up to 50% on National's brand of panty hose, compared to similar name-brand products. National was founded in 1952, publishes a 64-page catalog that shows control-top, support, sheer mesh, cotton-soled, and other panty hose styles, as well as stockings (support, sheer, and garterless) and knee highs. The "all-sheer" panty hose are offered in a good selection of beiges and browns, pastels, and deep fall and winter shades.

In addition to hosiery, National Wholesale sells bras, girdles, and body shapers by Exquisite Form, Glamorise, Kayser, and Playtex, slips by Figurefit and Pinehurst, dusters by Swirl, and cotton-knit vests, briefs, long-leg underpants, thermal underwear, and pants liners. Larger sizes are available, and note that hosiery is sold by the box (three to six pairs). National also offers an incontinence panty and a half-slip with a waterproof panel.

Special Factors: Satisfaction is guaranteed; only first-quality merchandise is sold; returns are accepted; orders are shipped worldwide.

THOS. OAK & SONS

**901 MAIN ST., DEPT. 807
SALEM, VA 24156
800-898-2929**

Catalog: free
Save: 25% average
Pay: check, MO, MC, V, AE, Discover
Sells: women's clothing and accessories
Store: mail order only

$ ☎

Thos. Oak & Sons, established in 1987, is one of the family of catalogs from the Home Shopping Network. It features moderately priced women's apparel and accessories chosen for comfort and easy care, which are shown in a 32-page, color catalog. You'll find easy-fitting dresses and activewear, including town-and-country dresses, around-the-house chemises, overshirts and loose jackets, pull-on pants and skirts, and robes, nightgowns, and foundation garments in the catalog. Shoes and slippers from Beacon, ComfortSteps, Daniel Green, Hush Puppies, Keds (including Grasshoppers), and Oldmaine Trotters are available, as well as a potpourri of household helpers and accessories.

Special Factors: Satisfaction is guaranteed; returns are accepted for exchange, refund, or credit.

PAGANO GLOVES, INC.

**3-5 CHURCH ST.
JOHNSTOWN, NY 12095-
  2196
518/762-8425**

Catalog: $3, refundable
Save: up to 50%
Pay: MO, MC, V
Sells: deerskin clothing and accessories
Store: same address; Monday to Friday 8–5,
  Saturday 9:30–3

 $$$ ☎ 🍁 🇺🇸

Pagano Gloves has been selling its deerskin clothing, gloves, and footwear since 1946, and offers a large part of its inventory through the 32-page color catalog. You'll find fashionable, streamlined coats and jackets, tailored and fringed Western models, motorcycle jackets, and other styles for men and women in the catalog, as well as fleece-lined slippers, slip-ons, and moccasins for men and women. The accessories include billfolds, keycases, tobacco pouches, handbags, and there are several pages of gloves, including lined and unlined dress gloves, mittens, and specialty gloves for driving and shooting. Custom sizes, lengths, and linings are also available at reasonable surcharges. The catalog includes instructions on how to care for deerskin garments and accessories.

Special Factors: Include measurements when ordering; guide included in the catalog.

THE PETTICOAT EXPRESS

318 W. 39TH ST.
NEW YORK, NY 10018-
1407
212/594-1276

Flyer: free
Save: 40% plus
Pay: check or MO
Sells: taffeta slips
Store: mail order only

$

Petticoat Express offers brides an easy way to cut 40% from the cost of an unseen necessity—the net and taffeta slip that creates the charming silhouette of a full-skirted bridal or attendant's gown. Petticoat Express, which has been in business since 1983, offers white, full-length half-slips: an A-line style for dresses of moderate flare ($19); a flounced, bouffant style for full skirts ($21); a double-ruffle bouffant ($26) for maximum fullness; and a style for tea-length (31″) skirts for $18. Sizes run from 3/4 to 19/20. The slips are made of taffeta and net, and are also ideal for full-skirted evening dresses.

Special Factor: C.O.D. orders are accepted.

QUINN'S SHIRT SHOP

RTE. 12
P.O. BOX 131
NORTH
 GROSVENORDALE, CT
 06255
508/943-7183

Price List: $2 and self-addressed, stamped envelope (see text)
Save: up to 60%
Pay: check or MO
Sells: Arrow shirts
Store: 245 W. Main St., Dudley, MA; Monday to Saturday 10–5

$$ ☎

Quinn's, a factory outlet for the Arrow Shirt company, offers slightly irregular shirts at up to 60% below the price of first-quality goods. The firm has been in business since 1956, and will send you a price list for $2 and a stamped, self-addressed envelope (the $2 charge is refundable with your first order). You can also call or write for a price quote on your favorite Arrow shirt (you must have the style number or code). Quinn's carries in regular, big, and tall sizes, 14½" to 20" neck, 31" to 38" sleeve. When you order, specify whether you want short sleeves or long (include the length if long). The shirts may be exchanged if the flaws are too apparent.

Special Factors: Satisfaction is guaranteed; price quote by phone or letter with SASE; returns are accepted for exchange; minimum order is 4 shirts per order; only C.O.D. orders are accepted.

ANTHONY RICHARDS

P.O. BOX 94503
CLEVELAND, OH 44101-
 4503
216/826-3008

Catalog: free
Save: up to 60%
Pay: check, MO, MC, V
Sells: moderately priced women's clothing
Store: mail order only

$$ ☎ ♦ ▬

The 48-page Anthony Richards catalog offers women comfortable, affordable clothing in a moderate price range—dresses at under $30, skirts for under $10, and jewelry at nominal prices. Anthony Richards is ideal for those of us on very tight budgets who need a number of outfits for the office or just an alternative to pants and sweaters for shopping and running errands. Most of the dresses are machine washable, are offered in missy (8–20) and half (14½–26½) sizes, and are stylish but not trendy. A small selection of nightwear and lingerie is offered, and several shoe styles were shown in the catalog we reviewed.

Special Factors: Satisfaction is guaranteed; minimum order is $10 with credit cards.

SAINT LAURIE LTD.

897 BROADWAY, DEPT. WBM92
NEW YORK, NY 10003
800-221-8660
212/473-0100
FAX: 212/473-2092

Style Sheets and Swatch Subscription: $10 (see text)
Save: 33% average
Pay: check, MO, MC, V, AE
Sells: executive clothing for men and women
Store: same address; Monday to Saturday 9:30–6, Thursday 9:30–7:30, Sunday 12–5 (closed Sunday in July and August)

$$$ ☎ 🍁

Saint Laurie has been manufacturing better suits since 1913 and began selling by mail in 1979. The ten-dollar subscription fee will bring you the spring and fall swatch collections, beautifully produced brochures of actual fabric samples with style brochures featuring line drawings of each garment, with notes on tailoring details. The swatch booklet describes the fiber content and lists which garments—suits, trousers, and skirts—that can be made up in each fabric. Membership in "The Swatch Club" is automatically extended for one year when you order.

The Saint Laurie look is expressed in conservatively styled suits, jackets, skirts, and trousers in fine fabrics: all-wool worsted, Italian and Moygashel linen, handwoven silks, gabardine, sharkskin, pinstripes, cotton seersucker, crepe, and glen plaids have all been offered in past mailings. Men's suits are available in short, regular, long, and extra-long lengths, to size 48; women's apparel is offered in petite, regular, and tall models, in sizes 2 to 18. Tailoring details (belt loop and trouser leg width, shoulder style, vents, pockets, lapels, etc.) are all described in the brochure; and pants are sent unhemmed. The prices are not low, but are as much as 30% below those charged by other firms for hand-tailored garments of this quality.

Every Saint Laurie garment is made on the premises, and visitors to the store will find clothing for all seasons in stock. If you're in New York, you can take advantage of Saint Laurie's made-to-measure services and have your suit custom-fitted. Even if you have your alterations made elsewhere, Saint Laurie will reimburse you up to $25 if you send the firm your bill.

Please note: Shipping charges on orders sent to Alaska, Hawaii, and Canada are twice the U.S. rate.

Special Factors: Returns of unworn, unaltered garments are accepted within 14 days; showroom is closed Sundays in July and August.

SARA GLOVE COMPANY, INC.

117 BENEDICT ST.
P.O. BOX 1940
WATERBURY, CT 06722-
 1940
203/574-4090
FAX: 203/574-3500

Catalog: $1
Save: up to 30%
Pay: check, MO, MC, V
Sells: work clothing and gloves
Store: same address; Monday to Friday
 8:30–4:30, Thursday 8:30–7

Work clothing and safety gear are showcased in the "Worldwide Outfitters" catalog from 20-year-old Sara Glove, at savings of up to 30%. Part of the 40-page catalog is devoted to gloves, gauntlets, and finger cots (tip protectors), including brown jersey and canvas chore gloves, warm fleece gloves, leather-and-canvas work gloves, and heat-resistant gloves of fabric and leather for "dry" work. If you work with solvents, caustics, oil, acids, grease, and chemicals, see the catalog for the line of gloves designed to resist these substances—there are vinyl, neoprene, nitrile, and latex models. Several of the gloves are USDA-approved for food handling, food processing, and related commercial uses. The catalog also features safety glasses and goggles, as well as ear plugs and muffs, respirators and other breathing filters, fire extinguishers, first-aid kits, and other safety equipment.

Most of the catalog is devoted to clothing, including work shirts in sizes to 5XL, pants, leather jackets and motorcycle apparel, Woolrich shirts, Carhartt work jackets and overalls, Dickies work clothing, lab coats, boots and footwear by Carolina Boots, Double-H, Herman Survivors, Kaufman, and Timberland. Sara Glove's custom department can personalize your work shirts, T-shirts, baseball jackets, and baseball caps with names and corporate logos, at a surcharge. Ray-Ban sunglasses and belts are also available.

Special Factors: Satisfaction is guaranteed; price quote by phone or letter; quantity discounts are available; C.O.D. orders are accepted; institutional accounts are available; orders are shipped worldwide.

SHOWCASE OF SAVINGS

L'EGGS BRANDS, INC.
P.O. BOX 748
RURAL HALL, NC 27098
919/744-1170
FAX: 919/744-1485

Catalog: free
Save: up to 50%
Pay: check, MO, MC, V, Discover
Sells: first-quality and "slightly imperfect" women's hosiery and underwear
Store: mail order only

$$$ ☎ 🏳

The 28-page color Showcase of Savings catalog brings you savings of up to 50% on your favorite panty hose—and some activewear and lingerie—from Bali, Hanes, Isotoner, L'eggs, and Underalls. The best buys are on the "slightly imperfect" irregulars, but first-quality nurses' hosiery is offered at 25% off list in three-packs.

The whole range of L'eggs is offered through Showcase of Savings: Sheer Energy, Sheer Elegance, Active Support, Silken Mist, Silken Support, L'eggs knee highs, Winter L'eggs, Summer L'eggs, and L'eggs Regular panty hose have been shown in past catalogs, in control-top styles, queen sizes, and a wide range of colors. (Just My Size and Sheer Energy Maternity panty hose are also sold, at savings of up to 50%.) Hanes hosiery—Silk Reflections, Hanes Too!, Hanes Alive, Ultra Silk, etc.—is also sold, as well as Isotoner panty hose, Bali bras and slips, and Hanes socks, T-shirts, and sweat shirts. See the detailed sizing guide in the catalog to be sure you get the best fit.

Special Factors: Satisfaction is guaranteed; "slightly imperfect" goods are clearly identified; returns are accepted; minimum order is $15 with credit cards.

THE SMART SAVER

**P.O. BOX 209
WASCO, IL 60183**

Catalog: free
Save: up to 30%
Pay: check or MO
Sells: intimate apparel
Store: mail order only

$$

The Smart Saver is a family-owned business that has specialized in women's intimate apparel since 1982, and sells Playtex foundations and styles by Exquisite Form, Lollipop, and Vanity Fair.

Bras, girdles, panties, and all-in-ones are shown in the 20-page catalog, which lists both the suggested retail and discount prices. Current offerings include a range of Playtex bras and girdles, Exquisite Form and Vanity Fair bras, and Lollipop panties. Bra and girdle size guides are given in the catalog. Smart Saver also offers its own line of girdles, at reasonable prices.

Special Factor: Only first-quality merchandise is sold, no seconds or irregulars.

SPORTSWEAR CLEARINGHOUSE

**P.O. BOX 317746-B2
CINCINNATI, OH 45231-
7746
513/522-3511**

Brochure: free
Save: up to 70%
Pay: check, MO, MC, V
Sells: printed sportswear overruns, hats, athletic socks, etc.
Store: mail order only

$$ ☎ ♦ 🏳

Forget about dayglo cycling shorts and $200 court shoes—you won't find these at Sportswear Clearinghouse. The fare is far more basic—T-shirts in sizes from youth to adult XL, sweats, shorts, socks, and hats, printed with corporate or institutional logos. If you succumb to the brochure, you can wind up wearing a T-shirt printed for the American Embassy at Sanaa Yemen, Notre Dame running shorts, and a hat emblazoned with an advertising message from a local welding shop. The Clearinghouse, which has been in business since 1976, offers T-shirts commemorating different events (the Boston Marathon and 1983 America's Cup were two seen in our brochure), sweatshirts, golf shirts (printed for the "staff" of different institutions), and T-shirts bearing the names of universities, corporations, and rock groups. Prices are hard to beat; T-shirts and shorts cost a few dollars, and hats and visors are priced under $2. Most of these items are sold in lots of three, six, or a dozen or more, and the selection of colors, logos, and slogans is up to the Clearinghouse. First-quality athletic socks and baseball hats embroidered with the replica logos of major league teams are also available, as well as belly/fanny packs and baseball/golf hats in neon colors.

Special Factors: Satisfaction is guaranteed; price quote by phone or letter; unused returns are accepted within 30 days for exchange, refund, or credit; C.O.D. orders are accepted (UPS delivery only); orders are shipped worldwide.

TAI, INC.

**90 DAYTON AVE.
PASSAIC, NJ 07055
201/777-0905**

Catalog: free
Save: quantity discounts (see text)
Pay: check, MO, MC, V, AE
Sells: silk-screened apparel and accessories
Store: same address; Monday to Friday
9–4:30, Saturday 11–4:30

TAI was founded in 1983 by Crown Art Products (see the firm's listing in "Art Materials"), which manufactures silk-screening supplies and equipment. TAI offers a line of clothing and accessories that are hand-screened with military insignias, at savings that run up to 30% (on goods bough in quantity). The catalog offers a range of items embellished with the motifs of military forces, including aprons, scarves, beach towels, laundry and duffel bags, T-shirts, pennants, decals, and bumper stickers. Choose from insignias of the Airborne divisions, Special Forces groups, the Marines, Rangers, the Foreign Legion, U.S.M.C. Recon, and other forces and divisions.

Special Factors: Price quote by phone or letter with SASE; quantity discounts are available; monthly specials are featured; minimum order is $25 with credit cards.

TODD UNIFORM, INC.

**3668 SOUTH GEYER
ST. LOUIS, MO 63127
800-458-3402
FAX: 314/984-5736**

Catalog: free
Save: up to 30%
Pay: check, MO, MC, V, AE, Discover
Sells: work clothing and uniforms
Store: Ripley, TN; Monday to Saturday
9–5:30

$$ ☎ ♦ ▀▀

Todd has been selling uniforms and work apparel since 1881, and the firm's 44-page color catalog brings you factory-direct savings—up to 30% below the competition. Quantity discounts of 5% to 30% enhance the savings. The clothing runs from the ubiquitous work shirt for men and women, which is offered in a range of colors, to jumpsuits, jackets, T-shirts, polo shirts, aprons, rainwear, and baseball hats. Your logo or slogan can be embroidered on the garments or on emblems, and the order form is designed to make it easy to specify even complicated orders. There are varying minimums for the custom work, but quantity discounts apply.

Special Factors: Satisfaction is guaranteed; price quote by phone or letter; quantity discounts are available; institutional accounts are available.

THE ULTIMATE OUTLET

**P.O. BOX 88251
CHICAGO, IL 60680-1251
800-332-6000**

Catalog: $2
Save: up to 70%
Pay: check, MO, MC, V, AE, Optima,
Spiegel Preferred Charge
Sells: clothing for men and women,
housewares
Store: 9 stores in Chicago area

$$$ ☎ ♦ ▀▀(see text)

The Ultimate Outlet is Spiegel's smart answer to the strong demand for its sales catalogs. A clearance outlet by mail, the upbeat catalog is as jaunty and fresh as the latest Spiegel edition, but The Ultimate Outlet boasts real sale prices on every page.

The issue we reviewed boasted several pages of chic women's shoes, many priced from $19.90 to $39.90. We found handsome Merino sweaters for $24.90, flannel blazers under $70, and a boardroom-worthy Chanel-style suit for under $80. Men are treated to a collection dominated by weekend wear—leather bomber jackets for $139, cotton argyle sweaters for $32, and corduroy pants for under $15 were all available. A selection of bed linens filled out the 112 pages. Since the offerings consist almost solely of Spiegel goods, you'll find many of the same brand names here, and The Ultimate Outlet has a similar sales policy. If all catalogs were like this, going through a recession might not seem so bad!

Please note: Deliveries to Alaska and APO/FPO addresses are made by USPS, *not* UPS.

Special Factors: Satisfaction is guaranteed; returns are accepted for exchange, refund, or credit.

WEARGUARD CORP.

**LONGWATER DR.
HINGHAM, MA 02061
800-388-3300
617/871-4100
FAX: 617/871-6239**

Catalog: free
Save: up to 30%
Pay: check, MO, MC, V, AE, Discover, Optima
Sells: work clothing, rugged casual wear, and accessories
Store: 53 outlets in CT, DE, MA, ME, MI, NH, NJ, NY, PA, and RI

$$$ ☎

WearGuard, which was founded in 1952, tells us that it supplies more than a million U.S. companies and consumers with work clothing. Prices run up to 30% below comparable retail, and quantity discounts are available. WearGuard may have the best selection of work shirts in the country—21 colors and patterns, in long or short sleeves, sized XS to XXXXXL, from about $16 to $21. In addition, T-shirts, polo shirts, chambray shirts, turtlenecks, Western and flannel shirts, jeans, gloves, thermal underwear and union suits, jumpsuits, coveralls, gabardine jackets, varsity-style jackets, and windbreakers are available. WearGuard's footwear includes Western boots, Durango Wellingtons, Timberland and Kodiak boots, work shoes, and boat moccasins. A similar range of apparel for women is offered, and there are specialty items for truckers and enforcement personnel.

WearGuard's custom department can provide designs on patches, emblems, T-shirts, and work shirts; stock logos and lettering is also available. The screen printing and direct embroidery are done "in house," which means WearGuard should be able to get your custom-embroidered job to you faster.

Special Factors: Satisfaction is guaranteed; price quote by phone; returns are accepted; quantity discounts are available; C.O.D. orders are accepted.

WORKMEN'S GARMENT CO.

**15205 WYOMING AVE.
DETROIT, MI 48238
313/834-7236**

Catalog: $2, refundable
Save: up to 75%
Pay: check or MO
Sells: new and reconditioned work clothing
Store: same address; Monday to Friday
8:30–4:30, Saturday 8:30–1

$$ ☎

Workmen's Garment, in business since 1954, can save you up to 75% on the cost of work clothing, much of which is suitable for outdoor wear as well. New and reconditioned goods are available.

Workmen's declares that "Big or Small, We Fit 'Em All," and really tries: The selection includes new blue denim jeans to size 66 waist, shop coats (to size 60), coveralls (to size 66 chest), work jackets,shirts to size 10XL, pants to size 76 waist, and shop aprons. Work clothing in brown duck and blue denim, painters' pants, and similar basics are featured, as well as other work clothing by well-known manufac-turers. The "Wear-Again" reconditioned clothing (washed, pressed, and sterilized) includes coveralls from $5, pants and shirts from $3, work jackets, lab coats, and many other items. And Workmen's also offers closeouts, at further savings. If you don't see what you're looking for, write—it may be available.

Special Factors: Satisfaction is guaranteed on new and "Wear-Again" clothing; shipping is included; returns are accepted within 10 days; minimum order is $15.

COMPANIES OUTSIDE THE U.S.A.

The following firms are experienced in dealing with customers in the U.S. and Canada. We've included them because they offer goods not widely available at a discount in the U.S., because they have a better selection, or because they offer the same goods at great savings.

Before ordering from any non-U.S. firm, please consult "The Complete Guide to Buying by Mail," page 573, for helpful tips. We recommend paying for orders from foreign firms with a credit card whenever possible, so you'll have some recourse if you don't receive your order. For more information, see "The Fair Credit Billing Act," page 612.

PITLOCHRY KNITWEAR AND MOFFAT WOOLLENS

**MAIL ORDER
  DEPARTMENT
BENMAR, MOFFAT
DUMFRIESSHIRE DG10
  9EP
SCOTLAND
011-44-387-683-20799
FAX: 011-44-387-683-
  21066**

Catalog: free
Save: up to 50%
Pay: check, IMO, MC, V, AE, Access, EC
Sells: Scottish knits and woven apparel
Store: same address; daily 9–5:30

$$$ ☎ 🍁 ▆

Pitlochry's 16-page color catalog shows a good selection of women's suits and coordinated skirt and sweater ensembles, in vibrant plaids and solids. These are the traditionally styled pleated and straight skirts, turtle-neck sweaters, and pullovers, cardigans, and blouses for which the British are so famous.

In addition to walking suits, Chesterfield coats, and waxed-cotton jackets, Pitlochry sells kilts, tams, scarves, and stoles in selected tartans, including a selection for children. There are sweaters in lambswool, Shetland wool, Aran wool, stunning intarsia patterns in rich color combinations, and even animal and thistle motifs. Several styles are offered in children's sizes, and there are two pages of sweaters and jackets for men. The prices, which are listed in pounds sterling, are from 20% to 35% below those of similar goods we found in the U.S., and all orders are sent by airmail. Please note that some of the clothing terms used in the catalog are British: "lumber" (jacket) for heavy buttoned cardigan, waistcoat for vest, and "rug" for blanket (as in "travel rug") are a few examples.

Special Factors: Satisfaction is guaranteed; returns are accepted within 14 days for exchange, refund, or credit.

RAMMAGERDIN

P.O. BOX 751
121 REYKJAVIK, ICELAND
011-354-1-11122
FAX: 011-354-1-627270

Catalog: $2, deductible
Save: 30% plus
Pay: check, IMO, MC, V, AE, DC, EC
Sells: Icelandic knitwear and yarns
Store: Hafnarstraeti 19, Reykjavik, Iceland;
Monday to Friday 9–6, Saturday 9–12;
also Hotel Loftleidir, Hotel Esja, and
Kringlan Shopping Centre, Reykjavik

$$$

You're probably familiar with Lopi, the soft, soft wool used to create Icelandic sweaters and accessories that are available in many catalogs. They're usually seen in cream, brown, and grey, in Nordic designs with snowflakes and reindeer. Rammagerdin used to sell those designs, but its current offerings are far more upbeat and stylish—but they're still made in that deliciously soft wool. Prices are routinely 30% less than those charged for the same goods in the U.S.

Rammagerdin's 24-page color catalog is devoted to cardigans, pullovers, skirts, vests, and zippered jackets for men and women, coats and delicate shawls, cardigans for children, and socks, slippers, caps, scarves, mittens, and blankets made of Icelandic wool. Most of the women's designs incorporate some traditional patterns, but use wonderful color combinations: an intarsia-knit pullover blended forest green, cherry red, magenta, tangerine, and burgundy quite success-fully, and there were lovely mergers of natural/pink/grey and rose/mint/baby blue. The men's designs are on the traditional side, but are quite handsome, and the fringed blankets (about 51" by 79") are offered in both bright and sober plaids and stripes.

Icelandic yarn can be bought here by the skein at prices much lower than those charged in specialty yarn stores in the U.S. Rammagerdin sells medium-weight, natural-colored and dyed yarn for $3.80 per 3½-ounce skein, shipped by airmail. All of the yarn is washed and mothproofed, and it's offered in both natural colors— creams, greys, charcoal, and browns—as well as heathery rose, moss, slate blue, and other poetic shades.

Special Factors: Shipping and insurance are included; orders are shipped worldwide.

W.S. ROBERTSON (OUTFITTERS) LTD.

**40/41 BANK ST.
GALASHIELS
SCOTLAND
011-44-1-896-2152**

Brochures and Price Lists: $5
Save: up to 30%
Pay: check, IMO, MC, V, Access
Sells: Scottish knitwear
Store: same address; Monday to Saturday 9–5:30

$$ ♦ ▦

W.S. Robertson sells Pringles, the cashmeres of cashmere, which have been Scotland's pride since 1815. Pringle's pullovers, cardigans, and vests are offered here at savings of up to 30% on U.S. prices—and they're also available in camel's hair, "lamaine" (a Merino wool), lambswool, and Shetland wool. Robertson also carries the stylish Lyle & Scott sweaters in cashmere, lambswool, and Botany wool, as well as knits by Ballantyne and Braemar, in cashmere, lambswool, and Shetland wool.

If you're having your order delivered to an address outside the United Kingdom, deduct 15% (the Value Added Tax, not charged on exported goods). The final figure is your cost. The prices are listed in pounds sterling, and the savings increase when the dollar is strong. If you're not paying in pounds, obtain the rate of exchange from your local bank on the day you order and use that figure to convert the pounds to dollars. Add shipping costs after you compute the export discount.

Special Factor: Price quote by phone or letter on styles not shown in the brochures.

MRS. MARY SPILLANE

**5 PORT RD.
KILLARNEY, CO. KERRY
IRELAND**

Catalog: free
Save: up to 35%
Pay: check, IMO, bank draft
Sells: Aran sweaters
Store: same address; Monday to Saturday
9:30–6

$$ ◆ ▇

Mrs. Spillane's catalog illustrates a variety of Aran-knit pullovers, cardigans, and vests for men, women, and children, all of which are knit by hand in Killarney. Prices run from about $65 to $125 for pullovers, and $67 and up for cardigans. Instead of pricing the sweaters individually, Mrs. Spillane gives the price *range* for each type of garment, and asks you to send the order form specifying the size, body style, neckline style, measurements, and color (white, cream, or natural black), and she'll send you a price quote. This may seem a cumbersome way to do business, but it's ideal if you want a special stitch worked into your sweater, need a very large size, or would like something unusual—three quarter sleeves, pockets, or a belt, for example.

Special Factors: Price quote by letter; orders are shipped worldwide.

SEE ALSO

Ace Leather Products, Inc. • handbags, attaché cases, and small leather goods • *LEATHER*
Atlantic Bridge Collection Corp. Ltd. • Aran handknits • *ART, ANTIQUES*
Austad's • golf apparel and shoes • *SPORTS*
Babouris Handicrafts • handknitted wool sweaters • *CRAFTS*
Bailey's, Inc. • wide range of outdoor apparel clothing for men • *TOOLS*
Bart's Water Ski Center, Inc. • water-skiing vests, T-shirts, swim trunks, and wet suits • *SPORTS*
Bass Pro Shops • boating and outdoor wear • *SPORTS*
Beauty Boutique • small selection of moderately priced women's apparel • *HEALTH*
Beauty by Spector, Inc. • wigs and hairpieces for men and women • *HEALTH*

Better Health Fitness • Danskin and Everlast sportswear • *SPORTS*

Bike Nashbar • bicycling and sports apparel, and sunglasses • *SPORTS*

Bowhunters Warehouse, Inc. • camouflage clothing • *SPORTS*

Bruce Medical Supply • dressing aids for the disabled, stoma scarves, incontinence products • *MEDICINE*

The Button Shop • replacement zippers for jeans, garment shoulder pads • *CRAFTS*

Cabela's Inc. • hunting and fishing wear, rugged outdoor clothing and footwear • *SPORTS*

Cambridge Wools, Ltd. • Aran-style sweaters • *CRAFTS*

Campmor • outdoor clothing and accessories for men, women, and children • *SPORTS*

Clothcrafters, Inc. • aprons, garment bags, and tote bags • *GENERAL MERCHANDISE*

The Company Store, Inc. • down-filled outerwear, cotton nightwear, and separates • *HOME: LINEN*

Custom Golf Clubs, Inc. • golf clothing and footwear • *SPORTS*

Cycle Goods Corp. • bicycling apparel and footwear • *SPORTS*

Defender Industries, Inc. • foul-weather wear and boating shoes • *AUTO*

Dharma Trading Co. • cotton clothing and silk scarves for fabric painting, etc. • *CRAFTS*

Direct Safety Company • protective and disposable industrial clothing, hats, and gloves • *TOOLS*

E & B Marine Supply, Inc. • foul-weather wear • *AUTO*

A. Feibusch Corporation • zippers of all types • *CRAFTS*

Gander Mountain, Inc. • hunting and fishing clothing, outdoor wear • *SPORTS*

Gettinger Feather Corp. • feather marabous and boas, loose feathers • *CRAFTS*

Goldberg's Marine Distributors • foul-weather wear and boating shoes • *AUTO*

Innovation Luggage • handbags and small leather goods • *LEATHER*

Lands' End, Inc. • casual clothing for men, women, and children • *GENERAL MERCHANDISE*

Las Vegas Discount Golf & Tennis • tennis and other sports apparel, tennis and golf shoes • *SPORTS*

Leather Unlimited Corp. • sheepskin mittens, hats, and bags • *LEATHER*

Lingerie for Less • Spenco breast forms • *MEDICINE*

D. MacGillivray & Coy. • Scottish knitwear, stock and custom-made kilts, etc. • *CRAFTS*

Mass. Army & Navy Store • government surplus clothing and gear, casual wear • *SURPLUS*

Mother Hart's Natural Products, Inc. • women's underwear, leotards, etc. • *HOME: LINEN*

New England Leather Accessories, Inc. • leather handbags and accessories • *LEATHER*

Omaha Vaccine Company, Inc. • Wells Lamont work gloves, Red Ball boots • *ANIMAL*

Overton's Sports Center, Inc. • boating and windsurfing apparel • *SPORTS*

Performance Bicycle Shop • cycling clothing, footwear, and helmets • *SPORTS*

Professional Golf & Tennis Suppliers, Inc. • golf, tennis, and running shoes and apparel • *SPORTS*

Pueblo to People • handwoven clothing and accessories from Central and South America • *GENERAL MERCHANDISE*

Racer Wholesale • auto racing suits and accessories • *AUTO*

Retired Persons Services, Inc. • support hosiery, slippers, socks, etc. • *MEDICINE*

Road Runner Sports • sports apparel and shoes • *SPORTS*

Ruvel & Co., Inc. • government surplus clothing and outdoor wear • *SURPLUS*

Sailboard Warehouse, Inc. • windsurfing apparel • *SPORTS*

Samuels Tennisport • court clothing, sport bags, and accessories • *SPORTS*

Script City • T-shirts and casual clothing with TV-theme logos, etc. • *BOOKS*

Shannon Duty Free Mail Order • Irish handknits • *HOME: TABLE SETTINGS*

Sierra Trading Post • outdoor clothing and accessories for men and women • *SPORTS*

Sport Shop • camouflage clothing • *SPORTS*

Sultan's Delight, Inc. • belly-dancing outfits, Arab headdresses and agals • *FOOD*

Surgical Products, Inc. • support hosiery, Enna Jettick shoes, therapeutic apparel • *MEDICINE*

Thai Silks • silk ties, scarves, handkerchiefs, lingerie, and blouses • *CRAFTS*

Utex Trading Enterprises • silk scarves and ties • *CRAFTS*

West Marine Products • foul-weather wear • *AUTO*

Wiley Outdoor Sports, Inc. • hunting (camouflage) clothing and accessories • *SPORTS*

Mother and Child

Clothing and accessories for the expectant and nursing mother, and infants and children; baby furniture, strollers, and related goods

The firms in this section offer maternity wear, clothing and accessories for infants and children, and even baby furniture and vehicles at savings of up to 60%. In addition, a number of the firms listed throughout this book sell goods for mother and baby. *Bennett Brothers* ("General Merchandise") offers a large selection of sterling baby keepsakes, Hedstrom nursery furnishings, car seats, playpens, high chairs, strollers, and toys. *Spiegel* ("General Merchandise") also carries maternity wear, children's clothing, and toys. *Chock Catalog Corp.* ("Clothing") features Carter's receiving blankets and crib sets, Curity diapers, and underwear and nightwear for newborn through toddler sizes. *Gohn Bros.* ("Clothing") sells Curity diapers and Gerber bibs, baby sleepers, waterproof pants, and shirts. *Campmor* ("Sports") offers baby buntings, Snuglis, and a diaper-changer backpack for the truly intrepid parent. And the *Consumer Information Center* and *Superintendent of Documents* ("Books") usually offer a number of publications devoted to baby-care advice and related information. For other tips on buying baby goods, see the publications list from Consumers Union in the current issue of *Consumer Reports*.

BABY BUNZ & CO.

**P.O. BOX 1717-WB92
SEBASTOPOL, CA 95473
707/829-5347**

Catalog: $1
Save: up to 30%
Pay: check, MO, MC, V
Sells: diapering supplies and layette items
Store: mail order only

$ ☎ ♦ 🇺🇸

If you use cloth diapers instead of disposables, you may be overwhelmed by all the prefolded diapers and diaper "systems" on the market. One of the most popular diapering methods among the cloth set is the use of a standard or fitted diaper with a natural-fiber cover.

Baby Bunz & Co. has been selling the best-known covers, Nikkys, since 1982. Nikkys are made in soft lambswool, waterproof cotton, and vinyl-lined cotton, and are available in sizes from newborn to three years (up to 34 pounds). Training pants are also offered, and prices of the Nikkys are up to 30% below retail. The colorful Baby Bunz brochure also shows the company's own line of diapers in three styles (contour, prefolded, and flat), which are sold at up to 22% below regular retail. (The brochure includes guides to folding diapers and diapering with Nikkys.) Dovetails biodegradable diapers are sold by Baby Bunz, as are Rubber Duckies nylon diaper and pants covers, adorable layettewear from WeeWear and Fix of Sweden, lambskin and wool booties, and bedding—pima cotton and Merino wool blankets, and a crib-sized lambskin. The natural theme is carried on with Weleda baby-care products, bath sponges, natural bristle baby brushes, a well-designed potty, and the ideal lovey, "First Doll." And Baby Bunz has added a cotton floral diaper bag/backpack to this winning collection of baby needs.

Canadian readers, please note: Only U.S. funds are accepted.

Special Factors: Satisfaction is guaranteed; unused returns are accepted within 30 days for replacement, refund, or credit; minimum order is $15 with credit cards.

BEN'S BABYLAND

**81 AVENUE A
NEW YORK, NY 10009
212/674-1353**

Brochure: 50¢
Save: up to 30%
Pay: check, MO, MC, V
Sells: baby furniture, wheeled goods, etc.
Store: same address; Monday to Friday
10–6, Saturday and Sunday 10–5

Ben's Babyland has been in business for about 75 years, selling furniture, strollers, walkers, and other goods for baby at Lower East Side prices—an average 20% to 30% off list.

Aprica strollers are the vehicle of choice among babies in New York City, and Ben's sells them at real discounts. You'll also find Simmons cribs and juvenile furniture, car seats, high chairs, strollers, playpens, walkers, or other goods by Graco and other top names here. If you're looking for crib quilts, bumpers, bath sets, or pillows, see the brochure or call Ben's Babyland—the firm sells baby bedding from several manufacturers. And cloth diapers and diaper covers (Dappi, Nikkys, and Rubber Duckies) are also available. Call or write (with specific model names, if possible) to check prices and availability of name-brand goods not listed in the brochure.

Special Factor: Price quote by phone or letter with SASE.

BOSOM BUDDIES

**P.O. BOX 6138, DEPT.
WBM
KINGSTON, NY 12401
914/338-2038**

Catalog: free
Save: up to 50% (see text)
Pay: check, MO, MC, V
Sells: nursing bras and clothing
Store: by appointment only

Bosom Buddies was founded in 1983 by a nursing mother who saw a market for "breastfeeding fashions." Her eight-page catalog includes a guide to taking your measurements so you're sure to order the right bra size.

Nursing bras by Decent Exposures, Leading Lady, Mary Jane, and Practical Elegance are offered, including many all-cotton styles. This is a great source for hard-to-find sizes—the Decent Exposures bras run up to size 42H, and other lines go up to 46K. Nightgowns and other clothing designed to make nursing easy are sold as well. Bosom Buddies also carries nursing pads and a full line of equipment for expressing and storing breast milk, and a number of helpful books. Not every item is discounted, but prices are reasonable, and savings run up to 50% on sale items.

Special Factor: Order sale merchandise promptly, since quantities may be limited.

MOTHER'S PLACE

P.O. BOX 94512
CLEVELAND, OH 44101-
    4512
800-829-0080

Catalog: free
Save: up to 60%
Pay: check, MO, MC, V
Sells: maternity clothing
Store: mail order only

At just 16 pages, the Mother's Place catalog may seem small, but it's big on answers to the problems of dressing attractively through pregnancy without going broke. The firm, which was founded in 1969, offers moderately priced dresses and separates to see you through work, play, and going out.

Dresses, jumpers, blouses and shirts, sweaters, jackets, activewear, and lingerie and nightwear are shown in the catalog, at great prices—$25 for a cotton/poly knit jumpsuit, $29 and $35 for great office ensembles, and less than $20 for activewear separates. The dresses are cut full enough to see you through all stages of pregnancy, and most are machine washable. If you're holding the line with expenses, Mother's Place will help you get through your pregnancy attractively and inexpensively.

Special Factors: Satisfaction is guaranteed; minimum order is $10 with credit cards.

MOTHERS WORK

DEPT. WB92
1309 NOBLE ST., 5TH FL.
PHILADELPHIA, PA 19123
215/625-9259
FAX: 215/440-9845

Catalog: free
Save: up to 30%
Pay: check, MO, MC, V, AE
Sells: maternity clothing
Store: 37 stores in CA, CO, CT, DC, FL, GA, IL, LA, MA, MD, MN, MO, NC, NJ, NY, OH, PA, TN, TX, and VA (locations listed in the catalog)

The expectant executive can put her tailor on a retainer as her waistline expands, or she can look here for suitable maternity wear. For $3, Mothers Work will send you a catalog with a set of fabric swatches for the different business separates. (The catalog fee is deductible from your order.)

The concept here is winningly simple: Take a business jacket (which you'll leave unbuttoned in late pregnancy), pair it with a maternity skirt and blouse in the early months, and switch to a jumper as your size increases. The jacket can be worn after the baby is born, and the jumper is a handsome solution to the problem of maintaining a polished look in late pregnancy without sacrificing comfort. Mothers Work also sells dresses in a variety of styles, and even lingerie and panty hose. Sizes run from 4 to 14.

Special Factors: Satisfaction is guaranteed; returns are accepted within 10 days for exchange, refund, or credit.

THE NATURAL BABY CO., INC.

**114 W. FRANKLIN AVE.,
SUITE WBMC
PENNINGTON, NJ 08534
800-358-BABY
609/737-2895
FAX: 609/737-7665**

Catalog: free
Save: up to 30%
Pay: check, MO, MC, V, AE
Sells: diapers and infants' clothing
Store: mail order only

$$$ ☎ 🍁 🇺🇸

The people behind The Natural Baby Co. really love children—and their parents. Everything in the firm's catalog has been chosen with an eye to making children comfortable and keeping them healthy, without costing Mom and Dad a bundle. The Natural Baby Co. began doing business in 1983, and is expanding its scope to include clothing for older children.

Diapers and covers are featured here—The Natural Baby's own "Rainbow" diaper, a fitted cloth style (pinless, foldless) made of flannel-lined terrycloth ($27 per dozen). If you're on a tight budget, you can get the "Natural Baby Diapers" of birdseye, for $16 a dozen. Several Nikky diaper covers are available in several styles, as well as the Natural Baby's own waterproof nylon covers ($3.95 each). Diaper pads and conventional (unfolded) cloth diapers are also sold. The catalog includes helpful sidebars on diapering with pinless covers, the cloth vs. disposables debate, and preventing diaper rash. A whole page is devoted to ideas on setting up a changing table using furniture you already have, supplemented by a $6 cushioned changing pad from Natural Baby. (The pad also comes as part of the "DiaperNapsac," a sturdy and capacious baby gear kit that rides on your back and costs $38.)

We were pleased to see a baby sling here, the Cozy Baby Carrier, which slips on quickly and can be used to hold a baby in nursing position, in front of or behind you, facing forward, or backward. The Cozy Baby Carrier will also help support older, heavier children who ride on their parents' hips. Sheepskin rugs and play balls, Faribo crib blankets, flannel buntings, and Storkenworks shoes are among the other goods available. The Natural Baby carries some clothing for older kids, including long johns and terry bathrobes, Nikky's heavyweight pants (in sizes to fit children up to 110 pounds), socks, sweaters, mittens, scarves, and other goods. Mothers are treated to Leading Lady bras, and nightwear designed to make nursing easier.

The other half of Natural Baby's business is a program called "The Incredible Toypack." It works like this: You send the company a check for $30 as a deposit, for which you receive a stack of manufacturers' catalogs. Go through them, make your selection (the minimum order is $60), and return the catalogs to Natural Baby within five weeks and you'll get your deposit check back, uncashed. You'll also save around 25% on what you order, which includes (at this writing) Selecta wood games and dolls, rocking horses, Baufix construction sets, Radio Flyer wagons and scooters, Campbell Villages dolls and toys, Galt Toys and art supplies, blocks, puppet theaters, children's furniture, and even books and tapes. Please note that the minimum order from the Toypack is $60, returns are not accepted (unless defective), and orders can take up to two months to be delivered. But even with those considerations, the Toypack is a wonderful way to save on "heirloom" toys and games—something to share with other parents.

The Natural Baby Co. is offering readers a discount of $2 on their first order. Be sure to identify yourself as a WBMC reader when you order. This WBMC reader discount expires February 1, 1993.

Special Factors: Price quote by phone or letter; C.O.D. orders are accepted.

HOLLY NICOLAS NURSING COLLECTION

**DEPT. W
P.O. BOX 7121
ORANGE, CA 92613-7121
714/639-5933**

Brochure with Swatches: $1
Save: up to 50%
Pay: check, MO, AE
Sells: nursing clothing
Store: mail order only

This business was founded in 1983 by a former fashion model, who began by creating nursing dresses for the mothers of her grandchildren, Holly and Nicolas. The clothes she produces are well designed, incorporating concealed openings for nursing into the lines of the garments.

The Holly Nicolas brochure shows pretty, feminine blouses, dresses, and nightgowns designed for the nursing mother. The styles are classic: A stylish, sailor-collar dress in dark blue Oxford cloth, a square-neck blouse in pink or blue striped shirting, and a sundress in lilac or blue cotton/rayon are among the offerings. Prices are very reasonable: $20 for the nightgown with hidden openings for nursing, to $65 for a fresh, flower-printed dress. Samples of the actual fabrics are included in the brochure.

Holly Nicolas is offering readers of this book a 20% discount on the "Transition Dress," a flattering style that will see you through the nine months and nursing afterward, thanks to concealed openings. It's self-belted and comes in a wool or cotton/poly blend. Identify yourself as a reader when you order to take the discount. This WBMC reader discount expires February 1, 1993.

Special Factors: Price quote by phone or letter; returns are accepted within 30 days for exchange or refund; orders are shipped worldwide.

RUBENS & MARBLE, INC.

P.O. BOX 14900-A
CHICAGO, IL 60614-0900
312/348-6200

Brochure: free with SASE
Save: up to 60%
Pay: check or MO
Sells: infants' clothing and bedding
Store: 2340 N. Racine Ave.; Monday to
Friday 9–3

$$$ 🇺🇸

Rubens & Marble has been supplying hospitals with baby clothes since 1890 and will sell you the same goods at up to 60% below regular retail prices. The babywear basics include undershirts in sizes from newborn to 36 months, with short, long, and mitten-cuff sleeves; they're offered in snap, tie, plain, and double-breasted slipover styles (many are seconds, with small knitting flaws). First-quality cotton/wool blend and preemie-sized cotton undershirts are available as well. Rubens & Marble also offers fitted bassinet and crib sheets, training and waterproof pants, kimonos, drawstring-bottom baby gowns, and terry bibs.

Special Factors: Send a self-addressed, stamped envelope for the price list; seconds are clearly marked; minimum order is 1 package (varying number depending on type of item).

THE WABBY COMPANY

Brochure: free
Save: up to 30% (see text)
Pay: check or MO
Sells: "breathable" diaper covers
Store: mail order only

**3331 GOLD RUN RD.
BOULDER, CO 80302
303/449-2120**

$

The Wabby Company sells its own diaper covers, "Wabbies," which are made of "breathable" Gore-Tex fabric. Because Gore-Tex allows vapors to escape but contains actual wetness, the Wabby should help you baby's bottom stay cooler than when it's doing a slow burn in rubber pants. Wabbies should outlast rubber pants, too, and can be rinsed out and machine washed and dried (see the brochure for use and care details). Wabbies are offered in sizes from newborn (up to 12 pounds) to XL (29 to 34 pounds), in white, yellow, or a print. The firm estimates you'll need four or five Wabbies per baby, and is selling them for $11.75 each. That's not cheap, but as far as we know, the Wabby is unique in its use of Gore-Tex and may help your baby feel more comfortable and happier. The Wabby Company also sells diaper-sack hampers, hats, booties, and long underwear.

Special Factor: Quantity discounts are available.

SEE ALSO

Alden Comfort Mills • down-filled crib comforters • *HOME: LINEN*
The Company Store • down-filled crib comforters and bedding •
    HOME: LINEN
Betty Crocker Enterprises • children's tableware, toys, games, and puzzles
    • *GENERAL MERCHANDISE*
Butternut Books • children's books • *BOOKS*
Clothcrafters, Inc. • cloth diapers and crib sheets • *GENERAL
    MERCHANDISE*
Michael C. Fina Co. • sterling silver baby gifts • *HOME: TABLE SETTINGS*
Showcase of Savings • maternity hosiery and underwear • *CLOTHING*
Spiegel, Inc. • children's clothing and maternity wear • *GENERAL
    MERCHANDISE*

Footwear

Shoes, boots, and slippers for men, women, and children

The firms in this section sell all kinds of footwear, from arctic boots to moccasins to nurses' shoes, at savings of up to 40%. The biggest problem in buying shoes by mail is getting a good fit. Here are some tips to improve the odds, and to make returns as easy as possible if necessary:

- Have your feet measured yearly, and order your true size.
- Buy from firms with liberal return policies, preferably an unconditional guarantee of satisfaction with a 30-day return period.
- Buy styles and shapes that have fit in the past.
- If the shoes you're buying are also available in a local store, try on a pair before ordering them.
- When the shoes arrive, unwrap them carefully and save the packaging.
- Try them on in the late afternoon, when your feet have swollen slightly.
- Walk around in a carpeted area to avoid scratching the soles.
- Leave the shoes on for at least half an hour, checking for rubbing and pinching after 20 minutes.
- If they fit, consider ordering a second pair *now,* while they're still in stock.
- If the shoes don't fit, return them according to the firm's instructions, indicating whether you want another size or a refund/credit.

Good maintenance is critical in preserving the looks and longevity of your shoes and boots. For helpful tips on caring for all types of footwear, see *The Butler's Guide* (Fireside/Simon & Schuster, 1980), by Stanley Ager and Fiona St. Aubyn, and *Taking Care of Clothes* (St. Martin's Press, 1982), by Mablen Jones. Some of the firms listed in "Leather" sell leather care products, as do a number of companies listed in the "See Also's" of that chapter. If your shoes and boots need professional help and you don't have a good repair service nearby, contact the Houston Shoe Hospital, at 5215 Kirby Dr., Houston, TX 77098, or 713/528-6268. This firm overhauls worn footwear at prices much lower than those charged by local repair shops we checked, and it handles mail-order repairs.

CLOVER NURSING SHOE COMPANY

**1948 EAST WHIPP RD., DEPT. WBM
KETTERING, OH 45440-2921
513/435-0025**

Brochure: free
Save: up to 40%
Pay: check, MO, MC, V
Sells: "Day Lites" shoes
Store: mail order only

Nurses look for comfort and good fit in their professional shoes, and many find both in Nurse Mates, a line of shoes manufactured by the Soft Spots company. Clover Nursing Shoe, in business since 1981, specializes in Day Lites—the same shoe. Clover sells the shoe at the best discounts around—up to 40% off regular retail, every day.

The Day Lites line includes over a dozen styles, from streamlined T-straps to sturdy blucher models. The shoes are made of soft leather and built up on lightweight wedge soles that sport a little blue heart. Some of the shoes are offered solely in "nurse white," but there are many available in black, navy, wine, brown, and other colors. Clover's prices are great, and the full range of sizes—from 5 to 12, slim (AA) to double-wide (EE)—is carried.

Special Factors: Satisfaction is guaranteed; only first-quality goods are sold; orders are shipped worldwide.

THE HANOVER SHOE CO.

**118 CARLISLE ST., DEPT.
  90036
HANOVER, PA 17331
800-426-3708**

Catalog: $1
Save: 25% average
Pay: check, MO, MC, V, AE, DC
Sells: men's footwear
Store: over 250 stores nationwide

$$$ ☎ 🇺🇸

The Hanover Shoe Company has been making shoes since 1899, and sells them through a 32-page color catalog and at hundreds of stores across the country. Hanover shoes incorporate construction details that make them comparable to similar styles from other firms that charge much more.

Hanover's top line of Shell Cordovan leather shoes includes classic wingtips, Oxfords, slip-ons, and other handsewn styles, all at under $180. Hanover's "Master Flex" shoes have a flexible leather sole, and are offered in several styles for under $140. Well-made calfskin brogues and wingtips are offered, as well as many other styles. Casual footwear by Clarks, New Balance, Rockport, and Timberland are also featured in the catalog.

Many of Hanover's own shoes are offered in sizes from 6 to 15, in widths from AA to EEE. Hosiery, belts, and shoe-care products are shown in the catalog, too. All purchases are backed by the Hanover guarantee of satisfaction, and please don't request discounts.

Special Factor: Satisfaction is guaranteed.

JUSTIN DISCOUNT BOOTS & COWBOY OUTFITTERS

**P.O. BOX 67-JWM
JUSTIN, TX 76247
800-677-BOOT
FAX: 817/648-3282**

Catalog: free
Save: 35% average
Pay: check, MO, MC, V
Sells: Western boots and clothing
Store: 101 W. Hwy. 156, Justin, TX;
  Monday to Saturday 9–6

$$$ ☎ 🍁 🇺🇸

This firm, although not owned by the Justin Boot Co., sells a number of the Justin boot lines in men's and women's styles. The 48-page color catalog includes a "compare at" price as well as the selling price for most items. We cross-checked several items, and found that the JDB prices were 20% to 40% less.

The footwear choices run from "ropers," comparatively plain, thick-soled boots with Western vamps that rise to mid-calf (about $90), to artful creations in exotic skins—ostrich, lizard, bull hide, and snakeskin. There are several pages of women's styles, including lizard Western boots, "fashion" ropers in Atlantis blue, pink, "gusto green," and "true purple," as well as traditional colors. Children can get their Justin Juniors in red, pink, navy, brown, and other colors, for under $50 a pair. Coordinating belts are available, and the custom embroidery department will embellish your boots with two initials for $6.50 per letter.

Real cowboys don't wear ostrich dress boots while mending fences, though—they wear work boots. JDB offers sturdy Justin styles with oil-tanned leather uppers and Vibram soles, and a number of specialty boots: insulated and all-weather models, snakeproof and steel-toed boots, and "engineer" boots (for oil field workers and motorcyclists). Justin Discount Boots also sells its own line of straw hats, German silver buckles and belt tips, David James coats, leather-care products, and Wrangler shirts, Carhartt jackets, and Wrangler jeans for men, women, and boys.

Special Factors: Satisfaction is guaranteed; price quote by phone or letter; unworn, unscuffed, unaltered returns are accepted for exchange, refund, or credit; C.O.D. orders are accepted; orders are shipped worldwide.

OKUN BROS. SHOES

**356 E. SOUTH ST.-WBM
KALAMAZOO, MI 49007
800-433-6344**

Catalog: free
Save: 18% average (see text)
Pay: check, MO, MC, V, Discover
Sells: dress, casual, and work shoes
Store: same address; Monday to Friday 8:30 A.M.–9 P.M., Saturday 8:30–7

Okun Bros. has been serving the footwear needs of Kalamazoo since 1920, and brings its shoe store to the rest of world through a 48-page catalog. Okun maintains that it can fit nearly any foot, and it has the largest stock of men's work and safety shoes available in Michigan. Some of the brands are rarely found sold at less than full retail. The typical discount is 18%, but heavy boots for sub-zero conditions have been sold here at up to 44% off, and specials in the sales flyers further the savings to 50%.

Casual shoes, plain pumps, athletic shoes for several sports, men's dress shoes, sandals, loafers and moccasins, deck shoes, nurses' shoes, bikers' boots, and work shoes and boots are all available through Okun. The brands and lines available here number over 200, including some of the most popular: Stacy Adams, Avia, Bates, Carolina Shoe Co., Clarks, Coleman, Converse, Dexter, Double H, Drew, Easy Spirit, Allen Edmonds, Etonic, Extra Depth, Florsheim, Foot-Joy, Freeman, French Shriner, Frye, Daniel Green, Harley-Davidson (motorcycle boots), Hi-Tec, Hush Puppies, Johnston & Murphy, Kaepa, KangaRoos, L.A. Gear, Minnetonka, New Balance, Nike, Nunn Bush, Nurse Mates, Propet, Red Bird, Red Wing, Reebok, Rockport, Rocky, Saucony, Sebago, Soft Spots, Sorel, Sperry Top-Sider, Sporto, Timberland, Tingley, and Wolverine. Thor-Lo "padded" specialty sport socks and Spenco insoles are also available.

Because only a fraction of the stock can be shown in the catalog, you should inquire about brands and styles not shown—they may be available.

Special Factors: Satisfaction is guaranteed; price quote by phone or letter with SASE; unworn returns are accepted; orders are shipped worldwide.

COMPANIES OUTSIDE THE U.S.A.

The following firm, A.W.G. Otten and Son, is experienced in dealing with customers in the U.S. and Canada. We've included Otten because the Dutch clogs it sells are not widely available at great savings in the U.S., especially in a wide selection of styles and sizes.

Before ordering from any non-U.S. firm, please consult "The Complete Guide to Buying by Mail," page 573, for helpful tips. We recommend paying for orders from foreign firms with a credit card whenever possible, so you'll have some recourse if you don't receive your order. For more information, see "The Fair Credit Billing Act," page 612.

A.W.G. OTTEN AND SON

**P.O. BOX 55655
1007 ND AMSTERDAM
THE NETHERLANDS**

Catalog: $1, cash
Save: up to 30%
Pay: IMO, MC, V, AE, DC, Access
Sells: wooden shoes and clogs
Store: 33 1st v.d. Helststraat, 1073 AC
    Amsterdam; Monday to Saturday 9–5:30

$$$ ☎ ♦

Wooden shoes, or *klompen,* are still worn in Holland by gardeners, fishermen, butchers, and dairy workers. Otten and Son's charming brochure tell us that in one part of Holland, a boy courting a girl would give her carved wooden shoes decorated with her initials. The *klompen* have even affected the language—there are several Dutch words that are derived solely from the sounds made by walking in wooden shoes.

Otten, which has been in business since 1898, makes seven shoe styles—including souvenir shoes with windmills carved on the toes. Most of Otten's shoes are painted in lively colors, and Otten makes a low-cut model that's easier to walk in than the traditional style. Wooden clogs with leather uppers, much like those made by Olof Daughters of Sweden, are also available. Prices for the shoes are easily 30% less than those charged in import and gift shops in the U.S. Sizes run from a child's size 4 to a man's size 14.

These shoes can be homes for lots of things other than feet—the large sizes can be used as doll beds, letter holders, planters, lamp bases, or even pencil holders. They make wonderful gifts, too.

Special Factor: Quantity discounts are available.

SEE ALSO

Austad's • golf apparel and shoes • *SPORTS*
Jos. A. Bank Clothiers, Inc. • fine quality, traditional men's shoes •
  CLOTHING
Bike Nashbar • bicycling footwear • *SPORTS*
Cabela's Inc. • hunting and fishing wear, rugged outdoor clothing and
  footwear • *SPORTS*

Cahall's Department Store • rugged footwear for men and women • CLOTHING

Campmor • rugged footwear for men, women, and children • SPORTS

Custom Coat Company, Inc. • deerskin moccasins • CLOTHING

Custom Golf Clubs, Inc. • golf clothing and footwear • SPORTS

Cycle Goods Corp. • bicycling apparel and footwear • SPORTS

D & A Merchandise Co., Inc. • Totes footwear • CLOTHING

The Deerskin Place • suede boots, moccasins, etc. • CLOTHING

Gander Mountain, Inc. • rugged boots and footwear • SPORTS

Gohn Bros. • sturdy work shoes and boots for men and women • CLOTHING

Golf Haus • golf shoes • SPORTS

Holabird Sports Discounters • shoes for sports activities • SPORTS

Huntington Clothiers • small selection of men's shoes • CLOTHING

Lands' End, Inc. • casual and sporty footwear for men and women • GENERAL MERCHANDISE

Las Vegas Discount Golf & Tennis • tennis and other sports apparel; tennis and golf shoes • SPORTS

Northern Hydraulics, Inc. • Northlake boots • TOOLS

Thos. Oak & Sons • moderately priced footwear for women • CLOTHING

Omaha Vaccine Company, Inc. • Wells Lamont work gloves, Red Ball boots • ANIMAL

Pagano Gloves, Inc. • moccasins • CLOTHING

Performance Bicycle Shop • cycling clothing, footwear, and helmets • SPORTS

Professional Golf & Tennis Suppliers, Inc. • golf, tennis, and running shoes and apparel • SPORTS

Anthony Richards • small selection of moderately priced women's shoes • CLOTHING

Road Runner Sports • sports apparel and shoes • SPORTS

Sara Glove Company, Inc. • work shoes and boots • CLOTHING

Sierra Trading Post • outdoor shoes for men and women • SPORTS

Spiegel, Inc. • fashion footwear for men, women, and children • GENERAL MERCHANDISE

Surgical Products, Inc. • support hosiery, Enna Jettick shoes, therapeutic apparel • MEDICINE

WearGuard Corp. • work shoes and boots • CLOTHING

Wholesale Veterinary Supply, Inc. • work shoes and boots • ANIMAL

Wiley Outdoor Sports, Inc. • hunting and outdoor footwear • SPORTS

CRAFTS AND HOBBIES

Materials, supplies, tools, and equipment for

every sort of craft and hobby

There are suppliers here that can outfit nearly any craft, including the needle arts, marquetry, miniatures, quilting, stenciling, basketry, clock making, wheat weaving, quilling, wood carving, spinning and weaving, batiking, decoy painting, jewelry making, and much more. Some of these firms have been in business for generations and specialize in avocations that your local crafts shop may not even know exist. If you have a problem with a material or technique, most can provide assistance by phone.

Placing an order will usually guarantee you a spot on the mailing list, which means you'll receive the sales flyers with savings of up to 70%. Be sure to save your catalogs—they're invaluable for comparison shopping, and are often valuable resources for technical information.

Home sewing is seeing a revival these days, especially among women who need good business wardrobes, but balk at the ludicrous prices of ready-to-wear. (The do-it-yourself home decorating market has undergone a similar revitalization, aided by shelter magazines that whetted appetites for fancy window treatments and upholstery, with layouts of goods that many found unaffordable.) Sewing it yourself can not only save you money, but if you're skilled you'll get a custom tailor job, with the fabric and details _you_ want. If you haven't dusted off your machine in years, you'll be glad to know that every aspect of sewing—from the fabric and notions to the patterns to the machines themselves—has been improved over the past decade. The sources here can help you find the right tools and materials for your clothing project, but see the listings in "Home: Decor" for decorator fabrics.

If you do needlework and use DMC floss, be sure you have the DMC Embroidery Floss Card in your files. This reference includes samples of each DMC floss color and a guide to which colors are available in pearl cotton in sizes 3, 5, and 8. (Most discount sources carry DMC floss, but few include color guides.) The American Needle-woman sells the DMC Floss Card; request the free catalog from The American Needlewoman, P.O. Box 6472-WBMC, Fort Worth, TX 76115.

If your craft or hobby involves the use of hazardous materials, it's essential to take precautions while you work. For more information, see the introduction to "Art Materials." For wooden toy parts, see the listings in "Tools." For lapidary equipment and findings, see the firms listed in "Jewelry."

FIND IT FAST

BASKETRY AND SEAT REWEAVING • **Caning Shop, Frank's Cane**
FEATHERS • **Gettinger**
FUN FUR • **Monterey Mills**
GENERAL CRAFTS • **Circle Craft, Craft King, Craft Resources, Vanguard**
LEATHERWORKING • **Veteran Leather**
MODELS • **Tower Hobbies**
NOTIONS AND SEWING TOOLS • **Button Shop, A. Feibusch, Home-Sew, Newark Dressmaker, Solo Slide, Taylor's, Thread Discount Sales**
TEXTILE ARTS, YARN, FABRIC • **Dharma Trading, Fiber Studio, Fort Crailo, Global Village, Great Northern Weaving, J & J, Smiley's Yarn, Straw Into Gold, Thai Silks, Utex, Webbs, Babouris, Maurice Brassard, Cambridge Wools, Stavros Kouyoumoutzakis, D. MacGillivray**

BUFFALO BATT & FELT CORP.

**3307 WALDEN AVE., DEPT. WBM92
DEPEW, NY 14043
716/683-4100
FAX: 716/683-8928**

Brochure and Samples: $1, refundable
Save: 40% plus
Pay: check, MO, MC, V
Sells: fiberfill, quilt batts, and pillow inserts
Store: mail order only

$$ ☎

Buffalo Batt's "Super Fluff" polyester stuffing is so springy and resilient, the snowy-white samples nearly bounced out of our brochure. The firm has been in business since 1913, and sells this craft and upholstery stuffing by the case at savings of 40% or more on regular retail prices.

Super Fluff is manufactured in rolls 27″ wide by 20 yards long and is the ideal filler for upholstery and crafts in which support and a downlike feel are desired. In addition to high loft and nonallergenic properties, Super Fluff is machine washable and dryable, mildew resistant, and easy to sew. Buffalo Batt also sells Super Fluff in one- and two-pound bags, bulk rolls, pillow inserts (from 12″ square to 18″ square), and "traditional" and two-inch-thick "comforter-style" quilt batts. The only negative is the minimum order of any two cases, which translates into 20 pounds of Super Fluff stuffing, or a total of 50 pillows in the 14″ size, for example—more than most single projects require, but manageable for a home-based crafts business, quilting circle, cooperative, or major decorating project.

Please note: Orders are shipped via UPS within the continental U.S. only.

Special Factors: Price quote by phone or letter; quantity discounts are available; minimum order is any 2 cases.

THE BUTTON SHOP

P.O. BOX 1065-HM
OAK PARK, IL 60304
708/795-1234

Catalog: free
Save: up to 50%
Pay: check, MO, MC, V
Sells: buttons and sewing supplies
Store: 7023 Roosevelt Rd., Berwyn, IL;
　　　　Monday to Friday 9–4, Saturday 10–2

The Button Shop may have sold only buttons when it was founded in 1900, but it now stocks closures of all kinds, as well as trims, sewing machine parts, scissors, and other sewing tools and notions at savings of up to 50% on list prices or regular retail.

Several pages of the 18-page catalog are devoted to buttons—anonymous white shirt buttons, clear waistband buttons, tiny buttons for doll clothes, classic four-hole coat and suit buttons, gilt heraldic buttons for blazers, designs for dressy clothing, Navy pea coat buttons, braided leather buttons for tweeds, and dozens of others, including baseball gloves and other novelty designs for children's clothing.

If you want to custom-cover buttons with your own fabric, you'll find Maxant and Prym kits, make-your-own fabric belt and buckle materials, gripper snaps and grommet sets, hooks and eyes of all types, zippers (including odd sizes to 108″), and Velcro by the inch and yard. You'll find all kinds of ricrac, bias tape, cording, white and black elastic (from ⅛″ to 3″), replacement jacket cuffs, elbow patches, trouser pockets, pressing cloth, tailor's chalk, fusible backing, garment shoulder pads, and pins and needles for hand and machine sewing. Thread in cotton, cotton-covered polyester, and polyester is offered. The brands represented include Dritz, Fiskars, Gingher, Oncore, Prym, Singer, Suisse, Talon, Wiss, and Wrights.

The Button Shop has a comparatively deep inventory of sewing machine supplies and parts, including bobbins, bobbin cases, needle plates, buttonholers, motors, foot controls, light bulbs, and belts. Please note that the catalog descriptions are brief and that line drawings are the only illustrations. If you're not sure an item is the right one and need more information, call or write before you order. You may also send a fabric swatch for the best color match if you're ordering trim, thread, or buttons.

Special Factors: Price quote by phone or letter; returns are accepted within 30 days for exchange, refund, or credit; minimum order is $3, $10 with credit cards; orders are shipped worldwide.

THE CANING SHOP

926 GILMAN ST., DEPT.
WBM
BERKELEY, CA 94710
415/527-5010

Catalog: $1, refundable
Save: up to 30%
Pay: check, MO, MC, V
Sells: seat-reweaving and basketry supplies
Store: same address; Tuesday to Friday 10–6, Saturday 10–2

$$ ☎ ♦ 🇺🇸

The Caning Shop stocks the materials, tools, and instructive materials you'll need to restore your woven-seat chairs—or weave a basket from scratch. The owner of this business coauthored *The Caner's Handbook,* and prides himself on offering the "highest quality materials that can be found in the jungles of Malaysia and Indonesia." Prices are lower here than those charged at some specialty shops, and a little higher than those charged by a discount source we used for comparison. But the selection is excellent, and it's worth paying more if you get materials that last longer.

The firm, which began business in 1971, carries 15 kinds of prewoven cane webbing, which is used in modern and mass-produced seating. Older chairs, which have holes in the frame around the seat opening, must be rewoven by hand. For this, The Caning Shop offers hanks of cane in several sizes and binder cane, and also sells Danish seat cord, rawhide lacing, fiber rush, Hong Kong grass (seagrass), ash splint, Shaker tape, whole reed (for wicker), wicker braid, rattan, pressed fiber (imitation leather) seats, and tools to aid in installation. Basketry buffs should look here for kits, materials, hoops, and handles. If you're a novice seat reweaver, there's help here: half of the 36-page catalog is devoted to volumes on caning and seat reweaving, as well as general furniture restoration and basketry. If you live in or near Berkeley, you can get help with your project at the shop, which also gives classes in a variety of crafts—"Seaweed Basketry," "Gourd Crafting," and "Advanced Plaiting" were among those in the brochure we received.

Canadian readers, please note: Payment for the catalog and goods orders must be in U.S. funds.

Special Factors: Satisfaction is guaranteed; price quote by phone or letter; C.O.D. orders are accepted; orders are shipped worldwide.

CHERRY TREE TOYS, INC.

P.O. BOX 369-140
BELMONT, OH 43718
800-848-4363
614/484-4363
FAX: 614/484-4388

Catalog: $1
Save: up to 50%
Pay: check, MO, MC, V
Sells: woodworking and crafts supplies
Store: I-70, Exit 208, Belmont, OH; Monday to Saturday 9–5, Sunday 11–5

$$$$ ☎ ♦ ▬

Cherry Tree Toys sells kits for delightful playthings, as well as scores of wooden parts for your own designs. The company was founded in 1981, and the prices are as much as 50% less than those charged for similar goods in toy and gift shops.

The 64-page color catalog shows kits for dozens of whirligigs, decorative clocks depicting motifs ranging from trains to football helmets, door harps, wooden wagons and sleds, pull toys, miniatures, dollhouses, "Wild West" wagons, and vintage cars. Clock movements and markers, music boxes, and hundreds of wooden parts—wheels, spindles, smokestacks, beads, knobs, pulls, pegs, etc.—are offered as well. Cherry Tree sells plans, kits, and books on making toys, dollhouses, whirligigs, clocks, and door harps, in addition to the supplies you'll need to finish the projects. We found a collection of brass stencils in a range of holiday motifs, as well as blank stencil sheets, Dover cut-and-use stencil sets, rubber stamps, and sets of gift tags, cards, and envelopes. If you're able to visit the factory outlet store in Belmont, you'll find discontinued catalog items and seconds at up to 75% off regular prices.

Special Factors: Satisfaction is guaranteed; price quote by phone or letter; returns are accepted within 10 days for exchange, refund, or credit; minimum order is $20 with credit cards; C.O.D. orders are accepted; orders are shipped worldwide.

CIRCLE CRAFT SUPPLY

P.O. BOX 3000
DOVER, FL 33527-3000
813/659-0992

Catalog: $1, refundable
Save: up to 30%
Pay: check or MO
Sells: general crafts supplies
Store: mail order only

The 152-page catalog from Circle Craft Supply lists everything, from "abaca shapes" to zip-lock bags, that you'll need to indulge in any of scores of arts, crafts, and hobbies. Circle Craft was founded in 1982, and sells at discounts that average 20%, and reach 30% on some items.

There are tools and materials here for a wide range of crafts and pastimes—jewelry making, basketry, flower making, drawing and painting, quick-count plastic canvas crafts, doll making, lamp making, clock making, Christmas ornaments, clay crafts, macrame, chenille crafts, crocheting, and much more. In addition to the supplies, Circle Crafts has an extensive bookshelf with guides on a wide range of arts and crafts.

Special Factors: Price quote by phone or letter; authorized returns are accepted within 10 days; C.O.D. orders are accepted; orders are shipped worldwide.

CRAFT KING, INC.

P.O. BOX 90637, DEPT. W
LAKELAND, FL 33804
813/686-9600
FAX: 813/688-5072

Catalog: $2
Save: up to 60%
Pay: check, MO, MC, V
Sells: general crafts supplies and projects
Store: 5675 New Tampa Hwy., Lakeland, FL; Monday to Saturday 9–5

$$ ☎ 🍁 ▦

Craft King's catalog is packed with supplies and kits for the kind of crafts that are popular in schools and camps, which also happen to make great after-school amusements. Craft King was established in 1979, and has no minimum order requirement.

The 128-page catalog lists tools and materials for every sort of pastime and craft, including painting, macrame, lamp-shade making, cross-stitch, beadwork, Christmas ornaments, felt crafts, pom-poms, doll making, miniatures, plastic canvas crafts, "fashion art," wood burning and carving, punch embroidery, quilting, and more. Patterns and kits for plastic canvas projects and instruction books for all types of crafts are also available, and prices average 30% to 60% off list.

Special Factors: Satisfaction is guaranteed; price quote by phone or letter; authorized returns are accepted for exchange, refund, or credit.

CRAFT RESOURCES, INC.

BOX 828
FAIRFIELD, CT 06880-0828
203/254-7702

Catalog: $1
Save: up to 50%
Pay: check, MO, MC, V
Sells: adult-oriented crafts kits
Store: mail order only

$ ☎ ▦

Craft Resources, founded in 1972, specializes in needlework projects in kit form and offers "the largest selection of adult-oriented crafts available." Craft Resources sells kits for projects in latch hooking, needlepoint, long stitch, crewel, stamped and counted cross-stitch, string art, basketry, copper punching, wood crafts, and "stained glass" (sun catchers). The kits range from very basic designs for the beginner to more complex patterns, but a patient novice should be able to tackle any of these projects, with reasonable to impressive results. Most yield purely decorative items, such as the latch-hook blocks, but there are kits to help you create small rugs, afghans, picture frames, baby bibs, pillows, and baskets.

Craft Resources also sells yarn, embroidery floss, needlestitch canvas, knitting needles and crochet hooks, embroidery hoops, pillow forms, fiberfill batts, stencils, picture mats, and frames. The best prices are on the kits sold by the dozen—the per-kit price can drop from $3 to $1.25. Therapists and instructors will find these bargains invaluable, but individuals should see the catalog if considering taking up any of the crafts mentioned. It's cheaper to buy a kit than it is to assemble the materials à la carte, and if you don't like the craft, you won't have made an investment that will be wasted.

Special Factors: Satisfaction is guaranteed; price quote by phone or letter; unused returns are accepted within 60 days; minimum order is $10 with credit cards.

DHARMA TRADING CO.

P.O. BOX 150916
SAN RAFAEL, CA 94915-
    0916
800-542-5227
FAX: 415/456-8747

Catalog: free
Save: up to 50%
Pay: check, MO, MC, V
Sells: textile art supplies
Store: 1604 Fourth St., San Rafael, CA;
    Monday to Saturday 10–6

$$ ☎ ♦ ▀

The "whole earth" movement may have peaked in 1969, the year this firm was founded, but Dharma Trading has survived even the pinstripes of the 1980s. The firm sells tools and materials for the textile arts—dyes, paints, resists, and fabrics. The informative, 88-page catalog provides helpful tips on the features of the dyes and paints, application techniques and suggested fabrics, and even metric conversion charts and a shrinkage "estimator." Prices are good, running up to 50% off list or comparable retail.

Coloring agents by Deka, Delta/Shiva, DyeHouse, Jacquard, Pabeo (Orient Express), Peintex, Procion, Sennelier (Tinfix), Setacolor, Versatex, and other firms are offered, as well as color remover, soda ash, urea, Synthrapol, gutta serti, and other resists. The tools include bottles and droppers for dye mixing and application, textile pens, tjantings, brushes (flat, foam, sumi), and steamers for setting dyes. Dharma Trading also stocks an extensive collection of all-cotton T-shirts, vests, skirts, pants, leggings, shorts, shirts, hats, shoes, rompers, and dresses, in sizes for adults and children, and silk scarves in a choice of silks and sizes. Undyed silk neckties and even silk charmeuse earring blanks await your creative impulses. Cotton, rayon, and silk fabrics that have yielded good results with dyeing and painting are listed; samples (silk or cotton/rayon) are available for 25¢ each. Selected books dealing with fabric design, painting, screening, direct dyeing, batiking, tie-dyeing, and other techniques are also sold.

Special Factors: Price quote by phone or letter; quantity discounts are available; orders are shipped worldwide.

A. FEIBUSCH CORPORATION

33 ALLEN ST.
NEW YORK, NY 10002
212/226-3964

Information: price quote
Save: up to 50%
Pay: check or MO
Sells: zippers, thread, notions, and garment hardware
Store: same address; Monday to Friday 9:30–5, Sunday 10–3:30

Feibusch has been helping New Yorkers zip up since 1941, handling requests from the mundane to the exotic. Unlike most specialty stores, the firm prices its enormous inventory at up to 50% below the going rate. Zippers of every conceivable size, color, and type are sold here—from minuscule dolls' zippers to heavy-duty closures for tents, luggage, and similar applications. If your requirements aren't met by the existing stock, Feibusch can have your zipper made to order. Talon and YKK zippers are available, and Feibusch also carries all-cotton and polyester thread in a full range of colors. There is no catalog, so *write* with your requirements: Describe what you're looking for or send a sample, specifying length desired, nylon or metal teeth, open or closed end, and other details. Enclose a scrap of fabric, if possible, to ensure a good color match. Be sure to include a self-addressed, stamped envelope with your correspondence if you want a reply.

Special Factors: Price quote by letter; orders are shipped worldwide.

THE FIBER STUDIO

P.O. BOX 637, DEPT.
WBMC
HENNIKER, NH 03242
603/428-7830

Catalog: $1 (see text)
Save: up to 40%
Pay: check, MO, MC, V, Discover
Sells: knitting, spinning, and weaving
  equipment and supplies
Store: 9 Foster Hill Rd., Henniker, NH;
  Tuesday to Saturday 10–4

The Fiber Studio has been serving the needs of knitters, spinners, and weavers since 1975 with a well-chosen line of tools and supplies, and yarn closeouts at great prices. The catalog lists looms, knitting machines, and spinning equipment and accessories by Ashford, Glimraka, Harrisville Design, Kyra, Leclerc, Louet, and Schacht. The prices aren't discounted, but shipping is included on some models (see "Special Factors," below). Natural dyes, mordants, and a good selection of spinning fibers from mohair tops to silk roving—are offered at competitive prices. (The sample card of current spinning fibers costs $4.) Scores of texts on knitting, spinning, and weaving are also available.

The bargains here are on yarns, which are sold in two ways: through the stock shown in the sample set, which costs $4, and through the yarn closeouts. The stock yarns include rug wools, natural yarns, Superwash wool, Irish linen, cotton, silk, Shetland wool, mercerized cotton, and others, priced up to 35% less at The Fiber Studio than at other sources we've checked. Quantity discounts on these yarns run from 10% on orders over $100 to 20% on orders over $200. *After* you order the yarn card from The Fiber Studio, you can send $1 and four #10 double-stamped, self-addressed envelopes and ask to be put on the mailing list for the quarterly closeouts. There are outstanding values here, and our mailing included dozens of types of yarns—loop mohair, 8/4 cotton, chenille yarn, silk and blends, bouclé, alpaca, Scottish Shetland, and many others. Color selection was good even among the closeout offerings, and excellent on the stock yarn.

Canadian readers, please note: Only U.S. funds are accepted.

Special Factors: Specify the *spinning fibers* or *yarns* sample set ($4 each); price quote by phone or letter; shipping is included on most models of Harrisville Design, Leclerc, and Schacht looms; quantity discounts are available; minimum order is $15 with credit cards; C.O.D. orders are accepted; orders are shipped worldwide.

FORT CRAILO YARNS COMPANY

**P.O. BOX G
NEWBURGH, NY 12550
914/562-2698**

Brochure and Samples: $2.80
Save: up to 35%
Pay: check, MO, MC, V, Discover
Sells: yarn for handweaving
Store: Broadway and Wisher Ave.,
  Newburgh, NY; Monday to Saturday
  9:30–5:30

$$ ☎

Fort Crailo Yarns, in business since 1963, sells four kinds of wool yarn and one of cotton, which are especially suited for handweaving. Prices run up to 35% below those of comparable yarns sold elsewhere.

The mothproofed, virgin wool yarns include Crailo Rya (570 yd./lb., 33 colors), Crailo-Spun (700 yd./lb., 30 colors), Crailo Lite-Spun (1,700 yd./lb., 28 colors), and the very fine Crailo Worsted (4,900 yd./lb., 27 colors). Fort Crailo's cotton yarn is sold in 8/2, 3, 4, 5, and 6 ply, in 17 colors, and is suitable for warp or weft, and all the yarns are sold on half-pound cones. The colors are clear and true, and the range of weights makes Fort Crailo a good source for weavers of anything from fine fabrics to rugs.

Special Factors: Price quote by phone or letter; quantity discounts are available.

FRANK'S CANE AND RUSH SUPPLY

7252 HEIL AVE., DEPT. WBMC
HUNTINGTON BEACH, CA 92647
714/847-0707
FAX: 714/843-5645

Catalog: free
Save: up to 40% (see text)
Pay: check, MO, MC, V
Sells: seat-reweaving supplies, furniture, kits, books, etc.
Store: mail order only

$$$ ☎ 🍁 🇺🇸

We requested the catalog from Frank's Cane and Rush because we were looking for a source for rattan—and we discovered a source for inexpensive furniture in the process. Frank's has been in business since 1975, and should be credited with having one of the most comprehensive catalogs of seat replacement materials that we've yet seen.

Frank's sells over a dozen weaves of cane webbing, as well as strand and binding cane, spline, fiber and wire-fiber rush, fiber wicker, Danish cord, oak and ash splints, round and flat reed, and fiber and real reed braid (often used as trim on wicker furniture). Frank's also sells the rattan we were looking for, basketry materials, raffia, seagrass, "tissue flex" (for rag coil baskets), wood hoops and handles, brass hardware, upholstery tools and supplies, dowels and wood crafts parts, and spindles and finials. Prices are competitive on these goods, and there are some bargains—Frank's is selling decorative upholstery nails for $3 per hundreds, and we paid $5.25 locally for the same number of the identical nail. The catalog also has six pages of books on seat reweaving, woodworking, basketry, and upholstery.

The furniture kits that so impressed us include hardwood Shaker-style arm and side chairs, rocking chairs, and stools. Prices are low: $10.95 for a stool kit, $25 for a child's ladderback chair kit, and $35 for an adult's chair. The top price is $110 for a finished, "old style porch rocker" with a woven cane back and seat—all you do is put on the rockers. (The other furniture comes in "kits" as nearly assembled furniture and enough fiber rush or flat fiber—your choice—to complete the seat.) The prices at Frank's are at least 30% below those charged for similar goods sold by several other firms we checked.

Special Factors: Price quote by phone or letter; minimum order is $10 with credit cards; C.O.D. orders are accepted; orders are shipped worldwide.

GETTINGER FEATHER CORP.

**16 W. 36TH ST.
NEW YORK, NY 10018
212/695-9470
FAX: 212/695-9471**

Price List and Samples: $2
Save: up to 75%
Pay: check or MO
Sells: feathers
Store: same address (8th floor); Monday to
Friday 9–4:30

Gettinger has been serving New York City's milliners and craftspersons since 1915 with a marvelous stock of exotic and common feathers. Even if you're not a "creative" type, you can add cachet to a tired hat with a few ostrich plumes, and Gettinger's feather boas are a dashing alternative to furs for gala occasions.

Raw or dyed pheasant, guinea hen, turkey, duck, goose, rooster, and peacock feathers are available here loose or sewn (lined up in continuous rows of even length), by the ounce or the pound, beginning at $5 (loose) and $8 (sewn) per ounce. Pheasant tail feathers, 6" to 8" long, cost $13 per hundred; yard-long peacock feathers are priced at $25 per hundred; and pheasant hides cost $9 and up per skin. Feather boas are available, sold in two-yard pieces, as well as ostrich and marabou fans. And if you're reviving old feather pillows, you may be interested in the bedding feathers, which cost $18 to $36 per pound, depending on the quality.

Gettinger Feather is offering readers a discount of 10% on their first order. Be sure to identify yourself as a WBMC reader when you order, and deduct the discount from the cost of the goods only. This WBMC reader discount expires February 1, 1993.

Special Factors: Price quote by phone or letter; minimum order is $20; orders are shipped worldwide.

GLOBAL VILLAGE IMPORTS

**1101 SW WASHINGTON, #140-W
PORTLAND, OR 97205**

Brochure and Swatches: $3.50, refundable
Save: up to 70%
Pay: check or MO
Sells: Guatemalan ikat fabrics
Store: mail order only

$$$ ☎ ♦ 🇺🇸

Ikat is a type of weaving that uses tie-dyed warp threads to create striated designs that blend into overall patterns, which may be as subtle as Zen or as colorfully riotous as a Mardi Gras parade. (Double ikats, in which both warp and weft threads are so dyed, represent a further refinement of the art.)

Global Village has been selling handwoven Guatemalan ikats since 1988, and donates a portion of its proceeds to groups working for "peace and justice in Central America" (including NISGUA and CAMP). The $3.50 sample fee (refundable with purchase) brings you an information packet and swatches of the single and double ikats currently available. The fabric is 36" wide, 100% cotton, and is woven by hand on large looms. We received stacks of over 30 stunning single ikats and seven double ikats, as well as a strip of white stickers. Global Village makes it easy to buy: Just cut the swatch of the desired fabric in half, put a sticker on that piece, and write on it the number of yards you're ordering. Prices for single ikats range from $8.99 for up to five yards, down to $5.99 for 31 yards or more. Double ikats run from $10.99 to $7.99. (Double ikats, hard to find at any price, are woven by the roll especially for Global Village.)

We found these prices to be nearly 50% below the rates prevailing in New York City specialty shops. Global Village also hopes to offer handwoven fabrics from around the world as its business grows. Fabric designers should take note of the company's custom weaving services, and wholesale inquiries are welcomed.

Special Factors: Minimum order is 1 yard; quantity discounts are available; C.O.D. orders are accepted; orders are shipped worldwide.

GREAT NORTHERN WEAVING

P.O. BOX 361-D
AUGUSTA, MI 49012
616/731-4487

Catalog and Samples: $1
Save: up to 50%
Pay: check or MO
Sells: rug-weaving supplies and tools
Store: mail order only

$$ ♦ 🇺🇸

The homey crafts of braiding and weaving rugs are served at Great Northern Weaving, where you can save up to 50% on supplies and tools. The firm has been in business since 1984, and prices most items competitively, and rags and filler up to 50% less than the going rate.

The 12-page catalog lists tools and materials for rug weaving, rug braiding, and shirret—Braid-Aids, Braidkins, Braid-Klamps, Fraser rag cutters, reed and heddle hooks, shuttles, and warping boards are all available. The materials include coned cotton warp (8/4 ply) in over two dozen colors, all-cotton rug filler in 15 shades, 16-ply rug roping, new cotton "rags" on rolls, and loopers in bulk (offered in white, cream, and grey). Reference books are also available.

Canadian readers, please note: Shipping charges on orders sent to Canada are paid C.O.D., and order payment must be made in U.S. funds.

Special Factors: Shipping is included on orders over $20; C.O.D. orders are accepted.

HOME-SEW

DEPT. WM2
BETHLEHEM, PA 18018-
    0099
215/867-3833
FAX: 215/867-9710

Catalog: 50¢
Save: up to 70%
Pay: check, MO, MC, V
Sells: sewing supplies and notions
Store: mail order only

$$ ☎ ♦(see text)

Home-Sew, which has been in business since 1960, offers savings of up to 70% on assorted laces and trims. The firm's 28-page catalog is well-organized and easy to use, with clear photographs of dozens of laces, braids, ribbons, and decorator fringes.

In addition to scores of laces, Home-Sew offers elastic, satin and velvet ribbon, ricrac, tape, and appliqués. Specialty thread—for general sewing, overlock machines, carpets, and quilting—is available on cones and spools. There are zippers, snaps, hooks and eyes, buttons, Velcro dots, belts and buckles, pins, needles, and scissors, as well as floss, adhesives, Styrofoam wreaths, spangles, beads, animal eyes, interfacings, and related items. If you're making your own curtains or slipcovers, check the prices on shirring and pleater tape, tasseled and moss fringe, cord filler, and related goods. Home-Sew's isn't the biggest catalog of its kind, but the products are very well chosen—just the things that can make your sewing and crafts projects easier, at the right price.

Canadian readers, please note: Send $1 (in Canadian funds) to Home-Sew Canada Inc., B.P. Box 1100, Dept. WBMC, Postal Station "E," Montreal, Quebec H2T 3B1, for the bilingual catalog.

Special Factors: Satisfaction is guaranteed; returns are accepted for exchange, refund, or credit; quantity discounts are available; shipping is included on orders over $35; minimum order is $5; orders are shipped worldwide.

J & J PRODUCTS LTD.

117 W. 9TH ST., SUITE 111
LOS ANGELES, CA 90015
213/624-1840
FAX: 213/624-0134

Swatch Cards: $3 each, refundable (see text)
Save: up to 40%
Pay: check, MO, MC, V
Sells: fine woolen fabrics
Store: mail order only

$$ ☎ ✦ ▬

Here are quality yard goods in beautiful colors, at competitive prices—gabardines, suitings, flannels, and other fine woolens. These are J & J's specialty, and each type of fabric is showcased in a swatch booklet that costs $3, refundable with a purchase from that line.

Each booklet includes a 2½″ by 4″ piece of fabric, with smaller snippets to show the choice of colors. "Gabardine," $18 per yard, is offered in 45 colors; the mid-weight "Flannel" is shown in 17 shades; "Lightweight Wool Suiting" is a wool broadcloth offered in 32 colors, including turquoise and true red; "Cashmere" features 20 fabrics, including a number of herringbones and tweeds, in beautiful shadings; "Crepe" features a fine-quality wool crepe in red and several neutrals; and the "Linings" swatch booklet shows 16 fashion colors and neutrals of the acetate material, at $2.59 per yard (prices and colors all subject to change). You can order the swatch booklets by name for $3 each; each is refundable with a purchase from that particular booklet, and ordering information is included. The fabric is not inexpensive, but it has the luster and hand of fine-quality goods that wear well.

Special Factors: Satisfaction is guaranteed; price quote by phone or letter.

MONTEREY MILLS OUTLET STORE

**P.O. BOX 271
JANESVILLE, WI 53547
800-438-6387**

Price List: free with SASE (see text)
Save: up to 60%
Pay: check, MO, MC, V
Sells: fake-fur fabric
Store: same address; Monday to Friday
8–4:30, Saturday 8–12 noon

Monterey Mills has been manufacturing deep-pile fabrics for a quarter of a century, and sells its deep-pile fabrics, popularly known as "fun fur," at prices up to 60% below the usual retail.

The Monterey Mills brochure describes the fiber content of the different furs and lists the available colors, pile height, and ounces per yard. In addition to plain plush and shag, you'll find patterns and colors simulating the pelts of bears, foxes, seals, tigers, and Dalmatians. Prices are given per cut yard, per yard on the roll (there are 12 to 15 yards per roll), and for quantity orders. Cut yards run from $6.95 to $12.50 per yard, and prices drop from there. You can buy the fabric in remnants (the Mill's choice of fur type), by the pound, or in cartons, for $3 a pound. Stuffing for crafts projects is available as well, at 59¢ a pound and up.

Please note: A set of samples is offered for $4, a worthwhile investment unless you're buying only remnants.

Special Factor: Minimum order is $25.

NEWARK DRESSMAKER SUPPLY, INC.

DEPT. WMD
6473 RUCH RD.
P.O. BOX 2448
LEHIGH VALLEY, PA 18001
215/837-7500
FAX: 215/837-9115

Catalog: $1
Save: up to 50%
Pay: check, MO, MC, V, Discover
Sells: sewing notions
Store: mail order only

$$$$ ☎ ♦ ▦

Newark Dressmaker has been in business since 1950 and is one of the best mail-order sources for home sewers, since it carries a huge array of notions and other supplies, from glass-headed pins to the material itself. The 56-page catalog features many hard-to-find goods, and the prices are very competitive—up to 50% below regular retail on some items we checked, and that doesn't count the 10% discount you can take if your order totals $50 or more.

Searching for specialty patterns, smocking guides, bear joints, alphabet beads, silk thread, or toy squeakers? Such requests are routine at Newark, which boasts an exhaustive inventory of materials and equipment for a range of crafts. If your local shop doesn't have what you're looking for, or if you'd like to save money, see this catalog for its pages of trims, appliqués, scissors, piping, ribbon, lace, braid, twill, zippers, sewing gadgets, knitting supplies, name tapes and woven labels, interfacing, buttons, thread, floss, bias tape, rhinestones, supplies for making dolls and stuffed bears, fabric, upholstery materials, books and manuals, and much more. Among the brands of goods stocked here, you'll find Boye, Coats & Clark's, Deka, Dritz, Lily, Prym, Sta-Flex, and Talon. "Sew Little" patterns for infants' and children's clothing are stocked, as well as "Great Fit" patterns for women's styles in sizes 38 to 60, and doll patterns from Putnam Pattern and other firms.

Canadian readers, please note: Only U.S. funds are accepted.

Special Factors: Satisfaction is guaranteed; minimum order is $5, $20 with credit cards; orders are shipped worldwide.

SMILEY'S YARNS

92-06 JAMAICA AVE.
WOODHAVEN, NY 11421
718/847-5038
718/849-9873 (STORE)

Brochure: free with self-addressed, stamped envelope
Save: up to 50% (see text)
Pay: check or MO
Sells: yarn for handknitting and crocheting
Store: same address; Monday to Saturday 10–5:30

$$

Smiley's, where "Yarn Bargains Are Our Business," has been selling first-quality yarns at a discount since 1935. Each month, Smiley's offers a different "Yarn of the Month" selection at discounts from 30% to as much as 80% on list prices. Among the manufacturers represented are Bernat, Bouquet, Bucilla, Caron, Coats & Clark's, Neveda, Novita, Patons, Phildar, Pingouin, Scheepjeswool, and Welcomme. You can call or write for a price quote on goods by these firms, or inquire about knitting and crocheting yarns by other manufacturers— they may be available. Smiley's also offers a complete selection of Boye knitting and crocheting accessories at 50% off. For samples of the current "Yarn of the Month" offering, send a long, stamped, self-addressed envelope.

Special Factors: Price quote by phone or letter with SASE; quantity discounts are available.

SOLO SLIDE FASTENERS, INC.

P.O. BOX 528
STOUGHTON, MA 02072
800-343-9670
FAX: 617/341-4705

Catalog: free
Save: up to 50%
Pay: check, MO, MC, V
Sells: dressmaking and dry-cleaning equipment and sewing supplies
Store: mail order only

Solo Slide is a family-run business that's been supplying dressmakers, cleaners, tailors, and other professionals with tools and equipment since 1954. Among the offerings in the firm's 30-page catalog are a number of items we've seen in the "hard-to-find" sections of notions catalogs, at prices as much as 50% less.

Solo offers an extensive selection of zippers by Talon and YKK, zipper parts (slides and stops), straight pins in several sizes, snaps, hooks and eyes, machine and hand needles, buttons (dress, suit, metal, leather, etc.), thread on cones and spools, knit collars and cuffs for jackets, shoulder pads, elbow patches, belting, elastic, and other notions. Fine-quality linings, including Bembergs, are stocked, as well as pocket material. There are scissors in the most useful models from Gingher, Marks, and Wiss, pressing boards for sleeves and hollow pressing, Qualitex pressing pads and other hams and rolls, and professional irons and steamers by Cissell, Hi-Steam/Namoto, and Sussman. The catalog also shows commercial/industrial sewing machines (blindstitch and lockstitch) and overlock machines by Babylock, Consew, Juki, Singer, and Tacsew.

Special Factors: Price quote by phone; authorized, unused returns (except custom-ordered or cut goods) are accepted within 30 days for credit; minimum order is $25; C.O.D. orders are accepted; orders are shipped worldwide.

STRAW INTO GOLD, INC.

**3006 SAN PABLO AVE.,
   DEPT. W4
BERKELEY, CA 94702
415/548-5247
FAX: 415/548-3453**

Catalog: free with double-stamped, self-addressed envelope
Save: up to 30%
Pay: check, MO, MC, V
Sells: textile crafts supplies and books
Store: same address; Tuesday to Friday 12–5:30, Saturday 10–5:30

Straw Into Gold, established in 1971, is a highly regarded mail-order source for textile crafts supplies and equipment, especially exotic and hard-to-find materials for spinners, weavers, and hand and machine knitters. Specials on fibers, yarns, books, and other goods appear regularly in flyers, at savings of up to 70%. The staff is helpful and informed, and classes in the textile arts are given at the shop.

The spinning fibers include silk of different types and silk blends, cotton, flax, ramie, wool, alpaca, mohair, camel's hair, goat's hair, and metallic fibers. Ashford spinning equipment and looms (not discounted), bamboo and steel knitting needles, wool winders, umbrella swifts, and other helpful tools are offered as well. Straw Into Gold sells Kaffe Fassett kits and yarns by Crystal Palace, Rowan Yarns, and Villawool, and a wide selection of other yarns and spun fibers. If you're a serious textile artist, investing in the sample books and cards is recommended. Straw Into Gold's bookshelf includes publications from Interweave Press, Bette Hochberg, and Shire (British), as well as videos and patterns by Rowan, Villawool, and Zimmerman.

Straw Into Gold is offering readers a discount of 10% on their first order. Be sure to identify yourself as a WBMC reader when you order, and deduct the discount from the cost of the goods only. This WBMC reader discount expires February 1, 1993.

Please note: The store is too busy to accept calls on Saturdays, so please phone during the week, Tuesday to Friday.

Special Factors: Send 2-4 double-stamped, self-addressed envelopes for catalog updates and flyers; quantity discounts are offered; orders are shipped worldwide.

TAYLOR'S CUTAWAYS AND STUFF

DEPT. WBMC-92
2802 E. WASHINGTON
URBANA, IL 61801-4699

$$

Brochure: $1
Save: up to 75%
Pay: check, MO, MC, V
Sells: cutaways and patterns
Store: mail order only

"Cutaways" are what's left when the pieces of a garment are cut from material. These scraps, sometimes running to a yard long, are perfect for doll clothing, piecework, quilting, and other crafts. Taylor's Cutaways, in business since 1977, offers bundles of polyesters, cottons, blends, calicos, and other assortments, as well as silk, satin, velvet, felt, and fake fur cutaways. The brochure lists a wide variety of patterns and project designs for such items as draft stoppers, puppets, dolls, Teddy bears, pigs, ducks, and other animals. Crocheting patterns for toys and novelties, iron-on transfer patterns, button and trim assortments, and toy eyes, joints, and squeakers are available.

The completely unskilled will appreciate Taylor's for its potpourris, already blended and scented, and the unscented dried flowers and plants, ground orris fixative, essential oils, and satin squares for making sachets. On the practical side, Taylor's sells "tea baglets," little fiber bags you fill with the tea of your choice and heat-seal with a household iron. (This is a great way to take a favorite loose tea with you when you travel.) Prices of these and most of the other goods average 50% below comparable retail, and savings can reach as high as 75%. This seems an especially good source for anyone who makes sachets and potpourris, dolls, toys, pieced quilts, and bazaar items.

Special Factor: Quantity discounts are available.

THAI SILKS

**252-W STATE ST.
LOS ALTOS, CA 94022
800-722-SILK
800-221-SILK
415/948-8611
FAX: 415/948-3426**

Brochure: free
Save: up to 50%
Pay: check, MO, MC, V, AE
Sells: imported silk fabric, scarves, and lingerie
Store: same address; Monday to Saturday 9–5:30

Beautiful, comfortable silk is also affordable at Thai Silks, where the home sewer, decorator, and artist can save up to 50% on yardage and piece goods (compared to average retail prices). Curiously, just 2% of the stock comes from Thailand—China, India, and Korea have contributed to this company's large selection, which includes sueded silk, jacquard weaves, crepe de chine, bouclé, pongee, China silk, silk satin, raw silk, noil, silk velvet, tapestry weaves, silk taffeta, prints, Dupioni silk, and upholstery weights, most of which are sold in a choice of colors. Hemmed white silk scarves and neckties for painting and batiking, Chinese embroidered handkerchiefs, silk lingerie, and blouses are also available.

If you're a serious sewer or textile artist, consider joining Thai Silk's "Silk Fabric Club." For $10 a year, you'll receive three swatched mailings of new silks, and samples of closeouts.

Special Factors: Satisfaction is guaranteed; price quote by phone or letter; quantity discounts are offered to firms and professionals; samples are available (details are given in the brochure); authorized returns are accepted; C.O.D. orders are accepted; minimum order is ¼ yard of fabric; orders are shipped worldwide.

THREAD DISCOUNT SALES

Catalog: free with long, stamped, self-addressed envelope

**P.O. BOX 2277
BELL GARDENS, CA
90201
213/562-3438
FAX: 213/560-8177**

Save: up to 50%
Pay: check, MO, MC, V, AE, Discover
Sells: coned thread, sewing machines
Store: 5960 East Florence, Bell Gardens, CA; Monday to Saturday 10–5

This firm sells machines and supplies for the serious sewer—sergers, overlock machines, and "coned" thread—at savings of up to 50% on list prices. Thread Discount, in business since 1962, offers a batch of photocopied sheets as its catalog; they feature White and Singer sewing and overlock machines at an average 50% discount on list or original prices. White's "computer" sewing machine models were among those we saw in our mailing, as well as Singer's "Magic Steam Press" ironing press.

Among the coned thread offered in the list we received were all-purpose polyester thread, 6,000 yards of overlock at under $3 a cone, and "woolly nylon" thread. J. & P. Coats general-purpose thread was offered at $1.99 for a 3,000-yard cone, which compares very favorably to the spool of just 325 yards selling for $1.29 in fabric shops. Most of the thread is offered in a full range of colors, which are listed by name and number (there are no samples or color guides). In addition, Thread Discount carries novelty metallics in a variety of colors and two sizes of nylon filament thread for "invisible" work.

Please note: A shipping surcharge is imposed on orders sent to Alaska, Hawaii, Puerto Rico, and Canada.

Special Factor: Minimum order is 6 cones of thread (on thread orders).

TOWER HOBBIES

DEPT. WBMC
P.O. BOX 778
CHAMPAIGN, IL 61824
800-637-4989
FAX: 217/356-6608

Catalog: $3, refundable
Save: up to 60%
Pay: check, MO, MC, V, Discover
Sells: radio-controlled models
Store: mail order only

$$$ ☎ 🍁 ▀

Tower Hobbies publishes a 290-page catalog of radio-controlled ships, planes, and other vehicles, which offer the pleasures of model building, electronics, piloting and driving, and tinkering. Tower has been satisfying hobbyists since 1971 with its great selection, deep discounts—up to 60%—and good service.

Tower Hobbies sells the newest releases from model manufacturers and state-of-the-art electronics. The catalog showcases kits for pickups, 4WDs, off-road cars, tractors, race cars, jeeps, and other vehicles by Kyosho, Team Losi, etc., and marine models—tugboats, yachts, hydroplanes, "swamp buggies," sailboats, cabin cruisers, and other ships—by Dumas, Kyosho, MRP, and other firms. And there are model planes from Ace, Airtronics, Cox, Flitecraft, Great Planes, Guillows, Kyosho, Lanier, Mark's, Royal, Sureflite, and Top Flite, among others. Tower doesn't let you down when it comes to getting things up and running: Every tool and material you need to build the models is available, as well as engines, radios, batteries, chargers, fuel, and related products. These goods are all sold at a discount. Tower's "combos," combinations of a model with appropriate charger or engine or other necessary components, afford even more savings. The catalog itself is worth over $3 for its tips and instructions, as well as coupons for savings throughout the year.

Special Factors: Satisfaction is guaranteed; price quote by phone or letter; returns of new, unused goods are accepted within 10 days; C.O.D. orders are accepted (by UPS delivery only); orders are shipped worldwide.

UTEX TRADING ENTERPRISES

**710 NINTH ST.
NIAGARA FALLS, NY
14301
716/282-8211**

Price List: free with SASE
Save: up to 50%
Pay: check or MO
Sells: imported silk fabric
Store: mail order only

$$ ☎ 🍁(see text) ▆

Utex trades in silk yard goods and sewing supplies, which it imports directly from China. Utex was established in 1980 and offers textile artists, decorators, designers, and home sewers something special— over 200 weights, weaves, and widths of silk.

The enormous inventory includes silk shantung, pongee, taffeta, twill, habotai, peau de soie, lamé, and suiting. Most of the fabrics are 100% silk, and the price list includes a guide that recommends appropriate fabrics for specific purposes. Unprinted scarves and ties, silk thread, floss, yarns, and fine brushes and dyes for hand-painting are also stocked.

Canadian readers, please note: Utex's Canadian address is 185 Spadina Ave., 5th Fl., Toronto, Ontario, M5V 2H1; the phone number is 416/596-7565.

Special Factor: Volume discounts are available.

VANGUARD CRAFTS, INC.

**P.O. BOX 340170, DEPT.
WMC
BROOKLYN, NY 11234-
0003
718/377-5188
FAX: 718/692-0056**

Catalog: $1, refundable
Save: up to 60%
Pay: check, MO, MC, V
Sells: crafts kits and materials
Store: 1081 E. 48th St., Brooklyn, NY;
Monday to Friday 10–6, Saturday 10–5

$$$ ☎ 🍁 ▆

Vanguard has been selling fun, in the form of crafts kits and projects, since 1959. The firm's 68-page color catalog is geared to educators and others buying for classroom use, but it's a great source for rainy-day project materials at home.

Past catalogs have shown kits and supplies for hundreds of crafts, including shrink art, foil pictures, grapevine wreaths, mosaic tiling, basic woodworking crafts, suncatchers, Styrofoam crafts, leather-working, fabric flowers, decoupage, copper enameling, needlepunch, pom-pom crafts, stenciling, string art, crafts sticks projects, Indian crafts, clothespin dolls, calligraphy, and other diversions. Vanguard recently added a line of kits inspired by the "spirit of the Southwest"—Santa Fe picture frames, "Pueblo" pottery, concho accessories, bead looms, kachina dolls, and more. Basic art supplies and tools—adhesives, scissors, paper, paint, pastels, hammers, craft knives, etc.—are also available. The prices are *very* reasonable, and the large selection makes it easy to meet the $25 minimum order.

Special Factors: Price quote by phone or letter; minimum order is $25; orders are shipped worldwide.

VETERAN LEATHER COMPANY, INC.

**204 25TH ST., DEPT. WBM
BROOKLYN, NY 11232
800-221-7565
718/768-0300
FAX: 718/768-8361**

Catalog: $2, refundable
Save: up to 50%
Pay: check, MO, MC, V
Sells: leatherworking supplies
Store: same address; Monday to Friday 8–5

Veteran Leather's 48-page catalog offers a wide range of kits, tools, and materials for novice and experienced leatherworkers, at prices up to 50% below those we found charged by crafts supply houses for similar goods.

The kits include classic Western-style billfolds, keycases, belts, wristbands, coasters, handbags, and even moccasins. Scores of belt buckles are available, including solid brass styles cast with relief images of deer, flying geese, trains, ships, trout, and similar themes. Veteran carries a full range of findings and hardware, including keyrings, key plates, conchos, money clips, bag locks, rivets, snap fasteners, and rings. Leather shears, bevelers, knives, pliers, chisels, punches, mallets, and stamps are sold, as well as Fiebing's dyes and leather finishes. Veteran offers the leather itself: oak, cowhide, cabretta, deerskin, suede (lamb, pig, and cow), skivers, cowhide embossed to resemble ostrich and alligator, and other types of splits and sides, and bundles of leather remnants, leather thread, and lacing. Books on a range of leather crafts are available to help you advance your craft.

Special Factors: Quantity discounts are available; minimum order is $25.

WEBBS

P.O. BOX 349
18 KELLOGG AVE.
AMHERST, MA 01004
413/253-2580
FAX: 413/253-4172

Price Lists and Samples: $2
Save: up to 80%
Pay: check, MO, MC, V
Sells: yarns and spinning and weaving equipment and books
Store: same address; Monday to Saturday 9:30–5:30

Knitters and weavers of all types—production, hand, and machine—will find inspiration in the yarns from Webbs. This firm has been doing business since 1980, selling all types of natural-fiber yarn at up to 80% below original prices. Webbs' mailings offer conventional and novelty yarns of cotton, wool, silk, rayon, and blends, sold in bags, coned, wound off, sometimes in balls, and in packs, unwound. (The packs come in assortments of 10, 25, and 100 pounds, at outstandingly low prices.)

Each set of samples is folded into a descriptive price sheet, which notes special considerations concerning supply, suitability for knitting or weaving, gauge, length per unit (e.g., yards per ball, cone, or pound), and prices and minimums. We've found some great buys in the past, including mohair in choice colors, ribbon yarn in several hues, fine-quality cotton yarns in different weights and fashion colors, and all-wool rug yarn. The stock includes Webbs exclusives, mill-ends, discontinued lines, and yarn overstock. Savings can be boosted with an extra 20% discount if your yarn order totals $60 or more, or 25% on orders over $120. (Take note of the exceptions, marked "no further discount" or "NFD" in the price sheets.) Don't overlook the "Naturals Collection," listed separately, which includes cotton, linen, wool, and blended yarns for dyeing, warping, and other purposes—also well priced.

Looms, spinning wheels, drum carders, and knitting machines are available at nondiscounted prices, although shipping is free on these items (which can be worth $25 to even $100, depending on where you live and the weight of the article).

Special Factors: Shipping is included on looms, spinning wheels, drum carders, and knitting machines; quantity discounts are available; authorized returns are accepted within 30 days (a 15% restocking fee may be charged).

COMPANIES OUTSIDE THE U.S.A.

The following firms are experienced in dealing with customers in the U.S. and Canada. We've included them because they offer goods not widely available at a discount in the U.S., because they have a better selection, or because they may offer the same goods at great savings.

Before ordering from any non-U.S. firm, please consult "The Complete Guide to Buying by Mail," page 573, for helpful tips. We recommend paying for orders from foreign firms with a credit card whenever possible, so you'll have some recourse if you don't receive your order. For more information, see "The Fair Credit Billing Act," page 612.

BABOURIS HANDICRAFTS

56 ADRIANOU ST.
105 55 ATHENS
GREECE
011-30-1-3247561

Price List and Samples: $5, deductible
Save: up to 50%
Pay: check, IMO, AE
Sells: handspun yarn and handknitted sweaters
Store: same address; Monday to Friday 11–3

Babouris Handicrafts, which has been doing business since 1959, sells yarn spun by hand from native wool at prices up to 50% below those charged in the U.S. for the same kinds of yarn. More than three dozen natural shades and brilliant fast-dyed colors are available, and airmail postage is included in the prices. There's a minimum order of 5kg (about 11 pounds) of yarn, but colors may be mixed to meet this requirement. Hand-knitted woolen pullovers and cardigans are also available; inquire for information.

Special Factors: Price quote by phone or letter; shipping is included; minimum order is 5kg of yarn; orders are shipped worldwide.

MAURICE BRASSARD & FILS INC.

████████████

C.P. 4
PLESSISVILLE, QUEBEC
 G6L 2Y6
CANADA
819/362-2408
FAX: 819/362-2408

Catalog: $5.95 (see text)
Save: 35% average
Pay: check or IMO
Sells: weaving yarns, looms, etc.
Store: 1972 Simoneau, Plessisville, Quebec; Monday to Friday 9–5

$$ 🍁

Maurice Brassard's catalog is a looseleaf binder with two dozen pages of yarn samples, all neatly tied and labeled. Many of the descriptions are in French as well as English, and measurements are mixed—some are in grams, others ounces, some meters, others in feet. The prices translate into savings of 30% and more, on average.

The yarns include cotton warp in 2/8, 2/16, 4/8, and bouclé, pearl cotton, polyester 2/8 and 2/16, Orlon, linen (natural, bleached, and dyed), silk noil, cotton slub, Merino and Superwash wools, and a variety of novelty yarns. The color selection is superb, and the quality of the goods first-rate. Brassard also sells cloth strips for weaving, braiding, and other crafts, in cotton, nylon, acetate, and acrylic. In addition to yarn, Brassard sells tools and equipment: cloth-cutting machines (to make strips), wool winders, a twisting device (for plying threads together), and looms and accessories by Leclerc.

The catalog and ordering instructions have been written for Canadian orders, so if you're buying from the U.S., we strongly suggest calling or writing to get exact shipping costs *before* ordering. If you wish to review Brassard's prices before purchasing the catalog, you may request the price list, which is free.

Please note: Letters to Canada require 40¢ in postage.

Special Factor: Quantity discounts are available.

CAMBRIDGE WOOLS, LTD.

██████████

**BOX 2572
AUCKLAND
NEW ZEALAND
011-64-9-390-769
FAX: 011-64-9-390-762**

Brochure and Samples: free
Save: up to 66%
Pay: IMO
Sells: wools and knitwear
Store: 40 Anzac Ave., Auckland; Monday to Friday 9–5

$$ ◆

We've found samples of two-ply wool knitting yarn selling locally for $2.50 to $3 an ounce that compare to Cambridge's yarn that's priced at $1 an ounce, or up to 66% less. This is native New Zealand wool, scoured and spun to the specifications of Cambridge Wools. Brightly colored two-ply (medium-weight) yarn costs $16 a pound in both all-wool and a mohair/wool blend, and a two-ply unscoured (greasy) yarn in natural colors is also priced at $16 a pound. These yarns serve the most popular applications: machine knitting, hand knitting, and weaving. Greasy and scoured spinning wools are sold uncarded in natural shades, and carded in natural and six rich colors.

The price list cites the availability of Aran handknitted pullovers and cardigans ($100), in natural yarn (white, grey, and black), in sizes to fit up to 42″. Sheepskins are also on offer, from "single" size (34″ by 21″, $40) to "quarto" size (66″ by 40″, $178). Car seat covers to fit seats in small and mid-sized cars cost $175 per pair. The good values here are not impaired by postage surcharges—shipping is included in the prices, and goods are sent by sea mail.

Special Factors: Satisfaction is guaranteed; returns are accepted for exchange or refund; shipping (by sea mail) is included; minimum order is $30.

STAVROS KOUYOUMOUTZAKIS

WORKSHOP SPUN WOOLS
166 KALOKERINOU AVE.
712-02 IRAKLION, CRETE GREECE
011-30-81-284-466

Price List and Samples: $1, cash, deductible
Save: up to 65%
Pay: check
Sells: Cretan and Australian yarn
Store: same address

$$

Mr. Kouyoumoutzakis sends out a price list thick with bundled snippets of lush yarn spun from the wools of Crete and Australia; they're suitable for knitting, weaving, and crafts. The Cretan yarns, in natural (undyed) shades of cream, grey, and dark brown, cost $5.20 per pound in "thick" and "medium" weights, $5.80 for "thin," and $6.20 for two-ply. The same wools, dyed in brilliant purples, golds, reds, blues, and greens, are offered in medium and thick weights, as is the creamy-colored Australian natural wool.

Prices are 10% higher if you order fewer than 20 pounds of wool, which is still a bargain. Airmail postage is included, and Mr. Kouyoumoutzakis believes that you should have your yarn within 20 to 30 days after your order is received in Greece. Remember to order enough of each color for your intended project, since dye lots are sure to differ. Please consult your customs office before ordering to get the current rates of duty.

Special Factor: Minimum order is 10 pounds (total).

D. MACGILLIVRAY & COY.

**BALIVANICH
BENBECULA
WESTERN ISLES PA88 5LA
SCOTLAND
011-44-870-2525**

Price Lists and Catalog: $4
Save: up to 50%
Pay: check, IMO, MC, V, AE, Access, EC
Sells: Scottish fabrics, knitwear, and handcrafts
Store: Balivanich, Benbecula

$$$ ❦ ▬

Four dollars will bring you MacGillivray's assortment of price lists and the catalog. MacGillivray offers everything from Hebridean perfumes to Highland dress accessories, but is best known for its bargains on woven goods.

The cream of the crop is the collection of authentic clan tartans. Three kinds of wools and weights are offered, from acrylic/wool blends at about $17 a yard to the all-wool, heavyweight worsted for about $29 a yard, in standard, ancient, and reproduction tartan colors. Also sold are many types of Harris tweeds, Scottish tweeds, suitings, coatings, linings, and dress fabrics, all preshrunk, from about $8 a yard. The muted tweeds are lovely, and the samples give an idea of the range of colors and textures available. (Samples of the tartans and other fabrics may be ordered from the catalog.)

Once made into garments, you can pair your tweeds with fine sweaters of lambswool, Shetland, or camel's hair, which are available in a palette of colors. The Fair Isle Aran sweaters are offered in jumper (pullover) and lumber jacket (high-necked cardigan) styles and as jerseys for children. Hand-knitted Harris wool sweaters for men and women begin at under $50. There are also shooting stockings, mohair stoles, heraldic wall shields, Harris tweed caps and ties, and hand-tailored kilts. Highland dress accessories, from bagpipes and skean dhus to waistcoats and bonnets, can be ordered. And MacGillivray will tailor clothing or make copies from illustrations, at prices at least 40% less than those charged by most dressmakers. The firm has been mailing orders to customers worldwide since 1942.

Special Factors: Satisfaction is guaranteed; returns (except made-to-measure and custom orders) are accepted within 14 days for exchange, refund, or credit.

SEE ALSO

American Science & Surplus • surplus material suitable for crafts • *SURPLUS*

Astronomical Society of the Pacific • charts, computer programs, tapes, slides, etc. on astronomy topics • *BOOKS*

Baron/Barclay Bridge Supplies • teaching and playing supplies for bridge • *TOYS*

The Bevers • wooden toy wheels, balls, etc. • *TOOLS*

Dick Blick Co. • crafts supplies • *ART MATERIALS*

BRE Lumber • cabinet-grade lumber • *HOME: MAINTENANCE*

Campmor • tent zippers, Eureka yard goods, grommet kits, etc. • *SPORTS*

Caprilands Herb Farm • potpourri ingredients, pomanders, essential oils, etc. • *FARM*

Ceramic Supply of New York & New Jersey, Inc. • ceramics and sculpting materials, music box parts • *ART MATERIALS*

Crown Art Products Co., Inc. • supplies and equipment for silk screening, stained glass, etc. • *ART MATERIALS*

Custom Golf Clubs, Inc. • supplies for making golf clubs, including stains, finishes, etc. • *SPORTS*

Derry's Sewing Center • sewing machines • *APPLIANCES*

Discount Appliance Centers • sewing machines and attachments • *APPLIANCES*

Eloxite Corporation • jewelry findings, lapidary equipment, and clock-making supplies • *JEWELRY*

Fabrics by Design • decorator fabrics • *HOME: DECOR*

Gohn Bros. • sewing notions, quilting batts, scissors, thread, yard goods, etc. • *CLOTHING*

Hong Kong Lapidaries, Inc. • scarabs, inlaid intaglios, beads, and other crafts materials • *JEWELRY*

House of Onyx • semiprecious and precious gems, cabochons • *JEWELRY*

Kicking Mule Records, Inc. • video music lessons • *BOOKS*

Leather Unlimited Corp. • leather, dyes, kits, etc. • *LEATHER*

Manny's Millinery Supply Co. • millinery supplies, feathers, bridal supplies, rhinestone beading, etc. • *CLOTHING*

Meisel Hardware Specialties • wooden craft parts and brass hardware, woodworking plans • *TOOLS*

Metropolitan Music Co. • violin wood, stain, varnish, tools, etc. • *MUSIC*

Original Paper Collectibles • vintage fruit-crate and other product labels for crafts use • *ART, ANTIQUES*

Plastic BagMart • zip-top plastic bags • *GENERAL: PACKAGING*
The Potters Shop Inc. • books on pottery and ceramics • *BOOKS*
Protecto-Pak • zip-top plastic bags • *GENERAL: PACKAGING*
Rammagerdin • Icelandic (Lopi) yarn • *CLOTHING*
San Francisco Herb Co. • dried flowers, other potpourri ingredients, potpourri recipes, etc. • *FOOD*
Ginger Schlote • economy jewelry findings • *JEWELRY*
Sewin' in Vermont • sewing machines and accessories • *APPLIANCES*
Shama Imports, Inc. • crewel-embroidered fabric • *HOME: DECOR*
Singer Sewing Center of College Station • sewing machines and sergers • *APPLIANCES*
R.C. Steele Co. • canine portrait needlework kits • *ANIMAL*
Suburban Sew 'N Sweep, Inc. • sewing and overlock machines • *APPLIANCES*
That Fish Place • aquarium supplies and equipment • *ANIMAL*
Triner Scale • pocket scale • *OFFICE*
University Products, Inc. • archival-quality collection storage, mounting, and display materials • *GENERAL: PACKAGING*
Weston Bowl Mill • unfinished wooden boxes, spool holders, etc. • *GENERAL MERCHANDISE*
Wood's Cider Mill • natural (undyed) yarns • *FOOD*
Woodworker's Supply of New Mexico • woodworking tools and equipment • *TOOLS*

FARM AND GARDEN

Seeds, bulbs, live plants, supplies, tools, and equipment

I f you buy your plants at the local florist or nursery, you may find the selection somewhat limited, and the prices noncompetitive. But the miracle of mail order can bring you bulbs, plants, flowers, herbs, and other growing things, as well as tools and equipment—often at considerable savings. Before you order growing materials, make sure the plants will survive in your climate or home environment. Soil test kits are offered by many mail-order garden suppliers, and among them the LaMotte kits are highly regarded. LaMotte has been manufacturing test kits, reagents, and apparatus for analyzing water, air, and soil for over 65 years. The best kit for the home gardener costs about $35 (although a simplified version that tests just pH levels is available for about $9). The deluxe kit comes with all the reagents and charts you'll need to perform about 30 pH tests and 15 tests for nitrogen, phosphorus, and potassium. The "LaMotte Soil Handbook" that comes with the kit is a fascinating guide to the elements of soil, including a definition of soil nutrients and a "pH preference guide" for over 600 plants, shrubs, and trees. The LaMotte kits can be found in the spring and summer catalogs from Gardener's Supply, 128 Intervale Rd., Burlington, VT 05401. Gardener's Supply is not a discount source, but it features a wealth of good and useful garden equipment and tools in its free catalog.

The business of preserving old plant varieties is the concern of *The Heirloom Gardener* (Sierra Club Books, 1984), by Carolyn Jabs. This is a wonderful guide to "living heirlooms"—endangered, rare, and nearly extinct fruit and vegetable varieties. (By some estimates, only a fraction of the varieties that existed at the turn of the century can be found today.) The book includes a brief history of the business of seeds, information on seed "savers" and seed exchanges, finding lost varieties, capsule histories of some select heirloom varieties, seed research resources, tips on harvesting seeds, and much other useful information. To buy the book, request the publications list from Sierra Club Mail-Order Service, 730 Polk St., San Francisco, CA 94109.

Kent Whealy's 422-page *Garden Seed Inventory* is something of a bible for vegetable seed savers. This book lists varieties alphabetically, describes each (height, appearance, variations, days to maturity), indicates which seed companies offer it, and also shows *how many* firms have offered that variety over the past few years. For example, the "Green Prolific" pickling cucumber was available from 23 firms in 1987, down from 34 who stocked the seed in 1981. The mandate is clear to seed savers: Buy, cultivate, and save those varieties! For price and ordering information on the current edition of the *Garden Seed Inventory,* send a request for the publication list with a long, self-addressed, stamped envelope to Seed Savers Exchange, RR 3, Box 239, Decorah, IA 52101.

If you're purchasing farm machinery, see the listing of Central Michigan Tractor & Parts in "Auto." In addition to the Department of Agriculture publications, university cooperative extensions also disseminate technical information of use to farmers and production growers. Among those in the "Small Farms Series," published by the Northeast Regional Agricultural Engineering Service, the 34-page *Used Farm Equipment: Assessing Quality, Safety, and Economics* is a clear and well-illustrated overview of points to consider before making such a purchase. Write to Northeast Regional Agricultural Engineering Service, Cornell University, 152 Riley-Robb Hall, Ithaca, NY 14853 for a list of current publications and prices.

The U.S. government operates an information clearinghouse staffed by agricultural pros who can advise you to on technical matters, including how to go organic ("sustainable agriculture" is part of the agency's mandate). Please note that you should turn here after consulting other sources, including your local extension agent; if you can't get help there, call ATTRA (Appropriate Technology Transfer for Rural Areas), at 800-346-9140, Monday to Friday, 8–5 CST.

If you're building your own greenhouse or cold frames, see the listing of Arctic Glass & Window Outlet ("Home: Maintenance") for thermopane panels. Other garden-related products are sold by some of the companies listed in "Tools."

BULBS, SEEDS, PLANTS • *Breck's, Butterbrooke, Caprilands, Carino, Dutch Gardens, Mellinger's, J.E. Miller, National Arbor Day, Park Seed, Pinetree Garden, R.H. Shumway, Van Bourgondien*
FARMING EQUIPMENT • *Central Tractor*
GREENHOUSES AND SUPPLIES • *Bob's Superstrong, Turner*
ROSES • *Nor'East, Rosehill Farm*

BOB'S SUPERSTRONG GREENHOUSE PLASTIC

BOX 42-WM92
NECHE, ND 58265
204/327-5540 (SEE TEXT)

Brochure: $1 or 2 first-class stamps
Save: up to 40%
Pay: check or MO
Sells: greenhouse plastic and fastening systems
Store: same address; by appointment

$$ ☎ 🍁(see text) 🇺🇸

Bob Davis and his wife, Margaret Smith-Davis, live on the Manitoba/North Dakota border. Resourceful gardeners, they experimented with different materials while trying to create an inexpensive greenhouse and discovered that woven polyethylene makes an ideal greenhouse skin, even in harsh climes. Their experiences with the material were so successful that they decided to market it themselves.

Their 12-year-old business, Bob's Superstrong Greenhouse Plastic (also known as Northern Greenhouse Sales), is a great source for other innovative gardeners who want to design their own greenhouses. The firm offers the "superstrong" woven poly and two anchoring systems. One is "Cinchstrap," a bright-white, flat, flexible poly strapping material that can be used for permanent anchoring, abrasion reduction in installation, and as a replacement for wood lathing in greenhouse assembly. The other, "Poly-Fastener," is a channel-system anchor that uses a flat spline to secure the poly. Prices for the woven poly run from 15¢ to 23¢ per square foot, depending on the quantity ordered; the standard width is ten feet, but Bob can heat-seal additional widths together to create a wider swath. The Poly-Fastener runs between 53¢ and 58¢ a linear foot in 300' and 100' rolls (or $1 per foot for cut pieces), and the Cinchstrap costs 11¢ a linear foot on 100' rolls.

The literature from this firm details the couple's experiences with these materials, and it discusses money-saving ideas. One is the use of "rebars," ("those long, rusty-colored iron rods placed in concrete to strengthen it") to create the greenhouse frame. There are many other tips, all of which are based on the experiences of the proprietors or those of their customers. The applications of the poly aren't limited to greenhouses and cold frames; woven poly has been used in solar collectors, vapor barriers, storm windows, pool covers, tent floors, and many other situations. Send $1 or two first-class stamps—or phone—for the charming and amazingly informative brochure. You may also speak to the proprietors by phone if you have questions; please note the phone hours, below.

Canadian readers, please note: Call or write to Box 1450WM, Altona, Manitoba R0G 0B0, for literature.

Special Factors: Price quote by phone or letter with SASE; calls are taken daily between 6 A.M. and 8 P.M., CST; minimum order is $1; C.O.D. orders are accepted; orders are shipped worldwide.

BRECK'S DUTCH BULBS

6523 N. GALENA RD.
PEORIA, IL 61632
309/691-4610, 4616
FAX: 309/691-2632

Catalog: free
Save: up to 50%
Pay: check, MO, MC, V, AE
Sells: Dutch flower bulbs
Store: mail order only

$$$ ☎

Breck's has been "serving American gardeners since 1818" with a fine selection of flower bulbs, imported directly from Holland. Discounts of up to 50% are offered on orders placed by July 31 for fall delivery and planting, and there are special savings on "samplers" and bulb collections.

The 60-page, color catalog shows many varieties of tulips, as well as a selection of crocuses, daffodils, hyacinths, irises, jonquils, anemones, and wind flowers. Blooming period, height, color and markings, petal formation, and scent are all described in the text. Each order is shipped with the Breck's "Dutch Bulb Handbook," which covers naturalizing, planting, indoor growing, bulb care, and related topics.

Special Factors: Satisfaction is guaranteed; early-order discounts are available; returns are accepted for exchange, replacement, or refund.

BUTTERBROOKE FARM SEED CO-OP

**78 BARRY RD.
OXFORD, CT 06483
203/888-2000**

Price List: free with long, self-addressed, stamped envelope
Save: up to 75%
Pay: check or MO
Sells: seeds
Store: mail order only

$$$ 🍁 🇺🇸

"Only pure, open-pollinated seeds will produce plants from which you can save seeds for planting another year." So says the straight-forward price list from Butterbrooke Farm Seed Co-Op, where becoming "seed self-reliant" is one of several gardening objectives.

Butterbrooke, established in 1978, is a seed cooperative whose members include organic farmers and seed savers. (Butterbrooke Farm was the "second farm in the State of Connecticut to be certified organic when the state adopted its certification program.") For just $12.50 per year, co-op members receive a 20% order discount, the quarterly Farm newsletter, "Germinations," advisory services, the opportunity to buy rare or heirloom seeds, and other benefits. This is no-frills gardening at its sensible best, from the selection of scores of seeds (a well-rounded kitchen-garden full) to the Farm's own "Home Garden Collection" for first-time planters—a group of vegetable favorites.

The packets are measured to reduce waste: the small size (50¢) will plant one to two 20-foot rows, and the large size ($1.25), three to four times that. All of the seeds are fresh, and they've been selected for short growing seasons. Butterbrooke also offers booklets on related topics—composting, making mulch, saving seeds—at nominal sums. You don't have to be a co-op member to buy from Butterbrooke, but the price of membership is low and the advice service alone should justify the expense.

Special Factors: C.O.D. orders are accepted; orders are shipped worldwide.

CAPRILANDS HERB FARM

**534 SILVER ST.
COVENTRY, CT 06238
203/742-7244**

Brochure: free
Save: up to 30%
Pay: check, MO, certified check
Sells: live herbs and country gifts
Store: same address; daily 9–5 except holidays

$ 🍁 ▀

Caprilands offers live and dried culinary and medicinal herbs and a potpourri of herbaceous gifts, seasonings, and rite materials. The Farm is run by Mrs. Simmons, a herbalist of sixty years' standing, who provides a legendary luncheon program for visitors to her 18th-century farmhouse. (Reservations are essential; details on the program are given in the brochure.)

Mrs. Simmons began her business in 1929, which has become a respected source among collectors of hard-to-find herbs and those who dabble in "natural magic." Over 300 kinds of standard culinary herbs and less common plants can be bought here, including Egyptian onions, rue, wormwood, mugwort, monardas, artemisia, santolinas, germander, lamb's ears, nepetas, ajuga, chamomile, woodruff, and many varieties of thyme, at $2 to $3 per plant. Scented geraniums, roses, and flowers are also offered. (The plants are available at the Farm only, not by mail.) Packets of seeds for herbs and herbal flowers are available by mail for $1 each. Mrs. Simmons' own guides to the cultivation and use of herbs are sold through the brochure, including one of the bibles of herbal horticulture—*Herb Gardening in Five Seasons.*

Caprilands offers a marvelous array of related goods: bronze sundials, wooden "good luck crows" for the garden, kitchen witches and costumed collectors' dolls, pomanders and sachet pillows, spice necklaces, wreaths, herbal hot pads, note paper and calendars, and much more. Amid this olfactory plenty is another great buy—rose buds and lavender flowers for $12 per pound, compared to $15 and $22 in other catalogs; essential oils are also sold.

Special Factors: Certain goods listed in the catalog are available only at the Farm; orders are shipped worldwide.

CARINO NURSERIES

BOX 538
INDIANA, PA 15701
800-223-7075
412/463-3350
412/463-7480

Catalog: free
Save: up to 65%
Pay: check, MO, MC, V
Sells: evergreen seedlings and transplants
Store: mail order only

$$$

Carino Nurseries has been supplying Christmas tree farmers, nursery owners, and others with evergreen seedlings since 1947, and its prices and selection are better than those we've seen elsewhere—savings of 60% are routine.

The 32-page catalog lists varieties of pine (Scotch, white, Mugho, Ponderosa, Japanese black, American red, and Austrian), fir (Douglas, Balsam, Grand, Fraser, and Concolor), spruce (Colorado blue, white, Englemann, Black Hills, Norway, and Serbian), and birch, dogwood, olive, Canadian hemlock, arborvitae, and other deciduous shrubs and trees.

Each catalog entry includes a description of the variety, age, and approximate height of the plants and the number of years spent in original and transplant beds. There are specials on ten-plant collections, but most of the seedlings are sold in lots of 100 at prices up to 65% below those of other nurseries. If you're buying 500 or more, Carino's prices drop 50%. Recommendations on selecting, planting, and shearing (for later harvest as Christmas trees) are given, and the shipping methods and schedule policies are detailed in the catalog as well.

Special Factors: Price quote by phone or letter; shipments are made by bus or UPS; minimum order is 10 or 100 plants (see text).

CENTRAL TRACTOR FARM & FAMILY CENTER

3915 DELAWARE AVE.
P.O. BOX 3330
DES MOINES, IA 50316
800-247-7508
FAX: 515/266-4229

Catalog: free
Save: 30% average
Pay: check, MO, MC, V, Discover
Sells: new, used, and rebuilt tractors and farm equipment
Store: 47 stores nationwide (locations are given in the catalog)

$$ ☎ ❦

The oversized, 172-page catalog from this firm opens with livestock supplies and closes with shop manuals for hundreds of farm machines. Central Tractor Farm & Family Center has been in business since 1935 and has over 170 outlets across the U.S. and Canada. The catalog and stores offer products for livestock and dairy farmers, water systems, fencing, accessories for pickup trucks, trailer hookups and parts, air compressors, tractor and implement paint, welding equipment, shop tools, and Homelite chain saws. We've listed Central Tractor for its extensive inventory of used parts for tractors made by Allis Chalmers, David Brown, Case, John Deere, Ferguson, Ford, International Harvester, Massey Ferguson, Minneapolis Moline, Oliver, and White. (Details of the warranty terms are given in the catalog.) New replacement parts are available, and there are illustrated shop manuals for these and other makes.

Canadian readers, please note: Inquire for shipping rates.

Special Factor: Quantity discounts are available.

DUTCH GARDENS

DEPT. WMC2
P.O. BOX 200
ADELPHIA, NJ 07710
908/780-2713
FAX: 908/780-7720

Catalog: free
Save: 30% average (see text)
Pay: check, MO, MC, V, AE, DC
Sells: Dutch flower bulbs
Store: mail order only

$$$ ☎

Dutch Gardens publishes one of the most beautiful bulb catalogs around—over 100 color pages of breathtaking flower "head shots" that approximate perfection. Dutch Gardens has been in business since 1961, and prices its bulbs well below other mail-order firms and garden supply houses—30% on average, and up to 50% on some bulbs and collections.

The fall planting catalog offers tulip, hyacinth, daffodil, narcissus, crocus, anemone, iris, snowdrop, allium, amaryllis, and other flower bulbs. The tulip selection alone includes single, double, fringed, parrot, lily, and peony types. The spring planting catalog we reviewed showed a dazzling array of lilies, begonias, dahlias, gladioli, peonies, tuberoses, anemones, freesia, and other flowers. Onions and shallots (for planting) were also available. Each Dutch Gardens catalog lists the size of the bulbs and the common and botanical names, height, planting zones, blooming period, and appropriate growing situations of each variety. A zone chart, guide to planting depth, hints on naturalizing, rock gardening, terrace planting, indoor growing, and forcing are included.

Special Factors: Bulbs are guaranteed to bloom (conditions are stated in the catalog); bulb bonuses or discounts are available on quantity orders; shipping is included on orders over $40; minimum order is $20.

FLORIST PRODUCTS, INC.

**2242 NORTH PALMER DR.
SCHAUMBURG, IL 60195
800-828-2242
FAX: 800-252-4022**

Catalog: free
Save: up to 50%
Pay: check, MO, MC, V, AE
Sells: greenhouse and gardening supplies
Store: mail order only

The 92-page catalog of "hobby growing supplies" from Florist Products should answer the needs of gardeners of all varieties, from the desultory to the dedicated. This firm has been in business since 1952, and prices its goods up to 50% below list or regular retail prices.

Serious horticultural pursuits are served here with greenhouses and greenhouse equipment (fans, heaters, watering and irrigation systems). Compression and hand sprayers, insecticides and fumigants, growth stimulators and hormones, plant food and fertilizers, soil testers, plant stands, propagation equipment, plastic pots and flats, hanging baskets, redwood planters, pruning shears and other garden tools, and weed barrier matting are also available. The brands are old favorites, including Corona, Felco, Jiffy, Peters, Safer, and Sudbury, among others. If you have a greenhouse or are an active grower, see this catalog before you buy your next round of supplies elsewhere.

Special Factors: Satisfaction is guaranteed; price quote by phone or letter with SASE; unused returns are accepted for exchange, refund, or credit.

MELLINGER'S INC.

DEPT. WBMC, W. SOUTH RANGE RD.
NORTH LIMA, OH 44452-9731
800-321-7444
IN OH 216/549-9861

Catalog: free
Save: up to 45%
Pay: check, MO, MC, V
Sells: seeds, bulbs, and garden equipment
Store: same address; Monday to Saturday 8:30–5 (July to March); 8–6 (April to June)

$$$ ☎ 🍁 ▄

Mellinger's publishes "the garden catalog for year-round country living," 120 pages of seeds, bulbs, live plants, reference books, greenhouses, garden equipment, and tools. Mellinger's, in business since 1927, offers many hard-to-find goods at savings of up to 45%. Like most of the firms listed in this chapter, Mellinger's has outstandingly low prices on some items, and offers nominal savings on others. (For example, we've found no better prices elsewhere on Blue Lake bush beans and Black-Seeded Simpson lettuce seeds, but no notable savings on the California Wonder pepper seeds.)

Mellinger's sells flower seeds and bulbs, potted trees and shrubs, shade tree and evergreen seedlings, herb plants, fruit trees, vegetable seeds and vines, tropical plants, and seeds for rare and unusual plants. Everything you'll need for successful cultivation is available, from seed flats to greenhouses. You'll find insect and animal repellants, plant fertilizers, soil additives, pruning and grafting tools, spades, cultivators, hoes, seeders, watering systems, cold frames, starter pots, planters and flower boxes, and related goods. In addition to chemical fumigants and insecticides, Mellinger's sells ladybugs, praying mantis egg cases, and other "natural" predators and beneficial parasites. Bird feeders and seed are also stocked.

Mellinger's also offers a wide variety of goods for hydroponic gardening, and poly-skin greenhouses in small and commercial sizes. Polyethylene is sold by the foot, and ventilation equipment, soil sterilizers, heaters, and thermostats are also available. Books on topics from plant propagation and insect control to flower pressing and food drying are offered, including the Brooklyn Botanic Garden Handbook manuals.

The catalog includes a guide to hardiness zones to help you make selections appropriate to your area and a statement of the terms of the warranty covering plant orders.

Special Factors: Plants are warrantied for 1 years (see the catalog for terms); authorized returns are accepted (a 10% restocking fee may be charged); minimum order is $10 with credit cards.

J.E. MILLER NURSERIES, INC.

■■■■■■■■

**5060 WEST LAKE RD.
CANANDAIGUA, NY
14424
800-836-9630
716/396-2647
FAX: 716/396-2154**

Catalog: free
Save: up to 50%
Pay: check, MO, MC, V, AE, Discover, Optima
Sells: plants, shrubs, trees, and nursery stock
Store: same address; Monday to Friday 8–4:30 (seven days during the spring)

$$$ ☎

Miller's spring and fall catalogs offer a full range of plants, seeds, bulbs, shrubs, and trees, at savings of up to 50%, compared to prices charged by nurseries and garden supply centers. Miller Nurseries has been in business since 1936, and publishes a fall sale catalog that features real bargains.

Miller's comprehensive selection includes russet apple, golden plum, grapes (including seedless varieties), red raspberry, blueberry, cherry, strawberry, and dozens of other fruit and nut trees, plants, and vines. Shade trees are offered, including poplar, locust, maple, and ash; and there are ornamental grasses and plants for the vegetable garden and some common flower bulbs as well. Garden supplies and equipment, including pruners, animal repellent, soil additives, wheel-barrows, mulch sheeting, etc., are also offered. The catalog includes horticultural tips, and each order is sent with Miller's 32-page planting guide. This firm has gotten rave reviews from several readers of this book, who've praised Miller's service and prices.

Please note: Orders are shipped to U.S. addresses only (not APO/FPO).

Special Factors: Trees and shrubs are sent as plants, guaranteed to grow; minimum order is $10 with credit cards.

NATIONAL ARBOR DAY FOUNDATION

100 ARBOR AVE.
NEBRASKA CITY, NE
68410
402/474-5655
FAX: 402/474-0820

Information: inquire
Save: 33% plus
Pay: check, MO, MC, V, AE
Sells: trees, plants, bulbs, etc.
Store: mail order only

$$$

The first Arbor Day was marked in Nebraska in 1872, when a newspaper editor petitioned the Board of Agriculture to designate a day for planting trees. Arbor Day is now celebrated in every state in the Union, and in over a dozen other countries. The Arbor Day Foundation exists to encourage tree planting and tree care, which it does in the most direct way: by selling trees (bare-root stock) at prices that are at least one-third lower than those charged by many nurseries. A membership costs $10, at this writing.

Among its other benefits, membership in the Foundation entitles you to the eight-page bimonthly publication, *Arbor Day,* and a copy of "The Tree Book," a catalog/guide to plant identification and cultivation. "The Tree Book" shows scores of shade and ornamental trees, flowering shrubs and trees, hedges, fruit trees, nut trees, evergreens, and evergreen windbreaks. All of these may be ordered from the Foundation, and bulbs and other goods are featured in every Foundation mailing.

Please note: Fall plant shipments are made between October 15 and December 10, and spring shipments are made between February

1 and May 31. Plants are *not* shipped to Alaska, Hawaii, California, or Arizona.

Special Factor: All horticultural products are guaranteed to grow.

NOR'EAST MINIATURE ROSES, INC.
━━━━━━━━━

**P.O. BOX 307-WB
ROWLEY, MA 01969
508/948-7964
FAX: 508/948-5487**

Catalog: free
Save: up to 30%
Pay: check, MO, MC, V
Sells: miniature roses
Store: 58 Hammond St., Rowley, MA; also
955 West Phillips St., Ontario, CA;
Monday to Friday 8–4, both locations

Nor'East publishes a 16-page catalog of its specialty, miniature roses, which are priced at $4.95 each, compared to over $7 for the same varieties sold elsewhere. (Nor'East does not tack on a per-plant handling fee, as do some of its competitors.) Dozens of types of miniature bush roses are available, including micro-minis (4″ to 8″ tall at maturity), climbers, and tree roses (miniatures budded to understocks). The varieties are grouped by colors, which include reds, pinks, yellows, oranges, apricots, whites, mauves, and blends. Among the fancifully named specimens are old favorites and new entries: Happy Go Lucky, Jim Dandy, Cupcake, Party Girl, Holy Toledo, Puppy Love, and Sunny Day, to name a few. The catalog descriptions include height of the mature plant, blooming pattern and coloring, scent, suitable growth situations, and other information.

Nor'East offers quantity discounts and specially priced bonuses for large orders. "We pick 'em" collections are also offered—prices drop to $3.79 per plant if you let the firm make the selection. Nor'East offers other collections, including easy-to-cultivate choices, fragrant types, and a beginners' kit that includes pots and potting mix. Planting and care directions are sent with each order. A selection of small vases and Sean McCann's book on miniature roses are also sold.

Special Factors: Returns of plants that fail to perform are accepted within 90 days for replacement; minimum order is $20 with credit cards.

PARK SEED CO.

**BN 950, COKESBURY RD.
GREENWOOD, SC 29647-
0001
803/223-7333
FAX: 803/223-6999**

Catalog: free
Save: up to 50%
Pay: check, MO, MC, V, AE, Discover
Sells: seeds, bulbs, garden equipment, etc.
Store: same address

$$$$ ☎ 🍁 ▓▓(see text)

Park is one of the most-cited sources among our gardening friends, some of whom rely on Park for all their growables. As one woman put it, the quality and reliability of Park's stock makes it a best buy among the big mail-order seed and bulb companies.

This venerable firm (established in 1868) has a broad range of flower and vegetable seeds—new varieties and old favorites—chosen for performance in the U.S. Herbs are another strong suit, and house plants and perennials are well represented. The thorough catalog descriptions include germination and cultivation information, and a 16-page gardening guide accompanies every order. Basic gardening tools and propagating devices are offered in every catalog. In addition to pricing its seeds and plants up to 20% below other firms offering the same quality, Park offers quantity discounts, early-order discounts, and bonuses.

Please note: No live stock—only seeds, tools, and supplies—are shipped to Canada and APO/FPO addresses.

Special Factors: Satisfaction is guaranteed; quantity discounts are available; returns are accepted within 1 year; minimum order is $20 with credit cards.

PINETREE GARDEN SEEDS

**RTE. 100
NEW GLOUCESTER, ME
   04260
207/926-3400
FAX: 207/926-3886**

Catalog: free
Save: up to 35%
Pay: check, MO, MC, V, AE
Sells: seeds, bulbs, plants, garden
   equipment, and books
Store: same address; Monday to Friday
   10–4 (April 15–November 8); see catalog
   for map and current hours

$$$ ☎   🍁   ▀▀▀

Pinetree Garden Seeds was established in 1979 to provide home gardeners with seeds in small packets, suitable for kitchen gardens or horticultural experiments. The firm has exceeded its goal, offering kitchen gadgets, gardening tools and supplies, books and other useful goods.

Pinetree's strength is the seeds that built the business—over 600 varieties of vegetable and flower seeds, just a handful of which are treated. Of special interest are the "vegetable favorites from around the world," including radicchio, fava beans, snow peas, entsai, burdock, flageolet, cardoons, epazotes, and chiles. You'll also find plants and tubers for shallots, asparagus, berries, and potatoes. The flower section features seeds, tubers, and bulbs for annuals, perennials, everlastings, and wildflowers.

The tools and equipment run from kitchen and canning helps to hand tools to the well-priced "Easylink" watering system from Suncast. Fertilizers, Havahart traps, netting, and related goods are offered. Over 30 pages of the catalog are devoted to books, including a number of gardening literature classics, cookbooks, garden planners, and the Garden Way Country Wisdom bulletins. Prices are quite competitive, and even the 35¢ seed packets are backed by Pinetree's ironclad guarantee of satisfaction.

Canadian and non-U.S. readers, please note: The catalog costs U.S.$1.50 if sent to a non-U.S. address.

Special Factors: Satisfaction is guaranteed; returns are accepted for exchange, refund, or credit; orders are shipped worldwide.

PRENTISS COURT GROUND COVERS

P.O. BOX 8662
GREENVILLE, SC 29604-
8662
803/277-4037

Brochure: 50¢
Save: up to 50%
Pay: check, MO, MC, V
Sells: live ground-cover plants
Store: mail order only

$$$ ☎

Here's an attractive, labor-efficient alternative to a conventional lawn—ground cover. Prentiss Court, established in 1978, offers a wide range of plants at up to 50% below nursery prices, and includes spacing and planting guides in the brochure.

The broad selection of plants here includes varieties of Cotoneaster, crownvetch, daylilies, Euonymus fortunei, fig vine, Hedera canariensis and helix, honeysuckle, hosta, jasmine, hypericum, Ophiopogon japonicus, Pachysandra terminalis, Parthenocissus, Trumpet creeper, and Vinca major and minor. In English, there are over 70 kinds of plants, including many types of ivy and flowering and berry-bearing ground cover. The plants are sold bare-root and/or potted, at an average price of 50¢ each. The brochure includes tips on planting and caring for ground covers.

Special Factors: Shipping is included; minimum order is 50 plants of the same variety.

ROSEHILL FARM

P.O. BOX 188
GALENA, MD 21635-0188
301/648-5538 UNTIL NOV.
1991
410/648-5538 AFTER NOV.
1991

Catalog: free
Save: 30% average (see text)
Pay: check, MO, MC, V
Sells: miniature roses
Store: Gregg Neck Rd., Galena, MD;
　　　Monday to Saturday 9–4

$$$ ☎

Rosehill Farm has been selling miniature roses since 1980 and brings out new varieties each year. The color catalog shows the standard-size minis, sweetheart sizes, micro-minis, climbers, and hanging basket types, including white, blush, yellow, gold, apricot, lavender, pink, orange, and red varieties. The catalog descriptions note special characteristics of each plant, height of the mature plant, suitable growing situations, color, and other useful information.

Rosehill's prices average about 30% below those of miniature roses we priced in local nurseries and other garden catalogs. Quantity discounts of 10% are given on orders of ten or more plants (15% on 15 or more). Real wholesale prices are available to not-for-profit organizations, nurseries, and garden centers. (Request the wholesale price list on your company letterhead.)

Special Factors: Quantity discounts are available; returns with tags are accepted within 60 days for replacement; minimum order is $20 with credit cards.

R.H. SHUMWAY SEEDSMAN

**P.O. BOX 1
GRANITEVILLE, SC 29829
803-663-9771**

Catalog: $1, refundable
Save: up to 50%
Pay: check, MO, MC, V
Sells: seeds, bulbs, and nursery stock
Store: Graniteville, SC; Monday to Saturday 8–4 (open Saturday in spring season only)

$$$ ☎   ❀   ▤

"Good Seeds Cheap" declares the cover of R.H. Shumway's catalog, which is full of old-fashioned *engravings* of flowers, fruits, and vegetables—there's not a photograph in sight. Shumway has been "The Pioneer American Seedsman" since 1870, and is notable for the number of old, open-pollinated seeds it carries, as well as new varieties.

The 64-page catalog opens with a good buy on flower seeds—six packets at under 80¢ each, mix or match. There are spring flower bulbs, over 50 types of roses, many pages of berries, fruit trees, vines, beans, vegetable seeds, corn, onions, squash, tomatoes, and Shumway specialties—lawn grasses, grasses for pasturage and hay, millet and other "forage" seed, sorghums, Sudan grasses, clover, legumes, and alfalfa. Market gardeners and other small commercial growers should check Shumway's wholesale prices on bulk seed orders. Special offers and bonuses are sprinkled liberally throughout the catalog, which also offers a small selection of well-priced garden helps.

Special Factors: Satisfaction is guaranteed; quantity discounts are available; returns are accepted within 90 days for exchange or replacement; minimum order is $15 with credit cards.

TURNER GREENHOUSES

DEPT. 131
P.O. BOX 1260
GOLDSBORO, NC 27533-
  1260
800-672-4770, EXT. 131
FAX: 919/736-4550

Catalog: free
Save: up to 35%
Pay: check, MO, MC, V
Sells: greenhouses and accessories
Store: mail order only

$$$ ☎ 🍁

Turner was founded in 1939 and has been producing greenhouses since 1957, and currently offers three basic models with a choice of options. Turner's prices average 25% less than the competition, and we've found similar greenhouses in other catalogs selling for 35% more.

Turner's greenhouses include a 7'-wide lean-to, and two freestanding models, 8' and 14' wide. The greenhouses come equipped with a ventilating system and aluminum screen door, and each can be expanded in length in 4' increments. You can choose from a polyethylene cover (6 mil), or fiberglass (warrantied for 20 years). Turner also sells electric and gas heaters, exhaust fans and air circulators, cooling units, greenhouse benches, thermometers, misters, sprayers, and insecticides. Don't miss the well-chosen books on composting, organic gardening, greenhouse growing, herb cultivation, and similar topics.

Special Factors: Satisfaction is guaranteed; price quote by phone or letter; authorized returns in original condition are accepted within 30 days for refund or credit (less freight); minimum order is $10.

K. VAN BOURGONDIEN & SONS, INC.

P.O. BOX A
BABYLON, NY 11702
800-873-9444
FAX: 516/669-1228

Catalog: free
Save: up to 40%
Pay: check, MO, MC, V, AE
Sells: flower bulbs and plants
Store: mail order only

$$$ ☎

The 64-page spring and fall catalogs from Van Bourgondien offer a wealth of growing things for home, lawn, and garden at up to 40% less than other suppliers. Both of the catalogs feature hosta and hybrid lilies, ground covers, a wide range of flowers, and supplies and tools. Van Bourgondien was founded in 1919, and offers early-order discounts.

Past fall catalogs have shown tulip, daffodil, hyacinth, iris, crocus, narcissus, anemone, allium, fritillaria, and other bulbs. Geraniums, delphiniums, shasta daisies, tiger lilies, lavender, flowering house plants, foxtails, black-eyed Susans, native ferns, and other greenery and flowers are usually offered. If you can't wait for the thaw, you can buy prepotted lilies of the valley, Aztec lily, paperwhites, amaryllis varieties, and crocus bulbs, which can all be forced. The spring catalog features begonias, gladiolus, dahlias, caladiums, perennials, cannas, ground cover, rhubarb, shallots, artichokes, and similar goods. Bulb planters and plant supplements are offered as well.

Special Factors: Goods are guaranteed to be "as described" and to be delivered in perfect condition; early-order and quantity discounts are available; bonuses are offered with large orders.

SEE ALSO

Arctic Glass & Window Outlet • glass panels for cold frames, greenhouses • *HOME: MAINTENANCE*
Central Michigan Tractor & Parts • used and reconditioned parts for tractors and combines • *AUTO*
Clothcrafters, Inc. • knee pads, gardening aprons, and porous plastic sheeting • *GENERAL MERCHANDISE*
Dairy Association Co., Inc. • liniment for livestock • *ANIMAL*

Daleco Master Breeder Products • kits for yard ponds • *ANIMAL*

Manufacturer's Supply • replacement parts for lawnmowers, rototillers, trimmers, tractors, etc. • *TOOLS*

Northern Hydraulics, Inc. • trimmers, NorTrac tractors, lawnmower parts, etc. • *TOOLS*

A.W.G. Otten and Son • wooden shoes and clogs for gardening • *CLOTHING: FOOTWEAR*

Fred Stoker and Sons, Inc. • sweet potato plants and tobacco seeds • *CIGARS*

That Fish Place • live aquarium plants • *ANIMAL*

WearGuard Corp. • chore coats, overalls, work clothes, shoes, etc. • *CLOTHING*

Zip Power Parts, Inc. • lawnmower parts • *TOOLS*

FOOD AND DRINK

Foods, beverages, and condiments

Herbs, spices, coffee, and tea are mail-order naturals, and all of them are available through the firms listed here. But these sources also offer you caviar and Italian truffles, Mexican and Lebanese foods, giant pistachio nuts, Vermont maple syrup at below-supermarket prices, and more—at savings that run to 80%.

But we can't spare you from the ordeal of the supermarket, a place that has made food shopping one of the most-loathed chores in our lives, according to a survey we saw recently. It's not just long waits at the checkout counter that turn us off—it's the bewildering array of choices, the misleading labeling, and the issues that once-innocuous products now raise. The roasting chicken, dozen eggs, peanut butter, apples, broccoli, sour cream, and paper towels in your shopping cart translate into a basket of anxiety—fears about salmonella, cholesterol, aflatoxin, alar, irradiation, saturated fats, and the environment. No wonder we're so reluctant to face those aisles! For help, try *The Goldbecks' Guide to Good Food* (New American Library, 1987), which we've found a fascinating and useful guide to everyday food shopping—from supermarkets to mail-order sources. Written by Nikki and David Goldbeck, the book covers nutrition bugaboos and the vocabulary of labeling and mislabeling, and includes extensive information on the organic market and additives and a wealth of other enlightening information on food.

Getting the most nutrition from your food dollars isn't easy, but *Nutrition Action Healthletter* can help. This 16-page newsletter is published ten times a year by the Center for Science in the Public Interest (CSPI), which takes a consumerist/advocacy position on matters of nutrition and food safety. A subscription to the newsletter is a benefit of membership in CSPI, which also publishes nutrition-related posters, books, pamphlets, software, and videotapes. For information, write to Center for Science in the Public Interest, 1875 Connecticut Ave., N.W., Suite 300, Washington, DC 20009-5728.

The Food and Drug Administration covers the same beat from the government's angle, with articles on food safety regulation and enforcement, new food processing technology, medical issues, and related topics. There are usually several hair-raising pages devoted to highlights of recent seizures, and a lively letters column. A subscription (ten issues) costs $12 at this writing, and can be ordered through the Consumer Information Center (see the listing in "Books").

When ordering foods, be mindful of the weather. Don't purchase such highly perishable or temperature-sensitive items as chocolate, soft cheese, fruits, vegetables, or uncured meats during the summer unless you have them shipped by an express service and plan to eat them immediately. (Most catalogs include caveats to this effect, and some firms just won't ship certain goods during warm weather under any circumstances.)

Consider the firms listed here when making out gift lists—whether you choose a packet of rare herbs or a year of gustatory delights provided by an "of-the-month" program, your presents will be remembered long after they're consumed. If you want to maximize your savings, choose a popular food gift such as pecans or dried fruit, buy it in bulk, and package it yourself!

FIND IT FAST

CHEESE • **Gibbsville**
COFFEE AND TEA • **Grandma's Spice Shop, The Maples, Northwestern Coffee Mills, Simpson & Vail**
GOURMET FOODS • **Caviarteria, The Chef's Pantry**
HERBS, SPICES, FLAVORINGS • **Bickford, The Chef's Pantry, Grandma's Spice Shop, E.C. Kraus, Mr. Spiceman, Pendery's, San Francisco Herb, The Spice House**
MAPLE SYRUP • **Palmer's, Elbridge C. Thomas**
NUTS, DRIED FRUITS • **Bates Bros., Durey-Libby, The Maples**
ORGANIC AND NATURAL FOODS • **Deer Valley, Jaffe Bros., Walnut Acres**
WINE- AND BEER-MAKING • **E.C. Kraus**

BATES BROS. NUT FARM, INC.

15954 WOODS VALLEY RD.
VALLEY CENTER, CA 92082
619/749-3333
FAX: 619/749-9499

Price List: free with self-addressed, stamped envelope
Save: up to 50%
Pay: check, MO, MC, V
Sells: nuts, dried fruits, and candy
Store: same address; every day 8–5; also Terra Nova Plaza, 358 E. H St., #604, Chula Vista, CA; every day, 10–7:30

$$

Nuts are the featured item at Bates, which grows some of what it sells. The nuts and other treats are generally priced below those of a number of Bates' competitors; our price checks showed possible savings of almost 50% on selected items.

The brochure lists the standard almonds, walnuts, peanuts, cashews, pecans, and mixes, as well as macadamia nuts, filberts, pignolias, sunflower seeds, and pistachios. You can buy them raw, roasted and salted, smoked, and saltless. The dried fruits include apricots, raisins, dates, papaya, figs, banana chips, pineapple, and coconut, as well as other sweets. These are the ingredients for trail mix, which Bates also sells ready-made, as well as granola, wheat germ snacks, popcorn, and old-fashioned candy—malted milk balls, English toffee, nut brittle, taffy, candy corn, and licorice ropes, among others. And look here for good prices on glacé fruit: fruitcake mix, cherries, colored pineapple wedges, orange and lemon peel, and citron. Gift packs are available year-round.

Special Factors: Price quote by phone or letter; C.O.D. orders are accepted; orders are shipped worldwide.

BICKFORD FLAVORS

19007 ST. CLAIR AVE.
CLEVELAND, OH 44117
800-283-8322

Price List: free
Save: up to 40% (see text)
Pay: check, MO, MC, V
Sells: flavorings
Store: same address; Monday to Friday 9–5

Bickford makes and sells its own concentrated flavorings, from naturally derived oils, leaving out the usual alcohol and sugar that you'll find in other "pure" essences. Over 100 flavorings are offered, from almond to wintergreen. Vanilla is sold here in white, dark, and regular versions. (The white vanilla won't tint your angel food cake or meringues.)

All of the flavorings are sold in one-ounce bottles for $1.99, which is competitive, but the bargain buys are pints ($15.75) and larger sizes. (Vanilla is also sold in bottles of two, four, and eight ounces.) In addition to an unparalleled selection of flavorings, Bickford also sells about 50 exotically flavored oils (ginger, peach, caramel, and sherry oil are all available), food colorings, carob syrup, and popcorn and popping oil.

Special Factors: Price quote by phone or letter; orders are shipped worldwide.

CAVIARTERIA INC.

29 E. 60TH ST.
NEW YORK, NY 10022
800-4-CAVIAR
IN NY 212/759-7410
IN CA 213/285-9773
FAX: 718/482-8985

Catalog: free
Save: up to 30%
Pay: check, MO, MC, V, AE, Optima
Sells: caviar and gourmet foods
Store: same address; also 247 N. Beverly Dr., Beverly Hills, CA; Monday to Saturday 9–6, both locations

Caviarteria, established in 1950, brings its line of caviar to the world through a 16-page catalog that's updated quarterly with newsletters. This family-run business stocks every grade of Caspian Beluga and

Sevruga caviar (fresh and vacuum-packed), plus American sturgeon, whitefish, and salmon caviar, at prices that begin at about $16 per ounce for Kamchatka bottom-of-the-barrel vacuum-packed and run up to about $275 for 3½ ounces of "Ultra" Beluga. We've compared prices of Caviarteria's Beluga Malassol with those of another caviar-by-mail firm and found savings of 40% here, and even Caviarteria's collection of caviar servers is offered at least 20% off list.

The catalog lists other gourmet treats: whole sides of smoked Scottish salmon, salmon steaks, Norwegian gravlax, fresh pâtés, foie gras from Israel and France, tinned white and black Italian truffles, as well as candied chestnuts and other delicacies. The Beverly Hills branch features party platters of caviar canapés and sliced Scottish salmon and lake sturgeon (delivered locally and shipped nationwide) and other food specialties prepared in the firm's commissary, and it will ship champagne anywhere in California.

Special Factors: Satisfaction is guaranteed; price quote by phone or letter; minimum order is $25 with credit cards; orders are shipped worldwide.

THE CHEF'S PANTRY

P.O. BOX 3
POST MILLS, VT 05058
800-TRY-CHEF
802/333-4141

Catalog: $1, refundable
Save: up to 50%
Pay: check, MO, MC, V
Sells: gourmet and specialty foods
Store: mail order only

$$$ ☎ 🍁 🇺🇸

Unless you're a food professional or live in a large city, you're unlikely to know where to find a good selection of the kinds of foodstuffs used by gourmet cooks, caterers, and serious home bakers. The Chef's Pantry, just three years old, remedies the problem with an 18-page catalog of condiments and delicacies, which it sells at prices as much as 50% below those charged by its competitors—and even lower on quantity purchases.

The catalog we reviewed featured the 11-pound bar of Callebaut bittersweet chocolate for $47.50 ($65 in other catalogs), Nielsen Massey vanilla extract at 25% below the competition, two grams of Mancha saffron for $12.75 ($16 elsewhere), and shallots from Brittany for just $2.45 per pound (in quantity). Other baking supplies—

candied fruits, flowers, extracts, and Brunet fruit purees, as well as vinegars, mustards, oils, preserved nuts and fruits, and other condiments and ingredients—are also stocked. Arborio rice, polenta, couscous, and "Cook-in-the-Kitchen" mixes for things like dilled tomato cream soup and lemon almond muffins are also offered. The Chef's Pantry selects preferred brands and varieties—Dauphi Noix nut oils, Italian porcini and Indian morels, and Raineri Olive Oil are a few examples. If you've got a gourmet cook on your gift list, check the roster of gift assortments available, which run from "Bakers Treat" to "Chocolate Crepe Party." If you don't see what you're looking for in the catalog, call or write.

The Chef's Pantry is offering readers a discount of 10% on their first order (of merchandise only). Be sure to identify yourself as a WBMC reader when you order, and deduct the discount from the cost of the goods only. This WBMC reader discount expires February 1, 1993.

Special Factors: Satisfaction is guaranteed; price quote by phone or letter with SASE; returns are accepted for exchange, refund, or credit.

DEER VALLEY FARM

**R.D. I, BOX 173
GUILFORD, NY 13780
607/764-8556**

Catalog: 50¢
Save: up to 40% (see text)
Pay: check or MO
Sells: organic and natural foods
Store: Rte. 37, Guilford, NY; Monday to Friday 8–5; 19B Ford Ave., Oneonta, NY; Monday to Saturday 9:30–5:30, Thursday 9:30–8:30; and 64 Main St., Cortland, NY; Monday to Saturday 9:30–5:30, Thursday 9:30–8:30

Deer Valley Farm, a respected name in organic and whole foods, has been in operation since 1947. The Farm, which has been certified organic by the State of New York, sells a full line of foods—from baked bread and cookies to wheat middlings. Whole grains, flours, cereals, nut butters, crackers, fruits, pasta, herbs and spices, tea, soy milk, preserves, and yeast and other baking ingredients are available. You can buy "organically grown" meats here at substantial savings:

Hamburger, typically priced at $4.50 to $6 per pound in health food stores, costs $3.05 per pound, and the trimmed sirloin is $6.19 a pound. Veal, pork, lamb, and even fish are also available (request the separate "Meat" list). Deer Valley also sells raw milk cheese, and the cheddar is only $3.29 to $4.39 per pound, less than some of the supermarket varieties. The only drawback here is the minimum order, $150, necessary to reap savings of 25% to 40% on the prices you'd pay if buying the same goods from your local health food store. But if you get your friends together, you can meet that amount easily with a combined order—just be prepared for an impromptu feast when the cartons arrive!

Special Factors: Price quote by phone or letter with SASE; deliveries are made by Deer Valley truck in the New York City area (elsewhere by UPS); minimum order is $10, $150 for wholesale prices.

DUREY-LIBBY EDIBLE NUTS, INC.

**P.O. BOX 345
CARLSTADT, NJ 07072
201/939-2775
FAX: 201/939-0386**

Flyer: free
Save: up to 50%
Pay: check or MO
Sells: nuts
Store: mail order only

$$

Durey-Libby, established in 1950, picks and processes "delicious fresh nuts you don't have to shell out a fortune for." You can't eat fancy tins, stoneware crocks, and rattan baskets, so if you're buying nuts, make sure you're paying for nuts.

The stock here includes walnuts, pecans, cashews, almonds, macadamia nuts, pistachios, and cocktail mixes, packed in bags and vacuum tins. The prices are up to 50% less than those charged by gourmet shops and many food catalogs. The smallest units are three-pound cans, which will give you enough for cooking and snacking.

If you identify yourself as a reader of this book when you order, you may deduct 10% from your order total (computed on the cost of the goods only). This WBMC reader discount expires February 1, 1993.

Special Factors: Satisfaction is guaranteed; price quote by phone or letter with SASE on quantity orders; shipping is included on orders within the contiguous U.S.; orders are shipped worldwide.

GIBBSVILLE CHEESE SALES
■■■■■■

W-2663 CTH-00
SHEBOYGAN FALLS, WI
53085
414/564-3242
414/564-2731
FAX: 414/564-6129

Price List: free
Save: up to 30%
Pay: check or MO
Sells: Wisconsin cheese and summer sausage
Store: same address; Monday to Saturday 7:30–5 (7:30–6 in December)

$$$ ☎ ❦(see text) ▆

Gibbsville Cheese Sales is a standout even in Wisconsin, the Dairy State, where *everyone* produces cheese. The company's prices are appetizingly low—as little as $2.30 a pound for mild cheddar in five-pound bulk packaging. Several types of summer sausage and beef sticks are also offered, in addition to well-priced gift packages for a variety of budgets and tastes.

Gibbsville produces the most popular kinds of cheese, including cheddar (mild, medium, aged, super-sharp white, garlic, and caraway), Colby (including salt-free), Swiss (baby, medium, aged, and lace), provolone, Muenster, Parmesan, Romano, mozzarella, Monterey Jack (including Jacks flavored with salami, hot pepper, dill, and vegetables), Gouda, flavored cold-pack cheese spreads (including sharp cheddar, Swiss almond, port wine, French onion, nacho, horseradish, garlic, etc.), and blue, Limburger, and string cheeses. You can buy cheddar and Colby in "economy" boxes of two or ten pounds, or in bulk with as little as a pound. Five pounds of rindless Colby cost $2.30 a pound, and prices of other cheese are just as reasonable. The price list indicates which cheeses are "lower in fat," and includes several "lite" versions of favorites.

Please note: Shipments are not made during summer months (approximately June to September).

Canadian readers, please note: Deliveries to Canada are made by UPS.

Special Factor: Price quote by phone or letter with SASE.

GRANDMA'S SPICE SHOP

DEPT. B
P.O. BOX 901
ELON COLLEGE, NC
27244
919/584-3616

Catalog: free
Save: up to 60%
Pay: check, MO, MC, V
Sells: herbs, spices, coffee, tea, etc.
Store: mail order only

$$$ ☎ ♦ ▀

There *is* a Grandma behind this shop: founder Catherine James, pictured in a rocking chair in front of a display of cookie cutters. The catalog offerings belie the old-fashioned image—it's one of the most sophisticated stock lists we've seen.

To wit: *Danish* breakfast coffee, Nougatine coffee (flavored with hazelnut oil), Jasmine tea from Fukien province, candied angelica, raspberry leaves, and peach butter are but a few of the uncommon brews and foodstuffs listed in the 16 pages. The inventory includes coffees (regular, flavored, and decaffeinated), loose teas (green, black, flavored, decaffeinated) and rare estate teas, Benchley teabags, a large herb and spice selection, potpourri blends and essential oils, cocoa, McStevens popcorn seasonings, McCutcheon preserves, and fruit-sweetened preserves. Spice racks, teapots, mortar and pestle sets, Belgian waffle irons, Rema bakeware, and Melitta travel sets are all available. The herbs and spices afford the best savings, up to 60% if bought in bulk (half or full pounds). Coffee and tea connoisseurs should see the catalog for the unusual and rare varieties (which are not sold at a discount).

Special Factors: Price quote by phone or letter with SASE; quantity discounts are available.

JAFFE BROS., INC.

**P.O. BOX 636-W
VALLEY CENTER, CA
92082-0636
619/749-1133
FAX: 619/749-1282**

Catalog: free
Save: up to 50%
Pay: check, MO, MC, V, Discover
Sells: organically grown food
Store: (warehouse) 28560 Lilac Rd., Valley
Center, CA; Sunday to Thursday 8–5,
Friday 8–3

 $$$ ☎ ✦ ▆

Jaffe Bros., established in 1948, sells organically and naturally grown nuts, seeds, beans, butters, fruit, and honey through its 20-page catalog. The prices average 30% below comparable retail, but there are greater savings on certain items, and quantity discounts are offered on many goods.

Jaffe's foods and goods are marketed under the Jaybee label, and virtually all of the products are grown "organically" (without fumigants or poisonous sprays but with "nonchemical" fertilizers) or "naturally" (similarly treated but not fertilized). You'll save on wholesome foods here—dried peaches, Black Mission figs, Monukka raisins, papaya, dates of several types, almonds, pine nuts, macadamias, nut butters, brown rice, whole-wheat pasta, flours and grains, seeds for eating and sprouting, 15 kinds of peas and beans, unheated honey, coconut, jams, juices, carob powder, salad oil, olives, mushrooms, herb teas, and much more. (Most of the produce is packed in five-pound units or larger.)

The current catalog also lists natural and dehydrated mushrooms, sun-dried tomatoes, canned organically grown olives, organic spaghetti sauce, low-salt dill pickles and sauerkraut, organic whole wheat pasta, kosher maple syrup, salt-free organic tortilla chips, organic applesauce, and even a biodegradable peppermint-and-castile soap/shampoo. If you'd like to bestow goodness upon a friend, be sure to see the group of gift assortments—nicely packaged selections of favorites, at reasonable prices.

Special Factors: Price quote by phone or letter; quantity discounts are available; authorized returns are accepted within 10 days; store is closed Saturdays; C.O.D. orders are accepted; orders are shipped worldwide.

E.C. KRAUS WINE & BEERMAKING SUPPLIES

**P.O. BOX 7850-WC
INDEPENDENCE, MO
64053
816/254-7448**

Catalog: free
Save: up to 40%
Pay: check, MO, MC, V
Sells: wine- and beer-making supplies
Store: 9001 E. 24 Hwy., Independence, MO; Monday to Friday 8–5:30, Saturday 9–1

$$$ ☎

E.C. Kraus, founded in 1967, can help you save up to half of the cost of wine and even more on liqueurs by producing them yourself. The firm's 16-page catalog features supplies and equipment for the home vintner and brewer, and even includes several beer recipes.

Kraus sells everything you'll need to produce your own beverages: malt and hops, fruit and grape concentrates, yeasts, additives, clarifiers, purifiers and preservatives, fruit acids, acidity indicators, hydrometers, bottle caps, rubber stoppers, corks and corkscrews, barrel spigots and liners, oak kegs, tubing and siphons, Mehu-Maya steam juicers, fermenters, fruit presses, dried botanicals, and much more. The T. Noirot extracts can be used to create low-priced liqueurs, and there are books and manuals to provide help if you want to learn more. If you're just getting started, you may find the Kraus "Necessities Box"—equipment and supplies for making five gallons of wine or four gallons of beer—just what you need.

Special Factors: Local ordinances may regulate production of alcoholic beverages; minimum order is $5 with credit cards.

THE MAPLES FRUIT FARM, INC.

**P.O. BOX 167
CHEWSVILLE, MD 21721
301/733-0777**

Catalog: free
Save: up to 50%
Pay: check, MO, MC, V
Sells: dried fruit, nuts, etc.
Store: 1875 Pennsylvania Ave., Hagerstown, MD; Monday to Thursday 9–6, Friday 9–7, Saturday 8–5

The 16-page catalog of dried fruits, nuts, coffee, tea, and sweets from Maples Fruit Farm pictures an early view of the Farm, which has been operated by the same family for 200 years. The prices here are mouth-watering—we found savings of 25% to 50% on the items we comparison-shopped.

The dried fruits include apricots, dates, pears, peaches, and pineapple. (Fruits prepared with sulphur dioxide are clearly indicated in the catalog.) Raw and roasted (salted and unsalted) nuts are offered, including cashews, almonds, peanuts, pecans, macadamia nuts, filberts, black walnuts, and a number of others, including trail mix. We compared several food catalogs and found that two pounds of raw pecans from Maples were 50% less expensive than those from a specialty pecan source, and the roasted macadamia nuts, honey-roasted peanuts, and cashews were all better buys here. Among sweets, Maryland grade-A amber maple syrup costs about 35% less than the syrup offered by competitors (who sold Canadian and New York state products). Maples Fruit Farm also sells 38 kinds of gourmet coffee and tea from Benchley, Celestial Seasonings, and Twining.

Reasonably priced gift baskets are available, and if you can stock up or share orders, check the *wholesale* prices on cases.

Special Factor: Satisfaction is guaranteed.

MR. SPICEMAN, INC.

169-06 CROCHERON AVE., DEPT. Q-1 AUBURNDALE, NY 11358 718/358-5020

Catalog: $1, deductible
Save: up to 94%
Pay: check, MO, MC, V
Sells: herbs, spices, seasonings, and candy
Store: same address; Friday 8–5 (8–noon in June, July, and August)

$$$ ☎ ✦ 🇺🇸

Mr. Spiceman publishes a catalog that runs from soup to nuts, but is best known for great buys on herbs, spices, and other seasonings. Founded in 1965, this firm supplies restaurants, delis, and fine food outlets, as well as consumers, at savings that average from 40% to 60%.

The catalog lists over 130 herbs and spices, available in small and bulk packaging, including ground allspice, cayenne pepper, ground cumin, curry powder, paprika, and other basics. Mr. Spiceman sells such unusual seasonings as achiote, juniper berries, cilantro leaves, and freeze-dried shallots, as well as marinade mixes, Mon Cheri chocolates, Ferrero Rocher confections, Tic Tac mints, crystallized ginger, Knorr soup and sauce mixes, Gravy Master flavoring, 4C products, and Virginia Dare extracts and flavorings. A number of kitchen gadgets are available, including an expanding spatula, a zucchini corer, and a pocket citrus peeler.

The prices are excellent, and Mr. Spiceman is bettering them for new customers. As a reader of this book, you may deduct 10% from your first order (computed on the goods total only). This WBMC reader discount expires February 1, 1993.

Special Factors: Call before visiting the retail location; minimum order is $25 with credit cards.

NORTHWESTERN COFFEE MILLS

Catalog: 50¢
Save: up to 40% (see text)
Pay: check, MO, MC, V, AE
Sells: coffee, tea, herbs, spices, and coffee filters
Store: same address

217 N. BROADWAY
MILWAUKEE, WI 53202
800-243-5283
414/276-1031

$$$ ☎ ♦ ▆

If coffee is America's drink, Wisconsin may be harboring a national treasure. It's the home of Northwestern Coffee Mills, which set up shop in 1875 in a town better known for a different sort of brew. Northwestern begins with top-quality Arabica, and roasts each type of bean separately to develop its optimum flavor.

The catalog describes each of the blends, straights, dark roasts, and decaffeinated coffees, noting relative strength, body, aroma, and flavor. Among the blends are American Breakfast, Fancy Dinner Blend (a strong, after-dinner coffee), Mocha Java, a New Orleans chicory blend, and "Stapleton's 1875 Blend," a favorite of local restaurateurs that "stands up well when heated for hours on end." There are fancy straights, including Brazil Santos (when available), Costa Rica Tarrazu, Kenya AA, Colombia Excelso, and Sumatra Lintong. Fully certified Jamaican Blue Mountain coffee from the Mavis Bank Estate is available, as well as estate-grown Java and Hawaiian Kona, Yemen Mocha Mattari (the *real* mocha from Yemen), Celebes Kalosi, and other rare straight coffees. Decaf drinkers can choose from solvent-processed or water-processed blends and straights. Coffee filters for all types of drip and percolator systems are sold, including Chemex, Filtropa, and the Wisconsin-made "Natural Brew" unbleached filters. Braun and Krups grinders and coffee makers are also available.

Although known for its coffee, Northwestern maintains a premium tea department. The catalog describes how tea is grown and processed, tea grading, and the types of teas it Northwestern sells: flavored, black, green, oolong, and decaffeinated. The varieties include Ceylon, Indian Assam, Indian Darjeeling, Irish Breakfast, Russian Caravan, Japan Sencha, "China Dragon Well Panfired Leaf," and Orange Spiced tea, among others. Last but not least, Northwestern sells herbs, spices, and other flavorings in supermarket sizes and in bulk. Several capsicums (peppers) are offered, and dried vegetables (garlic granules, horseradish powder, mushrooms, etc.), blended salt-free and salted seasonings, and natural extracts (vanilla, almond, cocoa, cinnamon, orange, etc.) are also listed. You can use these extracts, says Northwestern, to create flavored coffees (which it does not sell).

Northwestern's prices on single pounds of coffee or four-ounce packages of tea are market-rate, but the firm will sell both to consumers at bulk rates—something other distributors of premium coffees are reluctant to do. There are price breaks at 6 and 24 pounds, and discounts on coffee bought in bulk. Since coffee in whole-bean form will keep well for several months in the freezer, it makes sense to order as much as you can store. Do sample before buying, though—order half a pound of the intended brew to make sure it's what you want.

Special Factors: Satisfaction is guaranteed; quantity discounts are available; returns are accepted within 1 year for exchange, refund, or credit; orders are shipped worldwide.

PALMER'S MAPLE SYRUP

**BOX 246
WAITSFIELD, VT 05673-
9711
802/496-3696**

Brochure and Price List: free
Save: 33% plus (see text)
Pay: check, MO, AE
Sells: maple syrup
Store: same address; call for hours

$$ ☎

The Palmers have been sugaring since 1967, and in early spring they head for the woods to draw the sap that will be transformed into a season's worth of maple syrup. The brochure describes the entire process, including grading and canning, and gives the recipe for the raised doughnuts that Mrs. Palmer serves to visitors who drop by during the sugaring season.

And the Palmers are nice when it comes to the price, which at this writing is $11.40 a quart, compared to $16.95 for the same grade of Vermont syrup sold through a gourmet foods catalog we checked. Even the Palmers' highest per-ounce price, for half-pints, is lower by a third than what other mail-order firms are charging. The Palmers sell three grades of syrup—light amber (Fancy), medium amber (A), and dark amber (B)—at the same price. If you like a very delicate flavor, try the Fancy grade; grade B has a strong "mapley" flavor that suits some palates and purposes (cooking and baking) more than the other two grades. Maple cream and candies may also be available; see the price list for information.

Please note: "Log cabin" tins hold 16.9 ounces.

Special Factor: Price quote by phone or letter.

PENDERY'S INC.

304 E. BELKNAP ST., DEPT. W FT. WORTH, TX 76102-2296 800-533-1870 817/332-3871 FAX: 817/332-7230

Catalog: $2
Save: up to 75%
Pay: check, MO, MC, V, AE
Sells: herbs, spices, and Mexican seasonings
Store: same address; Monday to Friday 8:30–5:30, Saturday 9–5

$$$ ☎ 🍁 ▆

Pendery's has been spicing up drab dishes since 1870, and can add the authentic touch of real, full-strength chiles to your Tex-Mex cuisine for a fraction of the prices charged by gourmet shops. The firm's 32-page catalog describes the origins of the company and its contributions to the development of Tex-Mex chile seasonings. It's not a coincidence that "those captivating capsicums" occupy three catalog pages and include pods, ground peppers, and blends. Scores of general and specialty seasonings and flavorings are offered, including fajita seasoning, jalapeño peppers, and spice-rack standards from allspice to white pepper. Among the unusual or hard-to-find ingredients available here are masa harina, Mexican chocolate, annatto, horseradish powder, Worchestershire powder, dehydrated cilantro, corn shucks for tamales and cornhusk dolls, and dried diced tomatoes. The catalog also offers handsome, handblown Mexican glassware, dried flowers and other potpourri ingredients, and related gifts. Prices of the spices are far lower than those charged by gourmet stores and supermarkets—up to 75% less on some of the specialty seasonings.

Special Factor: Price quote by phone or letter with SASE.

SAN FRANCISCO HERB CO.

**250 14TH ST., DEPT. W
SAN FRANCISCO, CA
  94103
800-227-4530
IN CA 800-622-0768
415/861-7174
FAX: 415/861-4440**

Catalog with Recipes: free
Save: 50% plus
Pay: check, MO, MC, V
Sells: culinary herbs and spices and
  potpourri ingredients
Store: (wholesale outlet) same address;
  Monday to Friday 10–4

$$$ ☎ ◆ ▆

Reader-recommended San Francisco Herb is known for its excellent prices and selections of herbs, spices, potpourri ingredients, fragrance oils, botanicals, and teas. This 19-year-old firm is primarily a wholesaler, but if you can meet the minimum order of $30, you'll find San Francisco Herb a valuable source.

The culinary herbs and spices offered here range from the routine—allspice, cinnamon, marjoram, tarragon—to such uncommon seasonings as spice blends for Greek foods and cilantro leaf. Among the botanicals are alfalfa leaf, balsam fir needles, chamomile, kelp powder, lavender, nettle leaf, orris root, pine cones, rosebuds, pennyroyal, spearmint leaf, and yerba maté. (Some of these are suitable for consumption, and others aren't; check with a reliable information source before ingesting botanicals in any form.) Recipes for mulling spice blends, no-salt flavor enhancers, bouquet garni, and garam masala (a spice blend used in Indian cuisine) are all available.

The catalog also features dozens of recipes for sachets and simmering and jar potpourris. San Francisco Herb has sent us recipe samples of "Hollyberry Christmas Jar Potpourri," which has a delectable scent and lovely combination of colors, and "Plantation Peach," which is delightfully fruity. If you're not experienced in making potpourri, we strongly recommend trying some of the recipes to become more familiar with blending colors and fragrances.

The spices and botanicals are sold by the pound (selected items are available in four-ounce units), with quantity discounts of 10% on purchases of five pounds or more of the same item. San Francisco Herb also sells flavored teas in bulk, dehydrated vegetables, shelled nuts, sprouting seeds, and such miscellaneous food goods as arrowroot powder, bacon bits, and tapioca pearls. Prices of some of the items we checked were 70% below those of other sources, and satisfaction is guaranteed.

Special Factors: Satisfaction is guaranteed; volume discounts are available; authorized returns are accepted within 15 days (a 15% restocking fee may be charged); minimum order is $30; C.O.D. orders are accepted.

SIMPSON & VAIL, INC.

**P.O. BOX 309
38 CLINTON ST.
PLEASANTVILLE, NY
10570-0309
914/747-1336**

Catalog: free
Save: up to 30%
Pay: check, MO, MC, V
Sells: coffees, teas, brewing accessories, and gourmet foods
Store: same address; Monday to Friday 9–5:30. Saturday 9–4:30

Simpson & Vail, established in 1929, sells gourmet coffees at prices up to 30% less than those charged by many New York City bean boutiques. Over 50 coffees are offered, including American (brown), French, Viennese, and Italian roasts, Kenya AA, Tanzanian Peaberry, Hawaiian Kona, Sumatra Mandehling Kasho, and other straight coffees and blends. The water-process decaffeinated line includes American-style roast, espresso, Mocha Java, Tip of the Andes, and others. Coffee-making gear and supplies by Krups and Melitta are available.

The tea department features over 80 varieties, among them the classics of England and the East, blends, naturally flavored connoisseur teas (raspberry, vanilla, watermelon, coconut, etc.), and selected decaffeinated teas. You'll also find tea accessories—infusers and balls, strainers, and filters—as well as teapots, bone china mugs, tea cozies, warmers, canisters, tea bricks, and tea towels. The teapots range in capacity from one to ten cups, and include glass, terra cotta, and earthenware models.

Simpson & Vail also stocks such temptations as butter cakes from Vermont, Scottish shortbread, fudge sauces, soups by Abbott's, preserves, jams, marmalades, Patak Indian foods, Peloponnese Greek delicacies, and the delectable lines of Italian foodstuffs and condiments from Balducci's and Dean & Deluca.

Readers of this book may deduct 10% of the goods total from their first order only. Remember to identify yourself as a WBMC reader when you order. This WBMC reader discount expires February 1, 1993.

Special Factors: All beans are ground to order; gift packages are available; orders are shipped worldwide.

THE SPICE HOUSE

P.O. BOX 1633-W
MILWAUKEE, WI 53201
414/768-8799

Catalog: $1
Save: 35% average (see text)
Pay: check, MO, MC, V
Sells: seasonings
Store: 1048 N. Old World 3rd St.,
Milwaukee, WI; Monday to Saturday 10–5

$$$$ ☎ 🍁 ▀

The Spice House is a family-run firm that "grinds and blends our spices weekly to insure freshness," something no one else in the business seems to be doing. The selection is extraordinary—there are 11 forms and types of cinnamon, for example. The Spice House, established in 1957, prices even one-ounce sizes of seasonings at below-supermarket rates and offers savings of up to 40% on full pounds.

The informative, 24-page catalog begins with sweet California basil and ends with Tahiti vanilla beans. In between, you'll find Brady Street Cheese Sprinkle, Bicentennial "Rub" Seasoning (an early American blend), cassia buds from China, cardamom, chili peppers (rated for heat in Skoval units), tandoori chicken seasoning, fenugreek seeds, mulled wine spices, "Old World Seasoning," pot herbs for soups and stews, Spanish saffron, seasonings for salad dressings and homemade sausages, star anise, taco seasoning, French tarragon, and many other straight seasonings and blends. (Nearly three dozen are offered in salt-free versions, and The Spice House also offers a line of soup bases.) The descriptions include provenance, ingredients in the blends, and suggested uses.

The Spice House has also assembled some intriguing gift packages, including "Spicy Wedding," "Great Baker's Assortment," "Indian Curries," and a "Spice Replacement" set (when "the love of your life has left you taking all of your spices, maybe your house burned down or was just swept away by a tornado/hurricane"). Zassenhaus pepper mills and inexpensive jars for herb and spice storage are also available.

Special Factors: Satisfaction is guaranteed; price quote by phone or letter with SASE; returns are accepted for exchange, refund, or credit; orders are shipped worldwide.

SULTAN'S DELIGHT, INC.

P.O. BOX 140253
STATEN ISLAND, NY
10314-0014
718/720-1557

Catalog: free with a stamped, self-addressed envelope
Save: up to 50%
Pay: check, MO, MC, V
Sells: Middle Eastern foods and gifts
Store: mail order only

Authentic Middle Eastern food specialties are sold by Sultan's Delight at excellent prices—up to 50% below comparable goods in gourmet shops. The firm was established in 1980, and offers both raw ingredients and prepared specialties, including the Near East and Sahadi lines of foods. See the catalog if you're looking for canned tahini, couscous, tabouleh, fig and quince jams, stuffed grapevine leaves, bulghur, green wheat, orzo, fava beans, Turkish figs, or pickled okra. You'll also find olives, herbs and spices, jumbo pistachios and other nuts, roasted chick peas, halvah, Turkish delight, marzipan paste, olive oil, Turkish coffee, fruit leather, filo, feta cheese, and other specialties are offered as well. Cookbooks for Greek, Lebanese, and Middle Eastern cuisine are available, as are gifts, belly-dancing clothing and accessories, cookware, and related items.

Sultan's Delight is offering readers of this book a 10% discount on their first order (computed on the goods total only). Identify yourself as a reader when you order. This WBMC reader discount expires February 1, 1993.

Special Factors: Price quote by phone or letter with SASE; minimum order is $15; orders are shipped worldwide.

ELBRIDGE C. THOMAS & SONS

RTE. 4, BOX 336
CHESTER, VT 05143
802/263-5680

Brochure: $1
Save: up to 50% (see text)
Pay: check or MO
Sells: Vermont grade-A maple syrup
Store: mail order only

$$

Mr. Thomas makes and sells the nectar of New England—pure, grade-A Vermont maple syrup. He's been in business since 1938, and his prices on large sizes are as much as 50% lower than those of his competitors—and even better than those charged for lesser grades of non-Vermont syrup.

The stock is pure and simple: Vermont maple syrup, grade A, available in half-pint, pint, quart, half-gallon, and gallon tins. (Plastic containers are available upon request.) Maple sugar cakes, which make irresistible gifts, are also offered (by special order only). The brochure includes a number of suggestions for using maple syrup in your favorite foods—maple milk shakes, maple ham, frosting, and baked beans are just a few examples.

Special Factors: Quantity discounts are available; prices are subject to change without notice; orders are shipped worldwide.

WALNUT ACRES ORGANIC FARMS

PENNS CREEK, PA 17862
800-433-3998

Catalog: free
Save: up to 40%
Pay: check, MO, MC, V
Sells: organically grown foods, natural toiletries, cookware, etc.
Store: Penns Creek, PA; Monday to Saturday 8–5, Friday 9–8

$$

Walnut Acres Organic Farms, in business since 1946, sells organically grown foods, nutritional supplements, cookbooks, and related items. Most of the goods are produced at Walnut Acres, grown on "500 acres of chemical-free soil." The catalog presents the bounty in full, appetizing color: grains, cereals, granola, bread and pancake mixes, flours, seeds and nuts, nut butters, soups, salad dressings, sauces, pasta, dried fruits, juices, honeys, and other goods. Herbs and spices, relishes, dehydrated vegetables, canned fruits, vegetables, and beans, powdered milk, crackers, jams and preserves, cheeses, and baked goods are also offered. Walnut Acres sells nutritional supplements and some natural toiletries and unguents as well, and a variety of products "friendly to the environment."

Prices are not uniformly low, but most of those we spot-checked against two local health-food stores were at least 10% below the going rate for comparable items. We did find savings of 30% to 40%, however, on the dried fruits and nuts (compared to other mail-order sources). These were pound-for-pound comparisons; Walnut Acres sells its nuts, seeds, grains, cereals, and dried fruits in bulk packages (three and five pounds) at additional savings.

Special Factors: Products are guaranteed to be as represented; orders are shipped worldwide.

WOOD'S CIDER MILL

RD #2, BOX 477
SPRINGFIELD, VT 05156
802/263-5547

Brochure: free with SASE
Save: up to 50% (see text)
Pay: check or MO
Sells: cider jelly and syrup
Store: mail order only

$$ ✦ ▬▬

The Wood family has maintained a farm in Vermont since 1798 and today produces several wonderful treats for mail-order customers. The prices are better than reasonable—in fact, we've found Wood's cider jelly selling in other catalogs at prices nearly twice as high as those charged by the Woods themselves! Buying from the Woods directly gives you another benefit—the chance to order other wonderful things.

The Cider Mill is best known for its jelly, which is made of evaporated apple cider. From 30 to 50 apples are needed to make the cider that is concentrated in just one pound of jelly, but you'll understand why when you taste it on toast or muffins, or try it with pork and other meats as a condiment. Boiled cider is also available; it's a less-concentrated essence that is recommended as a base for a hot drink, as a ham glaze, and as a topping for ice cream and pancakes. For pancakes, however, our personal preference is the cider syrup, a blend of boiled cider and maple syrup. (We've also had outstanding success using it to baste Thanksgiving turkeys, and even roast chicken.) Straight maple syrup is also produced on the farm, and even the farm's sheep contribute to the offerings: natural and black two-ply yarns are sold through the brochure as well.

Special Factors: Satisfaction is guaranteed; returns are accepted for exchange or refund; quantity discounts are available; orders are shipped worldwide.

SEE ALSO

Cabela's Inc. • freeze-dried foods, trail packs • *SPORTS*

Campmor • dehydrated camping food, beef jerky, etc. • *SPORTS*

Caprilands Herb Farm • live and dried herbs, herbal vinegars, and teas • *FARM*

A Cook's Wares • gourmet vinegars, mustards, and other foods and condiments • *HOME: KITCHEN*

New England Cheesemaking Supply Co. • cheese-making supplies and equipment • *HOME: KITCHEN*

The Paper Wholesaler • catering supplies, restaurant paper goods, disposable tableware • *GENERAL MERCHANDISE*

Plastic BagMart • plastic food storage bags • *GENERAL: PACKAGING*

Protecto-Pak • zip-top plastic bags • *GENERAL: PACKAGING*

Fred Stoker and Sons, Inc. • popcorn and table syrup • *CIGARS*

Survival Supply Co. • dehydrated and "survival" food • *SPORTS*

Triner Scale • pocket scale • *OFFICE*

Weston Bowl Mill • sugar buckets and butter churns • *GENERAL MERCHANDISE*

Zabar's & Co., Inc. • gourmet foods and condiments • *HOME: KITCHEN*

GENERAL MERCHANDISE, BUYING CLUBS, GREAT SALES, AND GOOD VALUES

Firms and buying clubs offering a wide range of goods and services

Most of the firms listed in this chapter offer such a wide range of products that it might be confusing to put them elsewhere. So you'll find companies selling everything from mosquito netting to archival-quality document boxes. Go through the listings carefully, since there are some real finds here, and countless answers to the question of what to give for Christmas, birthdays, anniversaries, and other occasions.

We've added "great sales" to the scope of this chapter, because we wanted to be able to mention firms that don't sell at a *discount,* but run frequent catalog markdowns. Please note that many mail-order firms send their best sale catalogs or inserts to their best customers, so you may not receive more than one edition of a catalog—or the sale "book"—unless you place an order.

Shopping has become much easier thanks to 800 lines, but there's a lot more available through toll-free numbers than merchandise, including travel and lodging reservations, banking and investment assistance, product information and advice, and a wide range of services. The *AT&T Toll-Free 800 Consumer Directory* is a big help in finding 800 numbers quickly; it has over 50,000 listings, in categories ranging from accountants to yarn. The current (consumer) edition costs $9.95 (plus sales tax and handling), and can be ordered by calling 800-451-2100.

AMERICAN ASSOCIATION OF RETIRED PERSONS

**1909 K ST., N.W.
WASHINGTON, DC 20049
202/872-4700**

Information: inquire
Save: up to 40% (see text)
Pay: check, MO, MC, V
Sells: membership (see text)
Store: mail order only

$$$ ☎

The American Association of Retired Persons is a not-for-profit organization dedicated to improving the lives of older Americans, especially in the areas of finances and health. Membership is open to anyone aged 50 or older, retired or not, at a cost of just $5 a year. Among the benefits are subscriptions to the bimonthly *Modern Maturity* and the monthly *AARP News Bulletin,* the opportunity to buy low-cost supplemental health insurance, participation in AARP Federal Credit Union, the AARP Motoring Plan (affiliated with Amoco Motor Club), publications on health topics, discounts on hotels and car rentals, and access to a pharmacy-by-mail. (See the listing for Retired Persons Services in "Medicine" for more details.)

When you write to the AARP for membership information, you can request the group's publication, "Prescription for Action." This is a 68-page guide to approaching health care issues on a collective, community level. It gives guidelines and ideas for conducting price-comparison surveys of prescription drugs, compiling directories of physicians in your area who accept Medicare/Medicaid, cataloguing services for seniors, having a voice in government, and promoting proven alternative-care options and long-term home care. The book is a compendium of ideas, resources, and references—a great source for health-care activists.

Special Factor: Inquire for information.

BENNETT BROTHERS, INC.

30 E. ADAMS ST.
CHICAGO, IL 60603
312/263-4800
FAX: 312/621-1669
AND
211 ISLAND RD.
MAHWAH, NJ 07430
201/529-1900
FAX: 201/529-7855

Catalog: $5, redeemable
Save: up to 40%
Pay: check, MO, MC, V
Sells: jewelry, appliances, electronics, luggage, furnishings, etc.
Store: in Chicago: Monday to Friday 8:15–5 (see the catalog for holiday shopping hours); in New Jersey: Monday to Saturday 9–5:30

$$$ ☎

At the turn of the century, much of Bennett Brothers' business was in jewelry, gems, and watches. That's still a big part of the company's trade, but Bennett's current offerings, shown in the annual "Blue Book," also include giftware, leather goods, electronics, cameras, sporting goods, and toys.

The Blue Book is 450 color pages of name-brand goods, most of which make ideal gifts. (In fact, the firm's "Choose-Your-Gift" program is one of the easiest ways to deliver presents to employees and business associates.) Jewelry takes 200 pages of the catalog—wedding and engagement bands, pearls, pins and bracelets, necklaces, and other pieces featuring all kinds of precious and semiprecious gems, as well as charms, lockets, medallions, anniversary jewelry, Masonic rings, and crosses and religious jewelry. Traditional and contemporary looks are both featured, and there are moderately priced pieces. The watch department offers models from Armitron, Benrus, Citizen, Jules Jurgensen, Pulsar, Seiko, and Timex.

Bennett Brothers offers a fine selection of clocks, timepieces, and weather instrument stations. Silverware and chests, a beautiful collection of silver-plated and sterling silver giftware, tea sets, pewterware, and fine china are also sold. The catalog shows kitchen cutlery sets, cookware sets, small kitchen appliances, microwave ovens, barbecue grills, vacuum cleaners, air machines, exercise equipment, sewing machines, personal-care appliances, bed linens, towels, tablecloths, and luggage. The leather goods department is especially good, including briefcases and attaché cases and luggage from American Tourister, Elco, Monarch, Samsonite, and Winn.

The Blue Book also features a large group of personal electronics and office supplies—clock radios, portable cassette players, stereo systems and components, TVs and video equipment, phones and answering machines, CB equipment, home security systems, Casio keyboards, cameras, projectors, telescopes, binoculars, microscopes, pens, globes, cash registers, calculators, typewriters, safes, files, and office furnishings. Home furnishings are also available, including reproduction Victorian pieces, Couristan rugs, Douglas dinette sets, Lane chests, patio furniture, Stakmore and Kestell folding bridge tables and chairs, and other goods. The catalog includes Playskool toys, Bachman collectors' trains, Cox radio-controlled cars and planes, playing cards, and board games. There are also golf clubs, basket-balls, volleyballs and nets, gun cabinets, hunting knives, fishing rods, bocce ball and croquet game sets, dart boards, and sleeping bags. Metal detectors, flashlights and emergency beams, and even weather-vanes, lawnmowers, chain saws, and other power and hand tools are offered.

Bennett's prices are listed next to "suggested retail" prices throughout the book. After comparing prices of several types of goods, we concluded that Bennett's guideline prices (suggested retail) are fair and reliable. On that basis, we found that you can save between 30% and 40% here.

Special Factor: Authorized returns are accepted within 10 days for exchange or credit.

CLOTHCRAFTERS, INC.

P.O. BOX 176, DEPT.
  WM92
ELKHART LAKE, WI 53020
414/876-2112

Catalog: free
Save: up to 40%
Pay: check, MO, MC, V
Sells: home textiles
Store: mail order only

$$$ ☎ ▆

This firm, established in 1936, sells "plain vanilla" textile goods of every sort, from cheesecloth by the yard to flannel patches for cleaning guns. There are many inexpensive, useful items in the 16-page catalog, including a host of practical household goods: pot holders, red and white dish towels, chefs' hats, bouquet garni bags (12 for $3), salad greens bags, fabric coffee filters, striped denim place mats, cotton napkins ($9 per dozen), hot pads, and aprons. Clothcrafters has expanded its selection of well-priced kitchen tools, which include parchment paper, rubber spatulas, oven gloves, nut choppers, vegetable peelers, and other handy utensils.

You'll also find laundry bags, tote bags, flannel shoe bags, woodpile covers and firewood carriers, garment bags, cider-press liners, flannel polishing squares, and mosquito netting. The bed and bath department offers cotton duck shower curtains, lightweight cotton terry towels and bath wraps, terry tunics, beach mats, barbers' capes, cotton flannel sheets, pillowcases, sleeping bag liners, and crib sheets. Three kinds of cloth diapers are available. Textile artists should appreciate this source, since many of these items can be painted, embroidered, dyed, and otherwise embellished.

Gardeners will find the "PlyBan" porous plastic sheeting ideal for protecting newly planted rows from frost and insects ($8 for 4' by 50'). If you garden during the high insect season, you might want to add the mosquito-netting helmet to your order. While you're at it, consider the multi-pocketed apron—it has places for the trowel, seed packets, string, and all those stones that turn up. And don't overlook the denim knee pads—they fasten with Velcro, and are machine washable.

Canadian readers, please note: Only U.S. funds are accepted.

Special Factors: Satisfaction is guaranteed; shipping and insurance are included on orders over $15; returns are accepted for exchange, refund, or credit.

BETTY CROCKER ENTERPRISES

GENERAL MILLS, INC.
P.O. BOX 5347
MINNEAPOLIS, MN 55460
612/540-2464
FAX: 612/540-7995

Catalog: 50¢
Save: up to 77% (see text)
Pay: check, MO, MC, V
Sells: table settings, kitchenware, housewares, toys, etc.
Store: mail order only

$$$ ☎

Betty Crocker, one of the most successful marketing creations in the history of prepared foods, has an image built on helping homemakers make the most of their time and money. All of her mixes and snacks—from Hamburger Helper to Nature Valley Granola Bars—bear coupons good for "Betty Crocker Points," which can be collected and applied toward the purchase of items from the Betty Crocker catalog. And if you've never sent the 50¢ requested to get the catalog, do it now—the coupons you've been saving (or tossing out with the empty package) are worth real money on a wide range of goods.

Tableware is featured in the catalog, including Oneida Community flatware, china from Fiesta, Franciscan, Oneida, Pfaltzgraff, and Royal Albert, and pretty crystal stemware from Oneida. Silverware chests and zippered storage units for china are available, as well as Armetale pewter serving pieces, all sorts of bakeware, Regal cookware, cutlery, kitchen gadgets, a line of scissors, and the Betty Crocker cookbook collection. And there are pages of educational toys, games, and puzzles, several patterns of children's tableware, and home entertaining helps like Regal's coffee urns (55 and 101 cups), bridge tables and chairs, popcorn bowls, and teak snack tables.

Each item has three prices: the "regular" selling price (usually list), the reduced price if you include 3 Betty Crocker Points, and the lowest price, which you pay if you ante up a lot more Points. For example, Oneida silverplate flatware, with a suggested list price of $44.95 per place setting, costs just $12.25—plus 85 Betty Crocker Points. The "Learn to Tell Time" clock drops from $25.95 to $17.95 with 45 Points, and Mirro's kitchen timer costs $9.50 with 15 Points, $12.95 without. And the Points are easy to acquire—they're on all the Betty Crocker and General Mills products, and the catalog itself comes with 100 freebies, as well as $3 in food coupons!

Special Factors: Satisfaction is guaranteed; returns are accepted for exchange, refund, or credit; minimum order is $20 with credit cards.

DEWYNTERS LICENSING & DISTRIBUTION

116 W. 29TH ST., 12A
NEW YORK, NY 10001
212/268-6660
FAX: 212/268-6437

Catalog: free
Save: up to 30%
Pay: check or MO
Sells: Broadway show-theme gifts
Store: mail order only

$

Successful Broadway shows seem to inspire especially striking graphics and promotional art. If you've been struck by the image of a particular play—the mask of *The Phantom of the Opera,* or the little waif of *Les Misérables*—you'll be pleased to find them here at Dewynters on T-shirts, sweatshirts, mugs, and other useful items. Dewynters, which is the exclusive merchandiser for Broadway shows, also offers souvenirs of *Miss Saigon, Cats,* and *Black and Blue.* These gifts are less expensive here than they are through gift shops—T-shirts cost $13, Buddy Holly sunglasses are $6, and a Les Mis poster is $6 as well. New shows and gifts are added regularly, and if you're looking for items for a play or event not represented, call or write to see if they're available.

Special Factors: Price quote by phone or letter; C.O.D. orders are accepted.

GRAND FINALE

SUBSCRIPTIONS DEPT.
P.O. BOX 620049
DALLAS, TX 75262-0049
800-955-9595

Catalog: $3, year's subscription, refundable
Save: up to 60%
Pay: check, MO, MC, V, AE, Discover,
   Optima
Sells: upmarket and name-brand goods
Store: mail order only

$$$ ☎ ♣ ▆

Your catalog fee brings you a year of "luxury for less," 48 pages of special values, clearances, and closeouts from well-known catalogs. It's possible to save up to 70% on the original selling or list prices through Grand Finale.

Past catalogs have featured designer clothing, silver fish charm necklaces for cats, hand-embroidered table linens, leather desk sets, Hekman entertainment cabinets, cashmere sweaters, ceramic garden seats, needlepoint pillows, fashion jewelry, and Christmas decorations. Almost every catalog offers side tables, toys, Limoges bibelots, coasters, luggage, designer bed linens, rugs, cookware, flatware, fine china and crystal, and women's clothing. There's usually a sale section in the catalog featuring exceptional bargains; quantities of these items are limited, so order promptly. The quality is consistently high, and Grand Finale provides a gift boxing service ($2) and can forward presents to recipients directly.

Special Factors: Satisfaction is guaranteed; quantities are limited, so order promptly; returns are accepted for exchange, refund, or credit; orders are shipped worldwide.

LANDS' END, INC.

**LANDS' END LANE
DODGEVILLE, WI 53595-
0001
800-356-4444**

Catalog: free
Save: up to 40%
Pay: check, MO, MC, V, AE
Sells: clothing for men, women, and children
Store: 4320 New York St., Aurora, IL; 2241 and 2317 N. Elston Ave., Chicago, IL; 6131 Dempster, Morton Grove, IL; 15782 La Grange Rd., Orland Park, IL; 251 W. Golf, Schaumburg, IL; and #20 Yorktown Convenience Center, Lombard, IL; 6743 Odana Rd. and 411 S. State, Madison, WI

Lands' End began life in 1963, in the basement of a building on Chicago's waterfront. You can find the original store there still (as "Lands' End Outlet"), but the Lands' End of the well-priced buttondown is now doing business from the farmlands of Wisconsin. The firm sells good-quality, traditional and casual clothing and accessories for men, women, and children, as well as a popular line of canvas luggage and portfolios, bed linens, and other housewares. The monthly catalogs usually include "Lands' End Outlet," several pages of items featuring markdowns of up to 55%. We've had good experiences ordering from Lands' End and this section in particular, and suggest that you call if you're mailing your order in order to make sure stock is available. (Stock is checked automatically when you order by phone.) Good color selection is a strong feature here, as well as sizing—most women's wear runs to size 16, and many of the men's shirts are stocked in regular and long.

Special Factors: Satisfaction is guaranteed; returns are accepted.

LINCOLN HOUSE, INC.

300 GREENBRIER RD.-
  WBM92
SUMMERSVILLE, WV
  26651
304/872-3000

Catalog: free
Save: up to 40%
Pay: check, MO, MC, V
Sells: stationery, gifts, decorations, etc.
Store: mail order only

$$$ ☎ 🇺🇸

Lincoln House publishes a 48-page catalog of gifts, home accents, and stationery items that are offered at savings of up to 40% compared to goods of equal quality sold by other firms. Past catalogs have shown mug and place mat sets, brass candlesticks, scented candles, jewelry, memo boards, ceramic picture frames, kitchen gadgets, and recipe files. Stationery, gift wrappings, paperweights, and similar goods are always available, and the themes are cute and whimsical. The fall catalog includes a good selection of holiday items: Christmas ornaments, decorations, candles, decorated cookie tins, gift bags, and cards.

Lincoln House rewards dedicated shoppers with discounts of about 20% on purchases of 6 to 15 items, and up to 40% if the purchase numbers 16 or more items. Most of the goods are made by the firm's parent company, Bright of America, which has been in business since 1964.

Special Factors: Satisfaction is guaranteed; shipping and insurance are included; returns are accepted.

MATURE OUTLOOK

6001 N. CLARK ST.
CHICAGO, IL 60660-9977
800-336-6330

Information: inquire
Save: see text
Pay: check, MO, MC, V, Discover,
  SearsCharge
Sells: club memberships
Store: mail order only

$$ ☎

If you're over 50, you can enjoy the benefits of membership in Mature Outlook, one of the programs in the Sears umbrella of services.

Mature Outlook began life several years ago as a travel opportunities program, but in 1988 it was retools, with new perks, for the 50-plus age group.

A year of membership costs $9.95 and includes your spouse, regardless of age. You'll receive $100 in "Sears Money," coupons that can be redeemed with purchases at Sears stores or affiliates, travel discounts (last-minute tours and cruises), savings of 10% and 20% on dining and accommodations at any of the 1,400 participating Holiday Inns, discounts on car rentals (Avis, Hertz, National, Sears/Budget), and savings at Sears optical departments. You also receive the bimonthly *Mature Outlook,* a magazine with useful articles on travel, health, food, decorating and home improvement, and finances, and the *Mature Outlook Newsletter.* The price for all this, $9.95, seems more than reasonable. The only negative: If you pay for membership with a credit card, your card will be billed automatically for membership renewal each year. Mature Outlook makes no secret of this, but we know that some people dislike this feature. So if you'd like to receive subscription renewal notices (like those for magazine subscriptions) instead, simply pay by check or money order.

Special Factor: Memberships charged to credit cards are renewed automatically.

NEW ENGLAND BASKET CO.

P.O. BOX 1335
N. FALMOUTH, MA 02556
508/759-2000

Brochure and Price List: free
Save: up to 50%
Pay: check, MO, MC, V
Sells: baskets
Store: mail order only

$$ ☎ 🍁

New England Basket Co. sells a variety of baskets at prices up to 50% below those charged by some national housewares chains. The firm's 12-page, color brochure shows the kinds of baskets stocked at our local import shop: Tightly woven willow baskets in round, oval, and square shapes; bamboo trays, picnic hampers, rustic rattan baskets, and "country" baskets with a wash of white or soldier blue were among over 144 shown. Dimensions of each basket are given, and there are two prices—for one set or piece or one case. In addition to the obvious uses as decorative accents and a place for chips or rolls, don't overlook the possibilities of baskets as great gift containers, closet organizers, pet beds—the list is endless!

Special Factors: Price quote by phone or letter with SASE; quantity discounts are available; minimum order is $26.

THE PAPER WHOLESALER

**795 N.W. 72ND ST.
MIAMI, FL 33150
305/285-9229**

Catalog: $3
Save: up to 30%
Pay: check, MO, MC, V
Sells: party supplies, restaurant disposables
Store: (cash and carry warehouses) 2638 S.W. 28th Lane, Coconut Grove, 10101 NW 79th St., Hialeah, and 8259 W. Flagler, Miami, FL

$$

The Paper Wholesaler gives discounts of 30% on case lots of all kinds of party and entertaining supplies and related goods. The color catalog is full of table goods, decorations, and the little things that add fun to festive occasions: paper plates and napkins in vibrant colors and snappy designs, including ensembles for children's birthdays, wedding parties, and showers; plastic cutlery and cups, tablecloths, doilies, balloons, crepe paper, party hats, streamers and pennants, favors, and other novelties. Guest towels and toilet paper for the powder room are sold here, as well as a good selection of candles, hors d'oeuvre picks and drink stirrers, cocktail napkins with amusing slogans, wrapping paper, gift bags, bows and ribbon, and invitations in upbeat designs and colors.

The Paper Wholesaler has a "serious" section for restaurateurs and caterers, which includes a selection of cake-decorating supplies, cake pans, deli and bakery containers, commercial-sized rolls of foil and poly film, ice scoops and bar tools, carafes, syrup pitchers, ash trays, and even the brooms, mops, and buckets you'll need when the guests are gone. And there's food—restaurant-sized containers of Pepperidge Farm Goldfish, Hellmann's mayonnaise, Orville Redenbacher popcorn, Planter's peanuts, and other condiments and snacks. The catalog includes tips on party planning, and the order form even features shopping lists so you don't overlook anything.

Special Factors: Satisfaction is guaranteed; returns of unopened, unused goods are accepted within 30 days for exchange, refund, or credit.

PUEBLO TO PEOPLE

1616 MONTROSE BLVD.,
#5735
HOUSTON, TX 77006
713/523-1197
FAX: 713/523-1614

Catalog: free
Save: up to 40%
Pay: check, MO, MC, V, AE, Discover
Sells: handcrafts of Central and South America
Store: 1985 West Gray, Houston, TX; Monday to Thursday 10–6, Friday 10–7, Saturday 10–6, Sunday 12–5

$$$ ☎ ♦ ▀

Pueblo to People publishes a beautiful and fascinating catalog that is actually a mail-order cooperative, nearly half of whose proceeds go back to the people who produced its goods. Contrary to expectation, the prices here are quite low: We've compared scarves, fabric, toys, jewelry, and other items to similar goods available in import shops in New York City, and found the Pueblo to People prices up to 40% less.

The catalogs feature handsome handcrafts and goods native to South and Central America—organic Peruvian coffee, hand puppets, Guatemalan ikat pillows and jackets, and beautiful little fabric doves are a few of the goods shown in one catalog we reviewed. Pueblo to People sells dozens of books and tapes on the culture and problems of these countries, and the catalogs include extensive discussions of farming, nutrition, health, food aid, and the economic realities of life. If you're interested in the issues, you'll find names and addresses of other not-for-profit assistance groups peppered throughout the catalog, which may be helpful in getting involved. But even if you go no farther than ordering a scarf or tote bag from Pueblo to People, it's nice to know that a good portion of the price goes to help those in need.

Please note: Orders are shipped to U.S. and Canadian postal codes only.

Special Factors: Satisfaction is guaranteed; returns are accepted for exchange, refund, or credit; C.O.D. orders are accepted.

SPIEGEL, INC.

**P.O. BOX 6340
CHICAGO, IL 60680-6340
800-345-4500**

Catalog: $3
Save: up to 50% (see text)
Pay: check, MO, MC, V, AE, Optima
Sells: clothing, home furnishings, electronics, etc.
Store (outlet): Chicago, Villa Park, Countryside, Arlington, and Downers Grove, IL; Monday to Saturday 8–4

$$ ☎ ▆▆(see text)

Spiegel, in business since 1865, has reflected something of the changes in the country in its offerings: In the 1970s, the firm overhauled its image and began to feature clothing and home accessories targeted to the busy working woman. As we move into the more austere 1990s, the focus has shifted to more moderate apparel, though retaining the Spiegel style and verve.

Spiegel's oversized, seasonal catalogs feature clothing and accessories for the whole family, fashionable home furnishings and decorative accents, and appliances. We found a nice collection of labels in the catalog we reviewed—DKNY, Perry Ellis, Adrienne Vittadini, and other names in clothing, and Calico, Joyce, Nickels, and Pappagallo, among others, in the shoe department. The looks and prices speak to the career woman, and her male counterpart is courted with office and weekend wear from Alexander Julian, Perry Ellis, Ralph Lauren, Levi's, and other popular names. The catalog also offers jewelry and watches, leather goods and luggage, and electronics. Home furnishings and decorative accents are one of Spiegel's strong suits, and the catalog routinely offers everything from custom upholstery to copper mold magnets for the refrigerator: a Stanley reproduction Chippendale dining set, Hitchcock occasional furniture, Jay Yang sheets, lace curtains, T-Fal cookware, KitchenAid appliances, and Hoover and Eureka vacuum cleaners were among the nearly 300 pages of treats for the home we saw in the issue we reviewd. If you order from Spiegel regularly, you'll receive sale catalogs with markdowns of up to 60% on many of the goods, and Spiegel's easy-return policy has won it many loyal customers.

APO/FPO readers, please note: Freight deliveries (affecting certain items) cannot be made to APO/FPO addresses.

Special Factors: Ordering from the "big book" usually guarantees later mailings of sale catalogs; returns are accepted for exchange, refund, or credit.

THRIFT CLUB

P.O. BOX 9394
MINNEAPOLIS, MN 55440
800-328-0786
612/540-6122

Information: inquire
Save: up to 50%
Pay: check, MO, MC, V
Sells: memberships in buying club
Store: mail order only

$$$ ☎

The Thrift Club can help you save on everything from dog food to your next car through its various programs. Membership costs $49.95 per year, which can be recouped almost immediately through the "Coupon Exchange." (Membership comes with vouchers that allow you to request $50 in face-value coupons for 1,000 name-brand foods, cleaning products, and health and beauty aids. After claiming your free allotment, you can order new supplies at a cost under one third the face value.)

Couponing is a great way to save nickels and dimes, but Thrift Club membership gives you much more: prescription-filling services at a discount, savings on general merchandise (appliances, electronics, home furnishings, computers, jewelry, musical instruments, and even tapes and CDs), savings on Ryder truck rentals, long-distance service from U.S. Sprint, real estate broker referrals, a 15% discount at Pearle Vision Centers, car pricing and dealer referral services, and travel planning services. Discounts on car rentals from several agencies are possible, as well as savings on hotel accommodations (through the Entertainment program), and even a 5% rebate on air travel and Amtrak booked through Thrift Club's travel agency. Membership includes the quarterly, *Thrift Magazine,* which features an updated list of coupons, specials on household appliances and gifts available through the firm, and articles on saving time and money.

Thrift Club doesn't warehouse products itself, but has arrangements with different vendors to provide goods and services. (Please note that the firm derives no financial benefit from the sale of products or services—except memberships—and has no commission arrangements with the vendors.) The Club's staff can answer any questions you may have about services and membership.

Special Factor: Inquire for information.

LILLIAN VERNON CORPORATION

■■■■■■■■■

P.O. BOX 69-WBMC
MT. VERNON, NY 10551
914/662-5777
FAX: 914/699-7698

Catalog: free
Save: up to 50% (see text)
Pay: check, MO, MC, V, AE, Discover, DC
Sells: gifts, household accessories, personalized items, etc.
Store: 549 Main St., New Rochelle, NY; Monday to Saturday 10–6; also Loehmann's Plaza, 4000 Virginia Beach Blvd., Virginia Beach, VA; Monday to Friday 10–9, Saturday 10-6

$$$

What began with a $495 ad in *Seventeen Magazine* in 1951 has become a direct-mail fairy tale, with revenues of $140.6 million in 1989 and a name that's known to 29 million Americans: Lillian Vernon.

The business began with a personalized shoulder bag and belt, and the color catalogs still feature a number of items that can be engraved or printed with your initials. But Lillian Vernon's strength is in well-priced, well-designed gifts and home accessories. The typical catalog offers seasonal goods, bath accessories, closet organizers, toys and games, travel items, gardening gear, stationery, gift wrapping, and baby things. Customers appreciate the basic good values they find here (the average item costs $15), but there's something even better: *wholesale* pricing. If you're prepared to buy 15 or more of the same item, spending at least $250, you'll qualify for discounts of up to 50%. If you get together with friends, neighbors, and coworkers, you'll probably find a number of items you all want—especially if you're doing holiday shopping. There's no separate edition for the wholesale division; use the current Lillian Vernon catalog, and call or write for a quote. Businesses should note that Lillian Vernon offers a range of special services for corporate gift giving, including personalization.

Special Factors: Satisfaction is guaranteed; price quote by phone or letter with SASE; returns are accepted for exchange, refund, or credit; minimum order is $250, with a 15-piece minimum of each item.

WESTON BOWL MILL

P.O. BOX 218
WESTON, VT 05161
802/824-6219
FAX: 802/824-4215

Catalog: free
Save: up to 30%
Pay: check, MO, MC, V
Sells: woodenware and wooden household items
Store: Main St. (Rte. 100), Weston, VT; Monday to Saturday 9–5, Sunday 10–5

$$$ ☎ 🍁 🇺🇸

Weston is known for its bowls, but the Mill produces hundreds of other wooden items for use throughout the home. Prices of many of the goods in the catalog we reviewed were about 25% below comparable retail, and savings were even better on selected goods. Almost everything is available with and without finish (oil or lacquer).

The popular salad bowls, thick milled curves of wood, are offered in sizes from 6″ to 20″ across. You can save a good deal by buying the seconds (with small flaws that should not affect wear), which cost up to 20% less than the first-quality bowls. Weston sells much more for dining table and kitchen, including birch dinner plates and trays, maple and ash lazy Susans, salt-and-pepper shakers, cheese plates, knife racks, tongs, carving boards, cutting boards, and carbon steel knives.

The 16-page catalog offers a wide variety of other items for the home, including shelves with brackets, towel and tissue holders, spoon racks, pegged coat racks, door chimes, a large selection of wooden boxes, quilt racks, benches, stools, wooden fruits and vegetables, sugar buckets and churns, and baskets. Weston's bird feeders and whirligigs are well priced; likewise the delightful group of wooden toys—vehicles, tops, puzzles, game boards, cradles, and other classics—that are oil-finished. And the "country store" department includes "magic" massagers, lap boards, door stops and window props, outlet plates, spool holders, bells, yardsticks, and many other useful items.

Special Factors: Minimum order is $5, $20 with credit cards; orders are shipped worldwide.

SEE ALSO

Acme Premium Supply Corp. • premium merchandise • *TOYS*

The American Stationery Co., Inc. • custom-printed stationery, wedding invitations • *BOOKS*

Atlantic Bridge Collection Corp. Ltd. • Irish handcrafts and gifts • *ART, ANTIQUES*

Baron/Barclay Bridge Supplies • bridge-playing gifts • *TOYS*

Beauty by Spector, Inc. • wigs and hairpieces for men and women • *HEALTH*

Bruce Medical Supply • dining, dressing, bathing, and other aids for the disabled and motor-impaired • *MEDICINE*

Burden's Surplus Center • wide variety of tools, electrical components, security equipment • *SURPLUS*

Business Technologies • cash registers • *OFFICE*

Caprilands Herb Farm • herb charts, note cards, potpourri, pomanders, etc. • *FARM*

Caviarteria Inc. • gourmet gift assortments • *FOOD*

Current, Inc. • gifts, cards, stationery, etc. • *BOOKS*

The Dog's Outfitter • pet-related gifts • *ANIMAL*

The Emerald Collection • Irish gifts, tableware, and apparel • *HOME: TABLE SETTINGS*

Michael C. Fina Co. • silver and crystal giftware • *HOME: TABLE SETTINGS*

Gohn Bros. • Amish "general store" goods • *CLOTHING*

H & R Company • general surplus goods of all sorts • *SURPLUS*

House of Onyx • imported soapstone, onyx, and other stone art carvings and gifts • *JEWELRY*

D. MacGillivray & Coy. • Scottish tartans, Highland dress accessories, etc. • *CRAFTS*

A.W.G. Otten and Son • carved wooden shoes and clogs • *CLOTHING: FOOTWEAR*

Paradise Products, Inc. • wide variety of party goods • *TOYS*

Pendery's Inc. • potpourri ingredients and gifts • *FOOD*

La Piñata • piñatas • *TOYS*

Plexi-Craft Quality Products Corp. • Lucite and Plexiglas furniture, accessories, and gifts • *HOME: FURNISHINGS*

Rammagerdin • Icelandic yarns, knitwear, and souvenirs • *CLOTHING*

Rapidforms, Inc. • gift boxes and packing and shipping supplies • *OFFICE*

Rocky Mountain Stationery • handmade cards and notes • *BOOKS*

Nat Schwartz & Co., Inc. • bridal registry for gifts • *HOME: TABLE SETTINGS*

Shibui Wallcoverings • handmade wall coverings • *HOME: DECOR*

Albert S. Smyth Co., Inc. • giftware, bridal and gift registry • *HOME: TABLE SETTINGS*

Stecher's Limited • clocks, watches, and giftware • *HOME: TABLE SETTINGS*

R.C. Steele Co. • gifts for pets and owners • *ANIMAL*

Survival Supply Co. • "survivalist" gear, books, and food • *SPORTS*

TAI, Inc. • variety of cloth goods with silk-screened military insignias • *CLOTHING*

Thompson Cigar Company • smoking-related gifts • *CIGARS*

Packaging and Storage

Packing, packaging, and storage materials and equipment for consumer and business use

This section is devoted to things to put other things in—bags, boxes, and other containers, for use in home, office, and industry. We've also included wrapping paper and bows here, since many of the companies that sell them also sell packaging materials. We had hoped to bring you companies that sell recycled packing materials and boxes, but the *consumer* end of the industry is still characterized by outrageously high markups. As the use of recycled materials is mainstreamed and economies of scale kick in, the discounters will appear—and you'll find them here. (In the course of research, we did find a number of good business-to-business sellers. If you're a buyer for a business that wants to switch to environment-friendly mailing products and paper goods, please contact us for more information.)

CHISWICK TRADING, INC.

33 UNION AVE.
SUDBURY, MA 01776-0907
800-322-7772
FAX: 800/638-9899

Catalog: free
Save: up to 35%
Pay: check, MO, MC, V, AE
Sells: resale packaging
Store: mail order only

$$$ ☎ ♦

Chiswick, "America's Leading Supplier of Poly Bags," offers them in sizes from 2½" by 3" to 60" by 60", in zip-top styles and plain, for home and business packaging. Chiswick also sells paper and plastic shopping bags, gift boxes, bubble packaging and other shipping room supplies and equipment, poly film, antistatic packaging, labels, warehouse equipment, and related products. The prices on bulk orders drop by over 50%, and the selection of bag sizes and styles is hard to beat.

Special Factors: Satisfaction is guaranteed; minimum order is $50.

PLASTIC BAGMART

904 OLD COUNTRY RD.
WESTBURY, NY 11590
800-343-BAGS
516/997-3355

Price List: free with SASE
Save: up to 60%
Pay: check, MO, MC, V
Sells: plastic bags
Store: same address; Monday to Friday 9–5,
Saturday 9–3

$$$ ☎ 🍁(see text)

Plastic BagMart, established in 1980, offers plastic bags in sizes most frequently used in homes, offices, and industry. Prices are up to 60% less than those charged by supermarkets and variety stores for smaller lots.

The BagMart stocks plastic bags in sizes from 2″ square to 50″ by 48″, one to four mils thick. Garbage and trash cleanup bags, kitchen and office waste-can bags, food-storage bags, large industrial-type bags, zip-top styles, plastic shopping bags, and other types are available. The bags are sold in case lots only (100 to 1,000 bags per case, depending on the size). The price list features the most popular lines, but if you don't see what you need, write with particulars.

The BagMart is offering readers of this book a 5% discount on their *first* order (computed on the goods total only). This WBMC reader discount expires February 1, 1993.

Canadian readers, please note: Orders are shipped by UPS only.

Special Factors: Satisfaction is guaranteed; price quote by letter with SASE; returns are accepted within 10 days; minimum order is 1 case.

PROTECTO-PAK

**P.O. BOX 5096, DEPT. A
LONGVIEW, TX 75608
214/757-6092
214/297-3985**

Price List and Samples: $2, refundable
Save: up to 50%
Pay: check or MO
Sells: zip-top plastic bags
Store: mail order only

$$$ ◆ ▬

Protecto-Pak, established in 1983, offers heavy-duty plastic zip-top bags at savings that average 35% below comparable retail. The uses for these bags are almost endless, and they're great space-savers if storage is limited.

The bags run from 2″ square to 13″ by 15″; their seals make them relatively watertight. The suggested uses include storage of crafts supplies, spare parts from kits, polished silverware (wrapped in treated cloth), buttons and surplus trim for different garments, tobacco, daily doses of medications and dietary supplements, office supplies, photographs, hosiery and clothing in luggage and drawers, hardware, jewelry, and other items. Special sizes and thicknesses are available, and printing services are offered (minimum order 10,000). All of the bags are approved for food storage.

Special Factors: Price quote by phone or letter with SASE; quantity discounts are available; minimum order is $10.

UNIVERSITY PRODUCTS, INC.

517 MAIN ST.
P.O. BOX 101
HOLYOKE, MA 01041
413/532-9431
FAX: 413/532-9281

Catalog: free (see text)
Save: up to 40%
Pay: check, MO, MC, V, AE
Sells: archival-quality materials
Store: mail order only

$$$

You may not know it, but anarchy reigns on your bookshelves, in the pages of your photo albums, and among the works of art on your walls. It's sad but true that most of us store and display our precious belongings in materials and under conditions that damage them, sometimes irreparably.

Help is available from University Products, which publishes the comprehensive "Archival Quality Materials Catalog." University Products has been selling conservation and library supplies to institutions since 1968 and does business with preservation-minded individuals who want to protect their collectibles and other treasures. Both the materials used in display and storage and the conditions under which we keep them affect the long-term "health" of many collectibles. Problems with spotting, discoloration, and damage may also be seen in stamps, antique textiles, comic books, baseball trading cards, postcards, and even currency. To meet the need for safe storage of these goods, University Products makes acid-free manuscript boxes and interleaving pages, files, photo albums and Mylar page protectors, archival storage tubes, slide and microfiche storage materials, mounting materials and adhesives, an extensive selection of acid-free papers of all types, and related tools and supplies.

Most of the products are available in quantity, at prices up to 40% below those for single items. The catalog includes valuable information on conservation basics for a range of materials and collectibles. Since a "basic retouching" of an old photograph cost us $130, we are thoroughly convinced that each dollar spent in preservation can save a hundred in restoration—*if* restoration is possible.

Special Factors: Satisfaction is guaranteed; quantity discounts are available; institutional accounts are available.

U.S. BOX CORP.

1296 MCCARTER HWY.
NEWARK, NJ 07104
201/481-2000
718/387-1510
FAX: 718/384-3756

Catalog: $3
Save: up to 60%
Pay: check, MO, certified check
Sells: resale packaging
Store: mail order only

$$ ☎ 🍁 🇺🇸

U.S. Box Corp. has been selling packaging—boxes, bags, canisters, and displays—since 1948. This is primarily a business-to-business firm, but it offers products that consumers use routinely: wrapping paper, tape, gift boxes, ribbon, tissue paper, and mailing bags, for example. Prices are as much as 60% lower here than those charged for comparable items in variety and stationery stores. If you order thousands of units, savings per piece increase. Samples of the goods may be purchased at unit cost plus $2; this is recommended, since returns are not accepted.

U.S. Box's 88-page color catalog shows corrugated cardboard mailing boxes, packing and shipping tape and labels, shopping bags, gift and presentation boxes, poly bags, plastic display cases, showcase and window displays, and a full line of velvet boxes, inserts, and stands for jewelry sale and display. Both consumers and businesses should see the selection—and prices—of U.S. Box Corp.'s padded mailing envelopes, colored tissue paper, labels, candy boxes, gift totes, wooden "fruit" crates and baskets, ribbons, metallic stretch gift ties, bows, and cellophane and Mylar excelsior. If you're looking for dramatic home accents, see the line of "classical displays." These cast stone figures are modeled after Michelangelo's David, Diana, Apollo, and even King Tut and the Sphinx. Prices are reasonable, beginning at under $25. Please note that the minimum order is $150, so get friends together if you can't meet it yourself. And do send for product samples if you're not completely familiar with what you plan to buy.

Special Factors: Returns are not accepted; minimum order is $150; orders are shipped worldwide.

SEE ALSO

Current, Inc. • gift wrapping paper and ribbon • *BOOKS*
Turnkey Material Handling Co. • industrial containers and storage systems • *TOOLS*
Yazoo Mills, Inc. • shipping tubes • *ART MATERIALS*

HEALTH AND BEAUTY

_____

Cosmetics, perfumes, and toiletries; vitamins and

dietary supplements; and wigs and hairpieces

Y ou can save up to 90% on your cosmetic and beauty needs and still get the same name brands featured in beauty emporiums and department stores by buying by mail. But if your favorite perfume costs $160 an ounce, you might consider trying "copycat" scents, which are produced by two of the firms listed here. And because beauty comes from within, you'll find firms selling vitamins and dietary supplements listed here. What you take to augment your diet, if anything, is a question that you should take up with your physician.

If you're concerned about a specific issue, you can research it in consumer publications and in scientific medical journals (bibliographies and abstracts of articles can be obtained through computer services). Don't overlook the government pamphlets available through local health departments, and the commonsense health guides published by Consumers Union. And don't miss the *Consumer Reports Health Letter,* full of good reporting health and medical topics. For subscription information, see the current issue of *Consumer Reports,* or write to Consumers Union, 256 Washington St., Mount Vernon, NY 10553. The Public Citizen Health Research Group's *Health Letter* provides consumerist reporting on health issues in monthly, 12-page newsletters. For subscription information, write to Health Letter, Public Citizen Health Research Group, 2000 P St., N.W., Washington, DC 20036. Last but not least, no matter how much you read, please consult a physician about specific health problems or before embarking on a course of treatment for an existing condition.

For more firms selling related products, see the listings in "Medicine and Science."

EXERCISE EQUIPMENT • **Creative Health**
PERFUME AND BEAUTY PRODUCTS • **Beautiful Visions, Beauty**
  Boutique, Essential Products, Holbrook Wholesalers, Tuli-Latus
VITAMINS • **Freeda, Harvest of Values**
WIGS AND HAIRPIECES • **Beauty by Spector**

BEAUTIFUL VISIONS

**810 S. BROADWAY
HICKSVILLE, NY 11801
516/576-9000**

Catalog: free
Save: up to 90%
Pay: check, MO, MC, V
Sells: cosmetics and toiletries
Store: same address; Monday to Friday
  9:30–5, Saturday 9:30–4

$$

Beautiful Visions, which has been in business since 1977, sells beauty essentials from top manufacturers at up to 90% off list prices. Each issue of the 64-page catalog brings you cosmetics, skin-care products, and perfumes from Almay, Aziza, Biotherm, Charles of the Ritz, Coty, Diane Von Furstenberg, Jōvan, L'Oreal, Max Factor, Maybelline, Prince Matchabelli, Revlon, Vidal Sassoon, Vitabath, and other manufacturers. Current fashion shades are stocked, as well as the basics. The catalog also features grooming tools, fashion jewelry, and gifts, all at very reasonable prices.

Special Factors: Satisfaction is guaranteed; returns are accepted.

BEAUTY BOUTIQUE

**P.O. BOX 94520
CLEVELAND, OH 44101-
  4520
216/826-3008**

Catalog: free
Save: up to 90%
Pay: check, MO, MC, V
Sells: cosmetics and toiletries
Store: mail order only

$$ ☎ 🍁 🇺🇸

Before paying top dollar for cosmetics and perfumes, see the 56-page catalog from Beauty Boutique—you can save up to 90% on the original prices. You'll see page after page of name-brand cosmetics, toiletries, perfumes, and other goods by such firms as Elizabeth Arden, Elancyl, Giorgio, Jōvan, Estèe Lauder, Prince Matchabelli, Max Factor, Maybelline, Germaine Monteil, and Revlon. Cosmetic accessories, cases, makeup brushes, fashion jewelry, and even moderately priced clothing for women and housewares are usually available as well. This firm's parent company has been in business since 1969.

Special Factors: Satisfaction is guaranteed; minimum order is $10 with credit cards.

BEAUTY BY SPECTOR, INC.

**DEPT. WBMC-92
MCKEESPORT, PA 15134-
 0502
412/673-3259**

Catalog: free (see text)
Save: up to 50%
Pay: check, MO, MC, V
Sells: wigs and hairpieces
Store: mail order only

$$ ☎ ♦ ▆▆▆

Beauty by Spector, founded in 1958, offers the stylish Alan Thomas wigs and hairpieces at savings of up to 50% on salon prices, and the helpful sales staff can assist in making selections. The 20-page "Hairgoods Portfolio" features a number of designer styles for women. The wigs range from neat, softly coiffed heads to "Ginger," a youthful head of curls falling past the shoulders. These are contemporary styles—pretty, relaxed, and well shaped. Included in the Portfolio are wiglets, cascades, and falls that are ideal for everyday wear as well as dressy or special occasions, and a special line of "ultra-lightweight" wigs for women. Men's hairpieces, made with thermal-conductive and mesh bases, are offered in 55 base styles. Both wigs and hairpieces are made of several types of synthetic fibers and human hair, and are offered in a choice of dozens of colors and textures. Beauty by Spector will match your wig or piece to the closest shade if you provide a hair sample, or you may purchase the set of actual fiber samples.

Beauty by Spector offers readers of this book favorable prices (50% off suggested list), so be sure to identify yourself as a WBMC reader when you send for the catalog.

Special Factors: Specify men's or women's styles when requesting information; inquiries may be made by phone between 8 A.M. and 10 P.M., EST; orders are shipped worldwide.

CREATIVE HEALTH PRODUCTS

50 SADDLE RIDGE RD.
PLYMOUTH, MI 48170
800-742-4478
313/996-5900
FAX: 313/996-4650

Catalog: free
Save: 30% average
Pay: check, MO, MC, V, AE
Sells: fitness equipment, related medical devices
Store: mail order only (see text)

$$$ ☎ 🍁 🇺🇸

Creative Health Products has been selling health, fitness, and exercise equipment since 1976 and carries some of the best product lines available. Savings vary from item to item, but average 30% on list or regular retail prices.

The 12-page catalog lists current models of stationary bicycles, ergometers, rowers, treadmills, stair climbers, and accessories by Aerobics, Altero, Avita, Cateye, Marathon, Monark, Oglend-Bodyguard, Pacer, Quinton, Spirit, and Tunturi. There are pulse monitors from Biosig Instruments, CIC, Nissei, Polar, and Tunturi, and skin-fold calipers, body-fat analyzers, strength and flexibility testers, and professional scales by Detecto, Health-O-Meter, Metro, and Seca. Stethoscopes, blood pressure testers (sphygmomanometers), otoscopes, and ophthalmoscopes are also sold, and the catalog includes guides on buying different types of devices. Please note that this is professional equipment and, even with discounts, the prices are not low. Creative Health welcomes questions about any of the products it sells, and can help you find the best equipment for your needs. Although primarily a mail-order firm, Creative Health welcomes visitors, so drop by if you're in the area.

Special Factors: Price quote by phone or letter with SASE; quantity discounts are available; institutional accounts are available; C.O.D. orders are accepted; orders are shipped worldwide.

ESSENTIAL PRODUCTS CO., INC.

**90 WATER ST.
NEW YORK, NY 10005-
3587
212/344-4288**

Price List and Sample Cards: free with
SASE (see text)
Save: up to 90% (see text)
Pay: check or MO
Sells: "copycat" fragrances
Store: same address; Monday to Friday 9–6

$$$

"We offer our versions of the world's most treasured and expensive ladies' perfumes and men's colognes, selling them at a small fraction of the original prices." Essential was founded in 1895 and markets its interpretations of famous perfumes under the brand name of "Naudet."

Essential Products stocks 49 different copies of such costly perfumes as Beautiful, Coco, Eternity, Giorgio, Joy, L'Air du Temps, Obsession, Opium, Passion, Poison, White Linen, and Ysatis, as well as 20 "copycat" colognes for men, from Antaeus to Zizanie. A one-ounce bottle of perfume is $19 (¹/₂ ounce, $11), and four ounces of any men's cologne cost $10. When you write to Essential Products, please identify yourself as a WBMC reader, which entitles you to five free "scent cards" of Essential's best-selling fragrances. The sample cards give an idea of how closely the Naudet version replicates the original, but the product should be tried by the individual to evaluate it properly. You must also enclose a long, stamped, self-addressed envelope.

Special Factors: Satisfaction is guaranteed; returns are accepted within 30 days for refund; minimum order is $19; orders are shipped worldwide.

FREEDA VITAMINS, INC.

**36 E. 41ST ST.
NEW YORK, NY 10017
800-777-3737
212/685-4980**

Catalog: free
Save: up to 30%
Pay: check, MO, MC, V
Sells: dietary supplements
Store: Freeda Pharmacy, same address;
   Monday to Thursday 8:30–6:00, Friday
   8:30–4

$$$$ ☎ ✦ ▬

Freeda has been manufacturing vitamins and minerals in its own plant since 1928. This family-run operation is dedicated to providing the purest possible product. Its formulations are free of coal tar dyes, sulfates, starch, animal stearates, pesticides, sugar, and artificial flavorings, and are suitable for even the strictest vegetarian or Kosher diet. The Zimmermans, who run the firm, put an extra tablet in every bottle just to be nice, and we found savings of up to 30% on some of Freeda's supplements—and the WBMC reader discount makes this the best buy around.

The 48-page catalog lists vitamins, minerals, multivitamins, and nutritional products, which are available in a dizzying choice of combinations and strengths. The vitamin "families" include A and D, B, C, and E; among the minerals are calcium, iron, magnesium, potassium, selenium, and zinc; amino acids, proteins, and other dietary extras are offered. We've listed Freeda not for its megadose formulations, but because of its emphasis on quality production and additive-free goods. It's great to find a source for children's (and adults') vitamins made without sugar, coal tar dyes, sulfiting agents, animal stearates, sulfates, or artificial flavorings. (Freeda's chewable vitamins are naturally flavored, and there is an unflavored version for children on restricted diets. All of the Freeda vitamins are approved by the Feingold Association.) Needless to say, the Freeda catalog is free of the preposterous claims and misleading information often given by supplement sellers. And wonderful as all of this is, it's still important to check with your health-care professional before taking supplements and to avoid megadoses unless they're specifically recommended.

Freeda is offering readers of this book a special discount of 20% on all orders. You must mention WBMC to take the discount, which should be computed on the cost of the goods only, and can't be combined with other discounts and specials. This WBMC reader discount expires February 1, 1993.

Special Factors: Price quote by phone or letter; courtesy discounts are given to health-care professionals; orders are shipped worldwide.

HARVEST OF VALUES

HILLESTAD
  INTERNATIONAL INC.
1545 BERGER DR.
SAN JOSE, CA 95112
800-535-7742
IN CA 800-356-4190
408/298-0995

Catalog: free
Save: up to 40%
Pay: check, MO, MC, V
Sells: nutritional supplements, toiletries, and cleaning products
Store: same address; Monday to Friday 8–5

You can get "factory-direct" prices on vitamins, minerals, and other supplements by ordering from the manufacturer. The Harvest of Values products are made by Hillestad, its parent company, which was founded in 1959. Prices here are up to 40% less than those charged elsewhere for comparable goods.

A good selection of vitamins and nutritional supplements is offered here, listed in the comparatively hype-free, 32-page catalog. There are multivitamin and mineral formulations for adults, chewable versions for children, vitamins A, B-complex, C, and E; a "stress" formula; and chelated iron, bone meal, lecithin, alfalfa, amino acids, and protein powders. Harvest of Values also sells garlic concentrate in capsules, Co-Q-10, and an antacid that's free of sodium, aluminum, mineral oil, and corn syrup. Complete label data on most products are given in the catalog.

Harvest of Values also sells vitamin E cream and aloe body lotion, a pH-balanced cream rinse, conditioning shampoo, liquid "soapless" soap, and a biodegradable, phosphate-free cleanser for dishes, hand-washables, and general cleaning.

Special Factors: Satisfaction is guaranteed; all goods are guaranteed against defects in manufacturing; shipping is included on orders over $25; returns are accepted within 30 days.

HOLBROOK WHOLESALERS, INC.

1205 BROADWAY, RM. 204
NEW YORK, NY 10001
212/889-8681
FAX: 212/725-2562

Catalog: free
Save: up to 35%
Pay: check, MO, MC, V
Sells: perfumes and Lancôme products
Store: mail order only

$$$ ☎

You don't buy fragrances to put a sales commission in a stranger's pocket, you buy them because you like the way they make you—or someone else—smell. So if you don't need the "help" you'll get at the department store counter, skip it: Buy from Holbrook Wholesalers, and save up to 33% on the prices you usually pay.

Holbrook's 32-page catalog doesn't have glossy photos or provocative descriptions, it's just a no-frills list of men's and women's scents, their forms (perfume, cologne, after shave, etc.), and the retail and discount prices. The catalog we reviewed offered popular and hard-to-find fragrances among the hundreds, including Albert Nipon, Bibi de Jean Barthet, Decadence, Dunhill, Giorgio for Men, Sheherazade, Sybaris, That Man, and Zibeline. If you'd love to have a large "wardrobe" of scents but can't afford it even at a discount, see the listing of about 100 perfumes and colognes that are available in miniature bottles or sample sizes, from under $3. (They're also great for travel, stocking stuffers, and for the person who uses scent too rarely to justify a bigger bottle.) Lancôme's beauty treatment products for face and body are also available, as well as a selection of Lancôme cosmetics.

Please note: All orders are shipped via UPS.

Special Factors: Satisfaction is guaranteed; price quote by phone or letter; returns are accepted for exchange, refund, or credit.

TULI-LATUS PERFUMES LTD.

**146-36 13TH AVE.
P.O. BOX 422
WHITESTONE, NY 11357-
0422
718/746-9337**

Brochure: free
Save: up to 80% (see text)
Pay: check, MO, MC, V, AE, Optima
Sells: "copycat" fragrances
Store: mail order only

$$$ ☎ 🍁 ▰▰▰(see text)

Tuli-Latus, in business since 1970, sells its own versions of some of the world's finest, most expensive women's perfumes and men's scents, at up to 80% less than the cost of the originals.

Versions of 36 popular scents for women, including Chloé, Bal à Versailles, Joy, L'Air du Temps, Obsession, Patou's "1000," Opium, and Shocking are offered here. Men's scents, sold in perfume form, include a version of Russian Leather. Tuli-Latus also sells its own inspirations: "New Mown Hay" for men and "Jardin Exotique," a jasmine fragrance, and other florals for women. The brochure also shows necklaces of simulated pearls, and a line of facial creams and cleansers.

Tuli-Latus is offering readers of this book $5 off their *first* order (of nonsale items only). Identify yourself as a WBMC reader when you order. This WBMC reader discount expires February 1, 1993.

APO/FPO readers, please note: Orders are shipped to APO addresses only.

Special Factors: Returns of unused perfume are accepted within 15 days for refund or credit; minimum order is $15 with credit cards.

SEE ALSO

America's Pharmacy • vitamins and dietary supplements • *MEDICINE*
Better Health Fitness • exercise equipment • *SPORTS*
Caprilands Herb Farm • potpourri ingredients, essential oils, etc. •
  FARM
Dairy Association Co., Inc. • Bag Balm liniment • *ANIMAL*
The Eye Solution, Inc. • contact-lens solutions, travel kits, etc. •
  MEDICINE

Jaffe Bros., Inc. • Jaybee brand soap/shampoo • *FOOD*

D. MacGillivray & Coy. • Hebridean perfume • *CRAFTS*

Metacom, Inc. • motivational audio cassettes • *BOOKS*

Mother Hart's Natural Products, Inc. • Fuller Brush natural-bristle hairbrushes • *HOME: LINEN*

Retired Persons Services, Inc. • vitamins, beauty products, shampoo, etc. • *MEDICINE*

The Spice House • salt-free seasonings • *FOOD*

Walnut Acres Organic Farms • small selection of natural toiletries, additive-free nutritional supplements • *FOOD*

HOME

"Home" is a potent complex of the symbolic and concrete, a place in which physical shelter, the expression of personal aesthetics, the right to privacy, sensory pleasure, the ideology of family, and cultural dictums commingle. It's a fascinating merger of memory and expectation, circumstance and ingenuity. When the elements achieve the right balance, the result is the wonderful sense of comfort that we think of as "home."

Since this place often comes attached to a 30-year mortgage, its fiscal significance may seem to outweigh its psychological importance. But the right decisions—from buying a new lamp to adding a wing—can bring us pleasure while improving the equity in our homes, at the lowest possible cost. Veteran householders know that avoiding the infamous nightmares of redecorating and remodeling is a matter of good preparation, good budgeting, and good common sense.

Decor

Floor coverings, wall and window treatments, lighting, upholstery materials, tools, and services

Do-it-yourself home decor has always been an important part of the market, but in the last few years the distinctions between D-I-Y and to-the-trade (i.e., professional decorators) have begun to blur. Products once available to licensed designers exclusively are now offered by discounters and retail decorators, and they're selling to consumers who've shopped the showrooms and read the shelter magazines, and don't want any less than the best.

Unfortunately, success has a price. Manufacturers of decorating goods have begun threatening to pull their product lines from discounters if their brand names appear in ads, or even in unpaid editorial mentions like the listings in this book. Because of this, we've deleted those particular brands from *all* listings. So even if you don't see the name, the firm may carry the line—call or write to find out.

The following are a few of the resources and tips we've picked up over the years during the course of our own decorating projects:

Wallpaper and painting: Painting is one of the cheapest and easiest ways to give your home or a room a quick face-lift. Choosing the right type of paint for the job is half the battle; the other is preparing the surfaces properly. Both topics are covered in depth in *Paint and Wallpaper,* one of the volumes in the Time-Life "Home Repair and Improvement" series of books, which should be available at your local library. The same book addresses the selection of wallpaper, application techniques, and troubleshooting problems that may arise. Another good guide to selecting and hanging wallpaper, "How to Hang Wallcoverings," is published by the National Decorating Products Association, 1050 N. Lindbergh Blvd., St. Louis, MO 63132.

(It's also sent as part of the literature from Silver Wallcoverings, listed in this chapter.)

Upholstery and draperies: Pricing upholstery and drapery materials is sometimes tricky, since fabrics are commonly displayed on sample boards with the selvages—on which the manufacturer's name is usually printed—concealed. In fact, some mills print fake brand names on the selvages, which also thwarts attempts at comparison shopping. (Decorators and stores have keys to these names, but unless you do, there is no way to know that the fabric that reads "House 'n Home Fabrics & Draperies, Inc." is really from John Wolf.) There are different ways you can undermine these schemes, but perhaps the easiest route to accurate price quotes is with the fabric itself: Buy a yard, and send large pieces of it out with your price quote requests. Remember to state how many yards you intend to order, since that may affect the cost per yard.

The price spread on fabrics can be considerable from store to store, so compare at least five sources before deciding on your supplier. Buying off the shelf is almost always cheaper than having a shop special order a fabric, and if you're buying 25 yards or more of the same fabric, you should expect an extra price break. Even if you're working with a full-service upholsterer or draper, you'll probably get better value overall if you supply your own fabric, since you can get exactly what you want, without paying an extra markup. (This is known as a COM—"customer's own material"—job.)

If you go the professional route and engage a decorator, consider working out a cost-plus or per-hour payment arrangement. This advice comes to us from the president of a West Coast fabric store, where decorators buy at 50% off the tagged prices—and charge the client 100%.

Rugs and carpets: The Better Business Bureau publishes "Tips on Carpet and Rugs," a guide to selecting the best carpet for your needs. It's available from your local BBB office, or you can request the publications list and order form from: Council of Better Business Bureaus, Inc., 4200 Wilson Blvd., Suite 800, Arlington, VA 22203, Attn.: Publications Dept.

DECORATOR FABRIC • **Fabric Center, Fabrics by Design, Fabrics by Phone, Home Fabric Mills, Marlene's, Rubin & Green, Sanz, Shama, Silk Surplus, Tioga**
LIGHTING • **Golden Valley, King's Chandelier, Luigi Crystal, Main Lamp**
RUGS, CARPETING, FLOORING • **Bearden Bros., Floorcrafters Wholesale, Johnson's Carpets, National Carpet, Warehouse Carpets**
SLIPCOVERS • **Slipcovers of America**
WINDOW AND WALL TREATMENTS • **American Discount, Custom Window, Hang-It-Now, Harmony, Post Wallcoverings, Robinson's, Sanz, Shibui, Silver, Wells Interiors**

AMERICAN DISCOUNT WALLCOVERINGS

1411 FIFTH AVE., DEPT. WBM
PITTSBURGH, PA 15219
800-777-2737
FAX: 412/471-3347

Information: price quote
Save: up to 70%
Pay: check, MO, MC, V, Discover
Sells: wall coverings, fabrics, and window treatments
Store: same address; Monday to Friday 8:30–5, Saturday 8:30–1

$$$ ☎ ♦

American Discount Wallcoverings, whose parent firm was founded in 1916, offers savings of up to 70% on the best in decorator wall and window treatments. Custom bedspreads and draperies by a prominent manufacturer are also discounted 20%.

Most of the wall coverings are discounted 30% to 50%; upholstery and decorator fabrics are priced 10% to 35% below regular retail here. All of the goods are name-brand: Among the firms and designers represented are Boussac of France, David & Dash, Decorator's Walk, Eisenhart, Essex, Ginger Tree, Greeff, Imperial, Jonap, Josephson, Judscott, Katzenbach and Warren, Kravet, Ralph Lauren, Carey Lind, Quadrille, Sanitas, Van Luit, Westgate, Winfield, and York—and there are scores more. All of the custom window treatments made by Bali, Del Mar, Flexalum, Graber, HunterDouglas, Joanna, Kirsch, Levolor, LouverDrape, Nanik, and Verosol are discounted 25% to 70%.

American Discount is offering readers of this book a 65% discount on Graber mini blinds. (The discount is calculated on list price, and applies only to the Graber line.) This WBMC reader discount expires February 1, 1993.

Special Factors: Price quote by phone or letter with SASE; request order form when obtaining price quotes; all goods are first quality; returns (except cut rolls, borders, custom wall coverings, and custom window treatments) are accepted within 20 days (a 25% restocking fee is charged).

BEARDEN BROS. CARPET CORP.

3200 A DUG GAP RD.,
 DEPT. WC
DALTON, GA 30720
800-433-0074
FAX: 404/277-1754

Brochure and Samples: free
Save: up to 80%
Pay: check, MO, MC, V, AE, Discover, Optima
Sells: carpeting and padding
Store: same address; Monday to Friday 8–5:30, Saturday 9–4

$$$

Bearden Bros. set up shop in 1968 in Dalton, "Carpet Capital of the World," joining hundreds of other companies devoted to the manufacture of carpeting. Bearden sells lines from scores of mills, including Aldon, Armstrong, Beaulieu, Bigelow, Burlington, Cabin Craft, Citation, Collins & Aikman, Customweave, Galaxy, General Felt, Horizon, Interloom, J.P. Stevens, Lees, Masland, Mohawk, Monticello, Shaw, and World—and that's just a sample of the many brands available.

You can call with the manufacturer's name, style and color codes, and number of square yards you plan to buy and ask for a price quote, or send a carpet sample if you don't have that information. Bearden Bros. offers a generous guarantee of satisfaction, and publishes a brochure that includes a troubleshooting guide to carpet problems as well as consumer information hotlines that can handle your questions about the special "carpet protection" systems and the warranties provided by carpet manufacturers. Bearden will ship carpeting to all 50 states and Puerto Rico, and offers special discounts to religious institutions and carpet dealers.

Special Factors: Satisfaction is guaranteed; written confirmation of phone orders is required; quantity discounts are available.

CUSTOM WINDOWS & WALLS

**32525 STEPHENSON
HWY., DEPT. WM
MADISON HEIGHTS, MI
48071
800-772-1947
800-777-7747
FAX: 313/583-2863**

Brochure: free
Save: up to 75%
Pay: check, MO, MC, V, Discover
Sells: wall coverings and window treatments
Store: mail order only

$$ ☎

After deliberating over window treatments and wallpaper patterns, go the final step and get the best price. Custom Windows & Walls, which has been in business since 1908 and selling by mail since 1982, should definitely be on your list of sources.

Upon request, Custom will send you manufacturers' brochures that describe the available lines, along with discount prices. The firm offers window treatments by Bali, Del Mar, Kirsch, Levolor, and LouverDrape, as well as its own "Window Express" 1″ mini and ¹/₂″ micro blinds and vertical blinds in a choice of scores of colors and materials, at 50% to 75% below list prices. Measuring guides are included in the literature. Wall coverings and coordinating fabrics from a wide range of manufacturers are available, at prices discounted up to 50% below list. A price-quote form is included in the information packet.

Please note that all of the window treatments are made to order and can't be returned. Measure and *remeasure* carefully before ordering.

Special Factor: Price quote by phone or letter.

THE FABRIC CENTER, INC.

485 ELECTRIC AVE.
P.O. BOX 8212
FITCHBURG, MA 01420
508/343-4402

Catalog: $2
Save: up to 50%
Pay: check, MO, MC, V
Sells: decorator fabrics
Store: (showroom) same address; Monday
to Saturday 9–5:30

$$$ ☎ ❖

The Fabric Center has been in business since 1932, selling fine fabrics for home decorating at savings of up to 50% on suggested list prices. Decorator fabrics for upholstery and window treatments are available, including lines from Robert Allen, American Textile, Paul Barrow, Covington, George Harrington, Kravet, Peachtree, Thomas Strahan, and many others. The 132-page color catalog ($2) features hundreds of fabrics from a wide range of manufacturers, but if you know exactly what you want, you can call or write directly for a price quote.

Special Factors: Satisfaction is guaranteed; price quote by phone or letter; minimum order is 1 yard; orders are shipped worldwide.

FABRICS BY DESIGN

325 N.E. FIFTH AVE.
DELRAY BEACH, FL 33483
407/278-9700

Price List with Samples: $7.50
Save: 30% plus
Pay: check, MO, MC, V
Sells: decorator fabrics
Store: Woodland Fabrics (same address);
Monday to Saturday 9:30–5:30

$$ ☎ ❖

Fabrics by Design sells its own collection of decorator fabrics as well as selected lines from well-known firms. You'll save a solid 30% or more by buying from this source on the firm's collection of charming country prints and solids. Some of the patterns are reminiscent of the "traditional" lines in designer collections, but they cost a fraction as much as the name fabrics. All of the fabric is preshrunk cotton, treated with Scotchguard. Fabrics by Design also offers muslin,

Osnaburg, and professional-quality drapery lining in white and ivory. Designer fabrics are offered as well, including lines from Robert Allen, Anju, Bloomcraft, Cohama, Covington, Cyrus Clark, Greeff, P. Kaufmann, Spectrum, Stroheim & Romann, John Wolf, and Jay Yang. Be sure to get the swatch collection or prices of these fabrics if you're upholstering furniture or making slipcovers, curtains, or draperies.

Special Factors: Satisfaction is guaranteed; price quote by phone or letter with SASE; returns (except lengths under 5 yards and worn or laundered fabric) are accepted within 2 weeks; minimum order is 1 yard; orders are shipped worldwide.

FABRICS BY PHONE

P.O. BOX 309
WALNUT BOTTOM, PA
  17266
800-233-7012

Brochure and Samples: $3
Save: up to 50%
Pay: check, MO, MC, V
Sells: decorator fabrics
Store: Fabric Shop, 120 N. Seneca St., Shippensburg, PA

$$ ☎

Fabrics by Phone has been doing business since 1937, and represents a number of major lines and manufacturers. Robert Allen, Artmark, Design Craft, Fabricut, Kinney, Michaels Textiles, Warner, and Westgate are just a few of the names offered here—call or write for prices of specific fabrics. This firm also makes draperies and accessories to order. For more information on these services, send $3 for the literature, price list, and swatches.

Special Factors: Price quote by phone or letter with SASE; minimum order is 1 yard (on goods not in stock).

FLOORCRAFTERS WHOLESALE

P.O. BOX 644, DEPT. WBMC
UKIAH, CA 95482
707/468-0615, EXT. W92

Catalog: $1, refundable (see text)
Save: up to 75%
Pay: check, MO, MC, V, Discover
Sells: flooring, floor coverings, and window treatments
Store: mail order only

$$ ☎ ♦

Floorcrafters Wholesale has been selling flooring and floor coverings since 1987, offering deep discounts—up to 75%—on suggested list prices. The firm offers carpeting from Caladium, E.T.C., Galaxy, Horizon, Queen, Royalty, Tuftex, and Whitecrest. Vinyl sheeting from Congoleum and Tarkett is available, as well as hardwood flooring from Anderson and Bruce. Floorcrafters also sells window treatments (blinds) from Bali, Graber, and HunterDouglas. We didn't see the catalog, but if you know what you want, you may not need it—you can call or write if you know the manufacturer, style, color, and amount you need to get a price quote. The only drawback is the $100 minimum order, which you may not meet if you're buying floor coverings for a small area.

Please note: Orders to Canada and foreign countries are shipped freight-collect.

Special Factors: Price quote by phone or letter; minimum order is $100; orders are shipped worldwide.

GOLDEN VALLEY LIGHTING

274 EASTCHESTER DRIVE, #117A
HIGH POINT, NC 27262
800-735-3377
919/882-7330

Brochure: free (see text)
Save: up to 50%
Pay: check, MO, MC, V
Sells: floor, table, and wall lamps
Store: mail order only

$$

Golden Valley, a company founded and run by veterans of the lighting industry, offers savings of up to 50% on lamps and lighting fixtures from over 100 manufacturers.

You can send for the brochure, which urges you to shop around and call when you've decided what you want (have the manufacturer's name, model number, color, finish, and any other details at hand). You can also buy specific manufacturers' catalogs from Golden Valley Lighting for $5 each, and get the information that way. Please note that the firm's brochure includes a partial list of the manufacturers represented, so call and ask if you don't see the name you're looking for. When you're ready to order, you can make a deposit of 50% of the lamp's cost and pay the balance before shipment, or prepay the entire amount and expedite the order (details are given in the brochure).

Special Factor: Price quote by phone or letter with SASE.

HANG-IT-NOW WALLPAPER STORES

10,517F N. MAIN ST.
ARCHDALE, NC 27263
800-325-9494
919/431-6341
FAX: 919/431-0449

Information: price quote
Save: up to 50%
Pay: check, MO, MC, V, AE
Sells: wall coverings and decorator fabrics
Store: same address; Monday to Friday 9–6, Saturday 9–3; also 4620 W. Market St., Greensboro, and 759 Silas Creek Pkwy., Winston-Salem, NC

$$ ☎ ♦

Hang-It-Now Wallpaper is run by a couple who set up shop in 1981, and now have three stores selling name-brand wall coverings at savings of 30% to 65% on list prices. A limited selection of decorator fabrics is also available, at discounts of up to 40%.

All major brands of wall coverings (plus strings, grass cloth, and borders) are offered here, including Color House, Crutchfield, Eisenhart, Imperial, Katzenbach & Warren, Carey Lind, Sanitas, Sunwall, United, and Van Luit, among others. Hang-It-Now specializes in providing wall coverings to retail establishments, and has done numerous installations for furniture retailers and decorators. Regardless of the size of your order, the firm says that "service to the customer is still our number one aim."

Special Factors: Price quote by phone or letter; only first-quality goods are sold; orders are shipped worldwide.

HARMONY SUPPLY INC.

P.O. BOX 313
MEDFORD, MA 02155
617/395-2600
FAX: 617/396-8218

Information: price quote
Save: up to 60%
Pay: check, MO, MC, V
Sells: wallpaper and window treatments
Store: 18 High St., Medford, MA; Monday
  to Saturday 8–5:30, Thursday 8 A.M.–9 P.M.

$$ ☎

Harmony Supply, in business since 1949, can give your home a face-lift at a discount with saving of up to 60% on wallpaper, coordinating fabrics, and window treatments. Harmony carries over 2,500 designs and patterns of wallpaper, grass cloth, and string cloth, as well as mini, micro, vertical, and pleated shades and blinds by Bali, Flexalum, HunterDouglas, Kirsch, Levolor, Louverdrape, and Verosol. You'll save the most on goods that are currently in stock, but even special orders are discounted up to 60%. Call or write for a price quote, since there's no catalog or price list.

Special Factors: Price quote by phone or letter with SASE; returns (except custom blinds) are accepted within 30 days (a 25% restocking fee is charged on special-order goods).

HOME FABRIC MILLS, INC.

P.O. BOX 888
CHESHIRE, CT 06410
203/272-3529
FAX: 203/272-6686

Brochure: free
Save: up to 40%
Pay: check, MO, MC, V (see text)
Sells: decorator fabrics and custom services
Store: 882 South Main St., Cheshire, CT;
  also Rte. 202, Belchertown, MA; and 443
  Saratoga Rd., Rte. 50, Scotia, NY; Monday
  to Wednesday 10–9, Thursday to
  Saturday 10–5

We received a lovely color brochure from Home Fabric Mills, with samples of some of the firm's most popular upholstery and drapery materials. This company has been in business since 1968 and is a good source for the home decorator who's unsure of what type of fabric is best for a particular project or is trying to match a color.

The three Home Fabric Mills stores are stocked with thousands of bolts of upholstery and drapery materials, lining, trims, and workroom supplies from Robert Allen, Covington, Graber, Kaufmann, Kirsch, Lanscot-Arlen, Waverly, Wolf, and other manufacturers. Only first-quality goods are sold, and Home Fabric Mills will sell in half-yard increments—great to know if you're still deciding on your fabrics.

Please note: Credit card payments are accepted on out-of-state mail orders only.

Special Factors: Price quote by phone or letter; minimum order is 1/2 yard.

JOHNSON'S CARPETS, INC.

3239 S. DIXIE HWY.
DALTON, GA 30720
800-235-1079
404/277-2775
FAX: 404/277-9835

Brochure: free
Save: up to 80%
Pay: check, MO, MC, V, AE, Discover, Optima
Sells: name-brand floor treatments
Store: same address; Monday to Friday 8–5

$$$ ☎ ♦ ▆

Three-fourths of the carpeting produced in the U.S. is made in Georgia, states the Johnson's brochure. Johnson's has arrangements with over 40 carpet mills that allow it to offer carpet lines from a wide range of manufacturers, at prices up to 80% below those charged by department stores and other retail outlets.

If you've decided on the carpet you want to buy, call or write with the name of the manufacturer, the style name or number, and the square yardage required. Johnson's also creates its own "custom designer" rugs, and can produce designs to match wallpaper or furnishings—sample patterns are shown in the catalog (available on request). Padding, adhesives, and tack strips for installation are available.

A deposit is required when you place your order, and final payment must be made before shipment (common carrier is used). Both residential and commercial carpeting needs are served here—details on the products and sales policy are given in the brochure.

Special Factors: Price quote by phone or letter with SASE; orders are shipped worldwide.

KING'S CHANDELIER CO.

P.O. BOX 667, DEPT. WBM
EDEN, NC 27288
919/623-6188

Catalog: $3.50
Save: up to 50%
Pay: check, MO, MC, V
Sells: Czech, Venetian, and Strass chandeliers
Store: Hwy. 14 (Van Buren Rd.), Eden, NC; Monday to Saturday 10–4:30

The Kings have been designing and producing chandeliers since 1935 and offer many their designs through the 100-page catalog. There are light fixtures to suit every taste, at prices for all budgets.

The catalog shows page after page of chandeliers, candelabras, and wall sconces in a range of styles: Victorian, "Colonial," contemporary, and many variations on the classic lighting fixture dripping with prisms, pendalogues, faceted balls, and ropes of crystal buttons. Austere styles with brass arms and plain glass shades are also available, as well as the Kings' own magnificent designs made of Strass crystal. Prices begin at about $125 for a brass single sconce, and go up to $14,500 for the palatial Strass Royal Belvedere. Options include different finishes on the metal parts, hurricane shades or candelabra tapers, and candelabra bulb sockets. Individual and replacement parts for these lighting fixtures are stocked as well.

Since the black and white catalog photos can't show the chandeliers to best advantage, King's will creat a videotape of the lighting fixtures that interest you—preferably not more than six models. The VHS tapes is are available for a $25 deposit, refundable on return.

Special Factors: Satisfaction is guaranteed; returns are accepted within 5 days for refund or credit; minimum order is $15 on chandelier parts, $100 with credit cards; orders are shipped worldwide.

LUIGI CRYSTAL

**7332 FRANKFORD AVE.
PHILADELPHIA, PA 19136
215/338-2978**

Catalog: $1.50, refundable
Save: up to 50%
Pay: check, MO, MC, V, AE
Sells: crystal lighting fixtures
Store: same address; Monday to Saturday
9–5, Wednesday and Friday 9–7

$$$

Luigi Crystal may be located in the land of Main Liners, but its heart belongs to Tara. The firm has been creating crystal lighting fixtures since 1935, and the prices are surprisingly low—under $200 for a full-sized chandelier, for example. The 44-page catalog shows each candelabra, chandelier, sconce, and hurricane lamp in black-and-white photographs. Many of the styles are formal and ornate, heavily hung with prisms and pendalogues and set in marble or faceted crystal bases. Several lamps feature globe shades, gold cupid bases, "Aurora" crystal prism shades, and even stained glass. At the other end of the spectrum are simple "Williamsburg chimney lamps" for under $50 a pair, and several graceful five-arm chandeliers.

If you're searching for replacement parts for your own fixtures, see the catalog for glass chimneys, bobeches, strung button prisms, drop prisms in several styles (3″ to 8″ long), and pendalogues. In addition to those models, Luigi's workshops can produce designs to your specifications; call or write to discuss details and prices.

Special Factors: Price quote by phone or letter with SASE; orders are shipped worldwide ($1,000 minimum order).

MAIN LAMP/LAMP WAREHOUSE

**1073 39TH ST.
BROOKLYN, NY 11219
800-52-LITES
718/436-8500**

Information: price quote
Save: up to 50%
Pay: check, MO, MC, V, AE
Sells: lamps and ceiling fans
Store: same address; Monday, Tuesday, and
Friday 9–5:30, Thursday 9–9, Saturday
and Sunday 10–5

$$ ☎

Main Lamp/Lamp Warehouse, established in 1954, is noted for its comprehensive inventory of lamps, lighting fixtures, and name-brand ceiling fans that are all sold at a discount. Call or write for prices on lamps, lighting fixtures, and track lighting by American Lantern, Crystal Clear, Rembrandt, Stiffel, Thomas Industries, Waterford, and other major manufacturers. Ceiling fans by Casablanca, Emerson, and other firms are also stocked, and everything is sold at everyday discounts of up to 50%.

Special Factors: Price quote by phone or letter with SASE; store is closed Wednesdays; orders are shipped worldwide.

MARLENE'S DECORATOR FABRICS

**301 BEECH ST., DEPT. 2J
HACKENSACK, NJ 07601
800-992-7325**

Information: price quote
Save: up to 50%
Pay: check, MO, MC, V
Sells: decorator fabrics
Store: mail order only

$$ ☎ ♦ 🇺🇸

Marlene's Decorator Fabrics has been selling upholstery and drapery goods since 1951, and can save you up to 50% on the list prices of fabrics by Artmark, Paul Barrow, Berger, Brunschwig & Fils, Carole Fabrics, Duralee, Greeff, JAB, Kasmir, Kravet, Lee Jofa, Michaels, Peachtree, Stroheim & Roman, Westgate, and many other names. Write or call for a price quote, or send a fabric sample and a SASE if you're not sure of the manufacturer or pattern.

Special Factors: Price quote by phone or letter with SASE; minimum order is 1 to 3 yards, depending on the fabric.

NATIONAL CARPET

1384 CONEY ISLAND AVE.
BROOKLYN, NY 11230
718/253-5700

Catalog: $3 (see text)
Save: up to 40%
Pay: MO, MC, V
Sells: area carpets
Store: same address; Monday to
Wednesday 9–6, Thursday 9–8, Friday
9–4, Sunday 10:30–5

National sells Karastan rugs, and sends you the Karastan catalog sampler featuring the different lines for the $2 catalog fee. The rugs include the Karastan Originals Collection—reproductions of Tabriz, Heriz, Bokhara, Kasham, and other classic designs, the Williamsburg Collection, and the Garden of Eden Collection, a line featuring floral motifs. National has over half a century of experience in selling rugs, and offers discounts of up to 40% on suggested list prices.

Special Factor: Satisfaction is guaranteed.

PINTCHIK HOMEWORKS

2106 BATH AVE.
BROOKLYN, NY 11214
800-847-4199
718/996-5580
FAX: 718/996-1966

Brochure: free
Save: up to 60%
Pay: check, MO, MC, V
Sells: wall, window, and floor finishes and treatments
Store: 278 and 1555 Third Ave. and 2475 Broadway, New York, NY

$ ☎

This firm was founded in 1912 and is one of New York City's favorite sources for home-improvement items and decorative accessories. Pintchik stocks over 2,000 wallpaper patterns and window treatments; the brands include Bali, Del Mar, Duette, Graber, HunterDouglas, Joanna, Levolor, Louverdrape, and Verosol. The brochure includes a helpful guide to measuring your windows, as well as terms of Pintchik's lifetime warranty.

Paints by Pratt & Lambert, Benjamin Moore, Pittsburgh Paints, Luminall, Emalj, Red Devil, and other companies are also carried, and paint color chips are available upon request. Custom wallpaper designs, including logos, can be produced, and vertical shades can be laminated with fabrics or wallpaper. In addition, Pintchik sells flooring by Armstrong, Hartco, Kentile, Lees, and other well-known companies. Store shoppers will find a complete selection of other home-improvement and hardware items.

Special Factors: Price quote by letter with SASE; institutional and commercial accounts are available; returns are accepted within 3 weeks (a 20% restocking fee is charged).

POST WALLCOVERING
DISTRIBUTORS, INC.

P.O. BOX 7026
BLOOMFIELD HILLS, MI
  48013
800-521-0650

Information: inquire
Save: up to 75%
Pay: check, MO, MC, V
Sells: wall coverings, blinds, and
  coordinating fabrics
Store: mail order only

$ ☎ ▤

Post Wallcovering, in business since 1977, can save homeowners and decorators up to 75% on wall coverings and window treatments— wallpaper, borders, murals, and blinds are available. Before you call for a price quote on a wall covering, have the pattern number and book name at hand. If you're calling for a price quote on a window blind, have the manufacturer's name, style name, color name and number, width, and height written down.

Special Factor: Price quote by phone.

ROBINSON'S
WALLCOVERINGS

DEPT. 2LY
225 W. SPRING ST.
TITUSVILLE, PA 16354
800-458-2426
814/827-1893
FAX: 814/827-1693

Catalog and Samples: $2, refundable
Save: up to 50%
Pay: check, MO, MC, V, AE, Discover
Sells: wallpaper, decorator fabrics, and
  accessories
Store: 339 W. Spring St., Titusville; also
  3506 Liberty Plaza, Erie, and 2807
  Wilmington Rd., Rte. 18, New Castle, PA

$$$ ☎ ▤

Robinson's went into business in 1919, and its catalog prices still haven't caught up with the times. Robinson's specializes in wall coverings, but coordinating borders, fabrics, and home accessories are also available.

Among the wall coverings are patterns suitable for bathrooms, dining rooms, dens, bedrooms, nurseries, and kitchens. The designs range from the traditional to contemporary. Tools and supplies for installation are also offered. Complementary fabrics and borders are available for many wallpaper patterns, and Robinson's provides a number of color photographs in the catalog that show how different designs look when they're installed—a very helpful feature.

Robinson's also carries name-brand wall treatments, and can save you up to 50% on paper and fabric from popular manufacturers. Orders of the national brands are handled by the firm's Custom Order Sales Office; see the catalog for details.

Special Factors: Satisfaction is guaranteed; returns are accepted within 30 days for exchange or refund; minimum order is $15 with credit cards.

RUBIN & GREEN INC.

290 GRAND ST.
NEW YORK, NY 10002
212/226-0313
212/226-5015

Information: price quote
Save: 33% plus
Pay: check, MO, MC, V, AE
Sells: decorator fabrics
Store: same address; Sunday to Friday 9–5

$$$ 🍁(see text)

Rubin & Green, established in 1945, offers savings of up to 40% on a wide selection of decorator fabric. You can call or write for prices on lines by Robert Allen, David & Dash, Kravet, Stroheim & Romann, Jay Yang, and other firms and designers. The store staff can help advise you by phone if you can't get to the store. Rubin & Green can also create custom-made comforters, bedspreads, draperies, and other decorative accessories—inquire for information.

Canadian readers, please note: Deliveries to Canada are made by UPS only.

Special Factor: Price quote by phone or letter with SASE.

SANZ INTERNATIONAL, INC.

P.O. BOX 1794
HIGH POINT, NC 27261
919/886-7630
919/882-6212
FAX: 919/887-0145

Brochure: free with self-addressed, stamped envelope
Save: up to 80%
Pay: check, MO, MC, V
Sells: wallpaper and decorator fabrics
Store: 1183 E. Lexington Ave., High Point, NC; and four other locations

$$ ☎ 🍁

Sanz, established in 1978, offers decorator discounts of up to 80% on wall coverings and upholstery and drapery fabrics from hundreds of manufacturers and designers, which are listed in the brochure. They include Robert Allen, Charles Barone, Boussac of France, Brunschwig & Fils, Clarence House, Color House, Decorator's Walk, Ginger Tree, Greeff, Imperial, Lee Jofa, Katzenbach & Warren, Ralph Lauren, Milbrook, Quality House, Sanitas, Scalamandré, Sunwall, United, Warner, Woodson, and York. Imported grass cloth, papers in faux finishes, stripes, and other designs are available (see the brochure for information on how to order samples). Volume discounts are offered.

Special Factors: Price quote by phone or letter with SASE; quantity discounts are available; shipping is included on most items; returns are accepted within 30 days.

SHAMA IMPORTS, INC.

P.O. BOX 2900, DEPT.
WBM-92
FARMINGTON HILLS, MI
48333
313/478-7740

Brochure: free
Save: up to 50%
Pay: check, MO, MC, V
Sells: crewel fabrics and home accessories
Store: mail order only

$$$ ☎ 🍁 🇺🇸

Shama, which began business in 1982, offers excellent prices on Indian crewel fabrics and home accessories.

Crewel fabric, which is hand-embroidered on hand-loomed cotton, is offered here in traditional serpentine flower-and-vine motifs and other distinctive designs, in a range of colors. The eight-page color brochure that shows the patterns also includes decorating suggestions. Background (unembroidered) fabric is also available by the yard, and Shama stocks crewel chair and cushion covers, tote bags, bedspreads, and tablecloths as well. All of the fabric is 52″ wide and can be washed by hand or dry cleaned. Samples are available for $1 each; those showing one-fourth of the complete pattern cost $5 (refundable). The brochure lists the pattern repeats for all of the designs.

Special Factors: Satisfaction is guaranteed; uncut, undamaged returns are accepted within 30 days for refund or credit; C.O.D. orders are accepted.

SHIBUI WALLCOVERINGS

DEPT. WBM-92
P.O. BOX 1638
ROHNERT PARK, CA
  94928
800-824-3030
707/526-6170
FAX: 707/544-0719

Brochure and Samples: $4
Save: up to 50%
Pay: check, MO, MC, V
Sells: imported grass cloth and "natural" wall coverings
Store: mail order only

Shibui, which has been doing business since 1966, sells fine wall coverings made of natural materials—jute, grasses, strings, and textiles. Shibui stocks imported jute-fiber grass cloth, rush cloth, textile papers, textured weaves, and string wall coverings. The $4 brochure fee includes samples, and larger pieces are available upon request. The string wall coverings include several that look like silk but cost a fraction as much, and there are lots of wonderful wall coverings of woven grasses on paper of contrasting colors. Paper-hanging tool kits, adhesives, and lining paper are also available.

Special Factors: Satisfaction is guaranteed; price quote by phone or letter; shipping is included on orders over $100; single and double rolls can be cut from regular bolts (not returnable); returns are accepted within 30 days; C.O.D. orders are accepted; orders are shipped worldwide.

SILK SURPLUS

**235 EAST 58TH ST.
NEW YORK, NY 10022
212/753-6511**

Information: price quote
Save: up to 75% (see text)
Pay: check, MO, MC, V
Sells: discontinued decorator fabrics (see text)
Store: same address; Monday to Saturday 10–5:30; also 1147 Madison Ave., New York, 449 Old Country Rd., Westbury, 1210 Northern Blvd., Manhasset, and 281 Mamaroneck Ave., White Plains, NY

$

Silk Surplus is well-known to budget-minded New Yorkers who covet luxurious upholstery and drapery fabrics, because it's where they can save up to 75% (and sometimes even more) on sumptuous Scalamandré closeouts and fabrics from other mills: Silks, cottons, velvets, woolens, chintzes, brocades, damasks, and other weaves and finishes are usually available from Silk Surplus, which opened its doors in 1962.

Walk-in customers can select from among the bolts in any of the five Silk Surplus shops. But if you're buying by mail, you must know exactly which Scalamandré fabric you want, and in which color. If it's there, you're in luck. You may also send the store a fabric sample with a query. We emphasize that this is a great shopping stop on a trip to New York City, but only serious searchers for Scalamandré closeout fabrics should contact the store intending to buy by mail. If you're a design professional, you may ask for an additional trade discount.

Special Factors: Price quote by phone or letter with SASE; sample cuttings are free; all sales are final; orders are shipped worldwide.

SILVER WALLCOVERING, INC.

**3001-15 KENSINGTON AVE.
PHILADELPHIA, PA 19134
800-426-6600**

Brochure: $1, refundable
Save: up to 50%
Pay: check, MO, MC, V, AE, Discover
Sells: wall coverings and window
  treatments
Store: same address; Monday to Saturday
  8:30–5, Wednesday and Friday 8:30–8:30

$$$ ☎

Silver is a well-known source for name-brand wall and window treatments, which it sells by phone and by mail at savings of up to 50%. You can call for quotes on any style from Bali, Del Mar, Eisenhart, Imperial, Graber, Levolor, Reed, Sanitas, Seabrook, Sunworthy, Van Luit, Walltex, York, and *any other* wallpaper manufacturers. Borders and coordinating fabrics are also available. Silver has been in business since 1950, and includes the very useful "How to Hang Wallcoverings" in its information packet ($1).

Special Factor: Price quote by phone or letter with SASE.

SLIPCOVERS OF AMERICA

**P.O. BOX 590, DEPT. 131
BETHLEHEM, PA 18016-
  0590
215/868-7788**

Catalog: free
Save: up to 30%
Pay: check, MO, MC, V
Sells: slipcovers, curtains, and furniture
  throws
Store: mail order only

$$ ≡

The cost of reupholstering a couch or chair often approaches the purchase price of the furniture itself, which makes slipcovers very appealing. This firm sells "custom-look" slipcovers, looser "casually fitted" covers, coordinating pillows, curtains, tablecloths, and other accessories.

Slipcovers of America, which has been in business since 1915, publishes a 16-page color catalog of slipcovers that will stretch to fit dozens of couch and armchair styles. Velvet-look solids, bold florals, and country designs are offered, in throws and semi-fitted covers for nonstandard furniture, all at prices we found up to 30% below those charged by a major catalog company for similar goods. Slipcovers of America gives step-by-step instructions for measuring your furniture so you can be sure to get the best fit. If you want to coordinate the rest of your room, see the complementing curtains, valances, pillows, tablecloths, and other accents. You can also make your own—the fabric is sold in three-yard packs.

Special Factors: Satisfaction is guaranteed; no phone orders are accepted; returns are accepted.

SOUTH BOUND
MILLWORKS

**P.O. BOX 349
SANDWICH, MA 02563
508/477-2638**

Catalog: $1, refundable
Save: up to 50%
Pay: check, MO, MC, V
Sells: wooden and iron decorative
   hardware
Store: mail order only

$$ ☎ 🍁

South Bound Millworks' 26-page catalog shows line drawings of its birch curtain rod brackets, rod couplers for long rods, wooden finials, and wooden rings, all of which are carved in simple styles to blend in with many decorating modes. Coordinating shelf supports, towel racks, and even shower curtain supports are offered in sanded hardwood. The wrought iron fixtures produce a much more "country" effect. The curtain cranes (pivoting half-rods) are an old alternative to stationary rods, and decorative hold-backs have been used for centuries. Iron pot racks and kitchen fixtures, fireplace tools, candle stands, lamps, bathroom fixtures, plant hooks and cranes, and even an iron dinner chime are offered. South Bound also sells small wooden boxes, painted animal silhouettes, jointed wooden bears, and colorful draft stoppers.

Special Factor: Returns are accepted within 14 days for exchange, refund, or credit.

TIOGA MILL OUTLET STORES, INC.

DEPT. WBM-92
200 S. HARTMAN ST.
YORK, PA 17403
717/843-5139
FAX: 717/843-5139

Brochure: free (see text)
Save: up to 50%
Pay: check, MO, MC, V, Discover
Sells: decorator fabrics
Store: same address; Monday to Thursday
9:30–6, Friday 9:30–8, Saturday 9–5 (9–3
in July and August)

$$$

"When you think fabric, think Tioga!" urges the brochure from this source, which offers name-brand drapery and upholstery fabric at up to 50% off list prices. Tioga stocks material by Robert Allen, Bloomcraft, Covington, Fabricut, John Wolf, and many other designers and manufacturers. If you've selected your fabric, you can write or call Tioga for a price quote. If you're still shopping, you can avail yourself of the firm's decorating service by completing the "Special Project/Sample Request" portion of the order form and returning it with the $2 fee. Tioga will send you selected swatches, from which you may select your fabric. Drapery lining and upholstery supplies are also available, including tools, batting, linings (in widths of 48″, 54″, and 115″), gimp, burlap, and other goods.

Tioga Mill Outlet has been in business since 1970, and guarantees that all goods are first quality; flawed or damaged goods will be replaced or your money refunded. Returns due to customer error are not accepted, so *measure* and *remeasure* before you order.

Special Factors: Price quote by phone or letter with SASE; minimum order is ¼ yard; orders are shipped worldwide.

WAREHOUSE CARPETS, INC.

P.O. BOX 3233
DALTON, GA 30721
800-526-2229
404/226-2229
FAX: 404/278-1008

Brochure: free
Save: up to 50%
Pay: check or MO
Sells: carpeting, vinyl flooring, padding
Store: Walnut Ave. (Exit 136 off I-75),
Dalton, GA; Monday to Friday 8–5

$$ ☎ 🍁

Warehouse Carpets began life in 1977 as a carpeting wholesaler, and has since moved into the wonderful world of retail mail order. Warehouse Carpets offers customers savings of as much as 50% on the price of quality carpeting and floor coverings. Call for a quote if you're shopping for carpeting from Aladdin, Cabin Crafts, Columbus, Downs, Galaxy, Horizon, Interloom, Lees, Masland, Mohawk, Philadelphia, Salem, J.P. Stevens, World, or Wunda Weave, or vinyl flooring from Armstrong, Congoleum, Mannington, or Tarkett. And if you'd like to save an average of 50% on rug padding, Warehouse Carpets can provide several types.

You can call or write with the names of the manufacturer and style of the carpeting you want, and follow with a 50% deposit (check or money order). The balance is due when the goods are ready for shipment, which is made by common carrier, and the brochure and information sheet from Warehouse Carpets include complete details of the terms.

Special Factors: All goods are first quality; price quote by phone or letter with SASE; orders are shipped worldwide.

WELLS INTERIORS INC.

**7171 AMADOR PLAZA DR.
DUBLIN, CA 94568
800-547-8982**

Catalog: free
Save: up to 75%
Pay: check, MO, MC, V
Sells: window treatments and accessories
Store: same address; Monday to Friday 10–6, Saturday 10–5, Sunday 12–4; 17 other stores in CA and OR (see the catalog for locations)

$$$ ☎ ♣

Wells Interiors guarantees "the lowest prices" on its goods, and will beat any other dealer's price down to cost on a wide range of top brands. Discounts run up to 75% on retail prices, on Levolor's Riviera, Monaco, private-label blinds, and vertical lines (in all fabrics, materials, colors, and options offered by Levolor), HunterDouglas blinds, LouverDrape vertical blinds, and Del Mar woven woods, Duette blinds, Softlight shades, and metal blinds and verticals. Kirsch woven woods, pleated shades, decorator roller shades, verticals, and miniblinds are also available.

The catalog includes a helpful guide to the lines currently available, and includes instructions on measuring your windows and installing your blinds. Details of the firm's warranty are given in the catalog as well.

Special Factors: Price quote by phone or letter; written confirmation is required on phone orders.

SEE ALSO

Aristocast Originals Inc. • reproduction cast moldings, fireplace surrounds, architectural details, etc. • *HOME: MAINTENANCE*
BRE Lumber • flooring, cabinet-grade lumber, and paneling • *HOME: MAINTENANCE*
Buffalo Batt & Felt Corp. • throw pillow inserts and upholstery stuffing • *CRAFTS*
The Caning Shop • seat-weaving materials, replacement seats, upholstery supplies • *CRAFTS*

Cherry Hill Furniture, Carpet & Interiors • rugs, carpeting, and accessories • *HOME: FURNISHINGS*

CMC Music, Inc. • Howard Miller clocks • *MUSIC*

Crawford's Old House Store • reproduction Victorian lighting, relief wall coverings, etc. • *HOME: MAINTENANCE*

The Deerskin Place • sheepskins • *CLOTHING*

Defender Industries, Inc. • teak kitchen and bath accessories • *AUTO*

Eldridge Textile Co. • window treatments • *HOME: LINEN*

Goldberg's Marine Distributors • teak kitchen and bath accessories • *AUTO*

Home-Sew • upholstery supplies • *HOME: DECOR*

Leather Unlimited Corp. • sheepskin rugs • *LEATHER*

Loftin-Black Furniture Company • lamps, mirrors, etc. • *HOME: FURNISHINGS*

D. MacGillivray & Coy. • sheepskin rugs • *CRAFTS*

Murrow Furniture Galleries, Inc. • lamps • *HOME: FURNISHINGS*

Newark Dressmaker Supply, Inc. • upholstery supplies • *CRAFTS*

Quality Furniture Market of Lenoir, Inc. • lamps, decorator fabrics, etc. • *HOME: FURNISHINGS*

Shuttercraft • interior and exterior wooden window shutters • *HOME: MAINTENANCE*

Stuckey Brothers Furniture Co., Inc. • clocks, mirrors, etc. • *HOME: FURNISHINGS*

Sultan's Delight, Inc. • leather "camel" saddlebag hassocks • *FOOD*

Thai Silks • upholstery-weight silk fabrics • *CRAFTS*

Utex Trading Enterprises • upholstery-weight silk fabrics • *CRAFTS*

Furnishings

Household furnishings of all types, including outdoor furniture, office furnishings, and services

You can save as much as 50% on the suggested retail prices by ordering your furniture from North Carolina, the manufacturing center of the furnishing industry. The discounters don't take the staggering markups that make name-brand furnishings and home accessories prohibitively expensive in department and furniture stores, and that doesn't endear them to the furniture manufacturers;in fact, a number of manufacturers do everything they can to make it difficult for discounters to sell by mail, forbidding them to trade outside designated "selling areas" and sometimes even prohibiting the firms from having 800 lines. (Manufacturers elicit compliance by threatening to refuse to fill the discounters' orders.) This practice has the effect of limiting trade, and we find it reprehensible. To avoid creating problems for the discounters, we've *omitted brand names* in their listings. Most of these firms can take orders for furniture and accessories from hundreds of manufacturers, can supply catalogs, brochures, and swatches, and give decorating advice over the phone.

We strongly recommend using "in-home delivery service" when a firm offers it, since the furniture will be uncrated exactly where you want it. If there are any damages, you'll see them right away and can contact the company while the shipper is there to find out what you should do.

For listings of other firms that sell furnishings and decorative pieces for the home, see the "Decor" section of "Home," and "General Merchandise." Although some of the firms listed here also sell lines of office furniture, see "Office" for a more comprehensive selection.

BARNES & BARNES FINE FURNITURE

━━━━━━━

190 COMMERCE AVE.
SOUTHERN PINES, NC
  28387
800-334-8174
FAX: 919/692-3381

Brochure: free
Save: up to 55%
Pay: check, MO, MC, V
Sells: home furnishings
Store: same address; Monday to Friday 9–5,
  Saturday by appointment

$$ ☎

Barnes & Barnes has been selling home furnishings and accessories since 1980, and can save you up to 55% on the suggested retail prices on pieces from a long list of manufacturers. In addition to hundreds of furniture lines that include patio furniture, brass beds, and office furniture, Barnes & Barnes sells lamps, mirrors, clocks, and decorator fabric from a number of prominent firms. A deposit of 50% is required to place an order, and the rest is due upon delivery. Shipping charges are collected on delivery. For a roster of the available manufacturers and details on the firm's sales policy, request the free brochure.

Special Factor: Price quote by phone or letter.

CHERRY HILL FURNITURE, CARPET & INTERIORS

━━━━━━━

P.O. BOX 7405,
  FURNITURELAND
  STATION
HIGH POINT, NC 27264
800-328-0933
800-888-0933
919/882-0933
FAX: 919/882-0900

Brochure: free
Save: up to 50%
Pay: check or MO
Sells: home and office furniture and
  accessories
Store: mail order only

$$$ 🍁 ▤

Cherry Hill, in business since 1933, offers a wide range of home and office furnishings, accessories, and rugs and carpeting at prices that average 45% off list. The Contract Division serves the needs of developers, purchasing directors, architects, and others who are doing residential or commercial installations. Cherry Hill can supply lines from over 500 manufacturers, which are listed in the brochure that's sent upon request. A video catalog profiling popular lines is also available—call for information.

Special Factors: Price quote by phone or letter with SASE; inquiries are accepted over the 800 line; shipment is made by common carrier or van line.

FACTORY DIRECT TABLE PAD CO.

**1036 N. CAPITOL AVE.,
SUITE C-210
INDIANAPOLIS, IN 46204
800-428-4567**

Prices and Samples: $1
Save: up to 50%
Pay: check, MO, MC, V, Discover
Sells: custom-made table pads
Store: mail order only

$$

Factory Direct's brochure tells us that about half of the cost of a custom-made table pad is the fee paid to the person who measures the table. If you send for information, you'll receive a guide to doing this yourself, as well as a discount coupon for $100 off Factory Direct's retail prices. You'll also receive several sample chips of the table pad top, which can be made in pebble-grain or smooth finish, in plain colors or in wood grain, in different thicknesses. The pads are warrantied for 5, 10, 15, or 20 years, and complete details on the terms of sale are given in the literature.

Special Factors: Price quote by phone or letter; authorized returns are accepted within 15 days.

THE FURNITURE BARN

1190 HWY. 74 BYPASS
SPINDALE, NC 28160
704/287-7106
FAX: 704/287-8785

Brochure: free with SASE
Save: up to 55%
Pay: check, MO, MC, V, Discover
Sells: home furnishings and accessories
Store: same address; Monday to Saturday
9–5

$$$$ ☎ 🍁 ▥

The Furniture Barn is a family-owned firm that's been selling fine furnishings at great prices since 1970, and prides itself on prompt handling of orders and excellent delivery service. Furniture and decorative accessories can be bought here at savings of up to 55% on list prices. The Furniture Barn represents hundreds of manufacturers, listed in the brochure, which also includes details on the terms of sale. If you're in the Spindale area, drop by—there's a "mini-barn" for children and a 20,000-square-foot showroom.

Special Factors: Price quote by phone or letter with SASE; shipment is made by "a professional delivery specialist"; a 33% deposit is required.

GENADA IMPORTS

P.O. BOX 204, DEPT. W-92
TEANECK, NJ 07666
201/790-7522

Catalog: $1
Save: up to 40%
Pay: check, MO, MC, V
Sells: Danish and modern furniture
Store: mail order only

$$ 🍁 ▥

Genada sells Danish modern furniture in its most American incarnation: low-slung, teak-finished chairs and couches, with loose-cushion backs and seats of tweed-covered foam. The style has weathered fad and fatigue quite well, and the furniture's basic appeal is only enhanced by its low prices. Armchairs begin at under $100, and couches start at under $170 (armless divans from $120).

Genada isn't limited to Scandinavian design; the catalog shows reproductions of the Eames chair and other modern classics, folding chairs with woven rope seats and backs, knock-down bookcases and cabinets, butcher block table tops and bases, convertible foam-block chairs and sofas, gateleg tables with chairs that store in the base, and bentwood chairs. The catalog we reviewed also featured modern chairs by Paoli Chair Co., suitable for home of office, as well as several handsome styles in molded teak, walnut, and rosewood finishes, from about $300 and up. Imported armoires, freestanding wall units, computer work stations, desks, VCR carts, and bar stools are all available. If you're shopping for a bridge table with folding hardwood chairs, you'll find several reasonably priced styles here.

Special Factors: Price quote by phone or letter; specify upholstery and finish materials when ordering.

HARVEST HOUSE FURNITURE

P.O. BOX 1440
DENTON, NC 27239-1440
704/869-5181

Information: inquire (see text)
Save: up to 52%
Pay: check, MO, MC, V, Discover
Sells: home and office furnishings
Store: Hwy. 109 S., Denton, NC; Monday to Friday 9–5, Saturday 9–1

$$$ ☎ ♣

Harvest House has been doing business since 1977, selling name-brand home and office furnishings at savings that average 45% to 50% off list. During the periodic "sales," prices are up to 546% off manufacturers' suggested retail (with a minimum order of $400).

If you're still deciding which furniture to buy, you can send for the Harvest House brochure that includes a brands list and a question-naire, which you may complete and return with $6 (refundable with purchase). Harvest House will send you an information packet, with manufacturers' brochures selected to suit your tastes and needs. If you've chosen your furniture and are comparison shopping, you can call or write for a quote. Be sure to ask for the "Sales and Delivery Policy" sheet before you order, since it details the delivery terms and procedures.

Special Factors: Price quote by phone or letter with SASE; orders are shipped worldwide.

INTERIOR FURNISHINGS LTD.

P.O. BOX 1644
HICKORY, NC 28603
704/328-5683

Brochure: free
Save: up to 50%
Pay: check, MO, certified check
Sells: home furnishings and accessories
Store: 1308 Hwy. 70 S.W., Hickory, NC;
Monday to Friday 8:30–5, Saturday
8:30–12 noon

$$ ♦ ▭

The brands list from Interior Furnishings includes the names of some of North Carolina's best-known manufacturers, who produce home furnishings, bedding, lamps, mirrors, table pads, and other accessories. A deposit of one-third is required to place an order, and the balance is due before shipment is made. Only first-quality goods are sold, and Interior offers both common carrier and van line deliveries.

Special Factors: Price quote by phone or letter with SASE; orders are shipped worldwide.

LIBERTY GREEN

P.O. BOX 5035, STATION
1-WBM
WILMINGTON, NC 28403
800-255-9704
919/395-1440
FAX: 919/343-1170

Catalog: $3, refundable
Save: up to 60%
Pay: check, MO, MC, V, AE
Sells: country furnishings
Store: mail order only

$$$ ☎ ♦ ▭

Liberty Green is nestled deep in the land of furniture discounters, but takes a different approach from most: Instead of offering every line from every manufacturer in North Carolina, Liberty Green sells the work of its own craftsmen, at prices as much as 60% less than those of comparable goods bought from other furniture retailers.

The 12-page color catalog features "Plantation-style" furniture, which may be best described as simple country pine with a nod to the Shakers. Among its offerings are raised-panel entertainment centers, rush-seat ladderback chairs, a hutch in Welsh dresser style, pencil-post bed and coordinating bureaus and nightstands, wardrobes, lingerie chests, corner and jelly cupboards, hope chests, benches, and related pieces. The furniture is offered in a choice of stains with a satin lacquer or a "whitewashed" finish. A modified camel-back sofa and wing chair are also available, in a range of fabrics. As a finishing touch, Liberty Green will even affix a small brass plaque declaring your selection "custom crafted" for you if the piece costs over $200. If you like the country look but have been shocked at the prices in the catalogs catering to this style, you'll find this firm a pleasant relief. Liberty Green has been doing business since 1984, and guarantees your satisfaction with everything it produces.

Special Factors: Satisfaction is guaranteed; price quote by phone or letter; returns are accepted within 90 days for exchange, refund, or credit; orders are shipped worldwide.

LOFTIN-BLACK FURNITURE COMPANY

III SEDGEHILL DR.
THOMASVILLE, NC 27360
800-334-7398
919/472-6117
FAX: 919/472-2052

Brochure: free
Save: up to 50%
Pay: check, MO, MC, V
Sells: furnishings, bedding, and accessories
Store: same address; Monday to Saturday 8:30–5:30

$$$$ 🍁 ▄▄▄

Loftin-Black, founded in 1948, delivers selection, service, and savings. The firm offers fine home, office, and patio furniture and bedding, and accessories from hundreds of firms, including the top names in furnishings. Check here before ordering mirrors, table pads, and bedding—they're also available, at sizable savings. The brochure includes a brands listing and general sales information (a 50% deposit is required when ordering, and the balance is due upon delivery). Loftin-Black will provide in-home delivery and setup, although you can engage a common carrier if you prefer. If you're in the Thomasville area, drop in and see Loftin-Black's 14,000 square feet of furniture on display.

Special Factors: Price quote by phone or letter; delivery (in-home) is made by Loftin-Black's van service; orders are shipped worldwide.

MURROW FURNITURE GALLERIES, INC.

P.O. BOX 4337, DEPT. WBMC
WILMINGTON, NC 28406
919/799-4010
FAX: 919/791-2791

Brochure: free
Save: up to 50%
Pay: check or MO
Sells: home furnishings, bedding, and accessories
Store: 3514 S. College Rd., Wilmington, NC; Monday to Friday 8:30–5:30, Saturday 9–5:30

$$$ ☎ ♦

Murrow, founded in 1979, sells furnishings, bedding, and accessories from over 500 furnishings manufacturers (listed in the brochure). The extensive selection of brands and consistently good savings make this one of the best furniture discounters around. If you're able to visit the store in Wilmington, you'll find five gallery showrooms of 45,000 square feet, with fine furnishings and accessories on display. Delivery options and terms of sale are detailed in the brochure.

Special Factors: Price quote by phone or letter with SASE; deposit by check or money order is required; orders are shipped worldwide.

PLEXI-CRAFT QUALITY PRODUCTS CORP.

514 W. 24TH ST.
NEW YORK, NY 10011-1179
800-24-PLEXI
212/924-3244

Catalog: $2
Save: up to 50%
Pay: check, MO, MC, V
Sells: acrylic furnishings and accessories
Store: same address; Monday to Friday 9:30–5, Saturday 11–4

$$ ☎

Plexi-Craft manufactures its own line of Lucite® and Plexiglas® goods, which it sells at up to 50% below the prices charged for comparable products by department and specialty stores. Plexi-Craft, founded in 1972, also accepts orders for custom work.

Acrylic furnishings and accessories of all kinds are shown in the 16-page catalog. There are a number of tables—dining, cocktail, Parsons,

TV, snack, and side—and those with separate bases may be ordered with glass instead of acrylic tops. Several rolling bars are available, as well as chairs, pedestals, computer stands, vanities and stools, luggage racks, magazine units, and telephone tables. Desk sets, kitchen organizers and paper towel holders, and bathroom fixtures round out the selection. Antistatic cleaner and a polish formulated for acrylic are also available.

Special Factor: Price quote by phone or letter on custom work.

QUALITY FURNITURE MARKET OF LENOIR, INC.

2034 HICKORY BLVD. S.W.
LENOIR, NC 28645
704/728-2946
FAX: 704/726-0226

Information: price quote
Save: up to 47%
Pay: check, MO, MC, V
Sells: furnishings, bedding, and accessories
Store: same address; Monday to Saturday 8:30–5

$$$$ ✦

Quality Furniture Market, in business since 1953, takes its name seriously: You're invited to check the firm's ratings with Dun and Bradstreet, the Lyons listing, and the Lenoir Chamber of Commerce. The firm's magnificent selection is offered at prices that are 15% to 20% over cost, compared to the usual 110% to 125%.

Quality Furniture sells indoor and outdoor furniture, bedding, and home accessories by literally hundreds of firms. The list of brands is given in the brochure, as well as terms of sale and other conditions. We've received letters from readers who were very pleased with Quality's prices and the firm's in-home delivery service. If you're traveling near Lenoir, drop by and get lost in the three floors of furniture galleries and display rooms.

Special Factors: Price quote by phone or letter with SASE; all orders must be prepaid before shipment; shipment is made by common carrier or in-home delivery service.

QUEEN ANNE FURNITURE COMPANY, INC.

RTE. 2, BOX 427
TRINITY, NC 27370
919/431-2562
919/434-4990

Brochure with Swatches: $3 (see text)
Save: 45% average
Pay: check, MO, MC, V
Sells: home furnishings
Store: mail order only

$$ ☎

Queen Anne Furniture Company has found its inspiration as well as its name in "the Gallant Era of the 18th Century Splendor." The firm has been producing Queen Anne sofas, wing chairs, and other classics since 1983, at prices that average 45% below retail.

The six-page brochure shows clear, black-and-white photographs of the firm's sofas, loveseats, wing chairs, swivel rockers, Martha Washington chairs, slipper chairs, upholstered ottomans, and other seating. Dimensions of each piece are stated, and you can choose from three leg styles (cabriole with pad feet, Chippendale, or ball and claw), and cherry or oak stain and lacquer finish. Swatches of the firm's fabric come with the brochure as part of the $3 fee; you can use the firm's material or provide your own, in which case the prices are lower.

In addition to its own line, Queen Anne represents a number of well-known manufacturers of furniture and home accessories, which it also sells at a discount. See the brochure for a list of the available brands, or call for information and a price quote.

Please note: Pay the brochure/swatch fee by check or money order—not credit card.

Special Factor: Price quote by phone or letter with SASE.

SHAW FURNITURE GALLERIES, INC.

P.O. BOX 576
RANDLEMAN, NC 27317
919/498-2628

Brochure: free
Save: up to 45%
Pay: check, MO, MC, V
Sells: furnishings
Store: 131 W. Academy St., Randleman, NC; Monday to Friday 9–5:30, Saturday 9–5

$$$ ☎

The Shaw family has been selling furniture at a discount since 1940 and represents over 300 manufacturers; the large inventory can be seen in Shaw's showroom in Randleman. The brochure includes a partial listing of the available brands; inquire if you're pricing an item by a firm not mentioned, since it may be carried. The terms of sale are detailed in the brochure, and please note that final payments must be made by certified check or money order.

Special Factors: Price quote by phone or letter with SASE; shipments are made by van line or common carrier.

STUCKEY BROTHERS FURNITURE CO., INC.

RTE. 1, P.O. BOX 527
STUCKEY, SC 29554
803/558-2591
FAX: 803/558-9229

Information: price quote
Save: up to 50%
Pay: check, MO, certified check
Sells: indoor and outdoor furnishings and accessories
Store: same address; Monday to Friday 9–6, Saturday 9–5

$$ 🍁 ▬

Stuckey is South Carolina's answer to High Point—it sells a full line of furniture and accessories at North Carolina prices, and has been doing business by mail since 1946. Furnishings and accessories are available, including patio and nursery lines, from over 300 manufacturers. Clocks, lamps, mirrors, and bedding are available as well. Request the brochure that details the sales terms and shipping options (van line or common carrier).

Special Factors: Price quote by phone or letter with SASE; orders are shipped worldwide.

MARION TRAVIS

P.O. BOX 292
STATESVILLE, NC 28677
704/528-4424

Catalog: $1
Save: up to 50%
Pay: check, MO, MC, V
Sells: country chairs, benches, and tables
Store: 354 South Eastway Dr., Troutman, NC; Monday to Thursday 8–3:30, Friday 8–12 noon

$$$

You can pay hundreds of dollars for an oak pedestal table at your local antique shop, and search every tag sale in the state for a matched set of ladder-back chairs. Or you can send $1 to Marion Travis for the catalog that shows these and other furnishings.

You'll see ten pages with black-and-white photographs of country furniture, including a large selection of ladder-back chairs with woven cord seats. There are armchair and rocker styles and children's models, beginning at under $25. Plain, slat-seat kitchen chairs and a classic oak kitchen table with utility drawer are shown, as well as a deacon's bench, porch swing, and Kennedy-style rockers with cane backs and seats. The prices cited are for unfinished furniture, but Marion Travis will stain and finish your selection in natural, oak, or walnut.

Special Factor: Authorized returns of defective goods are accepted within 30 days.

TURNER TOLSON, INC.

P.O. DRAWER 1507
NEW BERN, NC 28560
800-334-6616
919/638-2121

Brochure: free
Save: up to 50%
Pay: check, MO, MC, V
Sells: home and office furnishings
Store: Hwy. 17 South, New Bern, NC; Monday to Saturday 10–6

$$$ ☎ 🍁

Turner Tolson, in business since 1887, is an authorized dealer for prominent names in home and office furnishings. The firm's brochure includes a partial roster of brands, and inquiries are invited on manufacturers not listed. Turner's prices are 40% to 50% lower than list, and shipping charges include in-home delivery and setup. A 25% deposit is required to place an order. You're invited to check the company's references with the New Bern Chamber of Commerce and the local bank. And if you make your purchase in person from the 36,000-square-foot showroom, Turner Tolson may pick up the check for your lodgings in New Bern—inquire for details.

Special Factors: Price quote by phone or letter with SASE; a 25% deposit is required when ordering.

ZARBIN & ASSOCIATES, INC.

**401 N. FRANKLIN ST.,
4TH FLOOR
CHICAGO, IL 60610
312/527-1570**

Information: price quote
Save: up to 40%
Pay: check, MO, certified check
Sells: furniture and bedding
Store: mail order only (see text)

$$

The Zarbin family has been selling furniture, bedding, and carpeting since 1963, and its mail-order department offers you a hassle-free way to save 40% on the best in home decor. Professional designers on staff can assist you in your selections by phone or mail, or guide you through the showroom of the Merchandise Mart in Chicago, where samples are displayed. Most of the goods are shipped from manufacturers' warehouses to the trucker; delivery charges and services include uncrating and setup.

Special Factor: Price quote by letter with SASE (include manufacturer's name, item stock number, and fabric and grade numbers, if applicable).

SEE ALSO

Alfax Wholesale Furniture • office and institutional furnishings • *OFFICE*
American Discount Wallcoverings • upholstery and decorator fabrics •
  HOME: DECOR

Barnes & Noble Bookstores, Inc. • folding beechwood bookshelves • *BOOKS*

Bennett Brothers, Inc. • small selection of home furnishings • *GENERAL MERCHANDISE*

Ben's Babyland • juvenile furniture • *CLOTHING: MOTHER AND CHILD*

Business & Institutional Furniture Company • office and institutional furniture • *OFFICE*

Cole's Appliance & Furniture Co. • home furnishings • *APPLIANCES*

Frank Eastern Co. • office furniture • *OFFICE*

The Fabric Center, Inc. • upholstery and decorator fabrics • *HOME: DECOR*

Fabrics by Design • upholstery and decorator fabrics • *HOME: DECOR*

Grayarc • small selection of office chairs and work stations • *OFFICE*

Harmony Supply Inc. • decorator fabrics • *HOME: DECOR*

Monarch • radiator enclosures • *HOME: MAINTENANCE*

Shama Imports, Inc. • crewel upholstery fabric and cushion covers • *HOME: DECOR*

Slipcovers of America • slipcovers • *HOME: DECOR*

Irv Wolfson Company • small selection of bedding, recliners, and dinette sets • *APPLIANCES*

Kitchen

___

Cookware, bakeware, restaurant equipment, and food storage

This chapter includes companies selling everything from measuring spoons to commercial ranges, frequently at discounts of 30% to 50% on the regular retail prices. For other kitchen electronics, see "Appliances"; for kitchen tools and linens, see the next chapter, "Linen"; and look in "Books" for cookbooks. In addition, a number of firms that sell specialty ingredients and cookware are listed in the "Food and Drink" chapter—including several that offer stupendous buys on herbs, spices, and other flavorings.

WINE STORAGE AND SERVING EQUIPMENT

It makes more sense to stock your wine cellar or bar by going to local sources, rather than buying by mail. Your local wine merchant can help you to choose wines to suit your palate as well as your pocket. (If you're interested in concocting your own liqueurs or becoming a small-scale vintner, see the listing for *E.C. Kraus* in "Food." The firm sells supplies and equipment for making beer and wine, as well as extracts that can be mixed with vodka to create cordials.)

Storing and serving wine properly require some basic equipment and tools. The storage area should be dark, cool (45 to 60 degrees F), and clean. The typical kitchen is the *worst* place for your wine rack. If you're unable to find a good spot in your house, you might consider purchasing a mini-cellar. *The Wine Enthusiast,* listed in this chapter, sells a variety of wine storage units and refrigerators, as well as wine-related accessories. *Bennett Brothers* (in "General Merchandise") sells a temperature-controlled unit, the "Wine Steward," for under $500; it holds up to 19 bottles and can be installed under a kitchen counter. *Plexi-Craft Quality Products* (in the "Furnishings" section) also sells conventional wine racks.

Serving equipment is available from a number of firms. Corkscrews are sold by *E.C. Kraus* and *Mr. Spiceman* (in "Food"). Ice and champagne buckets are sold by both *Bennett Brothers* and *Plexi-Craft,* and we've never seen a catalog from *Grand Finale* (in "General Merchandise") that *didn't* have cocktail napkins, glass coasters, and wine coasters.

FIND IT FAST

CHEESE-MAKING EQUIPMENT • **New England Cheesemaking Supply**
COMMERCIAL FIXTURES • **Fivenson, Kaplan Bros., Peerless**
GOURMET COOKWARE • **A Cook's Wares, Open House, Zabar's**

COLONIAL GARDEN KITCHENS

HANOVER, PA 17333-0066
717/633-3333

Catalog: free
Save: up to 40%
Pay: check, MO, MC, V, CB, DC, Discover
Sells: kitchen equipment and household helps
Store: mail order only

$$ ☎

Colonial Garden Kitchens is one of the Hanover House companies that offers moderately priced gadgets, as well as name-brand appliances that are offered at a discount. A third or more of the goods in the color catalog are usually on "sale," or priced 20% to 40% below their regular prices (and the "regular" prices don't appear to be inflated).

Each catalog features kitchen appliances, specialty cookware and utensils, work units and food storage containers, serving and entertaining equipment, and lots of things handy to have around the house. We've seen the KitchenAid food processor, commercial oven mitts, cast iron woks, a dinosaur muffin tin, insulated bakeware, microwave steamers, inexpensive bath towels, sock organizers, and cleaning products. Everything is backed by the firm's no-questions-asked guarantee of satisfaction.

Special Factors: Satisfaction is guaranteed; returns are accepted for exchange, refund, or credit; minimum order is $15 with credit cards.

A COOK'S WARES

**211 37TH ST.
BEAVER FALLS, PA 15010-
2103
412/846-9490**

Catalog: $2
Save: up to 50%
Pay: check, MO, MC, V, AE
Sells: cookware and kitchen utensils
Store: mail order only

$$$$ ☎ ▨

A Cook's Wares was founded in 1981, and is run by two devoted cooks. They choose the best in cookware and food preparation equipment, and sell it at savings of up to 50% through an informative, 46-page catalog.

The firm's stock includes cookware lines by All-Clad (the Cop-R Chef, anodized aluminum, and Master Chef lines), Chantal, Le Creuset, Cuisinart, Spring Copper, T-Fal, and Vollrath, and Mauviel's hotel-weight copper pots and pans. The Jacques Pepin Collection from Bourgeat is available, as well as bakeware by Apilco, Pillivuyt, Isabelle Marique Blue Steel, Kaiser, and Chicago Metallic (Village Baker and Silverstone-on-Steel). Cookie cutters from Ateco are listed in the catalog, as are molds for ladyfingers, petit fours, madeleines, macaroons, and other sweets. The cutlery and food preparation and serving equipment includes Kenwood and KitchenAid mixers and accessories, Hitachi automatic bread machines, Bron and Moha mandolines, barbecue equipment, Melior infusion coffee makers, Gaggia espresso makers, Krups equipment (coffee grinders, coffee makers, scales, and timers), Vitantonio and Mouli appliances, Tefal toasters, J.K. Adams wooden knife blocks, Rosti utensils and storage containers, Cuisinart food processors, and the complete Henckels cutlery and kitchen gadget lines. Also offered are goods by Atlas, William Bounds, Copco, F. Dick, DMT, Lola, Sparta, Victorinox, Westmark, Wusthof-Trident, and other makers, and cookbooks have just been added to the firm's impressive inventory.

A Cook's Wares has brought the same standards to its line of foodstuffs, primarily condiments: Paul Corcellet vinegars and mustards, Classic American mustards, Blanchard & Blanchard condiments, Select Origins herbs and spices, sun-dried tomatoes, olive spread, and other goods are available. Cooking and eating chocolate from Callebaut, Ghirardelli, and Lindt is offered, as well as Clearbrook Farms' dessert sauces, Tiptree preserves, and Vermont maple syrup.

Special Factors: Satisfaction is guaranteed; price quote by phone or letter with SASE on items not listed in the catalog; returns are accepted within 30 days.

FIVENSON FOOD EQUIPMENT, INC.

324 S. UNION ST.
TRAVERSE CITY, MI
  49684-2586
616/946-7761
IN MI 800-632-7342
FAX: 616/946-7126

Catalog: $3, refundable
Save: up to 60%
Pay: check, MO, MC, V, AE, Discover
Sells: commercial restaurant, bar, and concession equipment
Store: same address; Monday to Friday 8:30–5, Saturday 10–12

 $$$

Fivenson has been selling restaurant equipment to the food-service industry since 1937 and offers consumers the same products at prices up to 50% below list.

Fivenson's 16-page catalog features ranges, ovens, steamers, and fryers by Frymaster, Garland, Toastmaster, U.S. Range, and Vulcan, as well as Cleveland Range appliances, Idea and Wells warmers, Savoy toasters, and Amana Radarange microwave ovens. There are mixers from Dormont, Hamilton Beach, Hobart, Univex, and Waring, as well as Jackson dishwashers, cooling units of every description from Delfield, Kolpak, McCall, Northland, Raetone, and True, and sinks, lunchroom furniture, bakery racks, cleaning tools, chafing dishes, restaurant china, and other supplies. (The china and glassware are sold by the case only.) You can call or write for a price quote on specific models, or send for the catalog.

Special Factors: Price quote by phone or letter with SASE; kitchen layout and design services are available; orders are shipped worldwide.

KAPLAN BROS. BLUE FLAME CORP.

▬▬▬▬▬▬▬

523 W. 125TH ST.
NEW YORK, NY 10027-
3498
212/662-6990
FAX: 212/663-2026

Brochure: free with SASE
Save: up to 50%
Pay: check, MO, certified check
Sells: commercial restaurant equipment
Store: same address; Monday to Friday 8–5

$$

Kaplan Bros., established in 1953, sells commercial restaurant equipment at discounts of up to 50% on list prices and will send you manufacturers' brochures on request, if you supply a self-addressed, stamped envelope.

Kaplan is best known as a source for Garland commercial stoves, including the popular six-burner model that costs over $2,020 at list price, but $1,010 here. (Garland's Residential Range model is available.) Garland fryers, ovens, griddles, and salamanders are stocked, as well as Frymaster and Pitco fryers, PittWire modular wire shelving systems, and equipment by Blickman, Blodgett, and Vulcan.

Please note: Goods are shipped to "mainland U.S.A." only—no orders can be shipped to Alaska, Hawaii, Canada, or APO/FPO addresses.

Special Factors: Price quote by phone or letter with SASE; request brochures by name of manufacturer; if purchasing a stove for residential installation, have kitchen flooring, wall insulation, and exhaust system evaluated before ordering and upgrade if necessary.

KITCHEN ETC.

31 LAFAYETTE RD., DEPT. WBM92
P.O. BOX 1560
NORTH HAMPTON, NH 03862
800-232-4070
FAX: 603/964-5123

Catalog: free
Save: 40% average
Pay: check, MO, MC, V
Sells: tableware, kitchenware, and table linens
Store: Burlington and Natick, MA; Nashua and North Hampton, NH; and South Burlington, VT (see the catalog for locations)

$$$ ☎ 🍁 ▬

Kitchen Etc. has put together two great catalogs of fine china, cutlery, kitchenware, and serving pieces that bring you helpful buying information, as well as prices that are as much as 60% below regular retail. The firm has been doing business since 1983, and has five stores in New England.

The 92-page "Dinnerware Catalog" features several color pages of china patterns from Franciscan, International China, J.G. Durand, Johnson Brothers, Minton, Nikko, Noritake, Otagiri (Horizon), Pfaltzgraff, Royal Albert, Royal Doulton, and Wedgwood. The catalog also includes the available patterns, a guide to the shapes of each piece, present and future availability, and suggested list and discount prices. Stemware from Atlantis Block, J.G. Durand, Noritake, and Royal Doulton is sold, as well as Oneida stainless and silverplate.

The 36-page "Cook 'n Dine Catalog" offers kitchenware and serving pieces from some of the same manufacturers, as well as selected kitchen appliances by Atlas, Braun, Chantry, Krups, Melitta, and other well-known makers. There are spice racks and cookie jars, marble pastry slabs and lobster pots, soapstone griddles and iron kettles, all sold at a discount. If you're buying cookware or cutlery, check the prices on bakeware from Rema, Revere, Village Baker, and Wilton, the knives from Chicago Cutlery and Henckels, and the cookware from All-Clad, Berndes Bonanza, Calphalon, Corning Ware, Farberware, Le Creuset, Magnalite, Revere Ware, T-Fal, and Wagner (cast iron). The catalog includes a good deal of information on the materials and construction of the cookware, as well as illustrations of the different pots and pans.

Kitchen Etc. also offers a range of gifts and accessories, including frames from Burnes of Boston, Royal Doulton's Beatrix Potter china for children, wine buckets and candlesticks, pasta bowl sets, acrylic cutting boards, turkey platters, Mirro pressure cookers, and Joyce Chen woks. Special orders are accepted on some goods, so if you don't see what you're looking for in the catalog, call to see whether Kitchen Etc. can get it. Kitchen Etc. also maintains a bridal registry service.

Special Factors: Satisfaction is guaranteed; price quote by phone or letter; orders are shipped worldwide.

NEW ENGLAND CHEESEMAKING SUPPLY CO.

BOX 85, WBM
ASHFIELD, MA 01330
413/628-3808
FAX: 413/628-4061

Catalog: $1
Save: up to 80% (see text)
Pay: check, MO, MC, V
Sells: cheese-making supplies and
equipment
Store: Ashfield, MA; Monday to Friday 8–4
(call first)

$$ ☎ ♦

Making cheese at home is one of the few do-it-yourself endeavors with a nominal price tag that doesn't require a significant time or skills investment. New England Cheesemaking Supply, in business since 1978, can provide you with all the tools and materials you'll need to produce hard, soft, and semi-soft cheeses, at savings of up to 80% on the prices charged for the same kinds of cheeses.

Soft cheese is the easiest to make, and may be the cheapest, since you can get as much as two pounds of cheese from a gallon of milk. Milk is selling for $1.20 a half gallon in some parts of the country, and flavored soft cheeses often cost $4.50 to $7.00 per pound, or as much as $2.80 for packaged, four-ounce varieties. So, by using the "Gourmet Soft Cheese Kit," you can recoup the $15.95 cost, plus the price of the milk, after making as little as two pounds of soft cheese. This kit is designed for the beginner and comes with cheese starter, cheesecloth, a dairy thermometer, and recipes. It can be used to make *crème fraiche* as well as *fromage blanc*—generic soft cheese—in as little as ten minutes. (If you use skim milk, you can produce low-calorie, low-cholesterol cheese, and omit the salt for sodium-restricted diets.)

New England Cheesemaking Supply also sells a "basic" cheese kit (for ricotta, Gouda, Monterey Jack, cheddar, etc.), and others for making mozzarella and goat cheese. Rennet (animal and vegetable), a large selection of starter and direct-set cultures, lipase powders, mold powder, cheese wax, cheesecloth, thermometers, molds for shaping hard and soft cheese, and several books on cheese production are offered. Experienced cheese producers should see the 16-page catalog for the machinery as well: a home milk pasteurizer, Wheeler hard cheese press, and Deva nonelectric devices for making yogurt and soft cheese are all available. The couple who run this firm are experienced cheese producers, and can answer your questions by phone or letter.

Special Factors: Price quote by phone or letter with SASE; minimum order is $20 with credit cards; C.O.D. orders are accepted; orders are shipped worldwide.

OPEN HOUSE

**200 BALA AVE.
BALA-CYNWYD, PA 19004
215/664-1488**

Information: price quote
Save: up to 40%
Pay: check, MO, MC, V
Sells: flatware, stemware, cookware, etc.
Store: same address; Monday to Saturday 10–5

$$

Open House has been doing business since 1960, and prices its collection of tableware, cookware, cutlery, and linens at up to 40% below list or usual retail prices. There is no catalog, but you can call for a price quote on Arabia, Calphalon, Chantal, Le Creuset, Dansk, Fitz & Floyd, Guzzini, Libbey, Mikasa, Nikko, Retroneau, Schott-Zwiesel, Tri-Chef, and other brands. If you're trying to find the best price on name-brand cookware or table settings, give this firm a call—it may be available.

Open House is offering readers a discount of 10% on their first order. Be sure to identify yourself as a WBMC reader when you order, and deduct the discount from the cost of the goods only. This WBMC reader discount expires February 1, 1993.

Special Factor: Price quote by phone or letter with SASE.

PARIS INTERNATIONAL INC.

PARIS BREAD PANS
500 INDEPENDENCE
AVE., S.E.
WASHINGTON, DC 20003
202/544-6858

Price List: free with SASE
Save: up to 50%
Pay: check or MO
Sells: bakeware
Store: mail order only

$$$

After returning from a stay of several years in Paris, Clyde Brooks found himself longing for real French bread, for which he could find no substitutes. After some experimenting in the kitchen, he developed a recipe that captured the flavor, but couldn't find a pan that would give the bread its characteristic shape and texture. So he designed one himself, and Paris International was born. Mr. Brooks' pans compare to others sold for twice as much, and he's since developed other useful, well-priced baking equipment.

The Paris International French bread pans are made of nonstick quilted aluminum (two 18″ double-trough pans, $12, or a set of four for $18) for French baguettes and breads. Mr. Brooks has experimented with other breads since getting into the pan business in 1973, and offers a larger-trough pan for Italian loaves and San Francisco sourdough bread for $8. Recipes are included with all of the pans. Paris also sells the "Whole Oven Baking Sheet" in two sizes, for standard and wall ovens, which is useful for large batches of cookies, sweet rolls, and other baked goods. It costs $8 and comes with recipes for cookies and meringues. Mr. Brooks will forward any of these items to your favorite cook, enclosing your note or card if you so desire.

Canadian readers, please note: Only U.S. funds are accepted, and orders are sent via U.S. Postal Service.

Special Factor: Price quote by phone or letter with SASE.

PEERLESS RESTAURANT SUPPLIES

**1124 S. GRAND BLVD.
ST. LOUIS, MO 63104
800-255-3663
314/664-0400**

Catalog: $6
Save: 40% average
Pay: check or MO
Sells: commercial cookware and restaurant equipment
Store: Grand Blvd. (between I-64 and I-44), St. Louis, MO; Monday to Friday 8–5, Saturday 9–12 noon

$$ ☎ ♦

Six dollars brings you the whopping, 272-page Peerless catalog, which has everything you need to set up a professional kitchen or restaurant dining room—except the food. Since so many of the appliances and utensils can do double duty in home kitchens, the catalog makes a good investment if you're planning any significant kitchenware purchases.

Peerless represents over 2,000 manufacturers of everything from diner sugar shakers to walk-ins: tableware, trays and carts, bar accessories, restaurant seating, table linens and kitchen textiles, cookware, ranges and ovens, refrigerators, sinks, work tables, cleaning supplies and equipment, ice machines, dishwashers, and much more. The catalog we reviewed included pages of Libbey glassware, Hall and Buffalo china, cutlery by Chicago Cutlery and Dexter Russell, WearEver pots and pans, Vollrath stainless steel stock pots and chafing dishes, Rubbermaid's professional line of janitorial storage, and food-service containers, Detecto food scales, Hamilton Beach and Waring professional bar appliances, Peerless' own commercial cleaners and polishes, Seco wire shelves, Market Forge steamers, and Robot Coupe food processors. Peerless also offers cooking equipment by Castle, Dean, Frymaster, Hobart, Montague, Southbend, and Vulcan; commercial microwave ovens from MenuMaster and Panasonic, refrigeration from Delfield, Ice-O-Matic, Kelvinator, Raetone, Scotsman, Traulsend, and True; and Eagle sinks, In-Sink-Erator commercial disposers, ventilation equipment, and much more.

If you know what you want by manufacturer and model number, you can call or write for a price quote—but the catalog is worth the $6 fee if you're buying more than a couple of items. Food-service professionals will appreciate the services offered by Peerless, which include facility design, installation, construction supervision, concept development, and equipment leasing. Used kitchenware is also available at big savings, and if you get to St. Louis, stop in and check out the Peerless "Bargain Room," which features closeouts.

Special Factors: Price quote by phone or letter with SASE; quantity discounts are available; authorized returns are accepted within 30 days for exchange, refund, or credit (a 10% restocking fee may be charged, or 20% on special orders).

THE WINE ENTHUSIAST

404 IRVINGTON ST.
P.O. BOX 39
PLEASANTVILLE, NY
    10570-0039
800-356-8466
FAX: 800-833-8466
FAX: 914/747-0618

Catalog: free
Save: up to 30%
Pay: check, MO, MC, V, AE, Discover, Optima
Sells: wine storage units and accessories
Store: same address; Monday to Friday 9–6, Saturday 10–5

$$ ☎

The Wine Enthusiast dedicates itself to serving the oenophile with a 48-page color catalog of everything from corkscrews and stemware to refrigeration units. The firm has been in business since 1980, and sells at discounts of up to 30% on list prices.

Wine storage units are the featured line here, including stained oak modular racks, brass and black enameled steel wall grids, redwood wall systems, and several lines of refrigerated cellars—EuroCave, Sommelier, and Vinotheque, among others. Decanters, stemware, corkscrews, ice buckets and coolers, and books and videotapes on wine appreciation and history are available.

The Wine Enthusiast is offering readers a discount of 5% on all orders. Be sure to identify yourself as a WBMC reader when you order, and deduct the discount from the cost of the goods only. This WBMC reader discount expires February 1, 1993.

Special Factors: Satisfaction is guaranteed; price quote by phone or letter; returns (except food items, videotapes, and software) are accepted within 30 days for exchange, refund, or credit; orders are shipped worldwide.

ZABAR'S & CO., INC.

**2245 BROADWAY
NEW YORK, NY 10024
800-221-3347
212/787-2000**

Catalog: free
Save: up to 50%
Pay: check, MO, MC, V, AE, DC
Sells: gourmet food, cookware, and
   housewares
Store: same address; Monday to Friday
   8–7:30, Saturday 8 A.M.–midnight, Sunday
   9–6; housewares mezzanine 9–6 daily

$$ ☎ 🍁

Zabar's, thought of by many as New York City's ultimate deli, offers the better part of North America a sampling from its famed counters and housewares mezzanine via a 62-page catalog. Zabar's has been around since 1934, and offers savings of up to 50% on name-brand kitchenware, and competitive prices on foodstuffs.

Past catalogs have shown smoked Scottish, Norwegian, and Irish salmon, plum pudding, peppercorns, Brie, Bahlsen cookies and confections, pâtés, mustards, crackers, escargot, Lindt and Droste chocolate, Tiptree preserves, Dresden stollen, olive oil, prosciutto and other deli meats, and similar gourmet fare. The cookware selections include Mauviel hotel-weight copper pots and pans; Calphalon, Cuisinart, Farberware, Le Creuset, Magnalite, and Revere Ware equipment; Krups and Simac machines, Braun coffee makers, Robot Coupe food processors, Sharp microwave ovens, Mouli kitchen tools, and products by Melitta, Henckels, Toshiba, and other firms. Zabar's distinguishes itself among kitchenware vendors for the enormous selection of goods and the substantial discounts. The catalog features a representative selection from the store, but we regret that price quotes aren't given over the phone—if you don't see it in the catalog, you'll just have to visit the store.

Special Factors: Price quote by letter with SASE on cookware not shown in the catalog; minimum order is $10.

SEE ALSO

Bernie's Discount Center, Inc. • microwave ovens and large and small
   kitchen appliances • *APPLIANCES*

Betty Crocker Enterprises • cutlery, cookware, and kitchen gadgets • *GENERAL MERCHANDISE*

Bruce Medical Supply • food preparation equipment for those with limited strength and mobility • *MEDICINE*

Cabela's Inc. • camping cookware, stoves, implements • *SPORTS*

The Chef's Pantry • gourmet cooking ingredients • *FOOD*

CISCO • garbage disposers • *HOME: MAINTENANCE*

Clothcrafters, Inc. • pot holders, chefs' hats, coffee filters, greens bags, kitchen gadgets, etc. • *GENERAL MERCHANDISE*

Current, Inc. • canning labels, recipe boxes, etc. • *BOOKS*

Grandma's Spice Shop • spice racks, wine racks, mortar and pestle sets, teapots, etc. • *FOOD*

Jessica's Biscuit • cookbooks • *BOOKS*

Kitchen Etc. • bakeware, cookware, serving pieces, cutlery, etc. • *HOME: TABLE SETTINGS*

E.C. Kraus Wine & Beermaking Supplies • bottle washers, cherry pitters, funnels, corkscrews • *FOOD*

LVT Price Quote Hotline, Inc. • microwave ovens, major appliances, etc. • *APPLIANCES*

The New England Slate Company • salvaged slate for countertops • *HOME: MAINTENANCE*

The Paper Wholesaler • disposable bakeware and cake-decorating supplies • *GENERAL MERCHANDISE*

Percy's Inc. • major appliances • *APPLIANCES*

Plastic BagMart • garbage can liners • *GENERAL: PACKAGING*

Robin Importers, Inc. • kitchen cutlery, knife blocks, pepper mills, etc. • *HOME: TABLE SETTINGS*

S & S Sound City • microwave ovens • *APPLIANCES*

Simpson & Vail, Inc. • teapots, coffee makers, grinders, filters, etc. • *FOOD*

The Spice House • pepper mills and spice jars • *FOOD*

Sultan's Delight, Inc. • Turkish coffee pots and cups, mamoul and falafel molds, mortars and pestles • *FOOD*

Walnut Acres Organic Farms • cookware, bakeware, serving pieces, etc. • *FOOD*

Weston Bowl Mill • woodenware, knives, and kitchen helpers • *GENERAL MERCHANDISE*

The Wine Enthusiast • wine cellars, storage units, corkscrews, etc. • *FOOD*

Linen

Bed, bath, and table textiles, accessories, and services

Why wait for a white sale when you can buy your sheets, towels, pillows, and table linens from discounters who sell at savings of up to 60% every day, year-round? Some of the firms listed here offer both first-quality and irregular goods, and some sell only first-quality—ask before placing your order to be sure you're getting what you want. In addition to goods from the major mills, several of these firms provide sheets to fit waterbeds and oddly shaped mattresses, will rejuvenate down pillows and comforters, and make bed ruffles and coordinating lamp shades to match your sheets or bedroom fabric.

Caring for your bed, bath, and table textiles properly can mean they'll give you years more wear, so follow the manufacturers' care instructions. Although we've never seen it on a label, we've read that down-filled goods should never be stored in cedar or camphor, since they'll pick up those odors permanently. Some experts also advise against storing down-filled products in plastic—use a cloth bag or pillowcase instead. And if you keep your down-filled comforter slipcased in a duvet when it's in use, you won't have to have it cleaned as often, which will extend the its useful life.

ALDEN COMFORT MILLS

P.O. BOX 55
PLANO, TX 75086-0055
800-822-5336

Catalog: free
Save: up to 40%
Pay: check, MO, MC, V, AE, Discover, Optima
Sells: down-filled bedding, linens, and custom services
Store: 1708 14th St., Plano, TX; Monday to Friday 8–5, Saturday 9–4

$$ ☎ ▀▀▀

Alden Comfort Mills was founded in 1947 by Joe R. Pool, who later went into law and then became a member of the U.S. House of Representatives. Alden is still run by the Pool family, which offers its own line of down-filled comforters and pillows, as well as recovering and other custom services.

The 16-page color catalog features six comforter styles and weights, running from a summer-weight, channel-stitched style (full, $109.95) to the sumptuous "Newport," 64 ounces of down (full, $269). Featherbeds, crib comforters, and both bed and accent pillows filled with down and "featherfluff" feather mix are stocked, as well as well-priced dust ruffles, shams, cases, and duvet covers which can be made in Alden's stock fabric or your own material.

If your comforter cover has seen better days but the down itself still has good loft, it's a candidate for Alden's custom department, which can recover, refill, and even reconfigure the comforter to create a longer drop than the original (to suit the deeper mattresses being made today; more down will be required). Prices are reasonable for custom work and much lower than the cost of replacing good-quality bedding. Down and feather pillows can also be recovered and restuffed, and even old wool comforters can be given a facelift. Call for details, or see the catalog.

Special Factors: Satisfaction is guaranteed; price quote by phone or letter.

EZRA COHEN CORP.

307 GRAND ST.
NEW YORK, NY 10002
212/925-7800
FAX: 212/925-9767

Information: price quote
Save: up to 40%
Pay: check, MO, MC, V, AE, Optima
Sells: bed and bath linens
Store: same address; Sunday to Thursday
9–5, Friday 9–4

$$$ ☎ ▤

Ezra Cohen has been selling bed and bath linens on the Lower East Side since 1903 and stocks full lines from the major mills, as well as a wide range of accessories. Bed linens from Cannon (including the Versailles Charisma Collection), Fieldcrest, Martex (including Atelier), Revman, J.P. Stevens, and Wamsutta are available, including Laura Ashley, Katja, Adrienne Vittadini, Eileen West, and other designer lines. There are bath linens by Avanti, Fieldcrest's Royal Velvet towels and rugs and Charisma towels, and the lush Patrician towels by Martex. Comforters and bedspreads by Croscill, Crown Crafts, Dakotah, Dyne (down comforters), Nettlecreek, and Northern Feather are available. Call or write for prices on Fieldcrest bath carpeting, Regel scatter rugs, polyester and down bedding, and Ferncraft daybed covers. Cohen's custom department can produce shams, bed ruffles, and sheets for nonstandard mattresses.

Special Factors: Price quote by phone or letter with SASE; there is no catalog; store is closed Saturdays.

THE COMPANY STORE INC.

DEPT. A9010
500 COMPANY STORE RD.
LA CROSSE, WI 54601
800-323-8000
608/785-1400
FAX: 608/785-7037

Catalog: free
Save: up to 30%
Pay: check, MO, MC, V, AE, Discover
Sells: down-filled bedding and outerwear
Store: outlets in IL, MN, and WI (locations are given in the catalog)

$$$ ☎ 🍁 ▤

The Company Store publishes a color catalog of well-priced down bedding and a range of linen, and is known for its excellent selection of top-quality goods and prompt service.

Comforters of all weights, sizes, and types are offered here, including box, channel, and ring-stitched down-filled comforters, summer-weight down comforters, and all-cotton comforters. High fill power, natural down-proof materials, and hand-guided quilting are among the product features. Complementing pillows in baby/boudoir, neckroll, European, standard, queen, and king sizes and shapes are also available. The Company Store has a nice selection of all-cotton linens—sheets, bed ruffles, comforter covers, pillowcases, shams, and more, priced well below comparable products from other firms. The nursery department features bedding in pastel solids, crib comforters, bumper pads, and more. The "Custom Shop" can take your ideas for comforters, covers, pillows, and bed ruffles, and create them in your fabric or theirs. Comforter refurbishing and monogramming services are also available.

A portion of the catalog is devoted to the firm's extensive line of down-filled outerwear and accessories for men, women, and children. The offerings run from baby buntings to down-filled trenchcoats for men, and prices are very good.

Special Factors: Satisfaction is guaranteed; returns are accepted for exchange, refund, or credit.

DOMESTICATIONS

HANOVER, PA 17333-0040
717/633-3313

Catalog: $2
Save: up to 35%
Pay: check, MO, MC, V, CB, DC, Discover
Sells: bed and bath linens
Store: mail order only

$$ ☎

Domestications, a Hanover House Industries catalog, offers a colorful selection of linens for bed, bath, and table, plus well-priced home decorating items. Half of the 96-page catalog is devoted to sheets and bedding, with everything from paisley prints and cabbage roses to plush leopardskin and the Simpsons in evidence in the most recent edition. Selections from Bibb, Cannon, Fieldcrest, Martex, Dan River, J.P. Stevens, Utica, Wamsutta, and other firms have been offered in the past. All-cotton and blends are available, in sheet sets and individually. Blankets, bedspreads, and comforters from Barclay, Crown Crafts, Georgia Tufted, and Countess York have been featured, as well as pillows and mattress pads. Tablecloths, window treatment, lamps, decorative accents, and tableware are also featured, and prices run from market rate to bargain basement.

Special Factors: Satisfaction is guaranteed; returns are accepted; minimum order is $20 with credit cards.

ELDRIDGE TEXTILE CO.

**DEPT. L
277 GRAND ST.
NEW YORK, NY 10002
212/925-1523
FAX: 212/219-9542**

Catalog: $3 refundable
Save: up to 60%
Pay: check, MO, MC, V
Sells: bed, bath, and table linens
Store: same address; Sunday to Friday 9–5:30

$$ ☎ 🏳

Eldridge has been selling soft goods and housewares since 1940 and offers mail-order customers savings of up to 40% on bed, bath, and table linens by Laura Ashley, Beau Ideal, Cameo, Croscill, Crown Crafts, Dakotah, Faribo, Fieldcrest, Fashion Home, Innervisions, Jackson, Martex, Nettlecreek, Newmark (bath rugs), Northern Feather, Pacific Designs, Phoenix, André Richard, Saturday Knight, Springmaid, Utica, Wamsutta, and other firms. Some of the best-selling sheet and towel lines are listed in the brochure, but if you're shopping for bedspreads, shower curtains, or comforters, call or write for a price quote. Window treatments by DelMar, Graber, HunterDouglas, Levolor, and LouverDrape are available at savings of up to 60%.

Special Factors: Price quote by phone or letter with SASE; returns of unused goods are accepted for refund or credit; minimum order is $25.

HARRIS LEVY, INC.

**278 GRAND ST., DEPT.
WBM
NEW YORK, NY 10002
800-221-7750
212/226-3102
FAX: 212/334-9360**

Catalog: free
Save: up to 50%
Pay: check, MO, MC, V, AE, Optima
Sells: bed, bath, and table linens
Store: same address; Monday to Thursday
9–5:30, Friday and Sunday 9–4:30

$$$$ ☎

Levy, established in 1894, is one of the plums of New York City's Lower East Side—a firm that sells the crème de la crème of bed, bath, and table linens at savings of up to 50%. One-of-a-kind and imported items are available in the store, and *none* of the stock is seconds or discontinued.

Levy's imports include Egyptian cotton percale and linen sheets, Belgian kitchen towels, Irish damask tablecloths, and bedding from Switzerland, England, France, and Italy—all worth a trip to the store. Mail-order shoppers can call or write for the free catalog or price quotes on bed and bath linens from the major mills: Cannon, Fieldcrest, Martex, Revman, Dan River, Springmaid, J.P. Stevens, and Wamsutta. A large selection of bath accessories, shower curtains, rugs, and towels is also available. Levy's is known for its custom services and can provide monogramming and sheets in special sizes and shapes, tablecloths, dust ruffles, curtains, pillowcases, and other products from stock sheets or your own fabric. Closet organizers, travel accessories, and kitchen gadgets are also available in the store.

Please note: Phone orders are accepted Monday to Friday 10–4 only.

Special Factors: Price quote by phone, fax, or letter with SASE; minimum order is $25 with credit cards; orders are shipped worldwide.

MOTHER HART'S NATURAL PRODUCTS, INC.

P.O. BOX 4229
BOYNTON BEACH, FL
33424-4229
407/738-5866
407/738-0732

Catalog: free
Save: up to 70%
Pay: check, MO, MC, V
Sells: natural-fiber bed and bath linens and clothing
Store: mail order only

$$$ ☎ 🍁 🇺🇸

Mother Hart is the sort of firm we always enjoy finding, a small company run by decent people who sell worthwhile goods at very considerate prices. It's not uncommon to find savings of 50% to 70% on the products sold here, which are chiefly textiles for bed and bath, activewear, and underthings.

We've found stunning buys on flannel sheets and sheet blankets in all sizes in past catalogs, as well as down pillows and comforters, fleece mattress pads, cotton duvet covers in solids and prints, box spring covers and pads, and quilted cotton comforters. One of the best buys we've seen for awhile is in the line of untreated, all-cotton sheets, which don't have the resins that create a no-iron finish (and irritate some skins). Mother Hart's full-sized, untreated sheets cost $23.80 at this writing, while the same kind of sheet, in the same size, costs *$110* from a luxury linens catalog. (The upmarket firm does give you 210 threads per inch to Mother's 200, but how can ten little threads be worth over $86?)

Among the other goods we've seen in past catalogs are canvas luggage, shower curtains, natural-bristle hairbrushes, tote bags, handkerchiefs, cotton throws, and aprons. Leotards, tights, leg warmers, camisoles, sweaters, nightshirts, and other clothing has also been offered, at great savings. Note that some items may be available in limited quantities, so order promptly. All irregular goods are clearly indicated.

Special Factors: Satisfaction is guaranteed; price quote by phone or letter; unused returns are accepted within 30 days; orders are shipped worldwide.

J. SCHACHTER CORP.

85 LUDLOW ST.
NEW YORK, NY 10002
800-INTO-BED
212/533-1150
FAX: 718/384-7634

Catalog: $1
Save: up to 40%
Pay: check, MO, MC, V, Discover
Sells: down-filled bedding, linens, and custom services
Store: same address; Sunday to Thursday 9–5, Friday 9–2

$$ ☎ 🍁(see text) ▤

Schachter has been making comforters and pillows for the bedding industry and recovering old comforters for private customers since 1919. Custom work is featured in the 16-page catalog, but stock goods are also available.

Schachter specializes in custom jobs: Comforters, coverlets, bed ruffles, pillow shams, duvets, and shower curtains are popular requests. Filling choices for the comforters include lambswool, polyester, white goose down, and a nonallergenic synthetic down alternative. Schachter carries bed and bath linens by the major mills—Cannon, Croscill, Crown Craft (Kitan), Fieldcrest, Martex, Springs Industries, and Wamsutta—and labels from France, Germany, England, Switzerland, Italy, and Belgium—Bruna, Palais Royal, Peter Reed, Sferra, and Sufolla. Carter cotton bath rugs, Northern Feather pillows, Dyne comforters, and blankets by Chatham, Early's of Whitney, Faribo, Hudson Bay, and Northern are offered. Schachter's own stock comforters and accessories are all available, and the firm can recover and sterilize old down pillows and comforters.

Canadian readers, please note: Orders are delivered by UPS only.

Special Factors: Price quote by phone or letter with SASE; minimum order is $35 with credit cards; store is closed Saturdays; orders are shipped worldwide.

SPRINGMAID/WAMSUTTA MILL STORE

36 GROCE RD.
LYMAN, SC 29365
803/433-4645
OR
11 GATEWAY BLVD.
  SOUTH
SAVANNAH, GA 31419
912/921-0790
OR
1340 TUNNEL RD.
ASHEVILLE, NC 28805
704/298-3393
OR
3700 AVENUE OF THE
  CAROLINAS
FORT MILL, SC 29715
803/548-7444
OR
1110 MARKET ST.
CHATTANOOGA, TN
  37402
615/756-0805
OR
HIGHWAY 9
LANCASTER, SC 29720
803/286-2491

Information: price quote
Save: up to 50%
Pay: check, MO, MC, V
Sells: Springmaid and Wamsutta bed and
  bath linens and accessories
Store: same addresses; call for hours

$$$ ☎

Springmaid and Wamsutta, two respected home-textiles names owned by Spring Industries, have six mill stores that offer their products at prices up to 50% below suggested retail. Discontinued, first-quality sheets and towels are sold at reduced prices, and the irregulars are substantially discounted. The stores also carry complementing window treatments and a range of bath accessories.

There is no catalog, and you should call to see if what you want is in stock. Be sure you know the exact name of the style or pattern, the size needed, the color (and an alternative, if possible), and specify whether you want irregular or first-quality goods. (We've been told that the Lyman store tends to get more irregulars than the others, but all of them are worth trying if one is out of the desired item.)

Special Factor: Price quote by phone.

SEE ALSO

Atlantic Bridge Collection Corp. Ltd. • Irish double-damask table linens • *ART, ANTIQUES*

Ben's Babyland • nursery linen and bedding • *CLOTHING: MOTHER AND CHILD*

Bradbury's • table linens • *HOME: TABLE SETTINGS*

Campmor • sleeping bags, sleeping bag liners • *SPORTS*

Capital Cycle Corporation • goose-down comforters • *AUTO*

Clothcrafters, Inc. • plain cotton sheets, towels, table linens, etc. • *GENERAL MERCHANDISE*

Gettinger Feather Corp. • pillow feathers • *CRAFTS*

Gohn Bros. • flannel sheets, wool blankets • *CLOTHING*

Kitchen Etc. • table linens • *HOME: TABLE SETTINGS*

D. MacGillivray & Coy. • woven blankets and tartan bedspreads • *CRAFTS*

Plexi-Craft Quality Products Corp. • acrylic bathroom accessories • *HOME: FURNISHINGS*

Retired Persons Services, Inc. • waffle-type foam bed pads • *MEDICINE*

Robin Importers, Inc. • Carefree table linens • *HOME: TABLE SETTINGS*

Rubens & Marble, Inc. • bassinet and crib sheets • *CLOTHING*

Rubin & Green, Inc. • custom-made comforters, bedspreads, etc. • *HOME: DECOR*

Shama Imports, Inc. • crewel-embroidered bedspreads • *HOME: DECOR*

Shannon Duty Free Mail Order • linen damask and lace tablecloths • *HOME: TABLE SETTINGS*

Thai Silks • embroidered Chinese table linens • *CRAFTS*

Irv Wolfson Company • foreign-current electric blankets • *APPLIANCES*

Maintenance and Building

Hardware, tools, equipment, supplies, and materials

Maintaining your home—keeping it clean and in good repair—can involve an enormous amount of time and energy, often unnecessarily. *Make Your House Do the Housework* (Writer's Digest Books, 1986) can help you create the closest thing to a maintenance-free house, from selecting easy-care furniture and carpeting to eliminating gutters. You might not use every idea proposed by Don Aslett and Laura Aslett Simons, but their book has many time-saving tips and pointers we haven't seen elsewhere.

Consumers Union publishes a number of books to help you with everything from buying your next home to cleaning the windows. *Home Improvement Cost Guide, How to Buy a House, Condo, or Co-op, Home Security* (on locks, alarms, etc.), and *How to Clean Practically Everything* are among the titles available at this writing. See the current issue of *Consumer Reports* to order, or check your local bookstore.

For advice ranging from reviving linoleum to reshingling the roof, we turn to *The Old House Journal. OHJ* was founded in 1973 as a forum about rehabbing and restoring old (pre-1930) houses. The bimonthly magazine can be bought by subscription ($21 at this writing), back issue, or in bound yearbooks. *OHJ* books on plastering, Victorian decor, and the valuable *Old House Journal Catalog* are also available. Write to The Old House Journal Corporation, 435 Ninth St., Brooklyn, NY 11215, for subscription rates and book information. (Check the magazine clearinghouses in "Books," as well, since they may offer *OHJ* subscriptions at a better price.)

For related sources, see the listings in "Tools."

FIND IT FAST

ARCHITECTURAL DETAILS • *Aristocast Originals, Crawford's, Saco, Shuttercraft, Vintage Woodworks*

ARCTIC GLASS & WINDOW OUTLET

**RTE. 1-W
HAMMOND, WI 54015
715/796-2292
800-657-4656**

Catalog: $4, refundable
Save: up to 70%
Pay: MO, certified check, MC, V, Discover
Sells: exterior doors, windows, skylights, glass panels
Store: I-94 at Hammond Exit, 16 miles east of Minnesota/Wisconsin border; Monday 9–8, Tuesday to Saturday 9–5, Sunday 12–4

$$$ ☎ ♦

Joseph Bacon began his business after discovering that second-quality patio door panes doubled perfectly as passive solar panels in the greenhouse he was building—and cost up to 70% less. Since founding Arctic Glass in 1979, he's watched it outgrow several facilities, and increase revenues 2,000%.

Arctic Glass sells surplus and second-quality patio door panels from two of the best-known manufacturers in the business. Different types of double and triple panes are available (some with low E coating) and, except for the middle panes of triple-pane panels, most of the glass is 3/16″ thick; all of the panes are double-sealed. The flaws of the seconds shouldn't affect the performance of the panes, and suitable applications and uses are listed in the literature. Arctic also stocks Velux skylights and the complete line of Weather Shield skylights, doors, and windows—wood-framed casements, tilts, slider, direct-set, eyebrow, and fanlight windows and a variety of doors. Kolbe & Kolbe windows and doors are available, as well as goods from Caradco.

Prices are 40% to 70% below list, and all of the panels are guaranteed against leakage or failure for ten years. The warranty terms and installation instructions, including retrofitting, are detailed in the literature. And if you have any questions, you can talk them over with Mr. Bacon himself.

Arctic Glass & Window Outlet is offering readers a discount of 10% on their first order of insulated glass (with a maximum discount of $100). Be sure to identify yourself as a WBMC reader when you order, and deduct the discount from the cost of the goods only. This WBMC reader discount expires April 1, 1993.

Special Factors: Price quote by phone or letter with SASE; shipments are made to 49 of the 50 states; quantity discounts are available; minimum crating charge is $50 for mail orders; returns are accepted within 30 days for exchange, refund, or credit; minimum order is $50; orders are shipped worldwide.

ARISTOCAST ORIGINALS INC.

**6200 HIGHLAND PKWY., DEPT. 20
SMYRNA, GA 30082
404/333-9934**

Catalog: $3
Save: up to 50%
Pay: check, MO, MC, V, AE
Sells: architectural ornamentation
Store: same address; Monday to Friday 9–5

$$

Aristocast Originals has been selling architectural ornamentation and details since 1971, at savings of up to 50% on the prices charged elsewhere for similar goods. The line of niches, ceiling medallions, moldings and cornices is manufactured in England; fireplace surrounds, archways, corbels, and exterior details—porticoes, balustrades, canopies, corbels, columns, and door surrounds—are also available.

Aristocast offers a wide variety of styles in well-executed designs, something in poor supply in the do-it-yourself market. Aristocast's products are made of reinforced plaster, fiberglass, Herculite, and polyurethane (interior beans), and are easy to handle and install. Complete specifications and dimensions are listed for each item in the 28-page color catalog, and adhesives and other "fixing materials" are also available.

Special Factor: Authorized returns are accepted (a 20% restocking fee is charged).

BRE LUMBER

10741 CARTER RD.
TRAVERSE CITY, MI 49684
616/946-0043
FAX: 616/946-6221

Information: price quote
Save: up to 30%
Pay: check, MO, MC, V
Sells: lumber and flooring
Store: same address; Monday to Friday
8–5:30, Saturday 10–2

$$ ☎ 🍁 �merican flag▬

Home remodeling involves endless dilemmas, like realizing that prefinished parquet floor tiles have their merits, but you want a *real* floor. If that's out of line with the budget, BRE Lumber may be able to help.

BRE sells the genuine article, at a price better than those of other specialty dealers (though you won't beat the floor-in-a-box prices). BRE's stock includes cabinet-grade lumber flooring, wide-plank flooring, paneling, molding, and "dimensional lumber." The woods available in flooring include maple, padouk, bubinga, Brazilian cherry, and teak, among others, and the stock is "long and clear." You can save up to 30% on the delivered cost of the flooring (sometimes more depending on prices prevailing in your area). If you're planning to build or remodel, get BRE's current price list and samples ($15 plus shipping) and consider all the options before buying veneer-faced particle board.

Special Factors: Price quote by phone, fax, or letter with SASE; orders are shipped worldwide.

CISCO

1502 WEST CHERRY
CHANUTE, KS 66720
316/431-9290
FAX: 316/431-7354

Information: price quote
Save: up to 40%
Pay: check, MO, certified check
Sells: plumbing supplies and fixtures
Store: same address; Monday to Friday 8–5,
Saturday 8–12 noon

$$$ 🍁 ▬

CISCO, also known as Chanute Iron & Supply Co., stocks a full range of fixtures and equipment for plumbing, heating, and air conditioning.

A portion of CISCO's inventory is available by mail, at savings of 25% to 40%.

CISCO has been selling plumbing supplies, fixtures, and tools since 1941, and offers Delta and Moen faucets, Insinkerator garbage disposers, Wayne pumps, Burnham boilers, Miami Carey medicine chests and accessories, and whirlpools and fixtures by Aqua Glass, Benjamin, Owens-Corning, and Passport. There are Elkay and Polar sinks, Crane fixtures, swimming pool supplies and chemicals, tools by Rigid, and the professional line of tools by Makita. Replacement parts for all types of faucets are also stocked.

Please note: No catalog is available.

Special Factors: Price quote by phone or letter with SASE; minimum order is $10; orders are shipped worldwide.

CRAWFORD'S OLD HOUSE STORE

550 ELIZABETH ST.,
ROOM 104
WAUKESHA, WI 53186
800-556-7878

Flyer: free
Save: up to 30%
Pay: check, MO, MC, V, AE
Sells: doorstops, finials, corner protectors
Store: mail order only

$

Crawford's Old House Store offers a number of items that may come in handy if you're renovating an old house. The firm's oak and beech corner beads are quite popular, a welcome alternative to clear plastic corner protectors, and they're priced from under $11. Bullseye-design corner blocks, used at the top corners of door and window frames, cost $3 or less, depending on the quantity ordered. Oak newel post caps and other large finials are available as well.

Special Factor: Minimum order is $5, $15 with credit cards.

MONARCH

DEPT. WBMC
2744 ARKANSAS DR.
BROOKLYN, NY 11234
201/796-4117
FAX: 201/796-7717

Brochure: $1
Save: up to 35%
Pay: check, MO, MC, V
Sells: all-steel radiator enclosures
Store: mail order only

$$

If you've tired of looking at the exposed ribs of the radiators in your home, consider enclosures. They not only render the unsightly more decorative, but also help to direct the heat into the room.

Monarch sells enclosures in two dozen styles, ranging from simple models with plain grilles to designs that incorporate built-in cabinets and bookshelves. Unlike cheaper enclosures, these are constructed of heavy steel and come with closed backs. The tops of some are insulated, all the joints are welded, and the finishes include four stock enamel colors. Custom sizes and other colors, including woodgrain finishes, are available as well for a surcharge.

Monarch's literature includes a guide to measuring your radiator prior to ordering. (Please note that, like window treatments and other goods ordered to your own measurements, the enclosures are not returnable.) We've comparison shopped Monarch's enclosures, and found the prices up to 35% below those being charged for similar goods sold locally.

Special Factor: Inquiries from contractors and institutions are welcomed.

THE NEW ENGLAND SLATE COMPANY

R.D. #1, BURR POND RD.
SUDBURY, VT 05733
802/247-8809

Brochure: free
Save: up to 50%
Pay: check, MO, teller's check
Sells: new and recycled roofing and flooring
   slate
Store: same address; Monday to Friday
   8–4:30

$$$ ♣

The Taconic Overthrust, an area running along the Vermont-New York border, holds this country's only major deposits of colored slate.

Chuck Smid founded The New England Slate Company in 1975, after he had roofed his newly built home in slate salvaged from a nearby barn and figured there was a market in recycled (salvaged) slate.

The New England Slate Company sells both the characteristic slate of the area and recycled slate that had been reclaimed from buildings all over the Eastern seaboard. Grey, green, purple, brown, and the highly coveted red slate are available, as well as black slate from Maine, Vermont, and Pennsylvania. (The Maine slate, known as "monson" slate, is no longer actively quarried and can be obtained only through recyclers.) Slate is pricier than more commonly used roofing materials such as asphalt and fiberglass tile, but its 100-year-plus lifespan makes it much more cost effective. It's also the only appropriate choice for many historic properties, as well as universities and other public buildings. New England Slate's rooming line features new and salvaged slate in random widths and standard 3/16″ to 1/4″ thicknesses, in 12″ to 24″ lengths. Prices at this writing run from $195 for a square (100 square feet) of "semi-weathering green" in 12″ lengths to $1,300 for a square of new, "unfading red" in 24″ lengths. (Salvaged slate, when available, costs 20% to 25% less than newly quarried material.) Do-it-yourselfers can also buy the slate hammers, cutters, and rippers they'll need to do the job from New England Slate, as well as copper roofing nails, snow guards, roofing gloves, and even "the slater's bible," *Slate Roofs*. Custom cutting and color matching services can be provided.

The New England Slate Company also runs Vermont Cobble Slate, which offers salvaged slate for use in flooring, hearths, kitchen counters, bathrooms, and as veneer on vertical surfaces. This firm's brochure shows several installations in which the rich texture of the material and the interplay of colors are used to maximum effect, and the literature includes guidelines for setting and grouting the flooring and veneer. Boxes of ten square feet of random-size pieces cost $34, and are offered in black, purple, and mixed colors. The prices for salvaged materials are the best, but New England Slate is very competitive on newly quarried slate as well.

Special Factors: Satisfaction is guaranteed; price quote by phone or letter with SASE.

SACO MANUFACTURING & WOODWORKING

P.O. BOX 149-W
SACO, ME 04072
207/284-6613
FAX: 207/284-6613

Flyers: free with SASE (see text)
Save: up to 50%
Pay: check or MO
Sells: hand-turned newel posts, lampposts, and pine canisters
Store: 39 Lincoln St., Saco, ME; Monday to Friday 7–3:30

$$ ✦ 🇺🇸

Saco Manufacturing has been doing business since 1872, and although the firm has changed hands over the years, it still sells some of the same things it offered at the turn of the century.

One of these items is turned lampposts. These are center-bored, unfinished pine or poplar posts that are ready to be finished, wired, fitted with a lighting fixture, and installed outside your home. The posts are available in heights from 8′ to 12′, and are priced from $75 for the 8′ posts. Saco sells newel, porch, and mailbox posts in pine and other woods, in a choice of several finial styles. "Colonial Columns" and pilasters are also available; these custom-made supports can be created in Doric or Tuscan styles, or to the specifications of your contractor or architect.

Saco also sells large pine canisters to the offerings; they're 12″ across, come with fitted lids, and are made in 12″, 20″, and 30″ heights. They're handy as general-purpose storage containers, but can also be used as stools.

Please specify the literature you want when you send your self-addressed, stamped envelope: the flyer on lampposts, Colonial Columns, newel posts and finials, or canisters.

Special Factor: Price quote by letter with SASE on nonstandard sizes.

SHUTTERCRAFT

282 STEPSTONE HILL RD.
GUILFORD, CT 06437
203/453-1973

Brochure: free with SASE
Save: up to 30%
Pay: check, MO, MC, V
Sells: exterior house shutters and hardware
Store: same address; Monday to Friday 9–5

$$ ☎ ✦ 🇺🇸

Authentic, "historic" exterior wood shutters with movable louvers are sold here at prices well below those charged for custom-milled shutters. Shuttercraft's white pine and cedar shutters can be bought in widths up to 24", and in lengths to 108". Also available are fixed-louver shutters, exterior raised-panel shutters in Western cedar, interior styles, S-shaped holdbacks, and shutter hinges. Shuttercraft will prime, paint, trim, and rabbet your shutters for a fee; details are given in the brochure.

Special Factor: Shipping is included on shutters up to 60" long and on orders totaling $400 or more.

VINTAGE WOOD WORKS

**513 S. ADAMS
FREDERICKSBURG, TX
78624
512/997-9513**

Catalog: $2
Save: up to 30%
Pay: check, MO, MC, V, Discover
Sells: "Victorian gingerbread" architectural
details
Store: same address; also Hwy. 34, Quinlan,
TX

$$$ ☎ 🍁 ▦

Vintage Wood Works publishes a 60-page catalog of "Victorian and country gingerbread ... for Romantic Rooms & Pleasant Porches." The firm has been producing Victorian-style millwork since 1978, and charges up to 30% less than other firms do for the same kinds of goods.

The offerings include spandrels, cutwork grills and running trim, fan brackets and regular (support) brackets for shelves, decorative pieces to place over doors and windows, shelves, corbels, window cornices, gallery rails, porch posts, balusters, newel posts, finials, shingles, gable (roof-end) decorations, and individual components—spindles, balls, knobs, dowels, and even wooden toy parts. The catalog we reviewed introduced an expanded selection of staircase parts, including a line in oak for interior staircases. Each piece is described, with its dimensions, and the catalog includes suggestions for different uses and applications.

Special Factors: Satisfaction is guaranteed; quantity discounts are available; returns are accepted.

SEE ALSO

AAA-All Factory, Inc. • floor-care machines and supplies • *APPLIANCES*

ABC Vacuum Cleaner Warehouse • floor-care machines and supplies • *APPLIANCES*

Bob's Superstrong Greenhouse Plastic • super-strong woven polyethylene and anchoring straps • *FARM*

Discount Appliance Centers • floor-care machines and supplies • *APPLIANCES*

Clothcrafters, Inc. • mosquito netting and flannel polishing cloths • *GENERAL MERCHANDISE*

Grayarc • trash bags, wipes, door mats, etc. • *OFFICE*

Harry's Discounts & Appliances Corp. • vacuum cleaners • *APPLIANCES*

King's Chandelier Co. • replacement parts for chandeliers • *HOME: DECOR*

Manufacturer's Supply • woodburning furnaces and heaters • *TOOLS*

Midamerica Vacuum Cleaner Supply Co. • floor-care machines and janitorial supplies • *APPLIANCES*

Northern Wholesale Veterinary Supply, Inc. • Orvus WA Paste cleaner • *ANIMAL*

Oreck Corporation • Oreck vacuum cleaners and floor machines • *APPLIANCES*

Percy's Inc. • garbage disposals • *APPLIANCES*

Pintchik Homeworks • house paint • *HOME: DECOR*

Safe Specialties, Inc. • safes for home, office, and business • *OFFICE*

Sewin' in Vermont • vacuum cleaners • *APPLIANCES*

South Bound Millworks • wrought iron decorative hooks and bath fixtures • *HOME: DECOR*

Staples, Inc. • cleaning products, janitorial supplies, paper towels, brooms, trash bags, etc. • *OFFICE*

Value-tique, Inc. • safes for home, office, and business • *OFFICE*

Wholesale Veterinary Supply, Inc. • disinfectants and cleaning products • *ANIMAL*

Table Settings

China, crystal, glass, flatware, woodenware, and related goods

Buying current patterns of tableware is as easy as picking up the phone and calling one of the firms listed here. But if your pattern—in china, crystal, or silver—is discontinued, you'll have to turn to a specialist. Three of these firms—Beverly Bremer, Buschemeyer, and Midas—sell discontinued silver flatware (also called "estate" silver). If you're missing pieces of a china or crystal pattern, write to Replacements, Ltd., 302 Gallimore Dairy Rd., Greensboro, NC 27400-9723, or call 919/275-7224. Replacements has over 250,000 pieces in stock, and can help you identify your pattern if you're not sure of the name.

BARRONS

22790 HESLIP DR.
NOVI, MI 48050
800-538-6340
313/348-0816
FAX: 313/344-4342

Catalog: free
Save: up to 40%
Pay: check, MO, MC, V, Discover
Sells: tableware and giftware
Store: mail order only

$$$ ☎ 🍁 🇺🇸

Barrons has been selling fine tableware since 1975, and while it doesn't have a store, it does offer savings of up to 40% on the list prices of china, crystal, flatware, and gifts.

The 64-page, color catalog we received from Barrons showcased popular lines of china from Bernardaud Limoges, Block, Fitz & Floyd, Franciscan, Johnson Brothers, Lenox, Mikasa, Noritake, Royal

Doulton, Royal Worcester, Spode, Villeroy & Boch, and Wedgwood. Crystal from Atlantis, Baccarat, Gorham, Lenox, Mikasa, Noritake, Sasaki, and Wedgwood is offered, and you can save on stainless steel, silver plate, and sterling flatware from Dansk, Gorham, International, Kirk-Stieff, Lunt, Mikasa, Oneida, Reed & Barton, Towle, Wallace, and Yamazaki. Goebel and Royal Doulton figurines, Gorham crystal gifts, Towle silver serving pieces, and other collectibles and accessories are also sold at a discount. Barrons' holiday catalog offers great gifts— covered hatboxes, handknitted sweaters, clocks, jewelry and jewelry chests, and many other possibilities were shown in the issue we received.

Special Factors: Satisfaction is guaranteed; price quote by phone or letter with SASE; returns are accepted within 30 days for exchange, refund, or credit; orders are shipped worldwide.

BRADBURY'S

1627 WESTGATE RD.
EAU CLAIRE, WI 54703
715/834-4013
FAX: 715/834-3916

Brands List: free
Save: up to 50%
Pay: check, MO, MC, V
Sells: tableware and table linens
Store: mail order only

$$ ☎

Bradbury's, also known as Mid-America Tablewares, sells several lines of mid-priced china, at savings of up to 50% on list. The roster of manufacturers includes Blue Danube, Franciscan, Midwinter, Minton, Nikko, Royal Albert, and Royal Doulton. Both active and discontinued patterns of Johnson Brothers china are available as well. Bradbury's also sells Leacock table linens. Call or write for price information.

Special Factor: Price quote by phone or letter.

BEVERLY BREMER SILVER SHOP

Information: inquire (see text)
Save: up to 75%
Pay: check, MO, MC, V, AE
Sells: new and estate silver flatware, holloware, gifts, etc.
Store: same address; Monday to Saturday 10–5

DEPT. WBMC
3164 PEACHTREE RD.,
N.E.
ATLANTA, GA 30305
404/261-4009

$$ ☎

Beverly Bremer herself presides over this shop, which has an astounding inventory of things silver, from new sterling flatware to old loving cups. "The store with the silver lining," which opened in 1975, is worth a detour if you're traveling anywhere around Atlanta.

The briskest mail trade here is done in supplying missing pieces of sterling silverware, in new, discontinued, and hard-to-find patterns. If you know your pattern name, call to see whether the piece you want is in stock; you can also send a photocopy of both sides of a sample piece if you're unsure of the name.

Although the shop's specialty is flatware, the shelves and cases sparkle with vases, epergnes, picture frames, candlesticks, jewelry, christening cups, thimbles, and other treasures. Silver collectors should note that over 1,000 patterns are carried in stock here, "beautiful as new," and Ms. Bremer tells us that, unless noted, there are no monograms on the old silver. (She doesn't sell silver on which monograms have been *removed,* either.) Request a current inventory list of your flatware pattern.

Special Factors: Price quote by phone or letter; sterling silver pieces are bought; appraisals are performed.

BUSCHEMEYER & COMPANY

**515 S. FOURTH AVE.
LOUISVILLE, KY 40202
800-626-4555**

Information: price quote
Save: up to 40%
Pay: check, MO, MC, V, AE, DC, Discover
Sells: new and discontinued flatware
Store: mail order only

$$

Buschemeyer can help you save on purchases of new flatware—sterling, silverplate, and holloware. If you're looking for a discontinued pattern, Buschemeyer may have what you need. The firm stocks "all active and inactive sterling and silverplate flatware," and will put your name on a want list if the pattern you want isn't available. You can call or write for a price quote on current silver lines, and call (if you know the pattern name) about discontinued pieces, or send a photocopy of the front and back of a teaspoon or fork if you're not sure of the name.

Special Factor: Price quote by phone or letter with SASE.

CHINA CABINET, INC.

**24 WASHINGTON ST.
TENAFLY, NJ 07670
800-545-5353
201/567-2711**

Information: price quote
Save: up to 50%
Pay: check, MO, MC, V, Optima
Sells: tableware
Store: same address; Monday to Saturday
10–6, Thursday 10–8

$$

China Cabinet, in business since 1988, represents scores of manufacturers of fine china, crystal, and flatware. In addition to such widely available brands as Dansk, Gorham, Orrefors, and Wedgwood, China Cabinet offers goods from Colle, Arthur Court, Godinger, Jacques Jugeat, Royal Doulton, Silvestri, and Wilton, among others. Savings run up to 50%, and giftware from selected manufacturers is offered as well as place settings and serving pieces.

Special Factors: Price quote by phone or letter with SASE; minimum order is $25 with credit cards.

THE CHINA WAREHOUSE

P.O. BOX 21797
CLEVELAND, OH 44121
800-321-3212
216/831-2557

Catalog: free
Save: up to 40%
Pay: check, MO, MC, V
Sells: tableware and gifts
Store: mail order only

$$$ ☎ ♦

The China Warehouse has been in business since 1983 and offers "all major china and crystal lines," as well as flatware, decorative accessories, giftware, and collectible figurines. The brands include Armetale, Block, Gorham, Lenox, Noritake, Orrefors, Reed & Barton, Riedel, Royal Copenhagen, Royal Doulton, Sasaki, Spode, Towle, Wallace, Waterford, Wedgwood, and dozens of others in china, crystal, and stainless and sterling flatware. A catalog is available, but you can call or write for a price quote.

Special Factors: Price quote by phone or letter with SASE; orders are shipped worldwide.

COINWAYS/ANTIQUES LTD.

136 CEDARHURST AVE.
CEDARHURST, NY 11516
516/374-1970

Price List: free
Save: up to 75%
Pay: check, MO, MC, V, AE, DC, Discover,
Optima
Sells: new and used sterling flatware
Store: same address; Monday to Friday
10–5:30, Wednesday 10–7:30, Saturday
10–5

$$ ☎ ♦

Coinways/Antiques Ltd. should be on your list of firms to call when the garbage disposer claims one of your good teaspoons—especially if it's from an old or discontinued pattern. Coinways, which has been in business since 1980, sells both new and used ("estate") sterling flatware, by the piece or in full sets.

You'll save up to 75% on the suggested retail or market prices of silver manufactured by Alvin, Amston, Dominick & Haff, Durgin,

Easterling, Gorham, International, Kirk-Stieff, Lunt, Manchester, National, Oneida, Reed & Barton, Royal Crest, F.M. Smith, State House, Tiffany, Towle, Tuttle, Wallace, Westmoreland, F.M. Whiting, and other firms. If you're replacing a piece in an old pattern that's still active, try to find a piece of the same vintage. (Some manufacturers have reduced the amount of silver they use in each piece over the years, so that a fork made today will be lighter and feel less substantial than the same piece, circa 1930.) If you write to Coinways for a quote, note the name of the piece, its length and shape, and include a rubbing of the design if you don't know the pattern name.

Special Factors: Price quote by phone or letter with SASE; orders are shipped worldwide.

THE EMERALD COLLECTION

280 SUMMER ST., DEPT. DFCR
BOSTON, MA 02210
800-338-9790
FAX: 617/451-1167

Catalog: $2
Save: up to 35%
Pay: check, MO, MC, V, AE, Access
Sells: Irish collectibles and handcrafts
Store: Ballingeary, County Cork, Ireland

$$$ ☎ 🍁

Emerald, established in 1962, offers substantial savings on an extensive selection of Waterford crystal stemware and giftware. The 64-page color catalog shows tableware and gifts by Waterford and Belleek, Coalport, Royal Doulton, Royal Worcester, Spode, Villeroy & Boch, and Wedgwood. The complete lines of Beatrix Potter figurines, Bunnykins, and Peter Rabbit lamps and table settings are offered. Irish Dresden figurines are carried, as well as others by Belleek, Border Fine Arts, Goebel, Hummel, Irish Dresden, Lladró, and Royal Doulton. Caithness paperweights and other authentic Irish handcrafts round out this lovely catalog.

If you collect figurines or buy gifts frequently, you may find membership in Emerald's "Collector's Club" worthwhile. It includes newsletters with special offers, advance catalog mailings, and discount coupons—all for a $15 fee.

Special Factors: Satisfaction is guaranteed; authorized returns are accepted.

MICHAEL C. FINA CO.

**580 FIFTH AVE.
NEW YORK, NY 10036
212/869-8900
FAX: 212/575-4621**

Catalog: free
Save: up to 60%
Pay: check, MO, MC, V, AE, Optima
Sells: jewelry, tableware, and giftware
Store: same address; Monday to Friday
9:30–6, Thursday 9:30–7, Saturday
10:30–6

Nearly half of the Michael C. Fina holiday catalog is devoted to jewelry—rings embedded with diamonds and emeralds, strands of pearls and gold link necklaces, wedding bands, modern silver jewelry and accessories, and watches from Citizen, Omega, and Tissot were shown in the catalog we reviewed. Fina, which has been in business since 1935, is well known to New Yorkers for its jewelry, as well as the tableware it sells, at discounts of up to 60%.

Our catalog featured sample patterns in fine china by Aynsley, Bernardaud Limoges, Ceralene Raynaud Limoges, Fitz and Floyd, Gorham, Haviland Limoges, Lenox, Mikasa, Minton, Noritake, Pickard, Royal Crown Derby, Royal Doulton, Royal Worcester, Thomas, and Wedgwood. Crystal stemware from Atlantis, Baccarat, Gorham, Lenox, Miller Rogaska, Orrefors, St. Louis, and Stuart is available. Fina also sells flatware from Gorham, International, Kirk-Stieff, Lunt, Mikasa, Oneida, Reed & Barton, Retroneau, Towle, Wallace, and Yamazaki. Sterling silver baby gifts, picture frames, carriage clocks, Val St. Lambert candlesticks, and silver dressing table accessories were all shown in the catalog we reviewed. Fina also maintains a bridal registry.

Special Factors: Satisfaction is guaranteed; price quote by phone or letter; returns (except engraved or personalized items) are accepted within 3 weeks for exchange, refund, or credit; orders are shipped worldwide.

FORTUNOFF FINE JEWELRY & SILVERWARE, INC.

P.O. BOX 1550
WESTBURY, NY 11590
800-223-2326
516/294-3300
212/671-9300

Catalog: $2
Save: up to 50%
Pay: check, MO, MC, V, AE, DC
Sells: jewelry, tableware, and giftware
Store: 681 Fifth Ave., New York, and 1300 Old Country Rd., Westbury, NY; also Paramus Park Mall, Paramus, West Belt Mall, Wayne, and 441 Woodbridge Center Dr., Woodbridge, NJ

$$$ ☎

In addition to spectacular buys on fine jewelry and watches, Fortunoff is a top source for name-brand place settings in stainless, silverplate, and sterling silver. Attractive groups of silver giftware—chafing dishes, tea and coffee services, candlesticks, ice buckets, picture frames, and antique vanity accessories—appear frequently in the catalogs. Flatware from Empire Silver, International, Kirk-Stieff, Lauffer, Mikasa, Oneida, Reed & Barton, Retroneau, Roberts & Belk, Supreme, Towle, C.J. Vander, and Yamazaki is available—see the catalog or call for prices on specific patterns. Some of the Fortunoff stores carry a broader variety of products, including outdoor furniture, leather goods, decorative accents for the home, linens for bed and bath, organizers, and similar items.

Special Factors: Price quote on flatware by letter with self-addressed, stamped envelope; minimum order is $25; orders are not shipped outside the U.S.

THE JOMPOLE COMPANY, INC.

330 SEVENTH AVE.
NEW YORK, NY 10001
212/594-0442
FAX: 212/268-7312

Information: price quote
Save: up to 50%
Pay: check or MO
Sells: tableware, figurines, watches, and pens
Store: same address; Monday to Friday 9–5

$$ ✦

Jompole has been in business since 1913 and offers a fine selection of table settings, giftware, and writing instruments. You can save up to

50% here on china, flatware, crystal, and other tableware. The china lines include Bernardaud Limoges, Coalport, Denby, Franciscan, Hutschenreuther, Lenox, Mikasa, Minton, Pickard, Royal Copenhagen, Spode, and Wedgwood, among others. Crystal stemware is available from Baccarat, Fostoria, Gorham, Kosta Boda, Orrefors, Rosenthal, Val St. Lambert, and Waterford, and there's flatware from Alvin, Community, Fraser, International, Georg Jensen, Kirk-Stieff, Lauffer, Lunt, Oneida, Reed & Barton, Supreme Cutlery, Towle, Tuttle, Wallace, and other firms. Jompole may have figurines and collectibles by some of the same firms, as well as Hummel, Lladró, Norman Rockwell, and Swarovski.

You can call or write for prices on pens and pencils from Cross, Mont Blanc, Parker, and Waterman, or watches by Borel, Cartier, Heuer, Patek-Philippe, Rolex, or Seiko. Jompole also carries premium items for businesses—"from balloons and lollipops to diamonds and furs"—and invites inquiries from interested firms.

Special Factors: Price quote by phone or letter with SASE; institutional accounts are available; orders are shipped worldwide.

KAISER CROW INC.

3545 G. SO. PLATTE RIVER DR.
ENGLEWOOD, CO 80110
303/781-6888
FAX: 303/781-5982

Brochure: free
Save: up to 55%
Pay: check, MO, MC, V
Sells: flatware
Store: mail order only

$$

Kaiser Crow's business is flatware—stainless, silverplate, and sterling silver—from Gorham, International, Lunt, Oneida, Reed & Barton, Towle, Wallace, and other major manufacturers—which it sells at discounts of up to 55%. Kaiser Crow has been in business since 1985, and sent us a brochure showing specials on Oneida's Community, Heirloom, and gold-accented stainless flatware lines, at savings of more than 50% on list prices. Call or write for a price quote if you don't see what you're looking in the brochure.

Special Factors: Satisfaction is guaranteed; price quote by phone or letter; orders are shipped worldwide.

MAREL COMPANY

**6 BOND ST.
GREAT NECK, NY 11021
516/466-3118**

Information: price quote
Save: up to 50%
Pay: check or MO
Sells: tableware and giftware
Store: same address; Monday to Friday
9–5:30, Saturday 9–5

$$ 🇺🇸

Marel sells top brands in china, stemware, flatware, and giftware at savings of up to 50%. Call or write for prices on stainless, plated, and sterling silverware, holloware, and giftware by Gorham, Heirloom, International, Kirk-Stieff, Lunt, Oneida, Reed & Barton, Supreme, Towle, and Wallace. China, stemware, and crystal by Coalport, Franciscan, Haviland Limoges, Hutschenreuther, Lenox, Mikasa, Minton, Noritake, Rosenthal, Royal Doulton, Spode, Val St. Lambert, and Wedgwood is also offered. The stock includes current lines, and you can write or call for current prices.

Special Factor: Price quote by phone or letter with SASE.

MESSINA GLASS & CHINA CO. INC.

**P.O. BOX 307
ELWOOD, NJ 08217
609/561-1474**

Catalog: free (see text)
Save: up to 50%
Pay: check, MO, MC, V, AE, CHOICE,
Optima
Sells: tableware and collectibles
Store: Rte. 30, Elwood, NJ; Monday to
Friday (except Thursday) 10–5, Saturday
10–4 (closed Thursday and Sunday)

$$ ☎ ♦ 🇺🇸

Fine china and stoneware, stainless and sterling flatware, crystal stemware, and collectibles are among the offerings at Messina Glass & China, which has been in business since 1959. Although a catalog is sometimes available, calling or writing for a price quote is recommended. Messina carries tableware and gifts by Atlantis, Fitz & Floyd,

Galway, Gorham, Hummel, Lenox (including lamps), Noritake, Oneida, Reed & Barton, Royal Doulton, and Wedgwood, among others. If you're looking for a piece in a recently discontinued pattern, try here—it may be available. Messina also sells momogrammed barware, stemware, and crystal serving trays.

Messina is offering readers free shipping on orders sent within the 48 contiguous states. Be sure to identify yourself as a WBMC reader when you order to claim the exemption. This WBMC reader offer expires February 1, 1993.

Special Factors: Price quote by phone or letter with SASE; orders are shipped worldwide.

MIDAS CHINA & SILVER

**DEPT. WBMC-92
4315 WALNEY RD.
CHANTILLY, VA 22021
800-368-3153**

Catalog: free
Save: up to 70%
Pay: check, MO, MC, V, AE, Discover, Optima
Sells: tableware
Store: same address; Monday to Friday 10–6, Saturday 10–4; also 7223 Commerce St., Springfield, VA, and 1346-48 Gaskins Rd., Richmond, VA

Midas has been selling fine crystal, china, and silver giftware and table settings since 1965. The prices here are up to 70% less than full retail, and estate silver (including discontinued patterns) is also sold.

Midas sells china place settings and gifts by Aynsley, Coalport, Fitz and Floyd, Gorham, Hummel, Lenox, Lladró, Minton, Noritake, Orrefors, Rosenthal, Royal Crown Derby, Royal Doulton, Royal Worcester, Spode, and Wedgwood. Crystal gifts, barware, and stemware by Baccarat, Gorham, Orrefors, and Waterford are available at overseas prices. Sterling candelabra from Gorham, and stainless, plate, and sterling place settings by Alvin, Durgin, Easterling, Gorham, International Silver, Kirk-Stieff, Lunt, Manchester, National, Oneida, Reed & Barton, Royal Crest, Statehouse, Towle, Wallace, Westmoreland, Whiting, and Wiedlich are available, and Midas also sells silver chests and silver bags to keep your investment tarnish-free.

The catalog lists patterns and prices, but you can call or write for a quote. And contact the company if you plan to get married—Midas maintains a full-service bridal registry.

Special Factors: Price quote by phone or letter; returns (except special orders) are accepted within 30 days for exchange, refund, or credit; minimum order is $25.

ROBIN IMPORTERS, INC.

510 MADISON AVE.,
 DEPT. WBM
NEW YORK, NY 10022
212/753-6475

Brands List: free with SASE
Save: up to 50%
Pay: check, MO, MC, V, AE, DC, Optima
Sells: tableware, giftware, and kitchenware
Store: same address; Monday to Friday 9:30–5:30, Saturday 10–5

$$$ ☎ ♦

Robin offers an exhaustive range of tableware, kitchenware, and table and kitchen linens at prices up to 50% below list. The brochure lists the available brands, but no prices are given—call or write for a quote. The firm was established in 1957.

Robin carries china place settings and serving pieces by Adams, Arabia, Arzberg, Bernardaud Limoges, Block, Cartier, Coalport, Denby, Fitz and Floyd, Franciscan, Heinrich, Hutschenreuther, Meissen, Mikasa, Rosenthal, Spode, Villeroy & Boch, and other firms. Crystal stemware and gifts from Atlantis, Baccarat, Daum, Gorham, Iittala, Kosta Boda, Lalique, Orrefors, Riedel, Sasaki, Val St. Lambert, and Waterford are available. And the flatware and cutlery lines include Alessi, Dansk, W.M.F. Fraser, Georgian House, Gorham, Henckels, Lauffer, Lunt, Oneida, Retroneau, Ricci, Stanley Roberts, Supreme, Towle, Wallace, and Yamazaki. Robin completes the table with linens—Carefree cloths and napkins, in all sizes and colors, at 50% off list. Knives by Gorham, Henckels, and Wusthof-Trident are sold at savings, as well as knife blocks, salt-and-pepper mills, and other useful kitchen items.

Special Factors: Price quote by phone or letter with SASE; orders are shipped worldwide.

ROGERS & ROSENTHAL

22 W. 48TH ST., ROOM 1102
NEW YORK, NY 10036
212/827-0115

Information: price quote
Save: up to 50%
Pay: check or MO
Sells: tableware
Store: mail order only
$$ ≣

Rogers and Rosenthal, two old names in the silver and china business, represent the business of this firm: the best in table settings at up to 60% below list prices. Rogers and Rosenthal has been in business since 1960, selling flatware (stainless, plate, and sterling) by top manufacturers. The brands include 1847 Rogers, 1881 Rogers, Fraser, Gerber, Gorham, International, Jensen, Kirk-Stieff, Lauffer, Lunt, Oneida, Reed & Barton, Sasaki, Frank Smith, Supreme, Towle, Tuttle, Wallace, and Yamazaki. There are china and crystal lines by Arabia, Aynsley, Bernardaud Limoges, Block, Coalport, Fitz and Floyd, Franciscan, Gorham, Haviland Limoges, Hornsea, Hutschenreuther, Lauffer, Lenox, Mikasa, Noritake, Pickard, Portmeirion, Rosenthal, Royal Copenhagen, Royal Doulton, Royal Worcester, Spode, and Wedgwood. Also stocked are silver baby gifts, Lladró and Norman Rockwell figurines, and pewter holloware. Please write or call for a price quote—*there is no catalog.*

Special Factors: Price quote by phone or letter with SASE; returns are accepted for exchange.

RUDI'S POTTERY, SILVER & CHINA

176 RTE. 17
PARAMUS, NJ 07652
800-631-2526
201/265-6096
FAX: 265-2086

Information: price quote
Save: up to 50%
Pay: check, MO, MC, V, AE, Optima
Sells: tableware
Store: same address; Monday to Saturday 10–5:30, Tuesday and Thursday 10–9
$$$ ☎ ❦ ≣

Rudi's has been in business for 20 years, and in that time has expanded its stock to include some of the finest goods available, at savings of up to 60% on list prices. China, crystal, and flatware are stocked here; the silverware brands include Buccellati, Gorham, International, Kirk-Stieff, Lunt, Reed & Barton, Towle, Tuttle, and Wallace. Rudi's china dinnerware and crystal stemware lines include Arzberg, Baccarat, Belleek, Bernardaud Limoges, Coalport, Fitz and Floyd, Galway, Gorham, Kosta Boda, Lalique, Lenox, Mikasa, Minton, Noritake, Orrefors, Rosenthal, Royal Copenhagen, Royal Doulton, Royal Worcester, Sasaki, Spode, Stuart, Wedgwood, and Yamazaki. Call or write for a price quote on your pattern or suite.

Special Factors: Price quote by phone or letter with SASE; orders are shipped worldwide.

NAT SCHWARTZ & CO., INC.

**549 BROADWAY
BAYONNE, NJ 07002
800-526-1440**

Information: inquire
Save: up to 50%
Pay: check, MO, MC, V, Discover
Sells: tableware and giftware
Store: same address; Monday, Thursday, Friday 11–8, Tuesday and Saturday 11–5 (closed Wednesday and Sunday)

$$$ ☎

Schwartz, established in 1967, publishes a 48-page color catalog filled with fine china, crystal, flatware, and gifts that represent just a fraction of the firm's inventory. Schwartz's china and giftware department offers Belleek, Edward Marshall Boehm, Coalport, Fitz and Floyd, Lenox, Lladró, Mikasa, Minton, Noritake, Pickard, Royal Crown Derby, Royal Doulton, Royal Worcester, Spode, and Wedgwood. Crystal suites and gifts by Galway, Gorham, Lenox, Miller/Rogaska, Stuart, Waterford, and Wedgwood are available. Also featured are flatware and holloware by Gorham, International, Kirk-Stieff, Lunt, Oneida, Reed & Barton, Retroneau, Ricci, Towle, Tuttle, Wallace, and Yamazaki.

Schwartz offers a number of valuable services, including coordination of silver, crystal, and china patterns, gift and bridal registry, and a corporate gift program.

Special Factors: Satisfaction is guaranteed; price quote by phone; special orders are accepted with a nonrefundable 20% deposit (unless the order is canceled while still on back order); undamaged returns are accepted within 30 days (a restocking fee may be charged).

ALBERT S. SMYTH CO., INC.

DEPT. WM92
29 GREENMEADOW DR.
TIMONIUM, MD 21093
800-638-3333
301/252-6666
FAX: 301/252-2355

Catalog: free
Save: up to 65%
Pay: check, MO, MC, V, AE
Sells: tableware, giftware, and jewelry
Store: mail order only

$$$ ☎

All that gleams and glitters can be found at Smyth, at savings of up to 65% on comparable retail and list prices. Smyth has been doing business since 1914, and has a well-regarded customer service department.

The 24-page color catalog features a wide range of jewelry, including diamonds, strands of semiprecious beads, colored stone jewelry, and pearls. Watches by Movado, Omega, Pulsar, Rado, Seiko, and Raymond Weil have been offered in the past, as well as Mont Blanc pens, mahogany jewelry chests, Royal Doulton figurines, Virginia Metalcrafters gifts, and Kirk-Stieff pewter and silver gifts.

Tableware and home decorative accents are sold here at impressive savings, including such items as British carriage clocks, Baldwin brass gifts, and fine picture frames. You'll find pewter candlesticks, coffee sets, punch bowls, and place settings by Aynsley, Gorham, Kirk-Stieff, Lenox, Noritake, Reed & Barton, Royal Doulton, Spode, Towle, Villeroy & Boch, Wallace, Waterford, and Wedgwood among the offerings.

Smyth maintains a bridal registry, gift consultations, and a gift-forwarding service. The catalog shows a fraction of the inventory, so write or call for a price quote if you don't see what you're looking for.

Special Factors: Satisfaction is guaranteed; price quote by phone or letter with SASE; returns (except personalized and custom-ordered goods) are accepted within 30 days.

THURBER'S

**2158 PLAINFIELD PIKE
CRANSTON, RI 02921
800-848-7237
FAX: 401/942-5601**

Catalog: $1
Save: up to 50%
Pay: check, MO, MC, V, AE, Discover
Sells: tableware and giftware
Store: same address

$$$ ☎ 🍁 ▀

The Thurber's holiday catalog showcases both fine tableware and gifts, but you can call or write year-round for quotes on specific items. Thurber's has been in business since 1985, selling the accoutrements of gracious living at up to 50% off list prices.

The catalog Thurber's sent us offered a number of especially well-priced gifts, such as a sterling book mark for under $20, handsome lead crystal decanter for $30, and an ornate silver purse mirror for $15. Place settings and other tableware by Gorham, International, Kirk-Stieff, Lenox, Lunt, Minton, Noritake, Oneida, Reed & Barton, Royal Doulton, Royal Worcester, Tirschenreuth, Towle, Wallace, Wedgwood, and Yamazaki are available as well, at savings of up to 50%.

Special Factors: Price quote by phone or letter; orders are shipped worldwide.

COMPANIES OUTSIDE THE U.S.A.

The following firms are experienced in dealing with customers in the U.S. and Canada. We've included them because they offer goods not widely available at a discount in the U.S., because they have a better selection, or because they may offer the same goods at great savings.

Before ordering from any non-U.S. firm, please consult "The Complete Guide to Buying by Mail," page 573, for helpful tips. We recommend paying for orders from foreign firms with a credit card whenever possible, so you'll have some recourse if you don't receive your order. For more information, see "The Fair Credit Billing Act," page 612.

SHANNON DUTY FREE MAIL ORDER

Catalog: $2
Save: up to 40%
Pay: check, IMO, MC, V, AE, Access
Sells: tableware, Irish knits, and giftware
Store: same address

SHANNON FREE AIRPORT, DEPT. WM92 IRELAND
011-353-61-62610
FAX: 011-353-61-363182

$$$ ☎ ♦ ▆

Shannon has been doing business by mail since 1954, and the 54-page catalog features china and crystal, with clothing, table linens, gifts, and collectibles. The china firms represented include Adams, Aynsley, Belleek, Beswick, Coalport, Limoges, Masons, Midwinter, Royal Doulton, Royal Tara, Royal Worcester, Spode, and Wedgwood. The emphasis is on giftware, but select place settings and serving pieces are also offered. Savings are usually at least 30% on the U.S. retail prices, and are often more substantial.

Galway and Waterford crystal is also available at Shannon at savings of up to 40% off list prices. Several suites are offered, as well as serving and decorative pieces. In addition, Shannon carries Anri figurines, Royal Doulton character mugs, Royal Doulton's Bunnykins figures, Wedgwood's Beatrix Potter nursery accoutrements, Goebel collectibles, and lovely Claddagh jewelry. Genuine bargains can be found among the Irish linen handkerchiefs, Nottingham lace table-cloths, and double-damask table linens.

Shannon guarantees that orders shipped to addresses in the continental U.S. will be free of duty charges. Shipments to Alaska, Hawaii, and Puerto Rico may be assessed duty, which Shannon will refund or credit to a future order (see the catalog for details).

Canadian readers, please note: Shipping charges listed in the catalog are valid on orders sent to Canada. Prices are given in U.S. dollars, but Canadian funds are accepted. Use the rate of exchange in force on the day you order.

Special Factors: Satisfaction is guaranteed; returns are accepted within 30 days for exchange, refund, or credit; minimum order is $25 with credit cards; orders are shipped worldwide.

SKANDINAVISK GLAS

**4 NY ØSTERGADE
1101 COPENHAGEN K
DENMARK
011-45-3313-8095
FAX: 011-45-3332-3335**

Brochure and Price Lists: $3, refundable
Save: up to 33%
Pay: check, MO, MC, V, AE, DC
Sells: crystal and china table settings and giftware
Store: same address; Monday to Friday 9:30–5:30, Saturday 9:30–2

Skandinavisk Glas, formerly known as A.B. Schou, was founded in 1920 and sells the finest European crystal and porcelain. The firms represented include Herend, Hummel, Lladró, NAO, Royal Copenhagen, Royal Doulton, Wedgwood, and David Winter. The prices at Skandinavisk Glas, which *include* postage (surface) and insurance, are superb: place settings are priced 25% to 33% below New York City rates, and Lladró figurines cost about 30% below retail. The crystal collection is comparable; in addition to a comprehensive listing of Waterford stemware, vases, and giftware, Skandinavisk Glas sells decorative and service pieces by Baccarat, Daum, Hadeland, Iittala, Mats Jonassen, Kosta Boda, Nachtmann, Orrefors, and Swarovski.

Canadian readers, please note: Prices are listed in U.S. dollars. Add 25% to the prices if you're paying in Canadian funds.

Special Factors: Shipping and insurance are included; orders are shipped worldwide.

STECHER'S LIMITED

27 FREDERICK ST.
PORT-OF-SPAIN
TRINIDAD, WEST INDIES
809/62-35912, 32586
FAX: 809/627-8444

Brands List: free
Save: up to 40%
Pay: check or IMO
Sells: tableware, watches, jewelry, and giftware
Store: same address; Piarco International Airport; also Hilton Hotel, Long Circular Mall, and Westmall in Port-of-Spain; Gulf City Mall, San Fernando; Carrington Street, Scarborough, Tobago; and Arnos Vale Airport and Cobblestone Inn, Bay Street, Kingston in St. Vincent

Here in Trinidad is one of the world's best sources of luxury goods, which are sold at impressive discounts. Stecher's carries the best of the best in tableware, watches, clocks, pens, and lighters, at savings of up to 40%.

The stock includes crystal by Baccarat, Dartington, Daum, Hoya, Iittala, Kosta Boda, Lalique, Nybro, Orrefors, Riedel, Rosenthal, St. Louis, Schott-Zwiesel, Sevres, Swarovski, Val St. Lambert, Vannes Le Chatel, and Waterford. Place settings, gifts, and figurines from Aynsley, Belleek, Bing & Grøndahl, Capodimonte, Coalport, Hutschenreuther, Kaiser, Lladró, Minton, Noritake, Paragon, Rosenthal, Royal Albert, Royal Copenhagen, Royal Crown Derby, Royal Doulton, Royal Worcester, Spode, Villeroy & Boch, Wedgwood, and David Winter Cottages are available. The flatware lines include Georg Jensen and Wallace, among others.

This is an impressive list, but Stecher's is more frequently cited for its bargains on watches, clocks, jewelry, pens, and lighters. Again, the goods are first-rate: timepieces by Audemars Piguet, Cartier, Consul, Girard-Perregaux, Heuer (chronographs), Patek-Philippe, Seiko, and similar firms are offered, in addition to pens and lighters from Pierre Cardin, Cartier, Cross, Dunhill, Dupont, Lamy, Mont Blanc, Parker, Sheaffer, and Waterman, as well as a wide variety of fine jewelry (including cultured pearls) and leather goods, pipes, Swiss Army knives, and sunglasses by Porsche Carrera and Ray-Ban. Perfume is available in the Stecher's Airport Shop.

Stecher's doesn't have a catalog, but will send a list of brands and lines of merchandise currently available. The firm invites written inquiries concerning specific goods and manufacturers, and will send specific brochures and prices upon request. Stecher's has been doing business since 1946 and has satisfied the whims of such shoppers as Tony Curtis and Lena Horne.

Special Factor: Price quote by letter.

SEE ALSO

Atlantic Bridge Collection Corp. Ltd. • china and crystal tableware • ART, ANTIQUES

Betty Crocker Enterprises • china, stemware, and flatware • GENERAL MERCHANDISE

Bruce Medical Supply • dining aids and cutlery for those with limited strength or muscle control • MEDICINE

A Cook's Wares • cutlery and serving pieces • HOME: KITCHEN

Fivenson Food Equipment, Inc. • restaurant appliances, tableware, and serving pieces • HOME: KITCHEN

The Friar's House • china and crystal • ART, ANTIQUES

Harris Levy, Inc. • table linens • HOME: LINEN

Pendery's Inc. • Mexican glassware • FOOD

Ross-Simons Jewelers • china, crystal, and silver tableware • JEWELRY

Saxkjaers • Bing & Grøndahl and Royal Copenhagen place settings • ART, ANTIQUES

Weston Bowl Mill • wooden plates, trays, and tableware • GENERAL MERCHANDISE

The Wine Enthusiast • stemware and decanters • FOOD

JEWELRY, GEMS, AND WATCHES

Fine, fashion, and costume jewelry; loose stones, watches, and services

Whether you're looking for flea-market neck chains or investment-grade gems, you'll find them here, at savings of 20% to 75%, depending on the item. Before making a financial commitment of any magnitude, though, make sure you know what you're buying. The following may be of some assistance:

All About Jewelry: The One Indispensable Guide for Buyers, Wearers, Lovers, Investors, by Rose Leiman Goldenberg (Arbor House Publishing Co., 1983), covers precious and semiprecious stones, pearls, metals, and other materials used in jewelry. For an inside look at the business, try *Modern Jeweler's Consumer Guide to Colored Gemstones,* by David Federman (Modern Jeweler Magazine, 1990) (with dazzling color photographs by Tino Hammid). A gemlike production in its own right, it reveals the intrigue and chicanery that shape each stone's market, and discusses irradiation and heat treatment of gems. Write to Modern Jeweler, Vance Publishing Corporation, P.O. Box 1416, Lincolnshire, IL 60069-9958 for the current price and ordering information if you can't find it in a bookstore.

The FTC has established guidelines for the jewelry trade and publishes pamphlets for consumers that discuss the meanings of terms, stamps and quality marks, and related matters. Request "Gold Jewelry," "Bargain Jewelry," and "Guidelines for the Jewelry Industry" from the Federal Trade Commission, Public Reference Office, Washington, DC 20580.

If you need help in finding an appraiser, contact the American Society of Appraisers at 212/687-6305. The Society will locate an appraiser in your area and have that person contact you, at no charge.

(The Society's senior members have at least five years of experience and are required to pass an exam; they handle all "appraisables," not just jewelry.)

The Gemological Institute of America can tell you what should appear on a GIA report and confirm whether an appraiser has been trained by the organization. For more information, write to the Gemological Institute of America, Inc., 1180 Avenue of the Americas, New York, NY 10036. There is also a GIA office in California (P.O. Box 2110, 1660 Stewart St., Santa Monica, CA 90406).

The Jewelers' Vigilance Committee can tell you whether your dealer is among the good, the bad, or the ugly. This trade association monitors the industry and promotes ethical business practices. For more information, write to the Jewelers' Vigilance Committee, 1180 Avenue of the Americas, 8th Fl., New York, NY 10036.

DIAMONDS BY RENNIE ELLEN

15 W. 47TH ST., RM. 401
NEW YORK, NY 10036
212/869-5525

Catalog: $2
Save: up to 75%
Pay: check, MO, teller's check, bank draft
Sells: stock and custom-made jewelry
Store (factory): by appointment only
$$$

It's hard to believe that you can buy diamond engagement rings wholesale, but that's Rennie Ellen's business. You can save up to 75% on the price of similar jewelry sold elsewhere by buying here. Rennie Ellen is honest, reputable, and personable, and she's been cutting gems since 1960.

Rennie Ellen sells diamonds of all shapes, sizes, and qualities, set to order in platinum or gold. The color catalog shows samples of Ms. Ellen's design work, including rings, pendants, and earrings set with diamonds, rubies, sapphires, emeralds, and pearls. The factory is open to customers by appointment only.

Please note that the catalog ($2) includes information on both Diamonds by Rennie Ellen and her other concern, R/E Kane Enterprises (see that listing in this chapter).

Special Factors: Price quote by phone or letter with SASE; a detailed bill of sale is included with each purchase; returns are accepted within 5 working days; minimum shipping, handling, and insurance charge is $10.

ELOXITE CORPORATION

806 TENTH ST., DEPT. 4
WHEATLAND, WY 82201
307/322-3050
FAX: 307/322-3055

Catalog: 25¢
Save: up to 75%
Pay: check, MO, MC, V
Sells: jewelry findings
Store: same address; Monday to Friday
8:30–4, Saturday 8:30–3

$$$ ☎ 🍁 🇺🇸

Eloxite has been selling jewelry findings, cabochons, beads, and other lapidary supplies since 1955. Prices here are up to 75% less than those charged by other crafts sources for findings and jewelry components, and Eloxite also sells Crystalite cutting and grinding equipment for professional jewelers.

Jewelry findings with a Western flair are featured here: bola ties and slide medallions, belt buckles and inserts, and coin jewelry are prominent offerings. Also shown are pendants, rings, earrings, lockets, tie tacks, and pins made to be set with cabochons or cut stones, as well as jump rings, chains, pillboxes, screw eyes, and ear wires. The stones themselves are sold—cut cubic zirconia and synthetic gemstones and oval cabochons of abalone, agate, black onyx, garnet, opal, obsidian, jasper, and malachite. The catalog we reviewed included mother-of-pearl cameos and necklaces, loosely strung gemstone bead necklaces, and jewelers' tools and supplies.

Sandwiched between the pages of jewelry components are quartz clock movements and blanks for clock faces, clock hands, oil paints and palettes, and ballpoint pens and letter openers for desk sets. Discounts are available on most items, and specials are usually offered with orders of specified amounts.

Special Factors: Quantity discounts are available; undamaged returns are accepted within 15 days for exchange or refund (a $2 restocking fee may be charged); minimum order is $15; C.O.D. orders are accepted; orders are shipped worldwide.

HONG KONG LAPIDARIES, INC.

**2801 UNIVERSITY DR.
CORAL SPRINGS, FL
33065
305/755-8777
FAX: 305/755-8780**

Catalog: $3, refundable
Save: up to 50%
Pay: check, MO, MC, V
Sells: jewelry supplies and loose stones
Store: mail order only

$$$ ☎ 🍁 🇺🇸

Hong Kong Lapidaries, established in 1978, sells a wide range of precious and semiprecious stones in a variety of forms. The 44-page catalog shows items of interest to hobbyists as well, and the prices run as much as 70% below comparable retail.

Thousands of cabochons, beads, loose faceted and cut stones, and strung chips of pearl, garnet, amethyst, onyx, abalone, and other kinds of semiprecious stones are listed in the catalog, which comes with a separate foldout with color photos of representative pieces. Egyptian clay scarabs, coral, cameos, cubic zirconia, yellow jade, cloisonné jewelry and objets d'art, 14K gold-filled and sterling silver beads, and ball earrings are available. Hobbyists should note the thread—100% silk or nylon—in a score of colors and 16 *sizes*.

Special Factors: Satisfaction is guaranteed; price quote by fax; quantity discounts are available; returns are accepted within 12 days; minimum order is $50; orders are shipped worldwide.

HOUSE OF ONYX

**THE AARON BUILDING
GREENVILLE, KY 42345
800-626-8352
IN KY 800-992-3260
502/338-2363
FAX: 502/338-9605**

Catalog: free
Save: up to 60%
Pay: check, MO, MC, V
Sells: investment-grade stones, jewelry, and gifts
Store: same address; by appointment

$$$ ☎ 🍁 🇺🇸

The House of Onyx publishes a large tabloid catalog filled with reports on the gem industry and listings of diamonds and other precious stones, as well as specials on gifts and jewelry. The House of Onyx, which has gained over 50,000 clients worldwide since it opened its doors in 1967, enjoys a reputation for good service and prices.

Imported goods from Mexico, China, and India have been offered in the past, including Aztec onyx chess sets, ashtrays, bookends, vases, statuettes, candlesticks, and jewelry. There are cloisonné and vermeil beads, jewelry, and artware, and carvings of soapstone, rose quartz, tiger's eye, Burmese jadeite, lapis lazuli, carnelian, turquoise, and agate. The jewelry includes semiprecious bead necklaces, freshwater and cultured pearls, diamond rings, earrings, and pendants, from department-store grade to fine one-of-a-kind pieces. Collectors of crystals and mineral specimens should check here for amethyst, fluorite, quartz, pyrite, and others, and spheres of several minerals.

Vast quantities of choice, heavy, solid gold chains are stocked, and fine handmade jewelry can be produced to your specifications. The House also offers a wide range of investment-quality stones, with discounts of 50% and 60% offered on parcels of $2,000 to $12,500. The investment stones account for much of the business here, and the catalog is packed with useful information and commentary on the field.

Special Factors: Satisfaction is guaranteed; investment gemstones are sold with an unlimited time return guarantee and "100% purchase price refund" pledge; other returns are accepted within 30 days; minimum order is $25.

INTERNATIONAL GEM CORPORATION

3601 HEMPSTEAD TPK.
LEVITTOWN, NY 11756
516/796-0200
FAX: 516/796-0285

Catalog: $2
Save: up to 40%
Pay: check, MO, certified check
Sells: semiprecious stone jewelry
Store: mail order only

$$

International Gem Corporation, which has been selling to the trade since 1950, offers consumers the opportunity to buy jewelry and beads at wholesale prices—up to 40% below comparable retail.

The 18-page, color IGC catalog lists hand-knotted strands of 8mm balls of a variety of gemstones, in everything from aventurine to unikite. There are strands of beads and freshwater pearls, with gold bead and cloisonné spacers, in a choice of sizes and arrangements, and drop and stud earrings to match. And black onyx jewelry, beggars' beads, sumptuous ropes made of several strands of 4mm balls and pearls twisted together, and cloisonné jewelry and accessories are also offered. Options include the addition of gold spacer beads to some strands, custom lengths, and hand-knotting of loose strands.

Special Factors: Price quote by phone or letter with SASE on quantity orders; minimum order is $25; orders are shipped worldwide.

R/E KANE ENTERPRISES

**P.O. BOX 1745,
   ROCKEFELLER PLAZA
NEW YORK, NY 10185
212/869-5525**

Catalog: see text
Save: up to 75%
Pay: check, MO, teller's check
Sells: stock and custom-made cubic zirconia jewelry
Store: mail order only

$$$$

If you have diamond tastes but a rhinestone budget, consider the best alternative to the natural stone—cubic zirconia (C.Z.). C.Z., a synthetic stone, is the best impostor on the market. C.Z. weighs 80% more than diamonds; a 1.80-carat C.Z. stone is about the same size as a one-carat diamond.

This division of "Diamonds by Rennie Ellen" sells stock and custom-made C.Z. jewelry at just $10 a carat, including rings, earrings, bracelets, and necklaces, in both stock and custom designs. Please note that the catalog for R/E Kane is combined with the "Diamonds by Rennie Ellen" catalog. See the listing for that firm in this chapter for information on ordering the catalog.

Special Factors: Price quote by phone or letter with SASE; minimum shipping, handling, and insurance charge is $10.

ROSS-SIMONS JEWELERS

**9 ROSS-SIMONS DR.
CRANSTON, RI 02920-
9848**
800-556-7376
401/463-3100
FAX: 401/463-8599

Catalog: free
Save: up to 40%
Pay: check, MO, MC, V, AE, CB, DC,
Discover, Optima
Sells: jewelry, tableware, and giftware
Store: mail order only

$$$ ☎ ▨

Ross-Simons has 30 years of experience in the jewelry business, and showcases its gems and baubles in a color catalog. Half of each issue is devoted to fine china, flatware, and gifts. Prices are discounted up to 40% below suggested list and regular retail, and you can call directly for a quote if you're shopping for a specific name-brand item.

If you're looking for a good selection of stylish jewelry, you'll find it here. Diamond-encrusted necklaces and pins were prominent in the holiday catalog we reviewed, as well as gold bands with cabochon gems, gold mesh bracelets and chokers, necklaces of semiprecious gems, clasp bracelets of diamonds and rubies, a large collection of stud jackets, strands of cultured pearls, and more affordable versions in cubic zirconia, sterling silver, and 18K gold plate. Ross-Simons also sells watches, some of which are shown in the catalog. Call for a price if you're looking for a model by Audemars-Piguet, Bertolucci, Concord, Corum, Chopard, Ebel, Geneva, Movado, Omega, Piaget, Rado, Tissot, or Raymond Weil.

Fine china, crystal, silver, and gifts complete the catalog, which features patterns from Aynsley, Bernardaud, Block, Coalport, Fitz & Floyd, Gorham, Haviland, Johnson Brothers, Lenox, Mikasa, Minton, Noritake, Royal Copenhagen, Royal Doulton, Royal Worcester, Sasaki, Tirschenreuth, Villeroy & Boch, and Wedgwood. Crystal is available from some of the same manufacturers, as well as Atlantis, Baccarat, Miller Rogaska, Orrefors, St. Louis, and Waterford. And Ross-Simons sells flatware—stainless, silverplate, and new sterling—by Dansk, Fraser, Gorham, International, Kirk-Stieff, Lunt, Mikasa, Oneida, Reed & Barton, Retroneau, Sasaki, Towle, Wallace, and Yamazaki. Bing & Grøndahl and other commemoratives, music boxes, jewelry chests, and other gifts are also offered.

Special Factors: Satisfaction is guaranteed; price quote by phone or letter with SASE; returns (except personalized items) are accepted within 30 days for exchange, refund, or credit.

GINGER SCHLOTE

BOX 19523DD
DENVER, CO 80219

Catalog: $2.50
Save: up to 60%
Pay: check, MO, certified check
Sells: economy jewelry, mountings, and findings
Store: mail order only

$$ ✦ 🇺🇸

Mrs. Schlote started her business in 1981, bringing to it years of experience in her family's jewelry/mounting-parts business. She offers many bargains for the craftsperson on a budget, and runs specials regularly.

The 36-page catalog is crammed with economy chains, findings, and finished jewelry. Some of the items are gold-filled or sterling silver, but most are made of base metal with a white or yellow (golden) "lifetime" finish (Mrs. Schlote guarantees the finish against discoloration or tarnishing). Over three dozen chain styles are shown, starting at under 60¢ each, as well as novel pendants, rings, keyrings, bolas, cord tips, and tack pins. The jewelry and lapidary supplies include earring wires and clips, pendant mountings, bell caps, jump rings, clutchbacks, and pushnuts. Each catalog includes a number of bonus offers—freebies and extra discounts—and a coupon with which you can redeem the cost of the catalog. Be sure to mention this book to qualify for extra savings.

Special Factors: Satisfaction is guaranteed; shipping and insurance are included; returns are accepted within 10 days; orders are shipped worldwide.

SEE ALSO

Antique Imports Unlimited • antique jewelry and timepieces • *ART, ANTIQUES*

Atlantic Bridge Collection Corp. Ltd. • Claddagh jewelry • *ART,*
ANTIQUES
Beautiful Visions • small selection of fashion jewelry • *HEALTH*
Beauty Boutique • small selection of inexpensive fashion jewelry •
HEALTH
Bennett Brothers, Inc. • costume and fine jewelry and watches •
GENERAL MERCHANDISE
Berry Scuba Co. • underwater timepieces • *SPORTS*
Central Skindivers • underwater timepieces • *SPORTS*
Ceramic Supply of New York and New Jersey • jewelry findings • *ART*
MATERIALS
Circle Craft Supplies • economy jewelry findings, boxes, etc. • *CRAFTS*
Defender Industries, Inc. • waterproof watches • *AUTO*
Elderly Instruments • cloisonné pins of musical instruments • *MUSIC*
Fortunoff Fine Jewelry & Silverware, Inc. • fine jewelry and watches •
HOME: TABLE SETTINGS
The Jompole Company, Inc. • fine watches • *HOME: TABLE SETTINGS*
Manny's Millinery Supply Co. • hat pins • *CLOTHING*
Saxkjaers • Bing & Grøndahl pendants • *ART, ANTIQUES*
Nat Schwartz & Co., Inc. • fine jewelry • *HOME: TABLE SETTINGS*
Shannon Duty Free Mail Order • Claddagh and Irish jewelry • *HOME:*
TABLE SETTINGS
Albert S. Smyth Co., Inc. • fine jewelry and watches • *HOME: TABLE*
SETTINGS
Stecher's Limited • fine watches and clocks • *HOME: TABLE SETTINGS*

LEATHER GOODS

Small leather goods, handbags, briefcases, attaché cases, luggage, trunks, and services

The firms listed here stock everything you should need to tote your effects around town, to the office, and around the world. In addition to handbags, briefcases, suitcases, steamer and camp trunks, and small leather goods, some of the firms also sell cases for musical instruments and portfolios for models and artists.

If you're buying luggage, consider the different luggage materials available and the pros and cons of each before making your purchase. It's not advisable to buy luggage with attached wheels if you're doing any flying. The wheels tend to jam in conveyor systems and are usually ripped off by the time you've taken a few trips. Collapsible luggage carriers, which can be taken with you as hand baggage, solve the problem of getting bags around in huge, porterless terminals.

Other listings of firms that sell small leather goods and handbags can be found in "Clothing," portfolios and display cases and binders are available from a number of the companies listed in "Art Materials," and companies selling travel accessories are listed in "Travel."

ACE LEATHER PRODUCTS, INC.

**2211 AVE. U
BROOKLYN, NY 11229
800-DIAL ACE
718/891-9713**

Catalog: $1, refundable (see text)
Save: up to 40%
Pay: check, MO, MC, V, AE, Optima
Sells: luggage and leather goods
Store: 2211 and 2122 Ave. U, Brooklyn, NY; Monday to Saturday 10–6, Thursday 10–8

$$$ ☎ 🍁(see text)

Ace, which was established in 1960, sells luggage by American Tourister, Andiamo, Boyt, Amelia Earhart, French, Hartmann, Lark, Lucas, Members Only, Pegasus, Samsonite, Scully, Skyway, LeSport Sac, Tumi, and Ventura at discounts of up to 40%. Briefcases and attaché cases by Atlas, Bond Street, Boyt, Lodis, Renwick, Schlesinger, Scully, Tumi, and Yamani are available, as well as handbags and small leather goods by Etienne Aigner, Le Baron, Bond Street, Bosca, Garys, and Anne Klein. You'll find travel alarms, lighters, pens, and other small luxuries by Bulova, Colibri, Cross, Mont Blanc, Seiko, and Waterman in the store. The 36-page catalog (published during the holiday season) features gift merchandise, but price quotes are given throughout the year.

Canadian readers, please note: Orders to Canada are shipped via UPS.

Special Factor: Price quote by phone or letter with SASE.

AL'S LUGGAGE

**2134 LARIMER ST.
DENVER, CO 80205
303/295-9009
303/294-9045**

Catalog: $2, refundable
Save: up to 50%
Pay: check, MO, MC, V, AE, CHOICE, Discover
Sells: leather goods and luggage
Store: same address; Monday to Saturday 8:30–5:30

$$$ ☎ 🍁(see text)

The two dollars you send to this luggage discounter brings you a sheaf of photocopied materials from Samsonite, including price lists, ordering instructions, and shipping rate charts. Al's Luggage has been selling name-brand leather goods and luggage since 1965, and carries Diane Von Furstenberg, Jordache, Lion Leather, London Fog Luggage, Members Only, Platt, Stebco, Winn, and WK. In addition to current lines of suitcases, overnight bags, cosmetics cases, totes, wardrobes, duffels, and garment bags, Al's offers attaché cases, portfolios, and even camcorder carrying cases.

Please note that the catalog shows only Samsonite models, which are sold here for 30% to 50% below list prices. If you're shopping for an item by another manufacturer, you'll be better served by calling or writing for a price quote.

Canadian readers, please note: A minimum-order requirement may be imposed on orders to Canada; write for a shipping quote before sending order payment.

Special Factors: Price quote by phone or letter with SASE; C.O.D. orders are accepted; orders are shipped worldwide.

AMERICAN TOURISTER

**91 MAIN ST., DEPT. WB
WARREN, RI 92885-4301
800-879-2686
401/247-3201**

Information: price quote
Save: up to 70%
Pay: check, MO, MC, V, AE, Discover, Optima
Sells: American Tourister and Buxton products
Store: factory outlet stores nationwide; call for locations

$$$ ☎ ♦ ▀

American Tourister is one of the best-known names in the luggage business, and like many major manufacturers, it operates factory outlets to sell its overruns, closeouts, and discontinued styles and colors—at 40% to 70% off suggested list.

You can call for the location of the outlet nearest you, which can give you prices on luggage and leather goods by American Tourister and Buxton (you must have the style and color codes). American Tourister's luggage carries the company's "Gorilla Tough Guarantee," a three-year limited warranty.

Special Factors: Price quote by phone or letter; orders are shipped worldwide.

A TO Z LUGGAGE CO., INC.

**4627 NEW UTRECHT AVE.
BROOKLYN, NY 11219
800-342-5011
718/435-2880
FAX: 718/435-6317**

Catalog: free
Save: up to 50%
Pay: check, MO, MC, V, AE, CB, DC
Sells: luggage and leather goods
Store: same address; Sunday to Friday 9–6;
also 425 Fifth Ave., New York, NY;
Sunday to Friday 9–6; and 6 other New
York City locations

$$$ ☎ ♦ ▀

A to Z has been supplying New Yorkers with luggage and leather goods since 1945, discounting prices up to 50%. The catalog is published for the holiday season; calling or writing for price quotes is recommended.

A to Z sells luggage, briefcases and attaché cases, and other leather goods by Adolfo, American Tourister, Andiamo, Boyt, Amelia Earhart, Hartmann, Lark, Lucas, Members Only, Samsonite, Verdi, Wings, Zero Halliburton, and other designers and manufacturers. Artists' portfolios, steamer trunks, and related gifts are also available. And A to Z discounts pens by Cross, Mont Blanc, and Waterman. The 28-page catalog has dozens of gift ideas—desk and travel accessories, executive novelties, etc.—in addition to leather goods.

Special Factors: Price quote by phone or letter with SASE; service and repairs are available; orders are shipped worldwide.

CLASSIC DESIGNS

**P.O. BOX 994
MARION, MA 02738
508/748-2425**

Catalog: $1, refundable
Save: up to 40%
Pay: check, MO, MC, V
Sells: leather business and personal
accessories
Store: mail order only

$$$ ☎ ♦(see text)

Classic Designs, which was founded in the late 1970s, sells handcrafted leather goods at prices up to 40% less than those charged elsewhere for the same items. The briefcases, note pads, portfolios, planners, and other accessories are made of full-grain cowhide in "elegant, yet functional" styles with what the firm characterizes as a Down East look, and are very well priced: A six-ring personal planner with snap closure costs about $39 at this writing, briefcases and portfolios begin at under $100, and note pad covers cost $15 to $47. Everything is covered by Classic Designs' guarantee of satisfaction.

Canadian readers, please note: Request a shipping estimate before ordering.

Special Factors: Satisfaction is guaranteed; price quote by phone or letter.

INNOVATION LUGGAGE

**487 HACKENSACK AVE.
RIVER EDGE, NJ 07661
800-722-1800**

Information: price quote
Save: up to 50%
Pay: check, MO, MC, V, AE, DC
Sells: leather goods and luggage
Store: 14 locations in CT, NJ, and NY

$$$ ☎

Innovation, the "largest independent Samsonite dealer in the U.S.," has an excellent selection of luggage, briefcases, and other leather goods from a range of manufacturers. If you're looking for luggage, portfolios, briefcases and attaché cases, handbags, and small leather goods by American Tourister, Amelia Earhart, Hartmann, Invicta, Land, Lark, Samsonite, Skyway, Tumi, or Ventura, call or write Innovation for a price quote. Excellent savings can be found on one-of-a-kind items and closeouts that are sold in the stores only—ask for the location nearest you if you're in the tri-state area.

Special Factors: Price quote by phone or letter with SASE; minimum order is $15.

LEATHER UNLIMITED CORP.

DEPT. WBMC
7155 CTY. HWY. B
BELGIUM, WI 53004-9990
414/994-9464
FAX: 414/994-4099

Catalog: $2, refundable
Save: up to 50%
Pay: check, MO, MC, V
Sells: leathercraft supplies and equipment and finished products
Store: same address; Monday to Friday 7–3:30

$$$ ☎ ◆ ▬

Here's a catalog for the beginner, the seasoned leather worker, and the rest of us: It offers all sorts of leathercrafting supplies, from kits to raw materials, as well as leather cleaners and conditioners, a line of bags, attaché cases, and small leather goods, and even black powder supplies.

Leather Unlimited has been in business since 1971, and offers substantial savings on crafts supplies, beginning with leather—sold by the hide or in pieces. The weights run from fine lining grade to heavy belting leather, in a variety of finishes and colors. There are laces, belt blanks, shoe-repair pieces and soles, key tabs, and dozens of undyed embossed belt strips; these are matched by hundreds of belt buckles, which run from beautiful abalone inlays to a line with organization logos and sporting themes. The 64-page catalog features dozens of kits for making all sorts of finished goods, plus stamping tools, punches, carvers, rivets, screws, snaps, zippers, mallets, lacing needles, sundry findings, leather-care products and dyes by Fiebing's, and Missouri River patterns for making authentic frontier-style clothing.

Among the finished products available here are sheepskin rugs, slippers, mittens, hats, and purses made of sheepskin and deerskin, suede duffel and sports bags, leather totes, log carriers, and wineskins. Leather Unlimited is an authorized dealer for Harley-Davidson accessories—truckers' wallets, belts, keyrings, etc.—which are available. You'll also find top-grain belt leather attaché cases, briefcases, doctors' bags, portfolios, wallets, and other small leather goods listed in the catalog. The prices are outstandingly low—up to 50% below comparable retail on some items—and extra discounts are given on quantity or volume purchases.

Special Factors: Satisfaction is guaranteed; price quote by phone or letter with SASE; authorized returns are accepted within 10 days; minimum order is $30; orders are shipped worldwide.

THE LUGGAGE CENTER

**960 REMILLARD CT.
SAN JOSE, CA 95122
408/288-5363**

Information: price quote
Save: up to 50%
Pay: MO, MC, V, AE
Sells: luggage, business cases, and travel accessories
Store: locations in Bakersfield, Berkeley, Burlingame, Fresno, Los Gatos, Mountain View, Pleasant Hill, Redwood City, San Francisco, San Jose, San Lorenzo, San Rafael, Visalia, and Walnut Creek, CA

$$  ✿(see text)

The Luggage Center can save you up to 50% on the top names in luggage, and even more when the firm is running a sale. The firm stocks the latest lines from well-known firms, which include Atlantic, Atlas, Caribou, Halliburton, High Sierra, Lark, London Fog, Members Only, Pegasus, Ricardo, Samsonite, Skyway, and Ventura. Attaché cases, garment bags, and travel accessories are carried as well, and you can call or write for a price quote.

Canadian readers, please note: Orders to Canada are shipped via UPS.

Special Factors: Price quote by phone or letter with SASE; returns are accepted within 15 days.

NEW ENGLAND LEATHER ACCESSORIES, INC.

**11 PORTLAND ST.
ROCHESTER, NH 03867
603/332-0707
FAX: 603/332-4526**

Catalog and Samples: $54, refundable
Save: up to 30%
Pay: check, MO, MC, V, AE
Sells: leather handbags and accessories
Store: same address; Monday to Saturday 9–5; also North Country Leather, Rte. 1, Tidewater Mall, Kittery, ME; Monday to Saturday 10–6

$$$ ☎ ✿

The 12-page catalog from New England Leather is illustrated with line drawings of its handsome leather bags and accessories, which are priced up to 30% below comparable leather goods. The $5 you send for the catalog also brings you a handful of butter-soft leather samples that show you the color range—cobalt blue, hunter green, brown, wine, black—and the textures of the two leathers used here, deerskin and goatskin.

Dozens of handbags and small leather items are available, mainly classic envelopes, hobo bags, knapsacks, and variations on simple pouch designs. The bags are lined, constructed with brass and pewter hardware, treated to repel rain, and some styles are trimmed in cowhide. Prices run from $17 for a clutch purse to $170 for an enormous "mailbag." New England Leather has been in business since 1976, continuing on in the tradition of the region, which was once the leatherworking capital of the country. Everything produced by the firm is 100% American made.

New England Leather is offering readers a discount of 10% on all orders. Be sure to identify yourself as a WBMC reader when you order, and deduct the discount from the cost of the goods only. This WBMC reader discount expires February 1, 1993.

Special Factors: Returns are accepted; orders are shipped worldwide.

SEE ALSO

Bennett Brothers, Inc. • small leather goods, luggage, and luggage carts •
   GENERAL MERCHANDISE
Custom Coat Company, Inc. • deerskin handbags, gloves, billfolds, etc. •
   CLOTHING
Dairy Association Co., Inc. • Tackmaster leather balm • ANIMAL
The Deerskin Place • deerskin leather goods • CLOTHING
A. Feibusch Corporation • replacement luggage-weight zippers •
   CRAFTS
Gander Mountain, Inc. • backpacks and lightweight luggage • SPORTS
Holabird Sports Discounters • racquet-sports bags • SPORTS
IMPCO, Inc. • Lexol leather conditioner • AUTO
Justin Discount Boots & Cowboy Outfitters • leather-care preparations
   • CLOTHING: FOOTWEAR
Lands' End, Inc. • canvas luggage and attaché cases • GENERAL
   MERCHANDISE
Mother Hart's Natural Products, Inc. • cotton canvas luggage •
   HOME: LINEN

Pagano Gloves, Inc. • deerskin handbags, gloves, slippers, etc. • *CLOTHING*

Shannon Duty Free Mail Order • leather handbags • *HOME: TABLE SETTINGS*

United Pharmacal Company, Inc. • leather conditioner • *ANIMAL*

Veteran Leather Company, Inc. • leather-care products • *CRAFTS*

Wholesale Veterinary Supply, Inc. • leather-care products • *ANIMAL*

MEDICINE AND SCIENCE

Prescription and over-the-counter drugs, hearing aids, contact lenses and eyeglasses, and post-surgery supplies and equipment

Buying medication by mail is convenient, and it can be less expensive than having prescriptions filled at the local drugstore. Even generic drugs may be cheaper by mail, affording you savings of up to 60% on some commonly prescribed remedies. You can also save up to half on the usual cost of hearing aids, contact lenses, breast forms, and products for ostomates, diabetics, and convalescent patients by buying them from the firms listed here.

Do you hang on to your old eyeglasses after your prescription has changed? You can put them to good use by sending them to New Eyes for the Needy, P.O. Box 332, Short Hills, NJ 07078. Your castoff specs will go to buy new glasses for others who can't afford them, even at a discount.

The Lions Clubs International also run an eyeglass-collection project in conjunction with LensCrafters, the national eyewear chain. You can drop off your old glasses at any LensCrafters from Thanksgiving to New Year's Day. They'll be sorted by prescription, cleaned, sterilized, repaired, and restored, and then added to the thousands of pairs the LensCrafters/Lions Clubs team of optometrists and volunteers will use as part of the "Gift the Gift of Sight" program. Because it's illegal to dispense used eyeglasses in this country, the team goes to developing nations—most recently, Costa Rica—where thousand of poor patients are screened, free of charge, and fitted with glasses that exactly or nearly match their prescription. Many of the people who receive glasses from Give the Gift of Sight have never had an eye exam in their lives, so the program really does live up to its name.

Remember that the glasses are accepted during December—during the rest of the year, you can mail them to "New Eyes for the Needy," at the address above.

Want to keep up with government news on medicine and regulatory matters? Subscribe to *FDA Consumer*, published ten times yearly. You can order a subscription through the Consumer Information Catalog, which is available free upon request from the Consumer Information Center, Pueblo, CO 81002.

For related products, see the listings in "Health and Beauty."

FIND IT FAST

BREAST FORMS • **B & B Company, Lingerie for Less**
CONTACT LENSES AND SUPPLIES • **Contact Lens Replacement Center, The Eye Solution, National Contact Lens Center**
EYEGLASSES AND FRAMES • **Elite Eyewear, Hidalgo, Prism Optical**
FIRST-AID KITS • **Masuen**
HEARING AIDS • **Ric Clark**
INCONTINENCE PRODUCTS • **Medical Supply**
OSTOMY AND TRACHEOSTOMY SUPPLIES • **Bruce Medical**
PRESCRIPTION DRUGS • **America's Pharmacy, Medi-Mail, Pharmail, Retired Persons Services**

AMERICA'S PHARMACY

P.O. BOX 10490
DES MOINES, IA 50306-
0490
515/287-6872

Catalog: free
Save: up to 50%
Pay: check, MO, MC, V
Sells: OTC and prescription drugs and health aids
Store: mail order only

$

America's Pharmacy provides prescription-filling services by mail, including generics for up to 50% less than branded drugs. The firm also sells vitamins and dietary supplements, over-the-counter remedies, beauty aids, and other drugstore goods at a discount.

Generic prescription drugs, which are formula equivalents of name-brand products, are listed with trade names, chemical names, list prices, and the lower generic prices. The 52-page catalog also lists goods for diabetics, copycat fragrances, skin-care products, dietary supplements, pain relievers, cold and allergy remedies, nonprescription reading glasses, weight-control products, hearing aid batteries, Attends, condoms, and Spenco wraps. If you order prescription drugs from America's Pharmacy, you may request a printout of all of your prescriptions at the end of the year—a great help when you're doing your taxes.

Special Factors: Satisfaction is guaranteed; returns are accepted within 30 days; shipping and insurance are included; minimum order is $15.

B & B COMPANY, INC.

2417 BANK DR., SUITE 201
P.O. BOX 5731, DEPT. WC01
BOISE, ID 83705
208/343-9696

Brochure: free
Save: up to 50% (see text)
Pay: check, MO, MC, V
Sells: breast forms
Store: mail order only

$$

B & B produces a comfortable, reasonably priced breast form, weighted and shaped to ideal dimensions with cushioned pillows, each of which contains 1½ ounces of tiny glass beads. (The weight may be adjusted by adding or removing pillows.) The form itself is all-fabric (no silicone is used), made of nylon softened with fiberfill, with an all-cotton backing that rests next to your skin. Bosom Buddy is interchangeable (fits both left and right sides), available in sizes from 32AAA to 46DDD, and it costs $60 ($65 for sizes DD and DDD). These prices are about 50% below those of other silicone models. The brochure gives complete details, and B & B's staff can answer any questions you may have by phone.

Special Factors: Satisfaction is guaranteed; returns are accepted; C.O.D. orders are accepted; orders are shipped worldwide.

BRUCE MEDICAL SUPPLY

411 WAVERLY OAKS RD.,
DEPT. 10736
WALTHAM, MA 02154
800-225-8446
FAX: 617/894-9519

Catalog: free
Save: up to 60%
Pay: check, MO, MC, V
Sells: ostomy, tracheostomy, diabetic, and general medical products
Store: mail order only

$$$$ ☎ 🍁 🇺🇸

The Bruce Medical Supply catalog is a valuable aid to persons who have had tracheostomies, colostomies, ileostomies, or urostomies, as well as diabetics and anyone who needs general nonprescription medical supplies and equipment. Bruce Medical Supply, which has been in business since 1978, also stocks products designed to make all sorts of routine tasks easier.

The 56-page catalog offers a comprehensive range of ostomy supplies, including collection pouches, dressings, adhesives and removers, disks and seal rings, irrigators, lubricants, cleansing products, and disinfectants. Diabetes monitoring supplies and equipment, bathtub safety benches, tub grips, decubitus (bedsore) protection, wheelchairs, walkers, canes, crutches, magnifying glasses, nonprescription reading glasses, blood pressure kits, stethoscopes, compresses, and similar products are also stocked. Most of the goods are from well-known firms, including Ames, Hollister, Johnson & Johnson, Squibb, 3M, and United.

Books on related topics and general nursing and caretaker supplies are available. The catalog also features a good selection of dining, food preparation, dressing, grooming, and bathing aids for persons whose range of movement or strength is limited.

Special Factors: Satisfaction is guaranteed; price quote by phone or letter; goods are shipped in unmarked boxes; C.O.D. orders are accepted.

RIC CLARK COMPANY

36658 APACHE PLUME
DR.
PALMDALE, CA 93550
805/947-8598

Catalog: free
Save: 50% plus
Pay: check or MO
Sells: hearing aids
Store: mail order only

$$$ ❧ ▆

The Ric Clark Company's catalog features six hearing aid models, designed for varying degrees of hearing loss. Clark's aids are suitable for losses from mild to severe and include in-the-ear models, "compression" aids said to "cushion" sudden loud noises, and standard models. Prices are about half those charged by hearing-aid dealers. A $10 deposit entitles you to a month's free trial, after which you may return the aid for a complete refund or keep it and pay the balance. Batteries and repairs are also available.

Ric Clark Company recommends that you see a physician before buying an aid; you must sign a waiver if you don't provide a physician's note stating that you need an aid.

Special Factors: Satisfaction is guaranteed; all aids are warrantied; a budget payment plan is available; orders are shipped worldwide.

CONTACT LENS REPLACEMENT CENTER

P.O. BOX 1489, DEPT. 92
MELVILLE, NY 11747
516/491-7763

Price List: free with SASE
Save: up to 70%
Pay: check or MO
Sells: contact lenses and sunglasses
Store: mail order only

$$$ ☎ ❧ ▆

The Contact Lens Replacement Center can sell you lenses of every type at savings of up to 70%. The firm has been in business since 1986 and deals by mail only.

The replacement lenses offered by the Center include hard, soft, extended-wear, disposable, and gas-permeable types Toric and bifocal prescriptions are also available. Every major brand is available: American Hydron, American Optical, Barnes Hind/Hydrocurve,

Bausch & Lomb, Boston, Ciba, Coopervision, CSI/Sola, Johnson & Johnson (Acuvue), Softmate, Vistakon, and Wesley-Jessen (brown to blue). Please note: This is a *replacement* service—not for first-time lens wearers—and you must supply a current prescription. The prices are so low that it may make sense to discontinue your lens insurance and rely on this service if you lose or damage your contacts. All soft lenses are shipped in factory-sealed vials.

Contact Lens Replacement Center also sells fashion sunglasses by Randolph Engineering, Ray-Bank, Serengeti, and Vuarnet, at discount prices. Call with the model name or number for a price quote.

The Contact Lens Replacement Center is offering readers a discount of 50% on the *second pair* when they buy two pairs of hard or gas-permeable lenses. Be sure to identify yourself as a WBMC reader when you order, and deduct the discount from the cost of the goods only. This WBMC reader discount expires February 1, 1993.

Special Factors: Price quote by phone or letter with SASE; orders are shipped worldwide.

ELITE EYEWEAR

P.O. BOX 680030, DEPT. WC-22
NORTH MIAMI, FL 33168
305/754-5894, EXT. 22
FAX: 305/754-7352

Brochure and Price List: free
Save: up to 50%
Pay: check, MO, MC, V, AE, Discover
Sells: designer sunglasses and eyeglass frames
Store: mail order only

Elite Eyewear is an affiliate of Prism Optical (also listed in this chapter), which sells prescription eyeglasses by mail. Elite Eyewear, on the other hand, sells eyeglass frames and designer sunglasses. Elite's stock includes frames and sunglasses under labels of Geoffrey Beene, Bollé, Carrera, Cazal, Christian Dior, Gucci, Daniel Hunter, Anne Klein, Ted Lapidus, Logo, Mirari, Polo, Ray-Ban, Revo, Serengeti, and Vuarnet, among others. Elite's brochure tells you how to find the style numbers on frames you try on at your local optical shop, and how to calculate the frame size. When you receive your frames from Elite, you can have the lenses ground and the glasses fitted at the same shop where you tried on the frames—it's a nice way to thank the proprietors for use of their showroom. Since Elite's prices are up to 50% below regular retail, it's easy to save a good $50 simply by buying the frames at a discount. All purchases are backed by Elite's guarantee of satisfaction, and six-month manufacturers' warranties against breakage under normal use. Complete details are given in the free brochure.

Special Factors: Satisfaction is guaranteed; price quote by phone or letter with SASE; returns (in as-new condition) are accepted within 30 days for exchange, refund, or credit.

THE EYE SOLUTION, INC.

P.O. BOX 262-H
GALION, OH 44833
419/683-1608

Catalog: free
Save: up to 70%
Pay: check, MO, MC, V
Sells: contact lens solutions, accessories
Store: mail order only

$$$ ☎ 🇺🇸

If you wear contact lenses, we don't have to tell you about the high cost of care products. The Eye Solution remedies the problem by saving you up to 70% on the cost of cleaning, disinfecting, and lubricating preparations and equipment. We've priced The Eye Solution against *discount* drugstores, and almost invariably found The Eye Solution the better buy, sometimes beating the drugstore by 50%.

The catalog lists saline and rinsing solutions, daily and weekly cleaners, rewetting drops, and disinfection units (heat) and chemicals (cold) for soft lenses, and similar products for hard and gas-permeable lenses. The brands include Alcon, Allergan, Barnes-Hind, Bausch & Lomb, Blairex, Boston, Ciba Vision (AOSept), Coopervision, and Wesley-Jessen. A number of "introductory" and travel kits were shown in the catalog we reviewed, as well as cleaning machines and a special soap for contact lens wearers.

Special Factor: Minimum order is $30 with credit cards.

HIDALGO

DEPT. WB
45 LA BUENA VISTA
WIMBERLEY, TX 78676
512/847-5571
FAX: 512/847-2393

Catalog: free
Save: up to 60%
Pay: check, MO, MC, V, AE, CB, DC,
Discover, Optima
Sells: prescription eyeglasses, sunglasses,
etc.
Store: Wimberley North Too Shopping
Center, Wimberley, TX; Monday to Friday
9–5, Saturday 10–2

$$$ ☎ ♦ ▀

Hidalgo's 48-page catalog makes ordering your eyeglasses by mail seem so easy you'll wonder why you haven't tried it before. The firm has been in business since 1967 and understands the concerns of the person who's buying glasses by mail: The catalog includes detailed descriptions of the frames, lenses, and special coatings, and includes a "Consumers' Guide to Sunglasses" that answers every question we'd ever thought of. There are instructions on taking your "pupil distance" measurements, and a chart that shows the light transmission data on the lenses sold by Hidalgo. We really appreciate the "try-on program" that allows you to order up to three frames and try them out *before* ordering your glasses—a great feature for people who have a hard time finding frames that fit or flatter.

Hidalgo's own frames dominate the selection, and there are sunglasses by Bausch & Lomb and Ray-Ban, as well as replacement parts for the latter. The lens options include a choice of materials (glass, plastic, etc.), colors, coatings, and UV protection. Terms of Hidalgo's warranty are stated clearly in the catalog, as well as details on the "try-on" program. The prices are as much as 40% below regular retail on the nonprescription eyewear, and 50% or more on prescription glasses.

Special Factors: Price quote by phone or letter; returns in new, unused condition are accepted within 30 days for exchange, refund, or credit; orders are shipped worldwide.

LINGERIE FOR LESS

C & H SALES, INC.
11411 E. NORTHWEST
HWY.
DALLAS, TX 75218
214/341-9575

Leaflet: free with SASE
Save: up to 50%
Pay: check or MO
Sells: mastectomy breast forms
Store: same address; Monday to Friday
10–6, Sunday 1–4

$$$

Lingerie for Less sells a mastectomy form that's won praise from many women for its comfort as well as its price. It's Spenco's "Soft Touch Breast Form" (under $75), a molded gel breast form that has been compared favorably to others selling for more than three times as much. It's available in seven sizes and is designed to fit all types of brassieres. Name-brand lingerie is also available *(to in-store customers only)* at savings of up to 60%.

Special Factors: Breast forms are warrantied for 1 year (see the brochure for details); price quote by phone or letter with SASE (include size); returns are accepted.

MASUEN FIRST AID & SAFETY

P.O. BOX 901
TONAWANDA, NY 14151
800-831-0894
FAX: 800-222-1934

Catalog: free
Save: up to 30%
Pay: check, MO, MC, V, AE
Sells: first-aid kits, medical supplies
Store: mail order only

$$

Masuen, "Your Source for First Aid & Safety," publishes a 48-page catalog that's full of stock items for the medicine chest. Masuen's specialty is first-aid kits, and over a dozen are shown in the catalog, from small kits for the glove compartment to the "Masuen Portable First Aid Cabinet," which provides treatment for up to 120 persons. Masuen also sells resuscitators, sphygmomanometers, thermometers, all kinds of adhesive bandages and dressings, swabs, cotton rolls, splints, braces, antibiotic creams, soaps, analgesics, and protective clothing, eyewear, and gloves. Some of the prices are higher than those charged in local drugstores, but with quantity discounts you can realize savings of up to 30% on some items.

Special Factors: Price quote by phone or letter; quantity discounts are available; minimum order is $25.

MEDICAL SUPPLY CO., INC.

P.O. BOX 609
HEWITT, NJ 07421-0609
201/209-8448
FAX: 201/209-4788

Price List: free with SASE
Save: 30% average
Pay: check or MO
Sells: incontinence products
Store: mail order only

$

Coping with incontinence is easier now that Attends, Depends, and similar products have come onto the market. Unfortunately, alleviating anxiety can get to be expensive as time goes by, so it's great to find a source for incontinence products at a discount.

Medical Supply Co. has been in business since 1977 selling Depends briefs and Chux underpads at savings of up to 50%. For example, Depends selling for 90¢ each in a local drugstore are sold here as "Incontinence Pants" at 50¢ each (in cases of 50). The Chux underpads run from 13¢ to 41¢ each (sold in cases), depending on the size. Medical Supply accepts Medicaid (in New Jersey only) and does not charge shipping on orders delivered in Connecticut, New Jersey, New York, and Pennsylvania. (Customers in other states pay UPS charges collect.)

As a reader of this book, you may deduct 10% of the goods total from your *first* order. This WBMC reader discount expires February 1, 1993.

Special Factors: Shipping is included on deliveries to CT, NJ, NY, and PA; minimum order is 1 case.

MEDI-MAIL, INC.

**P.O. BOX 98520
LAS VEGAS, NV 89193-
8520
800-331-1458**

Brochure: free
Save: up to 80%
Pay: check, MO, MC, V
Sells: prescription drugs and health-care
products
Store: mail order only

$$ ☎ ▬ (see text)

Medi-Mail is a national membership pharmacy-by-mail that offers name-brand prescription drugs at competitive prices, and an additional 20% off the prices of *generic* drugs if you're a member of American Federation of Police, End Notch Discrimination, Hadassah, Pace Membership Warehouse, Seniors' Program for Lower Medical Costs, and other organizations—call to see if any of your affiliations may qualify. Medi-Mail also honors membership in the American Association of Retired Persons (AARP).

The firm's brochure answers general questions on buying prescription drugs by mail, and lists scores of generic over-the-countrer remedies, nutritional supplements, and beauty preparations. Among other services, Medi-Mail provides a refill slip (when appropriate) and itemized receipt with each prescription, and will send you a printout of your past orders on request.

Medi-Mail is offering you a gift of any Medi-Mail nonprescription item (health or beauty product) costing up to $5 with your first *prescription* order. Identify yourself as a reader when you order. This WBMC reader offer expires February 1, 1993.

Special Factors: Price quote by phone or letter with SASE; shipping is included; minimum order is $2.50, $10 with credit cards.

NATIONAL CONTACT LENS CENTER

3527 BONITA VISTA DR.
SANTA ROSA, CA 95404-
1506
800-326-6352
IN CA 707/545-6352
FAX: 707/545-6353

Brochure: free
Save: up to 75%
Pay: check, MO, MC, V
Sells: soft contact lenses
Store: same address (Santa Rosa Optometry Center); daily 6 A.M.–9 P.M.

$$$

The Santa Rosa Optometry Center runs this lens-by-mail service, which can save you up to 75% on your next pair. You must already be a lens-wearer to buy here, since the Center can't provide through the mail the fitting and monitoring services needed by first-time wearers.

The Center was established in 1974 and sells all the major soft contact lens brands, including lines by American Hydron, Aquaflex, Bausch & Lomb, Ciba, Coopervision, Hydrocurve, Johnson & Johnson (Acuvue), Wesley-Jessen (brown to blue), and Syntex. Colored, standard, and extended-wear lenses are offered, as well as toric (for astigmatism), bifocal, and aphakic (for cataracts) lenses. Hard and gas-permeable lenses are also available. Savings can reach 75%, depending on the lens and manufacturer. Every lens is backed by the Center's 30-day replacement guarantee.

Please note: National Contact Lens Center must have a copy of your lens prescription, or the original vials from your current lenses, to process your order.

Special Factors: Satisfaction is guaranteed; price quote by phone or letter with SASE; prescription is required for filling order; returns are accepted within 30 days for replacement, exchange, refund, or credit; orders are shipped worldwide.

PHARMAIL CORPORATION

P.O. BOX 1466
CHAMPLAIN, NY 12919-
    1466
800-237-8927
518/298-4922

Information: inquire
Save: 50% average
Pay: check, MO, MC, V
Sells: prescription drugs, vitamins, and
    health-care products
Store: 87 Main St., Champlain, NY; Monday
    to Thursday 10–3

$$ ☎

Pharmail wants you to be able to "pay 'insurance plan prices' for prescription drugs and enjoy benefits of scale on quantity purchases." This pharmacy has been dispensing prescription drugs, both name-brand and generic, since 1988.

You can request Pharmail's eight-page catalog, which is a partial list of the available drugs, or call for prices. The firm must have your physician's signed prescription to fill orders (authorized refills may be requested by phone), and birth date information is also required. There are no membership requirements, and Pharmail serves groups under preferential arrangements. Quantity prices are excellent, and if you're on a maintenance medication and can order a six-month supply, you'll save on the per-dose cost and spare yourself price increases. Pharmail can also provide a list of your purchases for the year, which is helpful at tax time. Request the catalog and literature for complete details and prices of commonly used name-brand and generic medications.

Pharmail is offering readers of this book a special savings on their *first order only*. If you're buying *three* new prescriptions (not refills), you may deduct one-half the cover price of this book; if you're ordering *five* new prescriptions, you may deduct the *entire* cover price. Identify yourself as a WBMC reader when ordering. This WBMC reader offer expires February 1, 1993.

Special Factors: Price quote by phone or letter with SASE; shipping is included; quantity discounts are available; minimum order is $4.99 per prescription, $10 per order.

PRISM OPTICAL, INC.

Catalog: $2, refundable
Save: up to 50%
Pay: check, MO, MC, V, AE, Discover
Sells: prescription eyeglasses
Store: same address; Monday to Friday 9–5

10992 N.W. 7TH AVE.,
DEPT. WC92
NORTH MIAMI, FL 33168
305/754-5894
FAX: 305/754-7352

$$

Prism Optical has been selling prescription eyeglasses by mail since 1959, and also carries Red Specs eye protectors for sports. The 12-page catalog shows dozens of eyeglass frames for men, women, and children, including designer styles, metal frames, and half-eye frames, discounted an average of 30% to 50%.

One of the benefits of ordering from Prism is being able to choose from a number of lens options. These include photochromic lenses, polycarbonate (ultra-thin) lenses, permanently tinted lenses, lenses with grey mirror-finish, and UV-filtering coating and scratch-resistant coating. The lens styles include single-vision and bifocal lenses, trifocals, and "invisible" bifocals, among others. Prism guarantees that the glasses will fit correctly, and the catalog provides guides to gauging the correct size of the temple and bridge pieces.

Prism is offering readers of this book a discount of 10% on their *first* order only. Identify yourself as a WBMC reader when you order. This WBMC reader discount expires February 1, 1993.

Special Factors: Satisfaction is guaranteed; price quote by phone or letter with SASE; returns are accepted within 30 days for refund or credit; C.O.D. orders are accepted.

RETIRED PERSONS SERVICES, INC.

500 MONTGOMERY ST.
ALEXANDRIA, VA 22314-
1563
703/684-0244

Catalog: free
Save: up to 80%
Pay: check or MO
Sells: prescription drugs, health and beauty aids, etc.
Store: stores in CA, CT, DC, FL, IN, MO, NV, NY, OR, PA, TX, and VA; locations are listed in the catalog

$$$

Retired Persons Services is the mail-order arm of the American Association of Retired Persons (AARP). Ordering from this pharmacy-by-mail is a benefit of membership in the AARP, which may be the smartest $5 you ever spend (see the listing for the AARP in "General Merchandise").

The 64-page catalog lists nutritional supplements, over-the-counter remedies, analgesics, supplies for diabetics, nail clippers and scissors, magnifying glasses, perfumes and products for skin and hair, sun blockers, liniments, razor blades, sphygmomanometers, support hosiery and foot-care products, dental-care items, hearing aid batteries, and much more. Prices for the generic and branded versions of about 75 prescription drugs are listed in the catalog, and you can complete the form enclosed in the catalog to request a price quote on your maintenance drugs if they're not listed, or telephone. Orders are filled on an invoice basis—you'll be billed for your order. The catalog features dozens of coupons worth 25¢ to 75¢ on selected items, and numerous articles on medical and general health topics.

Special Factors: Satisfaction is guaranteed; returns (except prescription drugs) are accepted for exchange, refund, or credit.

SURGICAL PRODUCTS, INC.

██████████

99 WEST ST.
P.O. BOX 500
MEDFIELD, MA 02052
800-229-2910
508/359-2910
FAX: 508/359-0139

Catalog: free
Save: up to 30%
Pay: check, MO, MC, V, AE
Sells: support hosiery and therapeutic apparel
Store: same address

$$ ☎ 🍁 ▐

This firm is better known under its catalog name, "Support Plus," since supportive hosiery and underwear for men and women are the catalog's chief focus. Discounts average about 15%, but we found some items selling for 30% less than regular retail.

If your physician recommends or prescribes support (elastic) hosiery, you'll find this catalog a helpful guide to what's available. Support Plus offers panty hose, stockings, knee-highs, and men's dress socks in different support strengths. (The compression rating for each style is given in the catalog descriptions.) Among the brands sold here are Bauer & Black, Berkshire, Futuro, Hanes, T.E.D., and Support Plus' own line. Maternity, cotton-soled, control-top, open-toe, and irregular styles are available.

Support Plus also sells posture pads for chairs and beds, joint "wraps" for applications of heat and cold, Curity sphygmo-manometers, Dale abdominal and lumbrosacral supports, Futuro braces and joint supports, and personal-care products and bathing aids—eating and dressing implements, bedding, underpads and disposable pants, bath seats and rails, and toilet guard rails. Women's foundation garments, Daniel Green shoes and slippers, and Isotoner gloves and slippers have been offered in past catalogs.

Special Factors: Unworn returns are accepted; minimum order is $20 with credit cards.

SEE ALSO

Astronomical Society of the Pacific • publications on astronomy topics • BOOKS
Astronomics/Christophers, Ltd. • telescopes • CAMERAS

Allyn Air Seat Co. • air-filled seats for wheelchairs • *SPORTS*

American Association of Retired Persons • pharmacy-by-mail services • *GENERAL MERCHANDISE*

Bailey's, Inc. • selection of first-aid kits • *TOOLS*

Bennett Brothers, Inc. • microscopes and telescopes • *GENERAL MERCHANDISE*

Campmor • snake bite kits, variety of first-aid kits • *SPORTS*

Clover Nursing Shoe Company • Nurse Mates nurses' shoes • *CLOTHING: FOOTWEAR*

Daleco Master Breeder Products • medicines for tropical fish • *ANIMAL*

Danley's • telescopes • *CAMERAS*

Defender Industries, Inc. • first-aid kits, marine safety gear • *AUTO*

Direct Safety Company • earplugs, safety goggles, stretchers, first-aid kits, etc. • *TOOLS*

Goldberg's Marine Distributors • first-aid kits, marine safety gear • *AUTO*

Kansas City Vaccine Company • livestock and pet biologicals and medications • *ANIMAL*

Leather Unlimited Corp. • leather doctors' bags • *LEATHER*

Mardiron Optics • telescopes • *CAMERAS*

Northern Wholesale Veterinary Supply, Inc. • animal biologicals and dietary supplements • *ANIMAL*

Okun Bros. Shoes • nurses' shoes • *CLOTHING: FOOTWEAR*

Omaha Vaccine Company, Inc. • biologicals and pharmaceuticals for livestock • *ANIMAL*

Orion Telescope Center • telescopes • *CAMERAS*

Plastic BagMart • zip-top plastic bags • *GENERAL: PACKAGING*

Scope City • telescopes • *CAMERAS*

United Pharmacal Company, Inc. • biologicals and instruments for animal care and treatment • *ANIMAL*

WearGuard Corp. • lab coats • *CLOTHING*

Wholesale Veterinary Supply, Inc. • biologicals and veterinary surgical supplies • *ANIMAL*

MUSIC

Instruments, supplies, and services

Professional musicians rarely pay full price for their instruments, and because you can buy from the same sources they use, neither should you. The firms listed here sell top-quality instruments, electronics, and supplies, and while they usually serve the knowledgeable, they can assist you even if you're a musical neophyte. If you catch the clerks during a lull in store trade, you can usually get the same kind of help over the phone—but please understand that they're usually very busy. Some of the stores take trade-ins, some rent instruments, and most sell used equipment.

By purchasing from these sources, you can save hundreds of dollars on top-rate equipment, and if you're equipping a band, you might save enough money to buy the van and pay the roadies. Get the best equipment you can—instruments can last a lifetime, and the resale market for quality pieces is good. Buy wisely today and you may be selling your "vintage" ax to Elderly Instruments or Mandolin Brothers 20 years down the road for several times what you paid!

FIND IT FAST

ACCORDIONS • **A.L.A.S.**
DRUMS • **Sam Ash, Lone Star**
FRETTED INSTRUMENTS • **Metropolitan Music, Shar, Weinkrantz**
GENERAL, SCHOOL, AND MARCHING BAND INSTRUMENTS • **Giardinelli, Interstate Music, Kennelly Keys, National Educational Music, West Manor**
GUITARS AND ELECTRONICS • **Sam Ash, Carvin, Discount Music, Kennelly Keys, Manny's**
PIANOS AND ORGANS • **Altenburg, CMC Music**
REEDS • **Discount Reed**

A.L.A.S. ACCORDION-O-RAMA

16 W. 19TH ST.
NEW YORK, NY 10011
212/675-9089
212/206-8344

Catalog: free (see text)
Save: up to 40%
Pay: check, MO, MC, V
Sells: accordions, accessories, and services
Store: same address (11th Floor); Tuesday
to Friday 9–4, Saturday 11–3

$$$

A.L.A.S., in business since 1950, has an extensive inventory of new and rebuilt accordions and concertinas that are all sold at a discount. A.L.A.S. is an authorized dealer and factory-service center for several leading brands, and can customize your instrument to meet your requirements—including MIDI. Concertinas and electronic, chromatic, diatonic, and piano accordions are offered here at considerable savings. A.L.A.S. carries its own line, as well as instruments by Arpeggio, Avanti, Cordovox, Crumar, Dellape, Elka, Excelsior, Farfisa, Ferrari, Gabbanelli, Galanti, Guerrinni, Hohner, Polytone, Sano, Scandalli, Solton, Sonola, Paolo Soprani, Vox, and other firms. The catalog features color photos of individual models with specifications. New and reconditioned models are stocked, and accordion synthesizers, amps, speakers, generators, organ-accordions, and accordion stands are available.

When you write for information, be sure to describe the type of accordion that interests you. In addition to price sheets and brochures, A.L.A.S. can send you a demonstration video for $25 (refundable deposit).

A.L.A.S. is offering readers of this book an extra 2% discount on purchases of new, full-size models. This WBMC reader discount expires February 1, 1993.

Special Factors: Price quote by letter with SASE; trade-ins are welcomed; orders are shipped worldwide.

ALTENBURG PIANO HOUSE, INC.

1150 EAST JERSEY ST.
ELIZABETH, NJ 07201
800-526-6979
IN NJ 800-492-4040
FAX: 908/527-9210

Brochure: free
Save: 35% minimum
Pay: check, MO, MC, V, AE
Sells: pianos and organs
Store: same address; Monday to Friday 9–9,
Saturday 9–6, Sunday 12–5

$$$ ☎ 🍁 🇺🇸

The Altenburg Piano House has been doing business since 1847, and it's run today by a descendant of the founder. Altenburg sells pianos and organs by "almost all" manufacturers, including lines by Baldwin, Hammond, Kawai, Kimball, Mason, and Yamaha. Prices are at least 35% below list or suggested retail, and if you write to Altenburg for literature, you'll receive information on its own line of pianos—upright, grand, and console models. Complete specifications are listed for each piano, including details on the encasing, keys, pinblock, bridges, soundboard, action, strings, hammer felt, and warranty. If you're pricing a name-brand model, call or write with the name of the piano or organ for price and shipping details.

Special Factors: Price quote by phone or letter with SASE; orders are shipped worldwide.

SAM ASH MUSIC CORP.

401 OLD COUNTRY RD.
CARLE PLACE, NY 11514
800-4-SAM ASH
516/333-8700
718/347-7757
FAX: 516/333-8767

Information: inquire
Save: up to 50%
Pay: check, MO, MC, V, AE, CB, DC,
Discover, Optima
Sells: instruments and electronics
Store: same address; Monday and Friday
10–9, Tuesday to Thursday, and Saturday
10–6; also Forest Hills, Huntington
Station, White Plains, Brooklyn, and New
York, NY; and Edison and Paramus, NJ

$$$ ☎ 🍁 🇺🇸

In 1924, violinist and bandleader Sam Ash opened a musical-instruments shop in Brooklyn. It's still family-run, but now boasts eight stores and patronage by superstars, schools and institutions, and the military, in addition to individuals. Regular half-off specials are a feature here, so don't buy anywhere else until you've given Ash a call.

Musical instruments, musical electronics, software, sound systems, recording equipment, digital home pianos, specialized lighting, and accessories are available from hundreds of manufacturers, including Akai, AKG, Alembic, Armstrong, Audio-Technica, Bach, Bose, Buffet, Bundy, Casio, Cerwin-Vega, Charvel, Conn, dbx, DeltaLab, Electro-Voice, Ensoniq, Fender, Gemeinhardt, Gibson, Guild, Hartke, Ibanez, Jackson, JBL, Karaoke (sing-along machines), Kawai, Kenwood, KLH, King, Kramer, Kurzweil, Leblanc, Ludwig, Marshall, Martin, Ovation, Pearl, Rickenbacker, Roland, Samson, Selmer, Sennheiser, Paul Reed Smith, Suzuki, Tama, Tascam, Technics, Toa, Washburn, Yamaha, and Zildjian. Sheet music is stocked, repairs and service are performed, and trade-ins are accepted at the stores.

Special Factors: Price quote by phone or letter with SASE; minimum order is $25; orders are shipped worldwide.

FRED'S STRING WAREHOUSE

███████████

212 W. LANCASTER,
*   DEPT. WM*
SHILLINGTON, PA 19607
800-677-2882
215/777-3733
FAX: 215/777-1007

Catalog: $1
Save: up to 40%
Pay: check, MO, MC, V, Discover
Sells: replacement strings for fretted instruments
Store: same address; Monday to Saturday 11–7

$$$ ☎ 🍁 🇺🇸

This firm, also known as Fred Bernardo's Music, offers strings for almost every sort of fretted instrument at savings of up to 40% off list or comparable retail. The catalog lists steel, brass, and bright-bronze and phosphor-bronze strings for all guitars, as well as a selection for pedal steel, mandolin, bass, banjo, violin, sitar, autoharp, and bouzouki. The brands include Aranjuez, Ernie Ball, Black Diamond, D'Addario, Darco, Fender, GHS, Gibson, Guild, Martin, John Pearse, Savarez, Dr. Thomastick-Infeld, and Vega. Picks, cables, harmonicas, DiMarzio pickups, Ibanez effects boxes, the Crybaby and other electronics, mikes, and capos are also available at a discount.

Special Factors: Price quote by phone or letter; authorized returns are accepted within 14 days; orders are shipped worldwide.

CARVIN

1155 INDUSTRIAL AVE.
ESCONDIDO, CA 92025
800-854-2235
FAX: 619/747-0743

Catalog: free
Save: up to 40%
Pay: check, MO, MC, V
Sells: Carvin instruments and accessories
Store: 7414 Sunset Blvd., Hollywood, CA;
Monday to Friday 11–8, Saturday 11–6

$$$ ▆▆▆

Carvin manufactures its own line of instruments and equipment, made to exacting standards. You'll find the specifications, features, and individual guarantees of each instrument noted in the color catalog; prices are up to 40% less than those of comparable models.

Mixers, amps, mikes, monitor systems, and electric guitars are offered here, as well as professional-quality guitars that designed for the requirements of contemporary music. All of the products are sold under a ten-day free trial arrangement; servicing and performance testing is done free of charge during the warranty period; and warranties range from one to five years, depending on the item.

Special Factors: Satisfaction is guaranteed; returns are accepted for refund.

CMC MUSIC, INC.

1385 DEERFIELD RD.
HIGHLAND PARK, IL
60035
708/831-3252

Information: price quote
Save: up to 50%
Pay: check, MO, MC, V, Discover
Sells: pianos, organs, keyboards, and clocks
Store: same address; Monday to Friday
10–6, Saturday 10–5:30

$$$ ☎

CMC Music, which is also known as Conn Music, sells pianos, organs, and other keyboard instruments at discounts of up to 50% on list prices. There is no catalog, but you can write for prices on pianos by Young Chang, Kimball, and Wyckoff, organs by Galanti, Kawai, and Technics, and keyboards by Bontempi, Kawai, Kurzweil, and Technics. Digital pianos, related electronics, and Howard Miller clocks are also available. Write for a price quote and shipping estimate.

Special Factors: Price quote by letter with SASE.

DISCOUNT MUSIC SUPPLY

41 VREELAND AVE., DEPT. WB
TOTOWA, NJ 07512-1120
201/942-9411
FAX: 201/890-7922

Catalog: free
Save: 35% average
Pay: check, MO, MC, V
Sells: guitars and rock electronics
Store: mail order only

$$$ ☎ ♦ ▬

Rock guitarists should get to know Discount Music Supply, whose 40-page catalog is packed with guitars, electronics, strings, and other accessories vital to the sound. Discount Music, in business since 1986, can save you an average of 35% on list prices, and much more on selected items and lines. Quantity discounts on strings, for example, can reduce list prices by nearly 70%.

DMS sells guitars and basses by Fender and Fernandes, amps and speakers by Boss, Celestion, Gorilla, and Venom; the Pignose amp, DiMarzio and Seymour Duncan pickups, Audio-Technica and Shure mikes, Sabine's Chromatic Autotuner, Conquest cables, Nady devices, Hamilton stands, guitar cleaning products, and effects boxes by Arion, Boss, DOD, Dunlop, Ibanez, and Rocktek. Studio systems and components by Boss, DigiTech, Rocktron, and Vestax are offered, as well as Hohner and Huang harmonicas, Casio and Fender picks. If you use strings by Augustine, Ernie Ball, La Bella, D'Addario, D'Angelico, Darco, Fender, GHS, Gibson, Guild, Kaman, Dean Markley, Martin, Maxima, S.I.T., and Vinci, see the catalog for enormous savings. Discount Music Supply doesn't list its entire inventory, so if you don't see what you're looking for, call, write, or fax your inquiry.

Please note: Inquire for information on left-handed guitar models.

Special Factors: Price quote by phone or letter; quantity discounts are available; authorized returns are accepted within 14 days for exchange, refund, or credit; minimum order is $10; C.O.D. orders are accepted.

DISCOUNT REED COMPANY

**SUITE 496; P.O. BOX 6010
SHERMAN OAKS, CA
91403
818/990-7962**

Price List: free with business-sized SASE
Save: up to 45%
Pay: check or MO
Sells: reeds for musical instruments
Store: mail order only

$$$ ◆ ▓

Discount Reed sells just that—"mail order reeds at fantastic savings." The woodwind reeds are sold by the box, priced up to 45% less than the per-box list prices—which represent really big savings if you're used to buying reeds one at a time. Since scrimping on reeds or pushing them beyond their natural life spans only impairs your music, it makes sense to buy by the box—and you'll always have spares.

Discount Reed, which began business in 1980, stocks reeds for all types of clarinets and saxophones, as well as oboes and bassoons, in strengths from 1 to 5½ (soft to hard). The brands include Grand Concert, Fred Hemke, Java, Jones (double reeds), Marca, Mitchell Lurie, La Mode, Olivieri, Rico, V-12, Vandoren, and La Voz. (If you're looking for a reed not listed in the flyer, call or write, since it may be available.) In addition, Discount Reed sells Harrison and Vandoren reed cases, reed trimmers, La Voz reed guards, Blue Note sax straps, swabs, and other accessories.

Special Factors: Satisfaction is guaranteed; price quote by phone or letter with SASE.

ELDERLY INSTRUMENTS

P.O. BOX 14210-WM92
LANSING, MI 48901
517/372-7890
FAX: 517/372-5155

Catalog: free (see text)
Save: 33% average
Pay: check, MO, MC, V, Discover
Sells: new and vintage musical instruments,
books, videotapes, and recordings
Store: 1100 North Washington, Lansing,
MI; Monday to Wednesday 11–7,
Thursday 11–9, Friday and Saturday 10–6

This wonderful company has an extraordinary selection of in-print, hard-to-find recordings of all types of music, from folk and bluegrass to jazz and classical, listed in a closely printed 96-page catalog. (For a sample of Elderly's picks, call "Dial-a-Ditty-a-Day," several minutes of an Elderly selection: call 517-372-1212.) Elderly Instruments also sells books on dance, repair and construction of instruments, music history, folklore, and even songbooks and videotapes.

Despite the impressive publication department, this firm made its name on its vintage instruments. Fenders, Martins, Dobros, Gibsons, and other electric and acoustic guitars have been offered in the past, as well as violins, mandolins, and other fretted instruments. And there are two additional catalogs—one for electric guitars and effects, and another for acoustic guitars and accessories. Elderly Instruments also sells new instruments, and lays claim to the title of world's largest dealer of new Martin guitars, and is among the top 20 Gibson dealers. You'll find a good selection of equipment here by Alvarez-Yairi, Boss, Crate, DiMarzio, Dobro, DOD, E.S.P., Gibson, Guild, Kahler, Kramer, Martin, Roland, Sigma, Stelling, Taylor, and Yamaha, among other firms. The monthly "used instruments list" is sent free with catalog orders, or you may subscribe for $5. Prices are as low as 50% off list, and everything is covered by the Elderly guarantee of satisfaction (see the catalog for details).

Please note: Mail-order hours are Monday to Saturday, 9–5.

Special Factors: Satisfaction is guaranteed; price quote by phone or letter with SASE; unused, authorized returns are accepted within 5 days for exchange, refund, or credit.

GIARDINELLI BAND INSTRUMENT CO., INC.

■■■■■■■■■■■■■■■

**7845 MALTLAGE DR.
LIVERPOOL, NY 13090
800-288-2334
FAX: 315/652-4534**

Catalog: free
Save: up to 50%
Pay: check, MO, MC, V, AE, Discover
Sells: brasses, woodwinds, and accessories
Store: same address; Monday to Friday
9–5:30, Saturday 9–1

$$$ ☎ ♦ ▆

Giardinelli has been selling fine brasses and woodwinds since 1948. The firm's 40-page catalog is an exhaustive listing of brass instruments, woodwinds, and accessories for both. Trumpets, flugelhorns, trombones, French horns, euphoniums, tubas, clarinets, flutes, piccolos, saxophones, oboes, and bassoons are all available. The brands include Bach, Besson, Buffet, Bundy, Courtois, DEG, Emerson, Farkas, Gemeinhardt, Getzen, Holton, Humes & Berg, Leblanc, Mercedes, Mirafone, Schilke, Selmer, Signet, Meinl Weston, Denis Wick, Yamaha, Yanigasawa, and others. Mouthpieces, mutes, reeds, metronomes, tuners, cases, stands, cleaning supplies, and books are also available. Giardinelli features its line of fine stock and custom mouthpieces for brasses. Savings run up to 50%, and the service department can assist you if you have questions or need advice.

Special Factors: Satisfaction is guaranteed; price quote by phone or letter with SASE; returns are accepted for exchange, refund, or credit; institutional accounts are available.

INTERSTATE MUSIC SUPPLY

■■■■■■■■■■■■■■■

**P.O. BOX 315
NEW BERLIN, WI 53151
800-837-BAND
FAX: 414/786-6840**

Catalog: free
Save: up to 60%
Pay: check, MO, MC, V
Sells: instruments, electronics, and
accessories
Store: Cascio Music Co., 13819 W.
National Ave., New Berlin, WI; Monday
to Thursday 10–8, Friday 10–5, Saturday
10–2

$$$ ☎ ♦ ▆

Interstate Music Supply is a division of Cascio Music Company, which has been in business since 1949. IMS serves the needs of schools and music teachers with a wide range of equipment, which is listed in the 164-page catalog. You'll find savings of up to 60% here on instruments, electronics, and accessories from major manufacturers.

Everything from woodwind reeds and corks to full lines of brass, woodwind, percussion, and stringed instruments is stocked here, including repair kits and parts, cleaning supplies, neckstraps, cases, storage units, music stands, stage lighting, sound systems, piano labs, and even riser setups for bands and orchestras. There are great buys on goods from Anvil, Bach, Blessing, Buffet, Bundy, Dynamic, Emerson, Engelhardt, Fender, Fostex, Franz, Gemeinhardt, Gibson, Holton, Korg, Kramer, Leblanc, Ludwig, Mesa-Boogie, Orff, Ovation, Pearl, Peavey, Roland, Sansui, Schilke, Seiko, Selmer, Trace-Elliot, Vandoren, Vito, Yamaha, and Zildjian. The catalog shows a fraction of the inventory, so call or write if you don't see what you're looking for.

Special Factors: Satisfaction is guaranteed; price quote by phone or letter with SASE; returns are accepted within 10 days for exchange, refund, or credit; institutional accounts are available; minimum order is $25.

KENNELLY KEYS MUSIC, INC.

**5030 208TH ST., S.W.
LYNNWOOD, WA 98036
800-426-6409
206/771-7020**

Catalog: free
Save: up to 50%
Pay: check, MO, MC, V, AE, Discover
Sells: musical instruments and accessories
Store: same address; Monday to Friday 8–5; also Bellevue, Everett, Mill Creek, Redmond, and Seattle, WA

$$$ ☎ 🍁

Marching bands, student musicians, guitarists—take note: Kennelly has an excellent selection of instruments and equipment for all of you, at savings of up to 50% on suggested list prices. Kennelly has been in business since 1960 and runs a repair department that offers its services to mail-order customers.

Woodwind, brass, and percussion instruments are available here, as well as guitars, speakers, amps, tuners, effects boxes, autoharps, mikes, stage lighting, mike cords, snakes, and more. The brands include AKG, Armstrong, Artley, Atlas, Bach, Blessing, Brilhart, Bose,

Buffet, Bundy, Conn, DEG, Emerson, Getzen, Gibson, Haynes, Holton, King, Korg, Larilee, Latin Percussion, Leblanc, Mitchell Lurie, Manhasset, McCormicks, Meyer, Mirafone, Muramatsu, Musser, Paiste, Pearl, Polytone, Remo, Rico, Roland, Selmer, Shure, Studio 49, Vandoren, Vito, and Zildjian.

Special Factors: Price quote by phone or letter with SASE; institutional accounts are available; authorized returns are accepted; minimum order is $25.

LONE STAR PERCUSSION

10611 CONTROL PL.
DALLAS, TX 75238
214/340-0835
FAX: 214/340-0861

Catalog: free with a long, self-addressed, stamped envelope
Save: 40% average
Pay: check, MO, MC, V
Sells: percussion instruments
Store: same address; Tuesday to Friday 9:30–5:30, Saturday 9:30–2

Concert, marching, jazz, and rock percussion—Lone Star stocks it all. This firm has been doing business with individuals and institutions worldwide since 1978, and publishes a 52-page catalog that lists drums and heads, drumsticks, keyboard mallets, cymbals, castanets, gongs, tambourines, triangles, wood blocks, bells, percussion for Latin music, and much more. The brands represented include American Drum, Balter, Bruno, Deschler, Feldman, Vic Firth, Tom Gauger, Grover, Hinger, Holt, Hyer, Latin Percussion, Linwood, Malletech, Musser (Ludwig), Payson, Pearl, Premier, Promark, Regal Tip, Remo, Ross, Sabian, Silverfox, Tama, Yamaha, and Zildjian. In the unlikely event you don't see what you're looking for among the thousands of items listed, call or write—it's probably available.

Special Factors: Satisfaction is guaranteed; price quote by phone or letter with SASE; authorized returns are accepted within 2 weeks (a restocking fee of up to 20% may be charged); institutional accounts are available; orders are shipped worldwide.

MANDOLIN BROTHERS, LTD.

**629 FOREST AVE.
STATEN ISLAND, NY
10310-2576
718/981-3226
FAX: 718/816-4416**

Catalog: free
Save: up to 35%
Pay: check, MO, MC, V, AE, Discover, Optima
Sells: new and vintage fretted instruments, electronics, and accessories
Store: same address; Monday to Saturday 10–6

$$$ ☎ 🍁 ▚

Mandolin Brothers has been selling vintage fretted instruments at good prices since 1971 and offers select new instruments at a standard discount of 35% from list prices. If you're in the Staten Island area, you can visit the well-stocked showroom and try out any of the instruments.

Mandolin Brothers' 60-page catalog is packed with listings of vintage guitars, mandolins, mandolas, banjos, electric basses, and other stringed instruments. A recent issue showed a number of early Martin and Gibson guitars, which were competitively priced. Part of the catalog is devoted to new equipment—guitars, mandolins, banjos, electronics, and accessories. The instrument lines include Alvarez-Yairi, Clevinger, Collings, Deering, Dobro, Epiphone, Flatiron, Franklin, Gibson, Guild, Heritage, Hohner Headless, Kentucky, Lowden, Martin, National Reso-Phonic, OME, Ovation, M.V. Pedulla, Jose Ramirez, Bart Reiter, Rickenbacker, Santa Cruz, Sierra, Sigma, Steinberger, Stelling, Stinger, Taylor, Wildwood, and Yamaha. There are amps, tuners, effects boxes, and other electronics by Boss, Crate (amps), DOD, Seymour Duncan, Fostex, Korg, Gallien Kreuger (amps), Ovation, and other firms; pickups by DeArmond, DiMarzio, and Seymour Duncan; and cables, strings, straps, frets, mutes, capos, books, videos, and more. Written instrument appraisals and repairs are available, and Mandolin Brothers ships in-stock instruments and amps on a three-day approval basis—and that includes vintage equipment.

Special Factors: Satisfaction is guaranteed; price quote by phone or letter with SASE; returns are accepted within 3 days; minimum order is $50 with credit cards; orders are shipped worldwide.

MANNY'S MUSICAL INSTRUMENTS & ACCESSORIES, INC.

**156 W. 48TH ST.
NEW YORK, NY 10036
212/819-0577**

Information: price quote
Save: up to 50%
Pay: check, MO, MC, V, AE, Discover
Sells: instruments, electronics, and accessories
Store: same address; Monday to Saturday 9–6

$$$ ☎ 🍁 ▊▊▊

Manny's has been selling musical instruments since 1935, and it's rare that this store on New York City's "Music Row" doesn't have a rock luminary or two checking out the equipment. Sales are run on a regular basis, bringing the standard 30% discounts up to 50%. Call for a price quote on instruments, electronics, and accessories, from amps and mixers to fine woodwinds and brass instruments. The roster of brands includes Atari, Bach, Bose, Buffet, Casio, Digitech, E-MZ, Fender, King, Gibson, Hohner, Ibanez, JBL, Korg, Leblanc, Ludwig, Marshall, Martin, Ovation, Pearl, Peavey, Roland, Shilke, Soundtech, Stewburger, Tascam, Washburn, and Yamaha. You'll find just about anything you need here, and if an item isn't stocked, Manny's can probably get it for you.

Special Factor: Price quote by phone, fax, or letter with SASE.

METROPOLITAN MUSIC CO.

**P.O. BOX 1415
STOWE, VT 05672
802/253-4814
FAX: 802/253-9834**

Catalog: free
Save: up to 50%
Pay: check or MO
Sells: stringed instruments and accessories
Store: mail order only

$$ 🍁 ▊▊▊

Metropolitan, in business since 1925, sells stringed instruments and accessories and maintains a workshop for repairs and adjustments. There are some "student" quality instruments here, but most of the models are chosen for professional musicians. Metropolitan carries

John Juzek violins, violas, cellos, and basses, and bows by F.N. Voirin, Glasser, and Emile Dupree. Bridges, Taperfit and other pegs, bow hair and parts, fingerboards, necks, chin rests, Resonans shoulder rests, Ibex tools, strings, cases, and bags are all stocked. This is an excellent source for the experienced musician who is familiar with the instruments and accessories. Books on instrument repair and construction are available, as well as a fine selection of wood, parts, and tools. The prices listed in the catalog are subject to discounts of 30% to 50%.

Special Factors: Price quote by phone or letter with SASE; minimum order is $15.

NATIONAL EDUCATIONAL MUSIC CO., LTD.

1181 RTE. 22
P.O. BOX 1130, DEPT. W-92
MOUNTAINSIDE, NJ 07092
800-526-4593
201/232-6700
FAX: 201/789-3025

Catalog: free
Save: up to 50%
Pay: check, MO, MC, V, AE
Sells: instruments and accessories
Store: mail order only

$$$

NEMC has been supplying school bands with instruments since 1959 and offers you the same equipment at savings of up to 50% on list prices. Brass, woodwind, and percussion instruments by Alpine, Amati, Bach, Blessing, Bundy, Decatur, DEG, Fox, Gemeinhardt, Getzen, Holton, John Juzek, Korg, Larilee, Leblanc, Ludwig, Meisel, Mirafone, Olds, Pearl, Schreiber, Selmer, Signet, Vito, and other firms are listed in the 32-page catalog. Imported master violins and violas are offered, as well as cases, stands, strings, bows, and other accessories. NEMC provides "the longest warranty in the industry" on woodwinds, drums, and brass and stringed (except fretted) instruments.

Special Factors: Price quote by phone or letter with SASE; returns (of instruments) are accepted within 7 days (a restocking fee may be charged); minimum order is $100 on accessories; orders are shipped worldwide.

PATTI MUSIC CORP.

414 STATE ST., DEPT. WC
MADISON, WI 53703
608/257-8829
FAX: 608/257-5847

Catalog: free
Save: 20% average
Pay: check, MO, MC, V, Discover
Sells: sheet music, music books, and
  metronomes
Store: same address; Monday to Saturday
  9:30–5:30

$$ ☎ ♦ ▅

One of the hardest items to find at a discount is sheet music, but that's the raison d'être of Patti Music Corp.'s mail-order department. The firm has been in business since 1936, and publishes a 64-page catalog of sheet music and books for piano and organ, and a selection of metronomes and tuners. Savings on the sheet music run around 15%, and the metronomes are discounted up to 33%.

Piano methods, ensembles, and solos are featured, from scores of music publishers. The catalog lists organ music for religious holidays, Christmas music and Broadway shoes, and flashcards, manuscript paper, theory books, and other teaching aids. The proficiency levels of the music and instructional material run from beginner to advanced. In addition to sheet music, there are key-wound, quartz, and electronic metronomes from Franz, Matrix, Seiko, and Wittner, and chromatic tuners by Seiko.

Special Factor: Discounts are available through the catalog only, not in the store.

RAINBOW MUSIC

RTE. 9, POUGHKEEPSIE
** PLAZA MALL**
POUGHKEEPSIE, NY
** 12601**
914/452-1900
FAX: 914/471-4085

Catalog: free
Save: up to 50%
Pay: check, MO, MC, V, AE, Discover
Sells: electronics and new and used vintage
  instruments
Store: same address; Monday to Saturday
  11–6

$$$ ☎ ♦ ▅

Rainbow's choice group of stringed instruments, electronics, MIDI, and percussion is featured in the catalog, which also shows a good selection of used and vintage equipment. Rainbow, which began business in 1976, invites inquiries about new equipment from Alembic, Crown, dbx, Fender, Fostex, Gibson, Guild, Ibanez, JBL, Kramer, Marshall, Martin, Ovation, Pearl, B.C. Rich, Rickenbacker, Roland, Steinberger, Subian, Tama, Tascam, Zildjian, and other manufacturers. Effects boxes, pickups, strings, keyboards, speakers, equipment cases, mixers, tape decks, and other goods are stocked, available at savings of up to 50%. Rainbow buys used guitars and amps, and accepts trade-ins.

Special Factors: Price quote by phone or letter with SASE; orders are shipped worldwide.

SHAR PRODUCTS COMPANY

P.O. BOX 1411
ANN ARBOR, MI 48106
313/665-7711
FAX: 313/665-0829

Catalog: free
Save: up to 50%
Pay: check, MO, MC, V, Discover
Sells: sheet music, stringed instruments, accessories
Store: 2465 S. Industrial Hwy., Ann Arbor, MI; Tuesday to Saturday 9–5

$$$ ☎ ❦(see text) ▆

"Shar is managed by knowledgeable string players and teachers, who are sympathetic to the needs of the string community." Shar has been in business since 1962, and prices its goods up to 50% below list or full retail prices.

The 64-page catalog gives equal time to stringed instruments and to the firm's extensive collection of classical music recordings and sheet music. If you play violin, viola, cello, or bass, see the catalog for the cases, bows, chin and shoulder rests, strings, bridges, tailpieces, pegs, music stands, humidifying tubes, endpipes, and other supplies and equipment. Student violins by Glaesel, Schroetter, and Suzuki are available, as well as fine violins by master violin makers.

The accessories catalog features hundreds of books of sheet music, manuals, videotapes, and audio cassettes. (The separate sheet music catalog, with thousands of titles, is available for $3.) Shar sells the Suzuki books and records line, videotapes of master artists (Casals, Segovia, Pavarotti, Heifetz, and others) in performance, classical recordings on cassette, and sheet music for a wide range of instruments. Not all goods are discounted, but savings overall average 30%, and selected lines are offered at further savings periodically.

Canadian readers, please note: Personal checks are not accepted.

Special Factors: Satisfaction is guaranteed; price quote by phone or letter with SASE; C.O.D. orders are accepted.

WEINKRANTZ MUSICAL SUPPLY CO., INC.

870 MARKET ST., SUITE 1265
SAN FRANCISCO, CA 94102-2907
415/399-1201
FAX: 415/399-1705

Catalog: free
Save: up to 50%
Pay: check, MO, MC, V
Sells: stringed instruments, parts, and supplies
Store: same address; Monday to Friday 9–5, PST

$$$ ☎ 🍁

Stringed instruments are the whole of Weinkrantz's business—violins, violas, cellos, and basses. Weinkrantz, founded in 1975, prices the instruments and parts 30% to 50% below suggested retail. The 40-page catalog lists the available instruments and outfits, cases, music stands, metronomes, bows, strings, and other supplies. There are several pages of strings alone, including Jargar, Kaplan, Pirastro, Prim, and Thomastik. Weinkrantz carries violins and violas by Helmut Mayer, T.G. Pfretzschner, Roth, Nagoya Suzuki, and Roman Teller. Cellos by these firms and Karl Hauser, Wenzel Kohler, and Anton Stohr are cataloged, as well as basses from Enesco, Roth, and Emanual Wilfer.

If you don't want to buy an outfit, you can order the bow, case or bag, rosin, string adjusters, and other equipment à la carte. Strings, bow hair, chin rests, bridges, metronomes, and tuners are all sold at a discount. Instrument cases by Gewa, Jaeger, and Winter are also available.

Canadian readers, please note: Orders must be paid in U.S. funds.

Special Factors: Satisfaction guaranteed (see the catalog for the policy on strings); price quote by phone or letter with SASE; minimum order is $10 with credit cards; orders are shipped worldwide.

WEST MANOR MUSIC

**831 EAST GUN HILL RD.
BRONX, NY 10467
212/655-5400**

Price List: free
Save: 40% average
Pay: check, MO, MC, V
Sells: musical instruments
Store: same address; Monday to Friday 9–4,
Saturday 10–3

$$$ ☎ ♦ ▆

West Manor Music has been supplying schools and institutions with musical instruments since 1956 and offers a wide range of instruments at an average discount of 40%. The 12-page catalog lists clarinets, flutes, piccolos, saxophones, oboes, trumpets, trombones, French horns, cornets, flugelhorns, euphoniums, Sousaphones, violas, violins, cellos, guitars, pianos, drums, cymbals, xylophones, glockenspiels, and other instruments. Drum stands and heads, strings, reeds, cases, music stands, metronomes, mouthpieces, and other accessories are sold. The brands represented include Alpine, Amati, Armstrong, Artley, Benge, Besson, Blessing, Buffet, Bundy, Conn, DEG, Fender, Fox, Gemeinhardt, Holton, King, Leblanc, Ludwig, Meisel, Noblet, Olds, Premier, Sabian, Selmer, Signet, Vito, and Zildjian, among others. All of the instruments sold are new, guaranteed for one year. West Manor also offers an "overhaul" service for popular woodwinds and brasses, and repairs can be performed.

Special Factors: Price quote by phone or letter with SASE; quantity discounts are available; minimum order is $50; orders are shipped worldwide.

SEE ALSO

Barnes & Noble Bookstores, Inc. • audio cassette cases and accessories • *BOOKS*
Bennett Brothers, Inc. • Casio musical keyboards, small selection of other instruments • *GENERAL MERCHANDISE*
Berkshire Record Outlet, Inc. • classical recordings on records, tapes, and CDs • *BOOKS*
Forty-Fives • original 45's from 1950 to the current year • *BOOKS*

Kicking Mule Records, Inc. • "Lark in the Morning" video music lessons
• *BOOKS*

Metacom, Inc. • audio cassettes • *BOOKS*

Wholesale Tape and Supply Company • tape duplicating machines and
equipment • *APPLIANCES*

OFFICE

Office machines, furniture, and supplies; printing and related services

If you're using a single source for your office supplies, chances are good you're not getting the best prices on supplies, printing, furnishings, and the countless items needed to keep the workplace running. You can begin a cost-control program by having the person you delegate as purchaser send for the catalogs listed here, so you can build a file of discount sources for all of your needs. And to avoid problems with questionable firms, consider making one simple rule: Don't buy from suppliers who solicit your firm by phone or fax.

If you're the head of a small business, you may find that your best buy on printed envelopes is the U.S. Postal Service. The USPS and the Stamped Envelope Agency, a private concern, offer envelopes with embossed stamps (postage) in windowed or plain styles, size 6¾ or 10, with up to seven lines of printing (maximum of 47 characters per line), at about the cost of the postage and a box of envelopes—which is like getting the printing free. Ask for PS Form 3203 from your local post office. You can also order stamps by mail or phone, from sheets of 25 to coils of 500. Ask for PS Form 3227 at your local post office, or call 800-STAMP-24 to order by phone (Discover, MasterCard, and VISA are accepted). There is a service fee of $3 at this writing, and the USPS promises delivery within five business days.

Several of the firms listed here sell computers and supplies, but hardware and software specialists are listed in the subsection of this chapter, "Computing." Look there for vendors of computers, peripherals, programs, furniture, paper goods, supplies, and services.

BUSINESS CARDS, STATIONERY, FORMS • **Brown Print, Business Envelope, Grayarc, L & D**
CASH REGISTERS • **Business Technologies, Quill**
GENERAL OFFICE SUPPLIES • **Franz Discount, Robert James, Mail Center USA, Quill, Reliable, Staples, Viking**
OFFICE FURNITURE • **Alfax, Business & Institutional Furniture, Factory Direct Furniture, Frank Eastern, National Business Furniture, Office Furniture Center, Quill, Viking**
OFFICE MACHINES • **Fax City, Lincoln, Quill, Staples, Typex**
POSTAL SCALES • **Triner Scale**
SAFES • **Safe Specialties, Value-tique**

ALFAX WHOLESALE FURNITURE

370 SEVENTH AVE., SUITE 1101
NEW YORK, NY 10001-3900
800-221-5710
212/947-9560

Catalog: free
Save: up to 50%
Pay: check, MO, MC, V
Sells: office and institutional furniture
Store: mail order only

$$ ☎

Alfax has been selling office furnishings since 1946 and does a brisk business with institutional and commercial buyers, especially schools and churches. The best discounts are given on quantity purchases, but even individual items are reasonably priced.

The 64-page color catalog shows furnishings for offices, nurseries (institutional), cafeterias, libraries, and conference rooms. Stackable chairs are offered in several styles, as well as a range of files and literature storage systems. P.A. systems, trophy cases, carpet mats, lockers, hat racks, park benches, heavy steel shelving, prefabricated office and computer stations and work stations are just a few of the institutional furnishings and fixtures available. Many products have home applications, and all of the equipment is designed for years of heavy use.

Special Factors: Satisfaction is guaranteed; institutional accounts are available.

BROWN PRINT & CO.

P.O. BOX 935
TEMPLE CITY, CA 91780
818/286-2106

Price List and Samples: $2
Save: up to 40%
Pay: check or MO
Sells: custom-designed business cards
Store: mail order only

$$ 🏳

Brown Print & Co. has been designing and printing business cards and stationery since 1966 and offers the person looking for something different just that. Mr. Brown, the proprietor, sent us a sample packet of dozens of cards, ranging from a photo backdrop of the Statue of Liberty at sunset to standard black and white cards with raised printing. Foils, embossed design, foldovers, and other options are available. Mr. Brown's talents would be wasted on someone who wanted a conventional card; his specialty is unusual design, and he enjoys working with his customers to create "the amusing, the novel, and other effective visual concepts."

Special Factors: Quantity discounts are available; minimum order is 500 cards.

BUSINESS ENVELOPE MANUFACTURERS, INC.

900 GRAND BLVD.
DEER PARK, NY 11729
516/667-8500
FAX: 516/586-5988

Catalog: free
Save: up to 75%
Pay: check, MO, MC, V
Sells: imprinted envelopes, stationery, forms, and office supplies
Store: mail order only

$$$ ☎

Business Envelope has been manufacturing envelopes and other office stationery for over 60 years, and can save you up to 75% on the usual prices on a wide range of supplies. The firm's 48-page catalog shows a full line of envelopes and letterhead, plain and imprinted, as well as commonly used business forms, copier paper, computer paper, labels, pens, pencils, literature organizers, bulletin boards, cash registers, mailing room supplies, rubber stamps, and much more. The prices on the printed stationery are about 50% below the going rate, and the choice of typefaces is better than what's usually offered by discounters.

Special Factors: Satisfaction is guaranteed; quantity discounts are available; minimum order is $20 with credit cards.

BUSINESS & INSTITUTIONAL FURNITURE COMPANY

611 N. BROADWAY
MILWAUKEE, WI 53202
800-558-8662
414/272-6080
FAX: 414/272-0248

Catalog: free
Save: up to 50%
Pay: check, MO, MC, V, Discover
Sells: office and institutional furnishings
Store: mail order only

$$$ ☎

Although the best prices at B & I are found on quantity purchases, even individual pieces are competitively priced. The catalog is geared for those who are furnishing offices, but many items are appropriate for home use as well. B & I has been in business since 1960, and offers a lowest-price guarantee (see the catalog for terms). Office furniture and machines are available, including desks, chairs, files, bookcases, credenzas, panels and panel systems (for office partitioning), and coin sorters. There are data and literature storage units, computer work stations, waste cans, mats, announcement boards, outdoor furniture, energy-saving devices, and much more. Over 250 brands are represented, and B & I can provide space planning and design services, free of charge.

Special Factors: "15-year, no-risk guarantee"; price quote by phone or letter; quantity discounts are available.

BUSINESS TECHNOLOGIES

**426 W. FIFTH ST.
DUBUQUE, IA 52001
800-397-5633
FAX: 319/557-1796**

Catalog: free
Save: 33% average
Pay: company check, MO, MC, V
Sells: cash registers and supplies
Store: same address

$$ ☎ 🍁 🇺🇸

Business Technologies makes ringing up sales its business, selling mainly Sanyo and Sharp cash registers, and supplies for these and virtually every other brand of cash register. The firm was established in 1985, and will send you manufacturers' brochures, a guide to selecting the right register for your needs, and a roster of optional accessories that will help you customize the register. Even the "simple" machines have programmable tax and percentage capabilities, and the top-of-the-line models are built-in bookkeepers and gofers: one system can enable a restaurant to keep track of employees' tips, track its guests' balances, and even transmit an order to the kitchen, where a small accessory printer unit types it out on a slip. Prices at Business Technologies are an average of 33% below list, and the firm can provide technical support, including free programming.

Special Factors: Price quote by phone, fax, or letter; minimum order is $10.

FACTORY DIRECT FURNITURE

**225 E. MICHIGAN ST.
MILWAUKEE, WI 53202-
　4900
414/289-9770**

Catalog: free
Save: up to 70%
Pay: check, MO, MC, V
Sells: office furniture and institutional
　equipment
Store: mail order only

$$$ ☎

Factory Direct Furniture sent us a 48-page catalog featuring some of the best buys around on office furniture, filing cabinets, bookcases, seating, work stations, storage units, office panel systems, and institutional furnishings. Savings of 40% are routine, and we found a number of items tagged 70% below manufacturers' list prices.

Factory Direct carries ergonomic seating for the executive as well as support staff, "barrister" bookcases, a full range of files, wood-veneer wall systems, computer work stations and work centers, bulletin and announcement boards, lockers, stacking chairs, folding and stacking conference tables, and a few office machines—time clocks and paper shredders. The manufacturers represented here include Accuride, Balt, Black, BPI (office panels), Buddy Products, Bush, Diversified, DMI, Durham, EckAdams, Edsal, Excel, FireKing, Foremost, Globe, Hale, Haskel, Hubbard, Inline Systems, Jefsteel, La-Z-Boy, Lee, MBF, Mill, MLP, National, O'Sullivan, Planto, SafCo, Samsonite, Sentry (safes), Signore, Stylex, and Thomasville Industries.

Please note: Factory Direct Furniture offers a five-year guarantee on everything it sells, normal wear and tear excepted. See the catalog for details on the warranty and the firm's "meet or beat" pricing policy.

Special Factors: Satisfaction is guaranteed; price quote by phone or letter; quantity discounts are available; institutional accounts are available.

FAX CITY, INC.

2711-B PINEDALE RD.
GREENSBORO, NC 27408
800-426-6499
919/288-2454
FAX: 919/288-1735

Brochure: free
Save: up to 50%
Pay: check, MO, MC, V, AE
Sells: fax machines and supplies
Store: same address; Monday to Friday
   8:30–5

Fax City, in business since 1986, sells facsimile machines, supplies, and related goods at savings of up to 50% on list or full retail prices. You can call or write for a quote, or see the price list for models by Avatek, Audiovox, Brother, Canon, Epson, Minolta, Murata, Nissei, Omnifax, Panafax, Panasonic, Ricoh, Samsung, Sanyo, Sharp, and Toshiba. Fax paper, line switches, surge suppressors, and laser printer peripheral interfaces are also available.

Fax City is offering readers of this book a discount of 20% on their first order of *fax paper only*. Identify yourself as a reader when you order. This WBMC reader discount expires February 1, 1993.

Special Factors: Price quote by phone or letter with SASE; orders are shipped worldwide.

FRANK EASTERN CO.

**599 BROADWAY
NEW YORK, NY 10012-
3258
212/219-0007**

Catalog: $1
Save: up to 50%
Pay: check, MO, MC, V
Sells: office, institutional, and computer furniture
Store: same address; Monday to Friday 9–5

$$$ ☎

Frank Eastern, in business since 1946, offers furnishings and equipment for business and home offices at discounts of up to 50% on list and comparable retail. Specials are run in every catalog.

The 72-page color catalog from Frank Eastern features desks, chairs, filing cabinets, bookcases, storage units, computer work stations, and wall systems and panels. Seating is especially well represented: ergonomic, executive, clerical, drafting, waiting room, conference, folding, and stacking models in wood, leather, chrome, and plastic, were all shown in the catalog we reviewed. Ergonomic seating is a Frank Eastern specialty, and the prices here are a good 25% less than those listed in two other office-supply catalogs we checked. Don't overlook good buys on solid oak bookcases, wall organizers, lateral filing cabinets, and mobile computer work stations.

Special Factors: Satisfaction is guaranteed; price quote by letter; quantity discounts are available; returns are accepted; minimum order is $75 with credit cards.

FRANZ DISCOUNT OFFICE PRODUCTS

1601 E. ALGONQUIN RD.
ARLINGTON HTS., IL
60005
800-323-8685
FAX: 800-242-0017

Catalog: free
Save: up to 85%
Pay: check, MO, MC, V, AE
Sells: office supplies, furniture, printing services, computer supplies, etc.
Store: same address; Monday to Friday 8–5

$$$ ☎ 🍁 🇺🇸

Franz has been in business since 1928 as a stationer to firms in the Chicago area, but a few years ago the management decided to venture into discount mail order. The company hit the ground running with a 48-page catalog that has rock-bottom prices on everyday office and computing supplies, as well as office furniture, files, and machines.

Some of the stock bears Franz's own label, but most is name brand—Avery, BASF, BIC, Canon, Curtis, Eldon, Globe, Hewlett-Packard, Hon, Meilink (safes), Murata, Pendaflex, Panasonic, Rolodex, Sentry (safes), Swingline, Texas Instruments, and Wilson Jones are all represented. The catalog is published eight times a year, and Franz will pay the shipping on orders over $25 that are delivered in the U.S.

Please note: Inquire for information on Franz's printing and rubber stamp services.

Special Factors: Satisfaction is guaranteed; price quote by phone or letter; shipping to U.S. addresses is included on orders over $25; quantity discounts are available; institutional accounts are available.

GRAYARC

GREENWOODS
INDUSTRIAL PARK
P.O. BOX 2944
HARTFORD, CT 06104
203/379-9941

Catalog: free (see text)
Save: up to 50%
Pay: check, MO, MC, V
Sells: business forms, office supplies, and equipment
Store: mail order only

$$$ ☎

Grayarc's business forms, machines, and office supplies are priced to save your company money and designed to expedite all kinds of business procedures. The 60-page catalog is packed with good values, and you can save up to 50% on some items.

Business forms are featured here: Reply messages, purchase orders, work proposals, invoices, statements, sales slips, insurance memos, bills of lading, receiving reports, and credit memos in carbon and carbonless sets are among the most popular types. Many are offered in designs and formats to suit different business situations. There are plain and windowed envelopes in several sizes and colors; inter-office envelopes; Tyvek, brown kraft, and white paper mailers; business letterhead, cards, and memos; and other necessities. Custom designs and printing services are available. Grayarc's equipment lines include printing calculators from Royal, Seiko, and Unitrex; Brother electronic typewriters; 3M compact copiers; cash registers, time clocks, literature racks, shelving, office chairs, and much more. The computer supplies are featured in a separate catalog, and include a wide range of forms and paper goods.

Special Factors: Satisfaction is guaranteed; specify "general supplies" or "computer forms" catalog (include make and model of your computer or word processor with the computer catalog request); returns are accepted within 30 days.

ROBERT JAMES CO., INC.

P.O. BOX 530, DEPT. FB91
MOODY, AL 35004
800-633-8296
205/640-7081
FAX: 205/640-7087

Catalog: free
Save: up to 60%
Pay: check, MO, MC, V, AE, Optima
Sells: office supplies
Store: 2201 Robert James Dr., Moody, AL

$$$ ☎ ▥

Robert James has been in business since 1939 and offers first-quality office supplies at job-lot prices through its 40-page Office Supply catalog. The firm also sells hotel goods through a 32-page Hospitality Supply catalog, making this an excellent source for office and institutional needs.

The Office Supply catalog offers printed and plain business envelopes, kraft envelopes, mailers, copier paper, labels, and forms. There are typing and word-processing ribbons, tapes, wheels, and elements, binders and binding machines, phones, answering machines, autodialers, desk organizers, literature racks, files and filing cabinets, shipping supplies, computer work stations, time clocks, paper shredders, chairs of all types, desks, and many other items. Savings are especially good on large quantities.

The Hospitality Supply catalog features hotel/motel supplies, including cotton towels, paper goods by the case, disposable razors, light bulbs, coat hangers, travel sizes of toothpaste, shampoo, and other toiletries. Stainless steel grab bars, rollaway beds, large-volume trash receptacles, park benches, vinyl-strap outdoor furniture, hand dryers, cribs, TV mounts, lamps, laundry and cleaning carts, and door viewers are among the other items available.

Robert James is offering readers a discount of 5% on their first order. Be sure to identify yourself as a WBMC reader when you order, and deduct the discount from the cost of the goods only. This WBMC reader discount expires February 1, 1993.

Special Factors: Satisfaction is guaranteed; specify catalog desired by name; price quote by phone or letter with SASE; quantity discounts are available; returns are accepted within 30 days.

L & D PRESS

**78 RANDALL ST., BOX 641
ROCKVILLE CENTRE, NY
11570
516/593-5058**

Price List: free
Save: up to 50%
Pay: check or MO
Sells: custom-printed stationery
Store: mail order only

L & D, founded in 1959, sells printed business cards, envelopes, and stationery. Prices on small orders of stationery are much better than those charged by similar firms. L & D has a good selection of business card styles in flat and raised thermographic print; colored stock and inks and 118 typefaces are available. Business letterhead, envelopes in a variety of styles and sizes, pressure-sensitive labels, and imprinted reply messages are offered at savings of up to 40%. Engraved business letterhead, envelopes, and cards can be provided, and dies may be made to order. Personal stationery is offered in Princess and Monarch sizes in ivory, white, and pale blue, and there are Embassy informals and notepads with self-sealing envelopes. L & D also sells the Boston personal paper shredder.

Special Factor: Inquire for information about custom services.

LINCOLN TYPEWRITERS AND MICRO MACHINES

111 W. 68TH ST.
NEW YORK, NY 10023
212/769-0606
FAX: 212/787-9397

Information: price quote
Save: up to 40%
Pay: check, MO, MC, V, AE, Optima
Sells: word processors, fax machines, calculators, etc.
Store: same address; Monday to Friday 9–6, Saturday 11–4

$$ ☎ 🍁 🇺🇸

Lincoln specializes in typewriters and calculators, runs a busy repair and service department, and accepts corporate accounts. Savings run up to 40% on many items; identify yourself as a reader of this book when requesting price quotes to get the best discounts. Lincoln stocks computer peripherals, typewriters, calculators, and other office machines by Brother, Hermès, IBM, Minolta, Olivetti, Olympia, Royal, SCM, Silver Reed, and other manufacturers. Ribbons, cartridges, cables, and other supplies are available in the store.

Special Factors: Price quote by phone or letter with SASE; manufacturers' warranties on some items will be extended by Lincoln; minimum order is $14.50.

MAIL CENTER USA

ONE DE ZAVALA CENTER
12734 CIMARRON PATH,
*   SUITE 104*
SAN ANTONIO, TX 78249
512/699-0311
FAX: 512/699-3419

Catalog: $5 (see text)
Save: up to 40% (see text)
Pay: check, MO, MC, V
Sells: office supplies and equipment
Store: mail order only

$$$ ☎

Mail Center USA runs a fleet of mailing centers in San Antonio and Austin, but is listed here for its mail-order office-supply business. You'll save 30% to 40% on *everything* in the big catalog ($5), and up to 70% on products featured in the quarterly sales catalogs, which are free.

The big catalog runs to 328 pages and offers everything in office needs, from accordion files to ZIP-code directories. The manufacturers represented include AccuFax, Bates, Canon, Curtis, Day Runner, Fellowes, G.E., Hewlett Packard, ITT, Ledu, Maxell, Mont Blanc, Panasonic, Pollenex, Qume, Rolodex, Stabilo, and Verbatim, among others. Mail Center USA offers great discounts: 30% on goods totals of $15 to $50, 35% on $50.01 to $100, and 40% on orders over $100. These discounts are computed on the catalog prices, which are not inflated, and cover printing services as well (greeting cards, order forms, checks, labels, business stationery, etc.).

Mail Center USA also publishes 78-page sale catalogs that feature closeouts of seasonal goods and office supplies at savings of up to 75%. You can request the current sale catalog, which is free; if you order from it, you'll receive the big catalog free.

Special Factors: Satisfaction is guaranteed; authorized returns are accepted for exchange, refund, or credit; institutional accounts are available; minimum order is $15.

NATIONAL BUSINESS FURNITURE, INC.

222 E. MICHIGAN ST.
MILWAUKEE, WI 53202
800-558-1010

Catalog: free
Save: up to 40%
Pay: check, MO, MC, V
Sells: office and computer furnishings
Store: mail order only

$$$ ☎

You can furnish your office for less through the 80-page NBF catalog, which offers everything from announcement boards to portable offices at savings of up to 40%. Whether you're shopping for a new chair or desk or planning a complete office installation, get the NBF catalog before you buy. The firm sells office systems, desks and tables for every purpose, credenzas, bookcases, shelving, computer work stations, desk organizers, literature racks, service carts, lockers, floor mats, reception furniture, and much more. The selection is super: There's a range of filing cabinets, and an extensive line of seating, including executive, clerical, luxury, ergonomic, conference, folding, stacking, and reception chairs. The manufacturers include Belcino, Chairworld, Fire King, Global, Globe, Haskell, High Point Furniture, Jansko, La-Z-Boy Chair, Meilink Safe, National Office Furniture,

O'Sullivan, Rubbermaid, Safco, Samsonite, Sauder, Signore, and Stylex, among others.

Special Factors: Price quote by phone or letter with SASE; quantity discounts are available.

OFFICE FURNITURE CENTER

**322 MOODY ST., DEPT. 6001
WALTHAM, MA 02154
800-343-4222
617/893-1505**

Catalog: free
Save: up to 50%
Pay: check, MO, MC, V
Sells: office furnishings and accessories
Store: same address; also 10 Spruce St., Nashua, NH; and 370 Seventh Ave., Suite 1101, New York, NY

$$$ ☎ ▀

The 32-page catalog from Office Furniture Center offers attractive chairs, desks, work stations, filing cabinets, bookcases, partition systems, and other business furniture and equipment. Office Furniture has been in business since 1985, and sells at discounts that averaged about 35% on the items we spot-checked, and reach 50% on some goods. The brands include Belcino, Bevis, Bush, DMI, Globe, Haskell, High Point, Independent Desk, Lee, Meilink, Signore, Stacor, and Stylex, among others. Office Furniture Center is distinguished among its competition by the fact that it maintains its own inventory of furniture and equipment, and should be able to get your goods to you much more quickly than companies that drop-ship from manufacturers. And if you're in the Boston metropolitan area, you might not even have to buy—you can lease furniture for terms of 24 to 60 months (the minimum lease order is $500).

Special Factor: Price quote by phone or letter.

QUILL CORPORATION

**100 SCHELTER RD.
LINCOLNSHIRE, IL 60197-
4700
708/634-4800
FAX: 708/634-5708**

Catalog: free (see text)
Save: up to 70%
Pay: check, MO, MC, V
Sells: office supplies and equipment
Store: mail order only

$$$ ☎ ♣

Quill, founded in 1956, offers businesses, institutions, and professionals savings of up to 70% on a wide range of office supplies and equipment. There are real buys on Quill's house brand of typing and computer supplies, which are comparable in performance and quality to name brands costing much more. The monthly 64-page catalogs feature general office supplies and equipment, including files, envelopes, mailers, and ribbons and elements for typewriters, word processors, and computer printers. There are labels, scissors, paper trimmers, pens and pencils, copiers and supplies, word processors, telephones, fax machines, binders and machines, dictating machines, accounting supplies, chairs, and much more. Quill also gives excellent discounts on custom-imprinted business stationery, labels, and forms. The computer lines include paper products and business programs, surge suppressors, disks, storage units, and related goods. The values are excellent, and delivery is prompt.

Please note: Quill does business with companies and professionals. In order to receive the catalog, *you must send your request on business letterhead*.

Special Factors: Satisfaction is guaranteed; request the catalog on business letterhead; institutional accounts are available; returns are accepted.

RAPIDFORMS, INC.

**301 GROVE RD.
THOROFARE, NJ 08086
800-257-8354
FAX: 800-422-8113**

Catalog: free (see text)
Save: up to 40%
Pay: check, MO, MC, V
Sells: business forms and products
Store: mail order only

$$

Rapidforms offers a range of over 3,500 business forms designed for every commercial purpose, which are formatted to expedite routine transactions. The firm has been doing business since 1939, and emphasizes prompt shipment as one of its strengths.

Six different catalogs are available here: The Manufacturing and Wholesale catalog features invoices, purchase orders, work orders, estimate and price quote forms, labels (in virtually every size, shape, design, and style), memos, stationery, personnel forms, "hazardous materials" products, and a large line of shipping products. The Retail catalog offers a complete line of sales slips, pricing guns and labels, gift certificates, and plastic designer shopping bags. The Repair Service catalog features service orders, job invoices, repair tags, and other service-related forms and goods. Auto service centers will find the Auto Repair Catalog handy for its complete line of automotive forms, including job work orders, estimate forms, repair orders, and other forms. The Contractors catalog offers a range of specialty forms for contractors, as well as a selection of standard forms. The Property Management catalog includes forms used in rental, real estate. Each catalog includes a line of continuous computer forms, with a compatibility index for numerous software packages.

Special Factors: Request the catalog desired *by title;* shipping is included on prepaid orders; quantity discounts are available; C.O.D. orders are accepted; orders are shipped worldwide.

THE RELIABLE CORPORATION

1001 W. VAN BUREN CHICAGO, IL 60607 800-869-6000 FAX: 800-326-3233

Catalog: free
Save: up to 50%
Pay: check, MO, MC, V, AE, Discover
Sells: home office equipment and supplies
Store: mail order only

$$$ ☎

We seldom see catalogs as glossy as Reliable's "Home Office" from discount suppliers, and rarely from a company that's been in business since 1917. Reliable has been recommended to us for its good prices, which are up to 50% below retail, and attention to service. The 52-page color catalog focuses on the home office, featuring products that have been chosen for their design quality as well as function and price: ergonomic chairs, compact file/desk units, halogen and fluorescent desk and floor lamps, oak computer carts, copiers, filing cabinets, "barrister" bookcases, drafting tables, wire grid organizers and wall units, phones, travel accessories, room intercoms, fax supplies, and even luggage and briefcases. There are usually some "fun" items—novelty phones, unusual desk organizers, keyless door locks, etc.—that help make this a great source for gifts and indulgences, at good prices.

Special Factors: Satisfaction is guaranteed; minimum order is $15 with credit cards.

SAFE SPECIALTIES, INC.

215 CENTER PARK DR., #650 KNOXVILLE, TN 37922 800-695-2815 IN TN 615/675-2815 FAX: 615/531-0101

Catalog: $1 with SASE
Save: 30% average
Pay: check, MO, MC, V, Discover
Sells: home and office safes
Store: mail order only

$$ ☎ 🍁

Safe Specialties, Inc. has been selling home and office safes since 1989, and offers popular home and office models at an average of

30% off list prices. SSI also manufactures the "Lockette Lockbox," a lockbox ideal for use in homes, office, hotel guest rooms, mobile homes, etc. (SSI can paint the box to blend with your existing decor, and produce custom sizes—call or write for information.)

If you're shopping for a safe made by any major manufacturer, give SSI a call; depository safes, pistol boxes, gun safes, secured boxes for RVs and trucks, data and diskette safes, in-wall and in-floor safes, fire-resistant file cabinets, and other models are available. If you live on the East Coast, SSI can have your safe installed for you, or provide directions on how to do it. Call of write if you're looking for a size or style not shown in the catalog.

Special Factors: Price quote by phone, fax, or letter; shipping is included on some models; orders are shipped worldwide.

STAPLES, INC.
■■■■■■■■■

150 CALIFORNIA ST.
P.O. BOX 160
NEWTON, MA 02195
617/965-7030

Catalog: free
Save: 50% average
Pay: check, MO, MC, V, Staples Charge
Sells: office supplies and furnishings, business machines
Store: 48 stores in CT, DC, MA, MD, NH, NJ, NY, OH, PA, RI, and VA (locations are listed in the catalog)

$$$ ☎

Staples brings us "The Price Revolution in Office Products" in the form of a superstore concept with deep discounts on every item. Staples has been in existence since 1986, and has earned a loyal following among buyers for small and home offices, as well as larger firms. Staples publishes a 112-page catalog of products with the "catalog list" prices and the Staples price. These are not closeouts, seconds, or unbranded goods, but first-quality products from Acco, Adams (forms), Alvin, AT&T, Bates, Brother, Canon, Casio, Cross, Curtis, Dennison Carter's, Eldon, Esselte, Faber Castell, GBC, Globe-Weis, Hammermill, Hewlett Packard, Maxell, Mont Blanc, Murata, Olympus (recorders), Panasonic, Parker, Pelikan (pens), Phone-Mate, Ricoh, Rolodex, Rubbermaid, SCM, Sentry (safes), Sharp, Sony, South-worth (paper), Texas Instruments, 3M, Vanguard, Velobind, Verbatim, Waterman (pens), and Wilson Jones, among others. You can order office furniture, computer supplies and programs, paper and forms, filing supplies, attaché cases, calendars, pens and pencils, adhesives, mailing room supplies, janitorial products, fax machines, copiers, phones and phone machines, and much more.

If there's a tradeoff for the savings and product choice, it's in *options,* like color or odd sizes. But we've been shopping at our local Staples for over years, and came away empty-handed only once, when we'd gone there to buy a Norton's "Utilities" program and learned that only those stores with Egghead Discount Software departments sell software (listed in the catalog).

Do sign up for the free, no-obligation membership card, since it entitles you to extra savings on selected items. A separate Staples charge card is also available. Please note that delivery charges are 5% of your order, with a minimum charge of $15.

Special Factors: Returns in original packaging are accepted within 30 days for exchange, refund, or credit; minimum order is $15 with credit cards.

TRINER SCALE

2842 SANDERWOOD
MEMPHIS, TN 38118
901/795-0746
FAX: 901/363-3114

Flyer: free
Save: 30% (see text)
Pay: check or MO
Sells: pocket scale
Store: same address; Monday to Friday 8–4:30

Triner Scale, which was founded in 1897, sells a pocket scale with all sorts of uses. It's a precision instrument that measures things that weight up to four ounces, and it comes packed in a pocket-sized case with a list of current postal rates tucked inside. A finger ring allows the scale to hang while measurements are taken; the thing to be weight is secured with an alligator clip. Suggested uses include postage determination, food measurement, lab use, craft and hobby use, and weighing herbs. It's a useful item to have on hand, and it can give you accurate readings of postage costs. Triner also sells a full line of mechanical and electronic postal scales that are competitively priced; inquire for information.

Special Factor: Shipping is included.

TURNBAUGH PRINTERS SUPPLY CO.

104 S. SPORTING HILL RD.
MECHANICSBURG, PA
17055-3057
717/737-5637

Catalog: $1
Save: see text
Pay: check or MO
Sells: printing supplies and new and used equipment
Store: same address; Monday to Friday 8–4

$$$ ☎ 🍁

Turnbaugh offers the printer working in the manner of Gutenberg new and used presses, type, and related equipment and supplies. Savings on used equipment are as much as 70% compared to the price of new goods. The stock is listed in *Printer's Bargain News,* a broadside that is published every two years.

Turnbaugh has been in business since 1931, and sells printing presses of every vintage, including hand, antique, treadle, and power (but not computerized) presses; offset machines, paper trimmers, stapling machines, folders, booklet stitchers, punching machines, numbering machines, and related equipment. Goods by Baltimore, Chandler & Price, Gordon, and Kelsey show up frequently. The catalog descriptions include the general condition and bed dimensions of the presses. Type, leads, rules, leaders, quoins, keys, spacers, gauge pins, printers' saws, composing sticks, cold padding cement, ink, type cleaner, rollers, type cabinets and cases, engraving tools, bone paper folders, embossing powder, paper stock, shipping tags, and other goods are offered as well.

Special Factors: Price quote by letter with SASE; *no printing services are available;* minimum order is $10; orders are shipped worldwide.

20TH CENTURY PLASTICS, INC.

3628 CRENSHAW BLVD.
LOS ANGELES, CA 90016
800-767-0777

Catalog: free
Save: up to 35%
Pay: check, MO, MC, V, AE
Sells: custom-imprinted binders and office products
Store: mail order only

$$ ☎

20th Century Plastics sells more than two dozen types of slide and transparency storage sheets, as well as video and audio cassette portfolios, magazine binders, static-proof computer disk storage, and portable key and business-card files. The firm carries a variety of binders that can be imprinted with your message or logo. Tab sets, file folders, report covers, presentation materials, time-management systems, records storage, and many other related products are shown in the catalog. Discounts are best on quantity purchases, but even individual items are competitively priced.

Special Factors: Satisfaction is guaranteed; returns are accepted within 30 days for exchange, refund, or credit.

TYPEX BUSINESS MACHINES, INC.

23 W. 23RD ST.
NEW YORK, NY 10010
800-221-9332
212/243-2500

Information: price quote with SASE
Save: up to 50%
Pay: check, MO, MC, V, Discover
Sells: typewriters, fax machines, copiers, etc.
Store: same address; Monday to Thursday 9:30–6, Friday 9:30–2

$$$ ☎ ▀▀

Typex, in business since 1979, offers the latest in office machines and supplies. Service and repairs are available in the store and to local customers. Specialty typewriters are featured, and savings average 30%. Call or write for prices on typewriters, word processors, calculators, answering machines, copiers, cash registers, fax machines, and supplies by and for Brother, Canon, IBM, Murata, Panasonic, Olympia,

Ricoh, Royal, Sharp, and Silver Reed. Brother and Smith Corona typewriters and word processors are a house specialty, with savings that average 35% to 50%. Foreign language typewriters are also available.

Special Factors: Price quote by phone or letter with SASE; SASE is required with all correspondence if a reply is desired; minimum order is $50 with credit cards.

VALUE-TIQUE, INC.

**P.O. BOX 67, DEPT. WBM
LEONIA, NJ 07605
201/461-6500**

Catalog: $1 (see text)
Save: 20% plus
Pay: check, MO, MC, V, AE, DC, Discover, Optima
Sells: Sentry safes
Store: 117 Grand Ave., Palisades Park, NJ; Monday to Friday 9–5, Saturday 9–1

$$

Value-tique has been selling home and office safes since 1968 and offers a range of well-known brands at discounts of 20% and more. Your savings are actually greater, because Value-tique also pays for shipping. And the $1 catalog fee buys a $5 credit certificate, good on any purchase. Value-tique sells Sentry Safes—a fireproof model camouflaged as a cabinet, the Media-Safe for computer disk storage, a standard office safe, and different wall safes. Centurion, Elsafe, Fichet-Bauche, Gardall, and Star safes are available, as well as Pro-Steel gun safes. Models include wall and in-floor safes, cash-drop safes, and many others for home and business use. If you're not sure of the best type for your security purposes, call Value-tique to discuss your needs. And before you order, *measure* to be sure the safe will fit into its intended location.

Special Factors: Price quote by phone or letter with SASE; shipping is included.

VIKING OFFICE PRODUCTS

**13809 SO. FIGUEROA ST.
LOS ANGELES, CA 90061
800-421-1222
FAX: 800-SNAPFAX**

Catalog: free (see text)
Save: up to 67%
Pay: check, MO, MC, V
Sells: office supplies, furniture, and
  computer supplies
Store: mail order only

$$ ☎

Viking Office Products began business in 1960, and sells office supplies, furnishings, and computer supplies at discounts of up to 67%. The company publishes a semi-annual, 240-page general catalog full of daily office needs, from pens and markers to ergonomic seating and filing cabinets, all of which are sold at a discount. Specials on selected goods are offered in the monthly sale catalogs. Both name brands and Viking's own label are represented, and shipping is free on orders of $25 or more (in the continental U.S. only).

Special Factors: Satisfaction is guaranteed; price quote by phone or letter with SASE; shipping is included on orders over $25 (to the continental U.S. only); returns are accepted.

VULCAN BINDER & COVER

**BOX 29
VINCENT, AL 35178
800-633-4526
205/672-2241
FAX: 205/672-7159**

Catalog: free
Save: up to 40%
Pay: check, MO, MC, V, AE
Sells: binders and supplies
Store: mail order only

 $$$ ☎ ❦

Three-ring binders can be quite pricey at stationery stores, which is why you should buy from the manufacturer. Vulcan can save you up to 40% on all of your binder needs, from light-duty binders with flexible covers to heavy-duty binders with 3″ D-rings. Vulcan's 48-page catalog also shows magazine files and binders, zippered binders, catalog binders, 19-ring binders, pocket sizes, tabbed inserts, notepad holders, report covers, page protectors, cassette cases, and even attaché cases and leather luggage. Custom imprinting is available on the binders and tabbed dividers.

Special Factors: Satisfaction is guaranteed; price quote by phone or letter with SASE; quantity discounts are available; returns are accepted within 15 days for exchange, refund, or credit; minimum order is $25.

SEE ALSO

Ace Leather Products, Inc. • attaché cases and briefcases • *LEATHER*

The American Stationery Co., Inc. • custom-printed stationery, notepads, and envelopes • *BOOKS*

A to Z Luggage Co., Inc. • attaché cases and briefcases • *LEATHER*

Barnes & Barnes • office furnishings • *HOME: FURNISHINGS*

Bennett Brothers, Inc. • corporate gift program • *GENERAL MERCHANDISE*

Bernie's Discount Center, Inc. • phones, phone machines, fax machines, copiers, calculators, etc. • *APPLIANCES*

Dick Blick Co. • flat files and display equipment • *ART MATERIALS*

Caviarteria Inc. • corporate gift program • *FOOD*

Cherry Hill Furniture, Carpet & Interiors • office furnishings • *HOME: FURNISHINGS*

Crutchfield Corporation • copiers, phone machines, fax machines, etc. • *APPLIANCES*

Famous Smoke Shop, Inc. • Mont Blanc and Waterford pens • *CIGARS*

Flax Artist's Materials • drafting furniture, supplies, and equipment • *ART MATERIALS*

Innovation Luggage • attaché cases and briefcases • *LEATHER*

Jerry's Artarama, Inc. • ergonomic chairs and flat files • *ART MATERIALS*

The Jompole Company, Inc. • pen and pencil sets, premiums, etc. • *HOME: TABLE SETTINGS*

Leather Unlimited Corp. • leather attaché cases, card cases, portfolios, etc. • *LEATHER*

Loftin-Black Furniture Company • office furnishings • *HOME: FURNISHINGS*

The Luggage Center • attaché cases • *LEATHER*

LVT Price Quote Hotline, Inc. • calculators, typewriters, phones, fax machines, pens, etc. • *APPLIANCES*

New York Central Art Supply Co. • Alvin drafting furniture, taborets, stools and chairs, lighting, etc. • *ART MATERIALS*

Plastic BagMart • trash can liners • *GENERAL: PACKAGING*

Plexi-Craft Quality Products Corp. • acrylic racks, desk accessories, etc.
• *HOME: FURNISHINGS*

Protecto-Pak • zip-top plastic bags • *GENERAL: PACKAGING*

S & S Sound City • phones and phone machines • *APPLIANCES*

Turner Tolson, Inc. • office furnishings • *HOME: FURNISHINGS*

Turnkey Material Handling, Inc. • parts bins, office and institutional
furnishings, and fixtures • *TOOLS*

University Products, Inc. • archival-quality storage supplies for microfiche
and microfilm; library supplies and equipment • *GENERAL: PACKAGING*

U.S. Box Corp. • product packaging for resale • *GENERAL: PACKAGING*

Wholesale Tape and Supply Company • labels, shipping envelopes •
APPLIANCES

Computing

Computers, peripherals, software, supplies, furniture, and accessories

If you're a first-time computer buyer or want to upgrade your current system, learn as much as you can from as many sources as possible. Attend demonstrations of new products, watch colleagues at work with different systems and programs, and ask questions. Don't assume that any software will perform as promised, no matter who's vouching for it. Evaluate your current and anticipated requirements as carefully as possible, since buying the right equipment the first time is the best money spent. Do you *need* 100 megabytes, a laser printer, or EGA monitor? What will you do with the computer? How much RAM will your software require? Is portability sufficiently important to make a laptop a good buy? Consult the repair shop of a large computer outlet to get an idea of how much repairs run on different types of equipment. Can you get by with a good 9-pin NLQ printer, and buy an ink-jet or 24-pin when the prices come down?

There are hundreds of publications on the market to guide you through the purchase of hardware and software and the use of specific systems, and many of them merit your attention. And there are tens of thousands of programs now in the public domain, which means they can be copied without infringement of copyright (hence the term "free programs"). They're sold at very low prices—often under $10—and can be as valuable as protected programs that cost $300 to $900 each. One word of caution, however: Viruses, which can damage your data, do crop up in the world of "shareware." If you want to protect yourself completely, don't use shareware or download programs from bulletin boards. And do remember to use a surge suppressor, and back up your disks!

CMO

101 REIGHARD AVE.
WILLIAMSPORT, PA 17701
800-233-8950
FAX: 717/327-1217

Information: price quote
Save: up to 40%
Pay: check, MO, MC, V, AE, Discover
Sells: computers, peripherals, and accessories
Store: same address

$ ☎ 🍁

CMO, formerly listed here as Computer Mail Order, sells computer systems, disk drives, boards, monitors, printers, modems, software, and accessories by a number of manufacturers, at savings of up to 40%. CMO also sells its own computers (XT, 286, and 386 models) under the "CMO Microsystems" label. You can save on goods by Amdek, AST, Bernoulli, C. Itoh, CMS, Curtis, Epson, Hewlett Packard, Juki, Kensington, Lotus, Magnavox, NEC, Okidata, Panasonic, Seagate, and Star Micronics at this firm—call or fax for a price quote on specific models.

Special Factors: Price quote by phone or letter with SASE; authorized returns are accepted (a restocking fee may be charged).

DAYTON COMPUTER SUPPLY

1220 WAYNE AVE.
DAYTON, OH 45410
800-331-6841
513/252-1247

Information: see text
Save: up to 60%
Pay: check, MO, MC, V, Discover
Sells: printer ribbons, fax paper, disks, etc.
Store: mail order only

$$ ☎ 🍁

Dayton Computer doesn't publish a catalog or brochure, but sells hundreds of types of printer ribbons, diskettes, tape, and paper for fax machines and printers. Dayton's prices on diskettes and tapes by 3M and Verbatim are competitive, and if you're buying your ribbons from your local stationer, or even a discounter, you're in for a shock when you check Dayton's prices—they're up to 60% below the going rate. Dayton sells unbranded ribbons for printers by Apple, Brother,

Commodore, Diablo, Epson, Hewlett Packard, IBM, Mannesman Tally, NEC, Okidata, Panasonic, Qume, Star Micronics, and other major manufacturers. Dayton also offers a good selection of continuous paper and labels. Call with the model number of your machine for current prices of ribbons, fax paper, disks, and other computer/fax supplies.

Special Factors: Satisfaction is guaranteed; price quote by phone; quantity discounts are available; C.O.D. orders are accepted.

DISK WORLD, INC.

DEPT. WBMC2
4215 MAIN ST.
SKOKIE, IL 60076-2046
800-255-5874
FAX: 708/673-6038

Catalog: free
Save: up to 50%
Pay: check, MO, MC, V, Discover
Sells: disks, printer ribbons, data cartridges, fax and computer paper, etc.
Store: mail order only

$$$ ☎ 🍁 ▆

Running out of disks and having to buy from a computer boutique at near-list price is entirely preventable, if you buy in bulk from Disk World. This firm has been in business since 1983, and sells disks, data cartridges (tape), storage units, printer ribbon, fax paper, and computer paper.

Disk World stocks 3½", 5¼", and 8" disks (as available) from Athana, BASF, Dysan, Fuji, Maxell, Nashua, and Verbatim, data cartridges from BASF and Nashua, and 5¼" and 8" Iomega Bernoulli cartridges (at savings of up to 38% off list). Prices average 45% to 55% off list, and Disk World's selection is excellent. In addition to name brands, the firm offers Super Star disks, which are made to its specifications and sold in standard tens, and at a lower price in bulk. Scores of unbranded printer ribbons are available, at prices among the lowest we could find *anywhere*. Disk sleeves, labels, and mailers are also available, as well as cleaning kits for laser printers, fax machines, dot-matrix printers, disk drives, surge suppressors, an inexpensive monitor stand, keyboard templates, a mini-vacuum cleaner, and a good selection of disk storage units. There are great buys on fax paper, green bar, plain white computer paper, laser printer supplies, and standard-grade VHS tapes for as little as $2.29 each. Warranty terms and return policies are stated clearly in the catalog.

Disk World is offering readers of WBMC a 4% discount on *first orders only,* so remember to mention this book when you place your first order. This WBMC reader discount expires February 1, 1993.

Special Factors: Satisfaction is guaranteed; price quote by phone or letter; returns are accepted within 30 days for exchange, refund, or credit; C.O.D. orders are accepted; orders are shipped worldwide.

EASTCOAST SOFTWARE

48 DERRYTOWN MALL
HERSHEY, PA 17033
800-877-1327

Catalog: free
Save: up to 35%
Pay: check, MO, MC, V
Sells: computer systems, software, disks, and peripherals
Store: same address; Monday to Friday 10–8, Saturday 10–4

Eastcoast's 24-page tabloid catalog lists thousands of educational, business, and recreational programs for Apple, Macintosh, Commodore 64, Amiga, and IBM-compatible computers. Blank disks, paper, peripheral covers, cables, printer stands, and some peripherals are also available, at savings of up to 35%. Both list and discount prices are given, and the terms of Eastcoast's "30-day replacement policy" are stated in the catalog.

Special Factors: Institutional accounts are available; returns are accepted within 30 days for exchange, refund, or credit.

EDUCALC CORPORATION

27953 CABOT RD.
LAGUNA NIGUEL, CA
92677
800/677-7001
FAX: 714/582-1445

Catalog: free
Save: up to 40%
Pay: check, MO, MC, V, AE, Discover, Optima
Sells: calculators, computer peripherals, books, and software
Store: same address; Monday to Friday 8–5

$$$

EduCALC specializes in portable computation, specifically calculators and peripherals that maximize the functions of the Hewlett Packard IL, 28S, 41, and 48SX series of hand-held computer/calculators. Canon, Casio, Franklin, Sharp, and Texas Instruments calculators are also carried, and used calculators are available. The savings average 25%, but some items are discounted up to 40%.

The HP calculators, when hooked up to the appropriate peripherals, can be linked to PCs, edit programs, save data on ram cards, develop programs, and analyze mathematical, scientific, engineering, and business data with the aid of software cards. The equipment currently available includes printer/plotters, optical wands, modules, interface units, cassette drives, couplers, disk drives, and adapters. EduCALC also sells personal (portable) dialers and diaries. Stands, covers, keyboard overlay systems, ribbons, printing paper, disks, plotter pens, and other supplies are offered as well. The 68-page catalog should be noted for its comprehensive bookshelf—both general and calculator-related reference texts on astronomy, navigation, engineering, higher mathematics and statistics, programming, and computer systems and languages are listed. The catalog descriptions are comprehensive, easy to understand, and include product specifications.

Canadian readers, please note: A $10 *per-item surcharge* is levied on orders shipped to Canada.

Special Factors: Satisfaction is guaranteed; price quote by phone or letter with SASE; returns are accepted within 15 days; orders are shipped worldwide.

800-SOFTWARE, INC.

**918 PARKER ST.
BERKELEY, CA 94710
800-888-4880
FAX: 415/644-8226**

Catalog: free
Save: up to 50%
Pay: check, MO, MC, V, AE
Sells: micro computers, software,
hardware, and network products
Store: same address; Monday to Friday 9–5,
Saturday 10–2

$$$$ ☎ ♦ ▀▀▀

800-Software has won recommendations from computer users who appreciate 800's prices, selection, and technical support. The company's well-designed, 72-page catalog lists programs for PCs, Macintosh computers, and some UNIX products, including databases, graphics, utilities, operating systems, personal finance programs, spreadsheets, desktop publishing programs, and word processing software. There are lines and products by Alpha, Amdek, Apple, Ashton-Tate, AST Research, Borland, Central Point Software, Computer Associates, Digital Research, Fox & Geller, Funk Software, Hayes, IMSI, Intel, Lotus, Micropro, Microsoft, Novell, Oasis Systems, Paperback Software, Quadram, Revelation Technology, Software Solutions, Toshiba, Word Perfect, XyQuest, and many others. You'll also find boards, buffers, graphics cards, keyboards, mice, monitors, printers, surge suppressors, modems, and other peripherals and accessories for PCs. Specials are run on a frequent basis, and the catalog is a great source for information on what's new in word processing, spreadsheet, data management, educational, and other types of programs.

Corporate and government buyers, please note: Free post-sale technical support is provided.

Special Factors: Products are guaranteed against manufacturing defects; price quote by phone or letter with SASE on items not listed in the catalog; institutional accounts are available; quantity discounts are available.

LYBEN COMPUTER SYSTEMS, INC.

P.O. BOX 1237
TROY, MI 48099-1237
313/649-4500
FAX: 313/649-2500

Catalog: free
Save: up to 70%
Pay: check, MO, MC, V
Sells: computer supplies
Store: 1150 Maplelawn, Troy, MI; Monday to Thursday 8:30–6, Friday 8:30–5, Saturday 9:30–2:30

Lyben offers a full range of computer supplies, and has especially good prices on software and diskettes—up to 70% off suggested list. The best prices here are on software, disks, ribbons, printer paper, and other computer supplies by BASF, Dysan, Maxell, Memorex, Sony, 3M, Verbatim, and other top manufacturers. All of the goods are sold by the box or carton. The 148-page catalog also shows daisy wheels, dust covers for peripherals, data storage units, maintenance products, strip outlets, surge suppressors, cables, data switches, buffers, modems, joysticks, ergonomic seating, power backup units, mice, forms feeders, fax paper, copier cartridges, mini-vacuum cleaners, and hundreds of other items.

Special Factors: Price quote by phone or letter with SASE; minimum order is $15; C.O.D. orders are accepted.

MACCONNECTION

14 MILL ST.
MARLOW, NH 03456
800-622-5472
FAX: 603/446-7791

Price List: free
Save: 25% to 40% average
Pay: check, MO, MC, V
Sells: Macintosh computer hardware, software, and accessories
Store: same address (pickup center for orders)

$$$$ ☎ 🍁 ▀

MacConnection, which has received resounding praise from readers and friends, was founded in 1984 by the same people who established PC Connection two years earlier. (See that firm's listing in this section for IBM-compatible products.) The firm stocks the latest versions of business and entertainment programs by scores of publishers, from Aatrix Software to Zedcor. Most of the listings indicate whether the software is copy-protected. MacConnection also sells modems, mice, keyboards, work stations, printers, monitors, maintenance and cleaning products, and disks by Fuji, Maxell, Sony, and Verbatim. You can subscribe to on-line services from CompuServe and Dow Jones through MacConnection as well. Savings here average 25% to 40%, and MacConnection is praised for its commitment to service—it provides warranty backup and support for everything it sells.

Special Factors: Price quote by letter; minimum order is $250 on "international" orders; orders are shipped worldwide.

MARYMAC INDUSTRIES, INC.

22511 KATY FRWY.
KATY, TX 77450-1598
713/392-0747
FAX: 713/574-4567

Brochure: free
Save: 15% plus
Pay: check, MO, MC, V, AE, DC, Discover, Optima
Sells: Radio Shack and Tandy products
Store: same address; Monday to Friday 8–6

Marymac lays claim to title of "world's largest independent authorized computer dealer," and is able to offer discounts of 15% and more on *anything* in the Radio Shack/Tandy catalog. (Get a copy from your local dealer, or request one from Tandy Catalog, 300 One Tandy Center, Fort Worth, TX 76102—Marymac doesn't have the catalog.)

Price quotes are given on computers, peripherals, fax machines, cellular phones, phone machines, TVs, audio components, and other goods under the Radio Shack and Tandy labels. Marymac has a "meet or beat" pricing policy, and will pay shipping and insurance on orders delivered within the continental U.S.

Special Factors: Price quote by phone or letter; shipping and insurance are included on orders sent within the continental U.S.; C.O.D. orders are accepted.

MEI/MICRO CENTER

**1100 STEELWOOD RD.
COLUMBUS, OH 43212
800-634-3478
FAX: 614/486-6417**

Catalog: free
Save: up to 75%
Pay: check, MO, MC, V
Sells: computer disks, ribbons, paper, etc.
Store: mail order only

$$$ ☎ ♦ ▬

MEI/Micro's 24-page catalog brings the prices of computer disks into the realm of reason, even on small orders—and if you buy in bulk, the prices of even double-density disks can drop to under 25¢ each. MEI/Micro has been in business since 1986, and backs everything it sells with an unconditional guarantee of satisfaction.

MEI/Micro's own disks, which are certified to meet or exceed ANSI standards, include both 3.5″ and 5.25″ disks in all formats, and in colors. Disks by Dysan, Precision, Sony, and 3M are also available at a discount, as well as labels, sleeves, and mailers. You'll find well-priced disk cases and bulk storage units, head-cleaning kits, surge suppressors, and stands for keyboard, monitor, and printer. Ribbons are sold at rock-bottom prices in packs of six, and paper and labels are also available in bulk.

Please note: MEI/Micro doesn't ship goods outside the U.S. and Canada, and does not ship boxes of paper by the U.S. Postal Service.

Special Factors: Satisfaction is guaranteed; price quote by phone or letter; returns are accepted for exchange, refund, or credit.

NEBS, INC.

**500 MAIN ST.
GROTON, MA 01470
508/448-6111**

Catalog: free (see text)
Save: up to 35%
Pay: check or MO
Sells: forms and supplies
Store: mail order only

$$ ☎

NEBS publishes two catalogs, "Business Forms and Supplies" and "Computer Forms," which offer those goods at prices up to 35%

below those charged by other office supply firms for the same or comparable items.

The general Business Forms catalog offers invoices, receipts, purchase orders, bookkeeping forms, and scores of other forms for small businesses. Labels, rubber stamps, shipping supplies, shopping bags, memos, business cards, stationery, and other office and business necessities are available.

The 54-page Computer Forms catalog features continuous-form stationery in several paper types, with raised or flat printing, and coordinating envelopes. Postcards, dozens of types of mailing labels, and all kinds of printout paper are stocked. NEBS has designed a number of forms to work with business software from Radio Shack, CYMA, Great Plains, BPI Systems, DAC Software, Star Software, and many other publishers. These forms (invoices, statements, payroll checks, job proposals, etc.) are offered in multipart designs, some with coordinating envelopes. NEBS also has good prices on ribbons and disks (in proprietary and name brands), disk storage units, and computer maintenance tools and dust covers. Prices are competitive, and most of the stock is available in small lots, as well as larger amounts at quantity discounts.

Special Factors: Satisfaction is guaranteed; specify "Business Forms" or "Computer Forms" catalog.

PC CONNECTION

6 MILL ST.
MARLOW, NH 03456
800-243-8088
FAX: 603/446-7791

Price List: free
Save: 25% to 40% average
Pay: check, MO, MC, V
Sells: IBM-compatible hardware, software, and supplies
Store: same address (pickup center for orders)

$$$$ ☎ ✦ ▀

Several of our friends who use Macintosh computers, as well as readers of this book, have commended MacConnection (listed earlier in this section) for superior pricing, stock, and service. The same people who operate MacConnection actually began with IBM-compatible systems in 1982 when they founded PC Connection— which they run with the same commitment to selection and service.

You can write to the firm for its current price list, see the ad in the current issue of *PC World,* or send for a price quote. The latest versions of software are carried by publishers that include Aldus, Ashton-Tate, Borland International, Broderbund, Electronic Arts, 5th Generation, Fox Software, Funk Software, Lotus, Microlytics, MicroPro, Microrim, Microsoft, Peter Norton, Sierra On-Line, Softlogic Solutions, Spinnaker, Springboard, Sublogic, Symantec, Word Perfect, Xerox, and XyQuest, among others. Most of the listings indicate whether the software is copy-protected. Hardware and accessories—computers, disk drives, emulation boards, printers, modems, monitors, joysticks, etc.—are also available; the brands represented at this writing include AST Research, Amdek, Curtis, DCA, Epson, Everex, Hayes, Intel, IOMEGA, Logitech, Magnavox, Mountain Computer, Practical Peripherals, Princeton Graphics, Seagate, Teac, Toshiba, and others. Disks by Fuji, Maxell, Sony, and Verbatim are offered, and you can also save on the CompuServe Subscription Kit and Grollier's OnLine Encyclopedia.

PC Connection provides warranty backup and support for everything it sells, and is a factory-authorized repair center for Epson and Iomega products.

Special Factors: Price quote by letter with SASE; minimum order is $250 on "international" orders; orders are shipped worldwide.

TELEMART

8804 N. 23RD AVE.
PHOENIX, AZ 85021
800-634-0402
FAX: 602/997-8737

Catalog: free
Save: up to 55%
Pay: check, MO, MC, V, AE, Discover
Sells: computer hardware and software
Store: 535 S. Dobson, Mesa; 2222 E. Indian
   School Rd., Phoenix; 13615 N. 35th Ave.,
   Glendale; and 1801 S. Alvernon, Tucson,
   AZ

Telemart has been selling computer hardware and programs since 1980, and features popular equipment and software at savings we found to be up to 56% below list. Telemart currently publishes a 16-page color catalog of software programs and a flyer featuring add-ons and other software, but you can also call for a price quote.

The equipment available at this writing includes boards, co-processors, monitors, keyboards, printers, scanners, mice, and other system components. Among the brands represented are ALPS, ALR, Amdek, AST, ATI, Bernoulli, Canon, Colorado Memory System, Epson, Everex, Hayes, Hercules, IBM, Intel, Logitech, NEC, Okidata, Panasonic, Seagate, Star Micronics, Teac, and Toshiba. The software catalog we saw ran from ATI's "Teach Me" series of system tutorials, to XTree's "ProGold" disk management program, and included business and database systems, windows, utilities, educational and reference tools (such as the electronic Random House encyclopedia), desktop publishing programs, CompuServe's membership kits (standard and DOS), and word processing programs, among others. The discounts on list price average 40%-plus, and you can send for the catalog or call for price quotes.

Special Factors: Satisfaction is guaranteed on software; price quote by phone or letter with SASE; authorized returns of software (in original packaging) are accepted within 30 days for exchange, refund, or credit; orders are shipped worldwide.

BEN TORRES RIBBON COMPANY

590 E. INDUSTRIAL RD., UNIT 15
SAN BERNARDINO, CA 92408
714/796-5559

Price List: free
Save: up to 40%
Pay: check or MO
Sells: refilled and new printer ribbons
Store: same address

$$

Ben Torres can sell you its own printer ribbons at prices about 40% below the going rate, or refill your used ribbon cartridges at savings of over 50%. Torres has been in business since 1979, and guarantees your "satisfaction with impressions" of the ribbons—whether new or refilled. Laser cartridges can be refilled as well, although you should check your printer's warranty or service contract before sending in your empties, to make sure using reconditioned cartridges doesn't violate its terms.

Torres' price list runs from Anadex to Xerox, and includes scores of printer models. New ribbons are available for most models, and all of the Torres ribbon cases are refillable (please note that some cartridges can't be opened without breaking them). Refilling, instead of throwing away the plastic cartridge and buying a whole new outfit, is a great way to save extra money—and it's environmentally smart, too!

Canadian readers, please note: Only U.S. funds are accepted.

Special Factors: Satisfaction is guaranteed; returns are accepted within 30 days for exchange, refund, or credit.

VISIBLE COMPUTER SUPPLY CORP.

**1750 WALLACE AVE.
ST. CHARLES, IL 60174
800-323-0628
FAX: 800-233-2016**

Catalog: free
Save: up to 60%
Pay: check, MO, MC, V, AE, CB, DC
Sells: office and computer supplies
Store: mail order only

$$$ ☎ 🇺🇸

Visible Computer's 270-page color catalog is packed with great buys on office essentials, and it's updated with a monthly catalog that features special promotions. This firm is a subsidiary of Wallace Computer Services, which has been in business since 1942.

The focus here is on computer support products, but there are scores of general office items shown in the catalog. You'll want to see the latest issue if you're shopping for phone message books, binding supplies, loose-leaf notebooks, pens and highlighters, labels, tape, Post-It notes, wastebaskets, files, records storage, telephones, phone machines, and shredders. The computer department stocks forms bursters, computer work stations, printer stands, continuous form paper, disks and disk storage, monitor screen filters, cables, outlet strips, and maintenance supplies and equipment. There are bonuses with minimum orders, and quantity discounts are available as well.

Special Factors: Satisfaction is guaranteed; price quote by phone or letter; returns are accepted within 30 days for exchange, refund, or credit; quantity discounts are available.

WESTERN S & G

P.O. BOX 12345
SAN LUIS OBISPO, CA
    93406-2345
800-233-9750
IN CA 800-843-8181

Price List: free
Save: up to 45%
Pay: check, MO, MC, V
Sells: computer software and disks
Store: mail order only

 $$ ☎ 🍁 🇺🇸

Western S & G offers great buys on IBM computer software, disks, and storage units. See the price list or call for the latest rates on disks and diskettes by Dysan, Fuji, Maxell, Memorex, and 3M. Western S & G also carries floppy-disk storage units, disk-saver kits, and head-cleaning diskette kits. The programs—business, entertainment, and word-processing—are listed in the catalog.

Special Factors: Price quote by phone; shipping is included; minimum order is 10 disks.

SEE ALSO

Astronomical Society of the Pacific • astronomy-related computer programs • BOOKS
Dick Blick Co. • computer work stations • ART MATERIALS
Business & Institutional Furniture Company • computer work stations • OFFICE
Crutchfield Corporation • PCs, word processors, software, and supplies • APPLIANCES
Frank Eastern Co. • computer work stations • OFFICE
Franz Discount Office Supplies • computer supplies, printers, etc. • OFFICE
Genada Imports • computer work stations • HOME: FURNISHINGS
Marv Golden Discount Sales, Inc. • aviation computers • AUTO
Grayarc • computer forms and paper goods • OFFICE
Robert James Co., Inc. • computer work stations • OFFICE
Jerry's Artarama, Inc. • computer work stations • ART MATERIALS
Lincoln Typewriters and Micro Machines • computer peripherals • OFFICE

Mail Center USA • computer peripherals, disks, and accessories • OFFICE

National Business Furniture, Inc. • computer work stations • OFFICE

Plexi-Craft Quality Products Corp. • acrylic computer stands • HOME: FURNISHINGS

Quill Corporation • computers, word processors, programs, work stations, paper products, disks, etc • OFFICE

Rapidforms, Inc. • continuous forms • OFFICE

The Reliable Corporation • computer accessories, work stations, etc. • OFFICE

Safe Sepcialties, Inc. • data and diskette safes, lockboxes, etc. • OFFICE

Staples, Inc. • computer disks, data binders, work stations, programs, etc. • OFFICE

20th Century Plastics, Inc. • static-proof disk storage • OFFICE

Viking Office Products • computer supplies, peripherals, and furniture • OFFICE

SPORTS AND RECREATION

Equipment, clothing, supplies, and services for all

kinds of sports and recreational activities

If the high price of recreation equipment seems unsporting to you, you've turned to the right place. Discounts of 30% are standard among many of the suppliers listed here, who sell clothing and equipment for cycling, running, golfing, skiing, aerobics, tennis and other racquet sports, skin and scuba diving, camping, hunting, hiking, basketball, triathloning, soccer, and other pleasures. Racquet stringing, club repairs, and other services are usually priced competitively as well. Buying your gear by mail may be the only sport that repays a nominal expenditure of energy with such an enhanced sense of well-being.

Before investing in a new athletic pursuit, find out if it's right for you. Joining a local team or group gives you a taste of the sport at minimal expense. If you've been sedentary for some time, you should have a complete physical before beginning any workout program or sport. Stop and cool down if you're in pain, but don't give up. You can make running, aerobics, and racquet sports easier on your joints by wearing properly fitted shoes, learning correct foot placement, and working out on a resilient surface. Low-impact aerobics, fast-paced walking, and swimming should be less stressful than running, calisthenics, and traditional sports. Getting fit should be a pleasure, and if you take the time to find an enjoyable, challenging sport or workout routine, cardiovascular health and vigor will be more easily won.

FIND IT FAST

CAMPING • Campmor, Gander Mountain, Survival Supply
CYCLING • Bike Nashbar, Cycle Goods, Performance Bicycle Shop

EXERCISE EQUIPMENT • **Better Health**
GOLF • **Austad's, Custom Golf Clubs, Golf Haus, Las Vegas, Professional Golf & Tennis, Telepro**
HUNTING • **Bass Pro Shops, Bowhunters Warehouse, Cabela's, Cheap Shot, Gander Mountain, Sport Shop, Wiley's**
RACQUET SPORTS • **Holabird, Las Vegas, Professional Golf & Tennis, Samuels Tennisport, The Tennis Co.**
SOCCER • **Soccer International**
VOLLEYBALL • **Spike Nashbar**
WATER SPORTS • **Bart's, Berry Scuba, Central Skindivers, Overton's, Sailboard Warehouse**

ALLYN AIR SEAT CO.

18 MILLSTREAM RD., DEPT. WBMC
WOODSTOCK, NY 12498
914/679-2051

Flyer: free with SASE
Save: up to 50%
Pay: check or MO
Sells: air-filled vehicle seat cushions
Store: mail order only

$$$ 🍁 🇺🇸

Allyn Air Seat sells air-filled cushions that should help you go the distance, whether you're traveling by bike, car, plane, truck, or wheelchair. The stock includes heavy-duty, air-filled seats for bicycles ($13), motorcycles ($35), standard and bucket auto seats, aircraft seats, wheelchairs, and trucks ($35). The cushions help absorb road vibration and bumps, making travel easier and less wearying. Allyn Air Seat also sells covers for lawn and garden tractors, ATVs, snowmobiles, and motorcycles. The firm's newest offering for cars and motorcycles is vinyl "pockettes," which hold maps and other items. Allyn Air, which was established in 1979, keeps its prices a good 30% below its competitors.

Special Factors: Price quote by phone or letter with SASE; C.O.D. orders are accepted; orders are shipped worldwide.

AUSTAD'S

DEPT. 10102
P.O. BOX 1428
SIOUX FALLS, SD 57196-
1428
800-759-4653 EXT. 10102

Catalog: free
Save: up to 40%
Pay: check, MO, MC, V, AE, DC
Sells: golf equipment and apparel
Store: 1600 Rte. 83, Oak Brook, IL; 7485
France Ave. South, Edina, and 648 NE
Hwy. 10, Blaine, MN; also Tenth and
Cleveland, Sioux Falls, SD

$$$ ☎ ♣

Austad's, established in 1963, devotes all 48 pages of its color catalog to the needs of the golfer. You can choose from the latest in equipment and gear—clubs for men, women, and junior players, and bags, carts, footwear, accessories, practice equipment, golfing video-tapes, and gifts for golfers are all available. Austad's represents the most popular names in golfing today—Dunlop, Spalding, Wilson, and Yamaha—as well as the offering its own private-label equipment. And Audstad's features its own line of comfortable clothing, "designed for golfers, by golfers."

Special Factors: All goods are unconditionally guaranteed against defects for 1 year; returns are accepted within 30 days for exchange, refund, or credit; orders are shipped worldwide.

BART'S WATER SKI CENTER, INC.

P.O. BOX 294-WBM
NORTH WEBSTER, IN
46555
800-348-5016
FAX: 219/834-4246

Catalog: free
Save: up to 40%
Pay: check, MO, MC, V, AE, Discover,
Optima
Sells: water-skiing gear and equipment
Store: same address; Monday to Saturday
9–6

$$$ ☎ ♣ ▆

The thrills of water skiing are cheaper at Bart's, where wet suits and skis cost up to 40% below list, and clearance items are offered at even greater savings. Bart's has been in business since 1971, and it backs every sale with a guarantee of satisfaction. The 48-page color catalog features water skis that range from beginners' to tournament models by Connelly, Jobe, Kidder, and O'Brien. Kneeboarders can choose from two pages of boards and accessories, and there is a large selection of floats, tubes, and other inflatables (called "toys" in the catalog). Ski vests and wet suits for men, women, and children are offered, in addition to wet suit accessories, swim trunks, T-shirts, and sunglasses. Gloves, slalom (tow) lines, boat hardware, and manuals and videotapes on water skiing are shown in the catalog.

Special Factors: Satisfaction is guaranteed; price quote by phone or letter; quantity discounts are available; returns are accepted within 60 days; orders are shipped worldwide.

BASS PRO SHOPS

1935 S. CAMPBELL
SPRINGFIELD, MO 65898
800-227-7776
FAX: 417/887-2531

Catalog: $3, refundable (see text)
Save: up to 40%
Pay: check, MO, MC, V, AE
Sells: fishing tackle, boating equipment, and hunting and camping gear
Store: same address; Monday to Saturday 7 A.M.–10 P.M., Sunday 9–6

The Bass Pro Shops catalog is something of an epic: In a past edition, the first page bore a photo of President Bush with the company's founder. A sweepstakes offer followed, then dozens of boats, and on page 43, an application for a Bass Pro Shops VISA card. Following that, over 400 full-color pages of rods, reels, lures, bait, hooks, books and videotapes, camping gear, clothing, boating equipment and electronics, and much more—all at discounts of up to 40%. Bass Pro Shops, which has been doing business since 1971, stocks the most popular brands and models. The big catalog costs $2, but comes with a $3 merchandise certificate. The 195-page sale seasonal catalogs are free, and are automatically sent to current customers. If your interests include a range of water sports, the $2 you spend for the big catalog is a worthwhile investment.

Please note: Orders must be paid in U.S. funds.

Special Factors: Satisfaction is guaranteed; price quote by phone or letter with SASE; returns are accepted; orders are shipped worldwide.

BERRY SCUBA CO.

DEPT. WBMC
6674 N. NORTHWEST
  HWY.
CHICAGO, IL 60631
800-621-6019
312/763-1626
FAX: 312/775-1815

Catalog: free
Save: up to 40%
Pay: check, MO, MC, V, AE, Discover, Optima
Sells: scuba-diving gear
Store: same address; also Lombard and Palatine, IL, and Atlanta, GA

$$

Berry, "the oldest, largest, and best-known direct-mail scuba firm in the country," carries a wide range of equipment and accessories for diving and related activities. Shop here for regulators, masks, wet suits, fins, tanks, diving lights, strobes, underwater cameras and housing, Citizen diving watches, pole spears, and other gear and accessories for underwater use. The brands include Arena, Bay Side, Chronosport, Citizen, Cyalume, Dacor, Deep Sea, Desco, E.B.S., Global, Henderson, Ikelite, Mako, Mares, Nikon, Parkway, Pennform, Scuba Systems, Seatec, Sherwood, Tabata, Tekna, Timex, Trident, Undersea Guns, Underwater Kinetics, U.S. Divers, U.S. Tech, Viking, and Wenoka. Berry does business on a price-quote basis, but also offers a complete 64-page catalog, free of charge.

Special Factor: Price quote by phone or letter with SASE.

BETTER HEALTH FITNESS

5201 NEW UTRECHT AVE.
BROOKLYN, NY 11219
718/436-4693
FAX: 718/854-3381

Catalog: free
Save: up to 50%
Pay: check, MO, MC, V, AE, Optima
Sells: exercise equipment
Store: same address; Monday to Wednesday 10–6, Thursday 10–8, Sunday 12–5 (closed Friday and Saturday)

$$$

Whether you're buying a stationary bicycle for rainy-day workouts or outfitting an entire gym, you can get equipment for less at Better

Health. The firm has been selling top-of-the-line models since 1978, and can provide design and layout services to local customers.

We were sent a lengthy list of *some* of the manufacturers Better Health represents, which include Altero Technologies, Alva (barres), Avita, Barracuda, Bodyguard by Oegland, Cal-Gym, Cat-Eye, Coffey, Everlast, Exercycle, Fitness Master, Healthometer, H.W.E. Massage, Life Fitness, Marcy Fitness, Monark (cycles), Pacemaster (treadmills), Paramount, Penco (lockers), Precor, Pro-Tec, Titan, Trotter (tread-mills), Tunturi, and Vectra. You can save up to 40% on the regular prices of equipment by these and other manufacturers. Call or write for quotes on multi-station units, free-weight benches, mats, dance studio equipment, hot tubs, locker room equipment, and related goods, or see the catalog for a partial listing. Better Health also carries Danskin and Everlast sportswear.

Better Health is offering readers of this book a discount of 5% on all orders. Identify yourself as a reader when you order. This WBMC reader discount expires February 1, 1993.

Special Factors: Satisfaction is guaranteed; price quote by phone or letter with SASE; authorized returns are accepted within 15 days for exchange, refund, or credit.

BIKE NASHBAR

4111 SIMON RD., DEPT. WBM2
YOUNGSTON, OH 44512
800-NASHBAR
FAX: 800-456-1223

Catalog: free
Save: up to 40%
Pay: check, MO, MC, V, Discover
Sells: bicycles, accessories, apparel, and equipment
Store: same address; also 4 other locations (listed in the catalog)

$$$ ☎ 🍁 ▆▆▆

Bike Nashbar, one of the country's top sources for the serious cyclist, publishes an 80-page catalog of everything from water bottles to top-of-the-line frames, sold at "guaranteed lowest prices."

Bike Nashbar sells its own line of road, touring, ATB, and racing bikes, which have features usually found on more expensive models. There are full lines of parts and accessories, including frames by Look; saddles from Avocet, Sella Italia, and Vetta; gears, brakes, chain wheels, hubs, pedals, derailleurs, handlebars, and other parts by

Campagnolo, Dura-Ace, Shimano, SR, Suntour, and other firms. Top-quality panniers and bags, racks, helmets, protective eyewear, gloves, tires and tubes, wheels, toe clips, locks (Citadel and Kryptonite), handlebar tape, grips, tire pumps, lights, and other accessories are offered. Bike Nashbar also features a large selection of cycling clothing under its own name as well as Descente, Hind, Tinley, and Tommaso, in styles for men and women. Shoes by Duegi, Look, and Sidi are carried as well.

Special Factor: Satisfaction is guaranteed.

BOWHUNTERS WAREHOUSE, INC.

**1045 ZIEGLER RD., BOX 158
WELLSVILLE, PA 17365
717/432-8611**

Catalog: free
Save: up to 40%
Pay: check, MO, MC, V
Sells: equipment for bow hunting, hunting, and archery
Store: same address; Monday to Friday 9–5, Wednesday 9–9, Saturday 9–1

Save up to 40% on a complete range of supplies for bow hunting, bow fishing, archery, and hunting through the 100-page catalog from this firm. Bowhunters Warehouse was established in 1978.

Bowhunters Warehouse features a large selection of bows and arrows, and also carries points, feathers, bow sights, rests, quivers, targets, bowhunting books and videotapes, optics, game calls, camouflage clothing and supplies, shooting equipment, and other gear for outdoor sports. Bear, Browning, Bushnell, Darton, Easton, Golden Eagle, Jennings, Martin, PSE, and other manufacturers are represented. Specifications are included with the information on the hunting equipment, making this a good reference catalog as well as a source for real savings.

Special Factors: Authorized returns are accepted (a restocking fee may be charged); minimum order is $10.

CABELA'S INC.

**812 13TH AVE.
SIDNEY, NE 69160
308/254-5505**

Catalog: free
Save: up to 40%
Pay: check, MO, MC, V, AE, Discover
Sells: hunting, fishing, and camping gear
Store: same address; Monday to Saturday
8–5:30

$$$ ☎ ♣

Cabela's, the "world's foremost outfitter" of fishing, hunting, and outdoor enthusiasts, has been praised by several readers who are involved in outdoor sports. Savings run up to 40% on some goods, and the firm is committed to its customers' satisfaction.

Cabela's sells rods, reels, and tackle from well-known manufacturers, including Berkley, Daiwa, Fenwick, Garcia, Mitchell, Shakespeare, and Shimano. Lures, line, tackle boxes, hooks, nets, and other fishing gear are stocked. The catalog shows pages of Minn Kota electric boat motors, boat covers, boat seats, dinghies, downriggers, winches, batteries, and trailer parts. Fishing is the strong suit in the spring and summer catalogs, but a comparable range of hunting equipment is offered in other issues.

General outdoor needs are served by the camping department: tents, sleeping bags and mats, gear bags, backpacks, cookware and kitchen equipment, heavy-duty flashlights, binoculars, sunglasses, knives, and related products are offered. And a good selection of outdoor clothing is sold, including waders, camouflage wear, fishing vests and hunting jackets, snakeproof boots, moccasins, bush jackets, parkas, jeans, and even stylish weekend wear for men and women.

Special Factors: Satisfaction is guaranteed; returns are accepted for exchange, refund, or credit.

CAMPMOR

P.O. BOX 997
PARAMUS, NJ 07653-0997
201/445-5000

Catalog: free
Save: up to 50%
Pay: check, MO, MC, V, AE, Discover
Sells: camping gear and supplies
Store: Rte. 17 N., Paramus, NJ; Monday,
Wednesday, Saturday 9:30–6; Tuesday,
Thursday, Friday 9:30–9

$$$ ☎ ♦ ▓

Campmor's 120-page catalog is full of great buys on all sorts of name-brand camping goods, bike touring accessories, and clothing. Campmor, established in 1946, offers savings of up to 50% on list prices. The catalog features clothing by Borglite Pile, Columbia Interchange System, Sierra Designs, Thinsulate, and Woolrich, and as well as duofold and Polypro underwear, Sorel and Timberland boots, and other outerwear. Swiss Victorinox knives are sold here at 30% off list, and there are Buck knives, Coleman cooking equipment, Sherpa snowshoes, Silva compasses, Edelrid climbing ropes, Eureka tents, and books and manuals on camping and survival. You'll also find sleeping bags by Coleman, The North Face, Slumberjack, and Wenzel, and backpacks by JanSport, Kelly Camp Trails, and Peak.

Special Factors: Returns are accepted for exchange, refund, or credit; minimum order is $20 on phone orders.

CENTRAL SKINDIVERS

160-09 JAMAICA AVE.
JAMAICA, NY 11432-6111
718/739-5772

Information: price quote
Save: up to 40%
Pay: check, MO, MC, V, AE, Discover
Sells: scuba-diving gear
Store: same address; Monday to Saturday
10–6:30

Central Skindivers, in business since 1952, sells name-brand diving gear at savings of up to 40%. The extensive inventory includes tanks from Dacor, Sherwood, and U.S. Divers, and a full range of regulators, masks, fins, gauges, computers, suits, and other gear. There are buoyancy jackets from Beuchat, Dacor, Seaquest, Seatec, Sherwood, Tabata, and U.S. Divers, and watches and timers from Chronosport, Citizen, Heuer, and Tekna. There is no catalog, so call for a price quote.

Special Factors: Price quote by phone; shipping is included; minimum order is $50, $75 with credit cards.

CHEAP SHOT INC.
▬▬▬▬▬▬

294 RTE. 980
CANONSBURG, PA 15317
412/745-2658
FAX: 412/745-4265

Catalog: free
Save: 33% plus
Pay: check or MO
Sells: ammunition
Store: Gun Runner, 950 S. Central Ave.,
   Canonsburg, PA; Monday to Friday 8–8,
   Saturday 8–5, Sunday 10–4

$$

Cheap Shot is "shooters serving shooters since 1976," at savings of 33% and more on the usual prices of ammo. The brands include CCI, Federal, Hornady, Nosler, Remington, and Winchester, and the 20-page catalog also offers a "reloading library," with several manuals on the subject.

Please note: Federal regulations on age and identification requirements are stated in the catalog, and you must provide signature and drivers' license number in order to purchase ammunition.

Special Factors: Price quote by phone or letter with SASE; authorized returns are accepted (a 20% restocking fee may be charged); C.O.D. orders are accepted (a 25% deposit is required).

CUSTOM GOLF CLUBS, INC.

■■■■■■■■■

10206 N.
INTERREGIONAL HWY.
35
AUSTIN, TX 78753
512/837-4810

Catalog: $1
Save: up to 50%
Pay: check, MO, MC, V, Discover
Sells: customized golf clubs, accessories, and repair equipment
Store: same address; Monday to Friday 7–7, Saturday 8–4, Sunday 9–5

$$$ ☎ ♦ 🇺🇸

The "Accessories" catalog from Custom Golf Clubs features its special line of "Golfsmith" clubs, made to order, and a full line of golfing accessories. The "Repairs" catalog shows over 160 pages of replacement parts and repair supplies. Custom Golf, which opened its doors in 1966, offers savings of up to 50% on the cost of comparable name-brand products.

The custom department can make golfing woods and irons in a choice of left- or right-handed models, men's or women's styles, in five degrees of flexibility and any length, weight, color, or grip size. All professional-quality, name-brand golf club lines are available as well, from such names as Dunlop, Hogan, MacGregor, Ping, PowerBilt, Spalding, Titleist, and Wilson. The Accessories catalog also features name-brand clothing, footwear, bags, carts, gloves, manuals, balls, club covers, and other golfing essentials, plus instructional videotapes and books. The Repairs catalog offers a line of replacement club heads, grips, refinishing supplies, and tools, as well as instruction manuals. Service and repairs are also available to mail-order customers, and if you'd like to learn how to become a professional club maker, check into the Custom Golf Training Program.

Canadian readers, please note: Orders must be paid in U.S. funds.

Special Factors: Request catalog desired by name ($1 each); orders are shipped worldwide.

CYCLE GOODS CORP.

**2801 HENNEPIN AVE. SO.
MINNEAPOLIS, MN 55408
800-328-5213
612/872-7600**

Catalog: $1
Save: up to 40%
Pay: check, MO, MC, V, AE, DC, Optima
Sells: cycling gear and equipment
Store: 2801 Hennepin Ave., Minneapolis,
   MN; Monday to Thursday 10–8, Friday
   10–6, Saturday 10–5, Sunday 12–4

$$$ ☎ ✦ ▰

Cycle Goods (also known as Cycl-Ology) publishes a 106-page catalog of cycling gear and supplies that includes valuable tips for improved performance and routine maintenance, along with detailed product information. The firm has been doing business since 1979.

Cycle Goods stocks a wide selection of racing and touring equipment, plus parts, tools, and clothing. Among the manufacturers represented here are Araya, Atom, Avocet, Berec, Bollé, Campagnolo, Cinelli, Citadel, Columbus, Cycle Pro, Descente, Guerciotti, Kingsbridge, Kirtland, Klein, Kryptonite, Lemond, Maillard, Mavic, Messinger, Michelin, Nike, Oakley, Rhode Gear, Rossin, Scott, Shimano, Sidi, Suntour, and Weinmann. Save up to 40% on equipment and accessories, and more on specials.

Special Factors: Price quote by phone or letter with SASE; orders are shipped worldwide.

GANDER MOUNTAIN, INC.

**P.O. BOX 6
WILMOT, WI 53192
800-554-9410**

Catalog: free
Save: up to 35%
Pay: check, MO, MC, V, Discover
Sells: hunting, fishing, camping, reloading,
   and boating gear
Store: Wilmot/Johnsburg Rd., Wilmot, and
   19555 West Bluemound Rd., Brookfield,
   WI; Monday to Friday 9–9, Saturday 9–6,
   Sunday 10–5

$$$ ☎ ✦ ▰

Gander Mountain has been recommended by several readers as a great source for outdoor sports gear and clothing, getting high marks for selection and service. Prices are also reliably low—we've found savings of up to 35% on different items.

Fishing and hunting needs are served here through a 172-page color catalog of equipment and clothing. The rod and reel department offers gear by Berkley, Browning, Daiwa, Eagle Claw, Fenwick, Garcia, Johnson, Liberty, Mitchell, Quantum, Ryobi, Shakespeare, Shimano, Sigma, and Zebco. There are lures by Bagley's, Mepps, Normark, and many other firms, and fishing line, nets, tackle boxes, rod cases, and other gear. Boat seats, covers, winches, bilge pumps, Minn Kota and other motors, Cannon downriggers, depth meters, recorders, radios, sonar devices, and Humminbird electronics are all offered as well.

Hunters will find a similar range of products for their sport: CVA blackpowder rifles, Lyman and MEC reloaders, Ram-line magazines and auto-loaders, Hastings replacement parts for shotguns, Gun Guard gun cases, Treadlok gun safes, Michaels holsters, practice equipment, shell boxes, and related goods. Spotting scopes, hunting binoculars, mounts, and tripods by Bushnell, Leupold, and Tasco are also available.

Gander's video department sells Warburton and other tapes on big game hunting, shooting and handling guns, game calls and hunting techniques, training hunting dogs, hunting wild birds, and fishing for bass, walleye, and trout. Specialty clothing for both hunting and fishing—waders, hunting and shooting jackets, camouflage wear—is carried, as well as rugged clothing suitable for outdoor wear. The catalog we reviewed offered chamois cloth shirts, rain suits, leather jackets, and footwear from American Eagle, Browning, Coleman, Danner, Hi-Tec, Long Haul, Tony Lama, Maine Classic, Minnetonka, Rocky, Sorel, and other firms. Bushnell sunglasses, backpacks and luggage, camp cookware, sleeping bags, tents, Buck knives, and other outdoor gear is available.

Special Factors: Satisfaction is guaranteed; orders are shipped worldwide.

GOLF HAUS

**700 N. PENNSYLVANIA
LANSING, MI 48906
517/482-8842**

Price List: free
Save: up to 60%
Pay: check, MO, MC, V
Sells: golf clubs, apparel, and accessories
Store: same address; Monday to Saturday
9–5:30

$$$$ ☎ ♦ ▤ (see text)

Golf Haus has "the absolute lowest prices on pro golf clubs" anywhere—up to 60% below list—and stocks goods by every possible manufacturer. All of the models sold here are available nationwide, which means that, unlike with the "exclusive models" offered by a number of discounters, the goods at Golf Haus can be price-shopped fairly. There are clubs, bags, putters, balls, and other golf equipment and supplies by Dunlop, Hogan, Lynx, MacGregor, Ping, PowerBilt, Ram, Spalding, Tiger Shark, Titleist, Wilson, and other firms. There are Bag Boy carts, Etonic shoes, gloves, umbrellas, spikes, scorekeepers, visors, rainsuits, tote bags, socks, and much more.

Golf Haus is offering readers of this book a gift of knit club head covers (for woods), with each purchase of a complete set of clubs (woods and irons). Identify yourself as a reader when you order. This WBMC reader discount expires February 1, 1993.

Special Factors: Price quote by phone or letter with SASE; shipping and insurance are included on orders shipped within the continental U.S.; minimum order is $50; orders are shipped worldwide.

HOLABIRD SPORTS DISCOUNTERS

**9008 YELLOW BRICK RD.
BALTIMORE, MD 21237
301/687-6400
FAX: 301/687-7311**

Brochure: free
Save: up to 40%
Pay: check, MO, MC, V, CHOICE
Sells: racquet sports equipment and
athletic footwear
Store: mail order only

$$$$ ☎ ♦ ▤

Buy here and get the "Holabird Advantage": equipment for racquet sports at up to 40% below list prices, service on manufacturers' warranties, and free stringing with tournament nylon on all racquets.

Holabird carries tennis racquets by scores of firms, including Donnay, Dunlop, Estusa, Fin, Fischer, Fox, Head, Mizuno, Prince, Pro-Kennex, Puma, Rossignol, Slazenger, Snauwaert, Spalding, Volkl, Wilson, Wimbledon, Yamaha, and Yonex. There are tennis balls by Dunlop, Penn, and Wilson, and ball machines by Lobster, Prince, and Tennis Tutor. The footwear department offers the newest styles from Adidas, Asahi, Asics Tiger, Avia, Brooks, Converse, Diadora, Ellesse, Etonic, Head, Ixspa, K-Swiss, Kaepa, Keds, L.A. Gear, Le Coq Sportif, Lotto, New Balance, Nike, Prince, Pro-Kennex, Reebok, Saucony, Sergio Tacchini, Tretorn, Turntec, and Wilson.

Racquetball players should check the prices on racquets by Ektelon, Head, Leach, Pro-Kennex, Spalding, Voit, and Wilson. The squash department features racquets by Black Knight, Donnay, Dunlop, Ektelon, Estca, Head, Pro-Kennex, Prince, Rossignol, Slazenger, Snauwaert, Spalding, Unsquashable, and Wilson, and eye guards by Bausch & Lomb, Ektelon, Leader, and Pro-Kennex. Pros can save their clubs sizable sums on court equipment and maintenance supplies, such as court dryers, tennis nets, ball hoppers, and stringing machines.

Holabird also stocks a full line of basketball, cross-training, aerobic, running, and walking shoes, as well as a complete line of name-brand T-shirts, socks, caps, sunglasses from Rayban and Serengeti, Casio and Timex sport watches, and table tennis (ping pong) supplies and equipment. See the monthly 8-page catalog for specials, or call or write for a price quote.

Special Factors: Price quote by phone or letter with SASE; authorized returns (except used items) are accepted within 7 days; orders are shipped worldwide.

LAS VEGAS DISCOUNT GOLF & TENNIS

4813 PARADISE RD.,
WBM-1
LAS VEGAS, NV 89109
702/798-6300
FAX: 702/798-1045

Catalog: free
Save: up to 40%
Pay: check, MO, MC, V, AE, CB, DC
Sells: golf, tennis, and racquetball gear
Store: 4813 Paradise Rd., Las Vegas, NV; also stores in AL, AZ, CA, CO, FL, GA, HI, IL, LA, MA, MD, NE, NV, NY, OK, OR, PA, TN, VA, Canada, France, Japan, and Spain (locations are listed in the catalog)

Las Vegas sells name-brand gear and equipment for golf, tennis, racquetball, and jogging at savings of up to 40%. The latest styles and models are featured. The 48-page, color catalog shows golf clubs (drivers, putters, wedges, chippers), bags, and balls by Ben Hogan, Lynx, MacGregor, Mizuno, PGA, Ping, Powerbilt, Ram, Spalding, Taylormade, Stan Thompson, Tiger Shark, Titleist, Wilson, Yamaha, and Yonex. The latest clothing from Difini, Foot-Joy, Hogan, Izod, Lamode, PGA Tour, St. Andrews, and other names is available, as well as instructional books and videotapes.

Las Vegas Discount also carries tennis racquets by Donnay, Dunlop, Head, Prince, Pro-Kennex, Spalding, Wilson, and Yamaha, as well as racquet strings and balls by Dunlop, Penn, Tretorn, and Wilson. There are lines of tennis shoes and apparel from several manufacturers, racquetball racquets from Ektelon, Head, and Wilson, and eye guards, Voit jump ropes, and miscellaneous sports accessories.

Special Factors: Price quote by phone or letter with SASE; orders are shipped worldwide.

OVERTON'S SPORTS CENTER, INC.

P.O. BOX 8228, DEPT. 48504
GREENVILLE, NC 27835
800-334-6541
FAX: 919/355-2923

Catalog: free
Save: up to 40%
Pay: check, MO, MC, V, AE, Discover
Sells: marine and water sports equipment, swimwear, and apparel
Store: 5343 S. Boulevard, Charlotte; 111 Red Banks Rd., Greenville; and 1331 Buck Jones Rd., Raleigh, NC

Overton's lays claim to title of "world's largest water sports dealer," selling equipment for boating, water skiing, snorkeling, and other avocations. Overton's was established in 1975, and sells at discounts of 40% and more. The firm's 108-page, color Water Sports catalog features skis and accessories ranging from junior trainers to experts' tricks, jumpers and slaloms by such companies as Connelly, EP, Jobe, Kidder, and O'Brien. Wetsuits, apparel, kneeboards, water toys, inflatables, snorkeling accessories, boating accessories, books, videotapes, and other goods are also offered.

The Overton's 128-page, color Discount Marine Catalog answers your boating needs with a wide range of products: boat seats and covers, safety equipment, instruments, electronics, hardware, cleaners, fishing equipment, clothing, fuel tanks, and performance accessories. The brands include Apelco, Aqua Meter, Brinkman, Eagle, Humminbird, Interphase, Ray Jefferson, Maxxima, Newmar, Power-Winch, Shakespeare, and Si-Tex, among others. The catalogs give the both the list or comparable retail, and Overton's discount prices.

Canadian readers, please note: Only U.S. funds are accepted.

Special Factors: Satisfaction is guaranteed; quantity discounts are available; unused returns are accepted within 30 days for exchange, refund, or credit; C.O.D. orders are accepted; orders are shipped worldwide.

PERFORMANCE BICYCLE SHOP

P.O. BOX 2741
CHAPEL HILL, NC 27514
919/933-9113
FAX: 919/967-3979

Catalog: free
Save: up to 40%
Pay: check, MO, MC, V, DC
Sells: bicycle parts and cycling apparel
Store: 13 stores in CA, CO, MD, NC, VA

Serious cyclists are familiar with Performance for its own line of high-end road and mountain bikes, which run from under $300 to about $1,000. The firm's parts department is well-stocked, and it carries components for maintenance and improvement by Bell, Campagnolo, Cinelli, Look, Time, Shimano, Sugino, and other firms. Performance offers cycling jerseys and shorts, as well as riding helmets, cycling shoes, gloves, panniers, and hundreds of products to enhance cycling performance.

If you find identical equipment advertised at a lower price elsewhere, you can send Performance a copy of the ad (or tell the phone operator where you saw it) and pay the lower price. Details on the "Price Protection Guarantee" are given in the catalog.

Special Factor: Satisfaction is guaranteed.

PROFESSIONAL GOLF & TENNIS SUPPLIERS, INC.

7825 HOLLYWOOD BLVD.
PEMBROKE PINES, FL
 33024
305/981-7283
FAX: 305/983-7033

Brochure: free with SASE
Save: 30% plus
Pay: check, MO, MC, V, AE, CB, DC, CHOICE, Discover, Optima
Sells: gear and apparel for golf and racquet sports
Store: same address; Monday to Sunday 9–6:30; other locations in AL and FL

$$$ ☎ ♦ ▆

This firm represents several divisions, which together offer an impressive array of equipment for golf, tennis, racquetball, and squash at savings of up to 40% on list prices. The quarterly catalog shows pro golf clubs by Acushnet, Jerry Barber, Browning, Dunlop, First Flight, Hagen, Ben Hogan, Lynx, MacGregor, Tony Penna, PGA, Ping, Pinseeker, PowerBilt, Ram, Rawlings, Sounder, Spalding, Stan Thompson, Taylor Made, Tiger Shark, Titleist, and Wilson. There are gloves, bags, shoes, balls, carts, and other golfing supplies as well.

Check Professional for buys on tennis racquets from Bancroft, Davis, Donnay, Dunlop, Durbin, Fila, Fischer, Head, Kneissl, Le Coq Sportif, Match Mate, P.D.P., Prince, Pro Group, Pro-Kennex, Rossignol, Scepter, Slazenger, Snauwaert, Spalding, Volkl, Wilson, Yamaha, and Yonex. Name-brand running and tennis shoes and balls, nets, ball machines, hoppers, stringing machines, bags, and other tennis goods are carried. The squash department offers racquets by Donnay, Dunlop, and Head; there are racquetball racquets by Ektelon, Head, Leach, Voit, and Wilson as well, plus name-brand shoes, bags, balls, and gloves.

Special Factors: Price quote by phone or letter with SASE; a 3% surcharge is levied on MasterCard and VISA orders; shipping and insurance are included on most items; orders are shipped worldwide.

ROAD RUNNER SPORTS

**6310 NANCY RIDGE RD.,
SUITE 101
SAN DIEGO, CA 92121-
3209
800-551-5558
FAX: 619/455-6470**

Catalog: free
Save: up to 35%
Pay: check, MO, MC, V, AE
Sells: running shoes and apparel
Store: same address; Monday to Friday 9–5,
Saturday 9–3

$$$ ☎ ♦ ▆

Road Runner Sports boasts "the absolute lowest running shoe prices," selling at a 10% markup on the wholesale cost, or up to 35% below list prices. The company has been in business for over 30 years and has thousands of pairs of shoes in stock.

Running shoes by Adidas, Asics, Avia, Brooks, Etonic, New Balance, Reebok, Saucony, and Turntec are stocked here, as well as running shorts, socks, T-shirts, Gore-Tex running suits, duffel bags, and other accessories. The 96-page color catalog features current best-sellers, and you can call or write for prices on styles not shown.

Special Factors: Price quote by phone or letter with SASE; orders are shipped worldwide.

SAILBOARD WAREHOUSE, INC.

**300 S. OWASSO BLVD.,
DEPT. WBMC
ST. PAUL, MN 55117
800-992-SAIL
FAX: 612/482-1353**

Catalog: free
Save: 35% average
Pay: check, MO, MC, V, AE
Sells: windsurfing equipment
Store: same address; Monday, Tuesday, and
Thursday 12–9, Wednesday and Friday
10–7, Saturday 9–2; also Hood River,
Oregon; Monday to Saturday 9–9, Sunday
9–6 (April 1–October 1)

$$$ ☎ ♦ ▆

Put wind and water together, and you have the prime ingredients for the nearly addictive sport of windsurfing, or sailboarding. The right equipment helps, which is what you'll find at Sailboard Warehouse—

at discounts that average 35%, but run much deeper on sale items. The firm has been in business since 1982, selling light to heavy wind sailboards, sails, masts, harnesses, fins, and a broad selection of windsurfing apparel. You'll find equipment by AHD, Bayley, Bic, Calvert, DaKine, Fanatic, F2, HiFly, HiTech, Kerma, Klepper, Maui Magic, Mistral, Naish, Neilpryde, O'Brien, Progressive Composites, Sailboard, Sea Trend, Tiga, Topsails, Weichart, West Wind, Windcatcher, Windsurfing Hawaii, and other manufacturers represented in the color catalog. The boards run from entry-level to custom models for pros, and the catalog we reviewed included several pages of helpful information on choosing equipment and evaluating construction and materials. Automaxi car racks, Bollé sunglasses, windsurfing books and videos, and wetsuits, drysuits, harnesses and other accessories by O'Neill and Ronny are also available.

Special Factors: Satisfaction is guaranteed; price quote by phone or letter with SASE; shipping is included on orders of 2 or more boards; authorized returns are accepted within 20 days for exchange, refund, or credit.

SAMUELS TENNISPORT

**7796 MONTGOMERY RD.
CINCINNATI, OH 45236
800-543-1153
IN OH 800-543-1152
513/791-4636
FAX: 513/791-4036**

Brochure: free
Save: up to 35%
Pay: check, MO, MC, V, AE, Discover, Optima
Sells: racquets, clothing, and equipment
Store: same address; Monday to Thursday 9–8, Friday 9–6, Saturday 10–5, Sunday 12–4

$$$ ☎ 🍁 ▥

Despite the firm's name, Samuels Tennisport offers equipment for racquetball and squash as well as court and platform tennis and badminton. Prices on the equipment are discounted up to 35%, but note that most of the clothing and accessories are sold at full retail.

The racquet department offers current tennis racquet models by Donnay, Dunlop, Fox, Head, Kneissl, MacGregor, Prince, Pro-Kennex, Puma, Rossignol, Wilson, Wimbledon, Yamaha, and Yonex. There are racquetball racquets by Ektelon, Head, and Pro-Kennex, and squash racquets by Donnay, Dunlop, Head, and Pro-Kennex. The badminton department has racquets by Black Knight, Carlton, HL, Victor, and Yonex, and string sets, shuttlecocks, and accessories. Custom stringing in nylon or gut is available at a surcharge. Ball machines, nets, court sweepers, Weathashade windscreens, and other court equipment is stocked.

The clothing and accessories department offers shoes and separates for on and off the court (including running shoes) by a number of prominent firms: Adidas, Asics, Avia, Brooks, Cerrutti, Diadora, Donnay, Ellesse, Fila, Foot-Joy, Head, K-Swiss, Le Coq Sportif, Nike, Fred Perry, Prince, Puma, Reebok, Rossignol, Saucony, Sergio Tacchini, Tretorn, Wilson, and Yonex. Bags from many of these firms are offered, and visors, wristbands, shoe repair products, insoles, eye guards, and gloves are available as well.

Special Factors: Satisfaction is guaranteed; price quote by phone or letter with SASE; minimum order is $25; C.O.D. orders are accepted; orders are shipped worldwide.

SIERRA TRADING POST

DEPT. WBMC-92
1625 CRANE WAY
SPARKS, NV 89431
702/355-3355
FAX: 702/355-3366

Catalog: free
Save: up to 60%
Pay: check, MO, MC, V
Sells: outdoor clothing for men and women
Store: same address

$$$ ☎ 🍁 🇺🇸

Sierra Trading Post brings you casual and outdoor clothing and camping gear in a catalog that reminded us of the ones we used to get from Banana Republic, *sans* the travelogue. Instead, you get down-filled clothing and outerwear, shoes for hiking and climbing, great pants and shorts, socks, sweaters, underwear, and even comfortable dresses that would be perfect for a post-hike trip into town. Name brands pepper Sierra's catalog—Hanes, Marmot, New Balance, The North Face, Patagonia, Sportif USA, Terramar, and Woolrich are among the manufacturers represented in past mailings. We've also found Acorn slippers, Icelandic sweaters, Bollé sunglasses, Conroy gloves, Asolo hiking shoes, alpaca blankets, and Sierra Designs sleeping bags and tents, all at savings of up to 60%.

Special Factors: Satisfaction is guaranteed; returns are accepted for exchange, refund, or credit.

SOCCER INTERNATIONAL, INC.

■■■■■■

**P.O. BOX 7222, DEPT. WBM-92
ARLINGTON, VA 22207-0222
703/524-4333**

Catalog: $2
Save: up to 35%
Pay: check or MO
Sells: soccer gear, accessories, and gifts
Store: mail order only

$$$ ☎ ▆

Soccer International, founded in 1976 by a rabid soccer buff, publishes a 16-page color catalog of game-related items ranging from professional equipment to novelties. The savings run up to 35%, and the catalog is a must-see for any soccer enthusiast or friend of one, since it's a great resource for gifts as well as gear.

You'll find a number of balls here from Brine, Mikasa, Mitre, and Umbro, and Soccer International's own line of jerseys and shorts, as well as English clothing imports. PVC leg shields and ankle guards, ball inflators, nets and goals, practice aids, and a great selection of books and videotapes on coaching, game strategy, and soccer history are available. You'll also find soccer-design pillows, soccer-theme radios, door mats, mugs, ties, belt buckles, and dozens of embroidered patches, bumper stickers, and theme T-shirts. Many of these items are hard to find at sports equipment stores and gift shops, but the prices we were able to check ran from 10% to 35% less from this firm.

Special Factors: Price quote by phone or letter on quantity orders; minimum order is $15.

SPIKE NASHBAR

4111 SIMON RD., DEPT. WBM-1
YOUNGSTOWN, OH 44512
800-937-7453
FAX: 800-456-1223

Catalog: free
Save: up to 40%
Pay: check, MO, MC, V, Discover
Sells: volleyball gear and apparel
Store: mail order only

 $$

Spike Nashbar is a newly formed sister company to Bike Nashbar (see the listing in this chapter) that offers savings of up to 40% on competition volleyball gear, clothing, and accessories. The 16-page color catalog offers over a dozen balls, for indoor and outdoor play, by Mikasa (including "King of the Beach" and "Sideout Sport" lines), Spalding, and Tachikara. Several nets and net systems are available, including one from Park and Sun for under $96 and "the best portable net system available," the Spectrum series, which costs about $236. There are volleyball shoes for men and women by Asics, Avia, K-Swiss, and Mizuno, beginning at under $40. Sportbras, socks, T-shirts, shorts, duffels, sport watches, and sun shields from Bausch & Lomb, Bollé, and Uvex are also sold, as well as vital knee protection from Asics and Body Glove. If you've ever watched or played serious volleyball, you'll know why they're part of the standard uniform of the game.

Canadian readers, please note: Only U.S. funds are accepted.

Special Factors: Satisfaction is guaranteed; returns are accepted for exchange, refund, or credit.

SPORT SHOP

**DEPT. WBMC
P.O. BOX 340
GRIFTON, NC 28530
919/746-8288
FAX: 919/746-8296**

Catalog: $1
Save: up to 50%
Pay: check, MO, MC, V, AE, Discover
Sells: hunting gear
Store: Hwy. 11 N., Grifton, NC; Monday to
 Saturday 8–5

$ ☎ ✦ ▆

The sport served here is bowhunting, for which Sport Shop offers a 64-page catalog of bows and hunting gear, at discounts of up to 50%. Sport Shop has been in business since 1955, and sells bows by Beamon, High Country, Holt, Jennings, Oneida, Pearson, and PSE, as well as Neet belt quivers, Easton arrows and shafts, vanes, straighteners, points, broadheads, sights, rests, releasers, strings, and targets. Bowfishing equipment and even some hunting items are sold—RWS and Thompson/Center blackpowder guns and blackpowder supplies, among other goods. Camouflage clothing and maintenance products are available, as are lures, game calls, and footwear by Rocky and Topline.

Special Factors: Price quote by phone or letter with SASE on goods not shown in the catalog; returns are accepted for exchange, refund, or credit; minimum order is $15 with credit cards; orders are shipped worldwide.

SURVIVAL SUPPLY CO.

**P.O. BOX 1745-WM
SHINGLE SPRINGS, CA
 95682
916/621-3836**

Catalog: free
Save: up to 30% (see text)
Pay: check, MO, MC, V
Sells: camping and outdoor gear, survival
 supplies, etc.
Store: mail order only

$$$ ☎ ✦ ▆

Survival Supply serves two distinct but overlapping markets: outdoors enthusiasts, and survivalists. The firm's 54-page catalog is heavy on emergency food and gear, and sells books on everything from combat ammunition to Caribbean tax havens. All of it is offered at prices that average 25% below regular retail (and quantity discounts are available on food items).

Survival Supply began business in 1987 and offers an extensive selection of dehydrated foods, including MRE rations and goods from Harvest Valley, Ready Reserves, Stone Mill Farms, and Weepak. (MRE rations are "Meals Ready to Eat," courtesy the U.S. government.) Survival Supply has also assembled survival kits that can keep one or two persons going for 3 to 30 days, as well as family assortments that can keep a party of four sustained for up to a year. A seven-day food kit for four costs about $250 at this writing, and includes water purification tablets, stoves and fuel, a cooking kit, 30 candles and waterproof matches, and much more—in addition to the food. Other kits and individual foods are also well-priced, and volume discounts apply to food purchases (from 5% on orders over $50 to 25% on orders over $600). In addition, Survival Supply offers a small selection of tents and sleeping bags, camp stoves and lanterns, mess kits, flashlights, camp saws and shovels, gas masks, knives, first-aid kits, solar-powered batteries and chargers, duffels, some military surplus clothing and camouflage BDU's, and survival guides—from genuine military manuals to handbooks on poaching.

Special Factors: Price quote by phone or letter; quantity discounts are available; C.O.D. orders are accepted; orders are shipped worldwide.

TELEPRO GOLF SHOP

**17622 ARMSTRONG AVE.
IRVINE, CA 92714-5791
800-333-9903**

Brochure: free
Save: up to 40%
Pay: check, MO, MC, V, Discover
Sells: golf clubs
Store: same address

Telepro, a division of Shamrock Golf Shops and an affiliate of Teletire (see "Auto"), sells first-quality golf clubs and accessories at savings of up to 40%. Telepro's informative brochure shows pro lines of clubs by Callaway, Cobra, Hogan, Lynx, Mizuno, Ping, Shamrock, Spalding, Taylormade, Wilson, Yonnex and other manufacturers. There are Wilson golf gloves, bags, Bag Boy carts, and other equipment, which are sold at various discounts. The brochure includes a questionnaire on your golfing style, which will help Telepro to determine the best clubs for your game.

Special Factors: Satisfaction is guaranteed; price quote by phone or letter with SASE; returns (except special orders) are accepted within 30 days (a 15% restocking fee may be charged).

THE TENNIS CO.

30610 SOUTHFIELD RD. SOUTHFIELD, MI 48076-1220
313/258-9366

Information: price quote
Save: up to 35%
Pay: check, MO, MC, V
Sells: squash and tennis equipment
Store: mail order only

$$$ ☎

The Tennis Co. sells tennis and squash equipment at savings of up to 35% on list. Call or write for prices on tennis racquets by Head, Prince, Pro-Kennex, and Wilson, and squash racquets by AMF Head, Donnay, Dunlop, Manta, Pro-Kennex, Slazenger, and Spalding. Merco squash balls and other supplies are stocked as well, and The Tennis Co. will also string your racquets.

Special Factor: Price quote by phone or letter with SASE.

WILEY OUTDOOR SPORTS, INC.

DEPT. WBMC 1992
P.O. BOX 5307
HUNTSVILLE, AL 35814
205/837-3931
FAX: 205/837-4017

Catalog: $3, refundable
Save: 30% average
Pay: check, MO, MC, V
Sells: hunting gear and equipment
Store: 1808 Sportsman Lane, Huntsville, AL

$$$ ☎ ♦ ▆

This family-run business has been outfitting hunters since 1953 with a full range of equipment and gear. Savings at Wiley average 30%, but can run as high as 50% on certain items and lines. Hunters will find everything from boots to blackpowder supplies in the 168-page catalog, including scopes, binoculars, and other optics from Aimpoint, Burris, J.B. Holden, Leupold, Nikon, Redfield, Simmons, Tasco, and Zeiss. Blackpowder rifles by Lyman and Thompson/Center are available, as well as reloading and bullet-casting equipment by Forster Products, Hornady, Lee, Lyman, and MEC. Holster, gun maintenance products, gun slings, tree stands, and related hunting accessories are stocked. There are game calls of all types, game scents, compasses, airguns for adults, and camping accessories. Clothing by Browning, Carhartt, Columbia, Hodgman, Mossy Oak, Remington, and Walls is sold, as well as duofold thermal underwear, footwear from Rocky Boots, and Serengeti sunglasses.

In addition to hunting needs, Wiley carries crossbows by Barnett, bowhunting gear, and an excellent selection of hunting and specialty knives by Al Mar, Browning, Buck, Case, Cold Steel, Gerber, Remington, Victorinox, and Wyoming Knife.

Special Factors: Satisfaction is guaranteed; unused returns are accepted within 10 days; minimum order is $25; C.O.D. orders (via UPS only) are accepted; orders are shipped worldwide.

SEE ALSO

Astronomics/Christophers, Ltd. • spotting scopes for bird watching • *CAMERAS*

Bruce Medical Supply • small selection of fitness equipment • *MEDICINE*

CISCO • swimming pool supplies • *HOME: MAINTENANCE*

Clothcrafters, Inc. • flannel gun-cleaning patches, mosquito netting, and sleeping bag liners • *GENERAL MERCHANDISE*

Creative Health Products • exercise equipment • *HEALTH*

Custom Coat Company, Inc. • custom tanning, dyeing, and tailoring of green hides • *CLOTHING*

Danley's • sports binoculars, rifle scopes, etc. • *CAMERAS*

E & B Marine Supply, Inc. • water skis • *AUTO*

Elite Eyewear • designer sunglasses • *MEDICINE*

Ewald-Clark • binoculars • *CAMERAS*

A. Feibusch Corporation • replacement tent zippers • *CRAFTS*

The Finals, Ltd. • swimwear, athletic wear, and accessories • *CLOTHING*

Leather Unlimited • black powder supplies, suede duffel bags • *LEATHER*

Mardiron Optics • binoculars and spotting scopes for hunting, bird watching, etc. • *CAMERAS*

Mass. Army & Navy Store • government surplus camping and survival gear • *SURPLUS*

Mr. Spiceman • beef jerky and other camp foods • *FOOD*

Newark Dressmaker Supply, Inc. • replacement zippers for sleeping bags and tents • *CRAFTS*

Okun Bros. Shoes • sports shoes • *CLOTHING: FOOTWEAR*

Orion Telescope Center • binoculars • *CAMERAS*

Pagano Gloves, Inc. • deerskin archers', hunters', and bowhunters' gloves • *CLOTHING*

Racer Wholesale • auto racing safety equipment and accessories • *AUTO*

Ruvel & Co., Inc. • government surplus camping supplies and survival goods • *SURPLUS*

Safe Specialties, Inc. • gun safes and pistol boxes • *OFFICE*

Scope City • field binoculars, spotting scopes • *CAMERAS*

Tower Hobbies • radio-controlled models and accessories • *CRAFTS*

Yachtmail Co. Ltd. • dinghies and boating equipment • *AUTO*

SURPLUS

—————

Surplus and used goods of every sort

This is the world of military overstock, obsolete electronics, and the 90% discount. Many of these dealers accept inquiries for goods not listed in their catalogs, but most people don't know what's available. *The Army/Navy Store Catalog* (Penguin Books, 1982), by Andrew I. Adler, Roger Adler, and William G. Thompson, provides a good guide to a wide range of popular items. It's illustrated with line drawings and features extensive listings of surplus suppliers in the U.S. and abroad. The firms in this chapter offer representative goods from all kinds of sources, combining the excitement of the unknown with the thrill of a bargain. If you have any questions about what an item is, though, call and ask before you order—you'll save yourself the hassle and expense of a return.

AMERICAN SCIENCE & SURPLUS
—————

601 LINDEN PL., DEPT. WBM-92
EVANSTON, IL 60202
708/475-8440
FAX: 708/864-1589

Catalog: 50¢
Save: up to 95%
Pay: check, MO, MC, V
Sells: industrial and military surplus goods
Store: 5696 Northwest Hwy., Chicago, IL; also 5430 W. Layton Ave., Milwaukee, WI; Monday to Friday 10–6, Thursday 10–9, Saturday 9–5, Sunday 11–5, both locations

$$$ ☎

American Science Center, formerly listed here as Jerryco, offers its surplus wares through witty catalogs that are published about six times yearly, and will send you four issues for 50¢. The American Science Center has been selling surplus since 1937 and offers that blend of the strange and useful that is catnip to fans of surplus goods: everything from "humongo scissors and son" (a big and a small pair of scissors), to steering wheels (black plastic, perfect for go carts, $7.50 each).

Past catalogs have shown small DC motors, staplers, heat guns, microscopes, farriers' tools, magnets, odd bottles, drill bits, dozens of kinds of tape, whet stones, silk thread, a dinosaur-shaped clock, telescoping antennas, pumps, casters, gray cue balls, piano hinges, Chinese riffler tools, and magnifying lenses. (Please *don't* expect to find these particular items in the catalogs you receive—these are surplus goods, and stock is limited.) The descriptions, which are droll and explicit, note the original and possible uses for the products, as well as technical data, when available. Savings on original and if-new prices can reach 95%.

Special Factors: Satisfaction is guaranteed; returns are accepted within 15 days; minimum order is $12.50.

BURDEN'S SURPLUS CENTER

1015 W. "O" ST.
LINCOLN, NE 68501-2209
800-488-3407
FAX: 402/474-5198

Catalog: free
Save: up to 85%
Pay: check, MO, MC, V, AE, Discover
Sells: new and surplus industrial goods, hardware, etc.
Store: same address; Monday to Saturday 9–6, Sunday 12–5

$$$ ☎ 🍁 ▆

Burden's, established in 1933, offers great buys on tools and hardware of all sorts. The 132-page catalog is dominated by industrial products—hydraulic equipment, motors, gas engines, blowers, compressors, air tools, winches, generators, transformers, and the like—but there are some consumer goods as well.

Past catalogs have offered pressure washers, electrical equipment and supplies, David White surveying equipment, plumbing equipment and tools, grinders, and other goods for commercial and industrial use, by Briggs & Stratton, Cessna, G.E., Gresen, Hypro, Kawasaki, and other manufacturers. The Burdex line of security and surveillance equipment is available, as well as other security components and alarms. You'll usually find Dremel and other hand tools, phones and accessories, halogen spotlights, Mag-Lite flashlights, Redington measuring wheels, casters, automotive products, propane heaters, and other useful goods in the catalog. Some, like the ammo boxes, are real government surplus, but most of the goods are like the $27.95 laptop carrying case: brand new bargains. If you have any questions about an item, you can call the staff technicians for information.

Special Factors: Authorized returns are accepted (a restocking fee may be charged); C.O.D. orders are accepted; orders are shipped worldwide.

E.T. SUPPLY

P.O. BOX 78190
LOS ANGELES, CA 90016-
  8190
213/734-2430
FAX: 213/734-1511

Catalog: free
Save: up to 90%
Pay: check, MO, MC, V
Sells: industrial surplus goods
Store: mail order only

$$$

E.T. Supply (no relation to extraterrestrials) has been in business since 1984, selling military and commercial surplus, with an emphasis on electrical components. Most of the 64-page catalog is devoted to accumulators, actuators, blowers, circuit breakers, generators, hydraulic cylinders, pumps, relays, rheostats, solenoids, switches, and similar items.

The catalogs usually feature several pages of tools, hardware, and parts that would be useful in vehicle repairs—wrench and socket sets, pliers, casters, tachometers, and aircraft instruments. The product descriptions often mention the manufacturer, and we've seen goods from Bendix, G.E., Kidde, Lear, Motorola, Pesco, Raytheon, Westinghouse, and Weston Electric in the past. Also noted in the catalog are the product's specifications, intended and possible functions, and price—up to 90% below original selling cost.

Special Factor: Price quote by phone or letter; authorized returns are accepted (a 15% restocking fee may be charged); orders are shipped worldwide.

H & R COMPANY

HERBACH & RADEMAN
401 E. ERIE AVE.
PHILADELPHIA, PA 19134-
   1187
215/426-1708
FAX: 215/425-8870

Catalog: free
Save: up to 50%
Pay: check, MO, MC, V
Sells: new and surplus electro-mechanical,
   robotic, and optical components
Store: same address; Monday to Friday
   8:30–4:45, Saturday 9:30–2

H & R Company (Herbach & Rademan), established in 1934, offers surplus bargains, chiefly electronics, robotics, optics, and intriguing mechanical devices. The 52-page catalog we received included capacitors, circuit breakers and interrupters, Protek and Triplett test equipment, relays, resistors, air and hydraulic cylinders, potentiometers, solenoids, transformers, and similar equipment. We also found pages of computer components, including monitors, keyboards, monitors, video and audio cables, disk drives, and power line filters.

H & R sells goods that nearly anyone, electro-mechanically inclined or not, can use: phone accessories, Pelouze scales (for kitchen, shipping room, and laboratory), heavy-duty outlet strips and surge suppressors, model trains and cars, Taylor weather instruments, 16mm projectors, goggles, robotics components, compasses, Bushnell and Tasco binoculars, educational products, cabinet slides, tool cases and cabinets, luggage carriers, magnets, flashlights, weather balloons, and reference books on computing and technical topics. Product specifications are given in the catalog, and item numbers are coded to indicate whether a product is in limited supply.

Special Factors: Satisfaction is guaranteed; price quote by phone or letter; returns with original packing materials are accepted within 30 days; minimum order is $20; orders are shipped worldwide.

MASS. ARMY & NAVY STORE

15 FORDHAM RD., DEPT.
   WBM92
BOSTON, MA 02134
617/783-1250
FAX: 617/254-6607

Catalog: free
Save: up to 40%
Pay: check, MO, MC, V, AE
Sells: government surplus apparel and accessories
Store: 895 Boylston St., Boston, and 1436 Massachusetts Ave., Cambridge, MA; also Central Surplus, 433 Massachusetts Ave., Cambridge, MA

Mass. Army & Navy offers both reproduction and genuine government surplus, presented as a fashion statement. The 52-page color catalog features camouflage clothing, Australian outback coats, pith helmets, leather pilots' caps, U.S. Air Force sunglasses, Canadian battle pants, Italian Army trenchcoats, survival manuals, and similar surplus. Mass. Army & Navy also offers casual footwear, bandannas, gloves, Lee and Levi's jeans, bomber jackets, pea coats, knapsacks, sleeping bags, air mattresses, backpacks, duffel bags, mess kits, night sticks, handcuffs, insignias and patches, and knives, among other useful items. And this firm also offers us the first bear militia we've seen—eight teddy bears in the uniforms of the U.S. Marine Corps, Army Airborne, Special Forces, and other services.

Special Factors: Price quote by phone or letter; returns are accepted for exchange, refund, or credit; orders are shipped worldwide.

RUVEL & CO., INC.

4128-30 W. BELMONT
   AVE., DEPT. WBMC
CHICAGO, IL 60641
312/286-9494

Catalog: $2
Save: up to 70%
Pay: check, MO, MC, V
Sells: government surplus
Store: same address; Monday to Friday 10–4:30, Saturday 10–2

Ruvel, established in 1965, is the source to check for good buys on government-surplus camping and field goods. U.S. Army and Navy surplus goods are featured in the 64-page catalog, including G.I. duffel bags, high-powered binoculars, leather flying jackets, mosquito netting, M65 field jackets, U.S. Marine Corps shooting jackets, dummy grenades, U.S. Army technical manuals, and similar items. Past catalogs have offered Israeli and M9 gas masks, Kevlar helmets, hammocks, snowshoes, strobe lights, mess kits, dinghies, night sticks, snowshoes, U.S. Army blankets, parade gloves, first-aid kits, and toxicological aprons.

Ruvel is noteworthy because of its low prices and extensive stock of real surplus—there are hundreds of "genuine" government-issue items available here, and many intriguing, useful surplus things that are increasingly hard to find these days.

Special Factors: Price quote by phone or letter with SASE; order promptly, since stock moves quickly.

SEE ALSO

All Electronics Corp. • surplus electrical components • *TOOLS*
Survival Supply Co. • surplus goods, survival gear and food, etc. •
  SPORTS

TOOLS, HARDWARE, ELECTRONICS, ENERGY, SAFETY, SECURITY, AND INDUSTRIAL GOODS

Materials, supplies, equipment, and services

This chapter offers the do-it-yourselfer, woodworker, hobbyist, logger, and small-time mechanic a wealth of tools and hardware, some of it at rock-bottom prices. Replacement parts for lawnmowers, trimmers, garden tractors, snowmobiles, snow throwers, blowers, go-carts, minibikes, and even plumbing and electrical systems are available from these companies. The tools run from hex wrenches and fine wood chisels to complete work benches and professional machinery, and the hardware includes hard-to-find specialty items as well as nuts and bolts.

When you're working, observe safety precautions and use goggles, dust masks, respirators, earplugs, gloves, and other protective gear as appropriate. Keep your blades sharpened and make sure your tools, hardware, and chemicals are kept out of the reach of children and pets. If you're using a chain saw, you may want to make sure that it's fitted with an approved antikickback device. Contact the manufacturer for recommendations.

For more tools and related products, see "Crafts and Hobbies," "General Merchandise," the "Maintenance" section of "Home," and "Surplus."

FIND IT FAST

ABRASIVES • **Red Hill**
LOGGING EQUIPMENT • **Bailey's, H & H, Zip Power Parts**
SAFETY GEAR • **Bailey's, Direct Safety**

ALL ELECTRONICS CORP.

P.O. BOX 567
VAN NUYS, CA 91408
800-826-5432
818/904-0524
FAX: 818/781-2653

Catalog: free
Save: up to 60%
Pay: check, MO, MC, V, Discover
Sells: surplus electronics and tools
Store: 905 S. Vermont Ave., Los Angeles,
CA; Monday to Friday 9–5, Saturday 9–4;
also 6228 Sepulveda Blvd., Van Nuys, CA;
Monday to Friday 9–5:30, Saturday 9–4

Electronics hobbyists will appreciate the 60-page catalog from All
Electronics, for the huge number of surplus parts, hardware items,
and tools.

Our latest All Electronics catalog offered semiconductors, trans-
ducers, heat sinks, sockets, cables and adapters, fans, collectors,
plugs, switches, solenoids, relays, capacitors, piezoelectric elements,
fuses, resistors, transformers, potentiometers, keyboards, computer
fans, and P.C. boards. While much of the stock is for electronics
hobbyists, the catalogs usually offer such items as telephone cords
and jacks, TV and video accessories, screwdrivers, soldering irons,
hemostats, and rechargable batteries. All Electronics, established in
1967, maintains a large inventory of stock items.

Special Factors: All parts are guaranteed to be in working order; price
quote by phone or letter with SASE; returns are accepted within 30
days; minimum order is $10; orders are shipped worldwide.

BAILEY'S, INC.

WESTERN DIVISION
44650, HWY. 101
P.O. BOX 550
LAYTONVILLE, CA 95454
707/984-6133
FAX: 707/984-8115
OR
SOUTHERN DIVISION
1520 S. HIGHLAND AVE.
P.O. BOX 9088
JACKSON, TN 38314
901/422-1300
FAX: 901/422-6118
OR
EASTERN DIVISION
3 SELINA DR.
P.O. BOX 14020
ALBANY, NY 12212
518/869-2131
FAX: 518/869-0725

Catalog: $2, year's subscription
Save: up to 70%
Pay: check, MO, MC, V
Sells: logging, woodcutting, and reforestation supplies and equipment
Store: same addresses; Monday to Friday 6 A.M.–9 P.M., Saturday 8–5 (CA); Monday to Friday 6–6, Saturday 8–5 (TN); and Monday to Friday 6–6, Saturday 8–5 (NY)

$$$$ ☎ 🍁 🇺🇸

Bailey's, one of the country's best sources for chain-saw parts and other logging gear, stocks a large number of goods everyone will find useful—boot dryers, leather conditioners, outdoor clothing, and safety gear. Savings run as high as 60% on goods in the general catalog, and even more on items offered in the sales flyers.

The 64-page catalog lists Oregon chain reels and bars for saws by Homelite, Husqvarna, McCulloch, Pioneer, and Stihl. Silvey chain grinders, spark plugs, tape measures, guide bars, bar and chain oil, bar wrenches and files, and other tools are available. Calked and heavy-duty boots by Chippewa, and Wesco are stocked, as well as climbing equipment, Duerr log splitters, Alaskan saw mills, winches, and other equipment. Bailey's is the place to call if you have questions about your chain saw. (Check for details on the firm's "Chain Saw Safety Awareness Program.") Orders are shipped promptly, the staff is quite helpful, and the toll-free order number is featured prominently in the catalog.

Campers and even urbanites will appreciate the well-priced outerwear (Filson jackets and pants, flannel shirts, rain slickers, etc.), and the first-aid kits and portable fire extinguishers. In addition, there are boot dryers, E.A.R. plugs and headset noise mufflers, and work gloves.

Special Factors: Quantity discounts are available; C.O.D. orders are accepted; orders are shipped worldwide.

THE BEVERS

P.O. BOX 12
WILLS POINT, TX 75169-
  0012
214/272-8370

Catalog: $2, refundable
Save: up to 50%
Pay: check, MO, MC, V
Sells: hardware and woodworking parts
Store: mail order only

$$$ ☎ 🇺🇸

The Bevers have been selling hardware and parts for household use and crafts projects since 1977. This is an excellent source for the hobbyist and do-it-yourselfer, and the Bevers are honest and committed to offering the best possible values.

The 44-page catalog offers goods for woodworking, construction, and household repairs: steel and brass wood screws with round and flat heads, lock and flat washers, a full range of eye bolts and squared screw hooks, Tap-Lok threads, machine screws with a choice of head styles, hex heads and carriage bolts, cotter pins, brass-plated hinges, picture hangers, lag screws, countersinks, doweling drill bits, clamps, and rotary and sandpaper drums for drills. There's a good selection of wooden parts for making toys and repairing furniture. including wood balls, toy wheels, Shaker pegs, peg boards, game pieces, golf tees, screw-hole buttons, knobs and pulls, and turned finials and spindles. The Bevers carry a number of hard-to-find items, so consult the catalog if you're having trouble locating a special screw or bolt.

Special Factor: Price quote by letter with SASE on quantity orders.

CAMELOT ENTERPRISES

P.O. BOX 65, DEPT. W
BRISTOL, WI 53104-0065
414/857-2695

Catalog: $1, refundable
Save: up to 60%
Pay: check, MO, MC, V
Sells: fasteners, tools, and hardware
Store: 8234 199 Ave., Bristol, WI; hours by
appointment only

$$$ ☎ ▄▄▄

Camelot, founded in 1983, sells "quality fasteners, hardware, and tools direct to the craftsman" at savings of up to 60%, through a 14-page catalog. Camelot carries a full range of nuts (hex, K-lock, wing, stop, etc.), bolts (hex-head, machine, carriage), screws (wood, lag, drywall, machine), washers, thread fittings, cotter pins, anchors, and other hardware. The tools include screwdrivers, punches, and other hand and power tools by Astro, Camelot, Chicago Tool, Continental, Ingersoll Rand, Lisle, Makita, Milton, Milwaukee, Rockford, and Truecraft, among others. Shop welders, Excalibur fastener sets, Gesipa pop rivets, and Camelot's own twist drills and fasteners are also sold at competitive prices.

Camelot is offering readers of this book a 5% discount on orders of $50 or more (excluding shipping and sales tax). Please identify yourself as a reader when you order. This WBMC reader discount expires February 1, 1993.

Special Factors: Satisfaction is guaranteed; price quote by phone or letter; returns are accepted within 10 days for replacement, refund, or credit; no collect calls are accepted.

DIRECT SAFETY COMPANY

7815 S. 46TH ST.
PHOENIX, AZ 85044
602/968-7009

Catalog: free
Save: up to 30%
Pay: check, MO, MC, V, AE
Sells: industrial safety equipment
Store: mail order only

$$$ ☎

Direct Safety sells a wide range of goods that are used routinely by hobbyists and in all types of industries. We've found gloves here priced 25% less here than comparable models sold elsewhere, quantity discounts are available.

Direct Safety offers protective gloves designed to resist solvents, acids, oils, knife cuts, heat, and PCBs. There are sulfur-free gloves, ideal for those who are allergic to natural rubber, and PVC gloves treated with a bacteria-controlling agent that helps to prevent the development of contact dermatitis in the wearer. A large selection of safety glasses and goggles, respirators, and protective head gear is offered. At least a dozen first-aid kits are available, as well as emergency showers and eyewash stations, fire extinguishers, flammable-materials containers and cabinets, security and emergency lights, voltage testers and electrical safety equipment, smoke detectors, hand-held metal detectors, emergency pilons and other vehicle safety equipment, antislip floor strips and coatings, and hazardous materials management gear. Monitors that measure the level of carbon monoxide in your home and car and devices that detect microwave leakage, radiation, pH levels, and blood alcohol levels (breath analyzers) are all available.

Special Factors: Satisfaction is guaranteed; quantity discounts are available; price quote by phone or letter with SASE; returns are accepted (a 15% restocking fee may be charged).

H & H MANUFACTURING & SUPPLY CO.

P.O. BOX 692
SELMA, AL 36701-0692
205/872-6067

Catalog: free
Save: up to 50%
Pay: check or MO
Sells: chain-saw parts and logging equipment
Store: 111 Hwy. 80 E., Selma, AL; Monday to Friday 7–5, Wednesday 8–12 noon

$$ ❦

H & H Manufacturing runs a mail-order firm known as "Saw Chain" that's been offering savings of up to 50% on saw chain and other logging needs since 1965. You can buy saw chain, guide bars, and sprockets here, for chain saws by Craftsman, John Deere, Echo, Homelite, Husqvarna, Jonsered, Lombard, McCulloch, Olympic, Pioneer, Poulan, Remington, Stihl, and other firms. The chain is sold in a range of pitches and gauges, and both gear-drive and direct-drive sprockets are stocked to fit all models. Swedish double-cut files, Esco rigging products, Windsor and Tilton saw chain and bars, wire rope, logging chokers, slings, and other logging equipment is also available. Remember to give all requested information when ordering chain and sprockets—make and model, chain pitch, gauge, number of drive links, type of bar, and length.

Special Factors: Price quote by phone or letter with SASE; chains, bars, files, and sprockets are guaranteed to last as long as or longer than any other make; returns are accepted for replacement; C.O.D. orders are accepted.

HARBOR FREIGHT TOOLS

3491 MISSION OAKS BLVD.
P.O. BOX 6010
CAMARILLO, CA 93011
800-423-2567
FAX: 805/388-0760

Catalog: free
Save: up to 80%
Pay: check, MO, MC, V, AE, Discover, Optima
Sells: tools, hardware, industrial equipment, machinery
Store: same address; also Bakersfield, Camarillo, Escondido, Fresno, Herperia, Lancaster, Ridgecrest, Salinas, Santa Maria, Stockton, and Visalia, CA, and Lexington, KY

Great prices can be found in Harbor Freight Tools' catalog, which offers toolbox necessities at savings of up to 80% on list and comparable retail. Specials are run frequently, making this a valuable source for the hobbyist, do-it-yourselfer, and professional shop.

Name-brand tools, machinery, and equipment are sold here at discount prices. Typical offerings from Harbor Freight Tools include air tools, hand tools, compressors, automotive tools, shop equipment, storehouses, power tools, drill bits, metal-working machinery, welding equipment, woodworking machines and accessories, engines, generators, pumps, safety equipment, and even home and garden tools and supplies.

Special Factor: Shipping is included on orders over $50.

MANUFACTURER'S SUPPLY

**P.O. BOX 167-WBMC-92
DORCHESTER, WI 54425-
0167
800-826-8563**

Catalog: free
Save: up to 50%
Pay: check, MO, MC, V
Sells: replacement parts for lawnmowers,
snowmobiles, chain saws, etc.
Store: mail order only

$$$ ☎ ◆ ▀

All machines give out eventually, but if you're handy, you can save a tidy sum on the cost of professional repairs by doing them yourself. Manufacturer's Supply is your source for the parts you'll need to get all kinds of things functioning again, and the prices here are up to 50% below list or comparable retail, which saves you yet more money.

Consult the 168-page bible from Manufacturer's for parts for chain saws, lawnmowers, motorcycles, snowmobiles, three-wheel vehicles, snow throwers, trimmers, trailers, and rototillers. There are sprockets and nose assemblies, chains, grinders, files, air filters, T-wrenches, starter springs, carburetor parts, and guide bars (for dozens of saw brands). Parts for standard and riding lawnmowers are stocked, as well as semi-pneumatic tires for mowers and shopping carts, wheelbarrows, and hand trucks.

Wheels, hubs, bearing kits, roller chains, sprockets, clutches, belts, and other goods are offered, for trailers, minibikes, go-carts, riding mowers, snow throwers, rototillers, garden tractors, and three-wheelers. The snowmobile parts include everything from lubricants to windshields—carburetors, fuel filters, cleats, tracks, pistons, gaskets, fan belts, suspension springs, and engines, among other items. Also available are wood-chopping tools, Woodchuck wood-burning furnaces, and Magic Heat air circulators and chimney cleaning brushes.

Special Factors: Price quote by phone or letter with SASE; authorized, unused returns are accepted within 30 days (a 20% restocking fee may be charged); minimum order is $10; C.O.D. orders are accepted.

MEISEL HARDWARE SPECIALTIES

P.O. BOX 70WM
MOUND, MN 55364
800-441-9870

Catalog: $1
Save: up to 40%
Pay: check, MO, MC, V
Sells: hardware, wood crafts parts and plans
Store: 4310 Shoreline Dr., Spring Park, MN; Monday to Friday 9–6, Saturday 9–5

Woodworkers, toy makers, and creative souls should appreciate this catalog of plans and project ingredients. Meisel offers a number of items we haven't seen in other catalogs, and prices of things like lamp harps, wood screws, and foam brushes are up to 40% below the going rate.

The 72-page catalog shows woodworking plans for toys, vehicles, lamps, playground equipment, yard ornaments, useful things for the home, kitchen projects, and dollhouses. There are parts and supplies for many projects, including ten sizes of wooden wheels, pegs and dowels, plastic eyes, turned spindles and posts, finials, wood furniture knobs, cork sheets, box hinges, clock movements and parts, push-button music boxes, and picture-hanging hardware. We found a number of items needed for projects languishing on our workshop shelves: small brass escutcheons and box corners, miniature box hasps, hardware for knock-down furniture, bread box tambour, and brass candle cups.

The catalog is also a good source for fix-up materials—turned spindles and legs for chairs and small tables, screw-hole buttons and furniture knobs, casters, magnetic cabinet catches, furniture glides, and picture frame wire are all available.

Special Factors: Satisfaction is guaranteed; returns are accepted for exchange, refund, or credit; minimum order is $15.

NORTHERN HYDRAULICS, INC.

■■■■■■

P.O. BOX 1499, DEPT.
  68075
BURNSVILLE, MN 55337
800-533-5545
612/894-8310
FAX: 612/894-0083

Catalog: free
Save: up to 50%
Pay: check, MO, MC, V, Discover
Sells: hydraulics, logging equipment, and
  machine parts
Store: Marietta and Norcross, GA;
  Burnsville, Fridley, Maplewood, Rochester,
  and Rogers, MN; Charlotte, Greensboro,
  Matthew, and Raleigh, NC; Greenville, SC;
  and Richmond, VA

$$$ ☎ ♦

Northern Hydraulics makes it easy to save up to 50% on hydraulics, gas and electric engines, logging equipment, trailer parts, air tools and compressors, winches, hand tools, farm and garden equipment, and much more. The 136-page catalog offers an enormous selection of log splitters, wedges, Homelite and McCulloch chain saws, Oregon chain and bars, files, and other logging gear. The hydraulic pumps include lines by J.S. Barnes and Parker, and there are Orbmark motors, motor valves, hydraulic tanks, strainers, hoses, and other parts and equipment. Gas engines for use with log splitters, lawn and riding mowers, rototillers, and other machines are stocked, including vertical- and horizontal-shaft models by Briggs & Stratton, Kohler, Onan, and Tecumseh. Air compressors and related equipment by American IMC and Campbell Hausfeld are offered, as well as air tools from Chicago Pneumatic, Ingersoll-Rand, and other firms.

Northern Hydraulics also sells go-cart parts and accessories, minibike parts, ATV tires and wheels, halogen tractor lamps, sandblasting equipment, pressure washers, air compressors, Aqua Siphon water heaters, propane tanks, and small hand tools. The farm and garden equipment includes filament trimmers, cultivators, NorTrac tractors, garden carts, agricultural pumps, mower tires, blowers, sprayers, tillers, and much more. And Dickies overalls, Northlake boots, and other useful items are also offered.

Special Factors: Price quote by phone or letter with SASE; authorized returns are accepted for exchange, refund, or credit (a 15% restocking fee may be charged); minimum order is $10.

RED HILL CORPORATION

P.O. BOX 4234
122 BALTIMORE ST.
GETTYSBURG, PA 17325
800-822-4003
717/337-1419
FAX: 717/337-3936

Catalog: free
Save: up to 50%
Pay: check, MO, MC, V
Sells: abrasives
Store: Chuck's Sporting Goods, 39 W. York
St., Biglerville, PA

$$$ ☎ 🍁 ▆

Red Hill's business is the rough stuff that gets things smooth—abrasives. The company, which was founded in 1978, offers a wide range of abrasives and refinishing products at prices up to 50% below those you'll pay at the hardware store.

The 12-page catalog includes belts (aluminum oxide on cloth backing) in 11 sizes, plain-back and pressure-sensitive sanding disks, paper disks for orbital sanders, sheets, sleeve and drums, rolls, and foam-core sanding blocks. In addition, the catalog we reviewed offered sanding pads for "jitterbug" sanders, RASKO's paper-backed steel wool sheets (to mount on sanders, for rubbing work), abrasive cords and tapes (for getting into carvings and crevices), tack cloths, and a stick for cleaning sanding belts when the grit gets clogged—a money saver in itself. And Red Hill carries glue guns, which home advice authority Martha Stewart believes will be the big appliance of the 1990s.

Special Factors: Price quote by phone or letter; quantity discounts are available; minimum order is $25; orders are shipped worldwide.

TOOLS ON SALE

**SEVEN CORNERS ACE
HARDWARE, INC.
216 W. SEVENTH ST.
ST. PAUL, MN 55102
800-328-0457
FAX: 612/224-8263**

Catalog: free
Save: up to 50%
Pay: check, MO, MC, V, AE, Discover
Sells: tools for contractors, masons, and woodworkers
Store: same address; Monday to Friday 7–5:30, Saturday 7–1

 $$$ ☎ ♦ ▆

If you can't get to St. Paul to visit Seven Corners Ace Hardware, where there are "over 35,000 items on the floor," you can do business with the firm's mail-order division, Tools on Sale. The parent company was founded in 1933, and specializes in tools for contractors and masons.

The Tools on Sale catalog is one of the last great freebies in America—960 pages of name-brand tools, at discounts of up to 50%. You'll find everything from air compressors to work benches here, from manufacturers that include Black & Decker (Elu), Bosch, Delta, Dremel, Freud, Hitachi, Jet, Jorgensen, Leigh, Makita, Milwaukee, Porter-Cable, Ryobi, Senco, and Skil, among others. If you're looking for stair templets, demolition hammers, moisture meters, water stones, mechanics' cabinets, or just want to *see* 29 pages of construction aprons and nail bags, look no farther. And there are ten pages of books and manuals on everything from making a hobbyhorse to building a home. Free freight on orders shipped to the U.S. (except Alaska and Hawaii) is an added bonus.

Special Factors: Price quote by phone or letter with SASE; shipping is included on orders shipped within the contiguous U.S.; authorized returns are accepted for exchange, refund, or credit (a 15% restocking fee may be charged); orders are shipped worldwide.

TREND-LINES, INC.

Catalog: $1
Save: up to 50%
Pay: check, MO, MC, V, AE, Discover
Sells: tools and hardware
Store: same address; call for hours

WOODWORKERS
WAREHOUSE OUTLET
375 BEACHAM ST.
CHELSEA, MA 02150
617/884-8951

$$ ☎ ♦

Trend-lines, which has been in business since 1981, markets complete lines of tools and a selection of hardware for the professional woodworker at savings of up to 50%. The 72-page color catalog offers a wide range of woodworking tools, including saws (jig, miter, band, reciprocating, scroll, radial-arm, and chain); drills, routers, trimmers, planers, jointers, sanders, nibblers, polishers, grinders, bits, blades, and other accessories. AEG, Black & Decker, Delta, Freud, Hitachi, Makita, Milwaukee, Porter-Cable, Ryobi, Shopcraft, Skil, and other popular names are represented. The catalog also shows full lines of parts and supplies, such as abrasives (sheets, belts, and disks), lubricants, adhesives, paste stains and varnishes, milk-based paint, wood plugs and buttons, Shaker pegs, dowels, toy wheels, and a number of dollhouse kits, as well as hand tools and cabinetry hardware. Woodworking manuals, plans, and instructive manuals are also offered.

We've found helpful and unusual items in the Trend-lines catalogs, including basswood shelf brackets in several styles, lint-free polishing cloth by the 90′ roll, wood moisture meters, ponyband clamps, corner chisels, and oak bath fixtures.

Special Factors: Satisfaction is guaranteed; returns (except custom-made or cut-to-size items) are accepted within 30 days for exchange, refund, or credit; minimum order is $20 with credit cards.

TURNKEY MATERIAL HANDLING CO.

P.O. BOX 1050
TONAWANDA, NY 14151-
1050
800-828-7540

Catalog: free
Save: up to 50%
Pay: check, MO, MC, V, AE
Sells: commercial and industrial furnishings,
storage units, etc.
Store: mail order only

$$$ ☎ ♦ ▤

Turnkey's line is geared for industrial and commercial applications, but there are many home uses for the sturdy storage units and other equipment sold here. Turnkey has been doing business since 1946, and publishes a 116-page catalog that features commercial shelving and metal storage bins in a huge selection of sizes and styles. You'll find everything from small parts bins ideal for hardware storage to 108-drawer steel wall cabinets, plus plastic bin-and-frame arrangements—all of which are appropriate for home use. The catalog also shows mats and runners, work benches, storage cabinets, stainless-steel rolling carts, office and folding chairs, suspension files, lockers, flat and roll files, moving pads, canvas tarps, security gates, hoists, ceiling fans, hand trucks, rolling ladders, trash cans, hydraulic lifts, first-aid kits and protective gear, power-failure lights, pumps, and many other product lines.

Special Factors: Satisfaction is guaranteed; price quote by phone or letter with SASE; authorized returns (except custom-made items) are accepted (a 20% restocking fee may be charged); minimum order is $25.

WHOLE EARTH ACCESS

822 ANTHONY ST.
BERKELEY, CA 94710
800-829-6300

Catalog: free
Save: up to 40%
Pay: check, MO, MC, V
Sells: hand and power tools and equipment
Store: same address; also Concord, San
Francisco, San Mateo, and San Rafael, CA

$$ ☎

Whole Earth Access was established in 1969 and offers woodworking tools and equipment at savings of up to 40% on list, with a "lowest prices nationwide" guarantee. See the catalog for details on the sales policy, and 48 pages of hand and power tools for woodworking—saws and sanders of all types, drills, routers, planers, and related machines. The brands include AEG, Black & Decker, Bosch, Clifton, Delta, Freud, Hitachi, Jorgensen, Makita, Milwaukee, Panasonic, Norton (abrasives), Porter-Cable, Ryobi, and Skil, among others. Whole Earth Access sells Emglo air compressors, surveying equipment by David White Instruments, Leigh dovetailing jigs, Bosch finish nailers, Lamello hand joining machines, Willson safety products, and Japanese woodworking tools, among other specialty items. You can order from the catalog, or call or write for price quotes on particular models.

Special Factors: Price quote by phone or letter with SASE; authorized returns are accepted.

WOODWORKER'S SUPPLY, INC.

5604 ALAMEDA PL. N.E.
ALBUQUERQUE, NM
  87113
800-645-9282
505/821-0500
FAX: 505/821-7331

Catalog: $2 (see text)
Save: up to 30%
Pay: check, MO, MC, V
Sells: woodworking tools and equipment
Store: same address; Monday to Friday
  8–5:30, Saturday 9–1

$$$

Woodworker's Supply publishes a 112-page, full-color catalog of woodworking tools and hardware, priced up to 30% below comparable goods sold elsewhere. The company has been in business since 1972, and will send you two years of catalogs for the $2 subscription fee.

   The catalog we reviewed offered basics from abrasives to rolling table shapers, as well as a number of hard-to-find items. We found drills (including cordless models), power screwdrivers, routers, saws (circular, jig, orbital, table, band, etc.), sanders (finish, belt, orbital, etc.), laminate trimmers, heat guns, biscuit joiners, power planes, grinders, jointers, drill presses, shapers, and other tools. The manufacturers represented include Bosch, Delta, Freud, Gerstner, Glit,

Jorgensen, Porter-Cable, Ryobi, Sioux, Skil, and Woodtek, among others. Drawer slides by Alfit, Delta, and Knape & Vogt are carried, as well as Grass and Blum hinges, coated-wire fixtures for custom kitchen cabinets, furniture and cabinet levelers, cassette storage tracks, halogen canister lights, wood project parts, veneers, butcher block, locks and latches, glue scrapers and injectors, steel wool-backed sheets for finish sanders, Preserve nontoxic wood finish, Haas knock-down joint fasteners, and a Japanese miter square. Like the best of such catalogs, Woodworker's Supply can give you as many ideas for new projects as it provides solutions to old woodworking problems.

Special Factors: Satisfaction is guaranteed; price quote by phone or letter; returns are accepted; minimum order is $5 ($25 to Canada); orders are shipped worldwide.

ZIP POWER PARTS, INC.

P.O. BOX 10308
ERIE, PA 16514-0308
800-824-8521
FAX: 814/898-0275

Catalog: free
Save: up to 45%
Pay: check, MO, MC, V
Sells: parts for chain saws, lawnmowers, snowmobiles, etc.
Store: 2008 E. 33rd St., Erie, PA; Monday to Friday 8–5, Saturday 9–1

$$$ ☎ ▓

If you own a chain saw, Zip Power Parts may be an old friend. In business since 1962, Zip Power Parts is one of the country's best sources for chain-saw parts, and it also sells other machinery components and outdoor power equipment.

The 32-page catalog shows chain saws by Homelite, Poulan, and Pro-Kut, as well as saw chain, bars, bar guards, and sprockets to fit all makes and models of chain saws. Saw chain grinders and chain saw repair parts, and small engine parts are all available, and Brush cutters, chain saws, table saws, and band saws are also stocked. There are shop tools for filing and grinding, wedges, lubricants, "mini-mills," hand tools, manuals, safety clothing and equipment, and woodcutting accessories. Additional parts for lawnmowers—mufflers, air filters, blades, starter rope and handles, fuel lines and filters, points, condensers, electronic ignitions, etc.—are listed in the catalog.

Special Factors: All products are guaranteed against defects in materials and workmanship; price quote by phone or letter; returns are accepted; C.O.D. orders are accepted; orders are shipped worldwide.

SEE ALSO

Alfax Wholesale Furniture • institutional furnishings and fixtures • *OFFICE*

American Science & Surplus • surplus tools, electronics, etc. • *SURPLUS*

Arctic Glass & Window Outlet • replacement patio door panes and passive solar panels • *HOME: MAINTENANCE*

Bennett Brothers, Inc. • home-security equipment • *GENERAL MERCHANDISE*

Business & Institutional Furniture Company • institutional furnishings and fixtures • *OFFICE*

Cahall's Department Store • work clothing and rugged footwear • *CLOTHING*

Central Tractor Farm & Family Center • shop and power tools, chain saws, welding equipment • *FARM*

Cherry Tree Toys, Inc. • wooden toy parts, hardware, etc. • *CRAFTS*

CISCO • professional power tools • *HOME: MAINTENANCE*

Clothcrafters, Inc. • shop aprons, woodpile covers, and tool holders • *GENERAL MERCHANDISE*

A Cook's Wares • Taylor Woodcraft work tables • *HOME: KITCHEN*

Crutchfield Corporation • security systems for car and home • *APPLIANCES*

Cycle Goods Corp. • bicycle repair tools • *SPORTS*

Defender Industries, Inc. • wood treatment products, marine hardware • *AUTO*

E.T. Supply • wrenches, socket sets, pliers, etc. • *SURPLUS*

Frank Eastern Co. • industrial and institutional supplies and furnishings • *OFFICE*

Goldberg's Marine Distributors • wood treatment products, marine hardware • *AUTO*

H & R Company • electrical and electronic components • *SURPLUS*

Metropolitan Music Co. • tools and supplies for making musical instruments • *MUSIC*

Okun Bros. Shoes • work and safety footwear • *CLOTHING: FOOTWEAR*

Oreck Corp. • beam flashlights and power-failure lights • *APPLIANCES*

S & S Sound City • surveillance equipment • *APPLIANCES*
Shuttercraft • shutter-hanging hardware • *HOME: MAINTENANCE*
Staples, Inc. • Falcon fire extinguishers • *OFFICE*
Todd Uniform, Inc. • work clothing and footwear for men and women •
   CLOTHING
WearGuard Corp. • protective gloves, tool kits, shop aprons, etc. •
   CLOTHING
Workmen's Garment Co. • work clothing and gloves • *CLOTHING*

TOYS AND GAMES

Juvenile and adult diversions

This isn't a large chapter, thanks to the fact that it's a seller's market and the large discount firms have no interest in entering the mail-order field (we know, we've asked them). We'll continue to search for firms that sell well-priced playthings, but at the same time we think it makes sense for parents to sit down with their children and talk about the items on their gift lists. There are ways of discussing the manipulative effects of advertising without turning your children into cynics or crushing the holiday spirit. You might be aided by *Zillions* (formerly known as *Penny Power*), published by Consumers Union. A "Consumer Reports for Kids," it's an ad-free guide to products, money management, and smart buying for shoppers from 8 to 13 years old. Help educate the next generation— buy a young friend a subscription. A year (six issues) costs $13.95 and can be ordered from Zillions, Subscription Dept., Box 51777, Boulder, CO 80322-0777. Good luck!

ACME PREMIUM SUPPLY CORP.

Catalog: free
Save: up to 50%
Pay: check, MO, MC, V
Sells: toys, novelties, and premium goods
Store: mail order only

DEPT. WBM
4100 FOREST PARK BLVD.
ST. LOUIS, MO 63108-
  2899
800-325-7888, EXT. 23
314/531-8880, EXT. 23
FAX: 314/531-2106

We've listed Acme Premium in this chapter because so much of what it offers is toys, games, and novelties. The 136-page color catalog is bursting with stuffed animals, balloons, games, and other diversions, but please note that Acme's targeted customers are businesses, clubs, churches, and carnivals; hence, the $100 minimum order. Acme also states that its merchandise "is not intended for use by children under 5 years of age."

We found a number of items everyone can use, at very good prices—glass and plastic tumblers, can openers, flashlights, and pens and pencils, for example. If you're throwing a party or organizing a bazaar, see the catalog for the wide selection of dart games, ball toss and hoop game equipment, bingo supplies and equipment, and similar goods. Imprinting is offered on T-shirts and windbreakers, visors, balloons, buttons, key rings, mugs, pens, and pencils. And of course, there are all kinds of stuffed toys: the entire Simpson menagerie, Mickey Mouse, the Noid from Pizza Hut, polka-dotted elephants, a gold-horned unicorn, Teenage Mutant Ninja Turtles, and a lavender seahorse, to name just a few. Complete details on the sales policy are given in the catalog.

Special Factors: Authorized returns are accepted (a restocking fee may be charged); minimum order is $100; orders are shipped worldwide.

BARON/BARCLAY BRIDGE SUPPLIES

3600 CHAMBERLAIN LANE, SUITE 230 LOUISVILLE, KY 40241-1989
800-274-2221
502/426-0410

Catalog: free
Save: up to 40% (see text)
Pay: check, MO, MC, V
Sells: playing and teaching materials for bridge
Store: mail order only

$$ ☎ ♦

Baron/Barclay Bridge Supplies carries materials and equipment for bridge players, from novices to old hands. We've listed the firm because it stocks hundreds of books on bridge, and sells them at quantity discounts of up to 25%. (Sale items are marked up to 40% below original selling prices.) Baron/Barclay has been in business since 1973, and specializes in teachers' materials.

Over half of the 44-page catalog is devoted to books—teaching manuals and texts, books on strategy and bidding, bridge history and reference texts, and complete courses in bridge. Videotapes and instructional software are also available, as well as playing cards, scoring cards and club forms, recap sheets, and a variety of gifts and equipment—bridge-motif china, magnetic card sets, timers, bumper stickers, pens and pencils, polo shirts, and even an electric card shuffler. You can also order subscriptions to *Bridge World* and other bridge-related magazines through Baron/Barclay's catalog.

Special Factors: Satisfaction is guaranteed; quantity discounts are available; returns are accepted within 10 days for exchange, refund, or credit (videotapes and software for exchange only); C.O.D. orders are accepted; orders are shipped worldwide.

PARADISE PRODUCTS, INC.

DEPT. WBM
P.O. BOX 568
EL CERRITO, CA 94530-
0568
800-227-1092

Catalog: $2
Save: up to 50%
Pay: check, MO, MC, V
Sells: party paraphernalia
Store: mail order only

$$ ☎ ◆

Paradise Products has been sponsoring bashes, wingdings, and festive events since 1952, when it began selling party products by mail. The 88-page catalog is a must-see for anyone throwing a theme event. The firm sells materials and supplies for over 120 different kinds of events, including Oktoberfest, the 50s, Roaring 20s, St. Patrick's Day, fiestas, "Las Vegas Night," Hawaiian luaus, pirate parties, Super Bowl celebrations, and July Fourth parties. Balloons, streamers, tissue balls and bells, party hats, banquet table coverings, crepe paper by the roll, pennants, garlands, and novelties are among the items available. Paradise's prices are as much as 50% below those charged by other party-supply stores.

Special Factors: Goods are guaranteed to be as represented in the catalog; shipments are guaranteed to arrive in time for the party date specified (terms are stated in catalog); minimum order is $30.

LA PIÑATA

NO. 2 PATIO MARKET,
OLD TOWN
ALBUQUERQUE, NM
87104
505/242-2400

Brochure: $1 or SASE
Save: up to 30%
Pay: check, MO, MC, V
Sells: piñatas and paper flowers
Store: same address; Monday to Saturday 10:30–5, Sunday 12–5 (winter); Monday to Saturday 9:30–9, Sunday 12–5 (summer)

$$ ☎ ◆

La Piñata is a marvelous source for piñatas, the hollow papier-mâché animals and characters that are traditionally filled with candy and broken by a blindfolded party guest. Prices here are low, and many of the items cost less than $10. The stock includes piñatas in the shapes of superheroes like Batman and Superman, Sesame Street characters, Spiderman, pumpkins, Santa, snowmen, witches, stars, reindeer, and other seasonal characters. And there are all sorts of animals, including bears, burros, cats, elephants, unicorns, frogs, pigs, kangaroos, and penguins. Most of the piñatas are offered in three sizes. La Piñata, which has been in business since 1955, also carries inexpensive, colorful paper flowers in several sizes.

La Piñata is offering readers a discount of 10% on all orders of piñatas only. Be sure to identify yourself as a WBMC reader when you order, and deduct the discount from the cost of the goods only. This WBMC reader discount expires February 1, 1993.

Special Factors: Price quote by phone or letter; minimum order is $10; C.O.D. orders are accepted.

SEE ALSO

American Science & Surplus • educational materials for elementary-grade sciences • *SURPLUS*

Bart's Water Ski Center, Inc. • water tubes and other inflatables • *SPORTS*

Bennett Brothers, Inc. • small selection of children's toys, board games, and cards • *GENERAL MERCHANDISE*

Betty Crocker Enterprises • educational toys, games, and puzzles • *GENERAL MERCHANDISE*

The Bevers • wooden wheels, balls, and other components for toy making • *TOOLS*

Butternut Books • children's books • *BOOKS*

Cherry Tree Toys, Inc. • wooden toy kits, parts, and plans • *CRAFTS*

Dover Publications, Inc. • cut-and-assemble projects, stickers, dioramas, etc. • *BOOKS*

A. Feibusch Corporation • zippers for doll clothing • *CRAFTS*

Gohn Bros. • "Dutch blitz" card game • *CLOTHING*

Home-Sew • dolls' eyes • *CRAFTS*

House of Onyx • Mexican onyx chess sets and boards • *JEWELRY*

D. MacGillivray & Coy. • woolen stuffed toys • *CRAFTS*

Meisel Hardware Specialties • wooden wheels and other toy parts, toy plans • *TOOLS*

The Natural Baby Co., Inc. • classical toys, games, furniture, and books • CLOTHING: MOTHER AND CHILD

Newark Dressmaker Supply, Inc. • supplies for making dolls and toys • CRAFTS

The Paper Wholesaler • party supplies • GENERAL MERCHANDISE

Pueblo to People • small selection toys and dolls from Central and South America • GENERAL MERCHANDISE

South Bound Millworks • jointed wooden bears • HOME: DECOR

R.C. Steele Co. • trivia game for dog lovers, dog-breed playing cards, etc. • ANIMAL

Taylor's Cutaways and Stuff • kits and patterns for making dolls and toys • CRAFTS

Tower Hobbies • radio-controlled vehicles • CRAFTS

Woodworker's Supply of New Mexico • wooden toy parts, plans, and dollhouse plans • TOOLS

TRAVEL

___

The business of getting from point A to point B seems simple enough, until you try to do it cheaply. But there are all kinds of ways to save on travel, depending upon the nature of the traveler and the trip. This chapter includes listings of information sources, discount travel brokers, money-saving accommodations, and travel-related services. In addition to these sources, you might consider checking your list of business and personal affiliations, so see whether membership in a professional organization, union, buying club, or other group entitles you to travel discounts and services. If you're interested in joining a buying club, shop for one with the best package of benefits for services you think you'll use during the year of membership. Check the listings in "General Merchandise" for the names of several clubs. And look for new luggage and travel gear among the companies listed in "Leather Goods."

CONSOLIDATORS/BUCKET SHOPS

Consolidators, also known as bucket shops, are travel wholesalers who buy cruise slots, blocks of rooms, and plane seats from airlines, hotels, and charter agents. They then resell them for less than the hotels, airlines, or often the charter operators themselves are willing to accept for individual tickets or rooms. Travel agents are big customers of consolidators, but individuals may buy from them too, which will often save them 20% to 30% on APEX fares and much more on full economy tickets.

Unitravel Corporation, one of the oldest consolidators in the business, books flights in the U.S. and Europe and sells directly to individuals. Contact Unitravel about a month before you anticipate traveling, and allow for some uncertainty, since tickets might not be available until shortly before the day of departure. Call 800-325-2222 or 314/727-8888 for more information.

Council Charter, another consolidator, enjoys an excellent reputation; it's been in business for over 40 years, and is affiliated with the Council on International Educational Exchange, a not-for-profit travel concern. For information on Council Charter's current offerings, call 800-223-7402 or 212/661-0311.

Nouvelle Frontiers is an off-price travel broker that sells to consumers as well as to travel agencies. For information, call 212/764-6494, or 415/781-4480. You can also try *Destinations Unlimited,* at 212/980-8220, and *European-American Travel,* at 800-848-6789, or 202/789-2255.

DISCOUNT TRAVEL AGENTS

Simple common sense tells you that commissions pegged to the selling price of a ticket may be something of a disincentive to getting travel agents to find you the lowest fare. On top of this problem is the real difficulty in getting "hard" information in a market that literally changes overnight, every night. Inexperienced and undermotivated travel agents can be impaired on both counts, for which you pay the price.

You can improve the odds of getting the lowest rate yourself by pricing your trip with at least three travel agents and asking for the cheapest fare. Make sure you know just what you're buying *before* you buy it. Ask for a statement of the agency's cancellation policy, and get it in writing if the travel agent is booking your trip through a tour operator.

The problems with agents make *Travel World* (also known as *Farefinders*) worth checking before your next trip. This travel agency is run by Annette Forest, who's been in the business for over a decade and uses a wide range of information sources to find the lowest fares. Travel World will search for the best rates on travel by air, train, or ship, as well as cruises and tours to any destination worldwide. You can buy your tickets and book reservations through Travel World, but it's optional—there's no obligation for the fare-finding services. Ms. Forest also teaches hands-on college classes for aspiring travel agents at Travel World, and invites inquiries on her course. Write to Travel World, 8621 Wilshire Blvd., Beverly Hills, CA 90211, or call 213/652-6305 for information.

If you're just interested in the best price on a cruise, give *Cruises Worldwide* a call. This travel agency will send you a printout of last—minute opportunities (from three-day getaways to 14 days on the high seas), as well as cruises scheduled up to a year from now. Discounts run from 5% to 50% on the published rates, and major lines are well represented—Carnival Princess, and Royal Viking were among those we saw in the listing we received. For information or the current printout, call 800-6-CRUISE, fax 714/975-1211, or write to Cruises Worldwide, 16585 Von Karman, Irvine, CA 92714.

STANDBY TRAVEL

If you can be flexible in your plans, consider the world of standby travel. It really is a last-minute affair, but it can be the cheapest way to fly—under $200 each way to Europe, at this writing.

Airhitch is an old friend among travelers who favor 11th-hour departures. The firm has offices in several large cities, but does most of its business by mail. You first phone for information, have a registration form sent to you, apply for the desired dates or range, send in a fee of $25, and then start calling for availability three days before your desired departure dates. The procedure is involved, but it works. The friendly phone system at Airhitch has been programmed to dispense all the details of the standby program. Make sure you have pen and paper at hand before calling 800-372-1234, or 212/864-2000.

Access International also books standby flights from New York to points in Europe. It works on a registration/fee basis, and publishes a brochure that describes the services. Call 212/333-7280 for information.

CONNECTIONS

Most travelers insist on the lowest possible prices for airline tickets, but squander comparatively large sums on the last leg of the journey—the trip from the airport to the hotel. Avoid this pitfall with the help of *Crampton's International Airport Transit Guide,* which lists schedules and rates of taxis, car services, trains, buses, car-rental agencies, and other connections from airports worldwide to nearby cities. The pocket-sized guide costs under $5, is updated yearly, and is sold by The Complete Traveller Bookstore (see "Other Resources," following). You may also contact the publisher, Salk International Travel Premiums, Inc., at P.O. Box 1388, Sunset Beach, CA 90742, or 213/592-3315, for more information.

EDUCATIONAL TRAVEL

Combining education with travel isn't a new concept, but *Elderhostel* brings it to a specific group—those 60 and over—and does it so successfully that it's created a loyal group of followers who plan their travel around Elderhostel programs. The organization was founded in 1981 and currently offers programs in hundreds of colleges in the U.S., Canada, and overseas—from Australia to West Germany. There are study cruises, "RV" programs for hostelers who are bringing their own accommodations (tent or RV), and "Intensive Studies" programs that offer more in-depth courses, as well as the popular courses held on campuses around the country. Previous catalogs have offered programs as diverse as "Ikebana: A Japanese Art" at South Georgia College, "The Role of the U.S. Intelligence in a Democracy" at Southern Utah University, "The Genius of Schubert," at the Peabody Institute of Johns Hopkins University in Maryland, and "Cults in America" at the Cape May Institute in New Jersey. The price is right: Programs in the U.S. currently run about $250 to $295 each, and include everything except transportation—classes, meals, lodging, and even entertainment. (The overseas programs cost more, since they include round-trip airfare, sightseeing, transfers, and all other costs.) Even the RV hostelers are bussed to the campus or course site, where they receive all their meals. Please note that you, or your spouse, must be at least 60 to participate, but there is no membership fee. These programs provide a wonderful avenue to new interests, friends, and travels, at a very reasonable price. For information, write to Elderhostel, 75 Federal St., 3rd Fl., Boston, MA 02110.

Imagine taking up painting on the coast of Cornwall, or embarking on a safari by jeep in New Mexico. These are two of hundreds of educational opportunities we read of in *Learning Vacations* (Peterson's Guides, 1986), by Gerson G. Eisenberg. Although some of the programs are limited to enrolled students, most are extension courses taught on campuses in the U.S., Canada, Europe, and as far afield as Tanzania. Prices for the courses vary considerably from program to program, usually depending on the type of accommodations. *Learning Vacations* is available from The Complete Traveller Bookstore, listed in the "Other Resources" section at the end of this chapter.

STUDENT TRAVEL

Like seniors, students can benefit from a variety of travel opportunities and savings. One of the best-known names in this field is

Council on International Educational Exchange (CIEE), which also runs Council Charter (see the previous section, "Consolidators/Bucket Shops"). If you're a high school or college student, CIEE can issue you an International Student Identity Card (ISIC), which you'll need to qualify for discounts on train and plane travel, admission to cultural and entertainment centers, and CIEE's own travel programs. The card costs $14, and comes with a brochure detailing available discounts. CIEE also publishes the highly recommended *Work, Study, Travel Abroad: The Whole World Handbook,* by Marjorie Cohen and Margaret Sherman ($10.95). For information on the identity card and other publications, write to Council on International Educational Exchange, 205 E. 42nd St., New York, NY 10017, or call 212/661-1414.

CAMPUS ACCOMMODATIONS

Staying on campus *sans* academics is often the cheapest alternative to everything but budget hotels. Rooms are usually available during college vacation periods, at prices as low as $19 a night. Amenities vary widely, but the rates are so good that it makes sense to consider this alternative when you're planning a trip.

Campus Holidays USA, Inc. has been arranging campus accommodations and other travel services since 1975. You can call or write for a list of the U.S. and British accommodations currently on offer, and purchase a book of coupons that can be used to pay for your stay. Campus Holidays can provide "lower-cost youth/student and teacher airfares," and tours of Europe, Asia, Africa, South America, and Australia for travelers who are 18 to 35 years old. Among these trips, its "Top Deck" tours are quite popular: British double-decker buses, which have been converted to hotels (sleeping quarters on top, dining and kitchen facilities below), take intrepid travelers on jaunts of 2 to 20 weeks. (The overland trek from London to Katmandu is a standout.) For information on what's currently available, write to Campus Holidays USA, Inc., 242 Bellevue Ave., Upper Montclair, NJ 07043; you can also call 201/744-8724, or fax 201/744-0531.

If you're interested in exploring the university option, don't miss the directory published by *Campus Travel Service,* "U.S. and Worldwide Travel Accommodations Guide." This 76-page book lists 600 universities in the U.S., and others in Canada, Australia, Ireland, England, Wales, Scotland, Scandinavia, Europe, Israel, Japan, Mexico, New Zealand, Africa, Asia, and Yugoslavia. The name, address, and phone number of each institution are given, as well as rates for singles and doubles, open dates, food service availability, nearby cultural and entertainment opportunities, whether children are accommodated, etc. The guide features listings of YMCA residences (51 in the U.S., 67 in Canada, and 23 overseas), including prices, amenities, restrictions, and booking policies. There are also several pages of valuable tips and references—on travel overseas, information on youth hostels, bargains for those under 30, travel opportunities for educators, toll-free airline numbers, bed-and-breakfast reservation services worldwide, home-exchange services, addresses of U.S. and foreign tourist offices, and some excellent health advice for travelers. All of this costs $13 ($11.95 plus $1.05 shipping); send a check or money order for the "Travel Accommodations Guide" to Campus Travel Service, P.O. Box 5007, Laguna Beach, CA 92652.

HOME EXCHANGES

One of the cheapest ways to save on hotel bills, especially if you're quartering a family, is to billet in someone else's home. There are a number of organizations that can help you effect a trade, either by arranging it or by providing a directory of like-minded parties with whom you negotiate.

Home Exchange International arranges the trades of homes of persons in the U.S., France, Italy, England, and other locations. To register, you pay a one-time fee of $50 and supply photographs of your home. When you've planned your vacation or narrowed your choices, contact the agency with details. Once a trade is arranged, you also pay a "closing fee" that runs from about $150 to $500, depending on the length of stay planned, type of home, etc. For more information, request a brochure from the Home Exchange International office nearer you: 185 Park Row, P.O. Box 878, New York, NY 10038 (212/349-5340); or 22458 Ventura Blvd., Suite E, Woodland Hills, CA 91364-1581 (818/992-8990).

Do-it-yourselfers may prefer dealing with *International Home Exchange Service/Intervac*, an organization that compiles three directories a year listing over 9,000 homes worldwide (most are outside the U.S.). A year's subscription costs $44 ($35 plus $9 for postage), and entitles you to one free listing. The apartments and houses in this directory are available for exchange *and* rent, so you don't necessarily have to exchange your own home to take advantage of a good deal.

For more information, write to International Home Exchange Service/Intervac, P.O. Box 190070, San Francisco, CA 94119, or call 415/435-3497.

THE TRAVELER WITH DISABILITIES

Travel can be especially trying for persons with disabilities, which is why *Access to the World* (Henry Holt and Company, 1986), by Louise Weiss, is such an important book. It lists hotels with accommodations for the handicapped, covers all aspects of travel by plane, bus, train, ship, car, and RV, and gives hundreds of references to *other* access guides, travel services for the disabled, and travel tips. *Access to the World* is available from The Complete Traveller Bookstore, listed in the "Other Resources" section at the end of this chapter.

Whole Person Tours, an enterprise providing tours for the disabled in Europe and the U.S., also publishes *The Itinerary,* a bimonthly magazine for the disabled traveler. The cost is $10 for one year, or $18 for two, from The Itinerary, P.O. Box 1084, Bayonne, NJ 07002.

DEALING WITH PROBLEMS ABROAD

No one plans to fall ill while traveling, but it happens. If you travel abroad frequently or want to play it safe on your vacation, consider becoming a member of the *International Association for Medical Assistance to Travelers (IAMAT).* Your $10 contribution to this not-for-profit organization nets you membership and a roster of English-speaking doctors in hundreds of foreign cities, as well as tips on staying healthy during your trip. For more information, write to IAMAT, 736 Center St., Lewiston, NY 14092.

The State Department "assists Americans in distress abroad," and may be able to provide information about the arrest, welfare, or whereabouts of a traveler through its Overseas Citizens Emergency Center. The State Department also issues travel advisories for countries afflicted by civil unrest, natural disasters, or outbreaks of serious diseases. All of this information, as well as visa requirements for travel to specific countries, may be obtained by calling 202/647-5225.

Planning the problems *out* of your trip is the best way to avoid them. Here are some pamphlets that can help ensure a pleasant experience: "Your Trip Abroad," "Travel Tips for Senior Citizens," "A Safe Trip Abroad," and "Tips for Americans Residing Abroad." Each booklet costs $1; request them by title from The Superintendent of Documents, U.S. Government Printing Office, Washington, DC 20402.

NEWSLETTERS

If you travel frequently, or would like to be able to afford to, you'll find the following newsletters of interest:

Consumer Reports Travel Letter, produced by Consumers Union, is a well-regarded "consumerist" publication for both business and recreational travelers. *CRTL* conducts in-depth comparisons of accommodations and prices in the U.S. and abroad, scrutinizes airline food, investigates travel scams, recommends methods of screening travel agents, and has probed the mare's nest of airline booking systems. Each monthly issue of *CRTL* runs around 12 pages; a year's subscription costs $37 at this writing. See the current *Consumer Reports* for an order form, or write to Circulation Department, Consumer Reports Travel Letter, 256 Washington St., Mount Vernon, NY 10553, for information. Single copies of back issues are available for $5 each.

Travel Smart is another newsletter that stays current with travel opportunities of all types, including discount fares and rates (including specials for seniors). Subscribers are offered deals on car rentals, cruises, accommodations, and air travel. And Travel Smart is full of great tips especially valuable to frequent travelers: A recent issue cited the end of an encephalitis alert in Florida, listed a number of short-term hotel bargains that were linked with bonus mileage offers, recommended restaurants in several cities for their moderately priced meals, and featured a two-season guide to cruises—along with the 800 numbers of dozens of cruise lines. A year of monthly issues costs $37; for more information, write to Travel Smart, 40 Beechdale Rd., Dobbs Ferry, NY 10522-9989.

OTHER RESOURCES

Whether your travels are confined to your armchair or you actually get up and go, you'll find travel guides a great help in planning your trip. The best-known series are *Fodor's, Fielding's, Frommer's, Baedeker's,* and *Birnbaum's.* These are reliable, general-purpose guide books to whole countries and major cities. The Frommer "$-A-Day" series is especially helpful if you're pinching pennies, but don't overlook the other books. If you're traveling abroad and want an informed guide to culturally and historically significant sites, see the *Blue Guide* series, which is highly recommended. The Zagats have entered the fray stateside with *Zagat's United States Hotel Survey,* a compilation on accommodations nationwide that have been rated by the Zagats' corps of paying guests and diners.

Many of the firms in "Books" sell travel guides and related literature, but specialty bookstores have far better stock and selection, and the staff can usually provide personal assistance in selecting the right book for your needs, even by mail.

The Complete Traveller Bookstore does a brisk mail-order trade through its 48-page catalog, which lists all the major guides, as well as *Insider's Guides,* the *Michelin* green and red guides, *Crown Insider's Guides* (written by expatriate Americans), the fascinating *Lonely Planet* books, which take you to the Cook Islands as well as Canada, and scores of specialty guides that cover everything from Alaskan hideaways to shopping in Seoul. Maps, foreign language tapes, and travel accessories are sold through the catalog as well. Store shoppers can peruse the collection of antiquarian travel books, including some early Baedekers, which are perched at the tops of the bookcases. For a copy of the catalog, send $1 to The Complete Traveller Bookstore, 199 Madison Ave., New York, NY 10016. Please note: This is *not* a discount bookseller.

The Forsyth Travel Library has an extensive selection of popular guides, road maps to cities and countries around the world, Berlitz phrase books, Audio-Forum language tapes, and Thomas Cook surface transit timetables. Through Forsyth, you can order rail passes to Europe and Britain (including "The Britainshrinkers" sightseeing tours), join American Youth Hostels (an application form is provided in Forsyth's brochure), and even subscribe to over a dozen travel publications, including *Consumer Reports Travel Letter.* Voltage converters and plug adapters, money belts, and other travel accessories are also available. Send 50¢ for the current brochure to Forsyth Travel Library, Inc., 9154 W. 57th St., Shawnee Mission, KS 66201-1375. Forsyth does *not* sell at a discount.

Book Passage publishes a 44-page catalog full of tantalizing reads: *Underwater Paradise: The World's Best Diving Sites, Muddling Through in Madagascar,* and *Doing Children's Museums* were just a few of the hundreds that caught our attention. In addition to the major travel guides and several language courses on tape, Book Passage offers titles on family travel, menu converters, railway timetables, shopping guides, maps, a number of guides to doing business abroad, and accessories—overnight bags, pocket-sized computer translators, fanny packs, etc. Request the catalog from Book Passage, 51 Tamal Vista Blvd., Corte Madera, CA 94925. Book Passage does *not* sell at a discount.

TravelBooks bills itself as "the compleat travel bookstore for domestic or international travel literature," and offers publications on adventure travel, trekking, hiking, student opportunities, and hundreds of maps. Write for the free catalog from TravelBooks, 113 Corporation Rd., Hyannis, MA 02601-2204, or call 800-869-3535.

Traveler's Checklist specializes in travel accessories, including money converters, adaptors and plugs, personal-care items, and related goods. Request a catalog from Traveler's Checklist, Cornwall Bridge Rd., Sharon, CT 06069. Please note that Traveler's Checklist does *not* sell at a discount.

Travel Accessories & Things has just that—those little items that can make life away from home a little easier. Inflatable pillows, personal "safes" of several types, eye masks, a folding cane, world-time alarm clocks, currency converters, and other useful travel aids have been offered in the past. Write to Travel Accessories & Things, P.O. Box 1178, Agoura Hills, CA 91301 for the current catalog.

SEE ALSO

Ace Leather Products, Inc. • travel clocks, gift items • *LEATHER*
Consumer Information Center • travel tips and related information •
BOOKS
Grandma's Spice Shop • Melitta coffee travel kit • *FOOD*
The Luggage Center • travel accessories • *LEATHER*
Mature Outlook • discounts on car rentals, air fares, tours, cruises, etc. •
GENERAL MERCHANDISE
The Reliable Corporation • pocket translators, leather luggage, travel
plugs, etc. • OFFICE
Superintendent of Documents • travel tips and related information •
BOOKS
Thrift Club • discounts on car rentals, air fares, tours, cruises, etc. •
GENERAL MERCHANDISE
The Lillian Vernon Corporation • travel accessories • *GENERAL*
MERCHANDISE

THE COMPLETE GUIDE TO BUYING BY MAIL

For U.S. Deliveries

Buying by mail has been made nearly effortless with the growth of 800 numbers and credit cards, but problems occasionally arise. The following is a guide to the basics of mail order—from sending for catalogs to getting credit for a return. Consult it to learn how to avoid problems—and to resolve them if they occur. If you're ordering from another country, having goods shipped abroad, or sent to an APO or FPO address, please see "Shipments Abroad," page 594, for special mail-order tips.

CATALOGS AND PRICE QUOTES

CATALOGS

Most mail-order firms publish some sort of catalog, which can be anything from a one-page list to a bound book. Some catalogs are still sent free of charge, but a fee, usually $1 to $5, if often charged. Firms sometimes ask for a SASE, which is a business-sized (#10), self-addressed, stamped envelope (SASE). If a SASE is requested and you don't send one, don't expect a response.

You'll need stamps to mail all those catalog requests, and you can order them, by mail, directly from the U.S. Postal Service. Both stamps and stamped envelopes are available; ask your postmaster or carrier for PS Form 3227, "Stamps by Mail," or request it from the Consumer Advocate, U.S. Postal Service, Washington, DC 20260. You can also call 800-STAMP-24 and charge your order to your MasterCard or VISA. (There is a $3 handling fee on all orders, and a $12.50 minimum on phone orders.) The stamps are usually delivered within a few days.

"Refundable" Catalogs: Some firms allow you to recoup the cost of the catalog when you place an order; this is indicated by the word "refundable" following the price of the catalogs listed in this book. Please note: If you don't place an order, you won't get the refund—"refundable" catalogs are not sold on an approval basis. Procedures for reimbursement vary, but many firms send a coupon with instructions to enclose it with your order and *deduct* the amount from the total. But often there is no coupon in the catalog, in which case you should deduct the amount from the order total *after* adding tax, shipping, and other surcharges, and note the reason for the deduction on the order form.

Often, a company will date the coupon, which means that you must order within a limited time period in order to recoup the fee.

Sending for Catalogs: Write a letter or postcard stating which catalog you want (some firms have several), mention any enclosures, and *always include your return address, printed clearly, in the letter.* Please refer to WBMC as your source, since it may qualify you for special discounts. Mention all enclosures so they're not overlooked. Keeping a log of dates on which catalog requests and orders are sent, inquiries made, and orders received is an excellent idea if you shop by mail frequently. Having complete records of mail-order correspondence will prove important if anything goes wrong.

If the catalog costs up to $1, you can send a dollar bill or coins taped securely between thick pieces of cardboard. For catalogs costing over a dollar, send a check or money order. *Never* send stamps unless asked, and don't use a credit card to pay for a catalog or a subscription unless the listing advises it.

Catalogs from Foreign Firms: When you send for a catalog from a foreign firm, use an international money order (IMO) or personal check if the catalog costs $5 or more, and cash or International Reply Coupons (see below) if it costs less than that. Money orders can be purchased at a bank or post office.

International Reply Coupons (IRCs) are certificates that can be exchanged for units of surface postage in foreign countries. They're available at the post office for 95¢ each, and are recommended when the catalog costs 75¢ or less.

You can save handling charges if the catalog costs $5 or less by sending cash through the mail. (In fact, several firms have requested it.) Technically it's risky and should be used only when you're dealing with currency. To conceal money and enclosures and remain within the half-ounce weight limit of a 50¢ stamp, slip the currency inside a piece of lacquered wrapping paper, or other kind of lightweight, opaque paper. This will camouflage the enclosure completely. Remember to mention enclosures in your letter.

Receiving Catalogs: Catalog publication schedules vary widely. Some firms publish new price lists weekly, while others bring out massive catalogs a decade. When firms run out of catalogs, are between printings, or issue catalogs seasonally, there can be a delay of months before you receive your copy. Some firms notify customers when this occurs, but most don't. Compounding the problem is the unusual demand a listing in a book like this occasions, when a firm may receive hundreds or even thousands of catalog requests over the course of a few weeks. Small firms are often swamped with bags of mail, and the fulfillment process is further slowed. If the catalog supply is exhausted, it may take weeks to get a print order filled, labels prepared, and catalogs sent. Bearing this in mind, please allow six to eight weeks to receive your catalog, and contact us if you have a problem (see "Feedback," page 616).

PRICE QUOTES

Some mail-order firms do not have catalogs, but sell their goods on a price-quote basis. Their name-brand goods can be identified by manufacturer's name, stock or model number, and color or pattern name or code. Cameras, appliances, audio and TV/video components, tableware, furniture, and sporting goods are commonly sold by discounters on a price-quote basis.

A price quote is simply the statement of the cost of that item from that firm. The company may guarantee that price for a limited period of time, or until stock is depleted. Some firms include tax, shipping charges, insurance, and handling in their price quotes, giving you one figure for the final cost. Don't accept such a price quote—make sure each fee or surcharge is itemized separately. The importance of this will become apparent if you have to return the item for a refund, in which case you probably won't be reimbursed for the shipping and handling charges.

Finding the Information: Before writing or calling for a price quote, you'll need to know the manufacturer's name, possibly the SKU ("storekeeping unit") code, product code (model or style number or pattern name), and size and color information, if applicable. These data can be found on the factory cartons or tags of goods in stores and in manufacturers' brochures. If you're pricing an item you found in a catalog, remember to look for the manufacturer's data, not the vendor's catalog code numbers. If you're using a buying guide or magazine as a source for information, verify the information before requesting price quotes—it may be out of date or contain typos.

Price Quotes by Letter: Most of the firms listed in this book will give quotes over the phone—in fact, many prefer it. But a letter is often cheaper, and it gives you a record of the quote. When you write requesting price quotes, include all of the available information about the item or items. Leave blanks next to each item so the person giving the quote can enter the price, shipping cost or estimate, and any related charges. Ask the firm to note how long it will honor the given prices, and ask for prices of no more than three items at a time. And you *must* include a SASE with your request if you want a response.

Price Quotes by Phone: Have all of the information in front of you when you call. *Don't* make collect calls, and don't use the "800" number for price quotes unless the listing recommends it. To avoid problems later, ask to speak to the manager, take down his or her complete name, and make notes of the conversation.

   NOTE: If you make a purchase over the phone using a credit card, some aspects of the transaction are not currently protected by the laws that regulate mail orders. For more information, see "The FTC Mail Order Rule," on page 597.

HOW TO ORDER

Before you order, make sure you're getting the best deal:

COST COMPARISONS

Your chief consideration is the *delivered* price of the product. Compute this from your price quotes and/or catalogs, then compare the figure to the *delivered* cost of the item if purchased from a local supplier. Consider such costs as mileage if you must drive to the local source, parking fees, sales and use tax, shipping and trucking, installation, etc. If you're buying a gift, compare the costs of having the mail-order firm wrap and send the item to the value of your own time, and materials and mailing costs. Finally, weigh the intangibles—

return policies, the prospect of waiting for a mail delivery versus getting the item immediately, the guarantees offered by the retailer and mail-order firm, etc. After contemplating costs and variables, you'll reach the bottom line and best buying option.

Before ordering any large item, measure all of the doorways through which the article must pass, allowing for narrow hallways, stairs, and the like. Some savvy shoppers even construct a carton dummy of the item by taping boxes together, and maneuver that through a dry-run delivery before ordering. Measure *before* you buy.

ORDERING

If the catalog is more than six months old, contact the company for a new edition and order from that (unless the listing indicates the catalog is published once a year)—prices can change without notice. (You may find yourself billed for the difference between the old price and the new if you order from an out-of-date catalog.) Use the catalog order form, along with the self-sticking address label on the catalog. If there's no order blank, use one from another catalog as a guide. Transcribe the code numbers, names of items, number of items ordered, units, prices, tax, and shipping charges—onto a separate piece of paper. Include your name, address, and phone number, the firm's name and address, and appropriate information if you're having the order sent to another address. Note any minimum-order requirements. Make a copy of the order, and file it with the catalog.

Second Choices and Substitutions: When the firm advises it and you're willing to accept them, give *second choices*. These usually refer to differences in color, not product. If you will accept *substitutions,* which may be different products that the firm considers comparable to what you ordered, you must give permission in writing on the order form. It's unlawful for a firm to make substitutions without written authorization from the buyer. If you don't want second choices and want to be sure the firm knows this, write "NO SECOND CHOICES OR SUBSTITUTIONS ACCEPTED" in red on the order form.

WBMC Reader Offers: If you wish to take advantage of a WBMC reader discount, rebate, bonus, or other special, be sure to comply with the conditions stated in the listing. Unless otherwise indicated, calculate discounts on the total cost of the *goods only,* not from the total that includes shipping, handling, insurance, and tax.

PHONE ORDERS

Many of the firms listed in this book take orders over the phone and have toll-free "800" numbers. Here's a brief description of how they work:

WATS Lines: The phone numbers with "800" area codes are WATS (Wide Area Telecommunication Service) lines. When you call a firm on its 800 line, no charge is made to your phone bill, even though the call *originated* from your phone. Instead, the cost of the call is billed (in terms of prepriced minutes) to the 800 number, where the call *terminates*.

A firm wishing to offer WATS to its customers chooses the calling areas it wants to serve from bands that include the contiguous 48 states, Alaska, Hawaii, Puerto Rico, the Virgin Islands, and Canada. Some companies have their own "in-house" 800 line, but others hire telemarketing firms to handle the orders, inquiries, and complaints. Telemarketers offer companies new to phone selling an opportunity to test the power of an 800 number without investing in line installation and operator training. Although telemarketing operators may not themselves be able to give you information on the products, they should be able to give you the order total, including the shipping and tax, and a good telemarketing service will have a statement of the firm's return policy in its data bank. *Don't* order from a firm whose service representative can't describe the terms of the policy, or when you're told that returns are not accepted under any circumstances—unless you're willing to take the gamble.

ORDERING

Before picking up the phone to place your order, follow this procedure:

1. Have your credit card ready
2. Make sure the card is one that's accepted by the firm, has not expired, and has a credit line sufficient for the purchase
3. Have the delivery name, address, and ZIP code available
4. Fill out the order form to use as a guide, and a record of the transaction. Include the catalog code numbers, units, colors, sizes, etc.
5. Have the catalog from which you're ordering at hand—the operator may ask for encoded information on the address label

When you place the call, ask the operator the following:

1. What is your name or operator number? (Operators are not a subspecies; they do have last names, and should provide them. If they won't, ask why—and reconsider purchasing from the firm if there is hesitation on this point.)
2. Are any of the items you're ordering out of stock? If yes, when is new stock expected?
3. When will the order be shipped?
4. Will any of the items be shipped separately?
5. What is the total, including shipping and tax, that will be charged to my account?
6. What are the terms of the return policy?

Every operator should answer questions 1, 5, and 6. Only those operators with stock information will be able to answer question 2, and, in all likelihood, only in-house operators can answer 3 and 4.

Many operators are required to ask for your home phone number, and sometimes your office number as well. This is done so they can verify that you are the person placing the order rather than a criminal who's obtained your card information from a carbon slip or stolen card. Since the firm may have to absorb the losses arising from fraud, it may refuse your order if you won't divulge your number, especially if you're buying certain types of goods and your order total is high.

While you're on the phone, the operator may try to "upsell" you, or get you to buy more goods. Beware of such unplanned purchases if you're trying to stick to a budget. On the other hand, you may be offered a real bargain on goods the firm wants to clear out. When this happens, the company's loss is your gain. Just make sure you really want the item—a bargain you'll never use is no bargain at all.

Once the transaction is completed and you've noted the operator's name or number, checked off the items you ordered, struck off those you didn't, entered the billing amount, and noted the time and date of the call, put this record in your file with the catalog. They may prove valuable later, if you have problems with your order.

The Pros and Cons of Phone Orders: Phone orders have certain advantages over mail orders. They're usually processed more quickly and, when the phone operator has stock information, you'll know right away whether an item is available. There are disadvantages, however, which relate to regulations governing shipment of goods. For more information, see "The FTC Mail Order Rule" on page 597.

ORDERING FROM FOREIGN FIRMS

Despite the fact that the world was supposed to be switching to the metric scale, many of the catalogs from Europe and elsewhere use the U.S. system—inches and pounds—in measurements. Converting metric measurements to U.S. equivalents is easy, though. Use the chart in any good dictionary.

There are confusing differences in sizing systems, color descriptions, and generic terms from one country to another. Sizes fall into three categories: U.S., British, and Continental, and the sizing chart on page 618 can be used as a general guide to equivalents. Always measure yourself before ordering clothing, and list the measurements on the order form if you're unsure of the proper size.

Color descriptions and terms are usually more poetic than precise, in both U.S. and foreign catalogs. Remember that color charts can resolve these questions, but you must allow for variations between photographic reproductions and the product itself. For a true match, write to the firm and ask for samples *before* you order, or at least make sure the firm will make refunds on returns.

There are some words used in Great Britain that have different meanings in the U.S. For example, the trunk of a car is called the "boot" in England; the hood is the "bonnet." A "jumper" is not a sleeveless dress worn over a blouse, it's a pullover sweater. Woven "rugs" are usually blankets sized to cover the top of a bed; a "torch" is a flashlight; a "spanner" is a wrench; a "beaker" is often a large cup, rather than a lab flask; a "cot" is a baby's crib. These are just a few; write to the firm before ordering if you have questions about a term.

The majority of foreign firms listed in this book give their prices in U.S. dollars. If they don't, you'll have to convert the firm's currency when you order. First, compute the total, including shipping, insurance, and other charges (but do not include duty). Next, convert this figure to dollars using the rate of exchange prevailing on the day you send the order. Get the rate from a bank, business newspaper, or the American Express office nearest you.

Before ordering, determine the rate of duty you'll be charged when the goods arrive and any shipping or transportation costs not included in the order total. See these sections for more information: "Paying for Goods from Foreign Firms," page 584; "Shipments from Foreign Countries," page 589; "Duty," page 593; and "Deliveries from Foreign Firms," page 600.

PAYMENT

There are two basic ways to pay for your order: now or later. You can *prepay*, using a check, money order, or debit card, or buy on *credit*. We make a distinction between these types of payments based on the rules that apply to refunds under the FTC Mail Order Rule, but some methods have characteristics of both categories.

Prepaid Orders: Payments made by check or money order are sometimes called "cash" by catalog companies, since the firm receives dollars instead of extending credit on the basis of a promise to pay. But with the exception of small catalog fees, *never* send currency through the mail.

Personal checks, accepted by most firms, are inexpensive and can be sent without going to the bank or post office. Since some firms wait until your check has cleared before sending your order, shipment may be delayed by as much as two weeks when you pay this way. Checks also provide you with a receipt (the canceled check), which is returned with your monthly statement. Use the "memo" space on your checks to jot down the firm's address, so if you lose track of the company in the future, you'll have a way to find it again.

Certified checks are guaranteed personal checks. You bring your check to the bank on which it's drawn, and pay a fee of about $5 to $9. The bank marks the check "certified" and freezes that sum in your account. Every company that accepts personal checks will accept a certified check, and the guarantee of funds should obviate the delay for clearance. The canceled certified check is returned with the other canceled checks in your statement. Firms that request certified checks for payment will usually accept a *bank check,* a *teller's check,* or a *cashier's check* instead.

Bank money orders are issued by banks for a fee, usually $1 to $3. Ask the teller for a money order in the desired amount and fill in the firm's name and your name and address. If the order isn't dated mechanically, insert the date. Most come with a carbon receipt; some have stubs that should be filled in on the spot before you forget the information.

Bank money orders are generally treated as certified checks (i.e., no waiting for clearance). If necessary, you can have the order traced, payment stopped, and a refund issued. You'll find this vital if your order is lost in the mail, since there's always a chance it's been intercepted.

Postal money orders, sold at the post office, are available in amounts up to $700 and cost from 75¢ to $1. They're self-receipting and dated, and can be replaced if the order is lost or stolen. Copies of the cashed money order can be obtained through the post office for up to two years after it's paid. This can prove helpful in settling disputes with firms that claim nonreceipt of payment. And, like stamped envelopes and stamps, money orders can be bought from postal carriers by customers who live on rural routes, or have limited access to the post office.

Bank international money orders, issued by banks, are used to pay foreign firms. You complete a form at the bank and, if the catalog prices are listed in foreign currency, the bank computes the amount in dollars based on the day's exchange rate. These orders cost from a few dollars or more, and they are receipted. Like domestic money orders, you send them to the firm yourself with the order. They are usually treated as immediate payment.

Postal international money orders are used to pay foreign firms; their cost varies, depending on the amount of the order. (For example, the service charge on a $200 postal IMO sent to Britain is $3 at this writing.) They're not for every transaction: ceilings on amounts to different nations vary from $200 to $500, they can't be sent to every country, and amounts of $400 or more must be registered. When you buy a postal IMO, you fill out a form with your name and address and the name and address of the firm, and you pay the order amount and surcharge. The post office forwards the information to the International Exchange Office in St. Louis, Missouri, which sends a receipt to you and forwards the money order, in native currency, directly to the firm (or to the post office nearest it, which sends it on). The entire procedure is supposed to take a few weeks; if you use postal IMOs, allow for this delay.

Bank drafts, or transfer checks, are the closest you can come to sending cash to a foreign firm through the mail. You pay the order amount, a mailing fee, and a service charge to your bank, then send one copy of the draft form to the firm and another to the firm's bank. You must have the name and address of the company's bank to do this. When the firm receives the form, it takes it to the bank, matches it to the other copy, and collects the funds. The forms will take five to ten days to reach the foreign country, provided they're sent airmail. Most banks charge $5 or more for bank drafts, depending on the amount of the check, but all foreign firms accept them.

Debit cards, which look like credit cards, are actually more like remote-control cash cards that are hooked into your checking account. See the following section for special caveats that apply to the use of debit cards when buying by mail.

Credit, Charge, and Debit Cards: Those wafers of plastic in your wallet have been important factors in the mail-order boom, and the pairing of 800 lines and credit cards has proven an irresistible combination for millions of consumers, creating phenomenal growth in phone orders.

Paying for an order with a credit card is simplicity itself—use a card accepted by the firm, make out the order form, and provide your account number, card expiration date, phone number, and signature in the blanks. If you're ordering from a catalog without a form, supply the same information on a sheet of paper. Using credit cards can make life easier if the shiiping costs aren't given or are difficult to calculate—they'll be added to the order total, and the order won't be held up as it might be if you paid by check or with a money order. Always check the minimum-order requirements when using a card, since they're often higher than those imposed on prepaid orders.

If you're low on cash but determined to order from a firm that doesn't accept cards, you can have Western Union send the company a money order and charge it to your MasterCard or VISA account. The surcharge is high—$14 to $37, and higher if you call in the order instead of placing it in person at a Western Union office. But it can be worth the expense if you might otherwise miss the buy of a lifetime.

The card companies, banks, and financial institutions that issue credit cards consider your past credit history, your current salary, and the length of time you've been at your current job when reviewing your application for a card. Minimums are raised when the interest rate climbs, but at this writing, a salary of about $20,000 and two years' employment with the same firm should net you a MasterCard or VISA account, provided you're credit-worthy in other respects. Getting an American Express, Diners Club, or debit card usually requires a higher salary and an excellent credit rating, and the issuers of "gold" accounts that offer larger credit lines and special programs geared for business and travel use usually look for an income of at least $40,000 and an excellent credit history.

Since there are thousands of card issuers and the market is considered saturated, the consumer is being wooed with reduced yearly fees and APRs, extended warranties, tie-ins with frequent-flyer programs, personal and auto insurance, discounts on lodging, and other benefits. If you need help comparing cards, Bankcard Holders of America, a not-for-profit consumer advocacy organization, can help you compare cards and find the one that best suits your buying habits. BHA publishes a list of banks with low APRs, and its bimonthly newsletters have useful information and updates on pending legislation that will affect bank card holders. For membership information and a publications list, write to Bankcard Holders of America, 560 Herndon Parkway, Suite 120, Herndon, VA 22070.

"Debit" cards deserve a special mention because they *look* like regular credit cards, but when the issuing bank receives the invoices for purchases, it *deducts* those amounts from your checking, savings, or money management account. This makes the debit card an electronic, instantly debited check, not a credit card, and it's important to bear in mind that the FTC views debit-card payments as *cash* payments. See the discussion of the FTC Mail Order Rule for more information on the debit-card issue.

Paying for Goods from Foreign Firms: You can usually pay for goods from foreign firms with a personal check, bank draft, or credit card. We recommend using a credit card (see "The Fair Credit Billing Act," page 612, for an explanation), but keep the following caution in mind:

If you use a credit card, the card issuer will charge you for the currency-conversion expense—a surcharge of 0.25% to 1%. The methods used by card companies to determine the rate of exchange vary widely, and are subject to the regulations existing in each foreign country. Your credit card statement should tell you the date the conversion was made and the surcharge. Check it carefully; the foreign currency total should be the same as your original order total, unless there was a price increase, short shipment, or shipping costs were higher than originally calculated. Check the *interbank* rate of exchange valid on the day the money was converted or the invoice was processed by the card company (your bank should be able to quote this). If there's a significant discrepancy between the interbank rate and the one the card firm used, write or call the customer-service department for an explanation.

Please read "Ordering from Foreign Firms," page 580, before ordering.

RETURN POLICIES

Most catalog firms guarantee satisfaction and will accept returns within 10, 14, or 30 days after you've received the order. Firms selling on a price-quote basis usually accept returns only if the product is defective. There are companies that don't accept returns under any circumstances, but they're not listed in this book.

Some goods—personalized or monogrammed, custom-made,

surplus, and sale items—are routinely exempted from full return policies. (If a firm has to special order an item for you, it may refuse to accept returns on that item—and may require you to buy a minimum number.) Health regulations usually prohibit returns of intimate apparel and bathing suits, but some companies will accept them. For more information, see "Returns," page 602.

Check the company's return policy before ordering. If you're shopping for a big-ticket item that carries a manufacturer's warranty, ask the mail-order firm for a copy *before* you buy, and see "Evaluating Warranties," page 607, for determining its value.

For more information, see "Returns," page 602.

CANCELING YOUR ORDER

When you order goods or services from a firm, whether by phone or mail, you enter into a contract of sale. You don't have the right to call the firm and rescind an order, nor do you have the right to stop payment on a check or money order on the basis of what an FTC staffer described as "buyer's remorse." (This term seems almost poetic in an industry that thrives on impulse purchases.) Different states have different laws governing matters of contract, but your second thoughts might give the firm cause to bring legal action against you. This is especially true if the company has undertaken action on an order, in what is termed "constructive acceptance of payment."

But if, after placing an order, you learn that the firm is in financial trouble or has a bad business record, stopping payment might be worth the possible risks. If you try to cancel, check the terms of the offer first. Magazine and book subscriptions are often sent on an approval basis, giving you a cancellation option. Goods offered with an unconditional guarantee of satisfaction can be sent back when they arrive. If these terms aren't offered and you're determined to cancel, contact the firm to discuss the matter.

SHIPPING, HANDLING, INSURANCE, SALES TAX, DUTY, AND SHIPMENTS ABROAD

When comparison shopping, consider shipping, insurance, tax, and handling as part of the total. (See "Cost Comparisons," page 576, for more information.) If you're having goods shipped to Canada, an APO or FPO address, or to another country, see "Shipments Abroad," page 594, for more information.

SHIPPING

This section addresses the concerns of consumers buying from U.S. firms who are having goods delivered to addresses in the U.S.

Shipping Computations: The largest ancillary cost of an order is usually shipping, calculated in a variety of methods. It's helpful to know how each works, so you can shop wisely.

Postpaid item prices, which include shipping charges, are popular because they spare customers the chore of extra computation—and they usually represent good buys. The shipping and packing costs are, however, passed along in the item price.

Itemized shipping costs are often seen as amounts in parentheses following the price or code number of the product. If you compare the UPS or USPS tape on the delivered parcel, you'll often find that the price you paid the firm for shipping was higher than what they paid to send it to you. That's because the fee you paid may include the costs of packing and materials, and it may also be prorated. For example, a California firm will compute all shipping charges based on the price of sending goods to Kansas, midway across the country. The windfall made on local deliveries winds up subsidizing the losses on shipments to the East Coast. And there are some firms that, quite simply, seem to be gouging the consumer with shipping charges that are far higher than their real costs. But even if the price you pay the firm is much higher than the actual shipping cost, don't ask the firm for the difference. Instead, suggest that it change its method of computing the charges, or at least place a ceiling on the shipping costs.

Numeric charges are based on the number of items you're ordering, as in "$2.50 for the first item; 75¢ each additional item." Firms structuring charges in this way often limit shipping to $7 to $12, so additional purchases made after you reach that limit are exempted from shipping charges entirely.

Flat order fees are simple dollar amounts charged on all orders, usually regardless of the number of items or weight. (Extra charges may apply if part of the order is shipped to another address.) A flat fee represents a bargain if you're placing a large order, but resist the temptation to order extra products just to make the shipping charge proportionately lower. And note that some firms selling on this basis will charge extra for heavy, outsized, or fragile items. Check the catalog carefully before ordering.

Free shipping is offered, often by smaller companies, on large orders. Customarily, orders under a certain dollar or item amount are charged shipping on some basis, but if your order exceeds a certain amount, no shipping is charged. The fact is often noted on the order blank—"on orders $100 and over, WE pay postage," or "free shipping on three dozen pairs or more same size, style, & color"—usually with the proviso that the order must be sent to one address. Again, don't order more than you need just to meet the minimum.

Sliding scales, tied to the cost of the order, are used by many companies. For example, if the goods total $15.00, you pay $2.75 for shipping; from $15.01 to $30.00, the charge is $3.50, etc. This is great if you're ordering many inexpensive, heavy items, but seems unfair when you're buying one, expensive thing. Some firms remedy this by using itemized shipping charges for small, high-ticket goods, and most limit the shipping charges to a maximum dollar amount, usually $7 to $12. Avoid padding your order to get the most from your shipping charge—you'll probably end up spending more dollars on dubious purchases than you save on postage.

Tables, based on the weight and sometimes delivery distance of the order, are still used by a number of prominent companies, as well as small firms. Tables require the most work on your part, since you must tally the shipping weights given with the item prices, find your zone or area on the rate chart, and then compute the shipping charges. Large, nonmailable goods will have to be shipped by truck; their catalog code numbers often have a suffix letter indicating this.

Some firms include in their catalogs all the rate charts you'll need to figure exact costs; others state at the bottom of the order form, "Add enough for postage and insurance. We will refund overpayment." When faced with this, you can consult a catalog that lists the weight of a comparable item both before *and* after packing, add the difference to the weight of the item you're ordering, and then call UPS or the post office for the rate. You can also call the firm itself and ask the shipping department to give you a quick calculation over the phone. You could send in the order without adding anything for shipping and ask the firm to bill you, but this may delay delivery.

The advantage to table computation is fairness of price. While you won't get the shipping "bargains" possible from firms using other methods to calculate those costs, neither will you find yourself paying exorbitant sums for shipment of small, light items.

Saving on Shipping Costs: When you have a chance to save on shipping by placing a large order, consult friends and neighbors to see if they want to combine orders with you. But unless you can view conferring, consolidating orders, and distributing the goods when they arrive as a social activity, count it as part of the cost of the order. Time is money, which is probably one of the reasons you shop by mail!

Carriers: No matter which method a firm uses to calculate shipping, it's going to send your goods by USPS, UPS, truck, or an overnight delivery service.

United Parcel Service (UPS): UPS is the delivery system many businesses prefer for mail order. UPS is cheaper, all costs considered, than USPS; it automatically insures each package for up to $100; and it also picks up the packages at the firm's office or warehouse. Unfortunately, we've received a number of complaints about UPS from readers who say that packages are often dumped on porches and left in vestibules, where they're vulnerable to theft. But our own experiences in the past year have shown improvement in service—our carrier *always* requires signature, and doesn't leave packages on doormats any longer. If you're having delivery problems, speak to the carrier about it, and then to a UPS supervisor if it's not corrected.

Under its Common Carrier Service, UPS handles packages weighing up to 70 pounds with a combined girth and length measurement of up to 108″ (with some qualifications). If your package exceeds the size/weight restrictions, it will be transported by a private trucking firm. UPS offers overnight delivery to certain states and ZIP codes through its Next Day Air service, and 2nd Day Air delivery to the 48 contiguous states and some parts of Hawaii. The delivery fee charged by UPS is determined by the delivery address, pickup location, the dimensions and weight of the package, and the service used.

United States Postal Service (USPS)—Parcel Post (PP): The costs for Parcel Post, or fourth-class mail, are somewhat higher than UPS charges, but Parcel Post offers one distinct advantage: *only packages sent by the U.S. Postal Service can be delivered to a post-office box.* (UPS must have a street address to deliver goods, although carriers will usually deliver to rural routes.) If you're having a package sent to a post-office box, write "DELIVERY BY PARCEL POST ONLY; UPS NOT ACCEPTABLE" in bold red letters on the order form, unless there's a box to check to indicate your preference. On the check, write "GOODS TO BE DELIVERED BY PARCEL POST ONLY." When the firm cashes the check, it's agreeing implicitly to this arrangement and should send the goods by Parcel Post.

While postal rates escalate by leaps and bounds, the size/weight restrictions remain relatively constant. USPS accepts parcels with a combined girth and length measurement of up to 84″ that weigh up to 70 pounds. Packages weighing under 15 pounds, with a combined girth/length measurement over 84″, are accepted at rates for 15-pound packages.

Truckers: When the firm specifies that an item must be sent by truck, or if you've ordered both mailable and nonmailable (outsized) goods, the entire order may be sent by truck. Sometimes firms indicate that goods are to be trucked with the term "FOB" or "freight," followed by the word "warehouse," "manufacturer," or the name of the city from which the goods are trucked. "FOB" stands for "free on board," and it means that the trucking charges will be billed from that point. When "manufacturer" follows FOB in the catalog, it means that the mail-order firm is probably having that item "drop-shipped," or sent from the manufacturer, instead of maintaining its own warehouse inventories of the product. If you're ordering nonmailable goods that you think will be drop-shipped, ask for the location of the manufacturer's warehouse so you can estimate the trucking costs. If you want the item quickly, you ask the mail-order company to verify that the manufacturer has the product in stock before placing the order, and whether the manufacturer can ship it by an overnight service.

Truck charges are usually collected upon delivery, and the additional expense is a real factor to consider when ordering very heavy items from a firm that's located far away. Truckers usually make "dump deliveries," meaning they unload the goods on the sidewalk in front of your home or business. For an additional fee (usually $10 to $20), you can usually have the goods delivered inside your house or apartment. Additional fees may be incurred if your order happens to be the only one the trucker is picking up from the firm that day or if the driver has to notify you of delivery. Before ordering an item you know will have to be trucked, get the price *plus* trucking charges and compare it to the cost of the same item if bought locally and delivered.

When the carrier arrives, you'll have to pay with cash or a certified check—personal checks and credit cards are seldom accepted.

SHIPMENTS FROM FOREIGN COUNTRIES

After your payment has been authorized or has cleared the bank, the firm should ship your order. Depending on the dimensions and weight of the package, it may be shipped by mail or sent by sea or air freight.

Mailable Orders: If the package weighs up to 20kg (about 44 pounds) and has a length of up to 1.5m (about 59") and a length/girth measurement of up to 3m (about 118") for surface mail or up to 2m (about 79") for airmail, it can be mailed. Almost everything you can buy from the foreign firms listed in this book will be mailable. Your decision when ordering will be choosing air, surface, or accelerated surface shipment (provided the firm offers all three). Mailed packages are delivered by your postal carrier, regardless of the service used by the company. Duty is collected by the carrier upon delivery.

Airmail is the most expensive service; airmailed packages generally take a week to ten days to arrive after they're posted, although some firms ask you to allow three weeks for delivery.

Surface mail, which includes both overland and boat shipment, is the cheapest service, but orders shipped by surface mail can take up to two months to reach you.

Accelerated surface mail is available in some countries; it's priced between standard surface and airmail rates, and hastens delivery time to about three weeks. It's known as "Fastmail" in some British catalogs, and represents the best shipping buy if you're neither desperate for an item nor prepared to wait a season for it.

Nonmailable Orders: In the unlikely event your order exceeds mail weight and/or size restrictions, it will have to be sent by an air or ship carrier.

Air freight is the best choice when the item or order just exceeds mail restrictions. Charges are based on the weight and size of the order, as well as the flight distance. The firm arranges to have the order sent to the airport with a U.S. Customs office that's closest to your delivery address. You pay the firm for air-freight charges, it sees the order to the airport, and sends you a Customs declaration form and invoice. When the airport apprises you of arrival, get right over with the forms, since most airports will charge a holding fee on goods still unclaimed five to ten days after delivery. In addition, you should make arrangements to have the package trucked to your home if it's too large to transport yourself. Once you clear Customs you can take the goods home or release them to the truckers you've hired and they'll make delivery.

Sea freight is much less expensive than air, but it can take months for an order to reach you. If you live near a port, you may want to handle Customs clearance yourself and hire a trucker to deliver the goods to your home. You can also hire an agent (customs broker) to clear Customs and arrange inland trucking. This service will cost from

$75 to $125, but it's the only practical way to deal with the process if you live far from the docking site and the foreign firm that sent the goods doesn't have arrangements with a U.S. agent who could take care of these details for you.

The procedure is similar to that of clearing an air shipment: You present the forms the firm has provided to the shipper and Customs officer, pay duty charges, and transport the goods home or release them to the truckers you've hired.

For information on duty rates, trademark regulations, and shipment of problematical or prohibited goods, see "Duty," page 593. For information on payment of duty on mailed goods, see "Deliveries from Foreign Firms," page 600.

HANDLING

Some firms charge an extra fee for handling or packing your order. The charge is usually not more than one or two dollars, and is often waived on orders over a certain dollar amount. The handling fee helps to cover the costs of labor and materials used in preparing your order for shipment. This surcharge, along with the shipping fee, may be taxed in certain states.

You can recoup part of this cost by reusing the carton and styrofoam peanuts or excelsior when you send gifts or pack fragile things for storage. If you're remailing the box, be sure to black out any marks made by the carrier, remove postage tapes, and delete addresses printed on the sides or top.

INSURANCE

Packages shipped by UPS are automatically for up to $100; you shouldn't have to pay extra insurance on those orders. (If you're buying from a firm that delivers via UPS but has a preprinted charge for insurance on the order form, don't pay it.) UPS charges 30¢ for each additional $100 in value on the same package—a fee usually covered in the shipping charge. The USPS does not insure automatically, so if you're having your package delivered by mail, not UPS, be sure to request insurance. Charges for postal insurance range from 70¢ for goods worth up to $50, to $5.00 for package contents worth from $400.01 to $500.00. Goods valued at more than $500 but under $25,000 must be registered as well as insured, and some goods can't be insured. If the item you're buying is uninsurable, have the firm arrange shipping with a carrier that will insure it. If you're not sure whether the firm will insure your goods, ask—*before you order*. The small fee is a worthwhile expense, something you know if you've ever had an uninsured order go awry. (See "Accepting Deliveries" for more information.)

Most insurance claims arise as a result of damage to or loss of goods. Procedures for claiming and reimbursement vary according to the carrier's rules and the firm's policy, but contact the firm as soon as you discover any damage to your shipment and ask the customer service department what to do. If there is documentation (signature of receipt on the UPS carrier's log or USPS insurance receipt), the claim can be verified and processed, and eventually you should be reimbursed or receive replacement goods. If there is no documentation and the worst happens—the goods never arrive—the firm may absorb the loss and send a replacement order. It may also refuse to do so, especially if its records indicate that the order was shipped. In such cases, it might be nearly impossible to prove that you didn't receive the order. (If you paid with a credit card, you may be able to get a chargeback. See "The Fair Credit Billing Act," page 612, for more information.) But if repeated entreaties for a refund or duplicate order meet resistance, state your case to the agencies listed in "Obtaining Help," page 611. And be sure to tell us—see "Feedback," page 616, for more information.

SALES TAX

You're supposed to pay sales tax on an order if you're having goods delivered to an address in the same state in which the mail-order firm, a branch office, or representative is located, and when the goods ordered are taxable under the laws prevailing in the area. Most states require payment of sales tax on handling, packing, and shipping charges.

Those are the general rules. The right of a state to create its own definition of "doing business" in that state, or "establishing nexus," rankles consumers who have to pay tax on what they perceive as out-of-state orders, and businesses that have to be tax collectors for 50 states. The issue of nexus is no stranger to the Supreme Court; one energetic individual took on both Sears and Montgomery Ward over 40 years ago and lost, and other mail-order firms have done battle with state governments and lost as well.

State governments are now trying to collect tax on *all* mail-order purchases delivered to residents of their states, calling such a tax a "use" tax (the actual sale takes place out of state, at the seller's place of business). Mail-order companies envision an accounting nightmare, and consumers stand to lose one of the benefits of shopping out-of-state: no sales tax on their purchases (unless nexus exists). Until the issue is resolved, keep paying sales taxes according to previously established guidelines.

DUTY

Orders from foreign firms are usually charged duty, which can't be prepaid. Duty is paid to the postal carrier who delivers your package or the Customs agent if the order is delivered by air or sea freight.

Assessment of Duty: U.S. duty is calculated on the transaction value, or actual price, of the goods being imported, on an *ad valorem* (percentage) or *specific* (per-unit) basis, and sometimes a combination of the two. Some goods—such as certified antiques, postage stamps, truffles, and original paintings—are imported duty-free. Check your local U.S. Customs office for current regulations, since rates and classifications are subject to change.

Prohibitions and Restrictions: Some goods can be imported only under certain conditions, and others are prohibited altogether. You can't import narcotics, pornography, fireworks, switchblade knives, absinthe, poison, or dangerous toys—and to our knowledge, none of the firms listed in this book sells them. If you wish to import animals, animal products, biologicals, petroleum products, plants, or seeds, you must make prior arrangements with certain agencies and obtain the necessary permits. And if you want to buy name-brand goods, be sure to check trademark restrictions. The manufacturers of certain goods register the trademarks with Customs, limiting the number of those items that an individual may import. Sometimes the manufacturer requires removal of the trademarked symbols or names, which is done by the Customs agent or the firm selling the goods. Goods that often fall under trademark restrictions include cameras, lenses, optics, tape recorders, perfumes, cosmetics, musical instruments, jewelry, flatware, and timepieces. Many foreign firms offer trademark-restricted goods in their catalogs, but don't inform you of U.S. regulations—find out before you order.

Obtaining Information: If you want to know more about duty rates and classifications, import restrictions, permits, and prohibitions, request the free booklet "Rates of Duty for Popular Tourist Items" from the Office of Information and Publications, Bureau of Customs,

1301 Constitution Ave., N.W., Rm. 6303, Washington, DC 20226. Use the brochure as a general guide only—contact your local Customs office for the latest rates. Provide a description of the goods you're ordering, including materials, composition, and decoration or ornamentation, since the classification of goods is more specific than indicated by the brochure.

If you want to import fruits, vegetables, or plants from abroad, write to Quarantines, Department of Agriculture, Federal Center Building, Hyattsville, MD 20782, and ask for an import permit application.

For more information on related matters, see "Ordering from Foreign Firms," page 580; "Paying for Goods from Foreign Firms," page 584; "Shipments from Foreign Countries," page 589; and "Deliveries from Foreign Firms," page 600.

SHIPMENTS ABROAD

Shipments to and from Canada: The U.S.–Canada Free Trade Agreement: The Free Trade Agreement (FTA) is a pact between the U.S. and Canada intended to promote trade and expand and enhance markets in both countries by removing some restrictions. The linchpin of the FTA is the mutual elimination of duties by 1998. Duties are being reduced in three ways: Some were eliminated when the FTA went into effect January 1, 1989; others are being reduced 20% a year over five years; and all others are being phased out over ten years. This tripartite formula permits industries that are ready for the increased competition to benefit from the new policy immediately, while protecting others that might be destabilized by the rapid abatement of tariffs.

The FTA affects an enormous range of raw materials and consumer goods—from fish and computers to ferrous alloys and plywood—but only those goods that are *produced* in the U.S. or Canada are entitled to free-trade treatment. (Tariffs on products of other countries are unaffected by the FTA, which is intended to benefit the U.S.–Canadian market.) The pact permits restrictions and quotas on products of certain industries and includes provisions dealing with "dumping" of goods at below-market prices and special considerations for government-subsidized products of both countries.

Despite the scope of the Free Trade Agreement, it's worth noting that *prior* to its enactment, more than 75% of the goods traded between the U.S. and Canada were exempted from tariffs. It may take a number of years for the effects of economies of scale and specialization to be discerned in the marketplace. Since only domestically produced goods are covered and phase-in periods may apply, mail-order shoppers must consult the nearest office of U.S. Customs or the Customs and Excise Office in Canada for rates and current information.

Shipments to APO/FPO Addresses: Over 60% of the firms listed in this book will send goods to APO and FPO addresses. Finding out which is easy: Look for the *stars and stripes* next to the maple leaf on the line with the dollar signs and phone and envelope symbols. (For more on the meanings of those symbols, turn to "The Listing Code," page xi.)

Mail-order firms generally ship orders via the USPS's PAL (parcel airlift) to the military mail dispatch center, where they are shipped overseas via SAM (space available mail). The size restrictions are 60″ in combined girth and length, and 30 pounds in weight. Firms sometimes charge additional handling fees for shipping to APO/FPO addresses, so read the catalog carefully and write for a shipping estimate *before* ordering if instructions aren't clear. Please note that neither UPS nor Federal Express makes APO/FPO deliveries, and that the USPS does not offer C.O.D. service to APO/FPO addresses.

Shipments Worldwide: Many of the companies that ship to Canada and U.S. military personnel also ship orders worldwide. (This is noted in the "Special Factors" section at the end of each listing.) If you're planning to have goods delivered to Japan, Israel, Europe, or any other address not in the U.S. or Canada, see the catalog (if available) for details on the firm's shipping policy. If it's not clear, or the firm sells on a price-quote basis, write or call the company before sending any funds and request a shipping quote. Since the employees of firms listed in this book are unlikely to be familiar with import restrictions and duty rates in other countries, please check these *before* placing your order to avoid unpleasant surprises. Most firms will request payment in U.S. funds; this may be most expeditiously handled by having your purchase charged to your credit card, but check with your issuing bank for rates and charges may apply to converting funds before you order. And please note that "The Complete Guide to Buying by Mail" has been compiled for readers who are having goods delivered to U.S. addresses, and will not apply in all parts to non-U.S. deliveries.

RECEIVING YOUR ORDER

What do you do when your order arrives? What steps do you take if it doesn't? The following section details your chief rights and responsibilities in this respect:

ACCEPTING DELIVERIES

When the postal or UPS carrier or trucker delivers your order, inspect the carton, bag, or crate before signing for it. If you're having someone else accept the package, ask that person to do the same. If the packaging is extensively damaged, you can refuse to sign for or accept the goods. This is not a procedure we wholly recommend, and the reasons are explained in "Returns," in this section.

If the box, bag, or carton is in good condition, accept it and open it as soon as possible. Unpack the goods carefully, putting aside the packing materials and any inserts until you've examined the contents. Most firms include a copy of your order form or a computerized invoice itemizing the order. If it's a printout or there's no invoice at all, get your file copy of the order you mailed or phoned in and check to make sure you've received what you ordered. Check the outside of the box, since some firms insert the invoice with the packing slip in a plastic envelope affixed to the top or side of the carton.

Check your order for the following: damaged goods, short shipments, unauthorized substitutions, wrong sizes, colors, styles, or models; warranty forms if the products carry manufacturers' warranties; missing parts; and instruction sheets if a product requires assembly. Since some firms return clothing modeled for catalog layouts to stock, examine the insides of collars for traces of makeup. Make sure ensembles are complete—that scarves, belts, hats, vests, ties, ascots, and other components have been included. Test electronic goods as soon as possible to make sure they function properly, and *do not* fill out the warranty card until you've tried the product and are satisfied that it is not defective. Try on clothing and shoes to make sure they fit. Check printed, engraved, or monogrammed goods for accuracy. If you decide to return a product, see "Returns" for more information.

If the goods are damaged, contact the seller immediately. Describe the condition of the goods and what you'd like done to correct the problem. If the firm asks you to file a complaint with the delivery service, request shipping information from the seller (the seller's shipping address, day of shipment, seller's account number, applicable shipment codes, and other relevant data). File the complaint with the delivery service, documenting your claim with photographs, if it seems necessary, and send a copy of the complaint to the seller. If you charged the purchase on a card with an extended warranty program, contact the issuer about the matter. Be persistent and methodical in your pursuit of a remedy, but be reasonable.

If you receive a short shipment (one or more items you ordered are not included in the package), the firm may have inserted a notice that the product is being shipped separately or an option notice if it's out of stock. (See "The Option Notice," page 598, for information on the latter.) Some companies don't back order, and will include a refund check with the order or under separate cover when a product is out of stock, or bill your account with the adjusted total if you used a credit card. If your shipment is short and there's no explanation, first check the catalog from which you ordered to see whether that item is shipped from the manufacturer or shipped separately by the firm. If there's no mention of special shipping conditions or delays in shipment in the catalog, contact the firm immediately.

DELAYED SHIPMENTS

What constitutes a real delay in receiving an order? What should you expect from the company if it has to delay shipping your order? The following section details your basic rights and responsibilities in this event:

The FTC Mail Order Rule: The Federal Trade Commission's "Mail Order Rule" addresses one of the biggest problems in the mail-order industry: late delivery. Mail-order shoppers should understand principles of the Rule, know what types of transactions are exempt from its protection, and understand what actions they're obliged to take to ensure protection under the regulations.

Please note: When a state or county has enacted laws similar in purpose to the functions of the FTC Mail Order Rule, the law that gives the consumer the most protection takes precedence.

General terms of the Rule: The Rule specifies that a firm, or "seller," must ship goods within 30 days of receipt of a *properly completed order,* unless the firm asks for more time in its catalog, advertisement, or promotional literature. The operative term here is "ship"—the firm does not have to have *delivered* the goods within 30 days under the terms of the Rule. And it must have received a *properly completed order:* Your check or money order must be good, your credit must be good if you're charging the order, and the firm must have all the information necessary to process the order. The 30-day clock begins ticking when the firm gets your check or money order made out in the proper amount, but stops if it's dishonored. If you're paying with a credit card, it begins when the firm charges your account. (An amendment to the Rule has been proposed under which the clock would begin ticking when data sufficient to process the order—credit card number, expiration date, etc.—are received.)

If your check or money order is insufficient to cover the order total or is dishonored by the bank, if your credit card payment is refused authorization, or if you neglect to include data necessary to the processing of your order (which could include size or color information, your address, etc.), the 30-day clock will not start until the problems are remedied—the firm receives complete payment, payment is honored by the bank, the credit card purchase is authorized, or you supply the missing data.

Exceptions to the Rule: The 30-day limit applies only when a firm does not ask you to allow more time for shipment. (Most qualifiers request extra time for *delivery,* which only confuses the issue.) Certain kinds of goods and purchases are not protected by the Rule. These include: mail-order photo finishing; seeds and growing plants; C.O.D. orders; purchases made under negative-option plans (such as book and record clubs); magazine subscriptions and other "serial deliveries," except for the first issue; and orders placed by phone that are paid by credit card. Genuinely "free" items don't fall under the Rule, but catalogs for which payment or compensation is requested are protected. The typical phone order is not protected by the Rule. See "The Rule and Phone Orders," following, for more information.

Assuming your order is covered under the Rule, the firm from which you're ordering must follow a specific procedure if it's unable to ship your order within 30 days. You must respond under the terms of the Rule if you want to retain all of your rights. Read on.

The option notice: If a firm is unable to ship within 30 days of receiving your properly completed order, or by the deadline it's given in its literature, it must send you an option notice. An option notice written in compliance with the Rule will tell you that there is a delay in shipping the item and may include a revised shipping date. If it does, and that date is up to 30 days later than the original deadline (either 30 days or a date specified by the firm), it should offer you the option of consenting to the delay or canceling the order and receiving a refund. The option notice must also state that *lack of response* on your part is *implied consent* to the delay. If you decide to cancel the order, the firm must receive the cancellation *before* it ships the order.

If the new shipping deadline is over 30 days after the original date, or the firm can't provide a revised shipping date, the option notice must say so. The notice should also state that your order will be automatically canceled unless the firm receives consent to the delay from you within 30 days of the original shipping date, and unless it's able to ship the order *within* 30 days after the original deadline and has not received an order cancellation from you as of the time of shipping.

The firm is required to send notices by first-class mail and to provide you with a cost-free means of response—a prepaid business-reply envelope or postcard. Accepting collect calls or cancellations over WATS lines is acceptable as long as the operators are trained to take them. If you want to cancel an order, get the response back to the firm as quickly as possible after you receive the option notice. Photocopy the card, form, or letter, and send it "return receipt requested" if you want absolute proof of the date of delivery. (If the firm ships your order the day after it received your cancellation, and you can prove it, you have the right to refuse delivery, have the order returned to the firm at its expense, and claim a prompt refund or credit.)

The renewed option notice: When a firm is unable to meet its revised shipping deadline, it must send you a renewed option notice in advance of the revised deadline. Unlike the first notice, second and subsequent notices must state that if you don't agree *in writing* to a new shipping date or indefinite delay, the order will be canceled. And the consent to a second delay must be received before the first delay period ends, or the order must be canceled, according to the Rule.

If you consent to an indefinite delay, you retain the right to cancel the order at any time before the goods are shipped. And the firm itself may cancel the order if it's unable to ship the goods within the delay period, and *must* cancel the order under a variety of circumstances.

The Rule and refunds: Under the terms of the Rule, when you or the firm cancel the order, you're entitled to a prompt refund. If your order was prepaid, the firm must send you a refund check or money order by first-class mail within seven working days after the cancellation. If you paid with a debit card, inform the firm when you cancel or when it notifies you that it's canceling the order that it must treat the payment as if it were cash, a check, or a money order, and reimburse your account within seven working days or send you a refund check. If you used a credit card, the Rule states that refunds must be made within one billing cycle. (We assume that these "refunds" are credits to your account, which will void the charge made for the goods.) The firm is *not* permitted to substitute credit vouchers for its own goods instead of making a reimbursement.

The Rule and phone orders: As mentioned previously in "Phone Orders," orders placed by phone and paid by credit card are not protected by the Rule. When the Rule was promulgated in 1975, phone orders were a much smaller part of the direct-mail industry than they are today.

The FTC is aware of consumers' concern and in 1990 entered the hearings phase of the rulemaking process on the Telephone Marketing Amendment, which is the proposed change to the Mail Order Rule that would protect transactions taking place by phone and via such newly developed technologies as interactive cable. Until changes are legislated, check to see if your state has laws protecting phone orders. If you order goods by phone and charge a deposit or partial payment to your credit card, but finalize the sale (complete payment) by *mailing* a check, money order, or credit card information to the company, the purchase is protected. (This practice is common in the furniture industry.) But you can't trigger protection by confirming a phone order in writing after you've called it in.

The Rule and the truth: Most mail-order firms operate in compliance with the Rule, in principle, but score low on detail. In industry parlance, the option notice is known as a "delay notice," and that's often what you receive: "The Wonder Duz-All you ordered is temporarily out of stock and will be sent as soon as it's available." But our reader feedback shows that a good number of large firms are acting in compliance with the Rule. However, if you're still being told that "It's on back order," without receiving an anticipated delivery date—or the option to cancel the order—tell us about it. See "Feedback," page 616, for information.

See "Complaint Procedures," page 610, for help in dealing with unresolved delivery problems.

DELIVERIES FROM FOREIGN FIRMS

The general guidelines outlined in "Accepting Deliveries," page 596, apply to deliveries from foreign firms. Please note, however, that *most* FTC regulations do not apply to shipments from non-U.S. firms.

The delivery procedure for foreign orders is determined by the shipping method the firm has used. For a complete discussion of carriers, see "Shipments from Foreign Countries," page 589.

You usually pay duty, or Customs charges, when you receive your order. The amount you pay is based on the value, type, and origin of the goods. See "Duty," page 593, for more information.

Most orders from foreign firms are mailable and are delivered by your postal carrier. Before your order reaches you, it's sent through Customs. Orders processed with the least delay are those with goods designated as duty-free because they qualify under certain provisions of Customs laws, or those worth under $50 that are marked "unsolicited gift." Some firms mark orders as gifts to save you money; this is not in keeping with Customs regulations, unless the order originates outside the U.S. Please don't ask a firm to send your order as an unsolicited gift, which can create problems.

The clearance procedure on dutiable goods includes entry, inspection, valuation, appraisal, and "liquidation," another term for determination of duty. Provided the necessary permits and entry papers have been filed with U.S. Customs and shipment of the goods violates no regulations, the Customs department will attach an entry form listing a tariff item number, rate of duty, and the amount of duty owed on the goods to the package. It will be sent to the post office and delivered to you by your postal carrier. He or she will collect the amount of duty and a "Customs Clearance and Delivery Fee," currently $3.25, as "postage due." Some foreign firms are annoyed by this term, since customers assume that the charge is for insufficient postage and complain to the company. Postal authorities have told us that the handling fee is not charged unless the order is assessed duty. But even if your order has dutiable goods, you may not have to pay any Customs charges—a high proportion of small orders are delivered fee-free.

If your parcel is held at the post office and you don't collect it within 30 days, it will be returned to the firm. If you disagree with the duty charge, you can challenge it within 90 days of receiving the order by sending the yellow copy of the mail-entry form to the Customs office named on the form, along with a statement explaining your reasons for contesting the charge.

DELAYED SHIPMENTS FROM FOREIGN FIRMS

You can reasonably expect your goods to arrive within six to eight weeks, provided you sent the order by air, are having it shipped by airmail or air freight, didn't order custom-made goods, and paid the correct amount—and as long as the country concerned is not at war. If you sent the order via surface mail and/or are having the goods shipped that way, are having any custom work done, or the country is in turmoil, don't hold your breath. We've been told that the delay for orders sent by surface mail averages three to six months.

Transactions with foreign firms generally come under the jurisdiction of international law. If your order doesn't arrive, write to the company, including photocopies of your order and proof of payment, and send the letter by registered airmail. Allow at least one month for a response, then try again. Put a stop on your check, or a tracer and a stop on a money order, if you paid with one. If the check or money order has been cashed, go to the post office and fill out an "International Inquiry" form. It will be sent to the postal service in the country concerned, which should investigate the matter. Notify the firm of your actions, and keep copies of all correspondence related to the affair, since you may need them at a later date.

If you paid with a credit card and you have not received your order, follow the querying procedure outlined above. If you don't hear from the company, but find that your credit card has been charged for the order, dispute the charge immediately under the provisions of the Fair Credit Billing Act. You may do this only if you have not received the goods at all and if the bank issuing the credit card is a U.S. bank. For more information, see "The Fair Credit Billing Act," page 612.

For more information on resolving problems with foreign companies, see "Complaints About Foreign Firms," page 614.

RETURNS, GUARANTEES, AND WARRANTIES

Your right to return goods is determined by the policy of the firm, the problem with the order, the conditions under which you made the return, and state and federal laws. See "Return Policies" and "Accepting Deliveries" for general information. Product warranties, whether written or implied, apply to many goods bought by mail. "Guarantees and Warranties," following, provides a comprehensive discussion of all types of warranties.

RETURNS

Return policies are often extensions of a firm's pledge of satisfaction. The policy determines how quickly you must return the product after receipt (if there's a time limit), acceptable causes for return, and what the firm will do to remedy the problem. Some companies will take anything back, but most exclude custom-made goods, personalized items, special orders, intimate apparel, bathing suits, and hats. Some also exempt sale items. Even a no-frills policy usually makes provisions for exchanges when the firm has erred or if the product is defective. It's important to read "Implied Warranties" for information on laws concerning product performance and rights you may have that are not stated in the catalog.

Obtaining Authorization: Before returning a product for any reason, check the inserts that may have been packed with the order as well as the catalog for instructions on return procedures. If there are no instructions, call or write to the firm for authorization to return the item. State the reason for the return, the item price and order number, date delivered, and the action you'd like taken. Depending on the firm's policy, you may request repairs or replacement of the item, an exchange, a refund check, credit to your charge account, or store credit for future purchases from the firm. Keep a photocopy of the letter for your files, or notes of your phone conversation.

Restocking Fees: Some firms impose a charge on returned goods to offset the labor and incidental costs of returning the item to inventory. Restocking fees, usually 10% to 15% of the price of the item, are most commonly charged by firms selling furniture, appliances, and electronics.

Sending the Item: Follow the mailing procedure outlined in the catalog, order insert, or authorization notice from the firm. When you send the goods back, include a dated letter with your name and address, the order number, authorization number or name of the person approving the return (if applicable), and a statement of what you want—repair, exchange, refund, or credit. Depending on the circumstances, you may have to enclose the invoice or sales slip. Keep file copies of your letter and invoices.

Pack the item in the original box and padding materials if requested, and insure it for the full value. Allow the firm at least 30 days to process the return or respond before writing or calling again.

Refunds and Credits: If you want your charge account credited for the return, be sure to provide the relevant data. Not every firm will issue a refund check or credit your account; some offer replacement or repair of the product, an exchange, or catalog credit only.

Exchanges: If you're exchanging the product for something entirely different, state the catalog code number, size, color, price, unit, etc. of the item you want in the letter you enclose with the return, or on the authorization form.

Postage Reimbursement: Some firms accept returns sent postage-collect, or will reimburse you for the shipping and insurance charges on a return. Most will not. Businesses are not required by federal law to refund the cost, even when you're returning goods as a result of the firm's error. State and local laws, however, may make provisions for this; check to see whether they do.

GUARANTEES AND WARRANTIES

Although the terms "guarantee" and "warranty" are virtually synonymous, we make a distinction between the two for the purpose of clarity. Here, a "guarantee" is the general pledge of satisfaction or service a firm offers on the sales it makes. Guarantees and related matters are discussed in "Return Policies," "Returns," and "Implied Warranties." A "warranty" is, generally, the written policy covering the performance of a particular product. Both guarantees and warranties are free; paid policies (including "extended warranties") are *service contracts*.

Warranties are regulated by state and federal law. Understanding policy terms will help you shop for the best product/warranty value; knowing your rights may mean the difference between paying for repairs or a replacement and having the firm or manufacturer do it.

The Magnuson-Moss Warranty—Federal Trade Commission Improvement Act: Also known as the Warranty Act, this 1975 law regulates warranties that are in print. Oral "warranties"—the sales-person's assurance of product performance and pledge of satis-faction—are worthless unless they're in writing.

The Warranty Act requires that warranties be written in "simple and readily understood language" that states all terms and conditions. If the product costs more than $15, a copy of the warranty must be available *before* purchase. In a store, it should be posted on or near the product, or filed in a catalog of warranties kept on the premises with a notice posted concerning its location. Mail-order firms comply with the law by making copies of warranties available upon request.

The Warranty Act requires the warrantor to use the term "full" or "limited" in describing the policy. A single product can have several warranties covering different parts, and each can be labeled separately as "full" or "limited." For example, a TV set may have a full one-year policy on the set and a limited 90-day policy on the picture tube. Generally speaking, the conditions stated here apply to warranties on goods costing over $15.

Full warranties provide for repair or replacement of the product at no cost to you, including the removal and reinstallation of the item, if necessary. The warranty may be limited to a certain length of time, and must state the period of coverage. Full warranties can't be limited to the original purchaser—the warrantor must honor the policy for the full term even if the item has changed hands. *Implied warranties* (see page 606) may not be limited in duration by the terms of the full warranty, and in some states may last up to four years.

The item should be repaired within a "reasonable" length of time after you've notified the firm of the problem. If, after a "reasonable" number of attempts to repair, the product is still not functioning properly, you may invoke the "lemon provision." This entitles you to a replacement or refund for the product.

Registering your product with the warrantor under a full warranty is voluntary, a fact that must be stated clearly in the terms. You can send the registration card to the firm, but this is at your discretion and not necessary to maintain the protection of the warranty.

Limited warranties provide less coverage than full warranties. Under them, you can be required to remove, transport, and reinstall a product; to pay for labor if repairs are made; and to return the warranty card to the firm in order to validate the policy. The warrantor can also limit the warranty to the original purchaser and give you prorated refunds or credits for the product. (The "lemon provision" doesn't apply to a limited warranty.)

Warrantors may also limit implied warranties (see the following section) to the length of *time* their policies run, but no less. If they limit the implied-warranty time, they must also state: "Some states do not allow limitations on how long an implied warranty lasts, so the above limitation may not apply to you." The warrantor may not limit the *extent* of protection you have under implied warranties, however.

Other provisions of the Warranty Act include the following:

- If you complain within the warranty period, the firm must act to remedy the problem within the terms of the warranty.
- If a *written* warranty is provided with the product, the warrantor can't exclude it from protection under implied warranties.

- A warrantor can exclude or limit *consequential damages* (see the following section) from coverage under both full and limited policies as long as the warranty states: "Some states do not allow the exclusion or limitation of incidental or consequential damages, so the above limitation or exclusion may not apply to you."
- All warranties must include information on whom to contact, where to bring or mail the product, and the name, address, or toll-free phone number of the warrantor.
- All warranties, full and limited, must state: "This warranty gives you specific legal rights, and you may have other rights that vary from state to state."

Implied Warranties: Implied warranties are state laws that offer protection against major hidden defects in products. Every state has these laws, which cover every sale unless the seller states that no warranties or guarantees are offered; that goods are sold "as is." But if a particular product sold by a firm with a no-guarantee policy carries a *written* warranty, the *implied* warranty of the state is also valid on that item. The terms of implied warranties differ from state to state, but many have similar sorts of provisions.

The warranty of merchantability is a common implied warranty. It means that the product must function properly for conventional use— a freezer must freeze, a knife must cut, etc. If the product does not function properly and your state has a warranty of merchantability, you're probably entitled to a refund for that item.

The warranty of fitness for a particular purpose covers cases in which the seller cites or recommends special uses for the product. For example, if a seller says that a coat is "all-weather," it should offer protection in rain and snow. If it claims that a glue will "bond any two materials together," the glue should be able to do that. When a salespersonmakes these assurances, check the printed product information to verify the recommendation or call the manufacturer. While the salesperson may have a direct incentive—commissions—to inveigle you into buying a product, the manufacturer should be more committed to your satisfaction and return business.

Consequential Damages: Incidental or consequential damages occur when a product malfunction causes damage to or loss of other property. The FTC uses the example of an engine block cracking when the antifreeze is faulty. Less extreme is the food spoilage caused by a refrigerator breakdown or the damage resulting from a leaky waterbed mattress.

Written warranties usually entitle you to consequential damages, but warrantors are allowed to exempt this coverage under both full and limited warranties. If the warrantor excludes consequential damages from coverage, the warranty must state: "Some states do not allow exclusion or limitation of incidental or consequential damages, so the above limitation or exclusion may not apply to you."

Provisions for consequential damages entitle you to compensation for the property damage or loss, as well as repair or replacement of the defective product. In the engine block example, the exemption of damages must be considered as a definite disadvantage when evaluating the product/warranty value.

Evaluating Warranties: Appraise the written warranty as thoroughly as you do the product's other features *before* you buy. In reading the warranty, bear in mind past experiences with products and warranty service from that manufacturer or seller, experiences with similar products, and your actual needs. Don't rush to buy the first model of a new product if you can wait. Later models are sure to be cheaper and better—just consider VCRs, CD players, and computers.

In evaluating a warranty, ask yourself these questions:

- Is the warranty full or limited?
- Does it cover the whole product, or specific parts?
- How long is the warranty period?
- Do you contact the manufacturer, seller, or a service center for repairs?
- Will you have to remove, deliver, and reinstall the product yourself?
- Do you have to have repairs done by an authorized service center or representative? If so, how close is the nearest facility?
- Will the warrantor provide a temporary replacement for use while your product is being serviced?
- Are consequential damages excluded? If the product turns out to be defective, could the consequential damages result in a significant loss?
- If reimbursement is offered on a pro-rata basis, is it computed on a time, use, or price schedule?
- Do you have the choice of a refund or replacement if the item can't be repaired?

Envision a worst-case scenario in which the product breaks down or malfunctions completely. What expenses could be incurred in consequential damages, supplying a substitute product or service, transporting the product to the service center or seller, and repair bills? Will returning the product be troublesome, and living without it while it's being repaired inconvenient? Your answers determine the value the warranty has for *you*. Consider that quotient along with the price and features of the product when comparison shopping to find your best buy.

Complying with Warranty Terms: Understanding and fulfilling the conditions of a warranty should be simple, but we've outlined a few tips that may make it easier:

- Read the warranty card as requested.
- Read the instructions or operations manual before using the product, and follow directions for use.
- Keep the warranty and dated receipt or proof of payment in a designated place.
- If the manufacturer offers a rebate on the product that requires sending the proof of payment, photocopy the receipt and keep the copy with the warranty.
- Abuse, neglect, and mishandling usually void the warranty. Other practices that may invalidate the policy include improper installation, repair or service by an unauthorized person or agency, use of the product on the wrong voltage, and commercial use. If others will be using the product, be sure they know how to operate it.
- Perform routine maintenance (cleaning, oiling, dusting, replacement of worn components, etc.) as required by the manual, but don't attempt repairs or maintenance that isn't required or permitted in the warranty or guide.

If you have a question about maintenance or use, contact the manufacturer or service center. If you void the warranty by violating its terms, you'll probably have to absorb the costs of repairs or replacement.

Obtaining Service: If the product breaks down or malfunctions, you'll find that you can expedite resolution if you follow these guidelines:

- Read the operating manual or instructions. The problem may be covered in a troubleshooting section, or you may find that you expected the product to do something for which it wasn't designed.
- Contact the warrantor, whose name, address, and/or phone number appear on the warranty, unless the seller offers service under warranty.
- Call, write, or visit as appropriate. State the nature of the problem, the date it occurred, and whether you want a repair, replacement, refund, and/or consequential damages. Bring a copy of the warranty and proof of payment when you visit, and include copies if you write. (Remember that your rights in respect to the nature and extent of compensation depend upon the terms of the warranty and laws prevailing in your area.)
- If you leave the product for repairs or have it picked up, get a signed receipt that includes the date on which it should be ready, an estimate of the bill if you have to pay for repairs, and the serial number of the product, if one is given.
- If you send the product, insure it for the full value. Include a letter describing the problem, the date on which it occurred, and how you'd like it resolved.
- After a call or visit, the FTC recommends sending a follow-up letter reiterating the conversation. Keep a photocopy, and send it by certified mail to the person or agency with which you spoke.
- Keep a log of all actions you take in having the warranty honored, including dates on which actions, visits, and calls were made, and a record of the expenses you incur in the process.
- If you've written to the seller or manufacturer concerning the problem and received no response after three to four weeks, write again. Include a photocopy of the first letter, ask for an answer within four weeks, and send the second letter by certified mail (keep a photocopy). Direct the letter to the head of customer relations or the warranty department, unless you've been dealing with an individual.
- If you've written to the manufacturer, it may help to contact the seller (or vice versa). A reputable firm doesn't want to merchandise through a seller who won't maintain good customer relations, and a responsible seller knows that marketing shoddy goods is bad for business. Bilateral appeals should be made after you've given the responsible party an opportunity to resolve the problem.

- If you have repairs done, ask to see the product demonstrated *before* you accept it, especially if you're paying for repairs. If there are indications that the problem may recur (e.g., it exhibits the same "symptoms" it had before it broke or malfunctioned), tell the service representative—it may be due to something that wasn't noticed during the repair.
- If you're paying for repairs, ask for a guarantee on parts and/or labor so you won't face another bill if the product breaks down shortly after you begin using it again.
- If the product keeps malfunctioning after it's repaired and it's under full warranty, you can probably get a replacement or refund under the "lemon provision." Write to the manufacturer or seller, provide a history of the problems and repairs, plus a copy of the warranty, and ask for a replacement or refund. If the warranty is limited, the terms may entitle you to a replacement or refund. Write to the manufacturer or seller with the product history and a copy of the warranty, and ask for a new product or compensation.
- Explore your rights under your state's implied-warranty and consequential-damages laws. They may offer you protections not given in the product warranty.
- If you've been injured by a malfunctioning product, contact an attorney.
- If, after acting in good faith and allowing the manufacturer or seller time to resolve the problem, you are still dissatisfied, contact your local consumer-protection agency for advice.

You may also report problems to other agencies and organizations. For more information, see "Obtaining Help," following.

COMPLAINTS

COMPLAINT PROCEDURES

A formal complaint is justified if you've notified the firm of a problem and asked for resolution, following procedures outlined in the catalog, warranty, or this guide, with unsatisfactory results. Give the firm one last chance to remedy the situation before asking for help from outside agencies. If your problem concerns nondelivery or dissatisfaction with a product and you paid with a credit card, you may be able to withhold payment or ask for a chargeback under the

Fair Credit Billing Act. See "The Federal Trade Commission," following, for more information.

The Complaint Letter: State your complaint clearly and concisely with a history of the problem and all the appropriate documentation: photocopies of previous letters, proof of payment, the warranty, repair receipts, etc. Don't send original documents—use photocopies and keep the originals in your file. Make sure your letter includes your name and address, the order or product number or code and descriptive information about the product, and the method of payment you used. Type or print the letter, and please don't be abusive. Tell the firm exactly what you want done. Give a deadline of 30 days for a reply or resolution, and note that if you don't receive a response by that time, you'll report the firm to the U.S. Postal Service, Better Business Bureau, Direct Marketing Association, Federal Trade Commission, or other appropriate agency. (See "Obtaining Help," following, for information.)

If the firm doesn't acknowledge the request or you're not satisfied by the response, take action.

OBTAINING HELP

There are several agencies and organizations that can help you with different types of problems. Some undertake investigations on a case-by-case basis, and others compile files on firms and act when the volume of complaints reaches a certain level.

When you seek help, provide a copy of your final complaint letter to the firm, as well as the documentation described in "The Complaint Letter."

Consumer Action Panels (CAPs): CAPs are third-party dispute resolution programs established by the industries they represent. They investigate consumer complaints, provide service information to consumers, and give their members suggestions on improving service to consumers.

MACAP helps with problems concerning major appliances. Write to Major Appliance Consumer Action Panel, 20 N. Wacker Dr., Chicago, IL 60606, or call 800-621-0477 for information.

Better Business Bureaus (BBBs): Better Business Bureaus are self-regulatory agencies, funded by businesses and professional firms, that monitor advertising and selling practices, maintain files on firms, help resolve consumer complaints, and disseminate service information to consumers. BBBs also perform the vital service of responding to inquiries about a firm's selling history, although they can't make recommendations. Most BBBs have mediation and arbitration programs, and are empowered to make awards (binding arbitration).

Whether you want to check a firm's record before ordering or file a complaint, you must contact the BBB nearest the *company*, not the office in your area. You can obtain a directory of BBB offices by sending your request and a SASE to the Council of Better Business Bureaus, Inc., 4200 Wilson Blvd., Suite 800, Arlington, VA 22203. Write to the appropriate office, and ask for a "consumer complaint" or "consumer inquiry" form, depending on your purpose.

Direct Marketing Association (DMA): The DMA is the largest and oldest trade organization of direct marketers and mail-order companies in existence. Over half of its members are non-U.S. firms; this gives it some clout in dealing with problematical foreign orders placed with member firms.

The DMA's *Mail Order Action Line (MOAL)* helps to resolve nondelivery problems with any direct-marketing firm, not just members. Upon receiving your *written* complaint, the DMA contacts the firm, attempts to resolve the problem, notifies you that it's involved, and asks you to allow 30 days for the firm to solve or act on the problem. To get help, send a copy of your complaint letter and documentation to Mail Order Action Line, DMA, 11 W. 42nd St., New York, NY 10163.

Consumers may also have their names added to or removed from mailing lists through the DMA. Request an "MPS" form from Mail Preference Service, Direct Marketing Association, 11 W. 42nd St., P.O. Box 3861, New York, NY 10163-3861.

The Federal Trade Commission (FTC): The FTC is a law-enforcement agency that protects the public against anticompetitive, unfair, and deceptive business practices. While it doesn't act on "individual" complaints, it does use your complaint letters to build files on firms. When the volume or nature of problems indicates an investigation is justified, the FTC will act. Several levels of action are possible, including court injunctions and fines of up to $10,000 for each day the violation is occurring. Report deviations from FTC regulations; your letter may be the one that prompts an investigation.

The Fair Credit Billing Act (FCBA), passed in 1975 under the FTC's Consumer Credit Protection Act, offers mail-order shoppers who use credit cards as payment some real leverage if they have a problem with nondelivery. The Act established a settlement procedure for *billing errors* that include, among other discrepancies, charges for goods or services not accepted or not delivered as agreed. The procedure works as follows:

- You must write to the creditor (phoning will not trigger FCBA protection) at the "billing error" address given on the bill.
- The letter must include your name and account number, the dollar amount of the error, and a statement of why you believe the error exists.
- The letter must be received by the creditor within 60 days after the first bill with the error was mailed to you. The FTC recommends sending it by certified mail, return receipt requested.
- The creditor has to acknowledge your letter, in writing, within 30 days of receipt, unless the problem is resolved within that time.
- You do not have to pay the disputed amount, the related portion of the minimum payment, or the related finance charges while it's being disputed.
- If an error is found, the creditor must write to you, explaining the correction—the amount must be credited to your account and related finance charges must be removed. If the creditor finds that you owe part of the amount, it must be explained in writing.
- If the creditor finds that the bill is correct, the reasons must be explained in writing and the amount owed stated. You will be liable for finance charges accrued during the dispute and missed minimum payments.
- You may continue to dispute at this point, but only if your state's laws give you the right to take action against the *seller* rather than the creditor. Write to the creditor within ten days of receiving the justification of the charge and state that you still refuse to pay the disputed amount. If you continue to challenge, contact your local consumer protection agency, since the creditor can begin collection proceedings against you and the agency may be able to recommend other means of handling the problem that don't jeopardize your credit rating.

Disputes over the *quality* of goods or services are covered under the FCBA if state law permits you to withhold payment from a *seller*. This applies to credit-card purchases over $50 that are made in your home state or within 100 miles of your mailing address. (The limits do not apply if the seller is also the card issuer, as is often the case with department stores.) Contact your local consumer protection agency for advice before taking action.

The United States Postal Service (USPS): The USPS takes action on complaints and resolves about 85% of the problems. This may be because, under provisions of the U.S. Code, it can go to court, get a restraining order, and withhold mail delivery to a company. (This is a very serious action and is never undertaken simply at a private citizen's request.) A number of our readers have told us that the USPS acts more swiftly, with better results, than do any of the other agencies we've cited here. You can send a copy of your final complaint letter and documentation to the Chief Postal Inspector, U.S. Postal Service, Washington, DC 20260—but readers have told us that writing directly to the Postmaster of the post office *nearest the firm* is what does the trick.

Bankruptcy Courts: Bankruptcy courts may offer information, if no actual compensation, on errant orders and refunds. If you've written to the company and received no response and its phone has been disconnected, contact the U.S. Bankruptcy Court nearest the firm. Tell the clerk why you're calling, and ask whether the company has filed for reorganization under Chapter 11. If it has, get the case number and information on filing a claim. Chapter 11 protects a business against the claims of its creditors; all you can do is file as one of them, and hope. As a customer, your claim comes after those of the firm's suppliers, utilities, banks, etc. The "take a ticket" approach is no guarantee that you'll get anything back, but if it's your only shot, take the trouble to file.

COMPLAINTS ABOUT FOREIGN FIRMS

For general information on dealing with complaints about foreign firms, see "Delayed Shipments from Foreign Firms," page 601.

The DMA may be able to undertake an investigation on your behalf. See page 612 for more information on the organization and its address.

The Council of Better Business Bureaus has affiliates in Canada, Mexico, Israel, and Venezuela. If the firm is located in any of those countries, write to the Council for the address of the office nearest the company, and contact that office with the complaint. See page 611 for more information and the Council's address.

The foreign trade council representing the firm's country may be able to provide information that could prove helpful. Contact the council and briefly describe your problem. Ask whether the organization can supply the name of a regulatory agency or trade organization in that country that might be of help. The councils have offices in New York City, and directory assistance can provide you with their phone numbers.

We'll try to help you to resolve problems with all of the firms, domestic and foreign, listed in this book. See "Feedback," following, for more information.

FEEDBACK

Consumers and businesses, we want to hear from you! Your suggestions, complaints, and comments help to shape each edition of *The Wholesale-by-Mail Catalog®*, and are valued highly. We thank every reader who's contacted us in the past and urge you to keep writing. You can help us by using the guidelines that follow.

Firms: If you'd like your company considered for inclusion in the next edition of WBMC, have your marketing director send us a copy of your current catalog or literature. Firms are listed at our discretion and must meet our criteria to qualify for inclusion.

Consumers: If you're writing a letter of complaint, please read the sections of "The Complete Guide to Buying by Mail" that may apply to your problem, and try to work it out yourself. If you can't remedy the situation on your own, write to us and include:

- a brief history of the transaction
- copies (not originals) of all letters and documents related to the problem
- a list of the dates on which events occurred, if applicable (the date a phone order was placed, goods were received, account charged, etc.)
- a description of what you want done (goods delivered, warranty honored, return accepted, money refunded or credited, etc.)

Include your name, address, and day phone number in your cover letter. We'll look into the matter, and while we can't guarantee resolution, we may be able to help you.

If you just want to sound off, we'd like to hear from you too. If you're moved to sing the praises of any mail-order company, please do so—let us know what has impressed you. And suggestions for the next edition of WBMC are welcomed. Send your postcard or letter to:

WBMC 1992
The Print Project
P.O. Box 505, Village Station
New York, NY 10014-0505

CHART

Clothing Sizes

Women's Garments

U.S.A	6	8	10	12	14	16	18	20
Great Britain	8	10	12	14	16	18	20	22
Europe	36	38	40	42	44	46	48	50

Women's Sweaters

U.S.A.	XS	S	M	M	L	L
Great Britian	34	36	38	40	42	44
Europe	40	42	44	46	48	50

Women's Shoes

U.S.A.	5	$5^{1}/_{2}$	6	$6^{1}/_{2}$	7	$7^{1}/_{2}$	8	$8^{1}/_{2}$	9	$9^{1}/_{2}$	10
Great Britain	$3^{1}/_{2}$	4	$4^{1}/_{2}$	5	$5^{1}/_{2}$	6	$6^{1}/_{2}$	7	$7^{1}/_{2}$	8	$8^{1}/_{2}$
Europe	36		37		38		39		40		41

Men's Suits and Sweaters

	S	S	M	M	L	XL
U.S.A.	34	36	38	40	42	44
Great Britain	34	36	38	40	42	44
Europe	44	46	48	50	52	54

Men's Shirts

U.S.A./G. Britain	14	$14^{1}/_{2}$	15	$15^{1}/_{2}$	$15^{3}/_{4}$	16	$16^{1}/_{2}$	17	$17^{1}/_{2}$	18
Europe	36	37	38	39	40	41	42	43	44	46

Men's Shoes

U.S.A.	$7^{1}/_{2}$	8	$8^{1}/_{2}$	9	$9^{1}/_{2}$	10	$10^{1}/_{2}$	11	$11^{1}/_{2}$	12	$12^{1}/_{2}$
Great Britain	6	$6^{1}/_{2}$	7	$7^{1}/_{2}$	8	$8^{1}/_{2}$	9	$9^{1}/_{2}$	10	$10^{1}/_{2}$	11
Europe	$39^{1}/_{2}$	40	$40^{1}/_{2}$	41	42	$42^{1}/_{2}$	43	44	$44^{1}/_{2}$	45	$45^{1}/_{2}$

COMPANY INDEX

AAA, *see* American Automobile Association
AAA-All Factory, Inc., 23
AAA Scale, *see* Triner Scale
AARP, *see* American Association of Retired Persons
ABC Vacuum Cleaner Warehouse, 24
Access International, 564
Ace Leather Products, Inc., 421
Acme Premium Supply Corp., 557
Adventures in Cassettes, *see* Metacom, Inc.
AHAM, *see* Association of Home Appliance Manufacturers
Airhitch, 564
A.L.A.S. Accordion-O-Rama, 447
Al's Luggage, 421
Alden Comfort Mills, 372
Alfax Wholesale Furniture, 466
All Electronics Corp., 539
Allyn Air Seat Co., 505
Altenburg Piano House, Inc., 448
America's Pharmacy, 430
American Animal Hospital Association, 3
American Association of Retired Persons, 282
American Automobile Association (AAA), 80
American Automobile Brokers, Inc., 81
American Cancer Society, 148
American Discount Wallcoverings, 319
American Family Publishers, 102
American Frame Corporation, 59
American Humane Education Society, 3
American Lung Association, 148
The American Needlewoman, 205
American Science & Surplus, 532
American Society of Appraisers, 411
The American Stationery Co., Inc., 103
American Tourister, 422
Amoco Motor Club, 80
Animal Health Insurance Agency, 2
Antique Imports Unlimited, 45

Appropriate Technology Transfer for Rural Areas (ATTRA), 239
Arctic Glass & Window Outlet, 382
Arctic Sheepskin Outlet, 156
Aristocast Originals Inc., 383
Arrow Shirt Co., *see* Quinn's Shirt Shop
Art Express, 60
Art Supply Warehouse, Inc., 61
Sam Ash Music Corp., 448
Association of Home Appliance Manufacturers (AHAM), 20
Astronomical Society of the Pacific, 104
Astronomics/Christophers, Ltd., 137
A to Z Luggage Co., Inc., 423
Atlantic Bridge Collection Corp. Ltd., 53
ATTRA, *see* Appropriate Technology Transfer for Rural Areas
The Audio Advisor, Inc., 24
Austad's, 506
Avian Referral Service, 2

B & B Company, Inc., 431
B & I, *see* Business & Institutional Furniture Company
Babouris Handicrafts, 231
Baby Bunz & Co., 189
Bailey's, Inc., 540
Jos. A. Bank Clothiers, Inc., 157
Barnes & Barnes Fine Furniture, 345
Barnes & Noble Bookstores, Inc., 105
Baron/Barclay Bridge Supplies, 558
Barrons, 391
Bart's Water Ski Center, Inc., 506
Bass Pro Shops, 507
Bates Bros. Nut Farm, Inc., 260
Bearden Bros. Carpet Corp., 320
Beautiful Visions, 307
Beauty Boutique, 307
Beauty by Spector, Inc., 308

Belle Tire Distributors, Inc., 82
Ben's Babyland, 190
Bennett Brothers, Inc., 283
Berkshire Record Outlet, Inc., 106
Bernie's Discount Center, Inc., 25
Berry Scuba Co., 508
Better Business Bureau, 2, 19, 79, 318
Better Health Fitness, 508
Betty Crocker Enterprises, 285
The Bevers, 541
Bickford Flavors, 261
Bike Nashbar, 509
Dick Blick Co., 62
Bob's Superstrong Greenhouse Plastic, 240
Book Passage, 570
BookWorld Services, Inc., 107
Bose Express Music, 108
Bosom Buddies, 190
Bowhunters Warehouse, Inc., 510
Bradbury's, 392
Maurice Brassard & Fils Inc., 232
BRE Lumber, 384
Breck's Dutch Bulbs, 241
Beverly Bremer Silver Shop, 393
Brodart Co., see Tartan Book Sales
Brown Print & Co., 467
Bruce Medical Supply, 432
Buffalo Batt & Felt Corp., 205
Burden's Surplus Center, 533
Buschemeyer & Company, 394
Business & Institutional Furniture Company,
    468
Business Envelope Manufacturers, Inc., 467
Business Technologies, 469
Butterbrooke Farm Seed Co-Op, 242
Butternut Books, 109
The Button Shop, 206

C & H Sales, Inc., see Lingerie for Less
Cabela's Inc., 511
Cahall's Brown Duck Catalog, see Cahall's
    Department Store
Cahall's Department Store, 158
The Caning Shop, 207
Cambridge Wools, Ltd., 233
Camelot Enterprises, 542
Campmor, 512
Campus Holidays USA, Inc., 566
Campus Travel Service, 566
Capital Cycle Corporation, 82
Caprilands Herb Farm, 243
Carino Nurseries, 244
Carvin, 450
Cascio Music Company, see Interstate Music
    Supply
Caviarteria Inc., 261
The Center for Auto Safety, 78
The Center for Safety in the Arts, 58
The Center for Science in the Public Interest
    (CSPI), 258

Central Michigan Tractor & Parts, 83
Central Skindivers, 512
Central Tractor Farm & Family Center, 245
Ceramic Supply of New York & New Jersey,
    Inc., 63
Chadwick's of Boston, Ltd., 159
Chanute Iron & Supply Co., see CISCO
Cheap Joe's Art Stuff, 64
Cheap Shot Inc., 513
The Chef's Pantry, 262
Cherry Auto Parts, 84
Cherry Hill Furniture, Carpet & Interiors, 345
Cherry Tree Toys, Inc., 208
China Cabinet, Inc., 394
The China Warehouse, 395
Chiswick Trading, Inc., 300
Chock Catalog Corp., 159
CIEE, see Council on International Educational
    Exchange
Cinema City, 46
Circle Craft Supply, 209
CISCO, 385
Ric Clark Company, 433
Clark's Corvair Parts, Inc., 85
Classic Designs, 423
Clothcrafters, Inc., 284
Clover Nursing Shoe Company, 198
CMC Music, Inc., 450
CMO, 490
Ezra Cohen Corp., 373
Coinways/Antiques Ltd., 395
Cole's Appliance & Furniture Co., 26
Colonial Garden Kitchens, 359
The Company Store Inc., 373
The Complete Traveller Bookstore, 564, 570
Computer Mail Order, see CMO
Conn Music, see CMC Music
Consumer Information Center, 110, 188, 259,
    430
Consumer Reports Travel Letter, 569
Consumers Union, 20, 188, 306, 556, 569
Contact Lens Replacement Center, 433
A Cook's Wares, 360
Coronet Books & CDs/Cassettes, 111
Council Charter, 563
Council on International Educational
    Exchange (CIEE), 563, 566
Craft King, Inc., 210
Craft Resources, Inc., 210
Crampton's International Airport Transit
    Guide, 564
Crawford's Old House Store, 385
Creative Health Products, 309
Crown Art Products Co., Inc., 65
CRTL, see Consumer Reports Travel Letter
Cruises Worldwide, 563
Crutchfield Corporation, 27
Crystal Sonics, 85
CSA, see Center for Safety in the Arts

CSPI, *see* Center for Science in the Public Interest
Current, Inc., 111
Curriculum Resources, *see* Craft Resources
Custom Coat Company, Inc., 160
Custom Golf Clubs, Inc., 514
Custom Windows & Walls, 321
Cycl-Ology, *see* Cycle Goods Corp.
Cycle Goods Corp., 515

D & A Merchandise Co., Inc., 161
Daedalus Books, Inc., 112
Dairy Association Co., Inc., 4
Daleco Master Breeder Products, 5
Danley's, 138
Dayton Computer Supply, 490
Deer Valley Farm, 263
The Deerskin Place, 162
Defender Industries, Inc., 86
Derry's Sewing Center, 29
Destinations Unlimited, 563
Dewynters Licensing & Distribution, 287
Dharma Trading Co., 211
Dial-a-Brand, Inc., 29
Diamonds by Rennie Ellen, 412
Direct Safety Company, 542
Discount Appliance Centers, 30
Discount Books & Video, Inc., 113
Discount Music Supply, 451
Discount Reed Company, 452
Disk World, Inc., 491
Disposable Supply, *see* Medical Supply Co.
The Dog's Outfitter, 6
Domestications, 374
Dover Publications, Inc., 114
Durey-Libby Edible Nuts, Inc., 264
Dutch Gardens, 245

E & B Marine Supply, Inc., 88
E.T. Supply, 534
Eastcoast Software, 492
Edgewood National, Inc., 89
Editions, 115
EduCALC Corporation, 493
800-Software, Inc., 494
Elderhostel, 565
Elderly Instruments, 453
Eldridge Textile Co., 375
Elite Eyewear, 434
Rennie Ellen, *see* Diamonds by Rennie Ellen
Eloxite Corporation, 413
The Emerald Collection, 396
Essential Products Co., Inc., 310
Euro-Tire, Inc., 90
European-American Travel, 563
Ewald-Clark, 139
Excalibur Bronze Sculpture Foundry, 47
Express Music, *see* Bose Express Music
Exxon Travel Club, 80
The Eye Solution, Inc., 435

The Fabric Center, Inc., 322
Fabrics by Design, 322
Fabrics by Phone, 323
Factory Direct Furniture, 469
Factory Direct Table Pad Co., 346
Famous Smoke Shop, Inc., 149
Farefinders, 563
Fax City, Inc., 470
Federal Trade Commission, 155, 411
A. Feibusch Corporation, 212
The Fiber Studio, 213
Michael C. Fina Co., 397
The Finals, Ltd., 163
Fivenson Food Equipment, Inc., 361
Flax Artist's Materials, 66
Floorcrafters Wholesale, 324
Florist Products, Inc., 246
Food and Drug Administration (FDA), 239, 430
The Forsyth Travel Library, 570
Fort Crailo Yarns Company, 214
Fortunoff Fine Jewelry & Silverware, Inc., 398
Forty-Fives, 116
Wally Frank Ltd., 150
Frank Eastern Co., 471
Frank's Cane and Rush Supply, 215
Franz Discount Office Products, 472
Fred Bernardo's Music, *see* Fred's String Warehouse
Paul Fredrick Shirt Company, 164
Fred's String Warehouse, 449
Freeda Vitamins, Inc., 311
The Friar's House, 54
A.I. Friedman, 67
F.R. Knitting Mills, Inc., 163
FTC, *see* Federal Trade Commission
The Furniture Barn, 347

Gallery Graphics, Inc., 48
Gander Mountain, Inc., 515
Gardener's Supply, 238
The Gemological Institute of America (GIA), 412
Genada Imports, 347
Gettinger Feather Corp., 216
GIA, *see* The Gemological Institute of America
Giardinelli Band Instrument Co., Inc., 454
Gibbsville Cheese Sales, 265
Global Village Imports, 217
Gohn Bros., 165
Goldbergs' Marine Distributors, 91
Marv Golden Discount Sales, Inc., 92
Golden Valley Lighting, 324
Goldman & Cohen Inc., 166
Golf Haus, 517
Grand Finale, 288
Grandma's Spice Shop, 266
Grayarc, 472
Great Northern Weaving, 218
Green Mt. Horse Products, *see* Dairy Association Co., Inc.

H & H Manufacturing & Supply Co., 543
H & R Company, 535
Edward R. Hamilton, Bookseller, 117
Hang-It-Now Wallpaper Stores, 325
Hanover House Industries, *see* Colonial
    Garden Kitchens, Domestications
The Hanover Shoe Co., 199
Harbor Freight Tools, 544
Harmony Supply Inc., 326
Harry's Discounts & Appliances Corp., 31
Harvest House Furniture, 348
Harvest of Values, 312
Herbach & Rademan, *see* H & R Corporation
Hidalgo, 436
Holabird Sports Discounters, 517
Holbrook Wholesalers, Inc., 313
Home Exchange International, 567
Home Fabric Mills, Inc., 326
Home Shopping Network, *see* Thos. Oak &
    Sons
Home-Sew, 218
Hong Kong Lapidaries, Inc., 414
House of Onyx, 414
Houston Shoe Hospital, 198
Humane Society, 1
Huntington Clothiers, 166

I Do I Do Bridal Salon, 167
IAMAT, *see* International Association for
    Medical Assistance to Travelers, *see*
    International Home Exchange
    Service/Intervac
Illinois Audio, Inc., 31
Images, 168
IMPCO, Inc., 93
Innovation Luggage, 424
Interior Furnishings Ltd., 349
International Association for Medical
    Assistance to Travelers (IAMAT), 568
International Gem Corporation, 415
International Home Exchange
    Service/Intervac, 567
Interstate Music Supply, 454
The Itinerary, 568

J & J Products Ltd., 219
J & R Music World, 32
J-B Wholesale Pet Supplies, Inc., 7
Jaffe Bros., Inc., 267
Robert James Co., Inc., 473
Jeffers Vet Supply, 8
Jerry's Artarama, Inc., 68
Jerryco, Inc., *see* American Science & Surplus
Jessica's Biscuit, 118
Jewelers' Vigilance Committee, 412
Johnson's Carpets, Inc., 327
The Jompole Company, Inc., 398
Justin Discount Boots & Cowboy Outfitters, 199

Kaiser Crow Inc., 399

Kansas City Vaccine Company, 9
Kaplan Bros. Blue Flame Corp., 362
The Kennel Vet Corp., 10
Kennelly Keys Music, Inc., 455
Kicking Mule Records, Inc., 119
King's Chandelier Co., 328
Kitchen Etc., 363
Stavros Kouyoumoutzakis, 234
E.C. Kraus Wine & Beermaking Supplies, 268

L & D Press, 474
Lands' End, Inc., 289
Las Vegas Discount Golf & Tennis, 518
Leather Unlimited Corp., 425
Lee-McClain Co., Inc., 168
LensCrafters, 429
Harris Levy, Inc., 376
Liberty Green, 349
Lincoln House, Inc., 290
Lincoln Typewriters and Micro Machines, 475
Lingerie for Less, 437
Loftin-Black Furniture Company, 350
Lone Star Percussion, 456
The Luggage Center, 426
Luigi Crystal, 329
LVT Price Quote Hotline, Inc., 33
Lyben Computer Systems, Inc., 495
Lyle Cartridges, 34

MACAP, *see* Major Appliance Consumer Action
    Panel
MacConnection, 495
MacGillivray & Coy., 235
Magazine Marketplace, 120
Magnum, 151
Mail Center USA, 475
Main Lamp/Lamp Warehouse, 329
Major Appliance Consumer Action Panel
    (MACAP), 22
Mandolin Brothers, Ltd., 457
Manny's Millinery Supply Co., 169
Manny's Musical Instruments & Accessories,
    Inc., 458
Manufacturer's Supply, 545
The Maples Fruit Farm, Inc., 269
Mardiron Optics, 140
Marel Company, 400
Marks Cigars, 151
Marlene's Decorator Fabrics, 330
Marymac Industries, Inc., 496
Mass. Army & Navy Store, 536
Master Animal Care, 11
Masuen First Aid & Safety, 437
Mature Outlook, 290
Medi-Mail, Inc., 439
Medical Supply Co., Inc., 438
MEI/Micro Center, 497
Meisel Hardware Specialties, 546
Mellinger's Inc., 247
Messina Glass & China Co. Inc., 400

Metacom, Inc., 120, 148
Metropolitan Music Co., 458
Mexican Chile Supply, *see* Pendery's Inc.
Midamerica Vacuum Cleaner Supply Co., 35
Midas China & Silver, 401
J.E. Miller Nurseries, Inc., 248
Miscellaneous Man, 49
Modern Jeweler, 411
Monarch, 386
Monterey Mills Outlet Store, 220
Mother Hart's Natural Products, Inc., 377
Mother's Place, 191
Mothers Work, 192
Mr. Slate, *see* The New England Slate
    Company
Mr. Spiceman, Inc., 270
Murrow Furniture Galleries, Inc., 351
Museum Editions New York Ltd., 50
Musiquarium Used CD Club, 121

National Arbor Day Foundation, 249
National Bird-Feeding Society, 2
National Business Furniture, Inc., 476
National Carpet, 331
National Contact Lens Center, 440
National Decorating Products Association, 317
National Educational Music Co., Ltd., 459
National Wholesale Co., Inc., 170
The Natural Baby Co., Inc., 193
NBF, *see* National Business Furniture, Inc.
NCA, *see* The Neighborhood Cleaners'
    Association
NEBS, Inc., 497
The Neighborhood Cleaners' Association
    (NCA), 155
NEMC, *see* National Educational Music Co.,
    Ltd.
New England Basket Co., 291
New England Business Service, *see* NEBS
New England Cheesemaking Supply Co., 364
New England Leather Accessories, Inc., 426
The New England Slate Company, 386
New Eyes for the Needy, 429
New York Ceiling Fan Center, *see* Main
    Lamp/Lamp Warehouse
New York Central Art Supply Co., 69
Newark Dressmaker Supply, Inc., 221
Holly Nicolas Nursing Collection, 194
Nor'East Miniature Roses, Inc., 250
Northeast Agricultural Engineering Service, 239
Northern Greenhouse Sales, *see* Bob's
    Superstrong Greenhouse Plastic
Northern Hydraulics, Inc., 547
Northern Wholesale Veterinary Supply, Inc., 11
Northwestern Coffee Mills, 271
Nouvelle Frontiers, 563

Office Furniture Center, 477
OHJ, *see* The Old House Journal Corporation
Okun Bros. Shoes, 200

The Old House Journal Corporation, 381
Omaha Vaccine Company, Inc., 12
Open House, 365
Oreck Corporation, 36
Original Paper Collectibles, 50
Orion Telescope Center, 141
A.W.G. Otten and Son, 202
Overseas Citizens Emergency Center, 568
Overton's Sports Center, Inc., 519
Owl Photo, 142

Pagano Gloves, Inc., 171
Pages/Booktraders, Ltd., 122
Palmer's Maple Syrup, 272
The Paper Wholesaler, 292
Paradise Products, Inc., 559
Paris Bread Pans, *see* Paris International Inc.
Paris International Inc., 366
Park Seed Co., 251
Patti Music Corp., 460
PC Connection, 498
Pearl Paint Co., 70
Peerless Restaurant Supplies, 367
Pendery's Inc., 273
Percy's, Inc., 37
Performance Bicycle Shop, 520
Pet Warehouse, 13
The Petticoat Express, 172
Pharmail Corporation, 441
La Piata, 559
Pinetree Garden Seeds, 252
Pintchik Homeworks, 332
Pitlochry Knitwear and Moffat Woollens, 182
Plastic BagMart, 301
Plexi-Craft Quality Products Corp., 351
Porter's Camera Store, Inc., 142
Post Wallcovering Distributors, Inc., 333
The Potters Shop Inc., 123
Prentiss Court Ground Covers, 253
Print's Graphic Design Book Store, 123
Prism Optical, Inc., 442
Professional Golf & Tennis Suppliers, Inc., 521
Protecto-Pak, 302
Publishers Clearing House, 124
Pueblo to People, 293

Quality Furniture Market of Lenoir, Inc., 352
Queen Anne Furniture Company, Inc., 353
Quill Corporation, 478
Quinn's Shirt Shop, 173

Racer Wholesale, 94
Rainbow Music, 460
Rammagerdin, 183
Rapidforms, Inc., 479
R/E Kane Enterprises, 416
Red Hill Corporation, 548
The Reliable Corporation, 480
Replacements, Ltd., 391
Retired Persons Services, Inc., 443

Anthony Richards, 173
Rick's Movie Graphics, Inc., 51
Iwan Ries & Co., 152
Road Runner Sports, 522
W.S. Robertson (Outfitters) Ltd., 184
Robin Importers, Inc., 402
Robinson's Wallcoverings, 333
Rocky Mountain Stationery, 125
Rogers & Rosenthal, 403
Rosehill Farm, 253
Ross-Simons Jewelers, 417
Rubens & Marble, Inc., 195
Rubin & Green Inc., 334
Rudi's Pottery, Silver & China, 403
Ruvel & Co., Inc., 536

S & S Sound City, 37
Saco Manufacturing & Woodworking, 388
Safe Specialties, Inc., 480
Sailboard Warehouse, Inc., 522
Saint Laurie Ltd., 174
Salk International Travel Premiums, Inc., 564
Samuels Tennisport, 523
San Francisco Herb Co., 274
Santa Rosa Optometry Center, see National
    Contact Lens Center
Sanz International, Inc., 335
Sara Glove Company, Inc., 175
Sara Lee, see Showcase of Savings
Saw Chain, see H & H Manufacturing &
    Supply Co.
Sax Arts & Crafts, 71
Saxkjaers, 55
J. Schachter Corp., 378
Ginger Schlote, 418
The Scholar's Bookshelf, 125
A.B. Schou, see Skandinavisk Glas
Nat Schwartz & Co., Inc., 404
Scope City, 143
Script City, 126
Seed Savers Exchange, 239
Seven Corners Ace Hardware, Inc., see Tools
    on Sale
Sewin' in Vermont, 38
Shama Imports, Inc., 335
Shannon Duty Free Mail Order, 407
Shar Products Company, 461
Shaw Furniture Galleries, Inc., 354
Shibui Wallcoverings, 336
Showcase of Savings, 176
R.H. Shumway Seedsman, 254
Shuttercraft, 388
Sierra Club Mail-Order Service, 239
Sierra Trading Post, 524
Silk Surplus, 337
Silver Wallcovering, Inc., 338
Simpson & Vail, Inc., 275
Singer Sewing Center of College Station, 39
Skandinavisk Glas, 408
Skipper Marine Electronics, Inc., 95

Skyline Color Lab, 144
Slipcovers of America, 338
The Smart Saver, 177
Smiley's Yarns, 222
Daniel Smith, 72
Albert S. Smyth Co., Inc., 405
Soccer International, Inc., 525
Solar Cine Products, Inc., 145
Solo Slide Fasteners, Inc., 222
South Bound Millworks, 339
The Spice House, 276
Spiegel, Inc., 294
Spike Nashbar, 526
Mrs. Mary Spillane, 185
Sport Shop, 527
Sporting Dog Specialties, see R.C. Steele Co.
Sportswear Clearinghouse, 177
Springmaid/Wamsutta Mill Store, 379
Stamped Envelope Agency, 465
Staples, Inc., 481
Stecher's Limited, 409
R.C. Steele Co., 14
Fred Stoker & Sons, Inc., 153
Strand Book Store, Inc., 127
Straw Into Gold, Inc., 223
Stu-Art Supplies, Inc., 73
Stuckey Brothers Furniture Co., Inc., 354
Suburban Sew 'N Sweep, Inc., 40
Sultan's Delight, Inc., 277
Superintendent of Documents, 128, 188, 569
Support Plus, see Surgical Products, Inc.
Surgical Products, Inc., 444
Survival Supply Co., 527

TAI, Inc., 178
Tartan Book Sales, 129
Taylor's Cutaways and Stuff, 224
Telemart, 499
Telepro Golf Shop, 528
Teletire, 96
The Tennis Co., 529
Thai Silks, 225
That Fish Place, 15
Elbridge C. Thomas & Sons, 278
Thompson Cigar Company, 154
Thos. Oak & Sons, 171
Thread Discount Sales, 226
Thrift Club, 295
Thurber's, 406
Tioga Mill Outlet Stores, Inc., 340
Titan Rubber International, 97
Todd Uniform, Inc., 179
Tomahawk Live Trap Company, 16
Tools on Sale, 549
Ben Torres Ribbon Company, 500
Tower Hobbies, 227
Travel Accessories & Things, 571
Travel Smart, 569
Travel World, 563
TravelBooks, 571

Traveler's Checklist, 571
Marion Travis, 355
Trend-lines, Inc., 550
Triner Scale, 482
Trumble Greetings, Inc., 130
Tuli-Latus Perfumes Ltd., 314
Turnbaugh Printers Supply Co., 483
Turner Greenhouses, 255
Turner Tolson, Inc., 355
Turnkey Material Handling Co., 551
20th Century Plastics, Inc., 484
Typex Business Machines, Inc., 484

The Ultimate Outlet, 179
United Pharmacal Company, Inc., 17
U.S. Box Corp., 304
The U.S. State Department, 568
United Supply Co., Inc., 74
Unitravel Corporation, 562
University Products, Inc., 136, 303
Utex Trading Enterprises, 228
Utrecht Art and Drafting Supply, 75

Value-tique, Inc., 485
K. Van Bourgondien & Sons, Inc., 256
Vanguard Crafts, Inc., 228
Vermont Cobble Slate, see The New England
    Slate Company
Lillian Vernon Corporation, 296
Veteran Leather Company, Inc., 229
Viking Office Products, 486
Vintage Wood Works, 389
Visible Computer Supply Corp., 501
Vulcan Binder & Cover, 486

The Wabby Company, 196
Walnut Acres Organic Farms, 278
Warehouse Carpets, Inc., 341
WearGuard Corp., 180
Webbs, 230
Weinkrantz Musical Supply Co., Inc., 462
WELL Associates, see Butternut Books
Wells Interiors Inc., 342
West Manor Music, 463
West Marine Products, 98
Western S & G, 502
Weston Bowl Mill, 297
Westside Camera Inc., 146
Whole Earth Access, 551
Whole Person Tours, 568
Whole Person Tours, see The Itinerary
Wholesale Tape and Supply Company, 40
Wholesale Veterinary Supply, Inc., 18
Wiley Outdoor Sports, Inc., 529
The Wine Enthusiast, 368
Wisconsin Discount Stereo, 41
Irv Wolfson Company, 42
Wood's Cider Mill, 279
Woodworker's Supply, Inc., 552
Workmen's Garment Co., 181

Yachtmail Co. Ltd., 99
Yazoo Mills, Inc., 76

Zabar's & Co., Inc., 369
Zarbin & Associates, Inc., 356
Zip Power Parts, Inc., 553
Zip-Penn, Inc., see Zip Power Parts

PRODUCT INDEX

abrasives, 548, 550, 551–553
accommodations
  campus, 566–567
  discount, 563
  home exchanges, 567–568
  YMCA, 567
accordions and concertinas, 447
air compressors, 547, 549, 552
air conditioners, 26, 29, 31, 33, 37, 38, 42
air-conditioning systems, 384–385
airbrushing supplies and tools, 60, 61, 63, 65, 69
airfare, discount, 562–563
Amish specialties, 165
animal biologicals, 6–8, 10–14, 17
animal traps, 16, 252
animal vaccines, 9, 10, 12, 17, 18
antiques, 45
archery supplies and equipment, 510
architectural ornaments, 383, 385, 388, 389
AT&T Toll-Free 800 Consumer Directory, 281
audio
  auto, 27–28, 31, 86
  bird song, 114
  blank audiotapes, 40
  components, 24–26, 27, 28, 31, 32, 34, 37, 40, 41
  language, 114, 120
  maintenance products, 25, 28, 34
  motivational, 113, 120
  old radio programs, 120
    bluegrass and blues, 118
    classical, 105, 106, 108, 111, 113, 121
    current, 108, 111, 113, 121
    vintage compilations, 120
auto parts
  Corvair, 85
  foreign, used and rebuilt, 84
  OEM Mercedes-Benz diesel, 93
auto price quotes/dealer referrals, 81
auto racing gear, 94

auto seat covers, sheepskin, 156
auto seat cushions, air-filled, 505
autos, domestic and foreign, 81
aviation supplies and gear, general, 92

badminton supplies and equipment, 523
Bag Balm, 4
balusters, 389
banjos, 457
barbecue grills, 283
barres, 509
basketry supplies, 215, 229
baskets, 291
bathing aids, 432, 444
batik supplies and equipment, 211–212
beadwork supplies, 210
bedding and mattresses, 349–352, 354, 356
beer, do-it-yourself supplies, 268
bicycle cushions, 505
bicycles, stationary, 509
bicycles and equipment, 509–510, 515, 520
binoculars, 137, 138, 140, 141, 143, 511, 516
birds, products for, 15, 17
blood pressure measuring devices, 432, 437, 443, 444
boating supplies and equipment, 86–88, 91, 95, 98, 99
  inflatable, 87, 88, 91, 98, 99
  yachting, 99
boats, 507
boilers, 384–385
books
  academic press, 107, 112, 125
  art, 105, 107, 112–115, 117, 124, 126, 127
  children's, 105, 107, 109, 112, 114, 127
  cookery, 105, 107, 112–115, 117–118, 127, 360
  copyright-free, 114
  educational, 109
  graphic arts, 123
  literary remainders, 112

movie and TV industry guides, 126
new, range of topics, 105, 107, 110, 112–114, 117, 126
on astronomy, 104
on ceramics and pottery, 123
on medical and nursing topics, 432
on photography, 145
on textile arts, 211, 223–224
out-of-print, 115, 122, 127
remaindered, 105, 112, 113, 117–118, 126, 127
reviewers' copies, current, 127
used, range of topics, 115, 122, 129
bow fishing supplies and equipment, 527
bow hunting supplies and equipment, 510, 527, 529–530
bowls, salad, 297
bread pans, French, 366
breast forms, 431, 437
bridal attire, 167
bridge-playing materials, 558
Broadway show memorabilia, 287
bulbs, flower, 241, 246, 247–249, 251, 252, 254, 256
business cards, 467, 474
buttons, 206, 219, 221, 223, 224

C.Z., see jewelry, cubic zirconia
cages and carriers, animal, 6–8, 10–14, 16–18
bird, 13, 16
calculators, 473, 475, 484, 493
calligraphy supplies and tools, 61, 68, 69, 71, 72
cameras and accessories, 142, 145, 146, 284
camping gear, 511, 512, 516, 524, 528, 530
candy, 260, 270
canes, 432
canvas (art), 60–62, 64, 66, 68–72, 74, 75
car seats, infants', 190
car, see auto
cards, greeting, 112, 125, 130, 290
cash registers, 467, 469, 473, 484
castanets, 456
caviar, 263
CDs (compact discs), 25, 105, 106, 108, 111, 113, 120, 121, 295
ceiling fans, 329–330, 551
cellos, 458–459, 461–463
ceramics supplies and equipment, 63, 71, 123
chain saws, 245, 540, 547, 553
parts, 540, 543, 545, 547, 553
chair reweaving supplies and equipment, 207–208, 215
chairs, ergonomic, 469–470, 471, 480, 486
chandeliers and parts, 328, 329
charts, star, 141, 143
cheese, 264, 265, 279
cheese-making supplies and equipment, 364
cider jelly, 279–280
cider-press liners, 285
cigars, 149–152, 154

cutters, 150, 151, 154
cleaning and maintenance equipment, 292
climbing supplies and equipment, 512, 524
clock-making supplies, 208–209, 413
clocks, 284, 345, 354
clothing
auto racing, 94
bridal, 167
children's, 160–164, 165, 176–178, 182, 183, 185, 189, 193, 195, 196
cycling, 164, 510, 515, 520
hosiery, 160, 161, 165, 166, 170, 176, 443, 444
hosiery, support, 443, 444
infants', underwear and sleepwear, 195
maternity, 166, 176, 191, 192
men's, 510, 512, 515, 516, 518–526
motorcycle , 160, 171, 175
nursing, 191, 195
T-shirts, 158, 175–180, 507, 518, 525, 526
uniforms, 179
women's, 156–185, 510, 512, 515, 516, 518–526
work, 158, 165, 175, 179–181
coffee, 266, 269, 271, 275
comforters, down, 83, 372–376, 378
computers and peripherals, 32, 475, 478, 482, 490, 493, 496, 499
supplies, 467, 472, 473, 478, 479, 482, 484
work stations, 468, 470, 471, 474, 476–478, 480, 482, 496, 501
condoms, 431
conservation supplies, 66, 303
construction tools and equipment, 549
consumer publications, in Spanish, 110
Consumer Reports Auto Price Service, 78–79
Consumer Reports Travel Letter, 569
Consumer's Resource Handbook, 20, 110
contact lenses, 433–434, 440
supplies, 435
cookware, commercial, 360, 367
copiers, 28, 33, 37, 473, 478, 480, 482, 484
supplies, 467, 473, 478
cosmetics, 307–308
court maintenance equipment, 517–518, 523–524
crafts projects, kits, 208, 210, 228, 229
crafts stuffing, 206, 220
cruises, discount, 563–564
crutches, 432
cycling, see bicycling

darkroom supplies and equipment, 142, 145, 146
decoupage supplies, 62, 209
diabetics, products for, 430, 432, 443
diamonds, custom-cut, 412
diapers and covers, 189, 190, 193, 196
discount buying organizations, 282, 290–291, 295
display materials, 304

dog parkas, 6
doll-making supplies, 209, 210, 221, 229
doors, 382
draperies, 319, 323, 334
   hardware and supplies, 327, 340
drawing supplies and materials, 60–62, 64,
   66–72
drugs, prescription, 430, 439, 441, 443
drums, *see* musical instruments, percussion
dyes, fabric, 65, 211, 213, 228

educational programs for seniors, 565
effects boxes, *see* electronics, musical
electrical components, 535, 539
electronics
   aviation, 92
   marine, 86–88, 91, 95, 98, 99
embroidery floss, 211, 219, 221, 228
envelopes, self-addressed with postage, 465
exercise equipment, 283, 309, 509
extracts, flavorings, 261, 262, 268, 271
eyeglasses, prescription, 434–435, 436, 442
eyewash stations, 542–543

fabric
   cashmere, 219–220
   cutaways, 224
   decorator, 217, 225, 228, 319, 321–323,
      325–327, 330, 333–336, 337, 340
   deep-pile (""fun fur"), 220
   ikat, 217
   lining, 219–220
   tartan, 235
   tweed, 219, 235
   wool flannel, 219–220
facsimile (fax) machines, 25, 27, 32, 33, 37,
   470, 478, 480–482, 484
factory repair manuals, 93
   Corvair, 85
   motorcycle, BMW, 83
   tractor, 245
FDA Consumer, 110
feather boas, 216
feathers
   bedding, 216
   loose, 216
   ostrich, 216
felt-crafts supplies, 210, 223
ferrets, supplies for, 17
figurines, collectible, 53–55, 392, 395, 396,
   399, 403, 405, 407–409
film, 142, 145, 146
filters, coffee, 271
first-aid kits, 175, 437, 541, 543, 551
fish, products for, 5, 13–16
fishing tackle, 507, 511, 516
flatware (silverware)
   replacement (discontinued patterns),
      391–395
flooring, 324, 332, 341

slate, 386–387
flue hole covers, 48
food
   bulk-packaged, 292, 528
   Mexican, 273
   Middle Eastern, 277
   organic, 263, 267, 278–279
food-handling supplies, 292
footwear
   athletic, 201, 518, 522
   cowboy and work boots, 200, 201
   men's, 156–158, 161, 162, 165, 167, 171,
      176, 180, 199–202, 510, 512, 515, 516,
      518–526
   moccasins, 162, 171, 201
   motorcycle boots, 200, 201
   nurses' shoes, 189, 201
   women's, 159, 171, 174, 180, 199–202, 510,
      512, 515, 516, 518–526
   wooden shoes, 202
   work, 158, 176, 180, 181
foreign-current appliances, 42
forms, business, 467, 472–476, 478, 479,
   481–481
foul-weather gear, 86–88, 99
four-wheel drive (4WD) vehicle parts, 89
fruit
   dried, 260, 263, 267, 269, 277, 279
furnaces, woodburning, 545
furniture
   art, 47
   nursery, 190
   unfinished, 355

games, 284, 286, 557, 559–560
garden carts, 547
Garden Way bulletins, 252
gardening supplies and equipment
   hydroponic, 247
gemstones, loose, 413–416
gerbils, supplies for, 13, 17
gift boxes, 304
gift wrapping and ribbon, 112, 290
globes, 284
gloves
   driving, 160, 171
   food handling, 175
   shooting, 160, 171
   work, 541, 543
go-cart parts, 545, 547
golfing clubs and gear, 506, 514, 517–519, 521,
   528–529
gongs, 456
graphic arts supplies and tools, 64, 66–68
greenhouses and supplies, 241, 246–248, 255,
   382
grey market, 136
guinea pigs, supplies for, 17
guitars, 449–451, 453–459
gun cabinets, 284

hamsters, supplies for, 13, 17
hand trucks, 551
shutter hardware, 389
harmonicas, 449, 451
hats, men's, straw, 200
hats, women's, 169
hearing aids, 433
    batteries, 431, 433, 443
heating fixtures, 384–385
herbs, 243, 247, 251
high chairs, 190
hoof softener, 4
horses, products for, 4, 8–10, 12, 17, 18
hotel (hospitality) supplies, 474
hotels, see accommodations
hunting supplies and equipment, 510, 511,
    513, 516, 524, 527–530
hydraulics, 547

incontinence products, adult, 432, 438, 444
ironing supplies and equipment, professional,
    223

jeeps, 81
jewelry, 53, 55, 283, 288, 293–296, 392, 397,
    398, 405, 407, 409, 412–418
    antique, 45
    boxes, presentation, 304
    cubic zirconia, 416
    findings, 413, 418
    Masonic, 283
    religious, 283
jewelry-making supplies, 63, 209

kilns, 62, 63, 71
kilts, custom-made, 235
kitchen cutlery, 286, 359, 360, 363, 365, 367,
    369, 402
kneeboards, 507, 519–520
knitting machines, 213, 231

labels
    return-address, 103
    vintage (original), 49, 50
    woven (name tapes), 221
lampposts, 388
lapidary supplies, 62, 413, 418
laser discs, music, current, 108
lawnmower parts, 545, 553
layette items, 160, 165, 189, 190, 194–196
leather conditioner, 4
leather tanning and coloring services, 160
leatherworking supplies and equipment, 62,
    228–229, 425
lighting fixtures, 324–325, 328, 329–330, 339,
    345, 349, 354
linen
    bed and bath, 283, 288, 289, 372–380
    crib, 195, 372, 374
livestock supplies, 4, 8, 9, 12, 17, 18, 245

logging supplies and equipment, 540, 545, 547
luggage
    canvas, 289

macrame supplies, 62, 209
magazines, by subscription, 102, 119, 124
mailing tubes, art, 76
mandolas, 457
mandolins, 453, 457
maple syrup, 267, 269, 272, 278, 280
    kosher, 267
maps, 570
marquetry supplies and equipment, 553
masonry tools and equipment, 549
mat board, 59, 69
meat, naturally raised, 263–264
metal detectors, 284, 543
metronomes, 454, 460, 462, 463
microscopes, 284
millinery supplies, 169
mineral specimens, 415
minibike parts, 545, 547
mirrors, 345, 349, 350, 354
models (hobby) and supplies, 227
moisture meters, 549, 550
motels, see accommodations
motorcycle parts
    BMW, 82–83
    seat cushions, 505
motors, 545, 547
music stands, 447, 451, 454–455, 459, 461–463
musical instrument accessories
    bows, 458–459, 461–462
    mouthpieces, 454
    reeds, 452, 455, 463
    strings, 449, 451, 457, 459, 461–463
musical instruments
    keyboard, 450–451
    vintage, 453, 457, 460–461

newel posts, 388, 389
nurses' shoes, 189, 201
nutritional supplements, 311, 132
nuts, 260, 1263, 264, 267, 269, 274, 277, 279

onyx carvings, 415
opera glasses, 140
organizers and agendas, 424
organs, 448, 450–451
ostomy supplies, 432
ovens
    commercial, 361, 362, 367
    conventional and microwave, 26, 29, 30, 33,
        37, 42

paint, house, 70, 332
painting (art) supplies and tools, 60–62, 64,
    66–75
paneling, 384
paper, art, 60, 61, 64, 66–75

paperweights, 53, 54, 396
papyrus, 72
parallel imports, *see* grey market
park benches, 466
party goods, 292, 557, 559–560
patio door panels, 382
patterns
    doll, 221
pens, 149, 284, 399, 405, 409, 467, 478, 481,
    486
perfume, 307, 310, 313, 314
pet jewelry, 6
pet supplies, 5–8,10–15, 17, 18
    food, 10
phones and phone machines, 26–28, 32, 33,
    38, 473, 478, 480–482
phonograph cartridges, styli, 34
photo processing, range of services, 139, 142,
    144, 145
photo storage supplies, 303, 484
    acid-free, 303
piatas, 559–560
pianos, 449–449, 450–451, 463
picture frames (sectional), 59, 73, 66, 67, 69, 75
picture frames (silver), 393, 397, 398, 405
pillows, 191, 211, 372, 374, 377, 378
plants
    fertilizer, 246–248, 252
    ground-cover, 253, 256
    house, 251, 256
    insecticide, 246–248, 255
    sweet potato, 153
planters, 246, 247
plastic bags, 300–302
platform tennis supplies and equipment, 523
playpens, 190
plumbing fixtures, 384–385
popcorn, 153
porch posts, 389
post-surgical supplies, 432
posters
    astronomy, 104
    movie, 46, 49, 51
    reproduction, 48, 50
    vintage (original), 46, 49, 51
potpourri ingredients, 225, 243, 273, 274
printing presses and printing supplies, 483
public address systems, 466
punch embroidery supplies, 210–211

quilt batts, 206

rabbits, supplies for, 8, 12, 17, 18
racquetball supplies and equipment, 517–518,
    518–519, 521, 523–524
radar detectors, 28, 32, 33, 37
radiator enclosures, 386
radio-controlled airplanes, cars, trains, boats,
    etc., 227, 284
rawhide bones, 6, 7, 10, 11, 14

recording equipment, 449
records, 45's, 116
refrigerators, commercial, 361, 367
restoration supplies, 303
roofing slate and tools, 386–387
roses, miniature, 250, 254
rototillers, 547
    parts, 545
rubber stamps, 467–468, 472
rug-making supplies and equipment, 218
rugs and carpeting, 320, 327, 331, 341

safes, 284, 480–481, 485
safety gear
    auto racing, 94
    ear plugs and muffs, 175, 541, 543
    glasses and goggles, 175, 543
    respirators, 175, 543
sailboarding, *see* windsurfing
scales, 482
scarves, undyed silk, 225, 228
scissors, sewing, 207, 219, 221
screenplays, movie and TV, 126
scuba-diving supplies and equipment, 508,
    512–513
sculpting equipment and supplies, 63, 69, 71,
    75
security equipment, 28, 284, 543, 551
seed saving, 242
seeds
    flower, 243, 247, 248, 251, 252, 254
    open-pollinated, 242, 254
    vegetable, 242, 247, 248, 251, 252, 254
sergers, 38, 39, 226
sewing machines, 29, 30, 38–40, 226
    commercial, 223
sewing notions, 165, 206–207, 212, 218–219,
    221, 223
sheet music, 449, 460, 461
shipping supplies, 304, 473–474, 479
    art, 76
shrink art supplies, 229
shrubs, 244, 247–249
shutters, wood, 389
silkscreening supplies and equipment, 61, 62,
    65, 69
silver chests, 391–392, 401
skylights, 382
slate, roofing, 386–387
slide storage supplies, 303, 484
slides, astronomy, 104, 137
slipcovers, 338
smoke detectors, 542–543
smoked fish, 263
smoking accessories, 149, 150, 152–154
snorkeling supplies and equipment, 519–520
snow thrower parts, 545
snowmobile parts, 545
snowshoes, 512
snuff, 153

soil test kits, 238, 246
sorghum syrup, 153
sound systems, 448–449, 450, 451, 455
sphygmomanometers , see blood pressure
    measuring devices
spinning supplies and equipment, 213,
    223–224, 230, 233
spotting scopes, 137, 138, 140, 143, 515–516
squash supplies and equipment, 517–518, 521,
    523–524, 529
stage lighting, 454–456
standby travel, 564
stationery
    business, 103, 467, 474, 476, 478, 479
    children's, 103
    novelty, 112, 290
    personal, 103
    wedding, 103
stethoscopes, 432
strollers, 190
sumi supplies, 61, 68
sunglasses, 176, 434, 436, 507, 511, 516, 518,
    523, 524
supports and braces, medical, 444
swimming accessories, 164
swimming pool supplies, 384–385

table pads, 346, 349, 350
tableware, restaurant, 361, 367
tambourines, 456
tape duplicating services, 40
tea, 263, 266, 267, 269, 271, 274, 275
telephones, see phones
telescopes and accessories, 137, 138, 140, 141,
    142
tennis supplies and equipment, 517–518,
    518–519, 521, 523–524, 529
thread, 165, 207, 212, 219, 221, 223, 226, 228
tires
    auto, 82, 90, 96, 97
    radial, 82–83
    RV, 96
    truck, 96
    van, 96
tobacco, 149, 150, 152–154
    cigar, 153
    cigarette, 153
    plug, 153
    seeds, 153
    snuff, 153
tours, discount, 562–563
toy-making parts, 208–209, 541, 546
toys, 194, 557–560
tractor and combine parts, 83, 245
trains, 284
travel
    accessories, 570–571
    agents, discount, 563
    bucket shops, 562–563
    consolidators, 562–563

guides, 569–571
medical assistance abroad, 568
newsletters, 569
standby, 564
student discounts, 565–566
U.S. State Department information on,
    568–569
with disabilities, 568
treadmills, 509
tree-climbing supplies and equipment, 540,
    547
trees
    evergreen, 244, 247, 249
    fruit, 247–249, 254
    shade, 246–248
trucks, 81
truffles, 263
trunks, 423
tuners, 454, 455–456, 460, 462
TV and video components, 26–29, 31–33, 37,
    38, 42
typewriters, 472–473, 475, 478, 484–485
    foreign-language, 484–485

upholstery fabric, see fabric, decorator
upholstery tools and supplies, 205, 215, 221

vacuum cleaners, floor machines, 23, 24, 26,
    29–31, 33, 35, 36, 38–40, 42
vans, 81
veneer, wood, 553
vet supplies, 6–12, 14, 16–18
Victorian architectural ornamentation, 389
videotapes
    blank, 31, 32, 40, 145
    educational, 113
    instructional, 113, 120
    movies, new and vintage , 105, 108, 113,
        127
    music, 108, 111
    on astronomy, 104
    vintage cartoons, 113, 120
violas, 459, 461–463
violins, 458–459, 461–463

walkers
    adults, 432
    infants, 190
wall coverings, 319, 321, 325, 326, 332, 333,
    335, 336, 338
watches, 283, 397–399, 405, 409, 417
water skiing supplies and equipment,
    506–507, 519–520
weaving supplies and equipment, 62, 71, 74,
    213, 214, 223, 230, 232–234
wet suits, 506–507, 508, 519, 522–523
wheelchairs, 432
    cushions, 505
wheels
    auto, 90, 96

performance, 97
whirlpools, 384–385
wigs and hairpieces for men and women, 308
window treatments, 319, 321, 326, 332, 333, 338, 342
windows, 382
windsurfing supplies and equipment, 522–523
wine
  do-it-yourself supplies, 268

serving and storage equipment, 368
wood-chopping tools, 545
woodburning supplies, 210
woodworking tools and equipment, 208–209, 541, 549–552

yarn, 211, 213, 214, 222, 224, 230–235

zippers and fasteners, 207, 212, 219, 221, 223, 224